D1822899

£10

860.2?

מַחֲזוֹר הַשָּׁלֵם
לְחַג הַשָּׁבוּעוֹת

מְתֻרְגָּם וּמְפֹרָשׁ
בְּתוֹסֶפֶת מָבוֹא
מֵאֵת

פַלְטִיאֵל בִּירְנְבּוֹים

בית ההוצאה העברי
ניו יורק

PRAYER BOOK

FOR

SHAVUOTH

*Translated and Annotated
with an Introduction*

by

PHILIP BIRNBAUM

HEBREW PUBLISHING COMPANY

NEW YORK

PRAYER BOOK FOR SHAVUOTH

Reprinted and bound July 1992
AG
Hebrew Publishing Company
P.O. Box 157
Rockaway Beach
New York 11693

M

Printed and bound in the United States of America

L

לזכרון
אבי מורי ר׳ אברהם יואל ב״ר ישראל
ואמי מורתי רווה בת ר׳ ראובן
ואחיותי דינה ולאה וצאצאיהן שנספו בשואה
תהא נפשם צרורה בצרור החיים

CONTENTS

הַתֹּכֶן

INTRODUCTION

I

Judaism demands from its adherents a knowledge of the Bible and the traditions based upon it. Many, however, lack the leisure or the aptitude for such study; hence, the Prayerbook has developed in a way that enables every worshiper to become familiar with the various forms of Jewish learning and religious expression. Since the Prayerbook is designed for all Jews, individual needs and private interests are often disregarded in the prescribed prayers. These are phrased in plural form and are meant to be the voice of all Israel. The diversified authorship of the Prayerbook, embracing prophets and psalmists, legalists and poets, proclaims that all Israel has a share in its making. For nearly two thousand years, the Hebrew prayers have helped to keep the Jews alive, saving them from losing their language and their identity.

The Hebrew Psalms, many of which form part of our daily and festival prayerbooks, stand out unique among the prayers of the entire world by their simplicity, power and majesty of diction. They have been described as the anatomy of all parts of the soul. All the sorrows, troubles, fears, doubts, hopes, pains, stormy outbreaks, perplexities by which the souls of men are tossed, are depicted in the Psalms, the hymnbook of the whole world. The Psalms are religion itself put into speech, the songs of the human soul, timeless and universal. The keynote of the Psalms is simplicity of heart, faith in God, and good conduct. In the Psalms we find the human heart in all its moods and emotions: in penitence, in danger, in desolation, and in triumph. They are as varied as is human life; they are enlightened in their ethics as they are lofty in their religious spirit.

It is frequently pointed out that our congregational prayers are meant to be petitions on behalf of the entire community of Israel. They are not primarily intended to give expression to our own personal feelings. How can millions of Jews feel alike every time they recite the prescribed daily prayers? Occasionally, however, traditional prayer helps us in a purely personal way, when pent-up emotion chokes our power of expression. Into its classical forms we manage to breathe our sentiments and our emotions. By means of congregational melodies, each worshiper adds his fervor to that of his neighbor, and receives in turn his neighbor's inspiration to add to his own devotion.

The sages of Israel constantly emphasized the importance of uniformity in synagogue service. In order to link the people closely together, they reconciled variant forms of prayer and sought to bring them into harmonious union. The well-known *Modim d'Rab-banan*, a constituent part of the *Shemoneh Esreh*, is so named because it consists of variant readings reported by a number of talmudic rabbis.

There is profound truth in the statement that from a man's prayers we can discover whether he is cultured or not. It is regrettable that the book, over which many generations have brooded and wept, has never been sufficiently appreciated as a vehicle of Jewish knowledge. People have learned to recite it by heart without giving adequate attention to its fine beauty and deep significance.

The Jewish concept of prayer is summed up as follows: "Prayer without devotion is not prayer. The man whose thoughts are wandering or occupied with other things ought not to pray. Before engaging in prayer, the worshiper ought to bring himself into a devotional frame of mind, and then he must pray quietly and with feeling, not like one who, carrying a load, unloads it and departs" (*Yad, Tefillah 4:16*). Since prayer must be regarded as "worship with the heart" (עבודה שבלב), the essential thing in prayer is designated by the sages as *kavvanah* (concentration, spirit of devotion). Hence, the proverbial saying: "Better is a little with *kavvanah* than much without it" (טוב מעט בכוונה מהרבות שלא בכוונה).

Many of our prayers are literary masterpieces with extraordinary power to elevate and to inspire. They make us intensely aware of human frailty. They keep reminding us that, according to Jewish tradition, there is no man who is absolutely free from sin and error; there are no perfect saints. Even Moses was denied admittance to the promised land because he had disobeyed a divine command.

The optimistic spirit of Judaism does not tolerate the idea that a man need ever despair and lose faith in himself. No one can sink so low that he cannot find his way back to God by self-discipline. Cheerfulness has remained a characteristic of the Jewish people until the present day.

The great poet-philosopher of twelfth-century Spain, Rabbi Yehudah Halevi writes: "Our Torah is based upon the principal emotions of man: fear, love, and joy. By each of these you may be brought into communion with God. Contriteness in the days of fasting does not bring you nearer to God than joy on Sabbaths and festivals. . . If joy in God excites you to the point of singing and dancing, it is a service to God." There is a passage in the Talmud to the effect that man will be called to account for every innocent enjoyment he has denied himself.

To be sure, the Maḥzor contains only a portion of the thirty-five thousand metrical compositions that were inspired by the synagogue services. The festival Prayerbook merely represents the kind and quality of the vast number of piyyutim that were intended to provide the worshipers with ever-new forms of religious expression and stimulating song. Much of the synagogal poetry was com-

posed by supremely gifted *hazzanim* or cantors, who pointed out
ingenious methods for the development of the Hebrew language
through a variety of new-style formations. Before long the divine
services gained an inner richness and the voice of song, which had
been silent since the destruction of the Temple, was heard once
again in the synagogue.[1]

The piyyutim were added to the old formulas of prayer in a
desire to give expression to the intense emotions and aspirations
of the people. They show us the Jewish heart laid before God in
all its moods: in penitence, in fear, in triumph. The worshiper
will always find something in the piyyutim in sympathy with his
own spiritual condition. They are adapted to old and young, and
are replete with midrashic lore conveyed in rhetorical figures.
Varied as life, their freshness is never lost.

All the youth of Israel who early learned to sing their religion
were apt to grow the most fruitfully in their faith. The singing of
hymns together planted the spirit of the Torah in their minds and
hearts forever. Most of the piyyutim are composed of biblical
phrases and midrashic interpretations. The payyetanim borrowed
language and meter from the Scriptures and drew their material
from the inexhaustible wealth of ideas dispersed in the Talmud and
Midrash. They wrote their prayer-hymns for the purpose of edify-

---

[1]The term *Mahzor*, originally designating the yearly cycle, was later
applied to the piyyutim composed for the entire cycle of the year. Finally, it
became the title of the prayerbook designed for the festivals of the year.

Though *piyyut* is derived from the Greek term for poetry, it denotes
specifically religious poetry; hence, *payyetan* signifies a liturgical poet.

Concerning the countless piyyutim yet to be found in unpublished manuscripts, Israel Davidson writes in the introduction to his *Thesaurus of Medieval
Hebrew Poetry:* "Many years will yet pass and much labor will have to be spent
before the contents of the innumerable manuscripts will be made accessible."
In his preface to the last volume of the *Thesaurus*, Davidson states that
"a rough enumeration brings up the number of poets to 2843. The religious
and secular Hebrew poems listed in Davidson's monumental work total 35,200.

ing and instructing the people. The hopes for a better future find their most eloquent expression in our liturgical poetry.

The most significant advancement of the piyyut was promoted by the ceaseless efforts of Rabbi Elazar ha-Kallir, a ḥazzan-payyetan of extensive learning who is said to have lived in Palestine during the eighth century. His numerous prayer-poems were introduced in all Jewish communities, where they were imitated by inspired payyetanim of succeeding generations.[1] The ḥazzan in the Middle Ages was often a combination of poet, composer and singer, many of whose melodies have been preserved down to our time. In the twelfth century, a famous author wrote: "If you cannot concentrate when you pray, search for melodies and choose a tune you like. Your heart will then feel what you say, for it is the song that makes your heart respond."[2]

The piyyutim have a timelessness about them that makes them the possession of each generation. They are filled with the prayers of men and women who have struggled to maintain life and turned to God in their distress. Perhaps nothing has come down to us in medieval literature that is more characteristically Jewish than these sublime utterances of the feelings of our people in many lands. Repeated expression is given in the piyyutim to the undying hope that God will finally put an end to the misfortunes and sufferings of Israel and humankind.

---

[1] Zunz informs us about the period of Rabbi Elazar ha-Kallir in the following terms: ...היה זה מנהגם של החונים לצרף אל התפלות שאמרו דברים שחברו בעצמם אחדים חיברו בקשות, שנועדו לעצמם בלבד, כדי לפתוח בהן את תפילתם... מיסדה של תקופה זו הוא ר' אלעזר בן יעקב קליר ... איש מופלא זה, שמפרטי חייו אין אנו יודעים כמעט כלום ... היה חזן בבית הכנסת, תפקיד שהיו נוהגים או לשימו לעתים קרובות, וביחוד בימי החגים, על שכמו של החכם הראשון במעלה ... שפתו הקשה של הקליר ... היא בנין ענקי, שמראהו מעלה על זכרוננו את הנפילים בני האלהים ואת תקופת הקדם המקודשת (הדרשות בישראל, pages 183-185).

[2] *Sefer Ḥasidim*, ed. Wistinetzki, page 8: חקור לך אחר ניגונים, וכשתתפלל אמור באותו ניגון שנעים ומתוק בעיניך ... ואו תתפלל בכוונה וימשך לבך אחר מוצא פיך.

Poetry seldom says directly what it means; it only hints at it under figures of speech. Some piyyutim are comparatively difficult to understand because they are couched in rare diction and allegorical terms. Quite often one is likely to miss the payyetan's thought by reason of the metaphorical imagery, conciseness and brevity, endless variations of rhyme and acrostics usually employed in the piyyut.[1] Biblical expressions are quoted at every turn, and talmudic-midrashic themes are continually intimated, so that without frequent reference to the ancient Hebrew classics the reader cannot fully appreciate the piyyutim. Once they are penetrated, they reveal themselves as immortal poems of extraordinary force. However, the best piyyutim combine simplicity and clarity and contain noble ideas about the basic problems of life on earth.

The Maḥzor contains prayer-poems which should be annotated but not translated. Such are the הוֹשַׁעֲנוֹת, replete with historical and midrashic allusions and constructed in an involved poetic fashion. They comprise many intricate acrostics and a variety of Hebrew synonyms which, if translated, are likely to create a wrong impression and confuse the reader. One of these prayer-poems is composed of an interesting alphabetic list of twenty-two Hebrew synonyms for the Temple; another presents an alphabetic description of Israel's qualities; a third enumerates types of locusts and destructive forces of nature mentioned in the Bible. It may well be said that the editions that have included the available English

---

[1]Alphabetical acrostics are quite frequent in biblical poetry. Psalms 25, 34 and 145, for example, are composed so that each verse begins with a different letter of the Hebrew alphabet in consecutive order. In Psalm 37 every other verse begins with one of the letters of the alphabet in regular order. Psalm 119 has twenty-two stanzas, each consisting of eight verses, each verse beginning with the same consecutive letter of the alphabet which forms the heading of the stanza. During the medieval period it became customary for the author to weave his name into the acrostic of his poem. The acrostic form was a practical aid to memory in the old days, before the invention of printing, when books were extremely rare and much had to be learned by heart.

translation of the *Hoshanoth* have not been enhanced by it. The *Hoshanoth* can be appreciated only in the Hebrew.

Ibn Ezra, who is best remembered for his brilliant commentary on the Bible written in the twelfth century, demands that prayer should be in lucid biblical Hebrew. He finds fault with the style of the payyetanim which is not always intelligible to those who are familiar with the language of the Bible. Belonging to the golden age of Jewish literary activity, and coming from a school of poets and philosophers quite different in spirit from Jews who studied the Talmud with greater zeal than the Bible, Ibn Ezra expresses harsh criticism of the Kallirian piyyutim which contain allusions to varied midrashic allegories and are replete with new grammatical forms based upon talmudic diction. He counsels that we should be contented with the regular ordained prayers, all of which have come down to us in simple Hebrew, instead of using piyyutim that blend old and new structures and are not easily understood.

Ibn Ezra writes: "Why should we not follow the example of king Solomon, the wisest man, whose prayer is explicitly clear? Everyone who knows Hebrew understands it, for it does not contain enigmas and allegories . . . Note how the prayers composed in ancient times . . . are free from allegoric expressions . . . Why should we not rather follow the example of the prescribed prayers, all of which are in pure Hebrew, instead of employing the dialects of the Medes, Persians, Greeks, and Arabs? . . . Our sages said: 'A literal interpretation of the Scriptures is indispensable'; if so, we ought to pray only in a literal sense and not in some mystical manner . . ."[1] In view of his strong opposition to the payyetanim and their style, it is difficult to explain why Ibn Ezra himself composed scores of piyyutim.

---

[1]Commentary on Koheleth 5:1.

Quite obviously, the poet cannot communicate his vision in ordinary language. The music of the sounds plays an important part in attuning the mind of the reader to receive the message.

II

Four times is the festival of *Shavuoth* (Weeks) mentioned in the Torah as the Feast of Weeks, referring to the forty-nine days, or seven weeks, carefully counted from the second day of *Pesaḥ* until *Shavuoth*, which occurs on the fiftieth day (Pentecost). In the Talmud, *Shavuoth* is called *Atsereth*, in the sense that it serves as a concluding festival of *Pesaḥ*. The Torah refers to *Shavuoth* as the Feast of the Harvest (*ḥag ha-katsir*) and the Day of First Fruits (*Yom ha-bikkurim*), observed by offering the best ripe produce of the field. The additional significance of *Shavuoth*, as the festival celebrating the giving of the Torah on Mount Sinai, completely overshadows the harvest significance. Milk dishes are the customary foods, symbolizing the Torah which is likened to milk, according to an allegorical interpretation of the Song of Songs (דבש וחלב תחת לשונך). In the observances of *Shavuoth*, the historical as well as the agricultural aspects are reflected. The Ten Commandments are read in the synagogue on the first day. They are preceded by the recital of the Aramaic poem *Akdamuth*, composed by Rabbi Meir ben Isaac of France, who lived in the eleventh century. The first night of the festival is spent in reading an anthology of sacred texts, known as *Tikkun Lel Shavuoth*. Plants and flowers, reminiscent of the slopes of Sinai, decorate the *bimah* (pulpit) and the *aron ha-kodesh* (holy ark). The story of Ruth, describing her acceptance of the faith of Israel during a summer harvest in Israel, is recited after *Hallel* on the second day.

"You shall count seven weeks, from the day when the sickle is first put to the standing grain. You shall then keep the Feast of Weeks in honor of the Lord your God, and the measure of your freewill offering shall be in proportion to the blessing that the Lord your God bestowed on you. You shall rejoice before the Lord your God with your son and daughter, your male and female servants, and the Levite of your community, as well as the stranger and the fatherless and the widow among you. . ." (Deuteronomy 16:9-11).

Referring to the joyous celebration of the festivals, Maimonides prescribes the following as a religious duty: "Women should have pretty clothes and trinkets bought for them, according to a man's financial means... And while one eats and drinks, it is his duty to feed the stranger, the orphan, the widow, and other poor and unfortunate people; for he who eats and drinks with his wife and family, without giving anything to eat and drink to the poor and the distressed—his meal is not a rejoicing divinely commanded, but a rejoicing of his stomach, a disgrace to those who indulge in it" (*Yad, Yom Tov 6:18*).

It is significant that the Jewish festivals are chiefly dedicated to the idea of joy. "You shall rejoice at your festival together with your son and daughter, your male and female servants, as well as the stranger, the orphan and the widow" (Deuteronomy 16:14). This rejoicing is designed to raise man above social afflictions at least during the festival days. The study of Torah has always been an essential part of festival rejoicing among our people. This intellectual joy has never degenerated into sensuality. As a result, the Jew has miraculously managed to preserve his equanimity and good humor, without which he would never have been able to rise from deep humiliation to lofty heights. The Jewish festivals are largely responsible for this miracle. Festive joy, being a religious duty, has proved a vital force in the consciousness of the Jew.

III

This Festival Prayerbook firmly abides by the wise counsel of Rabbi Judah of Regensburg, who wrote in the twelfth century: "He who copies a prayerbook . . . ought to copy every recurrent passage to the end, thereby dispensing with the worshiper's need of searching for it. . ." In this Mahzor, each of the services is arranged as a completely integrated unit so that the worshiper is not called upon to search from page to page and to commute from reference to reference. The directions are explicit, brief and to the point. The traditional text is left intact, carefully vocalized, and divided into sentences and clauses by the use of modern punctuation marks.

Every effort has been exerted to make the new translation of the Mahzor readily intelligible to the modern reader. Wherever necessary, an interpretive phrase has been inserted within square brackets, so that the reader may apprehend the thought immediately. No pronouns have been capitalized, because the frequent use of capitals makes for confusion. The example of English Bibles has been followed in this respect. The pronouns *thou* and *thee* have been retained where they are addressed to God, since they convey a more reverent feeling than the common *you*. The diction has not been allowed to reach the level of everyday English in view of the exalted literary tone of the Mahzor.

Since about the middle of the eighteenth century numerous attempts have been made to render the Mahzor into English on the basis of translations which began to appear as early as the fourteenth century. Their defects have been due largely to the word-for-word method and the evident supposition that the translator need not thoroughly understand the Hebrew text in order to translate it. On examining these versions one may detect at a glance the vast jungle of words from which a clear idea only rarely emerges.

They are the product of an age that scarcely believed help was needed or desirable for the understanding of the piyyutim, giving them to people without note or comment.

A great many editions of the Maḥzor have suffered from gross carelessness. In the first place, the Hebrew text has not been adequately provided with punctuation to indicate the logical relation of words to one another. The prayers have therefore remained unclear even to those who have a fair knowledge of Hebrew. Opinions are still divided as to the groupings of the words of one of the most popular prayers, the Kaddish.

Every student of Hebrew knows that בֶּן is not always the equivalent of *a son*. It frequently denotes age, membership in a definite class, or the possession of some quality. Similarly, אִישׁ and בַּעַל are often used interchangeably to characterize a person. Thus, אִישׁ לָשׁוֹן (Psalm 140:12) means *a slanderer*, and אִישׁ מִלְחָמָה (Exodus 15:3) *a warrior*. Hence, the rendering "the Lord is a man of war" is erroneous and nothing short of sacrilegious. "The children of thy covenant" is a mistranslation for *thy people of the covenant*. The term בַּר מִצְוָה is applied in the Talmud to every adult Israelite in the sense of *man of duty* and not "son of the commandment."[1] Similarly, בַּר דַּעַת is the counterpart of אִישׁ דַּעַת and signifies *a sensible man*. A telling argument against literalness is the awkward rendering of four Hebrew words (וּגְאָלוֹ מִיַּד חָזָק מִמֶּנּוּ): "and redeemed him from the hand of him that was stronger than he" (Jeremiah 31:10), meaning *he saved him from a stronger power*. This is typical of what has crept into the Maḥzor's translation as a result of copying from men unfamiliar with idiomatic Hebrew.

In examining the translations of the Maḥzor one encounters expressions like "As for me, may my prayer unto thee be in an acceptable time" instead of *I offer my prayer to thee at a time of grace*, alluding to the time of public worship. "The habitation of thy house," as redundant as "the tent of my house" (Psalm 132:3), simply means *thy abode* (אֹהֶל בֵּיתָ=מְעוֹן בֵּיתָ). "Answer me in the truth of thy salvation" hardly makes any sense. Proper translation would give *answer me with thy saving truth*. The word "truth" is often identical with mercy and kindness; for example, "thy kindness and thy truth shall ever preserve me" (Psalm 40:12).

Obvious errors found in current editions of the Maḥzor have been removed. Instead of לְכָל, the variant וְכָל has been adopted as the correct reading in the fifth verse of *Yigdal*. This verse is the poetic counterpart of Maimonides' fifth principle that the Creator is the only one to whom it is proper to address our prayers; hence, it is wrong to translate here: "To every creature he teacheth his greatness and his sovereignty." Through the change of a single character (וְכָל in place of לְכָל), the fifth verse of *Yigdal* corresponds exactly to the fifth principle of faith formulated by Maimonides: *Every creature must declare his greatness and his kingship;* that is, everyone must pray to God.

In the Baraitha of Rabbi Ishmael, enumerating the thirteen principles upon which the talmudic exposition of the Bible is based, the ninth principle as well as the tenth contains the word אַחֵר and not אֶחָד. The correct reading is found on the first page of *Sifra* and in some rare *Siddurim*, thus: כל דבר שהיה בכלל ויצא מן הכלל לטעון טען אחר שהוא כעניינו . . . כל דבר שהיה בכלל ויצא מן הכלל לטעון טען אחר שלא כעניינו.

Rabbi Jacob Emden of the 18th century called attention to a printer's error in the case of the parenthetical clause, "Our God and God of our fathers, be pleased with our rest," inserted in passages recited on festivals occurring on a Sabbath. Only the two words רְצֵה בִמְנוּחָתֵנוּ ("be pleased with our rest") directly apply to the Sabbath; the address to God applies to the remainder of the passage as well and should not be inserted in parentheses.

A running commentary has been provided in the present edition of the Maḥzor to explain various points of interest. Without accompanying illustrations even the best and most lucid translation cannot make clear, for example, the well-known tannaitic passage that lists the thirteen principles upon which the talmudic interpretation of the Bible is based. Included in the Maḥzor in order to complete the daily minimum of study required of every Jew, they are on the lips of countless worshipers. Yet very few have learned precisely what these important principles are, because the old translation is too obscurely worded for the student to make out its meaning.

Designed for laymen, the footnotes are written in non-technical style and contain no abbreviations. To save space they include references only to original sources which do not bear long titles.

The biblical references at the bottom of the English pages serve to indicate the central source of whatever has gone into the composition of the Maḥzor. The biblical phrases and expressions woven into the texture of the liturgical poems are indicated in the notes which, at the same time, contain biographical sketches of the authors.

PHILIP BIRNBAUM

עֵרוּב תַּבְשִׁילִין

Recited over food on the eve of a festival that is followed by a Sabbath

בָּרוּךְ אַתָּה, יְיָ אֱלֹהֵינוּ, מֶלֶךְ הָעוֹלָם, אֲשֶׁר קִדְּשָׁנוּ בְּמִצְוֹתָיו וְצִוָּנוּ עַל מִצְוַת עֵרוּב.

בְּדֵן עֵרוּבָא יְהֵא שָׁרֵא לָנָא לְמֵיפָא וּלְבַשָּׁלָא וּלְאַטְמָנָא, וּלְאַדְלָקָא שְׁרָגָא, וּלְמֶעְבַּד כָּל צָרְכָּנָא מִיּוֹמָא טָבָא לְשַׁבְּתָא, לָנוּ וּלְכָל הַדָּרִים בָּעִיר הַזֹּאת.

הַדְלָקַת נֵר שֶׁל יוֹם טוֹב

בָּרוּךְ אַתָּה, יְיָ אֱלֹהֵינוּ, מֶלֶךְ הָעוֹלָם, אֲשֶׁר קִדְּשָׁנוּ בְּמִצְוֹתָיו וְצִוָּנוּ לְהַדְלִיק נֵר שֶׁל (שַׁבָּת וְשֶׁל) יוֹם טוֹב.

בָּרוּךְ אַתָּה, יְיָ אֱלֹהֵינוּ, מֶלֶךְ הָעוֹלָם, שֶׁהֶחֱיָנוּ וְקִיְּמָנוּ וְהִגִּיעָנוּ לַזְּמַן הַזֶּה.

PARENTAL BLESSING

For daughters:

יְשִׂמֵךְ אֱלֹהִים כְּשָׂרָה, רִבְקָה, רָחֵל וְלֵאָה.

For sons:

יְשִׂמְךָ אֱלֹהִים כְּאֶפְרַיִם וְכִמְנַשֶּׁה.

יְבָרֶכְךָ יְיָ וְיִשְׁמְרֶךָ. יָאֵר יְיָ פָּנָיו אֵלֶיךָ וִיחֻנֶּךָ. יִשָּׂא יְיָ פָּנָיו אֵלֶיךָ, וְיָשֵׂם לְךָ שָׁלוֹם.

עֵרוּב תבשילין ("mixture of dishes") renders it permissible to prepare food on a holy day for use on the Sabbath which immediately follows it. The permission to prepare food on holy days is restricted to food required for those days; but if the preparation was begun before the holy day, it may be continued on the holy day itself. This is accomplished by symbolically singling out food for the Sabbath on the eve of the festival.

2

ERUV TAVSHILIN

Recited over food on the eve of a festival that is followed by a Sabbath

Blessed art thou, Lord our God, King of the universe, who hast sanctified us with thy commandments, and commanded us concerning the observance of *eruv*.

By means of this *eruv* may we be permitted to bake, cook, keep dishes warm, light Sabbath lights, and prepare during the festival all we need for the Sabbath—we and all Israelites that live in this town.

LIGHTING THE FESTIVAL LIGHTS

Blessed art thou, Lord our God, King of the universe, who hast sanctified us with thy commandments, and commanded us to light (the Sabbath and) the festival lights.

Blessed art thou, Lord our God, King of the universe, who hast granted us life and sustenance and permitted us to reach this season.

PARENTAL BLESSING

For sons:
May God make you like Ephraim and like Manasseh.

For daughters:
May God make you like Sarah and Rebekah, Rachel and Leah.

May the Lord bless you and protect you; may the Lord countenance you and be gracious to you; may the Lord favor you and grant you peace.[1]

ברכת הורים, the blessing of children by their parents on all important occasions, notably on the eve of Sabbath and festivals, is one of the most beautiful customs. The *Brantspiegel*, a treatise on morals published in 1602, mentions this in the following terms: "Before the children can walk they should be carried on Sabbaths and festivals to the father and mother to be blessed; after they are able to walk they shall go of their own accord with bowed body and shall incline their heads and receive the blessing." This custom has linked the generations together in mutual loyalty and affection.

[1] *Numbers* 6:24–26.

תְּפִלַּת מִנְחָה לְעֶרֶב יוֹם טוֹב

אַשְׁרֵי יוֹשְׁבֵי בֵיתֶךָ; עוֹד יְהַלְלוּךָ סֶּלָה.
אַשְׁרֵי הָעָם שֶׁכָּכָה לוֹ; אַשְׁרֵי הָעָם שֶׁיְיָ אֱלֹהָיו.

תהלים קמה

תְּהִלָּה לְדָוִד

אֲרוֹמִמְךָ, אֱלֹהַי הַמֶּלֶךְ, וַאֲבָרְכָה שִׁמְךָ לְעוֹלָם וָעֶד.

בְּכָל יוֹם אֲבָרְכֶךָ, וַאֲהַלְלָה שִׁמְךָ לְעוֹלָם וָעֶד.

גָּדוֹל יְיָ וּמְהֻלָּל מְאֹד, וְלִגְדֻלָּתוֹ אֵין חֵקֶר.

דּוֹר לְדוֹר יְשַׁבַּח מַעֲשֶׂיךָ, וּגְבוּרֹתֶיךָ יַגִּידוּ.

הֲדַר כְּבוֹד הוֹדֶךָ וְדִבְרֵי נִפְלְאֹתֶיךָ אָשִׂיחָה.

וֶעֱזוּז נוֹרְאוֹתֶיךָ יֹאמֵרוּ, וּגְדֻלָּתְךָ אֲסַפְּרֶנָּה.

זֵכֶר רַב טוּבְךָ יַבִּיעוּ, וְצִדְקָתְךָ יְרַנֵּנוּ.

חַנּוּן וְרַחוּם יְיָ, אֶרֶךְ אַפַּיִם וּגְדָל־חָסֶד.

טוֹב יְיָ לַכֹּל, וְרַחֲמָיו עַל כָּל מַעֲשָׂיו.

יוֹדוּךָ יְיָ כָּל מַעֲשֶׂיךָ, וַחֲסִידֶיךָ יְבָרְכוּכָה.

מנחה occurs in the Bible frequently in the sense of "gift" and "meal-offering." It is only in talmudic literature that *Minḥah* denotes afternoon service. *Minḥah* is one of the three daily services mentioned in Daniel 6:11 ("and three times a day he kneeled upon his knees, praying and giving thanks before his God"). According to tradition, the patriarchs Abraham, Isaac and Jacob were the authors of the three daily services. Both *Shaḥarith* and *Minḥah* correspond to the daily sacrifice (*Tamid*) which was offered in the Temple in the morning and in the afternoon. Since the recital of the *Shema* is obligatory only "when you lie down and when you rise up," it is not included in the

4

AFTERNOON SERVICE—EREV YOM TOV

Happy are those who dwell in thy house; they are ever praising thee. Happy the people that is so situated; happy the people whose God is the Lord.[1]

Psalm 145

A hymn of praise by David.

I extol thee, my God the King,
And bless thy name forever and ever.
Every day I bless thee,
And praise thy name forever and ever.
Great is the Lord and most worthy of praise;
His greatness is unsearchable.
One generation to another praises thy works;
They recount thy mighty acts.
On the splendor of thy glorious majesty
And on thy wondrous deeds I meditate.
They speak of thy awe-inspiring might,
And I tell of thy greatness.
They spread the fame of thy great goodness,
And sing of thy righteousness.
Gracious and merciful is the Lord,
Slow to anger and of great kindness.
The Lord is good to all,
And his mercy is over all his works.
All thy works praise thee, O Lord,
And thy faithful followers bless thee.

---

afternoon service. *Minḥah* may be recited at any time from noon (12:30) to sunset. The *Minḥah* service was postponed in the nineteenth century to very near sunset for the sake of convenience, so that *Minḥah* might be followed by *Ma'ariv* after a short interval.

[1] *Psalms* 84:5; 144:15.

כְּבוֹד מַלְכוּתְךָ יֹאמֵרוּ, וּגְבוּרָתְךָ יְדַבֵּרוּ.

לְהוֹדִיעַ לִבְנֵי הָאָדָם גְּבוּרֹתָיו, וּכְבוֹד הֲדַר מַלְכוּתוֹ.

מַלְכוּתְךָ מַלְכוּת כָּל עֹלָמִים, וּמֶמְשַׁלְתְּךָ בְּכָל דּוֹר וָדֹר.

סוֹמֵךְ יְיָ לְכָל הַנֹּפְלִים, וְזוֹקֵף לְכָל הַכְּפוּפִים.

עֵינֵי כֹל אֵלֶיךָ יְשַׂבֵּרוּ, וְאַתָּה נוֹתֵן לָהֶם אֶת אָכְלָם בְּעִתּוֹ.

פּוֹתֵחַ אֶת יָדֶךָ, וּמַשְׂבִּיעַ לְכָל חַי רָצוֹן.

צַדִּיק יְיָ בְּכָל דְּרָכָיו, וְחָסִיד בְּכָל מַעֲשָׂיו.

קָרוֹב יְיָ לְכָל קֹרְאָיו, לְכֹל אֲשֶׁר יִקְרָאֻהוּ בֶאֱמֶת.

רְצוֹן יְרֵאָיו יַעֲשֶׂה, וְאֶת שַׁוְעָתָם יִשְׁמַע וְיוֹשִׁיעֵם.

שׁוֹמֵר יְיָ אֶת כָּל אֹהֲבָיו, וְאֵת כָּל הָרְשָׁעִים יַשְׁמִיד.

תְּהִלַּת יְיָ יְדַבֶּר־פִּי; וִיבָרֵךְ כָּל בָּשָׂר שֵׁם קָדְשׁוֹ לְעוֹלָם וָעֶד.

Reader וַאֲנַחְנוּ נְבָרֵךְ יָהּ מֵעַתָּה וְעַד עוֹלָם; הַלְלוּיָהּ.

Reader:

יִתְגַּדַּל וְיִתְקַדַּשׁ שְׁמֵהּ רַבָּא בְּעָלְמָא דִּי בְרָא כִרְעוּתֵהּ;
וְיַמְלִיךְ מַלְכוּתֵהּ בְּחַיֵּיכוֹן וּבְיוֹמֵיכוֹן, וּבְחַיֵּי דְכָל בֵּית יִשְׂרָאֵל,
בַּעֲגָלָא וּבִזְמַן קָרִיב, וְאִמְרוּ אָמֵן.

יְהֵא שְׁמֵהּ רַבָּא מְבָרַךְ לְעָלַם וּלְעָלְמֵי עָלְמַיָּא.

יִתְבָּרַךְ וְיִשְׁתַּבַּח, וְיִתְפָּאַר וְיִתְרוֹמַם, וְיִתְנַשֵּׂא וְיִתְהַדָּר,
וְיִתְעַלֶּה וְיִתְהַלָּל שְׁמֵהּ דְּקֻדְשָׁא, בְּרִיךְ הוּא, לְעֵלָּא מִן כָּל
בִּרְכָתָא וְשִׁירָתָא, תֻּשְׁבְּחָתָא וְנֶחֱמָתָא, דַּאֲמִירָן בְּעָלְמָא,
וְאִמְרוּ אָמֵן.

אשרי The first two verses, which are taken from Psalms 84:5 and 144:15 and prefixed to Psalm 145, contain the word אשרי three times. *Ashre* is recited twice in the morning service and once in the afternoon service. The Talmud asserts that "whoever recites this psalm three times a day is assured of his share in the world to come" (Berakhoth 4b). This noble hymn of praise, calling upon all mankind to glorify God's greatness, celebrates his providential care

They speak of thy glorious kingdom,
And talk of thy might,
To let men know thy mighty deeds,
And the glorious splendor of thy kingdom.
Thy kingdom is a kingdom of all ages,
And thy dominion is for all generations.
The Lord upholds all who fall,
And raises all who are bowed down.
The eyes of all look hopefully to thee,
And thou givest them their food in due season.
Thou openest thy hand,
And satisfiest every living thing with favor.
The Lord is righteous in all his ways,
And gracious in all his deeds.
The Lord is near to all who call upon him,
To all who call upon him sincerely.
He fulfills the desire of those who revere him;
He hears their cry and saves them.
The Lord preserves all who love him,
But all the wicked he destroys.
My mouth speaks the praise of the Lord;
Let all creatures bless his holy name forever and ever.
   [1]We will bless the Lord henceforth and forever.
   Praise the Lord!

Reader:

Glorified and sanctified be God's great name throughout the world which he has created according to his will. May he establish his kingdom in your lifetime and during your days, and within the life of the entire house of Israel, speedily and soon; and say, Amen.

May his great name be blessed forever and to all eternity.

Blessed and praised, glorified and exalted, extolled and honored, adored and lauded be the name of the Holy One, blessed be he, beyond all the blessings and hymns, praises and consolations that are ever spoken in the world; and say, Amen.

---

for all his creation. It is an acrostic psalm, the successive lines beginning with the letters of the Hebrew alphabet taken in order. However, the letter *nun* is missing. The alphabetic arrangement is probably intended as an aid to memory.

---

[1] *Psalm* 115:18.

The *Shemoneh Esreh* is recited in silent devotion while standing, facing east.
The Reader repeats the *Shemoneh Esreh* aloud when a *minyan* holds service.

כִּי שֵׁם יְיָ אֶקְרָא, הָבוּ גֹדֶל לֵאלֹהֵינוּ.

אֲדֹנָי, שְׂפָתַי תִּפְתָּח, וּפִי יַגִּיד תְּהִלָּתֶךָ.

בָּרוּךְ אַתָּה, יְיָ אֱלֹהֵינוּ וֵאלֹהֵי אֲבוֹתֵינוּ, אֱלֹהֵי אַבְרָהָם,
אֱלֹהֵי יִצְחָק, וֵאלֹהֵי יַעֲקֹב, הָאֵל הַגָּדוֹל הַגִּבּוֹר וְהַנּוֹרָא, אֵל
עֶלְיוֹן, גּוֹמֵל חֲסָדִים טוֹבִים, וְקוֹנֵה הַכֹּל, וְזוֹכֵר חַסְדֵי אָבוֹת,
וּמֵבִיא גוֹאֵל לִבְנֵי בְנֵיהֶם לְמַעַן שְׁמוֹ בְּאַהֲבָה.

מֶלֶךְ עוֹזֵר וּמוֹשִׁיעַ וּמָגֵן. בָּרוּךְ אַתָּה, יְיָ, מָגֵן אַבְרָהָם.

אַתָּה גִּבּוֹר לְעוֹלָם, אֲדֹנָי; מְחַיֵּה מֵתִים אַתָּה, רַב לְהוֹשִׁיעַ.

מְכַלְכֵּל חַיִּים בְּחֶסֶד, מְחַיֵּה מֵתִים בְּרַחֲמִים רַבִּים, סוֹמֵךְ
נוֹפְלִים, וְרוֹפֵא חוֹלִים, וּמַתִּיר אֲסוּרִים, וּמְקַיֵּם אֱמוּנָתוֹ לִישֵׁנֵי
עָפָר. מִי כָמוֹךָ, בַּעַל גְּבוּרוֹת, וּמִי דוֹמֶה לָךְ, מֶלֶךְ מֵמִית
וּמְחַיֶּה וּמַצְמִיחַ יְשׁוּעָה.

וְנֶאֱמָן אַתָּה לְהַחֲיוֹת מֵתִים. בָּרוּךְ אַתָּה, יְיָ, מְחַיֵּה הַמֵּתִים.

When the Reader repeats the *Shemoneh Esreh*, the following *Kedushah* is said.

נְקַדֵּשׁ אֶת שִׁמְךָ בָּעוֹלָם כְּשֵׁם שֶׁמַּקְדִּישִׁים אוֹתוֹ בִּשְׁמֵי מָרוֹם,
כַּכָּתוּב עַל יַד נְבִיאֶךָ: וְקָרָא זֶה אֶל זֶה וְאָמַר:

שמונה עשרה is spoken of in the Talmud as *Tefillah*, the prayer par excellence, on account of its importance and its antiquity. According to tradition,
it was drawn up by the men of the Great Assembly. Originally, the *Shemoneh
Esreh* consisted of eighteen blessings; in its present form, however, there are
nineteen. The addition of the paragraph concerning the slanderers was made

Afternoon Service

SHEMONEH ESREH

The Shemoneh Esreh is recited in silent devotion while standing, facing east.
The Reader repeats the Shemoneh Esreh aloud when a minyan holds service.

When I proclaim the name of the Lord, give glory to our God![1]

O Lord, open thou my lips, that my mouth may declare thy praise.[2]

Blessed art thou, Lord our God and God of our fathers, God of Abraham, God of Isaac and God of Jacob; great, mighty and revered God, sublime God, who bestowest lovingkindness, and art Master of all things; who rememberest the good deeds of our fathers, and who wilt graciously bring a redeemer to their children's children for the sake of thy name.

O King, Supporter, Savior and Shield. Blessed art thou, O Lord, Shield of Abraham.

Thou, O Lord, art mighty forever; thou revivest the dead; thou art powerful to save.

Thou sustainest the living with kindness, and revivest the dead with great mercy; thou supportest all who fall, and healest the sick; thou settest the captives free, and keepest faith with those who sleep in the dust. Who is like thee, Lord of power? Who resembles thee, O King? Thou bringest death and restorest life, and causest salvation to flourish.

Thou art faithful to revive the dead. Blessed art thou, O Lord, who revivest the dead.

KEDUSHAH

When the Reader repeats the Shemoneh Esreh, the following Kedushah is said.

We sanctify thy name in this world even as they sanctify it in the highest heavens, as it is written by thy prophet: "They keep calling to one another:

---

toward the end of the first century at the direction of Rabban Gamaliel II, head of the Sanhedrin of Yavneh. The Talmud offers a variety of reasons for the number eighteen. It corresponds to the eighteen times God is mentioned in Psalm 29 as well as in the *Shema*. The three patriarchs Abraham, Isaac and Jacob are mentioned eighteen times in the Bible. This number also corresponds to the eighteen vertebrae of the spinal column (Berakhoth 28b).

[1] *Deuteronomy* 32:3.   [2] *Psalm* 51:17.

קָדוֹשׁ, קָדוֹשׁ, קָדוֹשׁ יְיָ צְבָאוֹת; מְלֹא כָל הָאָרֶץ כְּבוֹדוֹ.

לְעֻמָּתָם בָּרוּךְ יֹאמֵרוּ—

בָּרוּךְ כְּבוֹד יְיָ מִמְּקוֹמוֹ.

וּבְדִבְרֵי קָדְשְׁךָ כָּתוּב לֵאמֹר:

יִמְלֹךְ יְיָ לְעוֹלָם, אֱלֹהַיִךְ צִיּוֹן לְדֹר וָדֹר; הַלְלוּיָהּ.

Reader לְדוֹר וָדוֹר נַגִּיד גָּדְלֶךָ, וּלְנֵצַח נְצָחִים קְדֻשָּׁתְךָ נַקְדִּישׁ, וְשִׁבְחֲךָ אֱלֹהֵינוּ מִפִּינוּ לֹא יָמוּשׁ לְעוֹלָם וָעֶד, כִּי אֵל מֶלֶךְ גָּדוֹל וְקָדוֹשׁ אָתָּה. בָּרוּךְ אַתָּה, יְיָ, הָאֵל הַקָּדוֹשׁ.

אַתָּה קָדוֹשׁ וְשִׁמְךָ קָדוֹשׁ, וּקְדוֹשִׁים בְּכָל יוֹם יְהַלְלוּךָ סֶּלָה. בָּרוּךְ אַתָּה, יְיָ, הָאֵל הַקָּדוֹשׁ.

אַתָּה חוֹנֵן לְאָדָם דַּעַת, וּמְלַמֵּד לֶאֱנוֹשׁ בִּינָה. חָנֵּנוּ מֵאִתְּךָ דֵעָה, בִּינָה וְהַשְׂכֵּל. בָּרוּךְ אַתָּה, יְיָ, חוֹנֵן הַדָּעַת.

הֲשִׁיבֵנוּ אָבִינוּ לְתוֹרָתֶךָ, וְקָרְבֵנוּ מַלְכֵּנוּ לַעֲבוֹדָתֶךָ; וְהַחֲזִירֵנוּ בִּתְשׁוּבָה שְׁלֵמָה לְפָנֶיךָ. בָּרוּךְ אַתָּה, יְיָ, הָרוֹצֶה בִּתְשׁוּבָה.

סְלַח לָנוּ אָבִינוּ כִּי חָטָאנוּ, מְחַל לָנוּ מַלְכֵּנוּ כִּי פָשָׁעְנוּ, כִּי מוֹחֵל וְסוֹלֵחַ אָתָּה. בָּרוּךְ אַתָּה, יְיָ, חַנּוּן הַמַּרְבֶּה לִסְלֹחַ.

רְאֵה נָא בְעָנְיֵנוּ וְרִיבָה רִיבֵנוּ, וּגְאָלֵנוּ מְהֵרָה לְמַעַן שְׁמֶךָ, כִּי גוֹאֵל חָזָק אָתָּה. בָּרוּךְ אַתָּה, יְיָ, גּוֹאֵל יִשְׂרָאֵל.

קדושה, to which the Talmud (Sotah 49a) attaches unusual importance, is recited only when a *minyan* is present because it is said: "I shall be sanctified

> Holy, holy, holy is the Lord of hosts;
> The whole earth is full of his glory."[1]

Those opposite them say: Blessed—
Blessed be the glory of the Lord from his abode.[2]
And in thy holy Scriptures it is written:

> The Lord shall reign forever,
> Your God, O Zion, for all generations.
> Praise the Lord![3]

Reader:

Through all generations we will declare thy greatness; to all eternity we will proclaim thy holiness; thy praise, our God, shall never depart from our mouth, for thou art a great and holy God and King. Blessed art thou, O Lord, holy God.

———

Thou art holy and thy name is holy, and holy beings praise thee daily. Blessed art thou, O Lord, holy God.

Thou favorest man with knowledge, and teachest mortals understanding. O grant us knowledge, understanding and insight. Blessed art thou, O Lord, gracious Giver of knowledge.

Restore us, our Father, to thy Torah; draw us near, our King, to thy service; cause us to return to thee in perfect repentance. Blessed art thou, O Lord, who art pleased with repentance.

Forgive us, our Father, for we have sinned; pardon us, our King, for we have transgressed; for thou dost pardon and forgive. Blessed art thou, O Lord, who art gracious and ever forgiving.

Look upon our affliction and champion our cause; redeem us speedily for thy name's sake, for thou art a mighty Redeemer. Blessed art thou, O Lord, Redeemer of Israel.

among the children of Israel" (Leviticus 22:32), which implies that the proclamation of the holiness and kingship of God is to be made in public service only.

[1] *Isaiah* 6:3.   [2] *Ezekiel* 3:12.   [3] *Psalm* 146:10.

רְפָאֵנוּ יְיָ וְנֵרָפֵא, הוֹשִׁיעֵנוּ וְנִוָּשֵׁעָה, כִּי תְהִלָּתֵנוּ אָתָּה; וְהַעֲלֵה רְפוּאָה שְׁלֵמָה לְכָל מַכּוֹתֵינוּ, כִּי אֵל מֶלֶךְ רוֹפֵא נֶאֱמָן וְרַחֲמָן אָתָּה. בָּרוּךְ אַתָּה, יְיָ, רוֹפֵא חוֹלֵי עַמּוֹ יִשְׂרָאֵל.

בָּרֵךְ עָלֵינוּ, יְיָ אֱלֹהֵינוּ, אֶת הַשָּׁנָה הַזֹּאת וְאֶת כָּל מִינֵי תְבוּאָתָהּ לְטוֹבָה, וְתֵן בְּרָכָה עַל פְּנֵי הָאֲדָמָה, וְשַׂבְּעֵנוּ מִטּוּבֶךָ, וּבָרֵךְ שְׁנָתֵנוּ כַּשָּׁנִים הַטּוֹבוֹת. בָּרוּךְ אַתָּה, יְיָ, מְבָרֵךְ הַשָּׁנִים.

תְּקַע בְּשׁוֹפָר גָּדוֹל לְחֵרוּתֵנוּ, וְשָׂא נֵס לְקַבֵּץ גָּלֻיּוֹתֵינוּ, וְקַבְּצֵנוּ יַחַד מֵאַרְבַּע כַּנְפוֹת הָאָרֶץ. בָּרוּךְ אַתָּה, יְיָ, מְקַבֵּץ נִדְחֵי עַמּוֹ יִשְׂרָאֵל.

הָשִׁיבָה שׁוֹפְטֵינוּ כְּבָרִאשׁוֹנָה, וְיוֹעֲצֵינוּ כְּבַתְּחִלָּה; וְהָסֵר מִמֶּנּוּ יָגוֹן וַאֲנָחָה; וּמְלוֹךְ עָלֵינוּ, אַתָּה יְיָ לְבַדְּךָ, בְּחֶסֶד וּבְרַחֲמִים, וְצַדְּקֵנוּ בַּמִּשְׁפָּט. בָּרוּךְ אַתָּה, יְיָ, מֶלֶךְ אוֹהֵב צְדָקָה וּמִשְׁפָּט.

וְלַמַּלְשִׁינִים אַל תְּהִי תִקְוָה, וְכָל הָרִשְׁעָה כְּרֶגַע תֹּאבֵד, וְכָל אוֹיְבֶיךָ מְהֵרָה יִכָּרֵתוּ, וְהַזֵּדִים מְהֵרָה תְעַקֵּר וּתְשַׁבֵּר וּתְמַגֵּר וְתַכְנִיעַ בִּמְהֵרָה בְיָמֵינוּ. בָּרוּךְ אַתָּה, יְיָ, שׁוֹבֵר אוֹיְבִים וּמַכְנִיעַ זֵדִים.

עַל הַצַּדִּיקִים וְעַל הַחֲסִידִים, וְעַל זִקְנֵי עַמְּךָ בֵּית יִשְׂרָאֵל וְעַל פְּלֵיטַת סוֹפְרֵיהֶם, וְעַל גֵּרֵי הַצֶּדֶק וְעָלֵינוּ, יֶהֱמוּ נָא רַחֲמֶיךָ, יְיָ אֱלֹהֵינוּ; וְתֵן שָׂכָר טוֹב לְכָל הַבּוֹטְחִים בְּשִׁמְךָ בֶּאֱמֶת, וְשִׂים חֶלְקֵנוּ עִמָּהֶם, וּלְעוֹלָם לֹא נֵבוֹשׁ, כִּי בְךָ בָּטָחְנוּ. בָּרוּךְ אַתָּה, יְיָ, מִשְׁעָן וּמִבְטָח לַצַּדִּיקִים.

Heal us, O Lord, and we shall be healed; save us and we shall be saved; for thou art our praise. Grant a perfect healing to all our ills and wounds; for thou art a faithful and merciful God, King and Healer. Blessed art thou, O Lord, who healest the sick among thy people Israel.

Bless for us, Lord our God, this year and all its varied produce for the best. Bestow a blessing upon the face of the earth. Satisfy us with its goodness, and bless our year with the prosperity of good years, for thou art the good and beneficent God who dost bless the years. Blessed art thou, O Lord, who blessest the years.

Sound the great shofar for our freedom; lift up the banner to bring our exiles together; assemble us speedily from the four corners of the earth into our land. Blessed art thou, O Lord, who gatherest the dispersed of thy people Israel.

Restore our judges as at first, and our counselors as at the beginning; remove from us sorrow and sighing; reign thou alone over us speedily, O Lord, in kindness and mercy; clear us in righteousness and in justice. Blessed art thou, O Lord, who lovest righteousness and justice.

May the slanderers have no hope; may all wickedness perish instantly; may all thy enemies be soon cut down. Do thou speedily uproot and crush the arrogant; cast them down and humble them speedily in our days. Blessed art thou, O Lord, who breakest the enemies and humblest the arrogant.

May thy compassion, Lord our God, be aroused over the righteous and over the godly; over the leaders of thy people, the house of Israel, and over the remnant of their sages; over the true proselytes and over us. Grant a goodly reward to all who truly trust in thy name, and place our lot among them; may we never come to shame, for in thee we trust and on thy great kindness we faithfully rely. Blessed art thou, O Lord, who art the stay and trust of the righteous.

וְלִירוּשָׁלַיִם עִירְךָ בְּרַחֲמִים תָּשׁוּב, וְתִשְׁכּוֹן בְּתוֹכָהּ כַּאֲשֶׁר דִּבַּרְתָּ; וּבְנֵה אוֹתָהּ בְּקָרוֹב בְּיָמֵינוּ בִּנְיַן עוֹלָם; וְכִסֵּא דָוִד מְהֵרָה לְתוֹכָהּ תָּכִין. בָּרוּךְ אַתָּה, יְיָ, בּוֹנֵה יְרוּשָׁלָיִם.

אֶת צֶמַח דָּוִד עַבְדְּךָ מְהֵרָה תַצְמִיחַ, וְקַרְנוֹ תָּרוּם בִּישׁוּעָתֶךָ, כִּי לִישׁוּעָתְךָ קִוִּינוּ כָּל הַיּוֹם. בָּרוּךְ אַתָּה, יְיָ, מַצְמִיחַ קֶרֶן יְשׁוּעָה.

שְׁמַע קוֹלֵנוּ, יְיָ אֱלֹהֵינוּ; חוּס וְרַחֵם עָלֵינוּ, וְקַבֵּל בְּרַחֲמִים וּבְרָצוֹן אֶת תְּפִלָּתֵנוּ, כִּי אֵל שׁוֹמֵעַ תְּפִלּוֹת וְתַחֲנוּנִים אָתָּה; וּמִלְּפָנֶיךָ מַלְכֵּנוּ רֵיקָם אַל תְּשִׁיבֵנוּ, כִּי אַתָּה שׁוֹמֵעַ תְּפִלַּת עַמְּךָ יִשְׂרָאֵל בְּרַחֲמִים. בָּרוּךְ אַתָּה, יְיָ, שׁוֹמֵעַ תְּפִלָּה.

רְצֵה, יְיָ אֱלֹהֵינוּ, בְּעַמְּךָ יִשְׂרָאֵל וּבִתְפִלָּתָם; וְהָשֵׁב אֶת הָעֲבוֹדָה לִדְבִיר בֵּיתֶךָ, וְאִשֵּׁי יִשְׂרָאֵל וּתְפִלָּתָם בְּאַהֲבָה תְקַבֵּל בְּרָצוֹן, וּתְהִי לְרָצוֹן תָּמִיד עֲבוֹדַת יִשְׂרָאֵל עַמֶּךָ.

וְתֶחֱזֶינָה עֵינֵינוּ בְּשׁוּבְךָ לְצִיּוֹן בְּרַחֲמִים. בָּרוּךְ אַתָּה, יְיָ, הַמַּחֲזִיר שְׁכִינָתוֹ לְצִיּוֹן.

מוֹדִים אֲנַחְנוּ לָךְ, שָׁאַתָּה הוּא יְיָ אֱלֹהֵינוּ וֵאלֹהֵי אֲבוֹתֵינוּ לְעוֹלָם וָעֶד. צוּר חַיֵּינוּ, מָגֵן יִשְׁעֵנוּ אַתָּה הוּא. לְדוֹר וָדוֹר נוֹדֶה לְךָ, וּנְסַפֵּר תְּהִלָּתֶךָ, עַל חַיֵּינוּ הַמְּסוּרִים בְּיָדֶךָ, וְעַל נִשְׁמוֹתֵינוּ הַפְּקוּדוֹת לָךְ, וְעַל

When the Reader repeats the *Shemoneh Esreh*, the Congregation responds here by saying:

(מוֹדִים אֲנַחְנוּ לָךְ, שָׁאַתָּה הוּא יְיָ אֱלֹהֵינוּ וֵאלֹהֵי אֲבוֹתֵינוּ. אֱלֹהֵי כָל בָּשָׂר, יוֹצְרֵנוּ, יוֹצֵר בְּרֵאשִׁית. בְּרָכוֹת וְהוֹדָאוֹת לְשִׁמְךָ הַגָּדוֹל וְהַקָּדוֹשׁ עַל שֶׁהֶחֱיִיתָנוּ

מוֹדִים is based on נוֹדֶה לְךָ לְעוֹלָם, לְדוֹר וָדוֹר נְסַפֵּר תְּהִלָתֶךָ (Psalms 79:13; 55:18). אָשִׂיחָה

Return in mercy to thy city Jerusalem and dwell in it, as thou hast promised; rebuild it soon, in our days, as an everlasting structure, and speedily establish in it the throne of David. Blessed art thou, O Lord, Builder of Jerusalem.

Speedily cause the offspring of thy servant David to flourish, and let his glory be exalted by thy help, for we hope for thy deliverance all day. Blessed art thou, O Lord, who causest salvation to flourish.

Hear our voice, Lord our God; spare us and have pity on us; accept our prayer in mercy and favor, for thou art God who hearest prayers and supplications; from thy presence, our King, dismiss us not empty-handed, for thou hearest in mercy the prayer of thy people Israel. Blessed art thou, O Lord, who hearest prayer.

Be pleased, Lord our God, with thy people Israel and with their prayer; restore the worship to thy most holy sanctuary; accept Israel's offerings and prayer with gracious love. May the worship of thy people Israel be ever pleasing to thee.

May our eyes behold thy return in mercy to Zion. Blessed art thou, O Lord, who restorest thy divine presence to Zion.

We ever thank thee, who art the Lord our God and the God of our fathers. Thou art the strength of our life and our saving shield. In every generation we will thank thee and recount thy praise—for our lives which are in thy charge, for our souls which are in thy care, for thy miracles which are

When the Reader repeats the Shemoneh Esreh, the Congregation responds here by saying:

(We thank thee, who art the Lord our God and the God of our fathers. God of all mankind, our Creator and Creator of the universe, blessings and thanks are due to thy great and holy name, because thou hast kept us alive and sustained us; mayest

מודים דרבנן, recited by the Congregation in an undertone while the Reader repeats aloud the eighteenth benediction, is a composite of several phrases suggested by a number of talmudic rabbis (Sotah 40a).

נְסֶיךָ שֶׁבְּכָל יוֹם עִמָּנוּ, וְעַל | וְקִיַּמְתָּנוּ. כֵּן תְּחַיֵּנוּ וּתְקַיְּמֵנוּ,
נִפְלְאוֹתֶיךָ וְטוֹבוֹתֶיךָ שֶׁבְּכָל | וְתֶאֱסוֹף גָּלֻיּוֹתֵינוּ לְחַצְרוֹת
עֵת, עֶרֶב וָבֹקֶר וְצָהֳרָיִם. | קָדְשֶׁךָ לִשְׁמוֹר חֻקֶּיךָ וְלַעֲשׂוֹת
הַטּוֹב כִּי לֹא כָלוּ רַחֲמֶיךָ, | רְצוֹנֶךָ, וּלְעָבְדְּךָ בְּלֵבָב
וְהַמְרַחֵם כִּי לֹא תַמּוּ חֲסָדֶיךָ, | שָׁלֵם, עַל שֶׁאֲנַחְנוּ מוֹדִים לָךְ.
מֵעוֹלָם קִוִּינוּ לָךְ. | בָּרוּךְ אֵל הַהוֹדָאוֹת.)

וְעַל כֻּלָּם יִתְבָּרַךְ וְיִתְרוֹמַם שִׁמְךָ, מַלְכֵּנוּ, תָּמִיד לְעוֹלָם
וָעֶד.

וְכֹל הַחַיִּים יוֹדוּךָ סֶּלָה, וִיהַלְלוּ אֶת שִׁמְךָ בֶּאֱמֶת, הָאֵל,
יְשׁוּעָתֵנוּ וְעֶזְרָתֵנוּ סֶּלָה. בָּרוּךְ אַתָּה, יְיָ, הַטּוֹב שִׁמְךָ, וּלְךָ נָאֶה
לְהוֹדוֹת.

שָׁלוֹם רָב עַל יִשְׂרָאֵל עַמְּךָ תָּשִׂים לְעוֹלָם, כִּי אַתָּה הוּא
מֶלֶךְ אָדוֹן לְכָל הַשָּׁלוֹם, וְטוֹב בְּעֵינֶיךָ לְבָרֵךְ אֶת עַמְּךָ יִשְׂרָאֵל
בְּכָל עֵת וּבְכָל שָׁעָה בִּשְׁלוֹמֶךָ. בָּרוּךְ אַתָּה, יְיָ, הַמְבָרֵךְ אֶת
עַמּוֹ יִשְׂרָאֵל בַּשָּׁלוֹם.

After the *Shemoneh Esreh* add the following meditation:

אֱלֹהַי, נְצֹר לְשׁוֹנִי מֵרָע, וּשְׂפָתַי מִדַּבֵּר מִרְמָה; וְלִמְקַלְלַי
נַפְשִׁי תִדּוֹם, וְנַפְשִׁי כֶּעָפָר לַכֹּל תִּהְיֶה. פְּתַח לִבִּי בְּתוֹרָתֶךָ,
וּבְמִצְוֹתֶיךָ תִּרְדּוֹף נַפְשִׁי; וְכָל הַחוֹשְׁבִים עָלַי רָעָה, מְהֵרָה
הָפֵר עֲצָתָם וְקַלְקֵל מַחֲשַׁבְתָּם. עֲשֵׂה לְמַעַן שְׁמֶךָ, עֲשֵׂה לְמַעַן
יְמִינֶךָ, עֲשֵׂה לְמַעַן קְדֻשָּׁתֶךָ, עֲשֵׂה לְמַעַן תּוֹרָתֶךָ. לְמַעַן יֵחָלְצוּן
יְדִידֶיךָ, הוֹשִׁיעָה יְמִינְךָ וַעֲנֵנִי. יִהְיוּ לְרָצוֹן אִמְרֵי פִי וְהֶגְיוֹן לִבִּי
לְפָנֶיךָ, יְיָ, צוּרִי וְגוֹאֲלִי. עֹשֶׂה שָׁלוֹם בִּמְרוֹמָיו, הוּא יַעֲשֶׂה
שָׁלוֹם עָלֵינוּ וְעַל כָּל יִשְׂרָאֵל, וְאִמְרוּ אָמֵן.

daily with us, and for thy continual wonders and favors—evening, morning and noon. Beneficent One, whose mercies never fail, Merciful One, whose kindnesses never cease, thou hast always been our hope.

thou ever grant us life and sustenance. O gather our exiles to thy holy courts to observe thy laws, to do thy will, and to serve thee with a perfect heart. For this we thank thee. Blessed be God to whom all thanks are due.)

For all these acts, may thy name, our King, be blessed and exalted forever and ever.

All the living shall ever thank thee and sincerely praise thy name, O God, who art always our salvation and help. Blessed art thou, O Lord, Beneficent One, to whom it is fitting to give thanks.

O grant abundant peace to Israel thy people forever, for thou art the King and Lord of all peace. May it please thee to bless thy people Israel with peace at all times and at all hours. Blessed art thou, O Lord, who blessest thy people Israel with peace.

After the Shemoneh Esreh add the following meditation:

My God, guard my tongue from evil, and my lips from speaking falsehood. May my soul be silent to those who insult me; be my soul lowly to all as the dust. Open my heart to thy Torah, that my soul may follow thy commands. Speedily defeat the counsel of all those who plan evil against me, and upset their design. Do it for the glory of thy name; do it for the sake of thy power; do it for the sake of thy holiness; do it for the sake of thy Torah. That thy beloved may be rescued, save with thy right hand and answer me. May the words of my mouth and the meditation of my heart be pleasing before thee, O Lord, my Stronghold and my Redeemer.[1] May he who creates peace in his high heavens create peace for us and for all Israel. Amen.

אלהי נצור is taken substantially from the Talmud (Berakhoth 17a). עשה למען שמך and עושה שלום are later insertions.

---

[1] *Psalms* 60:7; 19:15.

יְהִי רָצוֹן מִלְּפָנֶיךָ, יְיָ אֱלֹהֵינוּ וֵאלֹהֵי אֲבוֹתֵינוּ, שֶׁיִּבָּנֶה בֵּית
הַמִּקְדָּשׁ בִּמְהֵרָה בְיָמֵינוּ, וְתֵן חֶלְקֵנוּ בְּתוֹרָתֶךָ. וְשָׁם נַעֲבָדְךָ
בְּיִרְאָה, כִּימֵי עוֹלָם וּכְשָׁנִים קַדְמוֹנִיּוֹת. וְעָרְבָה לַיְיָ מִנְחַת
יְהוּדָה וִירוּשָׁלָיִם, כִּימֵי עוֹלָם וּכְשָׁנִים קַדְמוֹנִיּוֹת.

Reader:

יִתְגַּדַּל וְיִתְקַדַּשׁ שְׁמֵהּ רַבָּא בְּעָלְמָא דִּי בְרָא כִרְעוּתֵהּ;
וְיַמְלִיךְ מַלְכוּתֵהּ בְּחַיֵּיכוֹן וּבְיוֹמֵיכוֹן, וּבְחַיֵּי דְכָל בֵּית יִשְׂרָאֵל,
בַּעֲגָלָא וּבִזְמַן קָרִיב, וְאִמְרוּ אָמֵן.

יְהֵא שְׁמֵהּ רַבָּא מְבָרַךְ לְעָלַם וּלְעָלְמֵי עָלְמַיָּא.

יִתְבָּרַךְ וְיִשְׁתַּבַּח, וְיִתְפָּאַר וְיִתְרוֹמַם, וְיִתְנַשֵּׂא וְיִתְהַדָּר,
וְיִתְעַלֶּה וְיִתְהַלָּל שְׁמֵהּ דְּקֻדְשָׁא, בְּרִיךְ הוּא, לְעֵלָּא מִן כָּל
בִּרְכָתָא וְשִׁירָתָא, תֻּשְׁבְּחָתָא וְנֶחֱמָתָא, דַּאֲמִירָן בְּעָלְמָא,
וְאִמְרוּ אָמֵן.

תִּתְקַבַּל צְלוֹתְהוֹן וּבָעוּתְהוֹן דְּכָל בֵּית יִשְׂרָאֵל קֳדָם אֲבוּהוֹן
דִּי בִשְׁמַיָּא, וְאִמְרוּ אָמֵן.

יְהֵא שְׁלָמָא רַבָּא מִן שְׁמַיָּא, וְחַיִּים, עָלֵינוּ וְעַל כָּל יִשְׂרָאֵל,
וְאִמְרוּ אָמֵן.

עֹשֶׂה שָׁלוֹם בִּמְרוֹמָיו, הוּא יַעֲשֶׂה שָׁלוֹם עָלֵינוּ וְעַל כָּל
יִשְׂרָאֵל, וְאִמְרוּ אָמֵן.

עָלֵינוּ לְשַׁבֵּחַ לַאֲדוֹן הַכֹּל, לָתֵת גְּדֻלָּה לְיוֹצֵר בְּרֵאשִׁית,
שֶׁלֹּא עָשָׂנוּ כְּגוֹיֵי הָאֲרָצוֹת, וְלֹא שָׂמָנוּ כְּמִשְׁפְּחוֹת הָאֲדָמָה;
שֶׁלֹּא שָׂם חֶלְקֵנוּ כָּהֶם, וְגֹרָלֵנוּ כְּכָל הֲמוֹנָם. וַאֲנַחְנוּ כּוֹרְעִים
וּמִשְׁתַּחֲוִים וּמוֹדִים לִפְנֵי מֶלֶךְ מַלְכֵי הַמְּלָכִים, הַקָּדוֹשׁ בָּרוּךְ
הוּא. שֶׁהוּא נוֹטֶה שָׁמַיִם וְיוֹסֵד אָרֶץ, וּמוֹשַׁב יְקָרוֹ בַּשָּׁמַיִם
מִמַּעַל, וּשְׁכִינַת עֻזּוֹ בְּגָבְהֵי מְרוֹמִים. הוּא אֱלֹהֵינוּ, אֵין עוֹד;

May it be thy will, Lord our God and God of our fathers, that the Temple be speedily rebuilt in our days, and grant us a share in thy Torah. There we will serve thee with reverence, as in the days of old and as in former years. Then the offering of Judah and Jerusalem will be pleasing to the Lord, as in the days of old and as in former years.[1]

Reader:

Glorified and sanctified be God's great name throughout the world which he has created according to his will. May he establish his kingdom in your lifetime and during your days, and within the life of the entire house of Israel, speedily and soon; and say, Amen.

May his great name be blessed forever and to all eternity.

Blessed and praised, glorified and exalted, extolled and honored, adored and lauded be the name of the Holy One, blessed be he, beyond all the blessings and hymns, praises and consolations that are ever spoken in the world; and say, Amen.

May the prayers and supplications of the whole house of Israel be accepted by their Father who is in heaven; and say, Amen.

May there be abundant peace from heaven, and life, for us and for all Israel; and say, Amen.

He who creates peace in his celestial heights, may he create peace for us and for all Israel; and say, Amen.

ALENU

It is our duty to praise the Master of all, to exalt the Creator of the universe, who has not made us like the nations of the world and has not placed us like the families of the earth; who has not designed our destiny to be like theirs, nor our lot like that of all their multitude. We bend the knee and bow and acknowledge before the supreme King of kings, the Holy One, blessed be he, that it is he who stretched forth the heavens and founded the earth. His seat of glory is in the heavens above; his abode of majesty is in the lofty heights. He is our God, there is none else;

---

[1] *Malachi* 3:4.

אֱמֶת מַלְכֵּנוּ, אֶפֶס זוּלָתוֹ, כַּכָּתוּב בְּתוֹרָתוֹ: וְיָדַעְתָּ הַיּוֹם
וַהֲשֵׁבֹתָ אֶל לְבָבֶךָ, כִּי יְיָ הוּא הָאֱלֹהִים בַּשָּׁמַיִם מִמַּעַל וְעַל
הָאָרֶץ מִתָּחַת, אֵין עוֹד.

עַל כֵּן נְקַוֶּה לְּךָ, יְיָ אֱלֹהֵינוּ, לִרְאוֹת מְהֵרָה בְּתִפְאֶרֶת עֻזֶּךָ,
לְהַעֲבִיר גִּלּוּלִים מִן הָאָרֶץ, וְהָאֱלִילִים כָּרוֹת יִכָּרֵתוּן; לְתַקֵּן
עוֹלָם בְּמַלְכוּת שַׁדַּי, וְכָל בְּנֵי בָשָׂר יִקְרְאוּ בִשְׁמֶךָ, לְהַפְנוֹת
אֵלֶיךָ כָּל רִשְׁעֵי אָרֶץ. יַכִּירוּ וְיֵדְעוּ כָּל יוֹשְׁבֵי תֵבֵל, כִּי לְךָ
תִּכְרַע כָּל בֶּרֶךְ, תִּשָּׁבַע כָּל לָשׁוֹן. לְפָנֶיךָ, יְיָ אֱלֹהֵינוּ, יִכְרְעוּ
וְיִפֹּלוּ, וְלִכְבוֹד שִׁמְךָ יְקָר יִתֵּנוּ, וִיקַבְּלוּ כֻלָּם אֶת עֹל מַלְכוּתֶךָ,
וְתִמְלֹךְ עֲלֵיהֶם מְהֵרָה לְעוֹלָם וָעֶד; כִּי הַמַּלְכוּת שֶׁלְּךָ הִיא,
וּלְעוֹלְמֵי עַד תִּמְלוֹךְ בְּכָבוֹד, כַּכָּתוּב בְּתוֹרָתֶךָ: יְיָ יִמְלֹךְ
לְעֹלָם וָעֶד. Reader וְנֶאֱמַר: וְהָיָה יְיָ לְמֶלֶךְ עַל כָּל הָאָרֶץ;
בַּיּוֹם הַהוּא יִהְיֶה יְיָ אֶחָד וּשְׁמוֹ אֶחָד.

MOURNERS' KADDISH

יִתְגַּדַּל וְיִתְקַדַּשׁ שְׁמֵהּ רַבָּא בְּעָלְמָא דִּי בְרָא כִרְעוּתֵהּ;
וְיַמְלִיךְ מַלְכוּתֵהּ בְּחַיֵּיכוֹן וּבְיוֹמֵיכוֹן, וּבְחַיֵּי דְכָל בֵּית יִשְׂרָאֵל,
בַּעֲגָלָא וּבִזְמַן קָרִיב, וְאִמְרוּ אָמֵן.

יְהֵא שְׁמֵהּ רַבָּא מְבָרַךְ לְעָלַם וּלְעָלְמֵי עָלְמַיָּא.

יִתְבָּרַךְ וְיִשְׁתַּבַּח, וְיִתְפָּאַר וְיִתְרוֹמַם, וְיִתְנַשֵּׂא וְיִתְהַדָּר,
וְיִתְעַלֶּה וְיִתְהַלַּל שְׁמֵהּ דְּקֻדְשָׁא, בְּרִיךְ הוּא, לְעֵלָּא מִן כָּל
בִּרְכָתָא וְשִׁירָתָא, תֻּשְׁבְּחָתָא וְנֶחֱמָתָא, דַּאֲמִירָן בְּעָלְמָא,
וְאִמְרוּ אָמֵן.

יְהֵא שְׁלָמָא רַבָּא מִן שְׁמַיָּא, וְחַיִּים, עָלֵינוּ וְעַל כָּל יִשְׂרָאֵל,
וְאִמְרוּ אָמֵן.

עֹשֶׂה שָׁלוֹם בִּמְרוֹמָיו, הוּא יַעֲשֶׂה שָׁלוֹם עָלֵינוּ וְעַל כָּל
יִשְׂרָאֵל, וְאִמְרוּ אָמֵן.

truly, he is our King, there is none besides him, as it is written in his Torah: "You shall know this day, and reflect in your heart, that it is the Lord who is God in the heavens above and on the earth beneath, there is none else."[1]

We hope therefore, Lord our God, soon to behold thy majestic glory, when the abominations shall be removed from the earth, and the false gods exterminated; when the world shall be perfected under the reign of the Almighty, and all mankind will call upon thy name, and all the wicked of the earth will be turned to thee. May all the inhabitants of the world realize and know that to thee every knee must bend, every tongue must vow allegiance. May they bend the knee and prostrate themselves before thee, Lord our God, and give honor to thy glorious name; may they all accept the yoke of thy kingdom, and do thou reign over them speedily forever and ever. For the kingdom is thine, and to all eternity thou wilt reign in glory, as it is written in thy Torah: "The Lord shall be King forever and ever."[2] And it is said: "The Lord shall be King over all the earth; on that day the Lord shall be One, and his name One."[3]

MOURNERS' KADDISH

Glorified and sanctified be God's great name throughout the world which he has created according to his will. May he establish his kingdom in your lifetime and during your days, and within the life of the entire house of Israel, speedily and soon; and say, Amen.

May his great name be blessed forever and to all eternity.

Blessed and praised, glorified and exalted, extolled and honored, adored and lauded be the name of the Holy One, blessed be he, beyond all the blessings and hymns, praises and consolations that are ever spoken in the world; and say, Amen.

May there be abundant peace from heaven, and life, for us and for all Israel; and say, Amen.

He who creates peace in his celestial heights, may he create peace for us and for all Israel; and say, Amen.

---

[1] *Deuteronomy* 4:39.   [2] *Exodus* 15:18.   [3] *Zechariah* 14:9.

עַרְבִית לְיוֹם טוֹב

On Sabbath:

תהלים צב

מִזְמוֹר שִׁיר לְיוֹם הַשַּׁבָּת. טוֹב לְהֹדוֹת לַיְיָ, וּלְזַמֵּר לְשִׁמְךָ
עֶלְיוֹן. לְהַגִּיד בַּבֹּקֶר חַסְדֶּךָ, וֶאֱמוּנָתְךָ בַּלֵּילוֹת. עֲלֵי עָשׂוֹר
וַעֲלֵי נָבֶל, עֲלֵי הִגָּיוֹן בְּכִנּוֹר. כִּי שִׂמַּחְתַּנִי יְיָ בְּפָעֳלֶךָ; בְּמַעֲשֵׂי
יָדֶיךָ אֲרַנֵּן. מַה גָּדְלוּ מַעֲשֶׂיךָ, יְיָ; מְאֹד עָמְקוּ מַחְשְׁבֹתֶיךָ.
אִישׁ בַּעַר לֹא יֵדָע, וּכְסִיל לֹא יָבִין אֶת זֹאת. בִּפְרֹחַ רְשָׁעִים
כְּמוֹ עֵשֶׂב, וַיָּצִיצוּ כָּל פֹּעֲלֵי אָוֶן, לְהִשָּׁמְדָם עֲדֵי עַד. וְאַתָּה
מָרוֹם לְעֹלָם, יְיָ. כִּי הִנֵּה אֹיְבֶיךָ, יְיָ, כִּי הִנֵּה אֹיְבֶיךָ יֹאבֵדוּ,
יִתְפָּרְדוּ כָּל פֹּעֲלֵי אָוֶן. וַתָּרֶם כִּרְאֵים קַרְנִי; בַּלֹּתִי בְּשֶׁמֶן רַעֲנָן.
וַתַּבֵּט עֵינִי בְּשׁוּרָי, בַּקָּמִים עָלַי מְרֵעִים תִּשְׁמַעְנָה אָזְנָי. צַדִּיק
כַּתָּמָר יִפְרָח, כְּאֶרֶז בַּלְּבָנוֹן יִשְׂגֶּה. שְׁתוּלִים בְּבֵית יְיָ, בְּחַצְרוֹת
אֱלֹהֵינוּ יַפְרִיחוּ. Reader עוֹד יְנוּבוּן בְּשֵׂיבָה, דְּשֵׁנִים וְרַעֲנַנִּים
יִהְיוּ. לְהַגִּיד כִּי יָשָׁר יְיָ; צוּרִי, וְלֹא עַוְלָתָה בּוֹ.

תהלים צג

יְיָ מָלָךְ, גֵּאוּת לָבֵשׁ; לָבֵשׁ יְיָ, עֹז הִתְאַזָּר; אַף תִּכּוֹן תֵּבֵל,
בַּל תִּמּוֹט. נָכוֹן כִּסְאֲךָ מֵאָז, מֵעוֹלָם אָתָּה. נָשְׂאוּ נְהָרוֹת, יְיָ,
נָשְׂאוּ נְהָרוֹת קוֹלָם, יִשְׂאוּ נְהָרוֹת דָּכְיָם. מִקֹּלוֹת מַיִם רַבִּים,
אַדִּירִים מִשְׁבְּרֵי יָם, אַדִּיר בַּמָּרוֹם יְיָ. Reader עֵדֹתֶיךָ נֶאֶמְנוּ
מְאֹד, לְבֵיתְךָ נַאֲוָה קֹּדֶשׁ, יְיָ, לְאֹרֶךְ יָמִים.

Mourners' Kaddish, page 19.

Psalm 92 was sung by the Levites in the Temple during the Sabbath offering. The psalmist reflects on the meaning of God's works, a meaning which
the foolish fail to perceive. The wicked seem to flourish only that they may

EVENING SERVICE FOR FESTIVALS

On Sabbath:

Psalm 92

A psalm, a song for the Sabbath day. It is good to give thanks to the Lord, and to sing praises to thy name, O Most High; to proclaim thy goodness in the morning, and thy faithfulness at night, with a ten-stringed lyre and a flute, to the sound of a harp. For thou, O Lord, hast made me glad through thy work; I sing for joy at all that thou hast done. How great are thy works, O Lord! How very deep are thy designs! A stupid man cannot know, a fool cannot understand this. When the wicked thrive like grass, and all evildoers flourish, it is that they may be destroyed forever. But thou, O Lord, art supreme for evermore. For lo, thy enemies, O Lord, for lo, thy enemies shall perish; all evildoers shall be dispersed. But thou hast exalted my power like that of the wild ox; I am anointed with fresh oil. My eye has gazed on my foes; my ears have heard my enemies' doom. The righteous will flourish like the palm tree; they will grow like a cedar in Lebanon. Planted in the house of the Lord, they·shall flourish in the courts of our God. They shall yield fruit even in old age; vigorous and fresh they shall be, to proclaim that the Lord is just! He is my Stronghold, and there is no wrong in him.

Psalm 93

The Lord is King; he is robed in majesty; the Lord is robed, he has girded himself with strength; thus the world is set firm and cannot be shaken. Thy throne stands firm from of old; thou art from all eternity. The floods have lifted up, O Lord, the floods have lifted up their voice; the floods lift up their mighty waves. But above the sound of many waters, mighty breakers of the sea, the Lord on high stands supreme. Thy testimonies are very sure; holiness befits thy house, O Lord, for all time.

Mourners' Kaddish, page 20.

---

be destroyed. The palm and cedar are long-lived and flourish during all seasons. They represent the enduring happiness of the faithful in contrast with the short-lived prosperity of the wicked.

For **מַעֲרָבוֹת**, recited by some congregations, see pages 351, 355.

Silent meditation:	Reader:

Reader:

בָּרְכוּ אֶת יְיָ הַמְבֹרָךְ.

Silent meditation:

יִתְבָּרַךְ וְיִשְׁתַּבַּח, וְיִתְפָּאַר וְיִתְרוֹמַם
וְיִתְנַשֵּׂא שְׁמוֹ שֶׁל מֶלֶךְ מַלְכֵי הַמְּלָכִים,
הַקָּדוֹשׁ בָּרוּךְ הוּא, שֶׁהוּא רִאשׁוֹן וְהוּא
אַחֲרוֹן, וּמִבַּלְעָדָיו אֵין אֱלֹהִים. סֶלוּ

Congregation and Reader:

בָּרוּךְ יְיָ הַמְבֹרָךְ לְעוֹלָם וָעֶד.

לָרֹכֵב בָּעֲרָבוֹת, בְּיָהּ שְׁמוֹ, וְעִלְזוּ לְפָנָיו; וּשְׁמוֹ מְרוֹמָם עַל כָּל בְּרָכָה וּתְהִלָּה. בָּרוּךְ שֵׁם כְּבוֹד מַלְכוּתוֹ לְעוֹלָם וָעֶד. יְהִי שֵׁם יְיָ מְבֹרָךְ מֵעַתָּה וְעַד עוֹלָם.

בָּרוּךְ אַתָּה, יְיָ אֱלֹהֵינוּ, מֶלֶךְ הָעוֹלָם, אֲשֶׁר בִּדְבָרוֹ מַעֲרִיב עֲרָבִים; בְּחָכְמָה פּוֹתֵחַ שְׁעָרִים, וּבִתְבוּנָה מְשַׁנֶּה עִתִּים; וּמַחֲלִיף אֶת הַזְּמַנִּים, וּמְסַדֵּר אֶת הַכּוֹכָבִים בְּמִשְׁמְרוֹתֵיהֶם בָּרָקִיעַ כִּרְצוֹנוֹ. בּוֹרֵא יוֹם וָלָיְלָה, גּוֹלֵל אוֹר מִפְּנֵי חֹשֶׁךְ וְחֹשֶׁךְ מִפְּנֵי אוֹר, וּמַעֲבִיר יוֹם וּמֵבִיא לָיְלָה, וּמַבְדִּיל בֵּין יוֹם וּבֵין לָיְלָה, יְיָ צְבָאוֹת שְׁמוֹ. Reader אֵל חַי וְקַיָּם, תָּמִיד יִמְלוֹךְ עָלֵינוּ, לְעוֹלָם וָעֶד. בָּרוּךְ אַתָּה, יְיָ, הַמַּעֲרִיב עֲרָבִים.

אַהֲבַת עוֹלָם בֵּית יִשְׂרָאֵל עַמְּךָ אָהָבְתָּ; תּוֹרָה וּמִצְוֹת, חֻקִּים וּמִשְׁפָּטִים, אוֹתָנוּ לִמַּדְתָּ; עַל כֵּן, יְיָ אֱלֹהֵינוּ, בְּשָׁכְבֵּנוּ וּבְקוּמֵנוּ נָשִׂיחַ בְּחֻקֶּיךָ, וְנִשְׂמַח בְּדִבְרֵי תוֹרָתֶךָ וּבְמִצְוֹתֶיךָ לְעוֹלָם וָעֶד. כִּי הֵם חַיֵּינוּ וְאֹרֶךְ יָמֵינוּ, וּבָהֶם נֶהְגֶּה יוֹמָם וָלָיְלָה; Reader וְאַהֲבָתְךָ אַל תָּסִיר מִמֶּנּוּ לְעוֹלָמִים. בָּרוּךְ אַתָּה, יְיָ, אוֹהֵב עַמּוֹ יִשְׂרָאֵל.

(When praying in private, add: אֵל מֶלֶךְ נֶאֱמָן)

דברים ו, ד—ט

שְׁמַע יִשְׂרָאֵל, יְיָ אֱלֹהֵינוּ, יְיָ אֶחָד.
בָּרוּךְ שֵׁם כְּבוֹד מַלְכוּתוֹ לְעוֹלָם וָעֶד.
וְאָהַבְתָּ אֵת יְיָ אֱלֹהֶיךָ בְּכָל לְבָבְךָ וּבְכָל נַפְשְׁךָ וּבְכָל מְאֹדֶךָ. וְהָיוּ הַדְּבָרִים הָאֵלֶּה, אֲשֶׁר אָנֹכִי מְצַוְּךָ הַיּוֹם, עַל

For Ma'aravoth, recited by some congregations, see pages 351,355.

Reader:	Silent meditation:
Bless the Lord who is blessed.	Blessed, praised, glorified, ex-
Congregation and Reader:	tolled and exalted be the name
Blessed be the Lord who is blessed	of the supreme King of kings, the Holy One, blessed be he,
forever and ever.	who is the first and the last, and

besides him there is no God. Extol him who is in the heavens—Lord is his name, and rejoice before him. His name is exalted above all blessing and praise. Blessed be the name of his glorious majesty forever and ever. Let the name of the Lord be blessed henceforth and forever.

Blessed art thou, Lord our God, King of the universe, who at thy word bringest on the evenings. With wisdom thou openest the gates of heaven, and with understanding thou changest the times and causest the seasons to alternate. Thou arrangest the stars in their courses in the sky according to thy will. Thou createst day and night; thou rollest away light before darkness, and darkness before light; thou causest the day to pass and the night to come, and makest the distinction between day and night— Lord of hosts is thy name. Eternal God, mayest thou reign over us forever and ever. Blessed art thou, O Lord, who bringest on the evenings.

Thou hast loved the house of Israel with everlasting love; thou hast taught us Torah and precepts, laws and judgments. Therefore, Lord our God, when we lie down and when we rise up we will speak of thy laws, and rejoice in the words of thy Torah and in thy precepts for evermore. Indeed, they are our life and the length of our days; we will meditate on them day and night. Mayest thou never take away thy love from us. Blessed art thou, O Lord, who lovest thy people Israel.

(*When praying in private, add:* God is a faithful King).

Deuteronomy 6:4–9

Hear, O Israel, the Lord is our God, the Lord is One.

Blessed be the name of his glorious majesty forever and ever.

You shall love the Lord your God with all your heart, and with all your soul, and with all your might. And these words which I command you today shall be in your heart. You shall

לְבָבֶךָ. וְשִׁנַּנְתָּם לְבָנֶיךָ, וְדִבַּרְתָּ בָּם בְּשִׁבְתְּךָ בְּבֵיתֶךָ, וּבְלֶכְתְּךָ
בַדֶּרֶךְ, וּבְשָׁכְבְּךָ וּבְקוּמֶךָ. וּקְשַׁרְתָּם לְאוֹת עַל יָדֶךָ, וְהָיוּ
לְטֹטָפֹת בֵּין עֵינֶיךָ. וּכְתַבְתָּם עַל מְזֻזוֹת בֵּיתֶךָ וּבִשְׁעָרֶיךָ.

דברים יא, יג–כא

וְהָיָה אִם שָׁמֹעַ תִּשְׁמְעוּ אֶל מִצְוֹתַי, אֲשֶׁר אָנֹכִי מְצַוֶּה אֶתְכֶם
הַיּוֹם, לְאַהֲבָה אֶת יְיָ אֱלֹהֵיכֶם, וּלְעָבְדוֹ בְּכָל לְבַבְכֶם וּבְכָל
נַפְשְׁכֶם. וְנָתַתִּי מְטַר אַרְצְכֶם בְּעִתּוֹ, יוֹרֶה וּמַלְקוֹשׁ, וְאָסַפְתָּ
דְגָנֶךָ, וְתִירֹשְׁךָ וְיִצְהָרֶךָ. וְנָתַתִּי עֵשֶׂב בְּשָׂדְךָ לִבְהֶמְתֶּךָ, וְאָכַלְתָּ
וְשָׂבָעְתָּ. הִשָּׁמְרוּ לָכֶם פֶּן יִפְתֶּה לְבַבְכֶם, וְסַרְתֶּם וַעֲבַדְתֶּם
אֱלֹהִים אֲחֵרִים, וְהִשְׁתַּחֲוִיתֶם לָהֶם. וְחָרָה אַף יְיָ בָּכֶם, וְעָצַר
אֶת הַשָּׁמַיִם וְלֹא יִהְיֶה מָטָר, וְהָאֲדָמָה לֹא תִתֵּן אֶת יְבוּלָהּ;
וַאֲבַדְתֶּם מְהֵרָה מֵעַל הָאָרֶץ הַטֹּבָה אֲשֶׁר יְיָ נֹתֵן לָכֶם. וְשַׂמְתֶּם
אֶת דְּבָרַי אֵלֶּה עַל לְבַבְכֶם וְעַל נַפְשְׁכֶם; וּקְשַׁרְתֶּם אֹתָם לְאוֹת
עַל יֶדְכֶם, וְהָיוּ לְטוֹטָפֹת בֵּין עֵינֵיכֶם. וְלִמַּדְתֶּם אֹתָם אֶת
בְּנֵיכֶם לְדַבֵּר בָּם, בְּשִׁבְתְּךָ בְּבֵיתֶךָ, וּבְלֶכְתְּךָ בַדֶּרֶךְ, וּבְשָׁכְבְּךָ
וּבְקוּמֶךָ. וּכְתַבְתָּם עַל מְזוּזוֹת בֵּיתֶךָ וּבִשְׁעָרֶיךָ.

לְמַעַן יִרְבּוּ יְמֵיכֶם וִימֵי בְנֵיכֶם, עַל הָאֲדָמָה אֲשֶׁר נִשְׁבַּע
יְיָ לַאֲבֹתֵיכֶם לָתֵת לָהֶם, כִּימֵי הַשָּׁמַיִם עַל הָאָרֶץ.

במדבר טו, לז–מא

וַיֹּאמֶר יְיָ אֶל מֹשֶׁה לֵּאמֹר: דַּבֵּר אֶל בְּנֵי יִשְׂרָאֵל וְאָמַרְתָּ
אֲלֵהֶם, וְעָשׂוּ לָהֶם צִיצִת עַל כַּנְפֵי בִגְדֵיהֶם לְדֹרֹתָם, וְנָתְנוּ עַל
צִיצִת הַכָּנָף פְּתִיל תְּכֵלֶת. וְהָיָה לָכֶם לְצִיצִת, וּרְאִיתֶם אֹתוֹ
וּזְכַרְתֶּם אֶת כָּל מִצְוֹת יְיָ, וַעֲשִׂיתֶם אֹתָם; וְלֹא תָתוּרוּ אַחֲרֵי
לְבַבְכֶם וְאַחֲרֵי עֵינֵיכֶם, אֲשֶׁר אַתֶּם זֹנִים אַחֲרֵיהֶם. לְמַעַן
תִּזְכְּרוּ וַעֲשִׂיתֶם אֶת כָּל מִצְוֹתָי, וִהְיִיתֶם קְדֹשִׁים לֵאלֹהֵיכֶם.

teach them diligently to your children, and you shall speak of them when you are sitting at home and when you go on a journey, when you lie down and when you rise up. You shall bind them for a sign on your hand, and they shall be for frontlets between your eyes. You shall inscribe them on the doorposts of your house and on your gates.

Deuteronomy 11:13-21

And if you will carefully obey my commands which I give you today, to love the Lord your God and to serve him with all your heart and with all your soul, I will give rain for your land at the right season, the autumn rains and the spring rains, that you may gather in your grain, your wine and your oil. And I will provide grass in your fields for your cattle, and you will eat and be satisfied. Beware lest your heart be deceived, and you turn and serve other gods and worship them; for then the Lord's anger will blaze against you, and he will shut up the skies so that there will be no rain, and the land will yield no produce, and you will quickly perish from the good land which the Lord gives you. So you shall place these words of mine in your heart and in your soul, and you shall bind them for a sign on your hand, and they shall be for frontlets between your eyes. You shall teach them to your children, speaking of them when you are sitting at home and when you go on a journey, when you lie down and when you rise up. You shall inscribe them on the doorposts of your house and on your gates—that your life and the life of your children may be prolonged in the land, which the Lord promised he would give to your fathers, as long as the sky remains over the earth.

Numbers 15:37-41

The Lord spoke to Moses, saying: Speak to the children of Israel and tell them to make for themselves fringes on the corners of their garments throughout their generations, and to put on the fringe of each corner a blue thread. You shall have it as a fringe, so that when you look upon it you will remember to do all the commands of the Lord, and you will not follow the desires of your heart and your eyes which lead you astray. It is for you to remember and do all my commands and be holy for your God.

אֲנִי יְיָ אֱלֹהֵיכֶם, אֲשֶׁר הוֹצֵאתִי אֶתְכֶם מֵאֶרֶץ מִצְרַיִם לִהְיוֹת
לָכֶם לֵאלֹהִים; אֲנִי Reader יְיָ אֱלֹהֵיכֶם–

אֱמֶת וֶאֱמוּנָה כָּל זֹאת, וְקַיָּם עָלֵינוּ כִּי הוּא יְיָ אֱלֹהֵינוּ וְאֵין
זוּלָתוֹ, וַאֲנַחְנוּ יִשְׂרָאֵל עַמּוֹ. הַפּוֹדֵנוּ מִיַּד מְלָכִים, מַלְכֵּנוּ
הַגּוֹאֲלֵנוּ מִכַּף כָּל הֶעָרִיצִים; הָאֵל הַנִּפְרָע לָנוּ מִצָּרֵינוּ,
וְהַמְשַׁלֵּם גְּמוּל לְכָל אֹיְבֵי נַפְשֵׁנוּ; הָעוֹשֶׂה גְדֹלוֹת עַד אֵין חֵקֶר,
וְנִפְלָאוֹת עַד אֵין מִסְפָּר; הַשָּׂם נַפְשֵׁנוּ בַּחַיִּים, וְלֹא נָתַן לַמּוֹט
רַגְלֵנוּ; הַמַּדְרִיכֵנוּ עַל בָּמוֹת אֹיְבֵינוּ, וַיָּרֶם קַרְנֵנוּ עַל כָּל שׂנְאֵינוּ;
הָעוֹשֶׂה לָנוּ נִסִּים וּנְקָמָה בְּפַרְעֹה, אוֹתוֹת וּמוֹפְתִים בְּאַדְמַת
בְּנֵי חָם; הַמַּכֶּה בְעֶבְרָתוֹ כָּל בְּכוֹרֵי מִצְרַיִם, וַיּוֹצֵא אֶת עַמּוֹ
יִשְׂרָאֵל מִתּוֹכָם לְחֵרוּת עוֹלָם. הַמַּעֲבִיר בָּנָיו בֵּין גִּזְרֵי יַם סוּף;
אֶת רוֹדְפֵיהֶם וְאֶת שׂוֹנְאֵיהֶם בִּתְהוֹמוֹת טִבַּע. וְרָאוּ בָנָיו
גְּבוּרָתוֹ; שִׁבְּחוּ וְהוֹדוּ לִשְׁמוֹ, וּמַלְכוּתוֹ בְּרָצוֹן קִבְּלוּ עֲלֵיהֶם–

מֹשֶׁה וּבְנֵי יִשְׂרָאֵל לְךָ עָנוּ שִׁירָה בְּשִׂמְחָה רַבָּה, וְאָמְרוּ
כֻלָּם:

מִי כָמֹכָה בָּאֵלִם, יְיָ; מִי כָּמֹכָה נֶאְדָּר בַּקֹּדֶשׁ, נוֹרָא תְהִלֹּת,
עֹשֵׂה פֶלֶא.

מַלְכוּתְךָ רָאוּ בָנֶיךָ, בּוֹקֵעַ יָם לִפְנֵי מֹשֶׁה; זֶה אֵלִי עָנוּ
וְאָמְרוּ:   יְיָ יִמְלֹךְ לְעֹלָם וָעֶד.

וְנֶאֱמַר: כִּי פָדָה יְיָ אֶת יַעֲקֹב, וּגְאָלוֹ מִיַּד חָזָק מִמֶּנּוּ. בָּרוּךְ
אַתָּה, יְיָ, גָּאַל יִשְׂרָאֵל.

הַשְׁכִּיבֵנוּ, יְיָ אֱלֹהֵינוּ, לְשָׁלוֹם; וְהַעֲמִידֵנוּ, מַלְכֵּנוּ, לְחַיִּים;
וּפְרוֹשׂ עָלֵינוּ סֻכַּת שְׁלוֹמֶךָ, וְתַקְּנֵנוּ בְּעֵצָה טוֹבָה מִלְּפָנֶיךָ,
וְהוֹשִׁיעֵנוּ לְמַעַן שְׁמֶךָ; וְהָגֵן בַּעֲדֵנוּ, וְהָסֵר מֵעָלֵינוּ אוֹיֵב, דֶּבֶר
וְחֶרֶב וְרָעָב וְיָגוֹן; וְהָסֵר שָׂטָן מִלְּפָנֵינוּ וּמֵאַחֲרֵינוּ, וּבְצֵל כְּנָפֶיךָ

I am the Lord your God who brought you out of the land of Egypt to be your God; I am the Lord your God.

True and trustworthy is all this. We are certain that he is the Lord our God, and no one else, and that we Israel are his people. It is he, our King, who redeemed us from the power of despots, delivered us from the grasp of all the tyrants, avenged us upon our oppressors, and requited all our mortal enemies. He did great, incomprehensible acts and countless wonders; he kept us alive, and did not let us slip.[1] He made us tread upon the high places of our enemies, and raised our strength over all our foes. He performed for us miracles and vengeance upon Pharaoh, signs and wonders in the land of the Hamites; he smote in his wrath all the first-born of Egypt, and brought his people Israel from their midst to enduring freedom. He made his children pass between the divided parts of the Red Sea, and engulfed their pursuers and their enemies in the depths. His children beheld his might; they gave praise and thanks to his name, and willingly accepted his sovereignty.

Moses and the children of Israel sang a song to thee with great rejoicing; all of them said:

"Who is like thee, O Lord, among the mighty? Who is like thee, glorious in holiness, awe-inspiring in renown, doing wonders?"[2]

Thy children saw thy majesty as thou didst part the sea before Moses. "This is my God!" they shouted, and they said:

"The Lord shall reign forever and ever."[3]

And it is said: "Indeed, the Lord has delivered Jacob, and rescued him from a stronger power."[4] Blessed art thou, O Lord, who hast redeemed Israel.

Grant, Lord our God, that we lie down in peace, and that we rise again, O our King, to life. Spread over us thy shelter of peace, and direct us with good counsel of thy own. Save us for thy name's sake; shield us, and remove from us every enemy and pestilence, sword and famine and grief; remove the adversary from before us and from behind us; shelter us in the shadow of thy

---

[1] *Job* 9:10; *Psalm* 66:9.   [2] *Exodus* 15:11.   [3] *Exodus* 15:18.   [4] *Jeremiah* 31:11.

תַּסְתִּירֵנוּ; כִּי אֵל שׁוֹמְרֵנוּ וּמַצִּילֵנוּ אָתָּה, כִּי אֵל מֶלֶךְ חַנּוּן
וְרַחוּם אָתָּה. וּשְׁמוֹר צֵאתֵנוּ וּבוֹאֵנוּ לְחַיִּים וּלְשָׁלוֹם, מֵעַתָּה
וְעַד עוֹלָם, Reader וּפְרוֹשׂ עָלֵינוּ סֻכַּת שְׁלוֹמֶךָ. בָּרוּךְ אַתָּה, יְיָ,
הַפּוֹרֵשׂ סֻכַּת שָׁלוֹם עָלֵינוּ, וְעַל כָּל עַמּוֹ יִשְׂרָאֵל, וְעַל יְרוּשָׁלָיִם.

On Sabbath:

(וְשָׁמְרוּ בְנֵי יִשְׂרָאֵל אֶת הַשַּׁבָּת, לַעֲשׂוֹת אֶת הַשַּׁבָּת לְדֹרֹתָם
בְּרִית עוֹלָם. בֵּינִי וּבֵין בְּנֵי יִשְׂרָאֵל אוֹת הִיא לְעוֹלָם, כִּי שֵׁשֶׁת
יָמִים עָשָׂה יְיָ אֶת הַשָּׁמַיִם וְאֶת הָאָרֶץ, וּבַיּוֹם הַשְּׁבִיעִי שָׁבַת
וַיִּנָּפַשׁ.)

וַיְדַבֵּר מֹשֶׁה אֶת מוֹעֲדֵי יְיָ אֶל בְּנֵי יִשְׂרָאֵל.

Reader:

יִתְגַּדַּל וְיִתְקַדַּשׁ שְׁמֵהּ רַבָּא בְּעָלְמָא דִי בְרָא כִרְעוּתֵהּ;
וְיַמְלִיךְ מַלְכוּתֵהּ בְּחַיֵּיכוֹן וּבְיוֹמֵיכוֹן, וּבְחַיֵּי דְכָל בֵּית יִשְׂרָאֵל,
בַּעֲגָלָא וּבִזְמַן קָרִיב, וְאִמְרוּ אָמֵן.

יְהֵא שְׁמֵהּ רַבָּא מְבָרַךְ לְעָלַם וּלְעָלְמֵי עָלְמַיָּא.

יִתְבָּרַךְ וְיִשְׁתַּבַּח, וְיִתְפָּאַר וְיִתְרוֹמַם, וְיִתְנַשֵּׂא וְיִתְהַדָּר,
וְיִתְעַלֶּה וְיִתְהַלָּל שְׁמֵהּ דְּקֻדְשָׁא, בְּרִיךְ הוּא, לְעֵלָּא מִן כָּל
בִּרְכָתָא וְשִׁירָתָא, תֻּשְׁבְּחָתָא וְנֶחֱמָתָא, דַּאֲמִירָן בְּעָלְמָא
וְאִמְרוּ אָמֵן.

<hr>

הפורש סכת שלום, instead of the weekday ending שומר עמו ישראל, is used to express the idea of peace which fills the Jewish home on Sabbath and festivals. This is the second of the two blessings that follow the recital of the *Shema* in the evening.

wings; for thou art our protecting and saving God; thou art indeed a gracious and merciful God and King. Guard thou our going out and our coming in, for life and peace, henceforth and forever. Do thou spread over us thy shelter of peace. Blessed art thou, O Lord, who spreadest the shelter of peace over us and over all thy people Israel and over Jerusalem.

On Sabbath:

(The children of Israel shall keep the Sabbath, observing the Sabbath throughout their generations as an everlasting covenant. It is a sign between me and the children of Israel forever, that in six days the Lord made the heavens and the earth, and on the seventh day he ceased from work and rested.)[1]

Moses announced the festivals of the Lord to the children of Israel. [2]

Reader:

Glorified and sanctified be God's great name throughout the world which he has created according to his will. May he establish his kingdom in your lifetime and during your days, and within the life of the entire house of Israel, speedily and soon; and say, Amen.

May his great name be blessed forever and to all eternity.

Blessed and praised, glorified and exalted, extolled and honored, adored and lauded be the name of the Holy One, blessed be he, beyond all the blessings and hymns, praises and consolations that are ever spoken in the world; and say, Amen.

---

[1] *Exodus* 31:16-17.   [2] *Psalm* 81:4-5.

אֲדֹנָי, שְׂפָתַי תִּפְתָּח, וּפִי יַגִּיד תְּהִלָּתֶךָ.

בָּרוּךְ אַתָּה, יְיָ אֱלֹהֵינוּ וֵאלֹהֵי אֲבוֹתֵינוּ, אֱלֹהֵי אַבְרָהָם,
אֱלֹהֵי יִצְחָק, וֵאלֹהֵי יַעֲקֹב, הָאֵל הַגָּדוֹל הַגִּבּוֹר וְהַנּוֹרָא, אֵל
עֶלְיוֹן, גּוֹמֵל חֲסָדִים טוֹבִים, וְקוֹנֵה הַכֹּל, וְזוֹכֵר חַסְדֵי אָבוֹת,
וּמֵבִיא גוֹאֵל לִבְנֵי בְנֵיהֶם לְמַעַן שְׁמוֹ בְּאַהֲבָה.

מֶלֶךְ עוֹזֵר וּמוֹשִׁיעַ וּמָגֵן. בָּרוּךְ אַתָּה, יְיָ, מָגֵן אַבְרָהָם.

אַתָּה גִבּוֹר לְעוֹלָם, אֲדֹנָי; מְחַיֵּה מֵתִים אַתָּה, רַב לְהוֹשִׁיעַ.

מְכַלְכֵּל חַיִּים בְּחֶסֶד, מְחַיֵּה מֵתִים בְּרַחֲמִים רַבִּים, סוֹמֵךְ
נוֹפְלִים, וְרוֹפֵא חוֹלִים. וּמַתִּיר אֲסוּרִים, וּמְקַיֵּם אֱמוּנָתוֹ לִישֵׁנֵי
עָפָר. מִי כָמוֹךָ, בַּעַל גְּבוּרוֹת, וּמִי דּוֹמֶה לָּךְ, מֶלֶךְ מֵמִית
וּמְחַיֶּה וּמַצְמִיחַ יְשׁוּעָה.

וְנֶאֱמָן אַתָּה לְהַחֲיוֹת מֵתִים. בָּרוּךְ אַתָּה, יְיָ, מְחַיֵּה הַמֵּתִים.

אַתָּה קָדוֹשׁ וְשִׁמְךָ קָדוֹשׁ, וּקְדוֹשִׁים בְּכָל יוֹם יְהַלְלוּךָ סֶּלָה.
בָּרוּךְ אַתָּה, יְיָ, הָאֵל הַקָּדוֹשׁ.

אַתָּה בְחַרְתָּנוּ מִכָּל הָעַמִּים, אָהַבְתָּ אוֹתָנוּ וְרָצִיתָ בָּנוּ,
וְרוֹמַמְתָּנוּ מִכָּל הַלְּשׁוֹנוֹת, וְקִדַּשְׁתָּנוּ בְּמִצְוֹתֶיךָ, וְקֵרַבְתָּנוּ
מַלְכֵּנוּ לַעֲבוֹדָתֶךָ, וְשִׁמְךָ הַגָּדוֹל וְהַקָּדוֹשׁ עָלֵינוּ קָרָאתָ.

אתה בחרתנו (thou hast chosen us) is a passage based on many biblical expressions that keep reminding the people of Israel that they have been chosen by God to be a beacon of light and truth to the nations of the earth: "You are a people holy to the Lord your God, who has chosen you from all the nations on the face of the earth to be his own possession . . ." (Deuteronomy 14:2). However much they may have fallen short of their duty, however much they may have neglected to remain faithful to their sacred task, they have not been deposed from the office to which they were appointed. The biblical term *am segullah* (God's own people) does not imply Israel's exclusive possession of divine love and favor. On the contrary, it means that God has exclusive claim to Israel's service, The most cherished ideal of Israel is that of universal brotherhood (S. R. Hirsch). Israel's character as the chosen people does not involve the infer-

O Lord, open thou my lips, that my mouth may declare thy praise.

Blessed art thou, Lord our God and God of our fathers, God of Abraham, God of Isaac and God of Jacob; great, mighty and revered God, sublime God, who bestowest lovingkindness, and art Master of all things; who rememberest the good deeds of our fathers, and who wilt graciously bring a redeemer to their children's children for the sake of thy name.

O King, Supporter, Savior and Shield! Blessed art thou, O Lord, Shield of Abraham.

Thou, O Lord, art mighty forever; thou revivest the dead; thou art powerful to save.

Thou sustainest the living with kindness, and revivest the dead with great mercy; thou supportest all who fall, and healest the sick; thou settest the captives free, and keepest faith with those who sleep in the dust. Who is like thee, Lord of power? Who resembles thee, O King? Thou bringest death and restorest life, and causest salvation to flourish.

Thou art faithful to revive the dead. Blessed art thou, O Lord, who revivest the dead.

Thou art holy and thy name is holy, and holy beings praise thee daily. Blessed art thou, O Lord, holy God.

Thou didst choose us from among all peoples; thou didst love and favor us; thou didst exalt us above all tongues and sanctify us with thy commandments. Thou, our King, didst draw us near to thy service and call us by thy great and holy name.

---

iority of other nations. "It was the *noblesse oblige* of the God-appointed worker for the entire human race" (Gudemann, *Das Judenthum*). The selection of Israel and the Oneness of God are closely related concepts which blend into one aspiration and ideal for a united mankind. Only in Israel did the ethical monotheism exist; and wherever else it is found later on, it has been derived directly or indirectly from Israel. The term *election* of Israel expresses a historical fact. Israel feels itself chosen, not as a master but as a servant. It separates itself from others only for the purpose of uniting them.

On Saturday night :

(וַתּוֹדִיעֵנוּ, יְיָ אֱלֹהֵינוּ, אֶת מִשְׁפְּטֵי צִדְקֶךָ, וַתְּלַמְּדֵנוּ לַעֲשׂוֹת חֻקֵּי רְצוֹנֶךָ. וַתִּתֶּן־לָנוּ, יְיָ אֱלֹהֵינוּ, מִשְׁפָּטִים יְשָׁרִים וְתוֹרוֹת אֱמֶת, חֻקִּים וּמִצְוֹת טוֹבִים; וַתַּנְחִילֵנוּ זְמַנֵּי שָׂשׂוֹן וּמוֹעֲדֵי קֹדֶשׁ וְחַגֵּי נְדָבָה, וַתּוֹרִישֵׁנוּ קְדֻשַּׁת שַׁבָּת וּכְבוֹד מוֹעֵד וַחֲגִיגַת הָרֶגֶל; וַתַּבְדֵּל, יְיָ אֱלֹהֵינוּ, בֵּין קֹדֶשׁ לְחֹל, בֵּין אוֹר לְחֹשֶׁךְ, בֵּין יִשְׂרָאֵל לָעַמִּים, בֵּין יוֹם הַשְּׁבִיעִי לְשֵׁשֶׁת יְמֵי הַמַּעֲשֶׂה. בֵּין קְדֻשַּׁת שַׁבָּת לִקְדֻשַּׁת יוֹם טוֹב הִבְדַּלְתָּ, וְאֶת יוֹם הַשְּׁבִיעִי מִשֵּׁשֶׁת יְמֵי הַמַּעֲשֶׂה קִדַּשְׁתָּ; הִבְדַּלְתָּ וְקִדַּשְׁתָּ אֶת עַמְּךָ יִשְׂרָאֵל בִּקְדֻשָּׁתֶךָ.)

וַתִּתֶּן־לָנוּ, יְיָ אֱלֹהֵינוּ, בְּאַהֲבָה (שַׁבָּתוֹת לִמְנוּחָה וּ)מוֹעֲדִים לְשִׂמְחָה, חַגִּים וּזְמַנִּים לְשָׂשׂוֹן, אֶת יוֹם (הַשַּׁבָּת הַזֶּה וְאֶת יוֹם) חַג הַשָּׁבֻעוֹת הַזֶּה, זְמַן מַתַּן תּוֹרָתֵנוּ (בְּאַהֲבָה) מִקְרָא קֹדֶשׁ, זֵכֶר לִיצִיאַת מִצְרָיִם.

אֱלֹהֵינוּ וֵאלֹהֵי אֲבוֹתֵינוּ, יַעֲלֶה וְיָבֹא, וְיַגִּיעַ וְיֵרָאֶה, וְיֵרָצֶה וְיִשָּׁמַע, וְיִפָּקֵד וְיִזָּכֵר, זִכְרוֹנֵנוּ וּפִקְדוֹנֵנוּ, וְזִכְרוֹן אֲבוֹתֵינוּ, וְזִכְרוֹן מָשִׁיחַ בֶּן־דָּוִד עַבְדֶּךָ, וְזִכְרוֹן יְרוּשָׁלַיִם עִיר קָדְשֶׁךָ, וְזִכְרוֹן כָּל עַמְּךָ בֵּית יִשְׂרָאֵל לְפָנֶיךָ, לִפְלֵיטָה וּלְטוֹבָה, לְחֵן וּלְחֶסֶד וּלְרַחֲמִים, לְחַיִּים וּלְשָׁלוֹם, בְּיוֹם חַג הַשָּׁבֻעוֹת הַזֶּה.

וְתוֹדִיעֵנוּ

is quoted in the Talmud (Berakhoth 33b) as a precious pearl (מרגניתא) and is attributed to Rav and Samuel, the founders of talmudic learning in Babylonia during the third century.

The paragraph וְתוֹדִיעֵנוּ is a good example of a formula transformed into a poem. In the course of time, several variations and additions have modified the original composition of this paragraph, which is quoted in the Talmud and by Maimonides somewhat differently.

וְתֶן לָנוּ mentions the pilgrim festivals חַגִּים וּזְמַנִּים (festive seasons). Since the terms *ḥaggim* and *zemannim* are employed as synonyms for festivals, the phrase זְמַן חֵרוּתֵנוּ does not mean that *Pesaḥ* is "the season of our freedom" but rather *our festival of freedom*.

On Saturday night:

(Thou, Lord our God, hast made known to us thy righteous judgments and taught us to perform thy pleasing statutes. Thou, Lord our God, hast given us right ordinances, true precepts and good laws. Thou hast granted us joyous holidays, holy festivals and feasts for freewill offerings; thou hast vouchsafed to us the holiness of the Sabbath, the glory of the festival and the pilgrimage of the festive season. Thou, Lord our God, hast made a distinction between the holy and the profane, between light and darkness, between Israel and the nations, between the seventh day and the six working days. Thou hast made a distinction between the holiness of the Sabbath and the holiness of the festival, and hast hallowed the seventh day above the six working days; thou hast distinguished and sanctified thy people Israel with thy holiness.)

Thou, Lord our God, hast graciously given us (Sabbaths for rest,) holidays for gladness, festive seasons for joy: (this Sabbath day and) this Feast of Weeks, our Festival of the Giving of the Torah, a holy convocation in remembrance of the exodus from Egypt.

Our God and God of our fathers, may the remembrance of us, of our fathers, of Messiah the son of David thy servant, of Jerusalem thy holy city, and of all thy people the house of Israel, ascend and come and be accepted before thee for deliverance and happiness, for grace, kindness and mercy, for life and peace, on this day of the Feast of Weeks.

According to Rashi (Betzah 17a), the title קדושת היום applies specifically to the paragraph ותתן לנו, which must have been known to the early authorities.

The prayer יעלה ויבא is based on the following passage in the Torah: "On your feasts and new moon festivals you shall sound the trumpets...they will serve as a reminder of you before your God" (Numbers 10:10). In the synagogues, it is customary to call out *Yaaleh v'Yavo* before the *Amidah* on the eve of *Rosh Ḥodesh* as a reminder to the congregation to insert this prayer in the proper place. Recited for the prosperity of the people and for deliverance and happiness, kindness and mercy, life and peace, *Yaaleh v'Yavo* refers also to Jerusalem, Messiah, and Israel. The Talmud (Berakhoth 29b) alludes to *Yaaleh v'Yavo*, referring to it by name in Sofrim 19:7. The Hebrew original of this prayer opens with a collocation of eight verbs, each of which heightens the cumulative effect. In English, however, it would be less pleasing to reproduce all of them.

The paragraph והשיאנו, containing the synonyms מועדים and זמנים, is a plea to God to grant us the true spiritual benefit of the festivals.

זָכְרֵנוּ, יְיָ אֱלֹהֵינוּ, בּוֹ לְטוֹבָה, וּפָקְדֵנוּ בוֹ לִבְרָכָה, וְהוֹשִׁיעֵנוּ
בוֹ לְחַיִּים; וּבִדְבַר יְשׁוּעָה וְרַחֲמִים חוּס וְחָנֵּנוּ, וְרַחֵם עָלֵינוּ
וְהוֹשִׁיעֵנוּ, כִּי אֵלֶיךָ עֵינֵינוּ, כִּי אֵל מֶלֶךְ חַנּוּן וְרַחוּם אָתָּה.

וְהַשִּׂיאֵנוּ, יְיָ אֱלֹהֵינוּ, אֶת בִּרְכַּת מוֹעֲדֶיךָ לְחַיִּים וּלְשָׁלוֹם,
לְשִׂמְחָה וּלְשָׂשׂוֹן, כַּאֲשֶׁר רָצִיתָ וְאָמַרְתָּ לְבָרְכֵנוּ. אֱלֹהֵינוּ
וֵאלֹהֵי אֲבוֹתֵינוּ, (רְצֵה בִמְנוּחָתֵנוּ) קַדְּשֵׁנוּ בְּמִצְוֹתֶיךָ וְתֵן חֶלְקֵנוּ
בְּתוֹרָתֶךָ, שַׂבְּעֵנוּ מִטּוּבֶךָ וְשַׂמְּחֵנוּ בִּישׁוּעָתֶךָ, וְטַהֵר לִבֵּנוּ
לְעָבְדְּךָ בֶּאֱמֶת; וְהַנְחִילֵנוּ, יְיָ אֱלֹהֵינוּ, (בְּאַהֲבָה וּבְרָצוֹן)
בְּשִׂמְחָה וּבְשָׂשׂוֹן (שַׁבָּת וּ)מוֹעֲדֵי קָדְשֶׁךָ, וְיִשְׂמְחוּ בְךָ יִשְׂרָאֵל
מְקַדְּשֵׁי שְׁמֶךָ. בָּרוּךְ אַתָּה, יְיָ, מְקַדֵּשׁ (הַשַּׁבָּת וְ)יִשְׂרָאֵל
וְהַזְּמַנִּים.

רְצֵה, יְיָ אֱלֹהֵינוּ, בְּעַמְּךָ יִשְׂרָאֵל וּבִתְפִלָּתָם; וְהָשֵׁב אֶת
הָעֲבוֹדָה לִדְבִיר בֵּיתֶךָ, וְאִשֵּׁי יִשְׂרָאֵל וּתְפִלָּתָם בְּאַהֲבָה
תְקַבֵּל בְּרָצוֹן, וּתְהִי לְרָצוֹן תָּמִיד עֲבוֹדַת יִשְׂרָאֵל עַמֶּךָ.

וְתֶחֱזֶינָה עֵינֵינוּ בְּשׁוּבְךָ לְצִיּוֹן בְּרַחֲמִים. בָּרוּךְ אַתָּה, יְיָ,
הַמַּחֲזִיר שְׁכִינָתוֹ לְצִיּוֹן.

מוֹדִים אֲנַחְנוּ לָךְ, שָׁאַתָּה הוּא יְיָ אֱלֹהֵינוּ וֵאלֹהֵי אֲבוֹתֵינוּ
לְעוֹלָם וָעֶד. צוּר חַיֵּינוּ, מָגֵן יִשְׁעֵנוּ אַתָּה הוּא. לְדוֹר וָדוֹר
נוֹדֶה לְּךָ, וּנְסַפֵּר תְּהִלָּתֶךָ, עַל חַיֵּינוּ הַמְּסוּרִים בְּיָדֶךָ, וְעַל
נִשְׁמוֹתֵינוּ הַפְּקוּדוֹת לָךְ, וְעַל נִסֶּיךָ שֶׁבְּכָל יוֹם עִמָּנוּ, וְעַל
נִפְלְאוֹתֶיךָ וְטוֹבוֹתֶיךָ שֶׁבְּכָל עֵת, עֶרֶב וָבֹקֶר וְצָהֳרָיִם. הַטּוֹב
כִּי לֹא כָלוּ רַחֲמֶיךָ, וְהַמְרַחֵם כִּי לֹא תַמּוּ חֲסָדֶיךָ, מֵעוֹלָם
קִוִּינוּ לָךְ.

Remember us this day, Lord our God, for happiness; be mindful of us for blessing; save us to enjoy life. With a promise of salvation and mercy spare us and be gracious to us; have pity on us and save us, for we look to thee, for thou art a gracious and merciful God and King.

Bestow on us, Lord our God, the blessings of thy festivals for life and peace, for joy and gladness, as thou didst promise to bless us. Our God and God of our Fathers, (be pleased with our rest) sanctify us with thy commandments and grant us a share in thy Torah; satisfy us with thy goodness and gladden us with thy help; purify our heart to serve thee sincerely. In thy gracious love, Lord our God, grant us thy holy (Sabbath and) festivals for gladness and joy; may Israel who sanctifies thy name rejoice in thee. Blessed art thou, O Lord, who hallowest (the Sabbath and) Israel and the festivals.

Be pleased, Lord our God, with thy people Israel and with their prayer; restore the worship to thy most holy sanctuary; accept Israel's offerings and prayer with gracious love. May the worship of thy people Israel be ever pleasing to thee.

May our eyes behold thy return in mercy to Zion. Blessed art thou, O Lord, who restorest thy divine presence to Zion.

We ever thank thee, who art the Lord our God and the God of our fathers. Thou art the strength of our life and our saving shield. In every generation we will thank thee and recount thy praise—for our lives which are in thy charge, for our souls which are in thy care, for thy miracles which are daily with us, and for thy continual wonders and favors—evening, morning and noon. Beneficent One, whose mercies never fail, Merciful One, whose kindnesses never cease, thou hast always been our hope.

מודים is based on Psalms 79:13 and 55:18, namely: ונודה לך לעולם, לדור. ערב ובקר וצהרים אשיחה and ודור נספר תהלתך. The phrase מודים אנחנו לך is taken from I Chronicles 29:13.

וְעַל כֻּלָּם יִתְבָּרַךְ וְיִתְרוֹמַם שִׁמְךָ, מַלְכֵּנוּ, תָּמִיד לְעוֹלָם וָעֶד.

וְכֹל הַחַיִּים יוֹדוּךְ סֶּלָה, וִיהַלְלוּ אֶת שִׁמְךָ בֶּאֱמֶת, הָאֵל,
יְשׁוּעָתֵנוּ וְעֶזְרָתֵנוּ סֶלָה. בָּרוּךְ אַתָּה, יְיָ, הַטּוֹב שִׁמְךָ, וּלְךָ נָאֶה
לְהוֹדוֹת.

שָׁלוֹם רָב עַל יִשְׂרָאֵל עַמְּךָ תָּשִׂים לְעוֹלָם, כִּי אַתָּה הוּא
מֶלֶךְ אָדוֹן לְכָל הַשָּׁלוֹם, וְטוֹב בְּעֵינֶיךָ לְבָרֵךְ אֶת עַמְּךָ
יִשְׂרָאֵל בְּכָל עֵת וּבְכָל שָׁעָה בִּשְׁלוֹמֶךָ. בָּרוּךְ אַתָּה, יְיָ, הַמְבָרֵךְ
אֶת עַמּוֹ יִשְׂרָאֵל בַּשָּׁלוֹם.

After the *Amidah* add the following meditation:

אֱלֹהַי, נְצֹר לְשׁוֹנִי מֵרָע, וּשְׂפָתַי מִדַּבֵּר מִרְמָה, וְלִמְקַלְלַי
נַפְשִׁי תִדּוֹם, וְנַפְשִׁי כֶּעָפָר לַכֹּל תִּהְיֶה. פְּתַח לִבִּי בְּתוֹרָתֶךָ,
וּבְמִצְוֹתֶיךָ תִּרְדּוֹף נַפְשִׁי; וְכֹל הַחוֹשְׁבִים עָלַי רָעָה, מְהֵרָה
הָפֵר עֲצָתָם וְקַלְקֵל מַחֲשַׁבְתָּם. עֲשֵׂה לְמַעַן שְׁמֶךָ, עֲשֵׂה לְמַעַן
יְמִינֶךָ, עֲשֵׂה לְמַעַן קְדֻשָּׁתֶךָ, עֲשֵׂה לְמַעַן תּוֹרָתֶךָ. לְמַעַן יֵחָלְצוּן
יְדִידֶיךָ, הוֹשִׁיעָה יְמִינְךָ וַעֲנֵנִי. יִהְיוּ לְרָצוֹן אִמְרֵי פִי וְהֶגְיוֹן לִבִּי
לְפָנֶיךָ, יְיָ, צוּרִי וְגוֹאֲלִי. עֹשֶׂה שָׁלוֹם בִּמְרוֹמָיו, הוּא יַעֲשֶׂה
שָׁלוֹם עָלֵינוּ וְעַל כָּל יִשְׂרָאֵל, וְאִמְרוּ אָמֵן.

יְהִי רָצוֹן מִלְּפָנֶיךָ, יְיָ אֱלֹהֵינוּ וֵאלֹהֵי אֲבוֹתֵינוּ, שֶׁיִּבָּנֶה בֵית
הַמִּקְדָּשׁ בִּמְהֵרָה בְיָמֵינוּ, וְתֵן חֶלְקֵנוּ בְּתוֹרָתֶךָ. וְשָׁם נַעֲבָדְךָ
בְּיִרְאָה, כִּימֵי עוֹלָם וּכְשָׁנִים קַדְמוֹנִיּוֹת. וְעָרְבָה לַיְיָ מִנְחַת
יְהוּדָה וִירוּשָׁלָיִם, כִּימֵי עוֹלָם וּכְשָׁנִים קַדְמוֹנִיּוֹת.

נְצוֹר לְשׁוֹנִי מֵרָע suggests a variety of Jewish ethical ideas, such as the
following:

According to Rabbi Akiva, the most comprehensive precept in the Torah
is the command: "You shall love your neighbor as yourself" (Leviticus

For all these acts may thy name, our King, be blessed and exalted forever and ever.

All the living shall ever thank thee and sincerely praise thy name, O God, who art always our salvation and help. Blessed art thou, O Lord, Beneficent One, to whom it is fitting to give thanks.

O grant abundant peace to Israel thy people forever, for thou art the King and Lord of all peace. May it please thee to bless thy people Israel with peace at all times and at all hours. Blessed art thou, O Lord, who blessest thy people Israel with peace.

After the Shemoneh Esreh add the following meditation:

My God, guard my tongue from evil, and my lips from speaking falsehood. May my soul be silent to those who insult me; be my soul lowly to all as the dust. Open my heart to thy Torah, that my soul may follow thy commands. Speedily defeat the counsel of all those who plan evil against me, and upset their design. Do it for the glory of thy name; do it for the sake of thy power; do it for the sake of thy holiness; do it for the sake of thy Torah. That thy beloved may be rescued, save with thy right hand and answer me. May the words of my mouth and the meditation of my heart be pleasing before thee, O Lord, my Stronghold and my Redeemer.[1] May he who creates peace in his high heavens create peace for us and for all Israel, Amen.

May it be thy will, Lord our God and God of our fathers, that the Temple be speedily rebuilt in our days, and grant us a share in thy Torah. There we will serve thee with reverence, as in the days of old and as in former years. Then the offering of Judah and Jerusalem will be pleasing to the Lord, as in the days of old and as in former years.[2]

19:18). Several talmudic proverbial sayings are to the effect that it is easy to acquire an enemy, but difficult to win a friend; he who turns his enemy into a friend is the bravest hero. The greater the man, the humbler he is. A person can forget in two years what he has learned in twenty. In prosperity, people feel brotherly to one another. He who studies but does not review his work is like one who sows but does not reap. Pay special attention to the poor, for it is from them that knowledge will come. Men should be careful not to give their wives any cause for tears, for God counts their tears.

---

[1] *Psalms* 60:7; 19:15.   [2] *Malachi* 3:4.

On Sabbath:

Reader and Congregation:

(וַיְכֻלּוּ הַשָּׁמַיִם וְהָאָרֶץ וְכָל צְבָאָם. וַיְכַל אֱלֹהִים בַּיּוֹם הַשְּׁבִיעִי מְלַאכְתּוֹ אֲשֶׁר עָשָׂה, וַיִּשְׁבֹּת בַּיּוֹם הַשְּׁבִיעִי מִכָּל מְלַאכְתּוֹ אֲשֶׁר עָשָׂה. וַיְבָרֶךְ אֱלֹהִים אֶת יוֹם הַשְּׁבִיעִי וַיְקַדֵּשׁ אֹתוֹ, כִּי בוֹ שָׁבַת מִכָּל מְלַאכְתּוֹ אֲשֶׁר בָּרָא אֱלֹהִים לַעֲשׂוֹת.

Reader:

בָּרוּךְ אַתָּה, יְיָ אֱלֹהֵינוּ וֵאלֹהֵי אֲבוֹתֵינוּ, אֱלֹהֵי אַבְרָהָם, אֱלֹהֵי יִצְחָק, וֵאלֹהֵי יַעֲקֹב, הָאֵל הַגָּדוֹל הַגִּבּוֹר וְהַנּוֹרָא, אֵל עֶלְיוֹן, קוֹנֵה שָׁמַיִם וָאָרֶץ.

מָגֵן אָבוֹת בִּדְבָרוֹ, מְחַיֵּה מֵתִים בְּמַאֲמָרוֹ, הָאֵל הַקָּדוֹשׁ שֶׁאֵין כָּמוֹהוּ, הַמֵּנִיחַ לְעַמּוֹ בְּיוֹם שַׁבַּת קָדְשׁוֹ, כִּי בָם רָצָה לְהָנִיחַ לָהֶם; לְפָנָיו נַעֲבֹד בְּיִרְאָה וָפַחַד, וְנוֹדֶה לִשְׁמוֹ בְּכָל יוֹם תָּמִיד מֵעֵין הַבְּרָכוֹת. Reader אֵל הַהוֹדָאוֹת, אֲדוֹן הַשָּׁלוֹם, מְקַדֵּשׁ הַשַּׁבָּת וּמְבָרֵךְ שְׁבִיעִי, וּמֵנִיחַ בִּקְדֻשָּׁה לְעַם מְדֻשְּׁנֵי עֹנֶג, זֵכֶר לְמַעֲשֵׂה בְרֵאשִׁית.

אֱלֹהֵינוּ וֵאלֹהֵי אֲבוֹתֵינוּ, רְצֵה בִמְנוּחָתֵנוּ. קַדְּשֵׁנוּ בְּמִצְוֹתֶיךָ, וְתֵן חֶלְקֵנוּ בְּתוֹרָתֶךָ; שַׂבְּעֵנוּ מִטּוּבֶךָ, וְשַׂמְּחֵנוּ בִּישׁוּעָתֶךָ; וְטַהֵר לִבֵּנוּ לְעָבְדְּךָ בֶּאֱמֶת; וְהַנְחִילֵנוּ, יְיָ אֱלֹהֵינוּ, בְּאַהֲבָה וּבְרָצוֹן שַׁבַּת קָדְשֶׁךָ, וְיָנוּחוּ בָהּ יִשְׂרָאֵל מְקַדְּשֵׁי שְׁמֶךָ. בָּרוּךְ אַתָּה, יְיָ, מְקַדֵּשׁ הַשַּׁבָּת.)

מגן אבות contains the substance of the seven benedictions constituting the *Amidah* for Sabbath-eve. It was originally added in order to prolong the service for the convenience of late-comers.

On Sabbath:

Reader and Congregation:

Va-y'chulu ha-shomayim v'ho-orets v'chol ts'vo-om
Va-y'chal elo-heem ba-yom ha-sh'vee-ee m'lach-to asher osoh
Va-yishbos ba-yom hash'vee-ee mikkol m'lach-to asher osoh.
Va-y'vorech eloheem es yom ha-sh'vee-ee va-y'kaddeysh oso
Kee vo shovas mikkol m'lach-to asher boro eloheem la-asos.

Blessed art thou, Lord our God and God of our fathers, God
of Abraham, God of Isaac and God of Jacob; great, mighty and
revered God, supreme God, Master of heaven and earth.

Mogeyn ovos bidvoro, m'cha-yey mey-seem b'ma-amoro,
Ho-eyl ha-kodosh she-eyn komohu,
Ha-meynee-ach l'ammo b'yom shabbas kodsho,
Kee vom rotsoh l'honee-ach lohem.

L'fonov na-avod b'yir-oh vofachad, v'nodeh lishmo
B'chol yom tomeed mey-eyn ha-b'rochos.
Eyl ha-hodo-os, adon ha-sholom, m'kaddeysh ha-shabbos,
Um'vo-reych shvee-ee, umeynee-ach bikdushoh
L'am m'dushney oneg zeycher l'ma-asey v-reyshees.

Reader:

Our God and God of our fathers, be pleased with our rest.

Kad'sheynu b'mits-vo-secho
V'seyn chelkeynu b'so-rosecho;
Sab'eynu mittu-vecho
V'sam-cheynu bee-shu-osecho.
V'ta-heyr libbeynu l'ovd'cho be-emes;
V'han-chee-leynu adonoy eloheynu
B'ahavoh uv'rotson shabbas kod'shecho
V'yo-nuchu voh yisro-eyl m'kad'shey sh'mecho.
Boruch attoh adonoy m'kaddeysh ha-shabbos.

Reader:

יִתְגַּדַּל וְיִתְקַדַּשׁ שְׁמֵהּ רַבָּא בְּעָלְמָא דִי בְרָא כִרְעוּתֵהּ;
וְיַמְלִיךְ מַלְכוּתֵהּ בְּחַיֵּיכוֹן וּבְיוֹמֵיכוֹן, וּבְחַיֵּי דְכָל בֵּית יִשְׂרָאֵל,
בַּעֲגָלָא וּבִזְמַן קָרִיב, וְאִמְרוּ אָמֵן.

יְהֵא שְׁמֵהּ רַבָּא מְבָרַךְ לְעָלַם וּלְעָלְמֵי עָלְמַיָּא.

יִתְבָּרַךְ וְיִשְׁתַּבַּח, וְיִתְפָּאַר וְיִתְרוֹמַם, וְיִתְנַשֵּׂא וְיִתְהַדָּר,
וְיִתְעַלֶּה וְיִתְהַלָּל שְׁמֵהּ דְּקֻדְשָׁא, בְּרִיךְ הוּא, לְעֵלָּא מִן
כָּל בִּרְכָתָא וְשִׁירָתָא, תֻּשְׁבְּחָתָא וְנֶחֱמָתָא, דַּאֲמִירָן בְּעָלְמָא,
וְאִמְרוּ אָמֵן.

תִּתְקַבֵּל צְלוֹתְהוֹן וּבָעוּתְהוֹן דְּכָל בֵּית יִשְׂרָאֵל קֳדָם אֲבוּהוֹן
דִי בִשְׁמַיָּא, וְאִמְרוּ אָמֵן.

יְהֵא שְׁלָמָא רַבָּא מִן שְׁמַיָּא, וְחַיִּים, עָלֵינוּ וְעַל כָּל יִשְׂרָאֵל,
וְאִמְרוּ אָמֵן.

עֹשֶׂה שָׁלוֹם בִּמְרוֹמָיו, הוּא יַעֲשֶׂה שָׁלוֹם עָלֵינוּ וְעַל כָּל
יִשְׂרָאֵל, וְאִמְרוּ אָמֵן.

עָלֵינוּ לְשַׁבֵּחַ לַאֲדוֹן הַכֹּל, לָתֵת גְּדֻלָּה לְיוֹצֵר בְּרֵאשִׁית,
שֶׁלֹּא עָשָׂנוּ כְּגוֹיֵי הָאֲרָצוֹת, וְלֹא שָׂמָנוּ כְּמִשְׁפְּחוֹת הָאֲדָמָה;
שֶׁלֹּא שָׂם חֶלְקֵנוּ כָּהֶם, וְגֹרָלֵנוּ כְּכָל הֲמוֹנָם. וַאֲנַחְנוּ כּוֹרְעִים
וּמִשְׁתַּחֲוִים וּמוֹדִים לִפְנֵי מֶלֶךְ מַלְכֵי הַמְּלָכִים, הַקָּדוֹשׁ בָּרוּךְ
הוּא, שֶׁהוּא נוֹטֶה שָׁמַיִם וְיוֹסֵד אָרֶץ, וּמוֹשַׁב יְקָרוֹ בַּשָּׁמַיִם
מִמַּעַל, וּשְׁכִינַת עֻזּוֹ בְּגָבְהֵי מְרוֹמִים. הוּא אֱלֹהֵינוּ, אֵין עוֹד;
אֱמֶת מַלְכֵּנוּ, אֶפֶס זוּלָתוֹ, כַּכָּתוּב בְּתוֹרָתוֹ: וְיָדַעְתָּ הַיּוֹם
וַהֲשֵׁבֹתָ אֶל לְבָבֶךָ, כִּי יְיָ הוּא הָאֱלֹהִים בַּשָּׁמַיִם מִמַּעַל וְעַל
הָאָרֶץ מִתָּחַת, אֵין עוֹד.

Reader:

Glorified and sanctified be God's great name throughout the world which he has created according to his will. May he establish his kingdom in your lifetime and during your days, and within the life of the entire house of Israel, speedily and soon; and say, Amen.

May his great name be blessed forever and to all eternity.

Blessed and praised, glorified and exalted, extolled and honored, adored and lauded be the name of the Holy One, blessed be he, beyond all the blessings and hymns, praises and consolations that are ever spoken in the world; and say, Amen.

May the prayers and supplications of the whole household of Israel be accepted by their Father who is in heaven; and say, Amen.

May there be abundant peace from heaven, and life, for us and for all Israel; and say, Amen.

He who creates peace in his celestial heights, may he create peace for us and for all Israel; and say, Amen.

ALENU

It is our duty to praise the Master of all, to exalt the Creator of the universe, who has not made us like the nations of the world and has not placed us like the families of the earth; who has not designed our destiny to be like theirs, nor our lot like that of all their multitude. We bend the knee and bow and acknowledge before the supreme King of kings, the Holy One, blessed be he, that it is he who stretched forth the heavens and founded the earth. His seat of glory is in the heavens above; his abode of majesty is in the lofty heights. He is our God, there is none else, truly, he is our King, there is none besides him, as it is written in his Torah: "You shall know this day, and reflect in your heart, that it is the Lord who is God in the heavens above and on the earth beneath, there is none else."[1]

עלינו, one of the most sublime prayers of antiquity, has been ascribed to various authors. According to an old tradition, it was composed by Joshua when he entered the Promised Land.

---

[1] *Deuteronomy* 4:39.

עַל כֵּן נְקַוֶּה לְּךָ, יְיָ אֱלֹהֵינוּ, לִרְאוֹת מְהֵרָה בְּתִפְאֶרֶת עֻזֶּךָ,
לְהַעֲבִיר גִּלּוּלִים מִן הָאָרֶץ, וְהָאֱלִילִים כָּרוֹת יִכָּרֵתוּן; לְתַקֵּן
עוֹלָם בְּמַלְכוּת שַׁדַּי, וְכָל בְּנֵי בָשָׂר יִקְרְאוּ בִשְׁמֶךָ, לְהַפְנוֹת
אֵלֶיךָ כָּל רִשְׁעֵי אָרֶץ. יַכִּירוּ וְיֵדְעוּ כָּל יוֹשְׁבֵי תֵבֵל, כִּי לְךָ
תִּכְרַע כָּל בֶּרֶךְ, תִּשָּׁבַע כָּל לָשׁוֹן. לְפָנֶיךָ, יְיָ אֱלֹהֵינוּ, יִכְרְעוּ
וְיִפֹּלוּ, וְלִכְבוֹד שִׁמְךָ יְקָר יִתֵּנוּ, וִיקַבְּלוּ כֻלָּם אֶת עֹל מַלְכוּתֶךָ,
וְתִמְלֹךְ עֲלֵיהֶם מְהֵרָה לְעוֹלָם וָעֶד; כִּי הַמַּלְכוּת שֶׁלְּךָ הִיא,
וּלְעוֹלְמֵי עַד תִּמְלֹךְ בְּכָבוֹד, כַּכָּתוּב בְּתוֹרָתֶךָ: יְיָ יִמְלֹךְ
לְעֹלָם וָעֶד. Reader וְנֶאֱמַר: וְהָיָה יְיָ לְמֶלֶךְ עַל כָּל הָאָרֶץ;
בַּיּוֹם הַהוּא יִהְיֶה יְיָ אֶחָד וּשְׁמוֹ אֶחָד.

MOURNERS' KADDISH

יִתְגַּדַּל וְיִתְקַדַּשׁ שְׁמֵהּ רַבָּא בְּעָלְמָא דִּי בְרָא כִרְעוּתֵהּ;
וְיַמְלִיךְ מַלְכוּתֵהּ בְּחַיֵּיכוֹן וּבְיוֹמֵיכוֹן, וּבְחַיֵּי דְכָל בֵּית יִשְׂרָאֵל
בַּעֲגָלָא וּבִזְמַן קָרִיב, וְאִמְרוּ אָמֵן.

יְהֵא שְׁמֵהּ רַבָּא מְבָרַךְ לְעָלַם וּלְעָלְמֵי עָלְמַיָּא.

יִתְבָּרַךְ וְיִשְׁתַּבַּח, וְיִתְפָּאַר וְיִתְרוֹמַם, וְיִתְנַשֵּׂא וְיִתְהַדָּר,
וְיִתְעַלֶּה וְיִתְהַלָּל שְׁמֵהּ דְּקֻדְשָׁא, בְּרִיךְ הוּא, לְעֵלָּא מִן כָּל
בִּרְכָתָא וְשִׁירָתָא, תֻּשְׁבְּחָתָא וְנֶחֱמָתָא, דַּאֲמִירָן בְּעָלְמָא
וְאִמְרוּ אָמֵן.

יְהֵא שְׁלָמָא רַבָּא מִן שְׁמַיָּא, וְחַיִּים, עָלֵינוּ וְעַל כָּל יִשְׂרָאֵל,
וְאִמְרוּ אָמֵן.

עֹשֶׂה שָׁלוֹם בִּמְרוֹמָיו, הוּא יַעֲשֶׂה שָׁלוֹם עָלֵינוּ וְעַל כָּל
יִשְׂרָאֵל, וְאִמְרוּ אָמֵן.

We hope therefore, Lord our God, soon to behold thy majestic glory, when the abominations shall be removed from the earth, and the false gods exterminated; when the world shall be perfected under the reign of the Almighty, and all mankind will call upon thy name, and all the wicked of the earth will be turned to thee. May all the inhabitants of the world realize and know that to thee every knee must bend, every tongue must vow allegiance. May they bend the knee and prostrate themselves before thee, Lord our God, and give honor to thy glorious name; may they all accept the yoke of thy kingdom, and do thou reign over them speedily forever and ever. For the kingdom is thine, and to all eternity thou wilt reign in glory, as it is written in thy Torah: "The Lord shall be King forever and ever."[3] And it is said: "The Lord shall be King over all the earth; on that day the Lord shall be One, and his name One."[2]

MOURNERS' KADDISH

Glorified and sanctified be God's great name throughout the world which he has created according to his will. May he establish his kingdom in your lifetime and during your days, and within the life of the entire house of Israel, speedily and soon; and say, Amen.

May his great name be blessed forever and to all eternity.

Blessed and praised, glorified and exalted, extolled and honored, adored and lauded be the name of the Holy One, blessed be he, beyond all the blessings and hymns, praises and consolations that are ever spoken in the world; and say, Amen.

May there be abundant peace from heaven, and life, for us and for all Israel; and say, Amen.

He who creates peace in his celestial heights, may he create peace for us and for all Israel; and say, Amen.

[1] *Exodus* 15:18. [2] *Zechariah* 14:9.

קִדּוּשׁ לְיוֹם טוֹב

On Sabbath eve:

(וַיְהִי עֶרֶב וַיְהִי בֹקֶר

יוֹם הַשִּׁשִּׁי. וַיְכֻלּוּ הַשָּׁמַיִם וְהָאָרֶץ וְכָל צְבָאָם. וַיְכַל אֱלֹהִים
בַּיּוֹם הַשְּׁבִיעִי מְלַאכְתּוֹ אֲשֶׁר עָשָׂה, וַיִּשְׁבֹּת בַּיּוֹם הַשְּׁבִיעִי מִכָּל
מְלַאכְתּוֹ אֲשֶׁר עָשָׂה. וַיְבָרֶךְ אֱלֹהִים אֶת יוֹם הַשְּׁבִיעִי וַיְקַדֵּשׁ
אֹתוֹ, כִּי בוֹ שָׁבַת מִכָּל מְלַאכְתּוֹ אֲשֶׁר בָּרָא אֱלֹהִים לַעֲשׂוֹת.)

סַבְרֵי מָרָנָן וְרַבּוֹתַי.

בָּרוּךְ אַתָּה, יְיָ אֱלֹהֵינוּ, מֶלֶךְ הָעוֹלָם, בּוֹרֵא פְּרִי הַגָּפֶן.

בָּרוּךְ אַתָּה, יְיָ אֱלֹהֵינוּ, מֶלֶךְ הָעוֹלָם, אֲשֶׁר בָּחַר בָּנוּ מִכָּל
עָם, וְרוֹמְמָנוּ מִכָּל לָשׁוֹן, וְקִדְּשָׁנוּ בְּמִצְוֹתָיו. וַתִּתֶּן־לָנוּ, יְיָ
אֱלֹהֵינוּ, בְּאַהֲבָה (שַׁבָּתוֹת לִמְנוּחָה וּ)מוֹעֲדִים לְשִׂמְחָה, חַגִּים
וּזְמַנִּים לְשָׂשׂוֹן, אֶת יוֹם (הַשַּׁבָּת הַזֶּה, וְאֶת יוֹם)

חַג הַשָּׁבֻעוֹת הַזֶּה, זְמַן מַתַּן תּוֹרָתֵנוּ,

(בְּאַהֲבָה) מִקְרָא קֹדֶשׁ, זֵכֶר לִיצִיאַת מִצְרָיִם. כִּי בָנוּ בָחַרְתָּ,
וְאוֹתָנוּ קִדַּשְׁתָּ מִכָּל הָעַמִּים, (וְשַׁבָּת) וּמוֹעֲדֵי קָדְשֶׁךָ (בְּאַהֲבָה
וּבְרָצוֹן) בְּשִׂמְחָה וּבְשָׂשׂוֹן הִנְחַלְתָּנוּ. בָּרוּךְ אַתָּה, יְיָ, מְקַדֵּשׁ
(הַשַּׁבָּת וְ)יִשְׂרָאֵל וְהַזְּמַנִּים.

Before the evening and morning meals on Sabbaths and festivals, *Kiddush*
(Sanctification) is recited over wine, the symbol of joy, for it is "wine that cheers
man's heart" (Psalm 104:15). The use of wine in connection with the *Kiddush* is
spoken of in the Talmud, where the biblical command "remember the Sabbath"
is interpreted to mean "remember it over wine" (Pesaḥim 106a). Wine is metaphorically represented as the essence of goodness. Israel is likened to a vine brought
from Egypt and planted in Eretz Yisrael, where it took deep root and prospered
(Psalm 80:9-11). When wine is not available, the *Kiddush* is recited over two
loaves of bread (*leḥem mishneh*) that commemorate the double portion of manna
that was gathered on Fridays.

46

KIDDUSH FOR FESTIVALS

On Sabbath Eve:

(There was evening and there was morning—

The sixth day. Thus the heavens and the earth were finished, and all their host. By the seventh day God had completed his work which he had made, and he rested on the seventh day from all his work in which he had been engaged. Then God blessed the seventh day and hallowed it, because on it he rested from all his work which he had created.)

Blessed art thou, Lord our God, King of the universe, who createst the fruit of the vine.

Blessed art thou, Lord our God, King of the universe, who hast chosen and exalted us above all nations, and hast sanctified us with thy commandments. Thou, Lord our God, hast graciously given us (Sabbaths for rest,) holidays for gladness and festive seasons for joy: (this Sabbath day and) this

Feast of Weeks, our Festival of the Giving of the Torah,

a holy convocation in remembrance of the exodus from Egypt. Thou didst choose and sanctify us above all peoples; in thy gracious love, thou didst grant us thy holy (Sabbath and) festivals for gladness and joy. Blessed art thou, O Lord, who hallowest (the Sabbath,) Israel and the festivals.

The origin of the *Kiddush* is traced back to the early period of the Second Temple, and is attributed to the men of the Great Assembly, who flourished at that time.

On Sabbath eve, the *Kiddush* begins with the phrase יום הששי (the sixth day) and continues with the words ויכלו השמים (the heavens were completed). The initial letters of these four Hebrew words make up the tetragrammaton, the divine name ('ה 'ו 'ה 'י) of four letters. This will explain why the *Kiddush* begins with the last two words (יום הששי) of the first chapter of the Torah and immediately continues with the beginning of the second chapter.

The phrase סברי מרנן is inserted in the *Kiddush* to call attention to the blessing about to be pronounced over the wine. Literally it means: Attention, Gentlemen. By responding *Amen*, and listening with attention to the recital of the *Kiddush*, they fulfill their duty of bearing witness that the universe is the creation of God. Since the *Kiddush* is a form of testimony, all stand up as witnesses who testify standing.

On Saturday night add:

בָּרוּךְ אַתָּה, יְיָ אֱלֹהֵינוּ, מֶלֶךְ הָעוֹלָם, בּוֹרֵא מְאוֹרֵי הָאֵשׁ.

בָּרוּךְ אַתָּה, יְיָ אֱלֹהֵינוּ, מֶלֶךְ הָעוֹלָם, הַמַּבְדִּיל בֵּין קֹדֶשׁ לְחֹל, בֵּין אוֹר לְחְשֶׁךְ, בֵּין יִשְׂרָאֵל לָעַמִּים, בֵּין יוֹם הַשְּׁבִיעִי לְשֵׁשֶׁת יְמֵי הַמַּעֲשֶׂה. בֵּין קְדֻשַּׁת שַׁבָּת לִקְדֻשַּׁת יוֹם טוֹב הִבְדַּלְתָּ. וְאֶת יוֹם הַשְּׁבִיעִי מִשֵּׁשֶׁת יְמֵי הַמַּעֲשֶׂה קִדַּשְׁתָּ; הִבְדַּלְתָּ וְקִדַּשְׁתָּ אֶת עַמְּךָ יִשְׂרָאֵל בִּקְדֻשָּׁתֶךָ. בָּרוּךְ אַתָּה, יְיָ, הַמַּבְדִּיל בֵּין קֹדֶשׁ לְקֹדֶשׁ.

בָּרוּךְ אַתָּה, יְיָ אֱלֹהֵינוּ, מֶלֶךְ הָעוֹלָם, שֶׁהֶחֱיָנוּ וְקִיְּמָנוּ וְהִגִּיעָנוּ לַזְּמַן הַזֶּה.

זכר ליציאת מצרים refers to *Pesah, Shavuoth* and *Sukkoth,* directly connected with the exodus from Egypt. The same phrase is elsewhere applied to the Sabbath on the basis of Deuteronomy 5:15 ("Remember that you were once a slave in the land of Egypt, and that the Lord your God brought you out from there by a mighty hand and an outstretched arm; hence the Lord your God has commanded you to observe the Sabbath day").

The termination מקדש ישראל והזמנים is in the festival benediction. The mention of Israel is due to the specifically Israel character of the festivals, whereas the Sabbath preceded the choice of Israel, and applies to all mankind.

On all festivals other than the last two days of Passover, the benediction שהחיינו is added to the *Kiddush:* "Blessed art thou, Lord our God . . . who hast granted us life and sustenance and permitted us to reach this festival." *Sheheheyanu* is omitted on the last two nights of *Pesah,* which commemorate the crossing of the Red Sea, to indicate that we must not rejoice over the misfortune that befell our foes.

Havdalah (distinction), marking the end of Sabbath and festivals, corresponds to the *Kiddush,* which proclaims the holiness of Sabbath and festivals. Both are attributed to the men, of the Great Assembly, who functioned during and after the Persian period of Jewish history, about 500-300 before the common era. The *Havdalah,* recited over wine, consists of four benedictions: over wine, spices, light, and the distinction between the sacred and the profane, between light and darkness, between Israel and the nations, between the seventh day and the six workdays.

According to Maimonides, the symbolic use of fragrant spices is to cheer the soul which is saddened at the departure of the Sabbath. When a festival follows immediately after Sabbath the spices are omitted, because the soul then rejoices

On Saturday night add:

Blessed art thou, Lord our God, King of the universe, who createst the light of the fire.

Blessed art thou, Lord our God, King of the universe, who hast made a distinction between the sacred and the profane, between light and darkness, between Israel and the nations, between the seventh day and the six working days. Thou hast made a distinction between the holiness of the Sabbath and the holiness of the festival, and hast hallowed the seventh day above the six working days; thou hast distinguished and sanctified thy people Israel with thy holiness. Blessed art thou, O Lord, who makest a distinction between the greater holiness and the lesser holiness.

Blessed art thou, Lord our God, King of the universe, who hast granted us life and sustenance and permitted us to reach this season.

---

with the incoming festival. The wine for the *Havdalah* is allowed to flow over as a symbol of the overflowing blessing expected in the coming week. It is customary to cup the hands around the *Havdalah*-candle and to gaze at the fingernails. The reflection of the light on the fingernails causes the shadow to appear on the palm of the hand, thus indicating the distinction "between light and darkness."

A twisted candle of several wicks is used, because the phrase *meoré ha-esh* (the lights of fire) is in the plural. The custom of dipping the finger in the wine of the *Havdalah* and passing it over the eyes alludes to Psalm 19:9, where God's commands are described as "enlightening the eyes." These usages are not applicable whenever the *Havdalah* is recited as part of the *Kiddush* for festivals. In addition to the *Havdalah* over wine, there is another *Havdalah* inserted in the fourth benediction of the *Shemoneh Esreh.*

In talmudic literature, great importance is attached to the *Havdalah;* future salvation as well as material blessings are promised to those who recite the *Havdalah* over the wine cup. "He who resides in Israel, he who teaches his children Torah, and he who recites the *Havdalah* at the conclusion of the Sabbath will enter the world-to-come" (Berakhoth 33a). According to a talmudic legend, fire was one of the things God had left uncreated when Sabbath set in; but after the close of the Sabbath, God endowed man with divine wisdom. "Man then took two stones, and by rubbing them together produced fire . . ." (Pesaḥim 53b).

The Midrash elaborates this as follows: "The light which God created on the first day lit up the world for man from the time he was created until the sunset of the following day; the surrounding darkness filled Adam with dread . . . Then God furnished him with two bricks which he rubbed together until fire was produced; whereupon he offered a benediction over the fire" (Genesis Rabbah 11:2).

בִּרְכוֹת הַשַּׁחַר

Upon entering the synagogue:

מַה טֹּבוּ אֹהָלֶיךָ יַעֲקֹב, מִשְׁכְּנֹתֶיךָ יִשְׂרָאֵל. וַאֲנִי בְּרֹב
חַסְדְּךָ אָבֹא בֵיתֶךָ, אֶשְׁתַּחֲוֶה אֶל הֵיכַל קָדְשְׁךָ בְּיִרְאָתֶךָ. יְיָ,
אָהַבְתִּי מְעוֹן בֵּיתֶךָ, וּמְקוֹם מִשְׁכַּן כְּבוֹדֶךָ. וַאֲנִי אֶשְׁתַּחֲוֶה
וְאֶכְרָעָה, אֶבְרְכָה לִפְנֵי יְיָ עֹשִׂי. וַאֲנִי תְפִלָּתִי לְךָ, יְיָ, עֵת רָצוֹן;
אֱלֹהִים, בְּרָב־חַסְדֶּךָ, עֲנֵנִי בֶּאֱמֶת יִשְׁעֶךָ.

Before putting on the *tallith*:

בָּרְכִי נַפְשִׁי אֶת יְיָ; יְיָ אֱלֹהַי, גָּדַלְתָּ מְאֹד, הוֹד וְהָדָר לָבָשְׁתָּ.
עֹטֶה אוֹר כַּשַּׂלְמָה, נוֹטֶה שָׁמַיִם כַּיְרִיעָה.

הִנְנִי מִתְעַטֵּף בְּטַלִּית שֶׁל צִיצִת כְּדֵי לְקַיֵּם מִצְוַת בּוֹרְאִי,
כַּכָּתוּב בַּתּוֹרָה: וְעָשׂוּ לָהֶם צִיצִת עַל כַּנְפֵי בִגְדֵיהֶם לְדֹרֹתָם.
וּכְשֵׁם שֶׁאֲנִי מִתְכַּסֶּה בְּטַלִּית בָּעוֹלָם הַזֶּה, כֵּן תִּזְכֶּה נִשְׁמָתִי
לְהִתְלַבֵּשׁ בְּטַלִּית נָאָה לָעוֹלָם הַבָּא בְּגַן עֵדֶן. אָמֵן.

משכנותיך, אהליך are interpreted in the Talmud (Sanhedrin 105b) to refer
to synagogues and schools. עת רצון is taken to mean the time of public worship (Berakhoth 8a).

ציצית is a continual reminder of our obligation to keep God's commands.
The purple-blue thread (פתיל תכלת) entwined in the *tsitsith* was originally its
chief distinction. When, however, it became impossible to procure the special
dye required, it was made permissible to use white threads alone. Why blue?
"Because this color resembles the sea, the sea resembles the sky ..." (Menaḥoth 43b).

Four threads are taken, of which one (the *shammash*) is considerably
longer than the rest, for each of the four corners of the *tallith*. The four threads
are drawn through a small hole or eyelet and the ends brought together.
A double knot is tied close to the margin of the *tallith;* the *shammash* is then

PRELIMINARY MORNING SERVICE

Upon entering the synagogue:

How goodly are your tents, O Jacob, your habitations, O Israel!

By thy abundant grace I enter thy house; I worship before thy holy shrine with reverence. O Lord, I love thy abode, the place where thy glory dwells. I will worship and bow down; I will bend the knee before the Lord my Maker. I offer my prayer to thee, O Lord, at a time of grace. O God, in thy abundant kindness, answer me with thy saving truth.[1]

Before putting on the tallith:

Bless the Lord, O my soul! Lord my God, thou art very great; thou art robed in glory and majesty. Thou wrappest thyself in light as in a garment; thou spreadest the heavens like a curtain.[2]

I am enwrapping myself in the fringed garment in order to fulfill the command of my Creator, as it is written in the Torah: "They shall make fringes for themselves on the corners of their garments throughout their generations."[3] Even as I cover myself with the tallith in this world, so may my soul deserve to be robed in a beautiful garment in the world to come, in Paradise. Amen.

---

twisted tightly 7 times round the remaining 7 threads, and another double knot is tied; then round 8 times, and a double knot; then round 11 times, and a double knot; and finally round 13 times, and a double knot. 7 and 8=15 equals the numerical value of י"ה, 11=ו"ה, and 13=אחד, meaning: The Lord is One. Furthermore, the numerical value of the word ציצית is 600, which with the 8 threads and the 5 knots makes a total of 613, the exact number of the positive (248) and negative (365) precepts of the Torah. This explains the talmudic statement that the wearing of the *tsitsith* is of equal merit with the observance of the whole Torah (Nedarim 25a).

---

[1] *Numbers* 24:5; *Psalms* 5:8; 26:8; 95:6; 69:14. [2] *Psalm* 104:1-2. [3] *Numbers* 15:38.

When putting on the *tallith*:

בָּרוּךְ אַתָּה, יְיָ אֱלֹהֵינוּ, מֶלֶךְ הָעוֹלָם, אֲשֶׁר קִדְּשָׁנוּ בְּמִצְוֹתָיו וְצִוָּנוּ לְהִתְעַטֵּף בַּצִּיצִת.

תהלים לו, ח–יא

מַה יָּקָר חַסְדְּךָ, אֱלֹהִים, וּבְנֵי אָדָם בְּצֵל כְּנָפֶיךָ יֶחֱסָיוּן. יִרְוְיֻן מִדֶּשֶׁן בֵּיתֶךָ, וְנַחַל עֲדָנֶיךָ תַשְׁקֵם. כִּי עִמְּךָ מְקוֹר חַיִּים, בְּאוֹרְךָ נִרְאֶה אוֹר. מְשֹׁךְ חַסְדְּךָ לְיֹדְעֶיךָ, וְצִדְקָתְךָ לְיִשְׁרֵי לֵב.

בְּטֶרֶם כָּל יְצִיר נִבְרָא.	אֲדוֹן עוֹלָם אֲשֶׁר מָלַךְ
אֲזַי מֶלֶךְ שְׁמוֹ נִקְרָא.	לְעֵת נַעֲשָׂה בְחֶפְצוֹ כֹּל
לְבַדּוֹ יִמְלוֹךְ נוֹרָא.	וְאַחֲרֵי כִּכְלוֹת הַכֹּל
וְהוּא יִהְיֶה בְּתִפְאָרָה.	וְהוּא הָיָה וְהוּא הֹוֶה
לְהַמְשִׁיל לוֹ לְהַחְבִּירָה.	וְהוּא אֶחָד וְאֵין שֵׁנִי
וְלוֹ הָעֹז וְהַמִּשְׂרָה.	בְּלִי רֵאשִׁית בְּלִי תַכְלִית
וְצוּר חֶבְלִי בְּעֵת צָרָה.	וְהוּא אֵלִי וְחַי גּוֹאֲלִי
מְנָת כּוֹסִי בְּיוֹם אֶקְרָא.	וְהוּא נִסִּי וּמָנוֹס לִי
בְּעֵת אִישַׁן וְאָעִירָה.	בְּיָדוֹ אַפְקִיד רוּחִי
יְיָ לִי וְלֹא אִירָא.	וְעִם רוּחִי גְּוִיָּתִי

אדון עולם treats of God's omnipotence and providence. This noble hymn has been attributed to various poets, particularly to Solomon ibn Gabirol who flourished in Spain during the eleventh century. In his famous hymn *Kether Malkhuth*, which is appended to the Sephardic liturgy for the evening service of Yom Kippur, Ibn Gabirol addresses God in terms which bear traces of the theme of *Adon Olam*.

When putting on the tallith:

Blessed art thou, Lord our God, King of the universe, who hast sanctified us with thy commandments, and commanded us to enwrap ourselves in the fringed garment.

Psalm 36:8–11

How precious is thy kindness, O God! The children of men take refuge in the shadow of thy wings. They have their fill of the choice food of thy house, and thou givest them to drink of thy stream of delights. For with thee is the fountain of life; by thy light do we see light. Extend thy love to those who know thee, and thy truth to the upright in heart.

ADON OLAM

He is the eternal Lord who reigned

Before any being was created.

At the time when all was made by his will,

He was at once acknowledged as King.

And at the end, when all shall cease to be,

The revered God alone shall still be King.

He was, he is, and he shall be

In glorious eternity.

He is One, and there is no other

To compare to him, to place beside him.

He is without beginning, without end;

Power and dominion belong to him.

He is my God, my living Redeemer,

My stronghold in times of distress.

He is my guide and my refuge,

My share of bliss the day I call.

To him I entrust my spirit

When I sleep and when I wake.

As long as my soul is with my body

The Lord is with me; I am not afraid.

יִגְדַּל אֱלֹהִים חַי וְיִשְׁתַּבַּח   נִמְצָא וְאֵין עֵת אֶל מְצִיאוּתוֹ.

אֶחָד וְאֵין יָחִיד כְּיִחוּדוֹ   נֶעְלָם וְגַם אֵין סוֹף לְאַחְדוּתוֹ.

אֵין לוֹ דְמוּת הַגּוּף וְאֵינוֹ גוּף   לֹא נַעֲרוֹךְ אֵלָיו קְדֻשָּׁתוֹ.

קַדְמוֹן לְכָל דָּבָר אֲשֶׁר נִבְרָא   רִאשׁוֹן וְאֵין רֵאשִׁית לְרֵאשִׁיתוֹ.

הִנּוֹ אֲדוֹן עוֹלָם וְכָל נוֹצָר   יוֹרֶה גְדֻלָּתוֹ וּמַלְכוּתוֹ.

שֶׁפַע נְבוּאָתוֹ נְתָנוֹ אֶל   אַנְשֵׁי סְגֻלָּתוֹ וְתִפְאַרְתּוֹ.

לֹא קָם בְּיִשְׂרָאֵל כְּמֹשֶׁה עוֹד   נָבִיא וּמַבִּיט אֶת תְּמוּנָתוֹ.

תּוֹרַת אֱמֶת נָתַן לְעַמּוֹ אֵל   עַל יַד נְבִיאוֹ נֶאֱמַן בֵּיתוֹ.

לֹא יַחֲלִיף הָאֵל וְלֹא יָמִיר   דָּתוֹ לְעוֹלָמִים לְזוּלָתוֹ.

צוֹפֶה וְיוֹדֵעַ סְתָרֵינוּ   מַבִּיט לְסוֹף דָּבָר בְּקַדְמָתוֹ.

גּוֹמֵל לְאִישׁ חֶסֶד כְּמִפְעָלוֹ   נוֹתֵן לְרָשָׁע רָע כְּרִשְׁעָתוֹ.

יִשְׁלַח לְקֵץ יָמִין מְשִׁיחֵנוּ   לִפְדּוֹת מְחַכֵּי קֵץ יְשׁוּעָתוֹ.

מֵתִים יְחַיֶּה אֵל בְּרֹב חַסְדּוֹ   בָּרוּךְ עֲדֵי עַד שֵׁם תְּהִלָּתוֹ.

יגדל is a summary of the thirteen principles of faith formulated by Maimonides in his commentary on the Mishnah (Sanhedrin 10:1). This poem
was composed by Daniel ben Judah of Rome (fourteenth century). One rhyme
runs through all its thirteen lines, each of which consists of sixteen syllables.
The variant reading וכל נוצר in the fifth line brings out the full meaning of
Maimonides' fifth principle that God alone must be worshipped. יורה is used
here in the sense of יניד, יספר (see Job 12 12:7–8; Psalm 145:6–12). In Erubin
65a, יורה is taken as the equivalent of יתפלל

    The Jewish philosophy of Moses Maimonides (1135–1204), summed up
in this poem, consists of the following principles: 1) There is a Creator.
2) He is One. 3) He is incorporeal. 4) He is eternal. 5) He alone must be
worshiped. 6) The prophets are true. 7) Moses was the greatest of all
prophets. 8) The entire Torah was divinely given to Moses. 9) The Torah

YIGDAL

1. Exalted and praised be the living God!
   He exists; his existence transcends time.

2. He is One—there is no oneness like his;
   He's unknowable—his Oneness is endless.

3. He has no semblance—he is bodiless;
   Beyond comparison is his holiness.

4. He preceded all that was created;
   The First he is though he never began.

5. He is the eternal Lord; every creature
   Must declare his greatness and his kingship.

6. His abundant prophecy he granted
   To the men of his choice and his glory.

7. Never has there arisen in Israel
   A prophet like Moses beholding God's image.

8. The Torah of truth God gave to his people
   Through his prophet, his own faithful servant

9. God will never replace, nor ever change
   His eternal Law for any other law.

10. He inspects, he knows all our secret thoughts;
    He foresees the end of things at their birth.

11. He rewards the godly man for his deeds;
    He repays the evil man for his evil.

12. At time's end he will send our Messiah
    To save all who wait for his final help.

13. God, in his great mercy, will revive the dead;
    Blessed be his glorious name forever.

---

is immutable. 10) God knows all the acts and thoughts of man. 11) He rewards and punishes. 12) Messiah will come. 13) There will be resurrection.

ראשון ואין ראשית לראשיתו is taken from חובות הלבבות, chapter 6.

אנשי סגולתו ותפארתו compare Exodus 19:5; Isaiah 46:13. נאמן ביתו see Numbers 12:7.

גומל ...איש חסד is taken from Proverbs 11:17, and רשע רע from Isaiah 3:11. The Book of Daniel ends with the phrase לקץ הימין.

In the Siddur of the Spanish-Portuguese Jews a fourteenth line is added to *Yigdal*, which reads: אֵלֶּה שְׁלֹשׁ עֶשְׂרֵה לְעִקָּרִים, הֵנָּם יְסוֹד דַּת אֵל וְתוֹרָתוֹ.

מסכת ברכות יא, א; ס, ב

בָּרוּךְ אַתָּה, יְיָ אֱלֹהֵינוּ, מֶלֶךְ הָעוֹלָם, אֲשֶׁר קִדְּשָׁנוּ בְּמִצְוֹתָיו
וְצִוָּנוּ עַל נְטִילַת יָדָיִם.

בָּרוּךְ אַתָּה, יְיָ אֱלֹהֵינוּ, מֶלֶךְ הָעוֹלָם, אֲשֶׁר יָצַר אֶת הָאָדָם
בְּחָכְמָה, וּבָרָא בוֹ נְקָבִים נְקָבִים, חֲלוּלִים חֲלוּלִים. גָּלוּי וְיָדוּעַ
לִפְנֵי כִסֵּא כְבוֹדֶךָ, שֶׁאִם יִפָּתֵחַ אֶחָד מֵהֶם אוֹ יִסָּתֵם אֶחָד מֵהֶם
אִי אֶפְשָׁר לְהִתְקַיֵּם וְלַעֲמוֹד לְפָנֶיךָ. בָּרוּךְ אַתָּה, יְיָ, רוֹפֵא כָל
בָּשָׂר וּמַפְלִיא לַעֲשׂוֹת.

בָּרוּךְ אַתָּה, יְיָ אֱלֹהֵינוּ, מֶלֶךְ הָעוֹלָם, אֲשֶׁר קִדְּשָׁנוּ בְּמִצְוֹתָיו
וְצִוָּנוּ לַעֲסוֹק בְּדִבְרֵי תוֹרָה.

וְהַעֲרֶב־נָא, יְיָ אֱלֹהֵינוּ, אֶת דִּבְרֵי תוֹרָתְךָ בְּפִינוּ, וּבְפִי
עַמְּךָ בֵּית יִשְׂרָאֵל, וְנִהְיֶה אֲנַחְנוּ וְצֶאֱצָאֵינוּ, וְצֶאֱצָאֵי עַמְּךָ בֵּית
יִשְׂרָאֵל, כֻּלָּנוּ יוֹדְעֵי שְׁמֶךָ וְלוֹמְדֵי תוֹרָתֶךָ לִשְׁמָהּ. בָּרוּךְ אַתָּה,
יְיָ, הַמְלַמֵּד תּוֹרָה לְעַמּוֹ יִשְׂרָאֵל.

בָּרוּךְ אַתָּה, יְיָ אֱלֹהֵינוּ, מֶלֶךְ הָעוֹלָם, אֲשֶׁר בָּחַר בָּנוּ מִכָּל
הָעַמִּים, וְנָתַן לָנוּ אֶת תּוֹרָתוֹ. בָּרוּךְ אַתָּה, יְיָ, נוֹתֵן הַתּוֹרָה.

במדבר ו, כד—כו

יְבָרֶכְךָ יְיָ וְיִשְׁמְרֶךָ. יָאֵר יְיָ פָּנָיו אֵלֶיךָ וִיחֻנֶּךָּ. יִשָּׂא יְיָ פָּנָיו
אֵלֶיךָ, וְיָשֵׂם לְךָ שָׁלוֹם.

קדשנו אשר ... אתה ברוך is an abrupt transition from the second person
singular to the third person. Such transitions occur frequently in biblical
poetry (compare Psalm 104:1-7; Isaiah 23:16; 47:8; 54:1; Jeremiah 49:4;
Micah 1:2). The phrase **ה' אתה ברוך** is borrowed from Psalm 119:12, while
העולם מלך is taken from Jeremiah 10:10.

Talmud Berakhoth 11a; 60b

Blessed art thou, Lord our God, King of the universe, who hast sanctified us with thy commandments, and commanded us concerning the washing of the hands.

Blessed art thou, Lord our God, King of the universe, who hast formed man in wisdom, and created in him a system of ducts and tubes. It is well known before thy glorious throne that if but one of these be opened, or if one of those be closed, it would be impossible to exist in thy presence. Blessed art thou, O Lord, who healest all creatures and doest wonders.

Blessed art thou, Lord our God, King of the universe, who hast sanctified us with thy commandments, and commanded us to study the Torah.

Lord our God, make the words of thy Torah pleasant in our mouth and in the mouth of thy people, the house of Israel, so that we and our descendants and the descendants of thy people, the house of Israel, may all know thy name and study thy Torah for ts own sake. Blessed art thou, O Lord, who teachest the Torah to thy people Israel.

Blessed art thou, Lord our God, King of the universe, who hast chosen us from all peoples and given us thy Torah. Blessed art thou, O Lord, Giver of the Torah.

Numbers 6:24–26

May the Lord bless you and protect you: may the Lord countenance you and be gracious to you; may the Lord favor you and grant you peace.

The expression נטילת ידים (literally, "uplifting the hands") is derived from the custom of lifting up one's hands immediately after washing them as a symbol of purification. The Targum renders שאו ידיכם (Psalm 134:2) by טולו ידיכון.

אשר יצר, referring to the complexity of the human body, concludes with רופא כל בשר and מפליא לעשות, a combination of two variants quoted in Berakhoth 60b.

לעסוק בדברי תורה is one of the various formulae quoted in the Talmud for use in connection with the study of the Torah. They are collated on this page as a compromise between the suggestions found in Berakhoth 11a–b.

ברכות השחר

פאה א, משנה א; מסכת שבת קכז, א

אֵלּוּ דְבָרִים שֶׁאֵין לָהֶם שִׁעוּר: הַפֵּאָה, וְהַבִּכּוּרִים, וְהָרֵאָיוֹן, וּגְמִילוּת חֲסָדִים, וְתַלְמוּד תּוֹרָה. אֵלּוּ דְבָרִים שֶׁאָדָם אוֹכֵל פֵּרוֹתֵיהֶם בָּעוֹלָם הַזֶּה וְהַקֶּרֶן קַיֶּמֶת לוֹ לָעוֹלָם הַבָּא, וְאֵלּוּ הֵן: כִּבּוּד אָב וָאֵם, וּגְמִילוּת חֲסָדִים, וְהַשְׁכָּמַת בֵּית הַמִּדְרָשׁ שַׁחֲרִית וְעַרְבִית, וְהַכְנָסַת אוֹרְחִים, וּבִקּוּר חוֹלִים, וְהַכְנָסַת כַּלָּה, וּלְוָיַת הַמֵּת, וְעִיּוּן תְּפִלָּה, וַהֲבָאַת שָׁלוֹם בֵּין אָדָם לַחֲבֵרוֹ; וְתַלְמוּד תּוֹרָה כְּנֶגֶד כֻּלָּם.

מסכת ברכות ס, ב

אֱלֹהַי, נְשָׁמָה שֶׁנָּתַתָּ בִּי טְהוֹרָה הִיא. אַתָּה בְרָאתָהּ, אַתָּה יְצַרְתָּהּ, אַתָּה נְפַחְתָּהּ בִּי, וְאַתָּה מְשַׁמְּרָהּ בְּקִרְבִּי, וְאַתָּה עָתִיד לִטְּלָהּ מִמֶּנִּי וּלְהַחֲזִירָהּ בִּי לֶעָתִיד לָבֹא. כָּל זְמַן שֶׁהַנְּשָׁמָה בְקִרְבִּי מוֹדֶה אֲנִי לְפָנֶיךָ, יְיָ אֱלֹהַי וֵאלֹהֵי אֲבוֹתַי, רִבּוֹן כָּל הַמַּעֲשִׂים, אֲדוֹן כָּל הַנְּשָׁמוֹת. בָּרוּךְ אַתָּה, יְיָ, הַמַּחֲזִיר נְשָׁמוֹת לִפְגָרִים מֵתִים.

בָּרוּךְ אַתָּה, יְיָ אֱלֹהֵינוּ, מֶלֶךְ הָעוֹלָם, אֲשֶׁר נָתַן לַשֶּׂכְוִי בִינָה לְהַבְחִין בֵּין יוֹם וּבֵין לָיְלָה.

בָּרוּךְ אַתָּה, יְיָ אֱלֹהֵינוּ, מֶלֶךְ הָעוֹלָם, שֶׁלֹּא עָשַׂנִי גוֹי.

בָּרוּךְ אַתָּה, יְיָ אֱלֹהֵינוּ, מֶלֶךְ הָעוֹלָם, שֶׁלֹּא עָשַׂנִי עָבֶד.

פאה part of the crop which the owner was required to leave for the benefit of the poor.(Leviticus 23:22). According to tradition, the minimum was one-sixtieth of the harvest (Mishnah Peah 1:2).

בכורים the earliest gathered fruits of the season brought to the Temple.

ראיון The nature and value of the offering which all male Israelites were required to present at the Temple is not defined in Deuteronomy 16:16–17.

גמילות חסדים There is no fixed limit to personal service and charity to all men. *Gemiluth hasadim* includes every kind of help.

Mishnah Peah 1:1; *Talmud Shabbath* 127a

These are the things for which no limit is prescribed: the corner of the field, the first-fruits, the pilgrimage offerings, the practice of kindness, and the study of the Torah. These are the things the fruits of which a man enjoys in this world, while the principal remains for him in the hereafter, namely: honoring father and mother, practice of kindness, early attendance at the schoolhouse morning and evening, hospitality to strangers, visiting the sick, dowering the bride, attending the dead to the grave, devotion in prayer, and making peace between fellow men; but the study of the Torah excels them all.

Talmud Berakhoth 60b

My God, the soul which thou hast placed within me is pure. Thou hast created it; thou hast formed it; thou hast breathed it into me. Thou preservest it within me; thou wilt take it from me, and restore it to me in the hereafter. So long as the soul is within me, I offer thanks before thee, Lord my God and God of my fathers, Master of all creatures, Lord of all souls. Blessed art thou, O Lord, who restorest the souls to the dead.

Blessed art thou, Lord our God, King of the universe, who hast given the cock intelligence to distinguish between day and night.

Blessed art thou, Lord our God, King of the universe, who hast not made me a heathen.

Blessed art thou, Lord our God, King of the universe, who hast not made me a slave.

תלמוד תורה is one of the duties to which there is no prescribed limit. We are to engage in Torah study at all times. The readings from the Bible and the Talmud which form part of the morning service are meant to enable every Jew to have a daily share in the study of the Torah.

לשכוי בינה is taken from Job 38:36, where שכוי is derived from שכה ("to see"). According to Berakhoth 60b and Rosh Hashanah 26a, שכוי signifies "cock", that is, the bird which foresees the approaching day. The worshiper expresses his appreciation of nature's super-senses and the exact timing of animals, for there are many kinds of "knowingness" in which animals far surpass us by means of their exquisite ability to "feel" things.

Women say:	Men say:

בָּרוּךְ אַתָּה, יְיָ אֱלֹהֵינוּ, מֶלֶךְ   בָּרוּךְ אַתָּה, יְיָ אֱלֹהֵינוּ, מֶלֶךְ

הָעוֹלָם, שֶׁעָשַׂנִי כִּרְצוֹנוֹ.   הָעוֹלָם, שֶׁלֹּא עָשַׂנִי אִשָּׁה.

בָּרוּךְ אַתָּה, יְיָ אֱלֹהֵינוּ, מֶלֶךְ הָעוֹלָם, פּוֹקֵחַ עִוְרִים.

בָּרוּךְ אַתָּה, יְיָ אֱלֹהֵינוּ, מֶלֶךְ הָעוֹלָם, מַלְבִּישׁ עֲרֻמִּים.

בָּרוּךְ אַתָּה, יְיָ אֱלֹהֵינוּ, מֶלֶךְ הָעוֹלָם, מַתִּיר אֲסוּרִים.

בָּרוּךְ אַתָּה, יְיָ אֱלֹהֵינוּ, מֶלֶךְ הָעוֹלָם, זוֹקֵף כְּפוּפִים.

בָּרוּךְ אַתָּה, יְיָ אֱלֹהֵינוּ, מֶלֶךְ הָעוֹלָם, רוֹקַע הָאָרֶץ עַל הַמָּיִם.

בָּרוּךְ אַתָּה, יְיָ אֱלֹהֵינוּ, מֶלֶךְ הָעוֹלָם, שֶׁעָשָׂה לִי כָּל צָרְכִּי.

בָּרוּךְ אַתָּה, יְיָ אֱלֹהֵינוּ, מֶלֶךְ הָעוֹלָם, הַמֵּכִין מִצְעֲדֵי גָבֶר.

בָּרוּךְ אַתָּה, יְיָ אֱלֹהֵינוּ, מֶלֶךְ הָעוֹלָם, אוֹזֵר יִשְׂרָאֵל בִּגְבוּרָה.

בָּרוּךְ אַתָּה, יְיָ אֱלֹהֵינוּ, מֶלֶךְ הָעוֹלָם, עוֹטֵר יִשְׂרָאֵל בְּתִפְאָרָה.

בָּרוּךְ אַתָּה, יְיָ אֱלֹהֵינוּ, מֶלֶךְ הָעוֹלָם, הַנּוֹתֵן לַיָּעֵף כֹּחַ.

בָּרוּךְ אַתָּה, יְיָ אֱלֹהֵינוּ, מֶלֶךְ הָעוֹלָם, הַמַּעֲבִיר שֵׁנָה מֵעֵינַי

וּתְנוּמָה מֵעַפְעַפָּי.

וִיהִי רָצוֹן מִלְּפָנֶיךָ, יְיָ אֱלֹהֵינוּ וֵאלֹהֵי אֲבוֹתֵינוּ, שֶׁתַּרְגִּילֵנוּ

בְּתוֹרָתֶךָ וְדַבְּקֵנוּ בְּמִצְוֹתֶיךָ; וְאַל תְּבִיאֵנוּ לֹא לִידֵי חֵטְא, וְלֹא

לִידֵי עֲבֵרָה וְעָוֹן, וְלֹא לִידֵי נִסָּיוֹן, וְלֹא לִידֵי בִזָּיוֹן; וְאַל תַּשְׁלֶט־

בָּנוּ יֵצֶר הָרָע; וְהַרְחִיקֵנוּ מֵאָדָם רָע וּמֵחָבֵר רָע; וְדַבְּקֵנוּ בְּיֵצֶר

שלא עשני אשה and the following two blessings are taken from **Menaḥoth** 43b. Men thank God for the privilege of performing many precepts **which** are incumbent only on male Israelites.

שעשני כרצונו is mentioned by David Abudarham (fourteenth century**) as** a recently introduced blessing to be recited by women.

הנותן ליעף כח is not derived from the Talmud but is found in **Maḥzor** Vitry, the liturgical work which was compiled in the eleventh century **by** Rabbi Simḥah of Vitry, France, a pupil of Rashi.

Men say:

Blessed art thou, Lord our God, King of the universe, who hast not made me a woman.

Women say:

Blessed art thou, Lord our God, King of the universe, who hast made me according to thy will.

Blessed art thou, Lord our God, King of the universe, who openest the eyes of the blind.

Blessed art thou, Lord our God, King of the universe, who clothest the naked.

Blessed art thou, Lord our God, King of the universe, who settest the captives free.

Blessed art thou, Lord our God, King of the universe, who raisest up those who are bowed down.

Blessed art thou, Lord our God, King of the universe, who spreadest forth the earth above the waters.

Blessed art thou, Lord our God, King of the universe, who hast provided for all my needs.

Blessed art thou, Lord our God, King of the universe, who guidest the steps of man.

Blessed art thou, Lord our God, King of the universe, who girdest Israel with might.

Blessed art thou, Lord our God, King of the universe, who crownest Israel with glory.

Blessed art thou, Lord our God, King of the universe, who givest strength to the weary.

Blessed art thou, Lord our God, King of the universe, who removest sleep from my eyes and slumber from my eyelids.

May it be thy will, Lord our God and God of our fathers, to make us familiar with thy Torah, and to cause us to adhere to thy precepts. Lead us not into sin, transgression, iniquity, temptation, or disgrace; let not the evil impulse have power over us; keep us far from an evil man and a bad companion; make us cling to

---

In the Talmud, the first יהי רצון is phrased in the singular (שתרגילני...ודבקני) while the second יהי רצון is reported in singular and plural (Berakhoth 60b; Shabbath 39b).

הַטּוֹב וּבְמַעֲשִׂים טוֹבִים; וְכֹף אֶת יִצְרֵנוּ לְהִשְׁתַּעֲבֶד־לָךְ.

Reader וּתְנֵנוּ הַיּוֹם וּבְכָל יוֹם לְחֵן וּלְחֶסֶד וּלְרַחֲמִים בְּעֵינֶיךָ

וּבְעֵינֵי כָל רוֹאֵינוּ, וְתִגְמְלֵנוּ חֲסָדִים טוֹבִים. בָּרוּךְ אַתָּה, יְיָ,

גּוֹמֵל חֲסָדִים טוֹבִים לְעַמּוֹ יִשְׂרָאֵל.

יְהִי רָצוֹן מִלְּפָנֶיךָ, יְיָ אֱלֹהַי וֵאלֹהֵי אֲבוֹתַי, שֶׁתַּצִּילֵנִי הַיּוֹם

וּבְכָל יוֹם מֵעַזֵּי פָנִים וּמֵעַזּוּת פָּנִים, מֵאָדָם רָע וּמֵחָבֵר רָע,

וּמִשָּׁכֵן רָע וּמִפֶּגַע רָע וּמִשָּׂטָן הַמַּשְׁחִית, מִדִּין קָשֶׁה וּמִבַּעַל דִּין

קָשֶׁה, בֵּין שֶׁהוּא בֶן־בְּרִית וּבֵין שֶׁאֵינוֹ בֶן־בְּרִית.

אֱלֹהֵינוּ וֵאלֹהֵי אֲבוֹתֵינוּ, זָכְרֵנוּ בְּזִכְרוֹן טוֹב לְפָנֶיךָ, וּפָקְדֵנוּ

בִּפְקֻדַּת יְשׁוּעָה וְרַחֲמִים מִשְּׁמֵי שְׁמֵי קֶדֶם; וּזְכָר־לָנוּ, יְיָ אֱלֹהֵינוּ,

אַהֲבַת הַקַּדְמוֹנִים, אַבְרָהָם יִצְחָק וְיִשְׂרָאֵל עֲבָדֶיךָ, אֶת הַבְּרִית

וְאֶת הַחֶסֶד, וְאֶת הַשְּׁבוּעָה שֶׁנִּשְׁבַּעְתָּ לְאַבְרָהָם אָבִינוּ בְּהַר

הַמּוֹרִיָּה, וְאֶת הָעֲקֵדָה שֶׁעָקַד אֶת יִצְחָק בְּנוֹ עַל גַּבֵּי הַמִּזְבֵּחַ,

כַּכָּתוּב בְּתוֹרָתֶךָ:

בראשית כב, א–יט

וַיְהִי אַחַר הַדְּבָרִים הָאֵלֶּה, וְהָאֱלֹהִים נִסָּה אֶת אַבְרָהָם,

וַיֹּאמֶר אֵלָיו: אַבְרָהָם, וַיֹּאמֶר הִנֵּנִי. וַיֹּאמֶר: קַח נָא אֶת בִּנְךָ,

אֶת יְחִידְךָ, אֲשֶׁר אָהַבְתָּ, אֶת יִצְחָק, וְלֶךְ לְךָ אֶל אֶרֶץ הַמֹּרִיָּה,

וְהַעֲלֵהוּ שָׁם לְעֹלָה עַל אַחַד הֶהָרִים אֲשֶׁר אֹמַר אֵלֶיךָ. וַיַּשְׁכֵּם

אַבְרָהָם בַּבֹּקֶר, וַיַּחֲבשׁ אֶת חֲמֹרוֹ, וַיִּקַּח אֶת שְׁנֵי נְעָרָיו אִתּוֹ

וְאֵת יִצְחָק בְּנוֹ; וַיְבַקַּע עֲצֵי עֹלָה, וַיָּקָם וַיֵּלֶךְ אֶל הַמָּקוֹם אֲשֶׁר

אָמַר לוֹ הָאֱלֹהִים. בַּיּוֹם הַשְּׁלִישִׁי, וַיִּשָּׂא אַבְרָהָם אֶת עֵינָיו וַיַּרְא

אֶת הַמָּקוֹם מֵרָחֹק. וַיֹּאמֶר אַבְרָהָם אֶל נְעָרָיו: שְׁבוּ לָכֶם פֹּה

עִם הַחֲמוֹר, וַאֲנִי וְהַנַּעַר נֵלְכָה עַד כֹּה, וְנִשְׁתַּחֲוֶה וְנָשׁוּבָה

נסה את אברהם Abraham's faith was put to the supreme test when he was commanded to sacrifice Isaac. This was the tenth and the greatest of the trials the good impulse and to good deeds, and bend our will to submit to thee. Grant us today, and every day, grace, favor and mercy, both in thy sight and in the sight of all men, and bestow loving-kindness on us. Blessed art thou, O Lord, who bestowest loving-kindness on thy people Israel.

May it be thy will, Lord my God and God of my fathers, to deliver me today, and every day, from impudent men and from insolence; from an evil man, a bad companion, and a bad neighbor, from an evil occurrence and from the destructive adversary; from an oppressive lawsuit and from a hard opponent, be he a man of the covenant or not.

Our God and God of our fathers, remember us favorably and visit us with mercy and salvation from the eternal high heavens. Remember in our favor, Lord our God, the love of our ancestors Abraham, Isaac and Israel thy servants. Remember the covenant, the kindness, and the oath which thou didst swear to our father Abraham on Mount Moriah, and the binding of Isaac his son on the altar, as it is written in thy Torah:

Genesis 22:1–19

And it came to pass after these things that God put Abraham to the test, and called to him: "Abraham!" He answered: "Here I am." Then he said: "Take your son, your only son, Isaac, whom you love; go to the land of Moriah and offer him there as a burnt-offering on one of the mountains that I will tell you." So Abraham rose early in the morning, saddled his ass, and took with him his two servants and his son Isaac; he cut wood for the burnt-offering and started for the place about which God had told him.

On the third day Abraham looked up and saw the place at a distance. Then Abraham said to his servants: "You stay here with the ass while I and the boy go yonder; we will worship and

---

he had to face, to prove that he was worthy of being the founder of the Jewish people. This narrative portrays also the faith and obedience of Isaac.

משטן המשחית is an allusion to the corrupting influence of Satan, the great adversary of man, who is often identical with the lower passions.

רבונו של עולם and זכרנו בזכרון טוב which immediately follows the biblical account of Abraham's willingness to sacrifice his son are both taken from the *Musaf* service for *Rosh Hashanah*. The *Akedah*, the intended sacrifice of Isaac, is regarded as a symbol of Israel's martyrdom.

אֲלֵיכֶם. וַיִּקַּח אַבְרָהָם אֶת עֲצֵי הָעֹלָה וַיָּשֶׂם עַל יִצְחָק בְּנוֹ,
וַיִּקַּח בְּיָדוֹ אֶת הָאֵשׁ וְאֶת הַמַּאֲכֶלֶת, וַיֵּלְכוּ שְׁנֵיהֶם יַחְדָּו. וַיֹּאמֶר
יִצְחָק אֶל אַבְרָהָם אָבִיו, וַיֹּאמֶר: אָבִי, וַיֹּאמֶר הִנֶּנִּי בְנִי;
וַיֹּאמֶר: הִנֵּה הָאֵשׁ וְהָעֵצִים, וְאַיֵּה הַשֶּׂה לְעֹלָה. וַיֹּאמֶר אַבְרָהָם:
אֱלֹהִים יִרְאֶה לּוֹ הַשֶּׂה לְעֹלָה, בְּנִי; וַיֵּלְכוּ שְׁנֵיהֶם יַחְדָּו. וַיָּבֹאוּ
אֶל הַמָּקוֹם אֲשֶׁר אָמַר לוֹ הָאֱלֹהִים, וַיִּבֶן שָׁם אַבְרָהָם אֶת
הַמִּזְבֵּחַ, וַיַּעֲרֹךְ אֶת הָעֵצִים, וַיַּעֲקֹד אֶת יִצְחָק בְּנוֹ, וַיָּשֶׂם אֹתוֹ
עַל הַמִּזְבֵּחַ מִמַּעַל לָעֵצִים. וַיִּשְׁלַח אַבְרָהָם אֶת יָדוֹ וַיִּקַּח אֶת
הַמַּאֲכֶלֶת לִשְׁחֹט אֶת בְּנוֹ. וַיִּקְרָא אֵלָיו מַלְאַךְ יְיָ מִן הַשָּׁמַיִם,
וַיֹּאמֶר: אַבְרָהָם, אַבְרָהָם, וַיֹּאמֶר הִנֵּנִי. וַיֹּאמֶר: אַל תִּשְׁלַח
יָדְךָ אֶל הַנַּעַר וְאַל תַּעַשׂ לוֹ מְאוּמָה, כִּי עַתָּה יָדַעְתִּי כִּי יְרֵא
אֱלֹהִים אַתָּה, וְלֹא חָשַׂכְתָּ אֶת בִּנְךָ אֶת יְחִידְךָ מִמֶּנִּי. וַיִּשָּׂא
אַבְרָהָם אֶת עֵינָיו וַיַּרְא וְהִנֵּה אַיִל, אַחַר, נֶאֱחַז בַּסְּבַךְ בְּקַרְנָיו;
וַיֵּלֶךְ אַבְרָהָם וַיִּקַּח אֶת הָאַיִל, וַיַּעֲלֵהוּ לְעֹלָה תַּחַת בְּנוֹ. וַיִּקְרָא
אַבְרָהָם שֵׁם הַמָּקוֹם הַהוּא: יְיָ יִרְאֶה, אֲשֶׁר יֵאָמֵר הַיּוֹם: בְּהַר יְיָ
יֵרָאֶה. וַיִּקְרָא מַלְאַךְ יְיָ אֶל אַבְרָהָם שֵׁנִית מִן הַשָּׁמַיִם. וַיֹּאמֶר:
בִּי נִשְׁבַּעְתִּי, נְאֻם יְיָ, כִּי יַעַן אֲשֶׁר עָשִׂיתָ אֶת הַדָּבָר הַזֶּה, וְלֹא
חָשַׂכְתָּ אֶת בִּנְךָ, אֶת יְחִידֶךָ. כִּי בָרֵךְ אֲבָרֶכְךָ, וְהַרְבָּה אַרְבֶּה
אֶת זַרְעֲךָ כְּכוֹכְבֵי הַשָּׁמַיִם, וְכַחוֹל אֲשֶׁר עַל שְׂפַת הַיָּם, וְיִרַשׁ
זַרְעֲךָ אֵת שַׁעַר אֹיְבָיו. וְהִתְבָּרְכוּ בְזַרְעֲךָ כֹּל גּוֹיֵי הָאָרֶץ, עֵקֶב
אֲשֶׁר שָׁמַעְתָּ בְּקֹלִי. וַיָּשָׁב אַבְרָהָם אֶל נְעָרָיו, וַיָּקֻמוּ וַיֵּלְכוּ יַחְדָּו
אֶל בְּאֵר שָׁבַע; וַיֵּשֶׁב אַבְרָהָם בִּבְאֵר שָׁבַע.

רִבּוֹנוֹ שֶׁל עוֹלָם, יְהִי רָצוֹן מִלְּפָנֶיךָ, יְיָ אֱלֹהֵינוּ וֵאלֹהֵי

בהר ה' יראה refers to the Temple which was afterwards established on this mountain (II Chronicles 3:1).

come back to you." So Abraham took the wood for the burnt-offering and laid it on his son Isaac, while he took in his hand the fire and the knife; and the two of them went off together.

Then Isaac spoke to Abraham his father and said: "My father"; and he answered: "Here I am, my son." And he said: "Here are the fire and the wood, but where is the lamb for a burnt-offering?" Abraham answered: "God will provide himself with the lamb for a burnt-offering, my son." So the two of them went on together. They came to the place of which God had told him, and Abraham built the altar there, arranged the wood, bound his son Isaac and laid him on the altar on top of the wood. Then Abraham put out his hand and took the knife to slay his son. But the angel of the Lord called to him from the heavens: "Abraham, Abraham," and he answered: "Here I am." He said: "Do not lay your hand on the boy, and do nothing to him; for I know now that you revere God, seeing that you have not refused me your son, your only son." Then Abraham looked up and saw behind him a ram caught in the thicket by its horns; so Abraham went and took the ram, and offered it as a burnt-offering instead of his son. Abraham called the name of that place Adonai-yireh, as it is said to this day: "The mount where the Lord reveals himself."

The angel of the Lord called to Abraham a second time from the heavens, and said: "By myself I swear," says the Lord, "that since you have done this, since you have not withheld your son, your only son, I will indeed bless you, and will surely make your descendants as numerous as the stars in the sky or as the sands on the seashore; your descendants shall possess the cities of their enemies, and through your descendants shall all the nations of the earth be blessed—because you have obeyed my voice." Abraham then returned to his servants, and they started together for Beersheba, for Abraham dwelt in Beersheba.

Master of the world! May it be thy will, Lord our God and

אֲבוֹתֵינוּ, שֶׁתִּזְכָּר־לָנוּ בְּרִית אֲבוֹתֵינוּ. כְּמוֹ שֶׁכָּבַשׁ אַבְרָהָם
אָבִינוּ אֶת רַחֲמָיו מִבֶּן־יְחִידוֹ, וְרָצָה לִשְׁחֹט אוֹתוֹ כְּדֵי לַעֲשׂוֹת
רְצוֹנֶךָ, כֵּן יִכְבְּשׁוּ רַחֲמֶיךָ אֶת כַּעַסְךָ מֵעָלֵינוּ, וְיִגֹּלּוּ רַחֲמֶיךָ
עַל מִדּוֹתֶיךָ, וְתִכָּנֵס אִתָּנוּ לִפְנִים מִשּׁוּרַת דִּינֶךָ, וְתִתְנַהֵג עִמָּנוּ,
יְיָ אֱלֹהֵינוּ, בְּמִדַּת הַחֶסֶד וּבְמִדַּת הָרַחֲמִים. וּבְטוּבְךָ הַגָּדוֹל,
יָשׁוּב חֲרוֹן אַפְּךָ מֵעַמְּךָ וּמֵעִירְךָ וּמֵאַרְצְךָ וּמִנַּחֲלָתֶךָ. וְקַיֶּם־
לָנוּ, יְיָ אֱלֹהֵינוּ, אֶת הַדָּבָר שֶׁהִבְטַחְתָּנוּ עַל יְדֵי מֹשֶׁה עַבְדֶּךָ,
כָּאָמוּר: וְזָכַרְתִּי אֶת בְּרִיתִי יַעֲקוֹב, וְאַף אֶת בְּרִיתִי יִצְחָק, וְאַף
אֶת בְּרִיתִי אַבְרָהָם אֶזְכֹּר, וְהָאָרֶץ אֶזְכֹּר.

לְעוֹלָם יְהֵא אָדָם יְרֵא שָׁמַיִם בַּסֵּתֶר וּבַגָּלוּי, וּמוֹדֶה עַל
הָאֱמֶת, וְדוֹבֵר אֱמֶת בִּלְבָבוֹ, וְיַשְׁכֵּם וְיֹאמַר:

רִבּוֹן כָּל הָעוֹלָמִים, לֹא עַל צִדְקוֹתֵינוּ אֲנַחְנוּ מַפִּילִים
תַּחֲנוּנֵינוּ לְפָנֶיךָ, כִּי עַל רַחֲמֶיךָ הָרַבִּים. מָה אֲנַחְנוּ, מֶה חַיֵּינוּ,
מֶה חַסְדֵּנוּ, מַה צִּדְקֵנוּ, מַה יְשׁוּעָתֵנוּ, מַה כֹּחֵנוּ, מַה גְּבוּרָתֵנוּ.
מַה נֹּאמַר לְפָנֶיךָ, יְיָ אֱלֹהֵינוּ וֵאלֹהֵי אֲבוֹתֵינוּ, הֲלֹא כָּל הַגִּבּוֹרִים
כְּאַיִן לְפָנֶיךָ, וְאַנְשֵׁי הַשֵּׁם כְּלֹא הָיוּ, וַחֲכָמִים כִּבְלִי מַדָּע,
וּנְבוֹנִים כִּבְלִי הַשְׂכֵּל, כִּי רֹב מַעֲשֵׂיהֶם תֹּהוּ, וִימֵי חַיֵּיהֶם הֶבֶל
לְפָנֶיךָ; וּמוֹתַר הָאָדָם מִן הַבְּהֵמָה אָיִן, כִּי הַכֹּל הָבֶל.

אֲבָל אֲנַחְנוּ עַמְּךָ בְּנֵי בְרִיתֶךָ, בְּנֵי אַבְרָהָם אֹהַבְךָ שֶׁנִּשְׁבַּעְתָּ
לוֹ בְּהַר הַמּוֹרִיָּה, זֶרַע יִצְחָק יְחִידוֹ שֶׁנֶּעֱקַד עַל גַּב הַמִּזְבֵּחַ,
עֲדַת יַעֲקֹב בִּנְךָ בְּכוֹרֶךָ, שֶׁמֵּאַהֲבָתְךָ שֶׁאָהַבְתָּ אוֹתוֹ, וּמִשִּׂמְחָתְךָ
שֶׁשָּׂמַחְתָּ בּוֹ, קָרָאתָ אֶת שְׁמוֹ יִשְׂרָאֵל וִישֻׁרוּן.

לעולם יהא and onwards forms an impressive setting for the *Shema*, the
acknowledgment of the unity of God. During the reign of Yezdejerd II (fifth
century) it was made unlawful for the Babylonian Jews to recite the *Shema*
as being a challenge to the Zoroastrian religion. Special government officials

God of our fathers, to remember in our favor the covenant of our fathers. Even as Abraham our father held back his compassion from his only son and desired to slay him in order to do thy will, so may thy mercy hold back thy anger from us; let thy compassion prevail over thy acts of retaliation. Be lenient with us, Lord our God, and deal with us kindly and mercifully. In thy great goodness, may thy fierce wrath turn away from thy people, thy city, thy land, and thy heritage. Fulfill, Lord our God, what thou hast promised us through Moses thy servant, as it is said: "I will remember my covenant with Jacob; also my covenant with Isaac and my covenant with Abraham will I remember; and I will remember the land."[1]

Man should ever be God-fearing in private as well as in public. He should acknowledge the truth, and speak the truth in his heart. Let him rise early and say:

Master of all worlds! It is not on account of our own righteousness that we offer our supplications before thee, but on account of thy great compassion. What are we? What is our life? What is our goodness? What is our virtue? What our help? What our strength? What our might? What can we say to thee, Lord our God and God of our fathers? Indeed, all the heroes are as nothing in thy sight, the men of renown as though they never existed, the wise as though they were without knowledge, the intelligent as though they lacked insight; most of their actions are worthless in thy sight, their entire life is a fleeting breath. Man is not far above beast, for all is vanity.

However, we are thy people, thy people of the covenant, the children of Abraham thy friend, to whom thou didst make a promise on Mount Moriah; we are the descendants of his only son Isaac, who was bound on the altar; we are the community of Jacob thy first-born, whom thou didst name Israel and Jeshurun because of thy love for him and thy delight in him.

---

were posted in the synagogues to watch the services. The rabbis of the time impressed upon the people the duty of reciting at least the first verse of *Shema* privately, in their homes, before proceeding to the synagogue for the morning service. לעולם יהא is an exhortation to the effect that Judaism must be practised in secrecy (בסתר) during religious persecution. The additional word ובנלוי is not found in early texts.

רבון כל העולמים is mentioned in Yoma 87b as a *Yom Kippur* prayer.

[1-2]*Leviticus* 26:12.

לְפִיכָךְ אֲנַחְנוּ חַיָּבִים לְהוֹדוֹת לְךָ וּלְשַׁבֵּחֲךָ וּלְפָאֶרְךָ,
וּלְבָרֵךְ וּלְקַדֵּשׁ וְלָתֵת שֶׁבַח וְהוֹדָיָה לִשְׁמֶךָ. אַשְׁרֵינוּ, מַה טּוֹב
חֶלְקֵנוּ וּמַה נָּעִים גּוֹרָלֵנוּ וּמַה יָּפָה יְרֻשָּׁתֵנוּ. Reader אַשְׁרֵינוּ,
שֶׁאֲנַחְנוּ מַשְׁכִּימִים וּמַעֲרִיבִים, עֶרֶב וָבְקֶר, וְאוֹמְרִים פַּעֲמַיִם
בְּכָל יוֹם:

שְׁמַע, יִשְׂרָאֵל, יְיָ אֱלֹהֵינוּ, יְיָ אֶחָד.

בָּרוּךְ שֵׁם כְּבוֹד מַלְכוּתוֹ לְעוֹלָם וָעֶד.

אַתָּה הוּא עַד שֶׁלֹּא נִבְרָא הָעוֹלָם, אַתָּה הוּא מִשֶּׁנִּבְרָא
הָעוֹלָם, אַתָּה הוּא בָּעוֹלָם הַזֶּה וְאַתָּה הוּא לָעוֹלָם הַבָּא. קַדֵּשׁ
אֶת שִׁמְךָ עַל מַקְדִּישֵׁי שְׁמֶךָ, וְקַדֵּשׁ אֶת שִׁמְךָ בְּעוֹלָמֶךָ,
וּבִישׁוּעָתְךָ תָּרוּם וְתַגְבִּיהַּ קַרְנֵנוּ. בָּרוּךְ אַתָּה, יְיָ, מְקַדֵּשׁ Reader
אֶת שִׁמְךָ בָּרַבִּים.

אַתָּה הוּא, יְיָ אֱלֹהֵינוּ, בַּשָּׁמַיִם וּבָאָרֶץ וּבִשְׁמֵי הַשָּׁמַיִם
הָעֶלְיוֹנִים. אֱמֶת, אַתָּה הוּא רִאשׁוֹן וְאַתָּה הוּא אַחֲרוֹן,
וּמִבַּלְעָדֶיךָ אֵין אֱלֹהִים. קַבֵּץ קוֹיֶךָ מֵאַרְבַּע כַּנְפוֹת הָאָרֶץ;
יַכִּירוּ וְיֵדְעוּ כָּל בָּאֵי עוֹלָם כִּי אַתָּה הוּא הָאֱלֹהִים לְבַדְּךָ לְכֹל
מַמְלְכוֹת הָאָרֶץ. אַתָּה עָשִׂיתָ אֶת הַשָּׁמַיִם וְאֶת הָאָרֶץ, אֶת
הַיָּם, וְאֶת כָּל אֲשֶׁר בָּם, וּמִי בְּכָל מַעֲשֵׂה יָדֶיךָ, בָּעֶלְיוֹנִים אוֹ
בַתַּחְתּוֹנִים, שֶׁיֹּאמַר לְךָ מַה תַּעֲשֶׂה. אָבִינוּ שֶׁבַּשָּׁמַיִם, עֲשֵׂה
עִמָּנוּ חֶסֶד בַּעֲבוּר שִׁמְךָ הַגָּדוֹל שֶׁנִּקְרָא עָלֵינוּ, וְקַיֶּם־לָנוּ, יְיָ
אֱלֹהֵינוּ, מַה שֶּׁכָּתוּב: בָּעֵת הַהִיא אָבִיא אֶתְכֶם, וּבָעֵת קַבְּצִי
אֶתְכֶם, כִּי אֶתֵּן אֶתְכֶם לְשֵׁם וְלִתְהִלָּה בְּכֹל עַמֵּי הָאָרֶץ, בְּשׁוּבִי
אֶת שְׁבוּתֵיכֶם לְעֵינֵיכֶם, אָמַר יְיָ.

קַדֵּשׁ אֶת שִׁמְךָ-בָּרַבִּים God manifests his divine power to the entire world by
delivering those who suffer martyrdom for his sake (Ezekiel 36:23; 39:7).

Therefore, it is our duty to give thanks to thee, to praise and glorify thee, to bless and hallow thy name, and to offer many thanksgivings to thee. Happy are we! How good is our destiny, how pleasant our lot, how beautiful our heritage! Happy are we who, early and late, morning and evening, twice every day, proclaim:

Hear, O Israel, the Lord is our God, the Lord is One.

Blessed be the name of his glorious majesty forever and ever.

Thou wast the same before the world was created; thou hast been the same since the world has been created; thou art the same in this world, and thou wilt be the same in the world to come. Reveal thy holiness to those who sanctify thy name; manifest thy holiness throughout thy world. May our strength rise and be exalted through thy deliverance. Blessed art thou, O Lord, who sanctifiest thy name in the presence of all men.

Thou, Lord our God, art in heaven and on earth and in the highest heavens. Truly, thou art the first and thou art the last; besides thee there is no God. O gather those who yearn for thee from the four corners of the earth. Let all mankind realize and know that thou alone art God over all the kingdoms of the earth. Thou hast made the heavens, the earth, the sea, and all that is in them. Who is there among all the works of thy hands, among the heavenly or the earthly creatures, that can say to thee, "What doest thou?" Our Father who art in heaven, deal kindly with us for the sake of thy great name by which we are called, and fulfill for us, Lord our God, that which is written: "At that time I will bring you home; at that time I will gather you; indeed, I will grant you fame and praise among all the peoples of the earth, when I bring back your captivity before your own eyes, says the Lord."[1]

---

[1] *Zephaniah* 3:20.

שמות ל, יז-כא

וַיְדַבֵּר יְיָ אֶל מֹשֶׁה לֵּאמֹר: וְעָשִׂיתָ כִּיּוֹר נְחֹשֶׁת, וְכַנּוֹ נְחֹשֶׁת,
לְרָחְצָה. וְנָתַתָּ אֹתוֹ בֵּין אֹהֶל מוֹעֵד וּבֵין הַמִּזְבֵּחַ. וְנָתַתָּ שָׁמָּה
מָיִם. וְרָחֲצוּ אַהֲרֹן וּבָנָיו מִמֶּנּוּ אֶת יְדֵיהֶם וְאֶת רַגְלֵיהֶם. בְּבֹאָם
אֶל אֹהֶל מוֹעֵד יִרְחֲצוּ מַיִם וְלֹא יָמֻתוּ; אוֹ בְגִשְׁתָּם אֶל הַמִּזְבֵּחַ
לְשָׁרֵת, לְהַקְטִיר אִשֶּׁה לַיְיָ. וְרָחֲצוּ יְדֵיהֶם וְרַגְלֵיהֶם וְלֹא יָמֻתוּ;
וְהָיְתָה לָהֶם חָק־עוֹלָם, לוֹ וּלְזַרְעוֹ לְדֹרֹתָם.

יְהִי רָצוֹן מִלְּפָנֶיךָ, יְיָ אֱלֹהֵינוּ וֵאלֹהֵי אֲבוֹתֵינוּ, שֶׁתְּרַחֵם
עָלֵינוּ וְתִמְחָל־לָנוּ עַל כָּל חַטֹּאתֵינוּ, וּתְכַפֶּר־לָנוּ עַל כָּל
עֲוֹנוֹתֵינוּ, וְתִסְלַח לְכָל פְּשָׁעֵינוּ, וְתִבְנֶה בֵּית הַמִּקְדָּשׁ בִּמְהֵרָה
בְיָמֵינוּ, וְנַקְרִיב לְפָנֶיךָ קָרְבַּן הַתָּמִיד, שֶׁיְּכַפֵּר בַּעֲדֵנוּ, כְּמוֹ
שֶׁכָּתַבְתָּ עָלֵינוּ בְּתוֹרָתֶךָ, עַל יְדֵי מֹשֶׁה עַבְדֶּךָ, מִפִּי כְבוֹדֶךָ,
כָּאָמוּר:

במדבר כח, א-ח

וַיְדַבֵּר יְיָ אֶל מֹשֶׁה לֵּאמֹר: צַו אֶת בְּנֵי יִשְׂרָאֵל וְאָמַרְתָּ
אֲלֵהֶם: אֶת קָרְבָּנִי לַחְמִי לְאִשַּׁי, רֵיחַ נִיחֹחִי, תִּשְׁמְרוּ לְהַקְרִיב
לִי בְּמוֹעֲדוֹ. וְאָמַרְתָּ לָהֶם: זֶה הָאִשֶּׁה אֲשֶׁר תַּקְרִיבוּ לַיְיָ:
כְּבָשִׂים בְּנֵי שָׁנָה תְמִימִם, שְׁנַיִם לַיּוֹם, עֹלָה תָמִיד. אֶת הַכֶּבֶשׂ
אֶחָד תַּעֲשֶׂה בַבֹּקֶר, וְאֵת הַכֶּבֶשׂ הַשֵּׁנִי תַּעֲשֶׂה בֵּין הָעַרְבָּיִם.
וַעֲשִׂירִית הָאֵיפָה סֹלֶת לְמִנְחָה, בְּלוּלָה בְּשֶׁמֶן כָּתִית רְבִיעִת
הַהִין. עֹלַת תָּמִיד, הָעֲשֻׂיָה בְּהַר סִינַי, לְרֵיחַ נִיחֹחַ, אִשֶּׁה לַיְיָ.
וְנִסְכּוֹ רְבִיעִת הַהִין לַכֶּבֶשׂ הָאֶחָד; בַּקֹּדֶשׁ הַסֵּךְ נֶסֶךְ שֵׁכָר לַיְיָ.

וידבר ... ועשית כיור According to the Talmud, God said: "Whenever they
recite the order of sacrifices, I will deem it as if they offered them before me
and I will forgive them all their sins" (Ta'anith 27b). The sacrificial system
symbolized self-surrender and devotion to the will of God. The peace-offering
with its communion-feast showed the idea of fellowship. It served to keep
alive the sense of dependence on God for the natural blessings of life, while

Exodus 30:17–21

The Lord spoke to Moses, saying: You shall make a bronze laver with a bronze base for washing, and place it between the tent of meeting and the altar, and put water in it, so that Aaron and his sons may wash their hands and feet in it. Whenever they enter the tent of meeting they must wash themselves with water, that they die not; or whenever they approach the altar to minister by burning a sacrifice to the Lord. They must wash their hands and feet, that they die not; this shall be a perpetual statute for them, for him and his descendants, throughout their generations.

May it be thy will, Lord our God and God of our fathers, to have mercy on us and pardon all our sins, iniquities and transgressions; may the Temple be restored speedily in our days, that we may offer before thee the daily offering to atone for us, as thou hast written in thy Torah through Moses thy servant, as it is said:

Numbers 28:1–8

The Lord spoke to Moses, saying: Command the children of Israel, and say to them: My food-offering, consumed by fire, a sweet savor to me, you shall be careful to offer me at its proper time. Say also to them: This is the fire-offering which you shall bring to the Lord: two yearling lambs without blemish, every day, as a daily burnt-offering. The one lamb you shall offer in the morning, and the other lamb towards evening, along with a tenth of an *ephah* of fine flour as a meal-offering, mixed with a fourth of a *hin* of oil from crushed olives. This is a daily burnt-offering, as instituted at Mount Sinai, for a sweet savor, a sacrifice to the Lord. Its drink-offering shall be the fourth part of a *hin* for the one lamb; in the holy place shall you pour out an oblation of

---

it had the social value of promoting the solidarity of the nation. The *Tamid*, or daily offering, symbolized Israel's pledge of unbroken service to God. The fragrant smoke of incense rising towards heaven was a natural symbol of prayer ascending to God. From Psalm 141:2 ("Let my prayer rise like incense before thee") it appears that the incense-offering symbolized prayer.

An *ephah* (a little over a bushel) was equivalent to three *seahs*, and a *seah* was equivalent to six *kabs*. A *hin* was equivalent to nearly two gallons. A *mina*, or *maneh*, was equal to 341 grams.

וְאֵת הַכֶּבֶשׂ הַשֵּׁנִי תַּעֲשֶׂה בֵּין הָעַרְבָּיִם; כְּמִנְחַת הַבֹּקֶר וּכְנִסְכּוֹ
תַּעֲשֶׂה, אִשֵּׁה רֵיחַ נִיחֹחַ לַיְיָ.

ויקרא א, יא

וְשָׁחַט אֹתוֹ עַל יֶרֶךְ הַמִּזְבֵּחַ צָפֹנָה לִפְנֵי יְיָ; וְזָרְקוּ בְּנֵי אַהֲרֹן
הַכֹּהֲנִים אֶת דָּמוֹ עַל הַמִּזְבֵּחַ סָבִיב.

יְהִי רָצוֹן מִלְּפָנֶיךָ, יְיָ אֱלֹהֵינוּ וֵאלֹהֵי אֲבוֹתֵינוּ, שֶׁתְּהֵא
אֲמִירָה זוֹ חֲשׁוּבָה וּמְקֻבֶּלֶת וּמְרֻצָּה לְפָנֶיךָ, כְּאִלּוּ הִקְרַבְנוּ
קָרְבַּן הַתָּמִיד בְּמוֹעֲדוֹ וּבִמְקוֹמוֹ וּכְהִלְכָתוֹ.

אַתָּה הוּא יְיָ אֱלֹהֵינוּ שֶׁהִקְטִירוּ אֲבוֹתֵינוּ לְפָנֶיךָ אֶת קְטֹרֶת
הַסַּמִּים בִּזְמַן שֶׁבֵּית הַמִּקְדָּשׁ הָיָה קַיָּם, כַּאֲשֶׁר צִוִּיתָ אוֹתָם עַל
יְדֵי מֹשֶׁה נְבִיאֶךָ, כַּכָּתוּב בְּתוֹרָתֶךָ:

שמות ל, לד–לו; ל ז–ח

וַיֹּאמֶר יְיָ אֶל מֹשֶׁה: קַח לְךָ סַמִּים, נָטָף וּשְׁחֵלֶת וְחֶלְבְּנָה,
סַמִּים וּלְבֹנָה זַכָּה; בַּד בְּבַד יִהְיֶה. וְעָשִׂיתָ אֹתָהּ קְטֹרֶת, רֹקַח
מַעֲשֵׂה רוֹקֵחַ, מְמֻלָּח, טָהוֹר קֹדֶשׁ. וְשָׁחַקְתָּ מִמֶּנָּה הָדֵק, וְנָתַתָּה
מִמֶּנָּה לִפְנֵי הָעֵדֻת בְּאֹהֶל מוֹעֵד אֲשֶׁר אִוָּעֵד לְךָ שָׁמָּה; קֹדֶשׁ
קָדָשִׁים תִּהְיֶה לָכֶם. וְנֶאֱמַר: וְהִקְטִיר עָלָיו אַהֲרֹן קְטֹרֶת סַמִּים
בַּבֹּקֶר בַּבֹּקֶר, בְּהֵיטִיבוֹ אֶת הַנֵּרֹת יַקְטִירֶנָּה. וּבְהַעֲלֹת אַהֲרֹן
אֶת הַנֵּרֹת בֵּין הָעַרְבַּיִם יַקְטִירֶנָּה; קְטֹרֶת תָּמִיד לִפְנֵי יְיָ
לְדֹרֹתֵיכֶם.

תלמוד בבלי, כריתות ו, א; תלמוד ירושלמי, יומא ד, ה

תָּנוּ רַבָּנָן, פִּטּוּם הַקְּטֹרֶת כֵּיצַד. שְׁלֹשׁ מֵאוֹת וְשִׁשִּׁים וּשְׁמוֹנָה
מָנִים הָיוּ בָהּ: שְׁלֹשׁ מֵאוֹת וְשִׁשִּׁים וַחֲמִשָּׁה כְּמִנְיַן יְמוֹת הַחַמָּה,
מָנֶה לְכָל יוֹם, פְּרָס בְּשַׁחֲרִית וּפְרָס בֵּין הָעַרְבָּיִם, וּשְׁלֹשָׁה
מָנִים יְתֵרִים שֶׁמֵּהֶם מַכְנִיס כֹּהֵן גָּדוֹל מְלֹא חָפְנָיו בְּיוֹם
הַכִּפֻּרִים, וּמַחֲזִירָם לְמַכְתֶּשֶׁת בְּעֶרֶב יוֹם הַכִּפֻּרִים, וְשׁוֹחֲקָן

strong drink unto the Lord. The other lamb you shall offer towards evening, with the same meal-offering and the same oblation as in the morning, to be a burnt-offering of sweet savor to the Lord.

Leviticus 1:11

He shall slaughter it on the north side of the altar before the Lord; and Aaron's sons, the priests, shall sprinkle its blood all around the altar.

May it be thy will, Lord our God and God of our fathers, that this recital be favorably regarded and accepted by thee as if we offered the daily offering at its proper time, its right place, and according to rule.

Thou art the Lord our God before whom our forefathers burned the incense of fragrant spices when the Temple was in existence, as thou didst command them through Moses thy prophet, as it is written in thy Torah:

Exodus 30:34–36; 30:7–8

The Lord said to Moses: "Take fragrant spices, stacte, onycha, and galbanum, aromatics along with pure frankincense; of each shall there be a like weight. And you shall make of it incense, a compound after the art of the apothecary, seasoned with salt, pure and holy. You shall pulverize some of it very fine, and place some of it in front of the ark in the tent of meeting, where I will meet with you; it shall be to you most holy." It is also said: "Aaron shall burn the incense of fragrant spices on the altar every morning; when he trims the lamps, he shall burn it. And when Aaron lights the lamps toward evening, he shall again burn it; this is a regular incense-offering before the Lord throughout your generations."

Babylonian Talmud, Kerithoth 6a; *Palestinian Talmud, Yoma* 4:5

The Rabbis have taught: How was the compounding of the incense performed? The [annual amount of] incense weighed three hundred and sixty-eight minas: three hundred and sixty-five corresponding to the number of the days of the solar year, one mina for each day—half a mina of incense being offered in the morning and half in the afternoon—and of the surplus three minas the high priest took two handfuls [to the Holy of Holies] on the Day of Atonement. These were ground again in a mortar on the eve

יָפֶה יָפֶה כְּדֵי שֶׁתְּהֵא דַקָּה מִן הַדַּקָּה. וְאַחַד עָשָׂר סַמָּנִים הָיוּ
בָּהּ, וְאֵלּוּ הֵן: הַצֳּרִי וְהַצִּפֹּרֶן, הַחֶלְבְּנָה, וְהַלְּבוֹנָה, מִשְׁקַל
שִׁבְעִים שִׁבְעִים מָנֶה; מוֹר וּקְצִיעָה, שִׁבֹּלֶת נֵרְדְּ, וְכַרְכֹּם,
מִשְׁקַל שִׁשָּׁה עָשָׂר שִׁשָּׁה עָשָׂר מָנֶה; הַקֹּשְׁטְ שְׁנֵים עָשָׂר, וְקִלּוּפָה
שְׁלֹשָׁה, וְקִנָּמוֹן תִּשְׁעָה. בְּרִית כַּרְשִׁינָה תִּשְׁעָה קַבִּין; יֵין
קַפְרִיסִין סְאִין תְּלָתָא וְקַבִּין תְּלָתָא; וְאִם אֵין לוֹ יֵין קַפְרִיסִין,
מֵבִיא חֲמַר חִוַּרְיָן עַתִּיק; מֶלַח סְדוֹמִית רֹבַע הַקַּב; מַעֲלֶה
עָשָׁן כָּל שֶׁהוּא. רַבִּי נָתָן אוֹמֵר: **אַף כִּפַּת הַיַּרְדֵּן כָּל שֶׁהוּא.**
וְאִם נָתַן בָּהּ דְּבַשׁ, פְּסָלָהּ; וְאִם חִסַּר אַחַת מִכָּל סַמָּנֶיהָ, חַיָּב
מִיתָה.

רַבָּן שִׁמְעוֹן בֶּן גַּמְלִיאֵל אוֹמֵר: הַצֳּרִי אֵינוֹ אֶלָּא שְׂרָף הַנּוֹטֵף
מֵעֲצֵי הַקְּטָף. בְּרִית כַּרְשִׁינָה לָמָה הִיא בָאָה, כְּדֵי לְיַפּוֹת בָּהּ
אֶת הַצִּפֹּרֶן, כְּדֵי שֶׁתְּהֵא נָאָה. יֵין קַפְרִיסִין לָמָה הוּא בָא, כְּדֵי
לִשְׁרוֹת בּוֹ אֶת הַצִּפֹּרֶן, כְּדֵי שֶׁתְּהֵא עַזָּה. וַהֲלֹא מֵי רַגְלַיִם יָפִין
לָהּ, אֶלָּא שֶׁאֵין מַכְנִיסִין מֵי רַגְלַיִם בָּעֲזָרָה מִפְּנֵי הַכָּבוֹד.

תַּנְיָא, רַבִּי נָתָן אוֹמֵר: כְּשֶׁהוּא שׁוֹחֵק, אוֹמֵר הָדֵק הֵיטֵב,
הֵיטֵב הָדֵק, מִפְּנֵי שֶׁהַקּוֹל יָפֶה לַבְּשָׂמִים. פִּטְּמָהּ לַחֲצָאִין,
כְּשֵׁרָה; לִשְׁלִישׁ וְלִרְבִיעַ, לֹא שָׁמָעְנוּ. אָמַר רַבִּי יְהוּדָה: זֶה
הַכְּלָל: אִם כְּמִדָּתָהּ, כְּשֵׁרָה לַחֲצָאִין; וְאִם חִסַּר אַחַת מִכָּל
סַמָּנֶיהָ, חַיָּב מִיתָה.

תַּנְיָא, בַּר קַפְּרָא אוֹמֵר: אַחַת לְשִׁשִּׁים אוֹ לְשִׁבְעִים שָׁנָה
הָיְתָה בָאָה שֶׁל שִׁירַיִם לַחֲצָאִין. וְעוֹד תָּנֵי בַּר קַפְּרָא: אִלּוּ
הָיָה נוֹתֵן בָּהּ קֹרְטוֹב שֶׁל דְּבַשׁ, אֵין אָדָם יָכוֹל לַעֲמוֹד מִפְּנֵי

of the Day of Atonement so as to make the incense extremely thin.

The incense was composed of the following eleven kinds of spices: balm, onycha, galbanum, and frankincense, seventy minas' weight of each; myrrh, cassia, spikenard, and saffron, sixteen minas' weight of each; twelve minas of costus; three minas of an aromatic bark; nine minas of cinnamon. [Added to the spices were] nine *kavs* of Karsina lye; three *seahs* and three *kavs* of Cyprus wine—if Cyprus wine could not be obtained, strong white wine might be substituted for it—a fourth of a *kav* of Sodom salt, and a minute quantity of *ma'aleh ashan* [a smoke-producing ingredient]. Rabbi Nathan says: A minute quantity of Jordan amber was also required. If one added honey to the mixture, he rendered the incense unfit for sacred use; and if he left out any of its ingredients, he was subject to the penalty of death.

Rabbi Simeon ben Gamaliel says: The balm required for the incense is a resin exuding from the balsam trees. Why was Karsina lye used? To refine the onycha. Why was Cyprus wine employed? To steep the onycha in it so as to make it more pungent. Though *mei raglayim* might have been good for that purpose, it was not decent to bring it into the Temple.

It has been taught: Rabbi Nathan says: While the priest was grinding the incense, his superintendent would say: "Grind it very thin, grind it very thin," because the [rhythmic] sound is good for the compounding of the spices. If the incense was compounded in two instalments, it is fit for use; but we have not heard that it is permissible to prepare it in portions of one-third or one-fourth [of the total required annually]. Rabbi Judah says: The general rule is that if it was well-proportioned, the incense was fit for use even though it was prepared in two instalments; if, however, one left out any of its ingredients he would be subject to the penalty of death.

It has been taught: Bar Kappara says: Once in sixty or seventy years a total of half the required amount came from the accumulated surpluses [the extra three minas of which the high priest took two handfuls on the Day of Atonement]. Bar Kappara moreover has taught: Had one mixed with the incense the smallest amount of honey, nobody could have resisted the scent. Then

רֵיחָהּ; וְלָמָה אֵין מְעָרְבִין בָּהּ דְּבַשׁ, מִפְּנֵי שֶׁהַתּוֹרָה אָמְרָה:
כִּי כָל שְׂאֹר וְכָל דְּבַשׁ לֹא תַקְטִירוּ מִמֶּנּוּ אִשֶּׁה לַיְיָ.

יְיָ צְבָאוֹת עִמָּנוּ, מִשְׂגָּב לָנוּ אֱלֹהֵי יַעֲקֹב, סֶלָה.

יְיָ צְבָאוֹת, אַשְׁרֵי אָדָם בֹּטֵחַ בָּךְ.

יְיָ, הוֹשִׁיעָה; הַמֶּלֶךְ יַעֲנֵנוּ בְיוֹם קָרְאֵנוּ.

אַתָּה סֵתֶר לִי, מִצַּר תִּצְּרֵנִי; רָנֵּי פַלֵּט תְּסוֹבְבֵנִי, סֶלָה.
וְעָרְבָה לַיְיָ מִנְחַת יְהוּדָה וִירוּשָׁלָיִם, כִּימֵי עוֹלָם וּכְשָׁנִים
קַדְמֹנִיּוֹת.

מסכת יומא לג, א

אַבַּיֵּי הֲוָה מְסַדֵּר סֵדֶר הַמַּעֲרָכָה מִשְּׁמָא דִגְמָרָא וְאַלִּבָּא
דְאַבָּא שָׁאוּל: מַעֲרָכָה גְדוֹלָה קוֹדֶמֶת לְמַעֲרָכָה שְׁנִיָּה שֶׁל
קְטֹרֶת, וּמַעֲרָכָה שְׁנִיָּה שֶׁל קְטֹרֶת קוֹדֶמֶת לְסִדּוּר שְׁנֵי גִזְרֵי
עֵצִים, וְסִדּוּר שְׁנֵי גִזְרֵי עֵצִים קוֹדֵם לְדִשּׁוּן מִזְבֵּחַ הַפְּנִימִי,
וְדִשּׁוּן מִזְבֵּחַ הַפְּנִימִי קוֹדֵם לַהֲטָבַת חָמֵשׁ נֵרוֹת, וַהֲטָבַת חָמֵשׁ
נֵרוֹת קוֹדֶמֶת לְדַם הַתָּמִיד, וְדַם הַתָּמִיד קוֹדֵם לַהֲטָבַת שְׁתֵּי
נֵרוֹת, וַהֲטָבַת שְׁתֵּי נֵרוֹת קוֹדֶמֶת לִקְטֹרֶת, וּקְטֹרֶת קוֹדֶמֶת
לְאֵבָרִים, וְאֵבָרִים לְמִנְחָה, וּמִנְחָה לַחֲבִתִּין, וַחֲבִתִּין לִנְסָכִין,
וּנְסָכִין לְמוּסָפִין, וּמוּסָפִין לְבָזִיכִין, וּבָזִיכִין קוֹדְמִין לְתָמִיד
שֶׁל בֵּין הָעַרְבָּיִם, שֶׁנֶּאֱמַר: וְעָרַךְ עָלֶיהָ הָעֹלָה, וְהִקְטִיר עָלֶיהָ
חֶלְבֵי הַשְּׁלָמִים. עָלֶיהָ הַשְׁלֵם כָּל הַקָּרְבָּנוֹת כֻּלָּם.

אָנָּא, בְּכֹחַ גְּדֻלַּת יְמִינְךָ תַּתִּיר צְרוּרָה.
קַבֵּל רִנַּת עַמְּךָ, שַׂגְּבֵנוּ, טַהֲרֵנוּ, נוֹרָא.

שלמים is here interpreted to imply completion (from שלם, "to be finished").
אנא בכח is a rhymed prayer. It has six words to each of its seven lines.
According to the Kabbalists, the forty-two words of this poem represent the
name of God which is composed of forty-two letters. Though it has been
credited to the *Tanna* Neḥunya ben ha-Kanah (first century) its author is
unknown.

why was no honey mixed with it? Because the Torah says: "You shall not present any leaven or honey as a fire-offering to the Lord."[1]

The Lord of hosts is with us; the God of Jacob is our fortress. Lord of hosts, happy is the man who trusts in thee.

O Lord, save us; may the King answer us when we call.

Thou art my shelter; from the foe thou wilt preserve me; with songs of deliverance thou wilt surround me.[2]

The offering of Judah and Jerusalem will be pleasing to the Lord, as in the days of old and as in former years.[3]

Talmud Yomu 33a

Abbaye recounted the daily order of the Temple service on the authority of tradition and according to Abba Saul: The large pile of wood was set on the altar prior to the second pile which supplied coal to be used for the incense; the second pile was arranged before placing two [additional] logs of wood [on the large pile]; the placing of the two logs of wood preceded the removing of the ashes from the inner altar; the removing of the ashes from the inner altar came before the trimming of the five lamps; the trimming of the five lamps preceded the sprinkling of the blood of the daily offering; the blood of the daily offering was sprinkled before the trimming of the two remaining lamps; the trimming of the two lamps preceded the incense offering; the incense offering preceded the offering of the sacrificial parts; the offering of the sacrificial parts preceded the meal-offering; the meal-offering preceded the offering of pancakes; the pancakes came before the libations; the libations preceded the additional offerings on sabbaths and festivals; the additional offerings preceded the removal of the two bowls of frankincense; the frankincense bowls preceded the daily afternoon-offering, as it is said: "And the priest shall arrange the burnt-offering on the altar, and burn on it the fat of the *shelamim*,"[4] which means that with the afternoon-offering all the offerings of the day are to be completed.

By the great power of thy right hand, O set the captive free.

Revered God, accept thy people's prayer; strengthen us, cleanse us.

[1] *Leviticus* 2:11.   [2] *Psalms* 46:8; 84:13; 20:10; 32:7.   [3] *Malachi* 3:4.   [4] *Leviticus* 6:5.

נָא, גִּבּוֹר, דּוֹרְשֵׁי יִחוּדְךָ כְּבָבַת שָׁמְרֵם.

בָּרְכֵם, טַהֲרֵם, רַחֲמֵם, צִדְקָתְךָ תָּמִיד גָּמְלֵם.

חֲסִין קָדוֹשׁ, בְּרֹב טוּבְךָ נַהֵל עֲדָתֶךָ.

יָחִיד גֵּאֶה, לְעַמְּךָ פְּנֵה, זוֹכְרֵי קְדֻשָּׁתֶךָ.

שַׁוְעָתֵנוּ קַבֵּל וּשְׁמַע צַעֲקָתֵנוּ, יוֹדֵעַ תַּעֲלֻמוֹת.

בָּרוּךְ שֵׁם כְּבוֹד מַלְכוּתוֹ לְעוֹלָם וָעֶד.

רִבּוֹן הָעוֹלָמִים, אַתָּה צִוִּיתָנוּ לְהַקְרִיב קָרְבַּן הַתָּמִיד
בְּמוֹעֲדוֹ, וְלִהְיוֹת כֹּהֲנִים בַּעֲבוֹדָתָם, וּלְוִיִּם בְּדוּכָנָם, וְיִשְׂרָאֵל
בְּמַעֲמָדָם; וְעַתָּה בַּעֲוֹנוֹתֵינוּ חָרַב בֵּית הַמִּקְדָּשׁ וּבָטֵל הַתָּמִיד,
וְאֵין לָנוּ לֹא כֹהֵן בַּעֲבוֹדָתוֹ, וְלֹא לֵוִי בְּדוּכָנוֹ, וְלֹא יִשְׂרָאֵל
בְּמַעֲמָדוֹ. וְאַתָּה אָמַרְתָּ: וּנְשַׁלְּמָה פָרִים שְׂפָתֵינוּ, לָכֵן יְהִי רָצוֹן
מִלְּפָנֶיךָ, יְיָ אֱלֹהֵינוּ וֵאלֹהֵי אֲבוֹתֵינוּ, שֶׁיְּהֵא שִׂיחַ שִׂפְתוֹתֵינוּ
חָשׁוּב וּמְקֻבָּל וּמְרֻצֶּה לְפָנֶיךָ כְּאִלּוּ הִקְרַבְנוּ קָרְבַּן הַתָּמִיד
בְּמוֹעֲדוֹ וְעָמַדְנוּ עַל מַעֲמָדוֹ.

On Sabbath:

וּבְיוֹם הַשַּׁבָּת שְׁנֵי כְבָשִׂים בְּנֵי שָׁנָה תְּמִימִם, וּשְׁנֵי עֶשְׂרֹנִים
סֹלֶת מִנְחָה בְּלוּלָה בַשֶּׁמֶן, וְנִסְכּוֹ. עֹלַת שַׁבָּת בְּשַׁבַּתּוֹ עַל עֹלַת
הַתָּמִיד וְנִסְכָּהּ.

The sacrificial system symbolized self-surrender and devotion to the will
of God. The peace-offering with its communion-feast showed the idea of
fellowship. It served to keep alive the sense of dependence on God for the
natural blessings of life, while it had a social value of promoting the solidarity
of the nation. The *Tamid*, or daily offering, symbolized Israel's pledge of

Almighty God, guard as the apple of the eye those who seek thee.
Bless them, cleanse them, pity them; ever grant them thy truth.
Mighty, holy God, in thy abundant grace, guide thy people.
Exalted God, turn to thy people who proclaim thy holiness.
Accept our prayer, hear our cry, thou who knowest secret thoughts.

Blessed be the name of his glorious majesty forever and ever.

Lord of the universe, thou hast commanded us to sacrifice the daily offering at its proper time with priests officiating, Levites [singing] on the platform, and lay representatives of Israel attending the Temple service. Now, through our sins the Temple is destroyed, the daily offering is abolished, and we have neither priest officiating, nor Levite [singing] on the platform, nor Israelite attending the Temple service. However, thou hast declared that we may substitute the prayer of our lips for the sacrifice of bullocks.[1] Therefore, may it be thy will, Lord our God and God of our fathers, that the prayer of our lips be favorably regarded and accepted by thee as if we offered the daily offering at its proper time and attended at its service.

On Sabbath:

On the Sabbath day two yearling male lambs without blemish [are to be offered], with two-tenths of an *ephah* of fine flour mixed with oil as a meal-offering, along with its libation. This is the burnt-offering of every Sabbath, in addition to the daily burnt-offering and its libation.[2]

---

unbroken service to God. From Psalm 141:2 ("Let my prayer rise like incense before thee") it appears that the incense-offering symbolized prayer.

It has been suggested that the fifth chapter of Mishnah Zevaḥim was selected to be used as part of the liturgy because it consists throughout of undisputed statements, whereas other Mishnah sections contain divergent opinions offered by various sages.

---

[1] *Hosea* 14:3.   [2] *Numbers* 28:9–10.

משנה זבחים, פרק ה

א. אֵיזֶהוּ מְקוֹמָן שֶׁל זְבָחִים. קָדְשֵׁי קָדָשִׁים שְׁחִיטָתָן בַּצָּפוֹן,
פַּר וְשָׂעִיר שֶׁל יוֹם הַכִּפּוּרִים שְׁחִיטָתָן בַּצָּפוֹן, וְקִבּוּל דָּמָן
בִּכְלִי שָׁרֵת בַּצָּפוֹן. וְדָמָן טָעוּן הַזָּיָה עַל בֵּין הַבַּדִּים וְעַל
הַפָּרֹכֶת וְעַל מִזְבַּח הַזָּהָב; מַתָּנָה אַחַת מֵהֶן מְעַכֶּבֶת. שְׁיָרֵי
הַדָּם הָיָה שׁוֹפֵךְ עַל יְסוֹד מַעֲרָבִי שֶׁל מִזְבֵּחַ הַחִיצוֹן; אִם לֹא
נָתַן, לֹא עִכֵּב.

ב. פָּרִים הַנִּשְׂרָפִים וּשְׂעִירִים הַנִּשְׂרָפִים שְׁחִיטָתָן בַּצָּפוֹן,
וְקִבּוּל דָּמָן בִּכְלִי שָׁרֵת בַּצָּפוֹן. וְדָמָן טָעוּן הַזָּיָה עַל הַפָּרֹכֶת
וְעַל מִזְבַּח הַזָּהָב; מַתָּנָה אַחַת מֵהֶן מְעַכָּבֶת. שְׁיָרֵי הַדָּם הָיָה
שׁוֹפֵךְ עַל יְסוֹד מַעֲרָבִי שֶׁל מִזְבֵּחַ הַחִיצוֹן; אִם לֹא נָתַן, לֹא
עִכֵּב. אֵלּוּ וָאֵלּוּ נִשְׂרָפִין בְּבֵית הַדָּשֶׁן.

ג. חַטֹּאת הַצִּבּוּר וְהַיָּחִיד, אֵלּוּ הֵן חַטֹּאת הַצִּבּוּר: שְׂעִירֵי
רָאשֵׁי חֳדָשִׁים וְשֶׁל מוֹעֲדוֹת, שְׁחִיטָתָן בַּצָּפוֹן, וְקִבּוּל דָּמָן בִּכְלִי
שָׁרֵת בַּצָּפוֹן. וְדָמָן טָעוּן אַרְבַּע מַתָּנוֹת עַל אַרְבַּע קְרָנוֹת.
כֵּיצַד, עָלָה בַכֶּבֶשׁ וּפָנָה לַסּוֹבֵב וּבָא־לוֹ לְקֶרֶן דְּרוֹמִית
מִזְרָחִית, מִזְרָחִית צְפוֹנִית, צְפוֹנִית מַעֲרָבִית, מַעֲרָבִית
דְּרוֹמִית. שְׁיָרֵי הַדָּם הָיָה שׁוֹפֵךְ עַל יְסוֹד דְּרוֹמִי. וְנֶאֱכָלִין
לִפְנִים מִן הַקְּלָעִים לְזִכְרֵי כְהֻנָּה, בְּכָל מַאֲכָל, לְיוֹם וָלַיְלָה,
עַד חֲצוֹת.

איזהו מקומן, the fifth chapter of Mishnah Zevahim, describing the places
where the sacrifices were offered in the Temple, forms part of the preliminary
morning service, in keeping with the following statement concerning the

Mishnah Zevaḥim, Chapter 5

1. Which were the places of sacrifice in the Temple? The most holy offerings were slaughtered on the north side of the altar, as were also the bullock and the he-goat for the Day of Atonement. Their blood, which was there received in a sacred vessel, had to be sprinkled over the space between the poles of the ark, towards the curtain of the Holy of Holies, and upon the golden altar. The omission of one of these sprinklings rendered the atonement ceremony invalid. The priest poured out the rest of the blood at the western base of the outer altar; if, however, he failed to do so, the omission did not invalidate the ceremony.

2. The bullocks and the he-goats which were to be burned were slaughtered on the north side of the altar; their blood, which was there received in a sacred vessel, had to be sprinkled towards the curtain and upon the golden altar. The omission of either of these sprinklings rendered the ceremony invalid. The priest poured out the rest of the blood at the western base of the outer altar; if, however, he failed to do so, the omission did not invalidate the ceremony. All these offerings were burnt at the place where the ashes were deposited.

3. The communal sin-offerings and those of individuals—the goats offered on new moon festivals and on major feasts are the communal sin-offerings—were slaughtered on the north side of the altar. Their blood, which was there received in a sacred vessel, required four sprinklings on the four corners of the altar. How was this done? The priest went up the ascent, and, having turned to the ledge bordering the altar, walked along it to the southeast, northeast, northwest and southwest corners, successively. The rest of the blood he poured out at the southern base. These offerings, prepared for food in any fashion, were eaten within the Temple court only by the males of the priesthood during that day and evening—until midnight.

---

substitution of prayer for sacrifices offered in ancient times: "Whenever they recite the order of sacrifices, I will deem it as if they offered them to me, and I will forgive them all their sins" (Ta'anith 27b).

ד. הָעוֹלָה קֹדֶשׁ קָדָשִׁים. שְׁחִיטָתָהּ בַּצָּפוֹן, וְקִבּוּל דָּמָהּ בִּכְלִי שָׁרֵת בַּצָּפוֹן. וְדָמָהּ טָעוּן שְׁתֵּי מַתָּנוֹת שֶׁהֵן אַרְבַּע; וּטְעוּנָה הַפְשֵׁט, וְנִתּוּחַ, וְכָלִיל לָאִשִּׁים.

ה. זִבְחֵי שַׁלְמֵי צִבּוּר וַאֲשָׁמוֹת, אֵלּוּ הֵן אֲשָׁמוֹת: אֲשַׁם גְּזֵלוֹת, אֲשַׁם מְעִילוֹת, אֲשַׁם שִׁפְחָה חֲרוּפָה, אֲשַׁם נָזִיר, אֲשַׁם מְצֹרָע, אָשָׁם תָּלוּי. שְׁחִיטָתָן בַּצָּפוֹן, וְקִבּוּל דָּמָן בִּכְלִי שָׁרֵת בַּצָּפוֹן, וְדָמָן טָעוּן שְׁתֵּי מַתָּנוֹת שֶׁהֵן אַרְבַּע. וְנֶאֱכָלִין לִפְנִים מִן הַקְּלָעִים לְזִכְרֵי כְהֻנָּה, בְּכָל מַאֲכָל, לְיוֹם וָלַיְלָה, עַד חֲצוֹת.

ו. הַתּוֹדָה וְאֵיל נָזִיר קָדָשִׁים קַלִּים. שְׁחִיטָתָן בְּכָל מָקוֹם בָּעֲזָרָה, וְדָמָן טָעוּן שְׁתֵּי מַתָּנוֹת שֶׁהֵן אַרְבַּע. וְנֶאֱכָלִין בְּכָל הָעִיר, לְכָל אָדָם, בְּכָל מַאֲכָל, לְיוֹם וָלַיְלָה, עַד חֲצוֹת. הַמּוּרָם מֵהֶם כַּיּוֹצֵא בָהֶם, אֶלָּא שֶׁהַמּוּרָם נֶאֱכָל לַכֹּהֲנִים, לִנְשֵׁיהֶם וְלִבְנֵיהֶם וּלְעַבְדֵּיהֶם.

ז. שְׁלָמִים קָדָשִׁים קַלִּים. שְׁחִיטָתָן בְּכָל מָקוֹם בָּעֲזָרָה, וְדָמָן טָעוּן שְׁתֵּי מַתָּנוֹת שֶׁהֵן אַרְבַּע. וְנֶאֱכָלִין בְּכָל הָעִיר, לְכָל אָדָם, בְּכָל מַאֲכָל, לִשְׁנֵי יָמִים וְלַיְלָה אֶחָד. הַמּוּרָם מֵהֶם כַּיּוֹצֵא בָהֶם, אֶלָּא שֶׁהַמּוּרָם נֶאֱכָל לַכֹּהֲנִים, לִנְשֵׁיהֶם וְלִבְנֵיהֶם וּלְעַבְדֵּיהֶם.

ח. הַבְּכוֹר וְהַמַּעֲשֵׂר וְהַפֶּסַח קָדָשִׁים קַלִּים. שְׁחִיטָתָן בְּכָל מָקוֹם בָּעֲזָרָה, וְדָמָן טָעוּן מַתָּנָה אֶחָת, וּבִלְבַד שֶׁיִּתֵּן כְּנֶגֶד הַיְסוֹד. שִׁנָּה בַּאֲכִילָתָן: הַבְּכוֹר נֶאֱכָל לַכֹּהֲנִים, וְהַמַּעֲשֵׂר לְכָל

4. The burnt-offering was one of the most holy sacrifices. It was slaughtered on the north side of the altar. Its blood, which was there received in a sacred vessel, required two sprinklings [at opposite angles of the altar] making four in all. This offering had to be flayed, severed into parts, and consumed by fire.

5. As to the communal peace-offerings and the guilt-offerings—the following are the guilt-offerings: for robbery, for making improper use of sacred objects, for violating a betrothed handmaid, the offering of a nazirite who has become ritually unclean, the offering of a leper at his cleansing, and the offering of a person in doubt whether an act he has committed requires a sin-offering— all these were slaughtered on the north side of the altar. Their blood, which was there received in a sacred vessel, required two sprinklings [at opposite angles of the altar] making four in all. These offerings, prepared for food in any fashion, were eaten within the Temple court only by the males of the priesthood that day and evening—until midnight.

6. The thanksgiving-offering and the ram offered by a nazirite [at the termination of his vow] were holy in a minor degree. These might be slaughtered anywhere in the Temple court. Their blood required two sprinklings [at opposite angles of the altar] making four in all. They might be eaten, prepared for food in any fashion, anywhere in the city by anyone during that day and evening— until midnight. The same rule applied to the priests' share, except that the priests' share might be eaten only by the priests, their wives, their children and their servants

7. The peace-offerings also were holy in a minor degree. These might be slaughtered anywhere in the Temple court. Their blood required two sprinklings [at opposite angles of the altar] making four in all. They might be eaten, prepared for food in any fashion, anywhere in the city by anyone during two days and one night. The same rule applied to the priests' share, except that the priests' share might be eaten only by the priests, their wives, their children and their servants.

8. The firstlings of animals, the tithe of cattle, and the paschal lamb were likewise holy in a minor degree. These migh be slaughtered anywhere in the Temple court. Their blood required one sprinkling only; this, however, had to be done at the base of the altar. The following difference prevailed as to the eating of them: the firstborn animal might be eaten only by the priests,

אָדָם. וְנֶאֱכָלִין בְּכָל הָעִיר, בְּכָל מַאֲכָל, לִשְׁנֵי יָמִים וְלַיְלָה
אֶחָד. הַפֶּסַח אֵינוֹ נֶאֱכָל אֶלָּא בַלַּיְלָה, וְאֵינוֹ נֶאֱכָל אֶלָּא עַד
חֲצוֹת, וְאֵינוֹ נֶאֱכָל אֶלָּא לִמְנוּיָיו, וְאֵינוֹ נֶאֱכָל אֶלָּא צָלִי.

ספרא, פתיחה

רַבִּי יִשְׁמָעֵאל אוֹמֵר: בִּשְׁלֹשׁ עֶשְׂרֵה מִדּוֹת הַתּוֹרָה נִדְרָשֶׁת:

א) מִקַּל וָחֹמֶר;

ב) וּמִגְּזֵרָה שָׁוָה;

ג) מִבִּנְיַן אָב מִכָּתוּב אֶחָד, וּמִבִּנְיַן אָב מִשְּׁנֵי כְתוּבִים;

ד) מִכְּלָל וּפְרָט;

ה) וּמִפְּרָט וּכְלָל;

ו) כְּלָל וּפְרָט וּכְלָל אִי אַתָּה דָן אֶלָּא כְּעֵין הַפְּרָט;

רבי ישמעאל בן אלישע, a contemporary of Rabbi Akiba, died as a martyr in the year 135 during the Roman persecutions. The *Baraitha d'Rabbi Ishmael*, which constitutes the introduction to the *Sifra* (tannaitic commentary on Leviticus), has been inserted here to complete the daily minimum of Bible and Talmud study required of every Jew. This section is prefaced (on page 57) by two blessings concerning Torah study.

ILLUSTRATIONS

1. If, for example, a certain act is forbidden on an ordinary festival, it is so much the more forbidden on Yom Kippur; if a certain act is permissible on Yom Kippur, it is so much the more permissible on an ordinary festival.

2. The phrase "Hebrew slave" (Exodus 21:2) is ambiguous, for it may mean a heathen slave owned by a Hebrew, or else, a slave who is a Hebrew. That the latter is the correct meaning is proved by a reference to the phrase "your Hebrew brother" in Deuteronomy 15:12, where the same law is mentioned (... "If your Hebrew brother is sold to you ...").

3. (a) From Deuteronomy 24:6 ("No one shall take a handmill or an upper millstone in pledge, for he would be taking a life in pledge") the Rabbis concluded: "Everything which is used for preparing food is forbidden to be taken in pledge." (b) From Exodus 21:26–27 ("If a man strikes the eye of his slave . . . and destroys it, he must let him go free in compensation for his eye. If he knocks out the tooth of his slave . . . he must let him go free . . .") the Rabbis concluded that when *any* part of the slave's body is mutilated by the master, the slave shall be set free.

4. In Leviticus 18:6 the law reads: "None of you shall marry anyone

while the tithe might be eaten by anyone. Both the firstling and the tithe might be eaten, prepared for food in any fashion, anywhere in the city during two days and one night. The paschal lamb, however, had to be eaten on that night only—and not later than midnight. It might be eaten only by those numbered for it; nor might it be eaten except when roasted.

TALMUDIC EXPOSITION OF THE SCRIPTURES

Sifra, Introduction

Rabbi Ishmael says: The Torah is interpreted by means of thirteen rules:

1.   Inference is drawn from a minor premise to a major one, or from a major premise to a minor one.

2.   From the similarity of words or phrases occurring in two passages it is inferred that what is expressed in the one applies also to the other.

3.   A general principle, as contained in one or two biblical laws, is applicable to all related laws.

4.   When a generalization is followed by a specification, only what is specified applies.

5.   When a specification is followed by a generalization, all that is implied in the generalization applies.

6.   If a generalization is followed by a specification and this in turn by a generalization, one must be guided by what the specification implies.

---

related to him." This generalization is followed by a specification of forbidden marriages. Hence, this prohibition applies only to those expressly mentioned.

5.   In Exodus 22:9 we read: "If a man gives to his neighbor an ass, or an ox, or a sheep, to keep, or *any* animal, and it dies . . ." The general phrase "any animal," which follows the specification, includes in this law all kinds of animals.

6.   In Exodus 22:8 we are told that an embezzler shall pay double to his neighbor "for anything embezzled [generalization], for ox, or ass, or sheep, or clothing [specification], or any article lost" [generalization]. Since the specification includes only movable property, and objects of intrinsic value, the fine of double payment does not apply to embezzled real estate, nor to notes and bills, since the latter represent only a symbolic value.

ז) מִכְלָל שֶׁהוּא צָרִיךְ לִפְרָט, וּמִפְּרָט שֶׁהוּא צָרִיךְ לִכְלָל;

ח) כָּל דָּבָר שֶׁהָיָה בִּכְלָל וְיָצָא מִן הַכְּלָל לְלַמֵּד, לֹא לְלַמֵּד עַל עַצְמוֹ יָצָא, אֶלָּא לְלַמֵּד עַל הַכְּלָל כֻּלּוֹ יָצָא;

ט) כָּל דָּבָר שֶׁהָיָה בִּכְלָל וְיָצָא לִטְעוֹן טְעַן אַחֵר שֶׁהוּא בְעִנְיָנוֹ, יָצָא לְהָקֵל וְלֹא לְהַחֲמִיר;

י) כָּל דָּבָר שֶׁהָיָה בִּכְלָל וְיָצָא לִטְעוֹן טְעַן אַחֵר שֶׁלֹּא כְעִנְיָנוֹ, יָצָא לְהָקֵל וּלְהַחֲמִיר;

יא) כָּל דָּבָר שֶׁהָיָה בִּכְלָל וְיָצָא לִדּוֹן בַּדָּבָר הֶחָדָשׁ, אִי אַתָּה יָכוֹל לְהַחֲזִירוֹ לִכְלָלוֹ עַד שֶׁיַּחֲזִירֶנּוּ הַכָּתוּב לִכְלָלוֹ בְּפֵרוּשׁ;

יב) דָּבָר הַלָּמֵד מֵעִנְיָנוֹ, וְדָבָר הַלָּמֵד מִסּוֹפוֹ;

---

7. In Leviticus 17:13 we read: "He shall pour out its blood, and *cover* it with *dust*." The verb "to cover" is a general term, since there are various ways of covering a thing; "with dust" is specific. If we were to apply rule 4 to this passage, the law would be that the blood of the slaughtered animal must be covered with nothing except dust. Since, however, the general term "to cover" may also mean "to hide," our present passage necessarily requires the specific expression "with dust"; otherwise, the law might be interpreted to mean that the blood is to be concealed in a closed vessel. On the other hand, the specification "with dust" without the general expression "to cover" would have been meaningless.

8. In Deuteronomy 22:1 we are told that the finder of lost property must return it to its owner. In the next verse the Torah adds: "You shall do the same . . . with his *garment* and with anything lost by your brother . . . which you have found . . ." *Garment*, though included in the general expression "anything lost," is specifically mentioned in order to indicate that the duty to announce the finding of lost articles applies only to such objects which are likely to have an owner, and which have, as in the case of clothing, some marks by which they can be identified.

9. In Exodus 35:2-3 we read: "Whoever does any work on the Sabbath shall be put to death; you shall not light a fire on the Sabbath day." The law against lighting a fire on the Sabbath, though already implied in "any work," is mentioned separately in order to indicate that the penalty for lighting a fire on the Sabbath is not as drastic.

10. According to Exodus 21:29-30, the proprietor of a vicious animal which has killed a man or woman must pay such compensation as may be im-

7. When, however, for the sake of clearness, a generalization necessarily requires a specification, or when a specification requires a generalization, rules 4 and 5 do not apply.

8. Whatever is first implied in a generalization and afterwards specified to teach us something new, is expressly stated not only for its own sake, but to teach something additional concerning all the instances implied in the generalization.

9. Whatever is first implied in a general law and afterwards specified to add another provision similar to the general law, is specified in order to alleviate, and not to increase, the severity of that particular provision.

10. Whatever is first implied in a general law and afterwards specified to add another provision which is not similar to the general law, is specified in order to alleviate in some respects, and in others to increase the severity of that particular provision.

11. Whatever is first implied in a general law and is afterwards specified to determine a new matter, the terms of the general law can no longer apply to it, unless Scripture expressly declares that they do apply.

12. A dubious word or passage is explained from its context or from a subsequent expression.

---

posed on him by the court. In a succeeding verse the Torah adds: "If the ox gores a slave, male or female, he must pay the master thirty shekels of silver." The case of a slave, though already included in the preceding general law of the slain man or woman, contains a different provision, the *fixed* amount of compensation, with the result that whether the slave was valued at more than thirty shekels or less than thirty shekels, the proprietor of the animal must invariably pay thirty shekels.

11. The guilt-offering which a cured leper had to bring was unlike all other guilt-offerings in this, that some of its blood was sprinkled on the person who offered it (Leviticus 14:13–14). On account of this peculiarity none of the rules connected with other offerings would apply to that brought by a cured leper, had not the Torah expressly added: "As the sin-offering so is the guilt-offering."

12. (a) The noun *tinshemeth* occurs in Leviticus 11:18 among the unclean birds, and again (verse 30) among the reptiles. Hence, it becomes certain that *tinshemeth* is the name of a certain bird as well as of a certain reptile. (b) In Deuteronomy 19:6, with regard to the cities of refuge where the manslayer is to flee, we read: "So that the avenger of blood may not pursue the manslayer . . . and slay him, *and he is not deserving of death.*" That the last clause refers to the slayer, and not to the blood avenger, is made clear by the subsequent clause: "inasmuch as he hated him not in time past."

יג) וְכֵן שְׁנֵי כְתוּבִים הַמַּכְחִישִׁים זֶה אֶת זֶה, עַד שֶׁיָּבוֹא הַכָּתוּב הַשְּׁלִישִׁי וְיַכְרִיעַ בֵּינֵיהֶם.

אבות ה, כג; מלאכי ג, ד

יְהִי רָצוֹן מִלְּפָנֶיךָ, יְיָ אֱלֹהֵינוּ וֵאלֹהֵי אֲבוֹתֵינוּ, שֶׁיִּבָּנֶה בֵּית הַמִּקְדָּשׁ בִּמְהֵרָה בְיָמֵינוּ, וְתֵן חֶלְקֵנוּ בְּתוֹרָתֶךָ. וְשָׁם נַעֲבָדְךָ בְּיִרְאָה, כִּימֵי עוֹלָם וּכְשָׁנִים קַדְמוֹנִיּוֹת.

קַדִּישׁ דְּרַבָּנָן

Mourners:

יִתְגַּדַּל וְיִתְקַדַּשׁ שְׁמֵהּ רַבָּא בְּעָלְמָא דִּי בְרָא כִרְעוּתֵהּ; וְיַמְלִיךְ מַלְכוּתֵהּ בְּחַיֵּיכוֹן וּבְיוֹמֵיכוֹן, וּבְחַיֵּי דְכָל בֵּית יִשְׂרָאֵל, בַּעֲגָלָא וּבִזְמַן קָרִיב, וְאִמְרוּ אָמֵן.

יְהֵא שְׁמֵהּ רַבָּא מְבָרַךְ לְעָלַם וּלְעָלְמֵי עָלְמַיָּא.

---

13. In Exodus 13:6 we read: "Seven days you shall eat unleavened bread," and in Deuteronomy 16:8 we are told: "Six days you shall eat unleavened bread." The contradiction between these two passages is explained by a reference to a third passage (Leviticus 23:14), where the use of the new produce is forbidden until the second day of Passover, after the offering of the *Omer*. If, therefore, the unleavened bread was prepared of the new grain, it could only be eaten six days of Passover. Hence, the passage in Exodus 13:6 must refer to unleavened bread prepared of the produce of a previous year.

קדיש דרבנן (Scholars' Kaddish) is recited after the reading of talmudic or midrashic passages. על ישראל ועל רבנן is a prayer for the welfare of the scholars.

The Kaddish

The essential part of the Kaddish consists of the congregational response: "May his great name be blessed forever and ever." Around this response, which is found almost verbatim in Daniel 2:20, the whole Kaddish developed. Originally, it was recited at the close of sermons delivered in Aramaic, the language spoken by the Jews for about a thousand years after the Babylonian captivity. Hence the Kaddish was composed in Aramaic, the language in which the religious discourses were held. At a later period the Kaddish was

13.   Similarly, if two biblical passages contradict each other, they can be harmonized only by a third passage.

Mishnah Aboth 5:23; *Malachi* 3:4

May it be thy will, Lord our God and God of our fathers, that the Temple be speedily rebuilt in our days; and grant us a portion in thy Torah. There we will serve thee with reverence, as in the days of old and as in former years.

KADDISH D'RABBANAN

Mourners:

Glorified and sanctified be God's great name throughout the world which he has created according to his will. May he establish his kingdom in your lifetime and during your days, and within the life of the entire house of Israel, speedily and soon; and say, Amen.

May his great name be blessed forever and to all eternity.

---

introduced into the liturgy to mark the conclusion of sections of the service or of the reading of the biblical and talmudic passages.

The Kaddish contains no reference to the dead. The earliest allusion to the Kaddish as a mourners' prayer is found in Maḥzor Vitry, dated 1208, where it is said plainly: "The lad rises and recites Kaddish." One may safely assume that since the Kaddish has as its underlying thought the hope for the redemption and ultimate healing of suffering mankind, the power of redeeming the dead from the sufferings of *Gehinnom* came to be ascribed in the course of time to the recitation of this sublime doxology. Formerly the Kaddish was recited the whole year of mourning, so as to rescue the soul of one's parents from the torture of *Gehinnom* where the wicked are said to spend no less than twelve months. In order not to count one's own parents among the wicked the period for reciting the Kaddish was later reduced to eleven months.

The observance of the anniversary of parents' death, the Jahrzeit, originated in Germany, as the term itself well indicates. Rabbi Isaac Luria, the celebrated Kabbalist of the sixteenth century, explains that "while the orphan's Kaddish within the eleven months helps the soul to pass from *Gehinnom* to *Gan-Eden*, the Jahrzeit Kaddish elevates the soul every year to a higher sphere in Paradise." The Kaddish has thus become a great pillar of Judaism. No matter how far a Jew may have drifted away from Jewish life, the Kaddish restores him to his people and to the Jewish way of living.

יִתְבָּרַךְ וְיִשְׁתַּבַּח, וְיִתְפָּאַר וְיִתְרוֹמַם, וְיִתְנַשֵּׂא וְיִתְהַדָּר,
וְיִתְעַלֶּה וְיִתְהַלָּל שְׁמֵהּ דְּקֻדְשָׁא, בְּרִיךְ הוּא, לְעֵלָּא מִן כָּל
בִּרְכָתָא וְשִׁירָתָא, תֻּשְׁבְּחָתָא וְנֶחֱמָתָא, דַּאֲמִירָן בְּעָלְמָא,
וְאִמְרוּ אָמֵן.

עַל יִשְׂרָאֵל וְעַל רַבָּנָן וְעַל תַּלְמִידֵיהוֹן, וְעַל כָּל תַּלְמִידֵי
תַלְמִידֵיהוֹן, וְעַל כָּל מָן דְּעָסְקִין בְּאוֹרַיְתָא, דִּי בְּאַתְרָא הָדֵן
וְדִי בְכָל אֲתַר וַאֲתַר, יְהֵא לְהוֹן וּלְכוֹן שְׁלָמָא רַבָּא, חִנָּא
וְחִסְדָּא וְרַחֲמִין, וְחַיִּין אֲרִיכִין, וּמְזוֹנֵי רְוִיחֵי, וּפֻרְקָנָא מִן קֳדָם
אֲבוּהוֹן דְּבִשְׁמַיָּא וְאַרְעָא, וְאִמְרוּ אָמֵן.

יְהֵא שְׁלָמָא רַבָּא מִן שְׁמַיָּא, וְחַיִּים טוֹבִים, עָלֵינוּ וְעַל כָּל
יִשְׂרָאֵל, וְאִמְרוּ אָמֵן.

עֹשֶׂה שָׁלוֹם בִּמְרוֹמָיו, הוּא בְּרַחֲמָיו יַעֲשֶׂה שָׁלוֹם עָלֵינוּ
וְעַל כָּל יִשְׂרָאֵל, וְאִמְרוּ אָמֵן.

During the geonic period it was suggested that the ten synonyms of praise contained in the Kaddish, glorifying "God's great name throughout the world which he has created according to his will," correspond to the ten divine utterances by which the world was created (Avoth 5:1). The seven words of the congregational response (...יהא שמיה רבא) are composed of twenty-eight letters, the numerical value of the word כח (power). This alludes to the first verse of the Torah, which consists of seven words composed of twenty-eight letters.

The prayer על הכל, recited on Sabbaths before the reading of the Torah, embodies part of the Kaddish in pure Hebrew. Genizah fragments have been found to contain a larger proportion of Hebrew in the Kaddish.

The Kaddish, like צדוק הדין ("acknowledgment of divine justice"), recited on the occasion of a death, seems to express the sentiment: "The Lord gave and the Lord has taken away; blessed be the name of the Lord" (Job 1:21).

The Kaddish has five different forms: 1) קדיש דרבנן, recited after the reading of passages from the Talmud; 2) קדיש שלם, the full-Kaddish, recited by the Reader at the end of the service; 3) חצי קדיש, the half-Kaddish, recited by the Reader between sections of the service; 4) קדיש יתום, the mourners' Kad-

Blessed and praised, glorified and exalted, extolled and honored, adored and lauded be the name of the Holy One, blessed be he, beyond all the blessings and hymns, praises and consolations that are ever spoken in the world; and say, Amen.

[We pray] for Israel, for our teachers and their disciples and the disciples of their disciples, and for all who study the Torah, here and everywhere. May they have abundant peace, loving-kindness, ample sustenance and salvation from their Father who is in heaven; and say, Amen.

May there be abundant peace from heaven, and happy life, for us and for all Israel; and say, Amen.

He who creates peace in his celestial heights, may he in his mercy create peace for us and for all Israel; and say, Amen.

---

dish, recited by the mourners after the service and after the recitation of certain psalms; 5) קדיש ל(את)חדתא, an expanded form of the mourners' Kaddish, recited at the cemetery after a burial.

לעלא מן כל...ושירתא תשבחתא refers to the hymns of praise contained in the Psalms of David; compare the expression על כל דברי שירות ותשבחות דוד.

נחמתא ("consolations"), occurring in the Kaddish as a synonym of praise, probably refers to prophetic works such as the Book of Isaiah, called Books of Consolation, which contain hymns of praise as well as Messianic prophecies.

עושה שלום, which repeats in Hebrew the thought expressed in the pre-ceding Aramaic paragraph, seems to have been added from the meditation recited at the end of the *Shemoneh Esreh*. The same sentence is also added at the end of the grace recited after meals. The three steps backwards, which formed the respectful manner of retiring from a superior, were likewise trans-ferred from the concluding sentence of the *Shemoneh Esreh*. On the other hand, the phrase "and say Amen," added at the end of the silent meditation after the *Shemoneh Esreh*, must have been borrowed from the Kaddish which is always recited in the hearing of no fewer than ten men.

שַׁחֲרִית לְיוֹם טוֹב

תהלים ל

מִזְמוֹר שִׁיר חֲנֻכַּת הַבַּיִת לְדָוִד. אֲרוֹמִמְךָ, יְיָ, כִּי דִלִּיתָנִי, וְלֹא שִׂמַּחְתָּ אֹיְבַי לִי. יְיָ אֱלֹהָי, שִׁוַּעְתִּי אֵלֶיךָ וַתִּרְפָּאֵנִי. יְיָ, הֶעֱלִיתָ מִן שְׁאוֹל נַפְשִׁי, חִיִּיתַנִי מִיָּרְדִי בוֹר. זַמְּרוּ לַיְיָ חֲסִידָיו, וְהוֹדוּ לְזֵכֶר קָדְשׁוֹ. כִּי רֶגַע בְּאַפּוֹ, חַיִּים בִּרְצוֹנוֹ; בָּעֶרֶב יָלִין בֶּכִי, וְלַבֹּקֶר רִנָּה. וַאֲנִי אָמַרְתִּי בְשַׁלְוִי, בַּל אֶמּוֹט לְעוֹלָם. יְיָ, בִּרְצוֹנְךָ הֶעֱמַדְתָּה לְהַרְרִי עֹז, הִסְתַּרְתָּ פָנֶיךָ, הָיִיתִי נִבְהָל. אֵלֶיךָ יְיָ אֶקְרָא, וְאֶל אֲדֹנָי אֶתְחַנָּן. מַה בֶּצַע בְּדָמִי, בְּרִדְתִּי אֶל שָׁחַת; הֲיוֹדְךָ עָפָר, הֲיַגִּיד אֲמִתֶּךָ. שְׁמַע יְיָ וְחָנֵּנִי; יְיָ, הֱיֵה עֹזֵר לִי. הָפַכְתָּ מִסְפְּדִי לְמָחוֹל לִי; פִּתַּחְתָּ שַׂקִּי וַתְּאַזְּרֵנִי שִׂמְחָה. Reader לְמַעַן יְזַמֶּרְךָ כָבוֹד, וְלֹא יִדֹּם; יְיָ אֱלֹהַי, לְעוֹלָם אוֹדֶךָּ.

MOURNERS' KADDISH

יִתְגַּדַּל וְיִתְקַדַּשׁ שְׁמֵהּ רַבָּא בְּעָלְמָא דִי בְרָא כִרְעוּתֵהּ; וְיַמְלִיךְ מַלְכוּתֵהּ בְּחַיֵּיכוֹן וּבְיוֹמֵיכוֹן, וּבְחַיֵּי דְכָל בֵּית יִשְׂרָאֵל, בַּעֲגָלָא וּבִזְמַן קָרִיב, וְאִמְרוּ אָמֵן.

יְהֵא שְׁמֵהּ רַבָּא מְבָרַךְ לְעָלַם וּלְעָלְמֵי עָלְמַיָּא.

יִתְבָּרַךְ וְיִשְׁתַּבַּח, וְיִתְפָּאַר וְיִתְרוֹמַם, וְיִתְנַשֵּׂא וְיִתְהַדָּר, וְיִתְעַלֶּה וְיִתְהַלָּל שְׁמֵהּ דְּקֻדְשָׁא, בְּרִיךְ הוּא, לְעֵלָּא מִן כָּל בִּרְכָתָא וְשִׁירָתָא, תֻּשְׁבְּחָתָא וְנֶחֱמָתָא, דַּאֲמִירָן בְּעָלְמָא, וְאִמְרוּ אָמֵן.

MORNING SERVICE FOR FESTIVALS

Psalm 30

A psalm, a song for the dedication of the house; by David.

I extol thee, O Lord, for thou hast lifted me up, and hast not let my foes rejoice over me. Lord my God, I cried to thee, and thou didst heal me. O Lord, thou hast lifted me up from the grave; thou hast let me live, that I should not go down to the grave. Sing to the Lord, you who are godly, and give thanks to his holy name. For his anger only lasts a moment, but his favor lasts a lifetime; weeping may lodge with us at evening, but in the morning there are shouts of joy. I thought in my security I never would be shaken. O Lord, by thy favor thou hadst established my mountain as a stronghold; but when thy favor was withdrawn, I was dismayed. To thee, O Lord, I called; I appealed to my God: "What profit would my death be, if I went down to the grave? Will the dust praise thee? Will it declare thy faithfulness? Hear, O Lord, and be gracious to me; Lord, be thou my helper." Thou hast changed my mourning into dancing; thou hast stripped my sackcloth and girded me with joy; so that my soul may praise thee, and not be silent. Lord my God, I will thank thee forever.

MOURNERS' KADDISH

Glorified and sanctified be God's great name throughout the world which he has created according to his will. May he establish his kingdom in your lifetime and during your days, and within the life of the entire house of Israel, speedily and soon; and say, Amen.

May his great name be blessed forever and to all eternity.

Blessed and praised, glorified and exalted, extolled and honored, adored and lauded be the name of the Holy One, blessed be he, beyond all the blessings and hymns, praises and consolations that are ever spoken in the world; and say, Amen.

יְהֵא שְׁלָמָא רַבָּא מִן שְׁמַיָּא, וְחַיִּים, עָלֵינוּ וְעַל כָּל יִשְׂרָאֵל,
וְאִמְרוּ אָמֵן.

עֹשֶׂה שָׁלוֹם בִּמְרוֹמָיו, הוּא יַעֲשֶׂה שָׁלוֹם עָלֵינוּ וְעַל כָּל
יִשְׂרָאֵל, וְאִמְרוּ אָמֵן.

הֲרֵינִי מְזַמֵּן אֶת פִּי לְהוֹדוֹת וּלְהַלֵּל וּלְשַׁבֵּחַ אֶת בּוֹרְאִי.

בָּרוּךְ שֶׁאָמַר וְהָיָה הָעוֹלָם, בָּרוּךְ הוּא. בָּרוּךְ עֹשֶׂה
בְרֵאשִׁית, בָּרוּךְ אוֹמֵר וְעוֹשֶׂה. בָּרוּךְ גּוֹזֵר וּמְקַיֵּם, בָּרוּךְ מְרַחֵם
עַל הָאָרֶץ, בָּרוּךְ מְרַחֵם עַל הַבְּרִיּוֹת, בָּרוּךְ מְשַׁלֵּם שָׂכָר טוֹב
לִירֵאָיו, בָּרוּךְ חַי לָעַד וְקַיָּם לָנֶצַח, בָּרוּךְ פּוֹדֶה וּמַצִּיל, בָּרוּךְ
שְׁמוֹ. בָּרוּךְ אַתָּה, יְיָ אֱלֹהֵינוּ, מֶלֶךְ הָעוֹלָם, הָאֵל, הָאָב
הָרַחֲמָן, הַמְהֻלָּל בְּפִי עַמּוֹ, מְשֻׁבָּח וּמְפֹאָר בִּלְשׁוֹן חֲסִידָיו
וַעֲבָדָיו. וּבְשִׁירֵי דָוִד עַבְדֶּךָ נְהַלֶּלְךָ, יְיָ אֱלֹהֵינוּ; בִּשְׁבָחוֹת
וּבִזְמִרוֹת נְגַדֶּלְךָ וּנְשַׁבֵּחֲךָ וּנְפָאֶרְךָ, וְנַזְכִּיר שִׁמְךָ וְנַמְלִיכְךָ,
מַלְכֵּנוּ, אֱלֹהֵינוּ. Reader יָחִיד, חֵי הָעוֹלָמִים, מֶלֶךְ, מְשֻׁבָּח
וּמְפֹאָר עֲדֵי עַד שְׁמוֹ הַגָּדוֹל. בָּרוּךְ אַתָּה, יְיָ, מֶלֶךְ מְהֻלָּל
בַּתִּשְׁבָּחוֹת.

דברי הימים א טז, ח-לו

הוֹדוּ לַייָ, קִרְאוּ בִשְׁמוֹ, הוֹדִיעוּ בָעַמִּים עֲלִילוֹתָיו. שִׁירוּ לוֹ,
זַמְּרוּ לוֹ, שִׂיחוּ בְּכָל נִפְלְאוֹתָיו. הִתְהַלְלוּ בְּשֵׁם קָדְשׁוֹ; יִשְׂמַח
לֵב מְבַקְשֵׁי יְיָ. דִּרְשׁוּ יְיָ וְעֻזּוֹ, בַּקְּשׁוּ פָנָיו תָּמִיד. זִכְרוּ נִפְלְאוֹתָיו
אֲשֶׁר עָשָׂה, מֹפְתָיו וּמִשְׁפְּטֵי פִיהוּ. זֶרַע יִשְׂרָאֵל עַבְדּוֹ, בְּנֵי
יַעֲקֹב בְּחִירָיו. הוּא יְיָ אֱלֹהֵינוּ, בְּכָל הָאָרֶץ מִשְׁפָּטָיו. זִכְרוּ
לְעוֹלָם בְּרִיתוֹ, דָּבָר צִוָּה לְאֶלֶף דּוֹר. אֲשֶׁר כָּרַת אֶת אַבְרָהָם,
וּשְׁבוּעָתוֹ לְיִצְחָק. וַיַּעֲמִידֶהָ לְיַעֲקֹב לְחֹק, לְיִשְׂרָאֵל בְּרִית
עוֹלָם. לֵאמֹר, לְךָ אֶתֵּן אֶרֶץ כְּנָעַן, חֶבֶל נַחֲלַתְכֶם. בִּהְיוֹתְכֶם

May there be abundant peace from heaven, and life, for us and for all Israel; and say, Amen.

He who creates peace in his celestial heights, may he create peace for us and for all Israel; and say, Amen.

Blessed be he who spoke, and the world came into being; blessed be he. Blessed be he who created the universe. Blessed be he who says and performs. Blessed be he who decrees and fulfills. Blessed be he who has mercy on the world. Blessed be he who has mercy on all creatures. Blessed be he who grants a goodly reward to those who revere him. Blessed be he who lives forever and exists eternally. Blessed be he who redeems and saves; blessed be his name. Blessed art thou, Lord our God, King of the universe, O God, merciful Father, who art praised by the mouth of thy people, lauded and glorified by the tongue of thy faithful servants. With the songs of thy servant David will we praise thee, Lord our God; with his hymns and psalms will we exalt, extol and glorify thee. We will call upon thy name and proclaim thee King, our King, our God. Thou who art One, the life of the universe, O King, praised and glorified be thy great name forever and ever. Blessed art thou, O Lord, King extolled with hymns of praise.

I Chronicles 16:8–36

Give thanks to the Lord, call upon his name; make known his deeds among the peoples. Sing to him, sing praises to him; speak of all his wonders. Take pride in his holy name; let the heart of those who seek the Lord rejoice. Inquire of the Lord and his might; seek his presence continually. Remember the wonders he has done, his marvels, and the judgments of his mouth, O descendants of Israel his servant, children of Jacob, his chosen. He is the Lord our God; his judgments are over all the earth. Remember his covenant forever, the word which he pledged for a thousand generations, the covenant he made with Abraham, and his oath to Isaac. He confirmed the same to Jacob as a statute, to Israel as an everlasting covenant, saying: "To you I give the land of Canaan as the portion of your possession." While they were but a few men,

---

ברוך שאמר is composed of eighty-seven words, a number suggesting the the numerical value of פז ("refined gold"). This hymn introduces the biblical selections entitled פסוקי דזמרא ("verses of praise"). It is included in the ninth century *Siddur* of Amram Gaon.

מְתֵי מִסְפָּר, כִּמְעַט וְגָרִים בָּהּ. וַיִּתְהַלְּכוּ מִגּוֹי אֶל גּוֹי, וּמִמַּמְלָכָה אֶל עַם אַחֵר. לֹא הִנִּיחַ לְאִישׁ לְעָשְׁקָם, וַיּוֹכַח עֲלֵיהֶם מְלָכִים. אַל תִּגְּעוּ בִמְשִׁיחָי, וּבִנְבִיאַי אַל תָּרֵעוּ. שִׁירוּ לַיְיָ כָּל הָאָרֶץ, בַּשְּׂרוּ מִיּוֹם אֶל יוֹם יְשׁוּעָתוֹ. סַפְּרוּ בַגּוֹיִם אֶת כְּבוֹדוֹ, בְּכָל הָעַמִּים נִפְלְאוֹתָיו. כִּי גָדוֹל יְיָ וּמְהֻלָּל מְאֹד, וְנוֹרָא הוּא עַל כָּל אֱלֹהִים. כִּי כָּל אֱלֹהֵי הָעַמִּים אֱלִילִים, וַיְיָ שָׁמַיִם עָשָׂה. הוֹד וְהָדָר לְפָנָיו, עֹז וְחֶדְוָה בִּמְקוֹמוֹ. הָבוּ לַיְיָ מִשְׁפְּחוֹת עַמִּים, הָבוּ לַיְיָ כָּבוֹד וָעֹז. הָבוּ לַיְיָ כְּבוֹד שְׁמוֹ, שְׂאוּ מִנְחָה וּבֹאוּ לְפָנָיו, הִשְׁתַּחֲווּ לַיְיָ בְּהַדְרַת קֹדֶשׁ. חִילוּ מִלְּפָנָיו כָּל הָאָרֶץ, אַף תִּכּוֹן תֵּבֵל בַּל תִּמּוֹט. יִשְׂמְחוּ הַשָּׁמַיִם וְתָגֵל הָאָרֶץ, וְיֹאמְרוּ בַגּוֹיִם יְיָ מָלָךְ. יִרְעַם הַיָּם וּמְלֹאוֹ, יַעֲלֹץ הַשָּׂדֶה וְכָל אֲשֶׁר בּוֹ. אָז יְרַנְּנוּ עֲצֵי הַיָּעַר, מִלִּפְנֵי יְיָ, כִּי בָא לִשְׁפּוֹט אֶת הָאָרֶץ. הוֹדוּ לַיְיָ כִּי טוֹב, כִּי לְעוֹלָם חַסְדּוֹ. וְאִמְרוּ, הוֹשִׁיעֵנוּ אֱלֹהֵי יִשְׁעֵנוּ, וְקַבְּצֵנוּ וְהַצִּילֵנוּ מִן הַגּוֹיִם, לְהֹדוֹת לְשֵׁם קָדְשֶׁךָ, לְהִשְׁתַּבֵּחַ בִּתְהִלָּתֶךָ. בָּרוּךְ יְיָ אֱלֹהֵי יִשְׂרָאֵל מִן הָעוֹלָם וְעַד הָעֹלָם; וַיֹּאמְרוּ כָל הָעָם אָמֵן וְהַלֵּל לַיְיָ.

רוֹמְמוּ יְיָ אֱלֹהֵינוּ, וְהִשְׁתַּחֲווּ לַהֲדֹם רַגְלָיו, קָדוֹשׁ הוּא. רוֹמְמוּ יְיָ אֱלֹהֵינוּ, וְהִשְׁתַּחֲווּ לְהַר קָדְשׁוֹ, כִּי קָדוֹשׁ יְיָ אֱלֹהֵינוּ.

וְהוּא רַחוּם, יְכַפֵּר עָוֹן וְלֹא יַשְׁחִית, וְהִרְבָּה לְהָשִׁיב אַפּוֹ, וְלֹא יָעִיר כָּל חֲמָתוֹ. אַתָּה, יְיָ, לֹא תִכְלָא רַחֲמֶיךָ מִמֶּנִּי, חַסְדְּךָ וַאֲמִתְּךָ תָּמִיד יִצְּרוּנִי. זְכֹר רַחֲמֶיךָ יְיָ, וַחֲסָדֶיךָ, כִּי מֵעוֹלָם הֵמָּה. תְּנוּ עֹז לֵאלֹהִים, עַל יִשְׂרָאֵל גַּאֲוָתוֹ, וְעֻזּוֹ בַּשְּׁחָקִים. נוֹרָא אֱלֹהִים מִמִּקְדָּשֶׁיךָ; אֵל יִשְׂרָאֵל, הוּא נֹתֵן עֹז וְתַעֲצֻמוֹת לָעָם; בָּרוּךְ אֱלֹהִים. אֵל נְקָמוֹת, יְיָ, אֵל נְקָמוֹת, הוֹפִיעַ. הִנָּשֵׂא שֹׁפֵט הָאָרֶץ, הָשֵׁב גְּמוּל עַל גֵּאִים. לַיְיָ הַיְשׁוּעָה, עַל עַמְּךָ בִרְכָתֶךָ

very few and strangers in it, when they went about from nation to nation and from realm to realm, he permitted no man to oppress them, and warned kings concerning them: "Touch not my anointed, and do my prophets no harm!" Sing to the Lord, all the earth; proclaim his salvation day after day. Recount his glory among the nations, and his wonders among all the peoples. For great is the Lord and most worthy of praise; he is to be feared above all gods. For all the gods of the peoples are mere idols, but the Lord made the heavens. Majesty and beauty are in his presence; strength and joy are in his sanctuary. Ascribe to the Lord, O families of peoples, ascribe to the Lord glory and strength. Give to the Lord the honor due to his name; bring an offering and come before him; worship the Lord in holy array. Tremble before him, all the earth; indeed, the world is firm that it cannot be shaken. Let the heavens rejoice, let the earth exult, and let them say among the nations: "The Lord is King!" Let the sea and its fulness roar; let the field and all that is therein rejoice. Then let the trees of the forest sing before the Lord, who comes to rule the world. Praise the Lord, for he is good; for his kindness endures forever. And say: "Save us, O God of our salvation, gather us and deliver us from the nations, to give thanks to thy holy name, to glory in thy praise." Blessed be the Lord, the God of Israel, from eternity to eternity. Then all the people said "Amen" and praised the Lord.

Exalt the Lord our God, and worship at his footstool—holy is he. Exalt the Lord our God, and worship at his holy mountain, for holy is the Lord our God. He, being merciful, forgives iniquity, and does not destroy; frequently he turns his anger away, and does not stir up all his wrath. Thou, O Lord, wilt not hold back thy mercy from me; thy kindness and thy faithfulness will always protect me. Remember thy mercy, O Lord, and thy kindness, for they have been since eternity. Give honor to God, whose majesty is over Israel, whose glory is in the skies. Feared art thou, O Lord, from thy sanctuary; the God of Israel gives strength and power to his people. Blessed be God! God of vengeance, O Lord, God of vengeance, appear! Arise, O Ruler of the world, and render to the arrogant what they deserve. Salvation belongs to the Lord; thy blessing be upon thy people. The Lord of hosts is with us; the

סֶלָה. יְיָ צְבָאוֹת עִמָּנוּ, מִשְׂגָּב לָנוּ אֱלֹהֵי יַעֲקֹב סֶלָה. יְיָ צְבָאוֹת,
אַשְׁרֵי אָדָם בֹּטֵחַ בָּךְ. יְיָ, הוֹשִׁיעָה; הַמֶּלֶךְ יַעֲנֵנוּ בְיוֹם קָרְאֵנוּ.

הוֹשִׁיעָה אֶת עַמֶּךָ, וּבָרֵךְ אֶת נַחֲלָתֶךָ, וּרְעֵם וְנַשְּׂאֵם עַד
הָעוֹלָם. נַפְשֵׁנוּ חִכְּתָה לַיְיָ, עֶזְרֵנוּ וּמָגִנֵּנוּ הוּא. כִּי בוֹ יִשְׂמַח
לִבֵּנוּ, כִּי בְשֵׁם קָדְשׁוֹ בָטָחְנוּ. יְהִי חַסְדְּךָ יְיָ עָלֵינוּ, כַּאֲשֶׁר יִחַלְנוּ
לָךְ. הַרְאֵנוּ יְיָ חַסְדֶּךָ, וְיֶשְׁעֲךָ תִּתֶּן־לָנוּ. קוּמָה עֶזְרָתָה לָּנוּ,
וּפְדֵנוּ לְמַעַן חַסְדֶּךָ. אָנֹכִי יְיָ אֱלֹהֶיךָ הַמַּעַלְךָ מֵאֶרֶץ מִצְרָיִם,
הַרְחֶב־פִּיךָ וַאֲמַלְאֵהוּ. אַשְׁרֵי הָעָם שֶׁכָּכָה לּוֹ, אַשְׁרֵי הָעָם שֶׁיְיָ
אֱלֹהָיו. Reader וַאֲנִי בְּחַסְדְּךָ בָטַחְתִּי, יָגֵל לִבִּי בִּישׁוּעָתֶךָ;
אָשִׁירָה לַיְיָ, כִּי גָמַל עָלָי.

לַמְנַצֵּחַ, מִזְמוֹר לְדָוִד. הַשָּׁמַיִם מְסַפְּרִים כְּבוֹד אֵל, וּמַעֲשֵׂה
יָדָיו מַגִּיד הָרָקִיעַ. יוֹם לְיוֹם יַבִּיעַ אֹמֶר, וְלַיְלָה לְּלַיְלָה יְחַוֶּה
דָּעַת. אֵין אֹמֶר וְאֵין דְּבָרִים, בְּלִי נִשְׁמָע קוֹלָם. בְּכָל הָאָרֶץ
יָצָא קַוָּם, וּבִקְצֵה תֵבֵל מִלֵּיהֶם; לַשֶּׁמֶשׁ שָׂם אֹהֶל בָּהֶם. וְהוּא
כְּחָתָן יֹצֵא מֵחֻפָּתוֹ, יָשִׂישׂ כְּגִבּוֹר לָרוּץ אֹרַח. מִקְצֵה הַשָּׁמַיִם
מוֹצָאוֹ, וּתְקוּפָתוֹ עַל קְצוֹתָם, וְאֵין נִסְתָּר מֵחַמָּתוֹ. תּוֹרַת יְיָ
תְּמִימָה, מְשִׁיבַת נָפֶשׁ; עֵדוּת יְיָ נֶאֱמָנָה, מַחְכִּימַת פֶּתִי. פִּקּוּדֵי
יְיָ יְשָׁרִים, מְשַׂמְּחֵי לֵב; מִצְוַת יְיָ בָּרָה, מְאִירַת עֵינָיִם. יִרְאַת יְיָ
טְהוֹרָה, עוֹמֶדֶת לָעַד; מִשְׁפְּטֵי יְיָ אֱמֶת, צָדְקוּ יַחְדָּו. הַנֶּחֱמָדִים
מִזָּהָב וּמִפַּז רָב, וּמְתוּקִים מִדְּבַשׁ וְנֹפֶת צוּפִים. גַּם עַבְדְּךָ נִזְהָר
בָּהֶם, בְּשָׁמְרָם עֵקֶב רָב. שְׁגִיאוֹת מִי יָבִין; מִנִּסְתָּרוֹת נַקֵּנִי. גַּם
מִזֵּדִים חֲשֹׂךְ עַבְדֶּךָ, אַל יִמְשְׁלוּ בִי; אָז אֵיתָם, וְנִקֵּיתִי מִפֶּשַׁע
רָב. Reader יִהְיוּ לְרָצוֹן אִמְרֵי פִי וְהֶגְיוֹן לִבִּי לְפָנֶיךָ, יְיָ, צוּרִי
וְגֹאֲלִי.

God of Jacob is our Stronghold. O Lord of hosts, happy is the man who trusts in thee. O Lord, save us; may the King answer us when we call. Save thy people and bless thy heritage; tend them and sustain them forever. Our soul waits for the Lord; he is our help and our shield. Indeed, our heart rejoices in him, for in his holy name we trust. May thy kindness, O Lord, rest on us, as our hope rests in thee. Show us thy kindness, O Lord, and grant us thy salvation. Arise for our help, and set us free for thy goodness' sake. I am the Lord your God, who brought you up from the land of Egypt; open your mouth and I will fill it. Happy the people that is so situated; happy the people whose God is the Lord. I have trusted in thy kindness; may my heart rejoice in thy salvation. I will sing to the Lord, because he has treated me kindly.[1]

Psalm 19

For the Choirmaster; a psalm of David. The heavens proclaim the glory of God; the sky declares his handiwork. Day unto day pours forth speech, and night unto night reveals knowledge. There is no speech, there are no words; unheard is their voice. Yet their message extends through all the earth, and their words reach the end of the world. In the heavens he has pitched a tent for the sun, which is like a bridegroom coming out of his chamber, like an athlete rejoicing to run the course. It sets out from one end of the heaven, and round it passes to the other end, and there is nothing hidden from its heat. The Lord's Torah is perfect, refreshing the soul; the Lord's testimony is trustworthy, teaching the simple man wisdom. The Lord's precepts are right, gladdening the heart; the Lord's commandment is clear, enlightening the eyes. The Lord's faith is pure, enduring forever; the Lord's judgments are true, they are altogether just. They are more desirable than gold, than much rare gold; sweeter are they than honey, than honey from the honeycomb. Thy servant is indeed careful with them; in keeping them there is great reward. Yet who discerns his own errors? Of unconscious faults hold me guiltless. Restrain thy servant also from wilful sins; let them not have dominion over me; then shall I be blameless, and I shall be clear of great transgression. May the words of my mouth and the meditation of my heart be pleasing before thee, O Lord, my Stronghold and my Redeemer.

השמים מספרים is not, according to Maimonides, a mere figure of speech. In his opinion, Psalm 19 contains a description of what the spheres actually do, and not what man thinks of them. (Guide 2:5).

[1] *Psalms* 99:5, 9; 78:38; 40:12; 25:6; 68:35–36; 94:1–2; 3:9; 46:8; 84:13 20:10; 28:9; 33:20–22; 85:8; 44:27: 81:11; 144:15; 13;6.

תהלים לד

לְדָוִד, בְּשַׁנּוֹתוֹ אֶת טַעְמוֹ לִפְנֵי אֲבִימֶלֶךְ, וַיְגָרְשֵׁהוּ וַיֵּלַךְ.

אֲבָרְכָה אֶת יְיָ בְּכָל עֵת; תָּמִיד תְּהִלָּתוֹ בְּפִי.

בַּיְיָ תִּתְהַלֵּל נַפְשִׁי; יִשְׁמְעוּ עֲנָוִים וְיִשְׂמָחוּ.

גַּדְּלוּ לַיְיָ אִתִּי, וּנְרוֹמְמָה שְׁמוֹ יַחְדָּו.

דָּרַשְׁתִּי אֶת יְיָ וְעָנָנִי, וּמִכָּל מְגוּרוֹתַי הִצִּילָנִי.

הִבִּיטוּ אֵלָיו וְנָהָרוּ, וּפְנֵיהֶם אַל יֶחְפָּרוּ.

זֶה עָנִי קָרָא וַיְיָ שָׁמֵעַ, וּמִכָּל צָרוֹתָיו הוֹשִׁיעוֹ.

חֹנֶה מַלְאַךְ יְיָ סָבִיב לִירֵאָיו וַיְחַלְּצֵם.

טַעֲמוּ וּרְאוּ כִּי טוֹב יְיָ; אַשְׁרֵי הַגֶּבֶר יֶחֱסֶה בּוֹ.

יְראוּ אֶת יְיָ, קְדֹשָׁיו, כִּי אֵין מַחְסוֹר לִירֵאָיו.

כְּפִירִים רָשׁוּ וְרָעֵבוּ, וְדֹרְשֵׁי יְיָ לֹא יַחְסְרוּ כָל טוֹב.

לְכוּ בָנִים, שִׁמְעוּ לִי, יִרְאַת יְיָ אֲלַמֶּדְכֶם.

מִי הָאִישׁ הֶחָפֵץ חַיִּים, אֹהֵב יָמִים לִרְאוֹת טוֹב.

נְצֹר לְשׁוֹנְךָ מֵרָע, וּשְׂפָתֶיךָ מִדַּבֵּר מִרְמָה.

סוּר מֵרָע וַעֲשֵׂה טוֹב, בַּקֵּשׁ שָׁלוֹם וְרָדְפֵהוּ.

עֵינֵי יְיָ אֶל צַדִּיקִים, וְאָזְנָיו אֶל שַׁוְעָתָם.

פְּנֵי יְיָ בְּעֹשֵׂי רָע, לְהַכְרִית מֵאֶרֶץ זִכְרָם.

צָעֲקוּ וַיְיָ שָׁמֵעַ, וּמִכָּל צָרוֹתָם הִצִּילָם.

קָרוֹב יְיָ לְנִשְׁבְּרֵי לֵב, וְאֶת דַּכְּאֵי רוּחַ יוֹשִׁיעַ.

רַבּוֹת רָעוֹת צַדִּיק, וּמִכֻּלָּם יַצִּילֶנּוּ יְיָ.

בשנותו את טעמו (Psalm 34) refers to the incident related in I Samuel 21:11–16 where the Philistine king, to whom David fled for refuge, is called Achish. Finding himself recognized as the slayer of Goliath, David feigned madness, and so escaped vengeance. The psalm is arranged alphabetically, except that the verse beginning with the letter ו is omitted and there is an additional verse at the end. יראו is pronounced ירו.

Psalm 34

A song of David, when he feigned madness before Abimelech,
who drove him out and he departed.

I bless the Lord at all times;
His praise is ever in my mouth.
My soul glories in the Lord;
The humble hear it and are glad.
Exalt the Lord with me,
And let us extol his name together.
I sought the Lord and he answered me,
And delivered me from all my fears.
Those who look to him are jubilant,
And they are never abashed.
This poor man cried, and the Lord heard him;
He saved him from all his troubles.
The angel of the Lord encamps
Around those who revere him, and rescues them.
Consider and see that the Lord is good;
Happy is the man who takes shelter with him.
Revere the Lord, you his holy people;
For those who revere him suffer no want.
Young lions may suffer want and hunger,
But those who seek the Lord shall lack nothing.
Come, children, listen to me;
I will teach you how to revere the Lord.
Who is the man that desires life,
And loves a long life of happiness?
Keep your tongue from evil,
And your lips from speaking falsehood.
Shun evil and do good;
Seek peace and pursue it.
The eyes of the Lord are toward the righteous
And his ears are open to their cry.
The Lord's anger is set against evildoers,
To cut off their name from the earth.
When they cry, the Lord listens,
And delivers them from all their troubles.
The Lord is near to the broken-hearted,
And saves those who are crushed in spirit
A good man may have many ills,
But the Lord delivers him from them all.

שׁוֹמֵר כָּל עַצְמוֹתָיו, אַחַת מֵהֵנָּה לֹא נִשְׁבָּרָה.

תְּמוֹתֵת רָשָׁע רָעָה, וְשֹׂנְאֵי צַדִּיק יֶאְשָׁמוּ.

Reader פּוֹדֶה יְיָ נֶפֶשׁ עֲבָדָיו, וְלֹא יֶאְשְׁמוּ כָּל הַחֹסִים בּוֹ.

תהלים צ

תְּפִלָּה לְמֹשֶׁה, אִישׁ הָאֱלֹהִים. אֲדֹנָי, מָעוֹן אַתָּה הָיִיתָ לָּנוּ בְּדֹר וָדֹר. בְּטֶרֶם הָרִים יֻלָּדוּ, וַתְּחוֹלֵל אֶרֶץ וְתֵבֵל, וּמֵעוֹלָם עַד עוֹלָם אַתָּה אֵל. תָּשֵׁב אֱנוֹשׁ עַד דַּכָּא, וַתֹּאמֶר שׁוּבוּ בְנֵי אָדָם. כִּי אֶלֶף שָׁנִים בְּעֵינֶיךָ כְּיוֹם אֶתְמוֹל כִּי יַעֲבֹר, וְאַשְׁמוּרָה בַלָּיְלָה. זְרַמְתָּם, שֵׁנָה יִהְיוּ; בַּבֹּקֶר כֶּחָצִיר יַחֲלֹף. בַּבֹּקֶר יָצִיץ וְחָלָף, לָעֶרֶב יְמוֹלֵל וְיָבֵשׁ. כִּי כָלִינוּ בְאַפֶּךָ, וּבַחֲמָתְךָ נִבְהָלְנוּ. שַׁתָּ עֲוֹנֹתֵינוּ לְנֶגְדֶּךָ, עֲלֻמֵנוּ לִמְאוֹר פָּנֶיךָ. כִּי כָל יָמֵינוּ פָּנוּ בְעֶבְרָתֶךָ, כִּלִּינוּ שָׁנֵינוּ כְמוֹ הֶגֶה. יְמֵי שְׁנוֹתֵינוּ בָהֶם שִׁבְעִים שָׁנָה, וְאִם בִּגְבוּרֹת שְׁמוֹנִים שָׁנָה, וְרָהְבָּם עָמָל וָאָוֶן, כִּי גָז חִישׁ וַנָּעֻפָה. מִי יוֹדֵעַ עֹז אַפֶּךָ, וּכְיִרְאָתְךָ עֶבְרָתֶךָ. לִמְנוֹת יָמֵינוּ כֵּן הוֹדַע, וְנָבִא לְבַב חָכְמָה. שׁוּבָה יְיָ, עַד מָתָי, וְהִנָּחֵם עַל עֲבָדֶיךָ. שַׂבְּעֵנוּ בַבֹּקֶר חַסְדֶּךָ, וּנְרַנְּנָה וְנִשְׂמְחָה בְּכָל יָמֵינוּ. שַׂמְּחֵנוּ כִּימוֹת עִנִּיתָנוּ, שְׁנוֹת רָאִינוּ רָעָה. Reader יֵרָאֶה אֶל עֲבָדֶיךָ פָעֳלֶךָ, וַהֲדָרְךָ עַל בְּנֵיהֶם. וִיהִי נֹעַם אֲדֹנָי אֱלֹהֵינוּ עָלֵינוּ, וּמַעֲשֵׂה יָדֵינוּ כּוֹנְנָה עָלֵינוּ, וּמַעֲשֵׂה יָדֵינוּ כּוֹנְנֵהוּ.

תהלים צא

יֹשֵׁב בְּסֵתֶר עֶלְיוֹן, בְּצֵל שַׁדַּי יִתְלוֹנָן. אֹמַר לַייָ, מַחְסִי וּמְצוּדָתִי, אֱלֹהַי אֶבְטַח בּוֹ. כִּי הוּא יַצִּילְךָ מִפַּח יָקוּשׁ, מִדֶּבֶר

Psalm 90 contrasts the eternity of God with the brevity of human life, and ends with a prayer for God's forgiveness and favor.

He protects all his limbs,
So that not one of them is broken.
Evil destroys the wicked,
And those who hate the righteous are doomed.
The Lord saves the life of his servants;
All who take shelter with him are never desolate.

Psalm 90

A prayer of Moses, the man of God. O Lord, thou hast been our shelter in every generation. Before the mountains were brought forth, before earth and world were formed—from eternity to eternity thou art God. Thou turnest man back to dust, and sayest: "Return, you children of man." Indeed, a thousand years in thy sight are like a day that passes, like a watch in the night. Thou sweepest men away and they sleep; they are like grass that grows in the morning. It flourishes and grows in the morning; in the evening it fades and withers. For we are consumed by thy anger; by thy wrath we are hurried away. Thou settest our iniquities before thee, and our guilty secrets are exposed in the light of thy presence. Indeed, all our days decline under thy displeasure; we spend our years like a fleeting sound. The length of our life is seventy years, or, by reason of strength, eighty years; their pride is only toil and futility, for it is speedily gone, and we fly away. Who knows the power of thy anger, to fear thee in proportion to thy displeasure? Teach us how to number our days, that we may attain a heart of wisdom. Relent, O Lord; how long? Relent as to thy servants. Satisfy us in the morning with thy kindness, that we may sing and rejoice throughout our days. Gladden us in proportion to the days wherein thou hast afflicted us, the years wherein we have seen evil. Let thy work be revealed to thy servants, and thy glory upon their children. May thy favor, Lord our God, rest on us; establish for us the work of our hands; the work of our hands establish thou.

Psalm 91

He who dwells in the shelter of the Most High abides under the protection of the Almighty. I say of the Lord: "He is my refuge and my fortress, my God, in whom I trust." Indeed, he will save you from the snare of the fowler, and from the destructive

---

Psalm 91 is termed שיר של פגעים, "a song against evil occurrences" (She-buoth 15b). It describes the safety of those who trust in God amid the perils of their journey through life. ארך ימים is repeated so that the number of verses of this psalm reaches a total of seventeen, the numerical value of טוב.

הַוּוֹת. בְּאֶבְרָתוֹ יָסֶךְ לָךְ, וְתַחַת כְּנָפָיו תֶּחְסֶה; צִנָּה וְסֹחֵרָה אֲמִתּוֹ. לֹא תִירָא מִפַּחַד לָיְלָה, מֵחֵץ יָעוּף יוֹמָם. מִדֶּבֶר בָּאֹפֶל יַהֲלֹךְ, מִקֶּטֶב יָשׁוּד צָהֳרָיִם. יִפֹּל מִצִּדְּךָ אֶלֶף, וּרְבָבָה מִימִינֶךָ; אֵלֶיךָ לֹא יִגָּשׁ. רַק בְּעֵינֶיךָ תַבִּיט, וְשִׁלֻּמַת רְשָׁעִים תִּרְאֶה. כִּי אַתָּה, יְיָ, מַחְסִי; עֶלְיוֹן שַׂמְתָּ מְעוֹנֶךָ. לֹא תְאֻנֶּה אֵלֶיךָ רָעָה, וְנֶגַע לֹא יִקְרַב בְּאָהֳלֶךָ. כִּי מַלְאָכָיו יְצַוֶּה לָּךְ, לִשְׁמָרְךָ בְּכָל דְּרָכֶיךָ. עַל כַּפַּיִם יִשָּׂאוּנְךָ, פֶּן תִּגֹּף בָּאֶבֶן רַגְלֶךָ. עַל שַׁחַל וָפֶתֶן תִּדְרֹךְ, תִּרְמֹס כְּפִיר וְתַנִּין. כִּי בִי חָשַׁק וַאֲפַלְּטֵהוּ; אֲשַׂגְּבֵהוּ כִּי יָדַע שְׁמִי. Reader יִקְרָאֵנִי וְאֶעֱנֵהוּ, עִמּוֹ אָנֹכִי בְצָרָה, אֲחַלְּצֵהוּ וַאֲכַבְּדֵהוּ. אֹרֶךְ יָמִים אַשְׂבִּיעֵהוּ, וְאַרְאֵהוּ בִּישׁוּעָתִי. אֹרֶךְ יָמִים אַשְׂבִּיעֵהוּ, וְאַרְאֵהוּ בִּישׁוּעָתִי.

הַלְלוּיָהּ, הַלְלוּ אֶת שֵׁם יְיָ; הַלְלוּ, עַבְדֵי יְיָ. שֶׁעֹמְדִים בְּבֵית יְיָ, בְּחַצְרוֹת בֵּית אֱלֹהֵינוּ. הַלְלוּיָהּ, כִּי טוֹב יְיָ; זַמְּרוּ לִשְׁמוֹ, כִּי נָעִים. כִּי יַעֲקֹב בָּחַר לוֹ יָהּ, יִשְׂרָאֵל לִסְגֻלָּתוֹ. כִּי אֲנִי יָדַעְתִּי כִּי גָדוֹל יְיָ, וַאֲדֹנֵינוּ מִכָּל אֱלֹהִים. כֹּל אֲשֶׁר חָפֵץ יְיָ עָשָׂה, בַּשָּׁמַיִם וּבָאָרֶץ, בַּיַּמִּים וְכָל תְּהֹמוֹת. מַעֲלֶה נְשִׂאִים מִקְצֵה הָאָרֶץ, בְּרָקִים לַמָּטָר עָשָׂה; מוֹצֵא רוּחַ מֵאוֹצְרוֹתָיו. שֶׁהִכָּה בְּכוֹרֵי מִצְרָיִם, מֵאָדָם עַד בְּהֵמָה. שָׁלַח אוֹתֹת וּמֹפְתִים בְּתוֹכֵכִי מִצְרָיִם, בְּפַרְעֹה וּבְכָל עֲבָדָיו. שֶׁהִכָּה גּוֹיִם רַבִּים, וְהָרַג מְלָכִים עֲצוּמִים. לְסִיחוֹן מֶלֶךְ הָאֱמֹרִי, וּלְעוֹג מֶלֶךְ הַבָּשָׁן, וּלְכֹל מַמְלְכוֹת כְּנָעַן. וְנָתַן אַרְצָם נַחֲלָה, נַחֲלָה לְיִשְׂרָאֵל עַמּוֹ. יְיָ, שִׁמְךָ לְעוֹלָם; יְיָ, זִכְרְךָ לְדֹר וָדֹר. כִּי יָדִין יְיָ עַמּוֹ, וְעַל עֲבָדָיו יִתְנֶחָם. עֲצַבֵּי הַגּוֹיִם כֶּסֶף וְזָהָב, מַעֲשֵׂה יְדֵי אָדָם. פֶּה לָהֶם וְלֹא יְדַבֵּרוּ, עֵינַיִם לָהֶם וְלֹא יִרְאוּ. אָזְנַיִם

pestilence. With his pinions he will cover you, and under his wings you will find refuge; his faithfulness is a shield and buckler. Fear not the terror of the night, nor the arrow that flies by day, nor the pestilence that stalks in darkness, nor the destruction that ravages at noon. Though a thousand fall at your side, and a myriad at your right hand, it shall not come near you. Only with your eyes will you gaze, and see the reward of evil men. Thou, O Lord art my refuge! When you have made the Most High your shelter, no disaster shall befall you, no calamity shall come near your tent. For he will give his angels charge over you, to guard you in all your ways. They will bear you upon their hands, lest you strike your foot against a stone. You can tread on lion and asp; you can trample young lion and serpent. "He clings to me, so I deliver him; I set him safe, because he loves me. When he calls upon me, I will answer him; I will be with him in trouble; I will rescue him and bring him to honor. With long life will I satisfy him, and let him see my saving power."

Psalm 135

Praise the Lord! Praise the name of the Lord; give praise, you servants of the Lord, who stand in the house of the Lord, in the courts of the house of our God. Praise the Lord, for the Lord is good; sing praise to his name, for it is pleasant. Surely, the Lord has chosen Jacob to be his, and Israel as his prized possession. I know that the Lord is great; our Lord is above all gods. The Lord does whatever he pleases, in heaven and earth, in the seas and all the depths. He makes clouds rise from the ends of the earth; he makes lightning for the rain, and brings forth the wind from his storehouses. It was he who smote the first-born of Egypt, both of man and beast. He sent signs and wonders into the midst of Egypt, on Pharaoh and on all his servants. It was he who struck down many nations, and slew mighty kings: Sihon, the king of the Amorites, Og, the king of Bashan, and all the kingdoms of Canaan. He gave their land as a heritage, a possession of his people Israel. O Lord, thy name is forever; O Lord, thy fame is for all generations. The Lord will do justice for his people; he will have compassion on his servants. Pagan gods are mere silver and gold, the work of men's hands. They have a mouth, but cannot speak; eyes have they, but cannot see; they have ears, but cannot

---

Psalm 135 is a hymn of praise particularly suitable for public worship, for it begins and ends with the liturgical *Halleluyah*. It is a mosaic of fragments from various biblical passages illustrating God's greatness. The first verse, for example, is identical with Psalm 113:1, except that the clauses are transposed.

לָהֶם וְלֹא יַאֲזִינוּ, אַף אֵין־יֶשׁ־רוּחַ בְּפִיהֶם. כְּמוֹהֶם יִהְיוּ
עֹשֵׂיהֶם, כֹּל אֲשֶׁר בֹּטֵחַ בָּהֶם. Reader בֵּית יִשְׂרָאֵל, בָּרְכוּ אֶת
יְיָ, בֵּית אַהֲרֹן, בָּרְכוּ אֶת יְיָ. בֵּית הַלֵּוִי, בָּרְכוּ אֶת יְיָ; יִרְאֵי יְיָ,
בָּרְכוּ אֶת יְיָ. בָּרוּךְ יְיָ מִצִּיּוֹן, שֹׁכֵן יְרוּשָׁלָיִם; הַלְלוּיָהּ.

תהלים קלו

כִּי לְעוֹלָם חַסְדּוֹ.	הוֹדוּ לַייָ כִּי טוֹב
כִּי לְעוֹלָם חַסְדּוֹ.	הוֹדוּ לֵאלֹהֵי הָאֱלֹהִים
כִּי לְעוֹלָם חַסְדּוֹ.	הוֹדוּ לַאֲדֹנֵי הָאֲדֹנִים
כִּי לְעוֹלָם חַסְדּוֹ.	לְעֹשֵׂה נִפְלָאוֹת גְּדֹלוֹת לְבַדּוֹ
כִּי לְעוֹלָם חַסְדּוֹ.	לְעֹשֵׂה הַשָּׁמַיִם בִּתְבוּנָה
כִּי לְעוֹלָם חַסְדּוֹ.	לְרוֹקַע הָאָרֶץ עַל הַמָּיִם
כִּי לְעוֹלָם חַסְדּוֹ.	לְעֹשֵׂה אוֹרִים גְּדֹלִים
כִּי לְעוֹלָם חַסְדּוֹ.	אֶת הַשֶּׁמֶשׁ לְמֶמְשֶׁלֶת בַּיּוֹם
כִּי לְעוֹלָם חַסְדּוֹ.	אֶת הַיָּרֵחַ וְכוֹכָבִים לְמֶמְשְׁלוֹת בַּלָּיְלָה
כִּי לְעוֹלָם חַסְדּוֹ.	לְמַכֵּה מִצְרַיִם בִּבְכוֹרֵיהֶם
כִּי לְעוֹלָם חַסְדּוֹ.	וַיּוֹצֵא יִשְׂרָאֵל מִתּוֹכָם
כִּי לְעוֹלָם חַסְדּוֹ.	בְּיָד חֲזָקָה וּבִזְרוֹעַ נְטוּיָה
כִּי לְעוֹלָם חַסְדּוֹ.	לְגֹזֵר יַם סוּף לִגְזָרִים
כִּי לְעוֹלָם חַסְדּוֹ.	וְהֶעֱבִיר יִשְׂרָאֵל בְּתוֹכוֹ
כִּי לְעוֹלָם חַסְדּוֹ.	וְנִעֵר פַּרְעֹה וְחֵילוֹ בְיַם סוּף
כִּי לְעוֹלָם חַסְדּוֹ.	לְמוֹלִיךְ עַמּוֹ בַּמִּדְבָּר
כִּי לְעוֹלָם חַסְדּוֹ.	לְמַכֵּה מְלָכִים גְּדֹלִים

Psalm 136 is called in the Talmud *Hallel ha-Gadol*, "the Great Hallel" (Pesaḥim 118a) to distinguish it from the "Egyptian Hallel" (Psalms 113–118) sung on festivals. It differs from all other psalms in that each verse closes with a refrain, probably designed to be sung in full chorus by the people.

hear; neither, indeed, is there any breath in their mouth. Those who make them will become like them—everyone who trusts in them. House of Israel, bless the Lord; house of Aaron, bless the the Lord; house of Levi, bless the Lord; you who revere the Lord, bless the Lord. Blessed from Zion be the Lord, who dwells in Jerusalem. Praise the Lord!

Psalm 136

Give thanks to the Lord, for he is good,
    His mercy endures forever;
Give thanks to the supreme God,
    His mercy endures forever;
Give thanks to the Lord of lords,
    His mercy endures forever;
To him who alone does great wonders,
    His mercy endures forever;
To him who made the heavens with wisdom,
    His mercy endures forever;
To him who spread the earth over waters,
    His mercy endures forever;
To him who made the great lights,
    His mercy endures forever;
The sun to rule by day,
    His mercy endures forever;
The moon and stars to rule by night,
    His mercy endures forever;
To him who smote Egypt's first-born,
    His mercy endures forever;
And brought out Israel from among them,
    His mercy endures forever;
With strong hand and with outstretched arm,
    His mercy endures forever;
To him who divided the Red Sea,
    His mercy endures forever;
And brought Israel through it,
    His mercy endures forever;
And drowned Pharaoh and his host in the Red Sea,
    His mercy endures forever;
To him who led his people through the wilderness,
    His mercy endures forever;
To him who struck down great kings,
    His mercy endures forever;

וַיַּהֲרֹג מְלָכִים אַדִּירִים	כִּי לְעוֹלָם חַסְדּוֹ.
לְסִיחוֹן מֶלֶךְ הָאֱמֹרִי	כִּי לְעוֹלָם חַסְדּוֹ.
וּלְעוֹג מֶלֶךְ הַבָּשָׁן	כִּי לְעוֹלָם חַסְדּוֹ.
וְנָתַן אַרְצָם לְנַחֲלָה	כִּי לְעוֹלָם חַסְדּוֹ.
נַחֲלָה לְיִשְׂרָאֵל עַבְדּוֹ	כִּי לְעוֹלָם חַסְדּוֹ.
שֶׁבְּשִׁפְלֵנוּ זָכַר לָנוּ	כִּי לְעוֹלָם חַסְדּוֹ.
וַיִּפְרְקֵנוּ מִצָּרֵינוּ	כִּי לְעוֹלָם חַסְדּוֹ.
נֹתֵן לֶחֶם לְכָל בָּשָׂר	כִּי לְעוֹלָם חַסְדּוֹ.
הוֹדוּ לְאֵל הַשָּׁמָיִם	כִּי לְעוֹלָם חַסְדּוֹ.

תהלים לג

רַנְּנוּ צַדִּיקִים בַּיְיָ, לַיְשָׁרִים נָאוָה תְהִלָּה. הוֹדוּ לַיְיָ בְּכִנּוֹר,
בְּנֵבֶל עָשׂוֹר זַמְּרוּ לוֹ. שִׁירוּ לוֹ שִׁיר חָדָשׁ, הֵיטִיבוּ נַגֵּן בִּתְרוּעָה.
כִּי יָשָׁר דְּבַר יְיָ, וְכָל מַעֲשֵׂהוּ בֶּאֱמוּנָה. אֹהֵב צְדָקָה וּמִשְׁפָּט,
חֶסֶד יְיָ מָלְאָה הָאָרֶץ. בִּדְבַר יְיָ שָׁמַיִם נַעֲשׂוּ, וּבְרוּחַ פִּיו כָּל
צְבָאָם. כֹּנֵס כַּנֵּד מֵי הַיָּם, נֹתֵן בְּאוֹצָרוֹת תְּהוֹמוֹת. יִירְאוּ מֵיְיָ
כָּל הָאָרֶץ, מִמֶּנּוּ יָגוּרוּ כָּל יֹשְׁבֵי תֵבֵל. כִּי הוּא אָמַר וַיֶּהִי, הוּא
צִוָּה וַיַּעֲמֹד. יְיָ הֵפִיר עֲצַת גּוֹיִם, הֵנִיא מַחְשְׁבוֹת עַמִּים. עֲצַת
יְיָ לְעוֹלָם תַּעֲמֹד, מַחְשְׁבוֹת לִבּוֹ לְדֹר וָדֹר. אַשְׁרֵי הַגּוֹי אֲשֶׁר
יְיָ אֱלֹהָיו, הָעָם בָּחַר לְנַחֲלָה לוֹ. מִשָּׁמַיִם הִבִּיט יְיָ, רָאָה אֶת
כָּל בְּנֵי הָאָדָם. מִמְּכוֹן שִׁבְתּוֹ הִשְׁגִּיחַ, אֶל כָּל יֹשְׁבֵי הָאָרֶץ.
הַיֹּצֵר יַחַד לִבָּם, הַמֵּבִין אֶל כָּל מַעֲשֵׂיהֶם. אֵין הַמֶּלֶךְ נוֹשָׁע
בְּרָב חָיִל, גִּבּוֹר לֹא יִנָּצֵל בְּרָב כֹּחַ. שֶׁקֶר הַסּוּס לִתְשׁוּעָה,

---

Psalm 33 contains a description of God's righteous rule and creative omnipotence. Israel's protection does not depend on military power but on God.
"He gathers the waters of the sea as a heap" refers to the appearance of the sea
from the shore. "He lays up the deeps in storehouses" refers to the vast sub-
terranean masses of water.

And slew mighty kings,
    His mercy endures forever;
Sihon, king of the Amorites,
    His mercy endures forever;
And Og, king of Bashan,
    His mercy endures forever;
And gave their land as a heritage,
    His mercy endures forever;
A heritage to Israel his servant,
    His mercy endures forever;
Who remembered us when we were downcast,
    His mercy endures forever;
And delivered us from our foes,
    His mercy endures forever;
Who gives food to all creatures,
    His mercy endures forever;
Give thanks to the God of heaven,
    His mercy endures forever.

Psalm 33

Rejoice in the Lord, you righteous; it is fitting for the upright to give praise. Give thanks to the Lord with the harp; sing to him with the ten-stringed lute. Sing a new song to him; play skillfully amid shouts of joy. The word of the Lord is right; all his work is done with faithfulness. He loves righteousness and justice; the earth is full of the Lord's kindness. By the word of the Lord the heavens were made, and all their host by the breath of his mouth. He gathers the waters of the sea as a heap; he places the deeps in storehouses. Let all the earth revere the Lord; let all the inhabitants of the world stand in awe of him. For he spoke, and the world came into being; he commanded, and it stood firm. The Lord annuls the counsel of nations; he foils the plans of peoples. But the Lord's purpose stands forever; his plans are through all generations. Happy is the nation whose God is the Lord, the people he has chosen for his possession. From heaven the Lord looks down; he sees all of mankind. From his abode he looks carefully on all the inhabitants of the earth. It is he who fashions the hearts of them all, he who notes all their deeds. A king is not saved by the size of an army; a warrior is not rescued by sheer strength. Vain is the horse for victory; nor does it afford escape by its great strength.

וּבְרֹב חֵילוֹ לֹא יִמָּלֵט. הִנֵּה עֵין יְיָ אֶל יְרֵאָיו, לַמְיַחֲלִים לְחַסְדּוֹ. לְהַצִּיל מִמָּוֶת נַפְשָׁם, וּלְחַיּוֹתָם בָּרָעָב. נַפְשֵׁנוּ חִכְּתָה לַיְיָ, עֶזְרֵנוּ וּמָגִנֵּנוּ הוּא. Reader כִּי בוֹ יִשְׂמַח לִבֵּנוּ, כִּי בְשֵׁם קָדְשׁוֹ בָטָחְנוּ. יְהִי חַסְדְּךָ יְיָ עָלֵינוּ, כַּאֲשֶׁר יִחַלְנוּ לָךְ.

תהלים צב

מִזְמוֹר שִׁיר לְיוֹם הַשַּׁבָּת. טוֹב לְהֹדוֹת לַיְיָ, וּלְזַמֵּר לְשִׁמְךָ עֶלְיוֹן. לְהַגִּיד בַּבֹּקֶר חַסְדֶּךָ, וֶאֱמוּנָתְךָ בַּלֵּילוֹת. עֲלֵי עָשׂוֹר וַעֲלֵי נָבֶל, עֲלֵי הִגָּיוֹן בְּכִנּוֹר. כִּי שִׂמַּחְתַּנִי יְיָ בְּפָעֳלֶךָ; בְּמַעֲשֵׂי יָדֶיךָ אֲרַנֵּן. מַה גָּדְלוּ מַעֲשֶׂיךָ, יְיָ; מְאֹד עָמְקוּ מַחְשְׁבֹתֶיךָ. אִישׁ בַּעַר לֹא יֵדָע, וּכְסִיל לֹא יָבִין אֶת זֹאת. בִּפְרֹחַ רְשָׁעִים כְּמוֹ עֵשֶׂב, וַיָּצִיצוּ כָּל פֹּעֲלֵי אָוֶן, לְהִשָּׁמְדָם עֲדֵי עַד. וְאַתָּה מָרוֹם לְעֹלָם, יְיָ. כִּי הִנֵּה אֹיְבֶיךָ, יְיָ, כִּי הִנֵּה אֹיְבֶיךָ יֹאבֵדוּ, יִתְפָּרְדוּ כָּל פֹּעֲלֵי אָוֶן. וַתָּרֶם כִּרְאֵים קַרְנִי; בַּלֹּתִי בְּשֶׁמֶן רַעֲנָן. וַתַּבֵּט עֵינִי בְּשׁוּרָי, בַּקָּמִים עָלַי מְרֵעִים תִּשְׁמַעְנָה אָזְנָי. צַדִּיק כַּתָּמָר יִפְרָח. כְּאֶרֶז בַּלְּבָנוֹן יִשְׂגֶּה. שְׁתוּלִים בְּבֵית יְיָ, בְּחַצְרוֹת אֱלֹהֵינוּ יַפְרִיחוּ. Reader עוֹד יְנוּבוּן בְּשֵׂיבָה, דְּשֵׁנִים וְרַעֲנַנִּים יִהְיוּ. לְהַגִּיד כִּי יָשָׁר יְיָ; צוּרִי, וְלֹא עַוְלָתָה בּוֹ.

תהלים צג

יְיָ מָלָךְ, גֵּאוּת לָבֵשׁ; לָבֵשׁ יְיָ, עֹז הִתְאַזָּר; אַף תִּכּוֹן תֵּבֵל, בַּל תִּמּוֹט. נָכוֹן כִּסְאֲךָ מֵאָז, מֵעוֹלָם אָתָּה. נָשְׂאוּ נְהָרוֹת, יְיָ, נָשְׂאוּ נְהָרוֹת קוֹלָם, יִשְׂאוּ נְהָרוֹת דָּכְיָם. מִקֹּלוֹת מַיִם רַבִּים, אַדִּירִים מִשְׁבְּרֵי יָם, אַדִּיר בַּמָּרוֹם יְיָ. Reader עֵדֹתֶיךָ נֶאֶמְנוּ מְאֹד, לְבֵיתְךָ נַאֲוָה קֹדֶשׁ, יְיָ, לְאֹרֶךְ יָמִים.

The eye of the Lord rests on those who revere him, those who hope for his kindness, to save them from death and to keep them alive in famine. Our soul waits for the Lord; he is our help and our shield. In him our heart rejoices; in his holy name we trust. May thy kindness, O Lord, rest on us, even as our hope rests in thee.

Psalm 92

A psalm, a song for the Sabbath day. It is good to give thanks to the Lord, and to sing praises to thy name, O Most High; to proclaim thy goodness in the morning, and thy faithfulness at night, with a ten-stringed lyre and a flute, to the sound of a harp. For thou, O Lord, hast made me glad through thy work; I sing for joy at all that thou hast done. How great are thy works, O Lord! How very deep are thy designs! A stupid man cannot know, a fool cannot understand this. When the wicked thrive like grass, and all evildoers flourish, it is that they may be destroyed forever. But thou, O Lord, art supreme for evermore. For lo, thy enemies, O Lord, for lo, thy enemies shall perish; all evildoers shall be dispersed. But thou hast exalted my power exceedingly;

I am anointed with fresh oil. My eye has gazed on my foes; my ears have heard my enemies' doom. The righteous will flourish like the palm tree; they will grow like a cedar in Lebanon. Planted in the house of the Lord, they shall flourish in the courts of our God. They shall yield fruit even in old age; vigorous and fresh they shall be, to proclaim that the Lord is just! He is my Stronghold, and there is no wrong in him.

Psalm 93

The Lord is King; he is robed in majesty; the Lord is robed, he has girded himself with strength; thus the world is set firm and cannot be shaken. Thy throne stands firm from of old, thou art from all eternity. The floods have lifted up, O Lord, the floods have lifted up their voice; the floods lift up their mighty waves. But above the sound of many waters, mighty breakers of the sea, the Lord on high stands supreme. Thy testimonies are very sure; holiness befits thy house, O Lord, for all time.

יְהִי כְבוֹד יְיָ לְעוֹלָם; יִשְׂמַח יְיָ בְּמַעֲשָׂיו. יְהִי שֵׁם יְיָ מְבֹרָךְ,
מֵעַתָּה וְעַד עוֹלָם. מִמִּזְרַח שֶׁמֶשׁ עַד מְבוֹאוֹ, מְהֻלָּל שֵׁם יְיָ. רָם
עַל כָּל גּוֹיִם יְיָ, עַל הַשָּׁמַיִם כְּבוֹדוֹ. יְיָ, שִׁמְךָ לְעוֹלָם; יְיָ, זִכְרְךָ
לְדֹר וָדֹר. יְיָ בַּשָּׁמַיִם הֵכִין כִּסְאוֹ, וּמַלְכוּתוֹ בַּכֹּל מָשָׁלָה.
יִשְׂמְחוּ הַשָּׁמַיִם וְתָגֵל הָאָרֶץ, וְיֹאמְרוּ בַגּוֹיִם יְיָ מָלָךְ. יְיָ מֶלֶךְ,
יְיָ מָלָךְ, יְיָ יִמְלֹךְ לְעֹלָם וָעֶד. יְיָ מֶלֶךְ עוֹלָם וָעֶד, אָבְדוּ גוֹיִם
מֵאַרְצוֹ. יְיָ הֵפִיר עֲצַת גּוֹיִם, הֵנִיא מַחְשְׁבוֹת עַמִּים. רַבּוֹת
מַחֲשָׁבוֹת בְּלֶב־אִישׁ, וַעֲצַת יְיָ הִיא תָקוּם. עֲצַת יְיָ לְעוֹלָם
תַּעֲמֹד, מַחְשְׁבוֹת לִבּוֹ לְדֹר וָדֹר. כִּי הוּא אָמַר וַיֶּהִי, הוּא צִוָּה
וַיַּעֲמֹד. כִּי בָחַר יְיָ בְּצִיּוֹן, אִוָּה לְמוֹשָׁב לוֹ. כִּי יַעֲקֹב בָּחַר לוֹ
יָהּ, יִשְׂרָאֵל לִסְגֻלָּתוֹ. כִּי לֹא יִטֹּשׁ יְיָ עַמּוֹ, וְנַחֲלָתוֹ לֹא יַעֲזֹב.
Reader וְהוּא רַחוּם, יְכַפֵּר עָוֹן וְלֹא יַשְׁחִית, וְהִרְבָּה לְהָשִׁיב
אַפּוֹ, וְלֹא יָעִיר כָּל חֲמָתוֹ. יְיָ, הוֹשִׁיעָה; הַמֶּלֶךְ יַעֲנֵנוּ בְיוֹם
קָרְאֵנוּ.

אַשְׁרֵי יוֹשְׁבֵי בֵיתֶךָ; עוֹד יְהַלְלוּךָ סֶּלָה.

אַשְׁרֵי הָעָם שֶׁכָּכָה לּוֹ; אַשְׁרֵי הָעָם שֶׁיְיָ אֱלֹהָיו.

תהלים קמה

תְּהִלָּה לְדָוִד

אֲרוֹמִמְךָ, אֱלוֹהַי הַמֶּלֶךְ, וַאֲבָרְכָה שִׁמְךָ לְעוֹלָם וָעֶד.

בְּכָל יוֹם אֲבָרְכֶךָ, וַאֲהַלְלָה שִׁמְךָ לְעוֹלָם וָעֶד.

גָּדוֹל יְיָ וּמְהֻלָּל מְאֹד, וְלִגְדֻלָּתוֹ אֵין חֵקֶר.

דּוֹר לְדוֹר יְשַׁבַּח מַעֲשֶׂיךָ, וּגְבוּרֹתֶיךָ יַגִּידוּ.

הֲדַר כְּבוֹד הוֹדֶךָ וְדִבְרֵי נִפְלְאֹתֶיךָ אָשִׂיחָה.

וֶעֱזוּז נוֹרְאֹתֶיךָ יֹאמֵרוּ, וּגְדֻלָּתְךָ אֲסַפְּרֶנָּה.

May the glory of the Lord be forever; may the Lord rejoice in his works. Blessed be the name of the Lord henceforth and forever. From the rising of the sun to its setting let the Lord's name be praised. High above all nations is the Lord; above the heavens is his glory. O Lord, thy name is forever; O Lord, thy fame is through all generations. The Lord has set up his throne in the heavens, and his kingdom rules over all. Let the heavens rejoice, let the earth exult, and let them say among the nations, "The Lord is King!" The Lord is King, the Lord was King, the Lord shall be King forever and ever. The Lord is King for evermore; the heathen have vanished from his land. The Lord annuls the counsel of nations; he foils the plans of peoples. Many are the plans in a man's heart, but it is the Lord's purpose that shall stand. The Lord's purpose stands forever; his plans are through all generations. For he spoke, and the world came into being; he commanded, and it stood firm. Surely, the Lord has chosen Zion; he has desired it for his habitation. Surely, the Lord has chosen Jacob to be his, and Israel as his prized possession. Surely, the Lord will not abandon his people, nor forsake his heritage. He, being merciful, forgives iniquity, and does not destroy; frequently he turns his anger away, and does not stir up all his wrath. O Lord, save us; may the King answer us when we call.[1]

Happy are those who dwell in thy house; they are ever praising thee. Happy the people that is so situated; happy the people whose God is the Lord.[2]

Psalm 145

A hymn of praise by David.

I extol thee, my God the King,
And bless thy name forever and ever.
Every day I bless thee
And praise thy name forever and ever.
Great is the Lord and most worthy of praise;
His greatness is unsearchable.
One generation to another praises thy works;
They recount thy mighty acts.
On the splendor of thy glorious majesty
And on thy wondrous deeds I meditate.
They speak of thy awe-inspiring might,
And I tell of thy greatness.

[1] *Psalms* 104:31; 113:2–4; 135:13; 103:19; *I Chronicles* 16:31; *Psalms* 10:16; 33:10; *Proverbs* 19:21; *Psalms* 33:11, 9; 132:13; 135:4; 94:14; 78:38; 20:10. [2] *Psalms* 84:5; 144:15.

זֵכֶר רַב טוּבְךָ יַבִּיעוּ, וְצִדְקָתְךָ יְרַנֵּנוּ.

חַנּוּן וְרַחוּם יְיָ, אֶרֶךְ אַפַּיִם וּגְדָל־חָסֶד.

טוֹב יְיָ לַכֹּל, וְרַחֲמָיו עַל כָּל מַעֲשָׂיו.

יוֹדוּךָ יְיָ כָּל מַעֲשֶׂיךָ, וַחֲסִידֶיךָ יְבָרְכוּכָה.

כְּבוֹד מַלְכוּתְךָ יֹאמֵרוּ, וּגְבוּרָתְךָ יְדַבֵּרוּ.

לְהוֹדִיעַ לִבְנֵי הָאָדָם גְּבוּרֹתָיו, וּכְבוֹד הֲדַר מַלְכוּתוֹ.

מַלְכוּתְךָ מַלְכוּת כָּל עֹלָמִים, וּמֶמְשַׁלְתְּךָ בְּכָל דּוֹר וָדֹר.

סוֹמֵךְ יְיָ לְכָל הַנֹּפְלִים, וְזוֹקֵף לְכָל הַכְּפוּפִים.

עֵינֵי כֹל אֵלֶיךָ יְשַׂבֵּרוּ, וְאַתָּה נוֹתֵן לָהֶם אֶת אָכְלָם בְּעִתּוֹ.

פּוֹתֵחַ אֶת יָדֶךָ, וּמַשְׂבִּיעַ לְכָל חַי רָצוֹן.

צַדִּיק יְיָ בְּכָל דְּרָכָיו, וְחָסִיד בְּכָל מַעֲשָׂיו.

קָרוֹב יְיָ לְכָל קֹרְאָיו, לְכֹל אֲשֶׁר יִקְרָאֻהוּ בֶאֱמֶת.

רְצוֹן יְרֵאָיו יַעֲשֶׂה, וְאֶת שַׁוְעָתָם יִשְׁמַע וְיוֹשִׁיעֵם.

שׁוֹמֵר יְיָ אֶת כָּל אֹהֲבָיו, וְאֵת כָּל הָרְשָׁעִים יַשְׁמִיד.

תְּהִלַּת יְיָ יְדַבֶּר־פִּי; וִיבָרֵךְ כָּל בָּשָׂר שֵׁם קָדְשׁוֹ לְעוֹלָם וָעֶד.

Reader וַאֲנַחְנוּ נְבָרֵךְ יָהּ מֵעַתָּה וְעַד עוֹלָם; הַלְלוּיָהּ.

תהלים קמז

הַלְלוּיָהּ; הַלְלִי נַפְשִׁי אֶת יְיָ. אֲהַלְלָה יְיָ בְּחַיָּי, אֲזַמְּרָה לֵאלֹהַי בְּעוֹדִי. אַל תִּבְטְחוּ בִנְדִיבִים, בְּבֶן־אָדָם שֶׁאֵין לוֹ תְשׁוּעָה. תֵּצֵא רוּחוֹ יָשֻׁב לְאַדְמָתוֹ; בַּיּוֹם הַהוּא אָבְדוּ עֶשְׁתֹּנֹתָיו. אַשְׁרֵי שֶׁאֵל יַעֲקֹב בְּעֶזְרוֹ, שִׂבְרוֹ עַל יְיָ אֱלֹהָיו. עֹשֶׂה שָׁמַיִם וָאָרֶץ, אֶת הַיָּם, וְאֶת כָּל אֲשֶׁר בָּם; הַשֹּׁמֵר אֱמֶת לְעוֹלָם. עֹשֶׂה מִשְׁפָּט לַעֲשׁוּקִים, נֹתֵן לֶחֶם לָרְעֵבִים; יְיָ מַתִּיר אֲסוּרִים. יְיָ

ואנחנו נברך is added from Psalm 115:18 so that אשרי, like the five subsequent psalms, may end with *Halleluyah*.

They spread the fame of thy great goodness,
And sing of thy righteousness.
Gracious and merciful is the Lord,
Slow to anger and of great kindness.
The Lord is good to all,
And his mercy is over all his works.
All thy works praise thee, O Lord,
And thy faithful followers bless thee.
They speak of thy glorious kingdom,
And talk of thy might,
To let men know thy mighty deeds,
And the glorious splendor of thy kingdom.
Thy kingdom is a kingdom of all ages,
And thy dominion is for all generations.
The Lord upholds all who fall,
And raises all who are bowed down.
The eyes of all look hopefully to thee,
And thou givest them their food in due season.
Thou openest thy hand,
And satisfiest every living thing with favor.
The Lord is righteous in all his ways,
And gracious in all his deeds.
The Lord is near to all who call upon him
To all who call upon him sincerely.
He fulfills the desire of those who revere him;
He hears their cry and saves them.
The Lord preserves all who love him,
But all the wicked he destroys.
My mouth speaks the praise of the Lord;
Let all creatures bless his holy name forever and ever.
　　[1]We will bless the Lord henceforth and forever.
　　Praise the Lord!

Psalm 146

Praise the Lord! Praise the Lord, O my soul! I will praise the Lord as long as I live; I will sing to my God as long as I exist. Put no trust in princes, in mortal man who can give no help. When his breath goes, he returns to the dust, and on that very day his designs perish. Happy is he who has the God of Jacob as his help, whose hope rests upon the Lord his God, Maker of heaven and earth and sea and all that is therein; who keeps faith forever, renders justice to the oppressed, and feeds those who are hungry. The Lord sets the captives free. The Lord opens the eyes of the

---

[1] *Psalm* 115:18.

פֹּקֵחַ עִוְרִים, יְיָ זֹקֵף כְּפוּפִים, יְיָ אֹהֵב צַדִּיקִים. יְיָ שֹׁמֵר אֶת
גֵּרִים, יָתוֹם וְאַלְמָנָה יְעוֹדֵד, וְדֶרֶךְ רְשָׁעִים יְעַוֵּת. Reader יִמְלֹךְ
יְיָ לְעוֹלָם, אֱלֹהַיִךְ צִיּוֹן לְדֹר וָדֹר: הַלְלוּיָהּ.

הַלְלוּיָהּ; כִּי טוֹב זַמְּרָה אֱלֹהֵינוּ, כִּי נָעִים, נָאוָה תְהִלָּה.
בּוֹנֵה יְרוּשָׁלַיִם יְיָ; נִדְחֵי יִשְׂרָאֵל יְכַנֵּס. הָרֹפֵא לִשְׁבוּרֵי לֵב,
וּמְחַבֵּשׁ לְעַצְּבוֹתָם. מוֹנֶה מִסְפָּר לַכּוֹכָבִים, לְכֻלָּם שֵׁמוֹת
יִקְרָא. גָּדוֹל אֲדוֹנֵינוּ וְרַב כֹּחַ, לִתְבוּנָתוֹ אֵין מִסְפָּר. מְעוֹדֵד
עֲנָוִים יְיָ, מַשְׁפִּיל רְשָׁעִים עֲדֵי אָרֶץ. עֱנוּ לַיְיָ בְּתוֹדָה, זַמְּרוּ
לֵאלֹהֵינוּ בְכִנּוֹר. הַמְכַסֶּה שָׁמַיִם בְּעָבִים, הַמֵּכִין לָאָרֶץ מָטָר,
הַמַּצְמִיחַ הָרִים חָצִיר. נוֹתֵן לִבְהֵמָה לַחְמָהּ, לִבְנֵי עֹרֵב אֲשֶׁר
יִקְרָאוּ. לֹא בִגְבוּרַת הַסּוּס יֶחְפָּץ, לֹא בְשׁוֹקֵי הָאִישׁ יִרְצֶה.
רוֹצֶה יְיָ אֶת יְרֵאָיו, אֶת הַמְיַחֲלִים לְחַסְדּוֹ. שַׁבְּחִי, יְרוּשָׁלַיִם,
אֶת יְיָ; הַלְלִי אֱלֹהַיִךְ, צִיּוֹן. כִּי חִזַּק בְּרִיחֵי שְׁעָרָיִךְ, בֵּרַךְ בָּנַיִךְ
בְּקִרְבֵּךְ. הַשָּׂם גְּבוּלֵךְ שָׁלוֹם, חֵלֶב חִטִּים יַשְׂבִּיעֵךְ. הַשֹּׁלֵחַ
אִמְרָתוֹ אָרֶץ; עַד מְהֵרָה יָרוּץ דְּבָרוֹ. הַנֹּתֵן שֶׁלֶג כַּצָּמֶר; כְּפוֹר
כָּאֵפֶר יְפַזֵּר. מַשְׁלִיךְ קַרְחוֹ כְפִתִּים; לִפְנֵי קָרָתוֹ מִי יַעֲמֹד.
יִשְׁלַח דְּבָרוֹ וְיַמְסֵם; יַשֵּׁב רוּחוֹ, יִזְּלוּ מָיִם. מַגִּיד דְּבָרָיו לְיַעֲקֹב,
חֻקָּיו וּמִשְׁפָּטָיו לְיִשְׂרָאֵל. Reader לֹא עָשָׂה כֵן לְכָל גּוֹי,
וּמִשְׁפָּטִים בַּל יְדָעוּם; הַלְלוּיָהּ.

הַלְלוּיָהּ; הַלְלוּ אֶת יְיָ מִן הַשָּׁמַיִם, הַלְלוּהוּ בַּמְּרוֹמִים.
הַלְלוּהוּ כָל מַלְאָכָיו, הַלְלוּהוּ כָּל צְבָאָיו. הַלְלוּהוּ שֶׁמֶשׁ
וְיָרֵחַ, הַלְלוּהוּ כָּל כּוֹכְבֵי אוֹר. הַלְלוּהוּ שְׁמֵי הַשָּׁמַיִם, וְהַמַּיִם
אֲשֶׁר מֵעַל הַשָּׁמָיִם. יְהַלְלוּ אֶת שֵׁם יְיָ, כִּי הוּא צִוָּה וְנִבְרָאוּ.

blind, raises those who are bowed down, and loves the righteous. The Lord protects the strangers, and upholds the fatherless and the widow; but the way of the wicked he thwarts. The Lord shall reign forever; your God, O Zion, for all generations. Praise the Lord!

Psalm 147

Praise the Lord! It is good to sing to our God, it is pleasant; praise is comely. The Lord rebuilds Jerusalem; he gathers together the dispersed people of Israel. He heals the broken-hearted, and binds up their wounds. He counts the number of the stars, and gives a name to each. Great is our Lord and abundant in power; his wisdom is infinite. The Lord raises the humble; he casts the wicked down to the ground. Sing thanks to the Lord; make melody upon the harp to our God, who covers the sky with clouds, provides rain for the earth, and causes grass to grow upon the hills. He gives food to the cattle, and to the crying young ravens. He cares not for [those who rely on] the strength of the horse; he delights not in [those who rely on] a warrior's legs. The Lord is pleased with those who revere him, those who yearn for his kindness. Praise the Lord, O Jerusalem! Praise your God, O Zion! He has indeed fortified your gates; he has blessed your children within. He establishes peace within your territory, and fills you with the finest of wheat. He sends forth his command to the earth; his word runs very swiftly. He gives snow like wool; he scatters hoarfrost like ashes. He casts forth his ice like crumbs; who can stand before his cold? He sends forth his word and melts them; he causes his wind to blow, and the waters flow. He declares his word to Jacob, his statutes and ordinances to Israel. He has not dealt so with heathen nations; his ordinances they do not know. Praise the Lord!

Psalm 148

Praise the Lord! Praise the Lord from the heavens; praise him in the heights. Praise him, all his angels; praise him, all his hosts. Praise him, sun and moon; praise him, all you stars of light. Praise him, highest heavens and waters that are above the heavens. Let them praise the name of the Lord; for he commanded and they were created. He fixed them fast forever and ever; he gave

וַיַּעֲמִידֵם לָעַד לְעוֹלָם, חָק־נָתַן וְלֹא יַעֲבוֹר. הַלְלוּ אֶת יְיָ מִן
הָאָרֶץ, תַּנִּינִים וְכָל תְּהֹמוֹת. אֵשׁ וּבָרָד, שֶׁלֶג וְקִיטוֹר, רוּחַ
סְעָרָה עֹשָׂה דְבָרוֹ. הֶהָרִים וְכָל גְּבָעוֹת, עֵץ פְּרִי וְכָל אֲרָזִים,
הַחַיָּה וְכָל בְּהֵמָה, רֶמֶשׂ וְצִפּוֹר כָּנָף. מַלְכֵי אֶרֶץ וְכָל לְאֻמִּים,
שָׂרִים וְכָל שֹׁפְטֵי אָרֶץ. בַּחוּרִים וְגַם בְּתוּלוֹת, זְקֵנִים עִם
נְעָרִים. יְהַלְלוּ אֶת שֵׁם יְיָ, כִּי נִשְׂגָּב שְׁמוֹ לְבַדּוֹ; הוֹדוֹ עַל אֶרֶץ
וְשָׁמָיִם. Reader וַיָּרֶם קֶרֶן לְעַמּוֹ, תְּהִלָּה לְכָל חֲסִידָיו, לִבְנֵי
יִשְׂרָאֵל עַם קְרֹבוֹ; הַלְלוּיָהּ.

תהלים קמט

הַלְלוּיָהּ; שִׁירוּ לַיְיָ שִׁיר חָדָשׁ, תְּהִלָּתוֹ בִּקְהַל חֲסִידִים.
יִשְׂמַח יִשְׂרָאֵל בְּעֹשָׂיו, בְּנֵי צִיּוֹן יָגִילוּ בְמַלְכָּם. יְהַלְלוּ שְׁמוֹ
בְמָחוֹל, בְּתֹף וְכִנּוֹר יְזַמְּרוּ לוֹ. כִּי רוֹצֶה יְיָ בְּעַמּוֹ, יְפָאֵר עֲנָוִים
בִּישׁוּעָה. יַעְלְזוּ חֲסִידִים בְּכָבוֹד, יְרַנְּנוּ עַל מִשְׁכְּבוֹתָם. רוֹמְמוֹת
אֵל בִּגְרוֹנָם, וְחֶרֶב פִּיפִיּוֹת בְּיָדָם. לַעֲשׂוֹת נְקָמָה בַגּוֹיִם,
תּוֹכֵחוֹת בַּלְאֻמִּים. Reader לֶאְסֹר מַלְכֵיהֶם בְּזִקִּים, וְנִכְבְּדֵיהֶם
בְּכַבְלֵי בַרְזֶל. לַעֲשׂוֹת בָּהֶם מִשְׁפָּט כָּתוּב; הָדָר הוּא לְכָל
חֲסִידָיו; הַלְלוּיָהּ.

תהלים קנ

הַלְלוּיָהּ; הַלְלוּ אֵל בְּקָדְשׁוֹ, הַלְלוּהוּ בִּרְקִיעַ עֻזּוֹ. הַלְלוּהוּ
בִגְבוּרֹתָיו, הַלְלוּהוּ כְּרֹב גֻּדְלוֹ. הַלְלוּהוּ בְּתֵקַע שׁוֹפָר, הַלְלוּהוּ
בְּנֵבֶל וְכִנּוֹר. הַלְלוּהוּ בְּתֹף וּמָחוֹל, הַלְלוּהוּ בְּמִנִּים וְעֻגָב.
הַלְלוּהוּ בְצִלְצְלֵי שָׁמַע, הַלְלוּהוּ בְּצִלְצְלֵי תְרוּעָה. Reader כֹּל
הַנְּשָׁמָה תְּהַלֵּל יָהּ; הַלְלוּיָהּ. כֹּל הַנְּשָׁמָה תְּהַלֵּל יָהּ; הַלְלוּיָהּ.

כל הנשמה is repeated because this verse marks the end of the Book of
Psalms.

a law which none transgresses. Praise the Lord from the earth, you sea-monsters and all depths; fire and hail, snow and vapor, stormy wind, fulfilling his word; mountains and all hills, fruit-trees and all cedars; wild animals and all cattle, crawling things and winged fowl; kings of the earth and all nations, princes and all earthly rulers; young men and maidens, old men and children; let them praise the name of the Lord, for his name alone is exalted; his majesty is above earth and heaven. He has raised the honor of his people, the glory of his faithful followers, the children of Israel, the people near to him. Praise the Lord!

Psalm 149

Praise the Lord! Sing a new song to the Lord; praise him in the assembly of the faithful. Let Israel rejoice in his Maker; let the children of Zion exult in their King. Let them praise his name with dancing; let them make music to him with drum and harp. For the Lord is pleased with his people; he adorns the meek with triumph. Let the faithful exult in glory; let them sing upon their beds. Let the praises of God be in their mouth, and a double-edged sword in their hand, to execute vengeance upon the nations, punishment upon the peoples; to bind their kings with chains, and their nobles with fetters of iron; to execute upon them the written judgment. He is the glory of all his faithful. Praise the Lord!

Psalm 150

Praise the Lord! Praise God in his sanctuary; praise him in his glorious heaven. Praise him for his mighty deeds; praise him for his abundant greatness. Praise him with the blast of the horn; praise him with the harp and the lyre. Praise him with the drum and dance; praise him with strings and flute. Praise him with re-sounding cymbals; praise him with clanging cymbals. Let everything that has breath praise the Lord. Praise the Lord!

בָּרוּךְ יְיָ לְעוֹלָם, אָמֵן וְאָמֵן. בָּרוּךְ יְיָ מִצִּיּוֹן, שֹׁכֵן יְרוּשָׁלָיִם;
הַלְלוּיָהּ. בָּרוּךְ יְיָ אֱלֹהִים, אֱלֹהֵי יִשְׂרָאֵל, עֹשֵׂה נִפְלָאוֹת לְבַדּוֹ.
Reader וּבָרוּךְ שֵׁם כְּבוֹדוֹ לְעוֹלָם; וְיִמָּלֵא כְבוֹדוֹ אֶת־כָּל הָאָרֶץ,
אָמֵן וְאָמֵן.

דברי הימים א כט, י‑יג

וַיְבָרֶךְ דָּוִיד אֶת יְיָ לְעֵינֵי כָּל הַקָּהָל, וַיֹּאמֶר דָּוִיד: בָּרוּךְ
אַתָּה יְיָ, אֱלֹהֵי יִשְׂרָאֵל אָבִינוּ, מֵעוֹלָם וְעַד עוֹלָם. לְךָ יְיָ
הַגְּדֻלָּה וְהַגְּבוּרָה וְהַתִּפְאֶרֶת וְהַנֵּצַח וְהַהוֹד, כִּי כֹל בַּשָּׁמַיִם
וּבָאָרֶץ; לְךָ יְיָ הַמַּמְלָכָה, וְהַמִּתְנַשֵּׂא לְכֹל לְרֹאשׁ. וְהָעֹשֶׁר
וְהַכָּבוֹד מִלְּפָנֶיךָ, וְאַתָּה מוֹשֵׁל בַּכֹּל, וּבְיָדְךָ כֹּחַ וּגְבוּרָה,
וּבְיָדְךָ לְגַדֵּל וּלְחַזֵּק לַכֹּל. וְעַתָּה אֱלֹהֵינוּ, מוֹדִים אֲנַחְנוּ לָךְ,
וּמְהַלְלִים לְשֵׁם תִּפְאַרְתֶּךָ.

נחמיה ט, ו‑יא

אַתָּה הוּא יְיָ לְבַדֶּךָ, אַתָּה עָשִׂיתָ אֶת הַשָּׁמַיִם, שְׁמֵי הַשָּׁמַיִם
וְכָל צְבָאָם, הָאָרֶץ וְכָל אֲשֶׁר עָלֶיהָ, הַיַּמִּים וְכָל אֲשֶׁר בָּהֶם,
וְאַתָּה מְחַיֶּה אֶת כֻּלָּם, וּצְבָא הַשָּׁמַיִם לְךָ מִשְׁתַּחֲוִים. Reader אַתָּה
הוּא יְיָ הָאֱלֹהִים, אֲשֶׁר בָּחַרְתָּ בְּאַבְרָם וְהוֹצֵאתוֹ מֵאוּר כַּשְׂדִּים,
וְשַׂמְתָּ שְּׁמוֹ אַבְרָהָם. וּמָצָאתָ אֶת לְבָבוֹ נֶאֱמָן לְפָנֶיךָ—
וְכָרוֹת עִמּוֹ הַבְּרִית לָתֵת אֶת אֶרֶץ הַכְּנַעֲנִי, הַחִתִּי, הָאֱמֹרִי,
וְהַפְּרִזִּי וְהַיְבוּסִי וְהַגִּרְגָּשִׁי, לָתֵת לְזַרְעוֹ; וַתָּקֶם אֶת דְּבָרֶיךָ, כִּי
צַדִּיק אָתָּה. וַתֵּרֶא אֶת עֳנִי אֲבֹתֵינוּ בְּמִצְרָיִם, וְאֶת זַעֲקָתָם
שָׁמַעְתָּ עַל יַם סוּף. וַתִּתֵּן אֹתֹת וּמֹפְתִים בְּפַרְעֹה וּבְכָל עֲבָדָיו
וּבְכָל עַם אַרְצוֹ, כִּי יָדַעְתָּ כִּי הֵזִידוּ עֲלֵיהֶם; וַתַּעַשׂ לְךָ שֵׁם
כְּהַיּוֹם הַזֶּה. Reader וְהַיָּם בָּקַעְתָּ לִפְנֵיהֶם, וַיַּעַבְרוּ בְתוֹךְ הַיָּם
בַּיַּבָּשָׁה; וְאֶת רֹדְפֵיהֶם הִשְׁלַכְתָּ בִמְצוֹלֹת, כְּמוֹ אֶבֶן בְּמַיִם
עַזִּים.

Blessed be the Lord forever. Amen, Amen. Blessed out of Zion be the Lord who dwells in Jerusalem. Praise the Lord! Blessed be the Lord God, the God of Israel, who alone works wonders; blessed be his glorious name forever. May the whole earth be filled with his glory. Amen, Amen.[1]

I Chronicles 29:10–13

David blessed the Lord before all the assembly, and David said: Blessed art thou, O Lord, God of Israel our Father, forever and ever. Thine, O Lord, is the greatness and the power, the glory and the victory and the majesty, for all that is in heaven and on earth is thine; thine, O Lord, is the kingdom, and thou art supreme over all. Riches and honor come from thee; thou rulest over all; in thy hand are power and might, and it is in thy power to make all great and strong. Hence, our God, we ever thank thee and praise thy glorious name. Blessed be thy glorious name, high above all blessing and praise.

Nehemiah 9:5–11

Thou art the Lord, thou alone. Thou hast made the heavens and the heaven of heavens with all their host, the earth and all the things upon it, the seas and all that is in them, and thou preservest them all; the host of the heavens worships thee. Thou art the Lord God, who didst choose Abram, and didst bring him out of Ur of the Chaldeans, and gavest him the name of Abraham. Thou didst find his heart faithful before thee, and didst make a covenant with him to give the land of the Canaanite, the Hittite, the Amorite, the Perizzite, the Jebusite, and the Girgashite—to give it to his descendants, and hast fulfilled thy words, for thou art righteous. Thou didst see the distress of our fathers in Egypt and hear their cry by the Red Sea; thou didst show signs and wonders on Pharaoh and all his servants and all the people of his land, for thou knewest that they dealt viciously against them; and so hast thou made a name for thyself to this day. The sea thou didst divide before them, so that they went through the middle of the sea on dry ground; and their pursuers thou didst cast into the depths, like a stone into the mighty waters.

---

[1] *Psalms* 89:53; 135:21; 72:18–19.

שמות יד, ל–לא

וַיּוֹשַׁע יְיָ בַּיּוֹם הַהוּא אֶת יִשְׂרָאֵל מִיַּד מִצְרָיִם; וַיַּרְא יִשְׂרָאֵל אֶת מִצְרַיִם מֵת עַל שְׂפַת הַיָּם. Reader וַיַּרְא יִשְׂרָאֵל אֶת הַיָּד הַגְּדֹלָה אֲשֶׁר עָשָׂה יְיָ בְּמִצְרַיִם, וַיִּירְאוּ הָעָם אֶת יְיָ, וַיַּאֲמִינוּ בַּיְיָ וּבְמֹשֶׁה עַבְדּוֹ.

שמות טו, א–יח

אָז יָשִׁיר מֹשֶׁה וּבְנֵי יִשְׂרָאֵל אֶת הַשִּׁירָה הַזֹּאת לַיְיָ, וַיֹּאמְרוּ לֵאמֹר: אָשִׁירָה לַיְיָ כִּי גָאֹה גָּאָה, סוּס וְרֹכְבוֹ רָמָה בַיָּם. עָזִּי וְזִמְרָת יָהּ, וַיְהִי לִי לִישׁוּעָה; זֶה אֵלִי וְאַנְוֵהוּ, אֱלֹהֵי אָבִי וַאֲרֹמְמֶנְהוּ. יְיָ אִישׁ מִלְחָמָה, יְיָ שְׁמוֹ. מַרְכְּבֹת פַּרְעֹה וְחֵילוֹ יָרָה בַיָּם, וּמִבְחַר שָׁלִשָׁיו טֻבְּעוּ בְיַם סוּף. תְּהֹמֹת יְכַסְיֻמוּ; יָרְדוּ בִמְצוֹלֹת כְּמוֹ אָבֶן. יְמִינְךָ יְיָ נֶאְדָּרִי בַּכֹּחַ, יְמִינְךָ יְיָ תִּרְעַץ אוֹיֵב. וּבְרֹב גְּאוֹנְךָ תַּהֲרֹס קָמֶיךָ; תְּשַׁלַּח חֲרֹנְךָ, יֹאכְלֵמוֹ כַּקַּשׁ. וּבְרוּחַ אַפֶּיךָ נֶעֶרְמוּ מַיִם, נִצְּבוּ כְמוֹ נֵד נֹזְלִים, קָפְאוּ תְהֹמֹת בְּלֶב יָם. אָמַר אוֹיֵב: אֶרְדֹּף אַשִּׂיג, אֲחַלֵּק שָׁלָל, תִּמְלָאֵמוֹ נַפְשִׁי, אָרִיק חַרְבִּי, תּוֹרִישֵׁמוֹ יָדִי. נָשַׁפְתָּ בְרוּחֲךָ, כִּסָּמוֹ יָם; צָלֲלוּ כַּעוֹפֶרֶת בְּמַיִם אַדִּירִים. מִי כָמֹכָה בָּאֵלִם יְיָ, מִי כָּמֹכָה נֶאְדָּר בַּקֹּדֶשׁ, נוֹרָא תְהִלֹּת, עֹשֵׂה פֶלֶא. נָטִיתָ יְמִינְךָ, תִּבְלָעֵמוֹ אָרֶץ. נָחִיתָ בְחַסְדְּךָ עַם–זוּ גָּאָלְתָּ; נֵהַלְתָּ בְעָזְּךָ אֶל נְוֵה קָדְשֶׁךָ. שָׁמְעוּ עַמִּים, יִרְגָּזוּן; חִיל אָחַז יֹשְׁבֵי פְּלָשֶׁת. אָז נִבְהֲלוּ אַלּוּפֵי אֱדוֹם, אֵילֵי מוֹאָב יֹאחֲזֵמוֹ רָעַד; נָמֹגוּ כֹּל יֹשְׁבֵי כְנָעַן. תִּפֹּל עֲלֵיהֶם אֵימָתָה וָפַחַד; בִּגְדֹל זְרוֹעֲךָ יִדְּמוּ כָּאָבֶן; עַד יַעֲבֹר עַמְּךָ יְיָ, עַד יַעֲבֹר עַם–זוּ קָנִיתָ. תְּבִאֵמוֹ וְתִטָּעֵמוֹ בְּהַר נַחֲלָתְךָ, מָכוֹן לְשִׁבְתְּךָ פָּעַלְתָּ, יְיָ, מִקְּדָשׁ, אֲדֹנָי, כּוֹנְנוּ יָדֶיךָ. יְיָ יִמְלֹךְ לְעֹלָם וָעֶד, יְיָ יִמְלֹךְ לְעֹלָם וָעֶד.

Exodus 14:30–31

Thus did the Lord save Israel that day from the power of the Egyptians; and Israel saw the Egyptians dead on the seashore. Israel saw the mighty act which the Lord had performed against the Egyptians, and the people revered the Lord; they believed in the Lord and in his servant Moses.

Exodus 15:1–18

Then Moses and the children of Israel sang this song to the Lord; they said: I will sing to the Lord, for he has completely triumphed; the horse and its rider he has hurled into the sea. The Lord is my strength and song, for he has come to my aid. This is my God, and I will glorify him; my father's God, and I will extol him. The Lord is a warrior—Lord is his name. Pharaoh's chariots and his army he has cast into the sea, and his picked captains are engulfed in the Red Sea. The depths cover them; they went down into the depths like a stone. Thy right hand, O Lord, glorious in power, thy right hand, O Lord, crushes the enemy. By thy great majesty thou destroyest thy opponents. Thou sendest forth thy wrath—it consumes them like stubble. By the blast of thy nostrils the waters piled up—the floods stood upright like a wall; the depths were congealed in the heart of the sea. The enemy said: "I will pursue them, I will overtake them, I will divide the spoil, my lust shall be glutted with them; I will draw my sword, my hand shall destroy them." Thou didst blow with thy wind—the sea covered them; they sank like lead in the mighty waters. Who is there like thee among the mighty, O Lord? Who is like thee, glorious in holiness, awe-inspiring in renown, doing marvels? Thou didst stretch out thy right hand—the earth swallowed them. In thy grace thou hast led the people whom thou hast redeemed; by thy power thou hast guided them to thy holy habitation. The peoples have heard of it and trembled; pangs have seized the inhabitants of Philistia. Then were the chieftains of Edom in agony; trembling seized the lords of Moab; all the inhabitants of Canaan melted away. Terror and dread fell on them. Under the great sweep of thy arm they are as still as a stone, till thy people pass over, O Lord, till the people thou hast acquired pass over. Thou wilt bring them in and plant them in the highlands of thy own, the place which thou, O Lord, hast made for thy dwelling, the sanctuary, O Lord, which thy hands have established. The Lord shall reign forever and ever. The Lord shall reign forever and ever.

כִּי לַיָי הַמְּלוּכָה, וּמֹשֵׁל בַּגּוֹיִם. Reader. וְעָלוּ מוֹשִׁיעִים בְּהַר צִיּוֹן לִשְׁפֹּט אֶת הַר עֵשָׂו, וְהָיְתָה לַיָי הַמְּלוּכָה. וְהָיָה יְיָ לְמֶלֶךְ עַל כָּל הָאָרֶץ; בַּיּוֹם הַהוּא יִהְיֶה יְיָ אֶחָד וּשְׁמוֹ אֶחָד.

נִשְׁמַת כָּל חַי תְּבָרֵךְ אֶת שִׁמְךָ, יְיָ אֱלֹהֵינוּ, וְרוּחַ כָּל בָּשָׂר תְּפָאֵר וּתְרוֹמֵם זִכְרְךָ, מַלְכֵּנוּ, תָּמִיד. מִן הָעוֹלָם וְעַד הָעוֹלָם אַתָּה אֵל, וּמִבַּלְעָדֶיךָ אֵין לָנוּ מֶלֶךְ גּוֹאֵל וּמוֹשִׁיעַ, פּוֹדֶה וּמַצִּיל וּמְפַרְנֵס, וּמְרַחֵם בְּכָל עֵת צָרָה וְצוּקָה; אֵין לָנוּ מֶלֶךְ אֶלָּא אָתָּה. אֱלֹהֵי הָרִאשׁוֹנִים וְהָאַחֲרוֹנִים, אֱלוֹהַּ כָּל בְּרִיּוֹת, אֲדוֹן כָּל תּוֹלָדוֹת, הַמְּהֻלָּל בְּרֹב הַתִּשְׁבָּחוֹת, הַמְנַהֵג עוֹלָמוֹ בְּחֶסֶד וּבְרִיּוֹתָיו בְּרַחֲמִים. וַיְיָ לֹא יָנוּם וְלֹא יִישָׁן, הַמְעוֹרֵר יְשֵׁנִים, וְהַמֵּקִיץ נִרְדָּמִים, וְהַמֵּשִׂיחַ אִלְּמִים, וְהַמַּתִּיר אֲסוּרִים, וְהַסּוֹמֵךְ נוֹפְלִים, וְהַזּוֹקֵף כְּפוּפִים. לְךָ לְבַדְּךָ אֲנַחְנוּ מוֹדִים.

אִלּוּ פִינוּ מָלֵא שִׁירָה כַּיָּם, וּלְשׁוֹנֵנוּ רִנָּה כַּהֲמוֹן גַּלָּיו, וְשִׂפְתוֹתֵינוּ שֶׁבַח כְּמֶרְחֲבֵי רָקִיעַ, וְעֵינֵינוּ מְאִירוֹת כַּשֶּׁמֶשׁ וְכַיָּרֵחַ, וְיָדֵינוּ פְרוּשׂוֹת כְּנִשְׁרֵי שָׁמָיִם, וְרַגְלֵינוּ קַלּוֹת כָּאַיָּלוֹת, אֵין אֲנַחְנוּ מַסְפִּיקִים לְהוֹדוֹת לְךָ, יְיָ אֱלֹהֵינוּ וֵאלֹהֵי אֲבוֹתֵינוּ, וּלְבָרֵךְ אֶת שְׁמֶךָ עַל אַחַת מֵאֶלֶף, אֶלֶף אַלְפֵי אֲלָפִים וְרִבֵּי רְבָבוֹת פְּעָמִים הַטּוֹבוֹת שֶׁעָשִׂיתָ עִם אֲבוֹתֵינוּ וְעִמָּנוּ. מִמִּצְרַיִם גְּאַלְתָּנוּ, יְיָ אֱלֹהֵינוּ, וּמִבֵּית עֲבָדִים פְּדִיתָנוּ; בְּרָעָב זַנְתָּנוּ וּבְשָׂבָע כִּלְכַּלְתָּנוּ; מֵחֶרֶב הִצַּלְתָּנוּ וּמִדֶּבֶר מִלַּטְתָּנוּ, וּמֵחֳלָיִם רָעִים וְנֶאֱמָנִים דִּלִּיתָנוּ. עַד הֵנָּה עֲזָרוּנוּ רַחֲמֶיךָ וְלֹא עֲזָבוּנוּ חֲסָדֶיךָ; וְאַל תִּטְּשֵׁנוּ, יְיָ אֱלֹהֵינוּ, לָנֶצַח. עַל כֵּן, אֵבָרִים שֶׁפִּלַּגְתָּ

נשמת was well known in the talmudic period. A portion of this poem is quoted as part of the prayer for rain (Berakhoth 59b; Ta'anith 6b). The phrase "countless millions of favors" probably refers to the drops of rain, each drop being a separate favor; indeed, the Talmud suggests that thanks

For sovereignty is the Lord's, and he governs the nations. Deliverers shall go up to Mount Zion to rule the hill country of Esau, and dominion shall be the Lord's. The Lord shall be King over all the earth; on that day shall the Lord be One and his name One.[1]

NISHMATH

The soul of every living being shall bless thy name, Lord our God; the spirit of all mortals shall ever glorify and extol thy fame, our King. From eternity to eternity thou art God. Besides thee we have no king who redeems and saves, ransoms and rescues, sustains and shows mercy in all times of woe and stress. We have no King but thee.

God of the first and of the last, God of all creatures, Lord of all generations, endlessly praised be he who guides his world with kindness and his creatures with mercy. The Lord neither slumbers nor sleeps; he rouses those who sleep and awakens those who slumber; he enables the speechless to speak and sets the captives free; he supports all who fall and raises all who are bowed down. To thee alone we give thanks.

Were our mouth filled with song as the sea [is with water], and our tongue with ringing praise as the roaring waves; were our lips full of adoration as the wide expanse of heaven, and our eyes sparkling like the sun or the moon; were our hands spread out in prayer as the eagles of the sky, and our feet as swift as the deer— we should still be unable to thank thee and bless thy name, Lord our God and God of our fathers, for one thousandth of the countless millions of favors which thou hast conferred on our fathers and on us. Thou hast delivered us from Egypt, Lord our God, and redeemed us from slavery. Thou hast nourished us in famine and provided us with plenty. Thou hast rescued us from the sword, made us escape the plague, and freed us from severe and lasting diseases. Until now thy mercy has helped us, and thy kindness has not abandoned us; mayest thou, Lord our God, never forsake us.

should be given for every drop of rain. *Nishmath* is identified in the Talmud (Pesaḥim 118a) with ברכת השיר, recommended by the Mishnah for the closing of the *Haggadah* service on Passover.

[1] *Psalm* 22:29; *Obadiah* 1:21; *Zechariah* 14:9.

בָּנוּ, וְרוּחַ וּנְשָׁמָה שֶׁנָּפַחְתָּ בְּאַפֵּינוּ, וְלָשׁוֹן אֲשֶׁר שַׂמְתָּ בְּפִינוּ, הֵן הֵם יוֹדוּ וִיבָרְכוּ, וִישַׁבְּחוּ וִיפָאֲרוּ, וִירוֹמְמוּ וְיַעֲרִיצוּ, וְיַקְדִּישׁוּ וְיַמְלִיכוּ אֶת שִׁמְךָ, מַלְכֵּנוּ. כִּי כָל פֶּה לְךָ יוֹדֶה, וְכָל לָשׁוֹן לְךָ תִשָּׁבַע, וְכָל בֶּרֶךְ לְךָ תִכְרַע, וְכָל קוֹמָה לְפָנֶיךָ תִשְׁתַּחֲוֶה, וְכָל לְבָבוֹת יִירָאוּךָ, וְכָל קֶרֶב וּכְלָיוֹת יְזַמְּרוּ לִשְׁמֶךָ, כַּדָּבָר שֶׁכָּתוּב: כָּל עַצְמוֹתַי תֹּאמַרְנָה, יְיָ מִי כָמוֹךָ, מַצִּיל עָנִי מֵחָזָק מִמֶּנּוּ, וְעָנִי וְאֶבְיוֹן מִגֹּזְלוֹ. מִי יִדְמֶה לָּךְ, וּמִי יִשְׁוֶה לָּךְ, וּמִי יַעֲרָךְ־לָךְ, הָאֵל הַגָּדוֹל, הַגִּבּוֹר וְהַנּוֹרָא, אֵל עֶלְיוֹן, קֹנֵה שָׁמַיִם וָאָרֶץ. Reader • נְהַלֶּלְךָ וּנְשַׁבֵּחֲךָ וּנְפָאֶרְךָ, וּנְבָרֵךְ אֶת שֵׁם קָדְשֶׁךָ, כָּאָמוּר: לְדָוִד, בָּרְכִי נַפְשִׁי אֶת יְיָ, וְכָל קְרָבַי אֶת שֵׁם קָדְשׁוֹ.

Reader:

הָאֵל בְּתַעֲצֻמוֹת עֻזֶּךָ, הַגָּדוֹל בִּכְבוֹד שְׁמֶךָ, הַגִּבּוֹר לָנֶצַח וְהַנּוֹרָא בְּנוֹרְאוֹתֶיךָ. הַמֶּלֶךְ הַיּוֹשֵׁב עַל כִּסֵּא רָם וְנִשָּׂא.

שׁוֹכֵן עַד, מָרוֹם וְקָדוֹשׁ שְׁמוֹ, וְכָתוּב: רַנְּנוּ צַדִּיקִים בַּיְיָ, לַיְשָׁרִים נָאוָה תְהִלָּה.

בְּפִי יְשָׁרִים תִּתְהַלָּל,

וּבְדִבְרֵי צַדִּיקִים תִּתְבָּרַךְ,

וּבִלְשׁוֹן חֲסִידִים תִּתְרוֹמָם,

וּבְקֶרֶב קְדוֹשִׁים תִּתְקַדָּשׁ.

וּבְמַקְהֲלוֹת רִבְבוֹת עַמְּךָ בֵּית יִשְׂרָאֵל בְּרִנָּה יִתְפָּאַר שִׁמְךָ, מַלְכֵּנוּ, בְּכָל דּוֹר וָדוֹר; שֶׁכֵּן חוֹבַת כָּל הַיְצוּרִים, לְפָנֶיךָ יְיָ

שוכן עד is borrowed from Isaiah 57:15. The initials of the four synonyms for "righteous" in בפי ישרים happen to form the acrostic יצחק; by re-arranging

Therefore, the limbs which thou hast apportioned in us, the spirit and soul which thou hast breathed into our nostrils, and the tongue which thou hast placed in our mouth, shall all thank and bless, praise and glorify, extol and revere, hallow and do homage to thy name, our King. Indeed, every mouth shall praise thee; every tongue shall vow allegiance to thee; every knee shall bend to thee, and every person shall bow before thee. All hearts shall revere thee, and men's inmost being shall sing to thy name, as it is written: "All my being shall say: O Lord, who is like thee? Thou savest the poor man from one that is stronger, the poor and needy from one who would rob him."[1] Who is like thee, who is equal to thee, who can be compared to thee, O great, mighty and revered God, supreme God, Master of heaven and earth? We will praise, laud and glorify thee and bless thy holy name, as it is said by David: "Bless the Lord, O my soul, and let my whole being bless his holy name."[2]

Reader:

Thou art God in thy tremendous power, great in thy glorious name, mighty forever and revered for thy awe-inspiring acts; thou, O King, art seated upon a high and lofty throne.

Thou who abidest forever, exalted and holy is thy name. It is written: "Rejoice in the Lord, you righteous; it is fitting for the upright to give praise."[3]

By the mouth of the upright thou art praised;
By the speech of the righteous thou art blessed;
By the tongue of the faithful thou art extolled;
Inside the holy thou art sanctified.

In the assemblies of the tens of thousands of thy people, the house of Israel, with ringing song shall thy name, our King, be glorified in every generation; for this is the duty of all creatures

---

the verbs תתרוממ, תתברך, תתקדש, תתהלל, the third letters spell רבקה. Such re-arrangement is found in the Sephardic *Siddur*.

[1] *Psalm* 35:10.　[2] *Psalm* 103:1.　[3] *Psalm* 33:1.

אֱלֹהֵינוּ וֵאלֹהֵי אֲבוֹתֵינוּ, Reader לְהוֹדוֹת, לְהַלֵּל, לְשַׁבֵּחַ, לְפָאֵר, לְרוֹמֵם, לְהַדֵּר, לְבָרֵךְ, לְעַלֵּה וּלְקַלֵּס עַל כָּל דִּבְרֵי שִׁירוֹת וְתִשְׁבְּחוֹת דָּוִד בֶּן־יִשַׁי עַבְדְּךָ מְשִׁיחֶךָ.

יִשְׁתַּבַּח שִׁמְךָ לָעַד, מַלְכֵּנוּ, הָאֵל הַמֶּלֶךְ הַגָּדוֹל וְהַקָּדוֹשׁ, בַּשָּׁמַיִם וּבָאָרֶץ. כִּי לְךָ נָאֶה, יְיָ אֱלֹהֵינוּ וֵאלֹהֵי אֲבוֹתֵינוּ, שִׁיר וּשְׁבָחָה, הַלֵּל וְזִמְרָה, עֹז וּמֶמְשָׁלָה, נֶצַח, גְּדֻלָּה וּגְבוּרָה, תְּהִלָּה וְתִפְאֶרֶת, קְדֻשָּׁה וּמַלְכוּת, Reader בְּרָכוֹת וְהוֹדָאוֹת, מֵעַתָּה וְעַד עוֹלָם. בָּרוּךְ אַתָּה, יְיָ, אֵל מֶלֶךְ גָּדוֹל בַּתִּשְׁבָּחוֹת, אֵל הַהוֹדָאוֹת, אֲדוֹן הַנִּפְלָאוֹת, הַבּוֹחֵר בְּשִׁירֵי זִמְרָה, מֶלֶךְ, אֵל, חֵי הָעוֹלָמִים.

Reader:

יִתְגַּדַּל וְיִתְקַדַּשׁ שְׁמֵהּ רַבָּא בְּעָלְמָא דִּי בְרָא כִרְעוּתֵהּ; וְיַמְלִיךְ מַלְכוּתֵהּ בְּחַיֵּיכוֹן וּבְיוֹמֵיכוֹן, וּבְחַיֵּי דְכָל בֵּית יִשְׂרָאֵל בַּעֲגָלָא וּבִזְמַן קָרִיב, וְאִמְרוּ אָמֵן.

יְהֵא שְׁמֵהּ רַבָּא מְבָרַךְ לְעָלַם וּלְעָלְמֵי עָלְמַיָּא.

יִתְבָּרַךְ וְיִשְׁתַּבַּח, וְיִתְפָּאַר וְיִתְרוֹמַם, וְיִתְנַשֵּׂא וְיִתְהַדָּר, וְיִתְעַלֶּה וְיִתְהַלָּל שְׁמֵהּ דְּקֻדְשָׁא, בְּרִיךְ הוּא, לְעֵלָּא מִן כָּל בִּרְכָתָא וְשִׁירָתָא, תֻּשְׁבְּחָתָא וְנֶחֱמָתָא, דַּאֲמִירָן בְּעָלְמָא, וְאִמְרוּ אָמֵן.

<table>
<tr><td>Silent meditation:</td><td>Reader:</td></tr>
</table>

Reader:

בָּרְכוּ אֶת יְיָ הַמְבֹרָךְ.

Silent meditation:

יִתְבָּרַךְ וְיִשְׁתַּבַּח, וְיִתְפָּאַר וְיִתְרוֹמַם וְיִתְנַשֵּׂא שְׁמוֹ שֶׁל מֶלֶךְ מַלְכֵי הַמְּלָכִים, הַקָּדוֹשׁ בָּרוּךְ הוּא, שֶׁהוּא רִאשׁוֹן וְהוּא אַחֲרוֹן, וּמִבַּלְעָדָיו אֵין אֱלֹהִים. סֹלּוּ

Congregation and Reader:

בָּרוּךְ יְיָ הַמְבֹרָךְ לְעוֹלָם וָעֶד.

לָרֹכֵב בָּעֲרָבוֹת, בְּיָהּ שְׁמוֹ, וְעִלְזוּ לְפָנָיו; וּשְׁמוֹ מְרוֹמָם עַל כָּל בְּרָכָה וּתְהִלָּה. בָּרוּךְ שֵׁם כְּבוֹד מַלְכוּתוֹ לְעוֹלָם וָעֶד. יְהִי שֵׁם יְיָ מְבֹרָךְ מֵעַתָּה וְעַד עוֹלָם.

towards thee, Lord our God and God of our fathers: to thank and praise, laud and glorify, extol and honor, bless and exalt and acclaim thee, even beyond all the songs of praise by David, son of Jesse, thy anointed servant.

Praised be thy name forever, our King, great and holy God and King, in heaven and on earth; for to thee, Lord our God and God of our fathers, pertain song and praise, hymn and psalm, power and dominion, victory, greatness and might, renown and glory, holiness and kingship, blessings and thanks, henceforth and forever. Blessed art thou, O Lord, most exalted God and King, Lord of wonders, who art pleased with hymns, thou God and King, the life of the universe.

Reader:

Glorified and sanctified be God's great name throughout the world which he has created according to his will. May he establish his kingdom in your lifetime and during your days, and within the life of the entire house of Israel, speedily and soon; and say, Amen.

May his great name be blessed forever and to all eternity.

Blessed and praised, glorified and exalted, extolled and honored-adored and lauded be the name of the Holy One, blessed be he, beyond all the blessings and hymns, praises and consolations that are ever spoken in the world; and say, Amen.

Reader:

Bless the Lord who is blessed.

Congregation and Reader:

Blessed be the Lord who is blessed forever and ever.

Silent meditation:

Blessed, praised, glorified, extolled and exalted be the name of the supreme King of kings, the Holy One, blessed be he, who is the first and the last, and besides him there is no God. Extol him who is in the heavens—Lord is his name, and rejoice before him. His name is exalted above all blessing and praise. Blessed be the name of his glorious majesty forever and ever. Let the name of the Lord be blessed henceforth and forever.

בָּרוּךְ אַתָּה, יְיָ אֱלֹהֵינוּ, מֶלֶךְ הָעוֹלָם, יוֹצֵר אוֹר וּבוֹרֵא
חֹשֶׁךְ, עֹשֶׂה שָׁלוֹם, וּבוֹרֵא אֶת הַכֹּל.

On festivals occuring on weekdays:

(הַמֵּאִיר לָאָרֶץ וְלַדָּרִים עָלֶיהָ בְּרַחֲמִים, וּבְטוּבוֹ מְחַדֵּשׁ
בְּכָל יוֹם תָּמִיד מַעֲשֵׂה בְרֵאשִׁית. מָה רַבּוּ מַעֲשֶׂיךָ, יְיָ; כֻּלָּם
בְּחָכְמָה עָשִׂיתָ, מָלְאָה הָאָרֶץ קִנְיָנֶךָ. הַמֶּלֶךְ הַמְרוֹמָם לְבַדּוֹ
מֵאָז, הַמְשֻׁבָּח וְהַמְפֹאָר וְהַמִּתְנַשֵּׂא מִימוֹת עוֹלָם. אֱלֹהֵי עוֹלָם,
בְּרַחֲמֶיךָ הָרַבִּים רַחֵם עָלֵינוּ, אֲדוֹן עֻזֵּנוּ, צוּר מִשְׂגַּבֵּנוּ, מָגֵן
יִשְׁעֵנוּ, מִשְׂגָּב בַּעֲדֵנוּ.

אֵל בָּרוּךְ גְּדוֹל דֵּעָה, הֵכִין וּפָעַל זָהֳרֵי חַמָּה, טוֹב יָצַר
כָּבוֹד לִשְׁמוֹ, מְאוֹרוֹת נָתַן סְבִיבוֹת עֻזּוֹ, פִּנּוֹת צְבָאָיו קְדוֹשִׁים,
רוֹמְמֵי שַׁדַּי, תָּמִיד מְסַפְּרִים כְּבוֹד אֵל וּקְדֻשָּׁתוֹ. תִּתְבָּרַךְ, יְיָ
אֱלֹהֵינוּ, עַל שֶׁבַח מַעֲשֵׂה יָדֶיךָ, וְעַל מְאוֹרֵי אוֹר שֶׁעָשִׂיתָ;
יְפָאֲרוּךָ סֶּלָה.) Continue תִּתְבָּרַךְ on page 133.

On Sabbath:

הַכֹּל יוֹדוּךָ וְהַכֹּל יְשַׁבְּחוּךָ, וְהַכֹּל יֹאמְרוּ אֵין קָדוֹשׁ כַּיְיָ.
הַכֹּל יְרוֹמְמוּךָ סֶּלָה, יוֹצֵר הַכֹּל, הָאֵל הַפּוֹתֵחַ בְּכָל יוֹם
דַּלְתוֹת שַׁעֲרֵי מִזְרָח, וּבוֹקֵעַ חַלּוֹנֵי רָקִיעַ, מוֹצִיא חַמָּה
מִמְּקוֹמָהּ, וּלְבָנָה מִמְּכוֹן שִׁבְתָּהּ, וּמֵאִיר לָעוֹלָם כֻּלּוֹ וּלְיוֹשְׁבָיו
שֶׁבָּרָא בְּמִדַּת רַחֲמִים. הַמֵּאִיר לָאָרֶץ וְלַדָּרִים עָלֶיהָ בְּרַחֲמִים,
וּבְטוּבוֹ מְחַדֵּשׁ בְּכָל יוֹם תָּמִיד מַעֲשֵׂה בְרֵאשִׁית. הַמֶּלֶךְ
הַמְרוֹמָם לְבַדּוֹ מֵאָז, הַמְשֻׁבָּח וְהַמְפֹאָר וְהַמִּתְנַשֵּׂא מִימוֹת
עוֹלָם. אֱלֹהֵי עוֹלָם, בְּרַחֲמֶיךָ הָרַבִּים רַחֵם עָלֵינוּ, אֲדוֹן עֻזֵּנוּ,
צוּר מִשְׂגַּבֵּנוּ, מָגֵן יִשְׁעֵנוּ, מִשְׂגָּב בַּעֲדֵנוּ. אֵין כְּעֶרְכְּךָ וְאֵין
זוּלָתֶךָ; אֶפֶס בִּלְתֶּךָ, וּמִי דּוֹמֶה לָּךְ. Reader • אֵין כְּעֶרְכְּךָ, יְיָ

תמיד is an alphabetic acrostic ending with אל ברוך גדול דעה.

Blessed art thou, Lord our God, King of the universe, who formest light and createst darkness, who makest peace and createst all things.

On festivals occurring on weekdays:

In mercy thou givest light to the earth and to those who dwell on it; in thy goodness thou renewest the work of creation every day, constantly. How great are thy works, O Lord! In wisdom hast thou made them all; the earth is full of thy creations. Thou alone, O King, hast ever been exalted, lauded and glorified and extolled from days of old. Eternal God, show us thy great mercy! Lord of our strength, thou art our secure Stronghold, our saving Shield, our Refuge.

The blessed God, great in knowledge, designed and made the brilliant sun. The Beneficent One created glory for his name. He placed luminaries round about his majesty. His chief hosts are holy beings that extol the Almighty. They constantly recount God's glory and holiness. Be thou blessed, Lord our God, for thy excellent handiwork and for the luminaries which thou hast made; they ever render thee glory.

Continue "Be thou blessed" on page 134.

On Sabbath:

All shall thank thee; all shall praise thee; all shall declare: There is none holy like the Lord! All shall forever extol thee, Creator of all. Thou, O God, openest daily the gates of the east and cleavest the windows of the sky; thou bringest forth the sun from its place, and the moon from its abode, and givest light to the whole world and to its inhabitants whom thou hast created in thy mercy.

In mercy thou givest light to the earth and to those who dwell on it; in thy goodness thou renewest the work of creation every day, constantly. Thou alone, O King, art ever exalted! Thou art lauded, glorified and extolled from days of old. Eternal God, show us thy great mercy. Lord of our strength, thou art our secure Stronghold, our saving Shield, our Refuge.

There is none to be compared to thee, and there is none besides thee; there is none but thee. Who is like thee? *There is none to be compared to thee*, Lord our God, in this world, *and there is none*

אֱלֹהֵינוּ, בָּעוֹלָם הַזֶּה; וְאֵין זוּלָתְךָ, מַלְכֵּנוּ, לְחַיֵּי הָעוֹלָם הַבָּא.
אֶפֶס בִּלְתְּךָ, גּוֹאֲלֵנוּ, לִימוֹת הַמָּשִׁיחַ; וְאֵין דּוֹמֶה לְךָ, מוֹשִׁיעֵנוּ,
לִתְחִיַּת הַמֵּתִים.

אֵל אָדוֹן עַל כָּל הַמַּעֲשִׂים	בָּרוּךְ וּמְבֹרָךְ בְּפִי כָּל נְשָׁמָה;
גָּדְלוֹ וְטוּבוֹ מָלֵא עוֹלָם	דַּעַת וּתְבוּנָה סוֹבְבִים אֹתוֹ.
הַמִּתְגָּאֶה עַל חַיּוֹת הַקֹּדֶשׁ	וְנֶהְדָּר בְּכָבוֹד עַל הַמֶּרְכָּבָה;
זְכוּת וּמִישׁוֹר לִפְנֵי כִסְאוֹ	חֶסֶד וְרַחֲמִים לִפְנֵי כְבוֹדוֹ.
טוֹבִים מְאוֹרוֹת שֶׁבָּרָא אֱלֹהֵינוּ	יְצָרָם בְּדַעַת בְּבִינָה וּבְהַשְׂכֵּל;
כֹּחַ וּגְבוּרָה נָתַן בָּהֶם	לִהְיוֹת מוֹשְׁלִים בְּקֶרֶב תֵּבֵל.
מְלֵאִים זִיו וּמְפִיקִים נֹגַהּ	נָאֶה זִיוָם בְּכָל הָעוֹלָם;
שְׂמֵחִים בְּצֵאתָם וְשָׂשִׂים בְּבוֹאָם	עוֹשִׂים בְּאֵימָה רְצוֹן קוֹנָם.
פְּאֵר וְכָבוֹד נוֹתְנִים לִשְׁמוֹ	צָהֳלָה וְרִנָּה לְזֵכֶר מַלְכוּתוֹ;
קָרָא לַשֶּׁמֶשׁ וַיִּזְרַח אוֹר	רָאָה וְהִתְקִין צוּרַת הַלְּבָנָה.

שֶׁבַח נוֹתְנִים לוֹ כָּל צְבָא מָרוֹם, תִּפְאֶרֶת וּגְדֻלָּה,
שְׂרָפִים וְאוֹפַנִּים וְחַיּוֹת הַקֹּדֶשׁ–

לָאֵל אֲשֶׁר שָׁבַת מִכָּל הַמַּעֲשִׂים בַּיּוֹם הַשְּׁבִיעִי; הִתְעַלָּה
וְיָשַׁב עַל כִּסֵּא כְבוֹדוֹ; תִּפְאֶרֶת עָטָה לְיוֹם הַמְּנוּחָה, עֹנֶג קָרָא
לְיוֹם הַשַּׁבָּת. זֶה שֶׁבַח שֶׁל יוֹם הַשְּׁבִיעִי, שֶׁבּוֹ שָׁבַת אֵל מִכָּל

אל אדון is an alphabetical hymn, generally attributed to the *Yorde Mer-*
kavah, mystics of the eighth century, who applied their minds to theosophy.
The *Tur* mentions a variant reading, והקטין instead of והתקין, according to
which the clause concerning the moon refers to the talmudic tradition that
God diminished the original size of the moon (Ḥullin 60b). *El Adon* is a praise
of God who created the seven seemingly "wandering" celestial bodies (כוכבי
לכת). Having spoken of the sun and the moon, the poet alludes to the five

besides thee, our King, in the life of the world to come; *there is none but thee,* our Redeemer, in the days of the Messiah; *and there is none like thee,* our Deliverer, during the revival of the dead.

God is the Lord of all creation;
Blessed and praised is he by every soul.
His greatness and goodness fill the universe;
Knowledge and wisdom surround him.

He is exalted above the celestial beings,
And adorned in glory above the chariot.
Purity and justice stand before his throne;
Kindness and mercy are in his glorious presence.

Good are the luminaries which our God has created;
He made them with knowledge, wisdom and insight;
He placed in them energy and power
To have dominion over the world.

Full of splendor, they radiate brightness;
Beautiful is their brilliance throughout the world.
They rejoice in their rising and exult in their setting,
Performing with reverence the will of their Creator.

Glory and honor do they give to his name,
And joyous song to his majestic fame.
He called forth the sun, and it shone;
He saw fit to regulate the form of the moon.

All the hosts of heaven give him praise;
All the celestial beings attribute glory and grandeur—

To God who rested from all the work of creation on the seventh day, and ascended to sit upon his throne of glory. He vested the day of rest with beauty, and called the Sabbath a delight. Such is the distinction of the seventh day, on which God rested from

---

planets Saturn (שבתאי) Venus (נוגה), Mercury (כוכב), Jupiter (צדק), and Mars (מאדים), by means of the initials of the words שבח נותנים כל צבא מרום.

לאל אשר שבת is found in the geonic liturgy. Like the other Sabbath additions to the *Yotser* benediction, it probably belongs to the talmudic period. According to the Midrash, Adam and the Sabbath sang in unison: "It is good to give thanks to the Lord"; hence ויום השביעי משבח ואומר.

מְלַאכְתּוֹ. וְיוֹם הַשְּׁבִיעִי מְשַׁבֵּחַ וְאוֹמֵר: מִזְמוֹר שִׁיר לְיוֹם
הַשַּׁבָּת, טוֹב לְהוֹדוֹת לַיָי. לְפִיכָךְ יְפָאֲרוּ וִיבָרְכוּ לָאֵל כָּל
יְצוּרָיו; שֶׁבַח, יְקָר וּגְדֻלָּה יִתְּנוּ לָאֵל מֶלֶךְ, יוֹצֵר כֹּל, הַמַּנְחִיל
מְנוּחָה לְעַמּוֹ יִשְׂרָאֵל בִּקְדֻשָּׁתוֹ בְּיוֹם שַׁבַּת קֹדֶשׁ. שִׁמְךָ יְיָ
אֱלֹהֵינוּ יִתְקַדָּשׁ, וְזִכְרְךָ מַלְכֵּנוּ יִתְפָּאַר, בַּשָּׁמַיִם מִמַּעַל וְעַל
הָאָרֶץ מִתָּחַת. תִּתְבָּרַךְ, מוֹשִׁיעֵנוּ, עַל שֶׁבַח מַעֲשֵׂה יָדֶיךָ, וְעַל
מְאוֹרֵי אוֹר שֶׁעָשִׂיתָ; יְפָאֲרוּךָ סֶּלָה.

תִּתְבָּרַךְ צוּרֵנוּ, מַלְכֵּנוּ וְגוֹאֲלֵנוּ, בּוֹרֵא קְדוֹשִׁים; יִשְׁתַּבַּח
שִׁמְךָ לָעַד מַלְכֵּנוּ, יוֹצֵר מְשָׁרְתִים, וַאֲשֶׁר מְשָׁרְתָיו כֻּלָּם
עוֹמְדִים בְּרוּם עוֹלָם, וּמַשְׁמִיעִים בְּיִרְאָה, יַחַד בְּקוֹל, דִּבְרֵי
אֱלֹהִים חַיִּים וּמֶלֶךְ עוֹלָם. כֻּלָּם אֲהוּבִים, כֻּלָּם בְּרוּרִים, כֻּלָּם
גִּבּוֹרִים, וְכֻלָּם עֹשִׂים בְּאֵימָה וּבְיִרְאָה רְצוֹן קוֹנָם. Reader וְכֻלָּם
פּוֹתְחִים אֶת פִּיהֶם בִּקְדֻשָּׁה וּבְטָהֳרָה, בְּשִׁירָה וּבְזִמְרָה,
וּמְבָרְכִים וּמְשַׁבְּחִים, וּמְפָאֲרִים וּמַעֲרִיצִים, וּמַקְדִּישִׁים
וּמַמְלִיכִים—

אֶת שֵׁם הָאֵל הַמֶּלֶךְ הַגָּדוֹל, הַגִּבּוֹר וְהַנּוֹרָא, קָדוֹשׁ הוּא.
וְכֻלָּם מְקַבְּלִים עֲלֵיהֶם עֹל מַלְכוּת שָׁמַיִם זֶה מִזֶּה, וְנוֹתְנִים
רְשׁוּת זֶה לָזֶה Reader לְהַקְדִּישׁ לְיוֹצְרָם. בְּנַחַת רוּחַ, בְּשָׂפָה
בְרוּרָה וּבִנְעִימָה קְדֻשָׁה, כֻּלָּם כְּאֶחָד עוֹנִים וְאוֹמְרִים בְּיִרְאָה:
קָדוֹשׁ, קָדוֹשׁ, קָדוֹשׁ יְיָ צְבָאוֹת; מְלֹא כָל הָאָרֶץ כְּבוֹדוֹ.
וְהָאוֹפַנִּים וְחַיּוֹת הַקֹּדֶשׁ, בְּרַעַשׁ גָּדוֹל מִתְנַשְּׂאִים לְעֻמַּת
שְׂרָפִים. Reader לְעֻמָּתָם מְשַׁבְּחִים וְאוֹמְרִים:
בָּרוּךְ כְּבוֹד יְיָ מִמְּקוֹמוֹ.

לָאֵל בָּרוּךְ נְעִימוֹת יִתֵּנוּ; לַמֶּלֶךְ, אֵל חַי וְקַיָּם, זְמִרוֹת
יֹאמֵרוּ, וְתִשְׁבָּחוֹת יַשְׁמִיעוּ; כִּי הוּא לְבַדּוֹ פּוֹעֵל גְּבוּרוֹת, עֹשֶׂה

all his work. The seventh day itself utters praise, saying: "A song of the Sabbath day—It is good to give thanks to the Lord." Therefore, let all God's creatures glorify and bless him; let them attribute excellence, glory and grandeur to God, the King and Creator of all, who in his holiness bestows rest upon his people Israel on the holy Sabbath day. Thy name, Lord our God, shall be hallowed; thy fame, our King, shall be glorified in heaven above and on earth beneath. Be thou blessed, our Deliverer, for thy excellent handiwork, and for the bright luminaries which thou hast made; they ever render thee glory.

Be thou forever blessed, our Stronghold, our King and Redeemer, Creator of holy beings; praised be thy name forever, our King, Creator of ministering angels, all of whom stand in the heights of the universe and reverently proclaim in unison, aloud, the words of the living God and everlasting King. All of them are beloved, all of them are pure, all of them are mighty, all of them are holy; they all perform with awe and reverence the will of their Creator; they all open their mouth with holiness and purity, with song and melody, while they bless and praise, glorify and reverence, sanctify and acclaim—

The name of the great, mighty and revered God and King; holy is he. They all accept the rule of the kingdom of heaven, one from the other, graciously granting permission to one another to hallow their Creator. In serene spirit, with pure speech and sacred melody they all acclaim in unison and with reverence:

Holy, holy, holy is the Lord of hosts;

The whole earth is full of his glory.[1]

Then the celestial spheres and the holy beings, rising with a loud sound toward the seraphim, respond with praise and say:

Blessed be the glory of the Lord from his abode.[2]

To the blessed God they offer melodies; to the King, the living and eternal God, they utter hymns and praises. Truly, he alone performs mighty acts and creates new things; he is a warrior who

---

[1] *Isaiah* 6:3.   [2] *Ezekiel* 3:12.

חֲדָשׁוֹת, בַּעַל מִלְחָמוֹת, זוֹרֵעַ צְדָקוֹת, מַצְמִיחַ יְשׁוּעוֹת, בּוֹרֵא
רְפוּאוֹת, נוֹרָא תְהִלּוֹת, אֲדוֹן הַנִּפְלָאוֹת, הַמְחַדֵּשׁ בְּטוּבוֹ בְּכָל
יוֹם תָּמִיד מַעֲשֵׂה בְרֵאשִׁית, כָּאָמוּר: לְעֹשֵׂה אוֹרִים גְּדֹלִים, כִּי
לְעוֹלָם חַסְדּוֹ. Reader אוֹר חָדָשׁ עַל צִיּוֹן תָּאִיר, וְנִזְכֶּה כֻלָּנוּ
מְהֵרָה לְאוֹרוֹ. בָּרוּךְ אַתָּה, יְיָ, יוֹצֵר הַמְּאוֹרוֹת.

אַהֲבָה רַבָּה אֲהַבְתָּנוּ, יְיָ אֱלֹהֵינוּ; חֶמְלָה גְדוֹלָה וִיתֵרָה
חָמַלְתָּ עָלֵינוּ. אָבִינוּ מַלְכֵּנוּ, בַּעֲבוּר אֲבוֹתֵינוּ שֶׁבָּטְחוּ בְךָ
וַתְּלַמְּדֵם חֻקֵּי חַיִּים, כֵּן תְּחָנֵּנוּ וּתְלַמְּדֵנוּ. אָבִינוּ הָאָב |הָרַחֲמָן,
הַמְרַחֵם, רַחֵם עָלֵינוּ וְתֵן בְּלִבֵּנוּ לְהָבִין וּלְהַשְׂכִּיל, לִשְׁמֹעַ
לִלְמֹד וּלְלַמֵּד, לִשְׁמֹר וְלַעֲשׂוֹת וּלְקַיֵּם אֶת כָּל דִּבְרֵי תַלְמוּד
תּוֹרָתֶךָ, בְּאַהֲבָה. וְהָאֵר עֵינֵינוּ בְּתוֹרָתֶךָ, וְדַבֵּק לִבֵּנוּ בְּמִצְוֹתֶיךָ,
וְיַחֵד לְבָבֵנוּ לְאַהֲבָה וּלְיִרְאָה אֶת שְׁמֶךָ, וְלֹא נֵבוֹשׁ לְעוֹלָם
וָעֶד. כִּי בְשֵׁם קָדְשְׁךָ הַגָּדוֹל וְהַנּוֹרָא בָּטָחְנוּ, נָגִילָה וְנִשְׂמְחָה
בִּישׁוּעָתֶךָ. Reader וַהֲבִיאֵנוּ לְשָׁלוֹם מֵאַרְבַּע כַּנְפוֹת הָאָרֶץ,
וְתוֹלִיכֵנוּ קוֹמְמִיּוּת לְאַרְצֵנוּ. כִּי אֵל פּוֹעֵל יְשׁוּעוֹת אָתָּה, וּבָנוּ
בָחַרְתָּ מִכָּל עַם וְלָשׁוֹן, וְקֵרַבְתָּנוּ לְשִׁמְךָ הַגָּדוֹל סֶלָה בֶּאֱמֶת,
לְהוֹדוֹת לְךָ וּלְיַחֶדְךָ בְּאַהֲבָה. בָּרוּךְ אַתָּה, יְיָ, הַבּוֹחֵר בְּעַמּוֹ
יִשְׂרָאֵל בְּאַהֲבָה.

ללמוד וללמד, to learn and teach, emphasizes one of the greatest Jewish
ideals and aspirations. Rabbi Jacob Anatoli of thirteenth-century Naples, in
his *Malmad ha-Talmidim*, writes to the effect that true wisdom is unselfish,
it craves to be shared. The truly wise man will freely dispense what he himself
has so generously received. Like the prophet of old, he will not be deterred
by any timidity or fear from the exercise of his powers. He will unshrinkingly
speak words of admonition and reproof to the strong and weak alike. For
truth need never tremble, even when great multitudes are arrayed against it.
Now *Torah* implies more than a body of ancient religious lore; it also signifies
a careful probing of the truth embodied in the text, which will disclose its

sows justice, produces triumphs, and creates healing. Revered in renown, Lord of wonders, in his goodness he renews the creation every day, constantly, as it is said: "He makes the great lights; truly, his mercy endures forever."[1] O cause a new light to shine upon Zion, and may we all be worthy soon to enjoy its brightness. Blessed art thou, O Lord, Creator of the lights.

With great love hast thou loved us, Lord our God; great and abundant mercy hast thou bestowed upon us. Our Father, our King, for the sake of our forefathers who trusted in thee, whom thou didst teach laws of life, be gracious to us and teach us likewise. Our Father, merciful Father, thou who art ever compassionate, have pity on us and inspire us to understand and discern, to perceive, learn and teach, to observe, do, and fulfill gladly all the teachings of thy Torah. Enlighten our eyes in thy Torah; attach our heart to thy commandments; unite our heart to love and reverence thy name, so that we may never be put to shame. In thy holy, great and revered name we trust—may we thrill with joy over thy salvation. O bring us home in peace from the four corners of the earth, and make us walk upright to our land, for thou art the God who performs triumphs. Thou hast chosen us from all peoples and nations, and hast truly brought us near to thy great name forever, that we may eagerly praise thee and acclaim thy Oneness. Blessed art thou, O Lord, who hast graciously chosen thy people Israel.

---

deeper meaning and wider application. And what branch of human wisdom is there that can be dispensed with in our endeavor to arrive at a fuller knowledge of God? The chief function of the Torah is to lead man into the path of righteousness. Biblical narratives are not mere reproductions of historical episodes; they teem with lessons of eternal truth. The Torah suggests to us not only our duty as truth-seekers, but also our responsibility as teachers and interpreters of the truth to the people.

יחד לבבנו let our heart be concentrated upon God, and not distracted by worldly desires. Such singleheartedness is frequently expressed by the phrases "a whole heart," "a perfect heart."

---

[1] *Psalm* 136:7.

(אֵל מֶלֶךְ נֶאֱמָן :When praying in private, add)

דברים ו, ד-ט

שְׁמַע יִשְׂרָאֵל, יְיָ אֱלֹהֵינוּ, יְיָ אֶחָד.

בָּרוּךְ שֵׁם כְּבוֹד מַלְכוּתוֹ לְעוֹלָם וָעֶד.

וְאָהַבְתָּ אֵת יְיָ אֱלֹהֶיךָ בְּכָל לְבָבְךָ וּבְכָל נַפְשְׁךָ וּבְכָל
מְאֹדֶךָ. וְהָיוּ הַדְּבָרִים הָאֵלֶּה, אֲשֶׁר אָנֹכִי מְצַוְּךָ הַיּוֹם, עַל
לְבָבֶךָ. וְשִׁנַּנְתָּם לְבָנֶיךָ, וְדִבַּרְתָּ בָּם בְּשִׁבְתְּךָ בְּבֵיתֶךָ, וּבְלֶכְתְּךָ
בַדֶּרֶךְ, וּבְשָׁכְבְּךָ וּבְקוּמֶךָ. וּקְשַׁרְתָּם לְאוֹת עַל יָדֶךָ, וְהָיוּ
לְטֹטָפֹת בֵּין עֵינֶיךָ. וּכְתַבְתָּם עַל מְזֻזוֹת בֵּיתֶךָ וּבִשְׁעָרֶיךָ.

דברים יא, יג-כא

וְהָיָה אִם שָׁמֹעַ תִּשְׁמְעוּ אֶל מִצְוֹתַי, אֲשֶׁר אָנֹכִי מְצַוֶּה אֶתְכֶם
הַיּוֹם, לְאַהֲבָה אֶת יְיָ אֱלֹהֵיכֶם, וּלְעָבְדוֹ בְּכָל לְבַבְכֶם וּבְכָל
נַפְשְׁכֶם. וְנָתַתִּי מְטַר אַרְצְכֶם בְּעִתּוֹ, יוֹרֶה וּמַלְקוֹשׁ; וְאָסַפְתָּ
דְגָנֶךָ, וְתִירֹשְׁךָ וְיִצְהָרֶךָ. וְנָתַתִּי עֵשֶׂב בְּשָׂדְךָ לִבְהֶמְתֶּךָ; וְאָכַלְתָּ
וְשָׂבָעְתָּ. הִשָּׁמְרוּ לָכֶם פֶּן יִפְתֶּה לְבַבְכֶם, וְסַרְתֶּם וַעֲבַדְתֶּם
אֱלֹהִים אֲחֵרִים, וְהִשְׁתַּחֲוִיתֶם לָהֶם. וְחָרָה אַף יְיָ בָּכֶם, וְעָצַר
אֶת הַשָּׁמַיִם וְלֹא יִהְיֶה מָטָר, וְהָאֲדָמָה לֹא תִתֵּן אֶת יְבוּלָהּ;
וַאֲבַדְתֶּם מְהֵרָה מֵעַל הָאָרֶץ הַטֹּבָה אֲשֶׁר יְיָ נֹתֵן לָכֶם. וְשַׂמְתֶּם
אֶת דְּבָרַי אֵלֶּה עַל לְבַבְכֶם וְעַל נַפְשְׁכֶם; וּקְשַׁרְתֶּם אֹתָם לְאוֹת
עַל יֶדְכֶם, וְהָיוּ לְטוֹטָפֹת בֵּין עֵינֵיכֶם. וְלִמַּדְתֶּם אֹתָם אֶת
בְּנֵיכֶם לְדַבֵּר בָּם, בְּשִׁבְתְּךָ בְּבֵיתֶךָ, וּבְלֶכְתְּךָ בַדֶּרֶךְ, וּבְשָׁכְבְּךָ
וּבְקוּמֶךָ. וּכְתַבְתָּם עַל מְזוּזוֹת בֵּיתֶךָ וּבִשְׁעָרֶיךָ.

The initial letters of אל מלך נאמן form the word אמן. There are 245 words
in the *Shema*. When the Reader repeats ה' אלהיכם אמת the number of words is

SHEMA

(*When praying in private, add:* God is a faithful King.)

Deuteronomy 6:4–9

Hear, O Israel, the Lord is our God, the Lord is One.

Blessed be the name of his glorious majesty forever and ever.

You shall love the Lord your God with all your heart, and with all your soul, and with all your might. And these words which I command you today shall be in your heart. You shall teach them diligently to your children, and you shall speak of them when you are sitting at home and when you go on a journey, when you lie down and when you rise up. You shall bind them for a sign on your hand, and they shall be for frontlets between your eyes. You shall inscribe them on the doorposts of your house and on your gates.

Deuteronomy 11:13–21

And if you will carefully obey my commands which I give you today, to love the Lord your God and to serve him with all your heart and with all your soul, I will give rain for your land at the right season, the autumn rains and the spring rains, that you may gather in your grain, your wine and your oil. And I will provide grass in your fields for your cattle, and you will eat and be satisfied. Beware lest your heart be deceived, and you turn and serve other gods and worship them; for then the Lord's anger will blaze against you, and he will shut up the skies so that there will be no rain, and the land will yield no produce, and you will quickly perish from the good land which the Lord gives you. So you shall place these words of mine in your heart and in your soul, and you shall bind them for a sign on your hand, and they shall be for frontlets between your eyes. You shall teach them to your children, speaking of them when you are sitting at home and when you go on a journey, when you lie down and when you rise up. You shall inscribe them on the doorposts of your house and on your gates—

---

raised to 248, corresponding to the 248 parts of the human frame. On reciting the *Shema* privately, however, one is required to add the three words אל מלך נאמן in order to complete the number 248.

לְמַעַן יִרְבּוּ יְמֵיכֶם וִימֵי בְנֵיכֶם, עַל הָאֲדָמָה אֲשֶׁר נִשְׁבַּע
יְיָ לַאֲבֹתֵיכֶם לָתֵת לָהֶם, כִּימֵי הַשָּׁמַיִם עַל הָאָרֶץ.

במדבר טו, לז-מא

וַיֹּאמֶר יְיָ אֶל מֹשֶׁה לֵּאמֹר: דַּבֵּר אֶל בְּנֵי יִשְׂרָאֵל וְאָמַרְתָּ
אֲלֵהֶם, וְעָשׂוּ לָהֶם צִיצִת עַל כַּנְפֵי בִגְדֵיהֶם לְדֹרֹתָם, וְנָתְנוּ עַל
צִיצִת הַכָּנָף פְּתִיל תְּכֵלֶת. וְהָיָה לָכֶם לְצִיצִת, וּרְאִיתֶם אֹתוֹ
וּזְכַרְתֶּם אֶת כָּל מִצְוֹת יְיָ, וַעֲשִׂיתֶם אֹתָם; וְלֹא תָתוּרוּ אַחֲרֵי
לְבַבְכֶם וְאַחֲרֵי עֵינֵיכֶם, אֲשֶׁר אַתֶּם זֹנִים אַחֲרֵיהֶם. לְמַעַן
תִּזְכְּרוּ וַעֲשִׂיתֶם אֶת כָּל מִצְוֹתָי, וִהְיִיתֶם קְדֹשִׁים לֵאלֹהֵיכֶם.
אֲנִי יְיָ אֱלֹהֵיכֶם, אֲשֶׁר הוֹצֵאתִי אֶתְכֶם מֵאֶרֶץ מִצְרַיִם לִהְיוֹת
לָכֶם לֵאלֹהִים; Reader אֲנִי יְיָ אֱלֹהֵיכֶם—

אֱמֶת וְיַצִּיב, וְנָכוֹן וְקַיָּם, וְיָשָׁר וְנֶאֱמָן, וְאָהוּב וְחָבִיב, וְנֶחְמָד
וְנָעִים, וְנוֹרָא וְאַדִּיר, וּמְתֻקָּן וּמְקֻבָּל, וְטוֹב וְיָפֶה הַדָּבָר הַזֶּה
עָלֵינוּ לְעוֹלָם וָעֶד. אֱמֶת, אֱלֹהֵי עוֹלָם מַלְכֵּנוּ, צוּר יַעֲקֹב מָגֵן
יִשְׁעֵנוּ. Reader לְדֹר וָדֹר הוּא קַיָּם, וּשְׁמוֹ קַיָּם, וְכִסְאוֹ נָכוֹן,
וּמַלְכוּתוֹ וֶאֱמוּנָתוֹ לָעַד קַיֶּמֶת. וּדְבָרָיו חָיִים וְקַיָּמִים, נֶאֱמָנִים
וְנֶחֱמָדִים, לָעַד וּלְעוֹלְמֵי עוֹלָמִים, עַל אֲבוֹתֵינוּ וְעָלֵינוּ, עַל
בָּנֵינוּ וְעַל דּוֹרוֹתֵינוּ, וְעַל כָּל דּוֹרוֹת זֶרַע יִשְׂרָאֵל עֲבָדֶיךָ.

עַל הָרִאשׁוֹנִים וְעַל הָאַחֲרוֹנִים דָּבָר טוֹב וְקַיָּם לְעוֹלָם
וָעֶד, אֱמֶת וֶאֱמוּנָה, חֹק וְלֹא יַעֲבֹר. Reader אֱמֶת, שָׁאַתָּה הוּא
יְיָ אֱלֹהֵינוּ וֵאלֹהֵי אֲבוֹתֵינוּ, מַלְכֵּנוּ מֶלֶךְ אֲבוֹתֵינוּ, גֹּאֲלֵנוּ גֹּאֵל
אֲבוֹתֵינוּ, יוֹצְרֵנוּ צוּר יְשׁוּעָתֵנוּ, פּוֹדֵנוּ וּמַצִּילֵנוּ; מֵעוֹלָם שְׁמֶךָ,
אֵין אֱלֹהִים זוּלָתֶךָ.

אמת ויציב is mentioned in the Mishnah (Tamid 5:1) among the prayers
used in the Temple. The fifteen synonyms, ויציב–ויפה, correspond to the fifteen
words in the last sentence of the *Shema*, beginning with אני.

That your life and the life of your children may be prolonged in the land, which the Lord promised he would give to your
fathers, as long as the sky remains over the earth.

Numbers 15:37–41

The Lord spoke to Moses, saying: Speak to the children of
Israel and tell them to make for themselves fringes on the corners
of their garments throughout their generations, and to put on the
fringe of each corner a blue thread. You shall have it as a fringe,
so that when you look upon it you will remember to do all the
commands of the Lord, and you will not follow the desires of your
heart and your eyes which lead you astray. It is for you to remember and do all my commands and be holy to your God.
I am the Lord your God who brought you out of the land of Egypt
to be your God; I am the Lord your God.

True and certain, established and enduring, right and steadfast,
beloved and precious, pleasant and sweet, revered and glorious,
correct and acceptable, good and beautiful is this faith to us forever and ever. True it is that the eternal God is our King, the
Stronghold of Jacob and our saving Shield. He exists throughout
all generations; his name endures; his throne is firm; his kingship and his truth are forever established. His words are living
and enduring, faithful and precious, forever and to all eternity, as
for our fathers so also for us, for our children and future generations, and for all generations of the seed of Israel his servants.

Alike for the first and the last generations this faith is good
and valid forever and ever; it is true and trustworthy, a law that
will not pass away. True it is that thou art the Lord our God and
the God of our fathers, our King and the King of our fathers, our
Redeemer and the Redeemer of our fathers, our Maker and saving
Stronghold, our Deliverer and Rescuer. Thou art eternal; there is
no God besides thee.

The rule is not to interrupt the connection between אלהיכם ה׳ and אמת,
as if these three words formed one sentence, meaning: "The Lord your God
is true" (Mishnah Berakhoth 2:2).

הדבר הוה refers to the *Shema* as a solemn profession of the Oneness of God.
The *Shema* is the watchword of Israel's faith, and it is the desire of every
loyal Jew to have it upon his lips when he dies.

עֶזְרַת אֲבוֹתֵינוּ אַתָּה הוּא מֵעוֹלָם, מָגֵן וּמוֹשִׁיעַ לִבְנֵיהֶם
אַחֲרֵיהֶם בְּכָל דּוֹר וָדוֹר. בְּרוּם עוֹלָם מוֹשָׁבֶךָ, וּמִשְׁפָּטֶיךָ
וְצִדְקָתְךָ עַד אַפְסֵי אָרֶץ. אַשְׁרֵי אִישׁ שֶׁיִּשְׁמַע לְמִצְוֹתֶיךָ,
וְתוֹרָתְךָ וּדְבָרְךָ יָשִׂים עַל לִבּוֹ. אֱמֶת, אַתָּה הוּא אָדוֹן לְעַמֶּךָ,
וּמֶלֶךְ גִּבּוֹר לָרִיב רִיבָם. אֱמֶת, אַתָּה הוּא רִאשׁוֹן וְאַתָּה הוּא
אַחֲרוֹן, וּמִבַּלְעָדֶיךָ אֵין לָנוּ מֶלֶךְ גּוֹאֵל וּמוֹשִׁיעַ. מִמִּצְרַיִם
גְּאַלְתָּנוּ, יְיָ אֱלֹהֵינוּ, וּמִבֵּית עֲבָדִים פְּדִיתָנוּ. כָּל בְּכוֹרֵיהֶם
הָרָגְתָּ, וּבְכוֹרְךָ גָּאָלְתָּ, וְיַם סוּף בָּקַעְתָּ, וְזֵדִים טִבַּעְתָּ, וִידִידִים
הֶעֱבַרְתָּ; וַיְכַסּוּ מַיִם צָרֵיהֶם, אֶחָד מֵהֶם לֹא נוֹתָר. עַל זֹאת
שִׁבְּחוּ אֲהוּבִים וְרוֹמְמוּ אֵל, וְנָתְנוּ יְדִידִים זְמִירוֹת, שִׁירוֹת
וְתִשְׁבָּחוֹת, בְּרָכוֹת וְהוֹדָאוֹת לַמֶּלֶךְ, אֵל חַי וְקַיָּם. רָם וְנִשָּׂא,
גָּדוֹל וְנוֹרָא, מַשְׁפִּיל גֵּאִים וּמַגְבִּיהַּ שְׁפָלִים, מוֹצִיא אֲסִירִים
וּפוֹדֶה עֲנָוִים, וְעוֹזֵר דַּלִּים, וְעוֹנֶה לְעַמּוֹ בְּעֵת שַׁוְּעָם אֵלָיו.
תְּהִלּוֹת לְאֵל עֶלְיוֹן, בָּרוּךְ הוּא וּמְבֹרָךְ.

מֹשֶׁה וּבְנֵי יִשְׂרָאֵל לְךָ עָנוּ שִׁירָה בְּשִׂמְחָה רַבָּה, וְאָמְרוּ כֻלָּם:
מִי כָמֹכָה בָּאֵלִם, יְיָ; מִי כָּמֹכָה נֶאְדָּר בַּקֹּדֶשׁ, נוֹרָא תְהִלֹּת,
עֹשֵׂה פֶלֶא.

שִׁירָה חֲדָשָׁה שִׁבְּחוּ גְאוּלִים לְשִׁמְךָ עַל שְׂפַת הַיָּם; יַחַד
כֻּלָּם הוֹדוּ וְהִמְלִיכוּ וְאָמְרוּ:
יְיָ יִמְלֹךְ לְעוֹלָם וָעֶד.

צוּר יִשְׂרָאֵל, קוּמָה בְּעֶזְרַת יִשְׂרָאֵל, וּפְדֵה כִנְאֻמְךָ יְהוּדָה
וְיִשְׂרָאֵל. Reader גֹּאֲלֵנוּ יְיָ צְבָאוֹת שְׁמוֹ, קְדוֹשׁ יִשְׂרָאֵל. בָּרוּךְ
אַתָּה, יְיָ, גָּאַל יִשְׂרָאֵל.

Thou wast the help of our fathers from of old, and hast been a Shield and Savior to their children after them in every generation. In the heights of the universe is thy habitation, and thy justice and righteousness reach to the furthest ends of the earth. Happy is the man who obeys thy commands and takes thy Torah and thy word to heart. True it is that thou art the Lord of thy people, and a mighty King to champion their cause. True it is that thou art the first and thou art the last, and besides thee we have no King who redeems and saves. From Egypt thou didst redeem us, Lord our God, and from the house of slavery thou didst deliver us; all their first-born thou didst slay, but thy first-born thou didst redeem; thou didst divide the Red Sea and drown the arrogant, but thy beloved people thou didst take across; the water covered their enemies, not one of them was left.

For this, the beloved people praised and extolled God; they offered hymns, blessings and thanksgivings to the King, the living and eternal God. He is high and exalted, great and revered; he brings low the arrogant, and raises up the lowly; he frees the captives, and delivers the afflicted; he helps the poor, and answers his people whenever they cry to him. Praised be the supreme God; be he ever blessed.

Moses and the children of Israel sang a song to thee with great joy; all of them said:

"Who is like thee, O Lord, among the mighty?

Who is like thee, glorious in holiness,

Awe-inspiring in renown, doing wonders?"[1]

The redeemed people sang a new song of praise to thy name at the seashore; they all, in unison, gave thanks and proclaimed thy sovereignty, and said:

"The Lord shall reign forever and ever."[2]

Protector of Israel, arise to the aid of Israel; deliver Judah and Israel, as thou hast promised. Our Redeemer, thou art the Lord of hosts, the Holy One of Israel. Blessed art thou, O Lord, who hast redeemed Israel.

---

[1] *Exodus* 15:11.   [2] *Exodus* 15:18.

The *Amidah* is recited in silent devotion while standing, facing east.

אֲדֹנָי, שְׂפָתַי תִּפְתָּח, וּפִי יַגִּיד תְּהִלָּתֶךָ.

בָּרוּךְ אַתָּה, יְיָ אֱלֹהֵינוּ וֵאלֹהֵי אֲבוֹתֵינוּ, אֱלֹהֵי אַבְרָהָם,
אֱלֹהֵי יִצְחָק, וֵאלֹהֵי יַעֲקֹב, הָאֵל הַגָּדוֹל הַגִּבּוֹר וְהַנּוֹרָא, אֵל
עֶלְיוֹן, גּוֹמֵל חֲסָדִים טוֹבִים, וְקוֹנֵה הַכֹּל, וְזוֹכֵר חַסְדֵי אָבוֹת,
וּמֵבִיא גוֹאֵל לִבְנֵי בְנֵיהֶם לְמַעַן שְׁמוֹ בְּאַהֲבָה.

מֶלֶךְ עוֹזֵר וּמוֹשִׁיעַ וּמָגֵן. בָּרוּךְ אַתָּה, יְיָ, מָגֵן אַבְרָהָם.

אַתָּה גִּבּוֹר לְעוֹלָם, אֲדֹנָי; מְחַיֵּה מֵתִים אַתָּה, רַב לְהוֹשִׁיעַ.

מְכַלְכֵּל חַיִּים בְּחֶסֶד, מְחַיֵּה מֵתִים בְּרַחֲמִים רַבִּים, סוֹמֵךְ
נוֹפְלִים, וְרוֹפֵא חוֹלִים, וּמַתִּיר אֲסוּרִים, וּמְקַיֵּם אֱמוּנָתוֹ לִישֵׁנֵי
עָפָר. מִי כָמוֹךָ, בַּעַל גְּבוּרוֹת, וּמִי דּוֹמֶה לָךְ, מֶלֶךְ מֵמִית
וּמְחַיֶּה וּמַצְמִיחַ יְשׁוּעָה.

וְנֶאֱמָן אַתָּה לְהַחֲיוֹת מֵתִים. בָּרוּךְ אַתָּה, יְיָ, מְחַיֵּה הַמֵּתִים.

אַתָּה קָדוֹשׁ וְשִׁמְךָ קָדוֹשׁ, וּקְדוֹשִׁים בְּכָל יוֹם יְהַלְלוּךָ סֶּלָה.
בָּרוּךְ אַתָּה, יְיָ, הָאֵל הַקָּדוֹשׁ.

When the Reader repeats the Shemoneh Esreh, the following Kedushah is said:

נְקַדֵּשׁ אֶת שִׁמְךָ בָּעוֹלָם כְּשֵׁם שֶׁמַּקְדִּישִׁים אוֹתוֹ בִּשְׁמֵי מָרוֹם,
כַּכָּתוּב עַל יַד נְבִיאֶךָ: וְקָרָא זֶה אֶל זֶה וְאָמַר:

קָדוֹשׁ, קָדוֹשׁ, קָדוֹשׁ יְיָ צְבָאוֹת; מְלֹא כָל הָאָרֶץ כְּבוֹדוֹ.

אָז בְּקוֹל רַעַשׁ גָּדוֹל, אַדִּיר וְחָזָק, מַשְׁמִיעִים קוֹל; מִתְנַשְּׂאִים
לְעֻמַּת שְׂרָפִים, לְעֻמָּתָם בָּרוּךְ יֹאמֵרוּ:

בָּרוּךְ כְּבוֹד יְיָ מִמְּקוֹמוֹ.

מִמְּקוֹמְךָ מַלְכֵּנוּ תוֹפִיעַ וְתִמְלֹךְ עָלֵינוּ, כִּי מְחַכִּים אֲנַחְנוּ
לָךְ. מָתַי תִּמְלֹךְ בְּצִיּוֹן, בְּקָרוֹב בְּיָמֵינוּ לְעוֹלָם וָעֶד תִּשְׁכֹּן.

The Amidah is recited in silent devotion while standing, facing east.

O Lord, open thou my lips, that my mouth may declare thy praise.[1]

Blessed art thou, Lord our God and God of our fathers, God of Abraham, God of Isaac and God of Jacob; great, mighty and revered God, sublime God, who bestowest lovingkindness, and art Master of all things; who rememberest the good deeds of our fathers, and who wilt graciously bring a redeemer to their children's children for the sake of thy name.

O King, Supporter, Savior and Shield. Blessed art thou, O Lord, Shield of Abraham.

Thou, O Lord, art mighty forever; thou revivest the dead; thou art powerful to save.

Thou sustainest the living with kindness, and revivest the dead with great mercy; thou supportest all who fall, and healest the sick; thou settest the captives free, and keepest faith with those who sleep in the dust. Who is like thee, Lord of power? Who resembles thee, O King? Thou bringest death and restorest life, and causest salvation to flourish.

Thou art faithful to revive the dead. Blessed art thou, O Lord, who revivest the dead.

Thou art holy and thy name is holy, and holy beings praise thee daily. Blessed art thou, O Lord, holy God.

When the Reader repeats the *Shemoneh Esreh*, the following *Kedushah* is said:

We sanctify thy name in this world even as they sanctify it in the highest heavens, as it is written by thy prophet: "They keep calling to one another:

Kodosh kodosh kodosh adonoy ts'vo-os
M'lo chol ho-orets k'vodo.[2]

Boruch k'vod adonoy mim-komo.[3]

Mim-kom'cho malkeynu so-fee-ah v'sim-loch oleynu
Kee m'chakkeem anachnu loch.

ממקומך מלכנו is included in the weekday *Kedushah* in the *Siddur* of Amram Gaon with some variations: ... בקרוב בימינו ובחיינו תשכן ... תופיע ותושיענו.

[1]*Psalm* 15:11.   [2]*Isaiah* 6:3.   [3]*Ezekiel* 3:12.

תִּתְגַּדַּל וְתִתְקַדַּשׁ בְּתוֹךְ יְרוּשָׁלַיִם עִירְךָ לְדוֹר וָדוֹר וּלְנֵצַח נְצָחִים. וְעֵינֵינוּ תִרְאֶינָה מַלְכוּתֶךָ, כַּדָּבָר הָאָמוּר בְּשִׁירֵי עֻזֶּךָ, עַל יְדֵי דָוִד מְשִׁיחַ צִדְקֶךָ:

יִמְלֹךְ יְיָ לְעוֹלָם, אֱלֹהַיִךְ צִיּוֹן לְדֹר וָדֹר; הַלְלוּיָהּ.

Reader:

לְדוֹר וָדוֹר נַגִּיד גָּדְלֶךָ, וּלְנֵצַח נְצָחִים קְדֻשָּׁתְךָ נַקְדִּישׁ, וְשִׁבְחֲךָ אֱלֹהֵינוּ מִפִּינוּ לֹא יָמוּשׁ לְעוֹלָם וָעֶד, כִּי אֵל מֶלֶךְ גָּדוֹל וְקָדוֹשׁ אָתָּה. בָּרוּךְ אַתָּה, יְיָ, הָאֵל הַקָּדוֹשׁ.

אַתָּה בְחַרְתָּנוּ מִכָּל הָעַמִּים, אָהַבְתָּ אוֹתָנוּ וְרָצִיתָ בָּנוּ, וְרוֹמַמְתָּנוּ מִכָּל הַלְּשׁוֹנוֹת, וְקִדַּשְׁתָּנוּ בְּמִצְוֹתֶיךָ, וְקֵרַבְתָּנוּ מַלְכֵּנוּ לַעֲבוֹדָתֶךָ, וְשִׁמְךָ הַגָּדוֹל וְהַקָּדוֹשׁ עָלֵינוּ קָרָאתָ.

וַתִּתֶּן־לָנוּ, יְיָ אֱלֹהֵינוּ, בְּאַהֲבָה (שַׁבָּתוֹת לִמְנוּחָה וּ)מוֹעֲדִים לְשִׂמְחָה, חַגִּים וּזְמַנִּים לְשָׂשׂוֹן, אֶת יוֹם (הַשַּׁבָּת הַזֶּה וְאֶת יוֹם) חַג הַשָּׁבֻעוֹת הַזֶּה, זְמַן מַתַּן תּוֹרָתֵנוּ, (בְּאַהֲבָה) מִקְרָא קֹדֶשׁ, זֵכֶר לִיצִיאַת מִצְרָיִם.

אֱלֹהֵינוּ וֵאלֹהֵי אֲבוֹתֵינוּ, יַעֲלֶה וְיָבֹא, וְיַגִּיעַ וְיֵרָאֶה, וְיֵרָצֶה וְיִשָּׁמַע, וְיִפָּקֵד וְיִזָּכֵר, זִכְרוֹנֵנוּ וּפִקְדוֹנֵנוּ, וְזִכְרוֹן אֲבוֹתֵינוּ, וְזִכְרוֹן מָשִׁיחַ בֶּן־דָּוִד עַבְדֶּךָ, וְזִכְרוֹן יְרוּשָׁלַיִם עִיר קָדְשֶׁךָ, וְזִכְרוֹן כָּל עַמְּךָ בֵּית יִשְׂרָאֵל לְפָנֶיךָ, לִפְלֵיטָה וּלְטוֹבָה, לְחֵן וּלְחֶסֶד וּלְרַחֲמִים, לְחַיִּים וּלְשָׁלוֹם, בְּיוֹם חַג הַשָּׁבֻעוֹת הַזֶּה. זָכְרֵנוּ, יְיָ אֱלֹהֵינוּ, בּוֹ לְטוֹבָה, וּפָקְדֵנוּ בוֹ לִבְרָכָה, וְהוֹשִׁיעֵנוּ בוֹ לְחַיִּים; וּבִדְבַר יְשׁוּעָה וְרַחֲמִים חוּס וְחָנֵּנוּ, וְרַחֵם עָלֵינוּ וְהוֹשִׁיעֵנוּ, כִּי אֵלֶיךָ עֵינֵינוּ, כִּי אֵל מֶלֶךְ חַנּוּן וְרַחוּם אָתָּה.

וְהַשִּׂיאֵנוּ, יְיָ אֱלֹהֵינוּ, אֶת בִּרְכַּת מוֹעֲדֶיךָ לְחַיִּים וּלְשָׁלוֹם, לְשִׂמְחָה וּלְשָׂשׂוֹן, כַּאֲשֶׁר רָצִיתָ וְאָמַרְתָּ לְבָרְכֵנוּ. אֱלֹהֵינוּ וֵאלֹהֵי אֲבוֹתֵינוּ, (רְצֵה בִמְנוּחָתֵנוּ) קַדְּשֵׁנוּ בְּמִצְוֹתֶיךָ וְתֵן חֶלְקֵנוּ

Mosai tim-loch b'tsee-yon
B'korov b'yomeynu l'olom vo-ed tish-kon.
Tis-gaddal v'sis-kaddash b'soch y'rusholayim eer-cho
L'dor vodor ul'neytsach n'tsocheem.
V'ey-neynu sir-enoh malchu-secho
Ka-dovor ho-omur b'sheerey uzecho
Al y'dey Dovid m'shee-ach tsid-kecho.

Yimloch adonoy l'olom, elohayich tsee-yon l'dor vodor. Hallelu-yoh.

Reader:

Through all generations we will declare thy greatness; to all eternity we will proclaim thy holiness; thy praise, our God, shall never depart from our mouth, for thou art a great and holy God and King. Blessed art thou, O Lord, holy God.

Thou didst choose us from among all peoples; thou didst love and favor us; thou didst exalt us above all tongues and sanctify us with thy commandments. Thou, our King, didst draw us near to thy service and call us by thy great and holy name.

Thou, Lord our God, hast graciously given us (Sabbaths for rest,) holidays for gladness, festive seasons for joy: (this Sabbath day and) this Feast of Weeks, our Festival of the Giving of the Torah, a holy convocation in remembrance of the exodus from Egypt.

Our God and God of our fathers, may the remembrance of us, of our fathers, of Messiah the son of David thy servant, of Jerusalem thy holy city, and of all thy people the house of Israel, ascend and come and be accepted before thee for deliverance and happiness, for grace, kindness and mercy, for life and peace, on this day of the Feast of Weeks.

Remember us this day, Lord our God, for happiness; be mindful of us for blessing; save us to enjoy life. With a promise of salvation and mercy spare us and be gracious to us; have pity on us and save us, for we look to thee, for thou art a gracious and merciful God and King.

Bestow on us, Lord our God, the blessings of thy festivals for life and peace, for joy and gladness, as thou didst promise to bless us. Our God and God of our Fathers, (be pleased with our rest)

בְּתוֹרָתֶךָ, שַׂבְּעֵנוּ מִטּוּבֶךָ, וְשַׂמְּחֵנוּ בִּישׁוּעָתֶךָ, וְטַהֵר לִבֵּנוּ
לְעָבְדְּךָ בֶּאֱמֶת; וְהַנְחִילֵנוּ, יְיָ אֱלֹהֵינוּ (בְּאַהֲבָה וּבְרָצוֹן)
בְּשִׂמְחָה וּבְשָׂשׂוֹן (שַׁבָּת וּ)מוֹעֲדֵי קָדְשֶׁךָ, וְיִשְׂמְחוּ בְךָ יִשְׂרָאֵל
מְקַדְּשֵׁי שְׁמֶךָ. בָּרוּךְ אַתָּה, יְיָ, מְקַדֵּשׁ (הַשַּׁבָּת וְ)יִשְׂרָאֵל
וְהַזְּמַנִּים.

רְצֵה, יְיָ אֱלֹהֵינוּ, בְּעַמְּךָ יִשְׂרָאֵל וּבִתְפִלָּתָם; וְהָשֵׁב אֶת
הָעֲבוֹדָה לִדְבִיר בֵּיתֶךָ, וְאִשֵּׁי יִשְׂרָאֵל וּתְפִלָּתָם בְּאַהֲבָה
תְקַבֵּל בְּרָצוֹן, וּתְהִי לְרָצוֹן תָּמִיד עֲבוֹדַת יִשְׂרָאֵל עַמֶּךָ.

וְתֶחֱזֶינָה עֵינֵינוּ בְּשׁוּבְךָ לְצִיּוֹן בְּרַחֲמִים. בָּרוּךְ אַתָּה, יְיָ,
הַמַּחֲזִיר שְׁכִינָתוֹ לְצִיּוֹן.

מוֹדִים אֲנַחְנוּ לָךְ, שָׁאַתָּה
הוּא יְיָ אֱלֹהֵינוּ וֵאלֹהֵי אֲבוֹתֵינוּ
לְעוֹלָם וָעֶד. צוּר חַיֵּינוּ, מָגֵן
יִשְׁעֵנוּ, אַתָּה הוּא. לְדוֹר וָדוֹר
נוֹדֶה לְּךָ, וּנְסַפֵּר תְּהִלָּתֶךָ, עַל
חַיֵּינוּ הַמְּסוּרִים בְּיָדֶךָ, וְעַל
נִשְׁמוֹתֵינוּ הַפְּקוּדוֹת לָךְ, וְעַל
נִסֶּיךָ שֶׁבְּכָל יוֹם עִמָּנוּ, וְעַל
נִפְלְאוֹתֶיךָ וְטוֹבוֹתֶיךָ שֶׁבְּכָל
עֵת, עֶרֶב וָבְקֶר וְצָהֳרָיִם.
הַטּוֹב כִּי לֹא כָלוּ רַחֲמֶיךָ,
וְהַמְרַחֵם כִּי לֹא תַמּוּ חֲסָדֶיךָ,
מֵעוֹלָם קִוִּינוּ לָךְ.

*While the Reader recites Modim,
the Congregation reads:*

מוֹדִים אֲנַחְנוּ לָךְ, שָׁאַתָּה
הוּא יְיָ אֱלֹהֵינוּ וֵאלֹהֵי
אֲבוֹתֵינוּ. אֱלֹהֵי כָל בָּשָׂר,
יוֹצְרֵנוּ, יוֹצֵר בְּרֵאשִׁית,
בְּרָכוֹת וְהוֹדָאוֹת לְשִׁמְךָ
הַגָּדוֹל וְהַקָּדוֹשׁ עַל שֶׁהֶחֱיִיתָנוּ
וְקִיַּמְתָּנוּ. כֵּן תְּחַיֵּנוּ וּתְקַיְּמֵנוּ,
וְתֶאֱסוֹף גָּלֻיּוֹתֵינוּ לְחַצְרוֹת
קָדְשֶׁךָ לִשְׁמוֹר חֻקֶּיךָ וְלַעֲשׂוֹת
רְצוֹנֶךָ, וּלְעָבְדְּךָ בְּלֵבָב
שָׁלֵם, עַל שֶׁאֲנַחְנוּ מוֹדִים לָךְ.
בָּרוּךְ אֵל הַהוֹדָאוֹת.

sanctify us with thy commandments and grant us a share in thy Torah; satisfy us with thy goodness and gladden us with thy help; purify our heart to serve thee sincerely. In thy gracious love, Lord our God, grant us thy holy (Sabbath and) festivals for gladness and joy; may Israel who sanctifies thy name rejoice in thee. Blessed art thou, O Lord, who hallowest (the Sabbath and) Israel and the festivals.

Be pleased, Lord our God, with thy people Israel and with their prayer; restore the worship to thy most holy sanctuary; accept Israel's offerings and prayer with gracious love. May the worship of thy people Israel be ever pleasing to thee.

May our eyes behold thy return in mercy to Zion. Blessed art thou, O Lord, who restorest thy divine presence to Zion.

We ever thank thee, who art the Lord our God and the God of our fathers. Thou art the strength of our life and our saving shield. In every generation we will thank thee and recount thy praise—for our lives which are in thy charge, for our souls which are in thy care, for thy miracles which are daily with us, and for thy continual wonders and favors—evening, morning and noon. Beneficent One, whose mercies never fail, Merciful One, whose kindnesses never cease, thou hast always been our hope.

While the Reader recites Modim, the Congregation reads:

(We thank thee, who art the Lord our God and the God of our fathers. God of all mankind, our Creator and Creator of the universe, blessings and thanks are due to thy great and holy name, because thou hast kept us alive and sustained us; mayest thou ever grant us life and sustenance. O gather our exiles to thy holy courts to observe thy laws, to do thy will, and to serve thee with a perfect heart. For this we thank thee. Blessed be God to whom all thanks are due.)

וְעַל כֻּלָּם יִתְבָּרַךְ וְיִתְרוֹמַם שִׁמְךָ, מַלְכֵּנוּ, תָּמִיד לְעוֹלָם וָעֶד.

וְכֹל הַחַיִּים יוֹדֽוּךָ סֶּלָה, וִיהַלְלוּ אֶת שִׁמְךָ בֶּאֱמֶת, הָאֵל, יְשׁוּעָתֵנוּ וְעֶזְרָתֵנוּ סֶלָה. בָּרוּךְ אַתָּה, יְיָ, הַטּוֹב שִׁמְךָ, וּלְךָ נָאֶה לְהוֹדוֹת.

Priestly blessing recited by the Reader:

אֱלֹהֵֽינוּ וֵאלֹהֵי אֲבוֹתֵֽינוּ, בָּרְכֵֽנוּ בַבְּרָכָה הַמְשֻׁלֶּֽשֶׁת בַּתּוֹרָה, הַכְּתוּבָה עַל יְדֵי מֹשֶׁה עַבְדֶּֽךָ, הָאֲמוּרָה מִפִּי אַהֲרֹן וּבָנָיו, כֹּהֲנִים עַם קְדוֹשֶֽׁךָ, כָּאָמוּר: יְבָרֶכְךָ יְיָ וְיִשְׁמְרֶֽךָ. יָאֵר יְיָ פָּנָיו אֵלֶֽיךָ וִיחֻנֶּֽךָּ. יִשָּׂא יְיָ פָּנָיו אֵלֶֽיךָ, וְיָשֵׂם לְךָ שָׁלוֹם.

שִׂים שָׁלוֹם, טוֹבָה וּבְרָכָה, חֵן וָחֶֽסֶד וְרַחֲמִים, עָלֵֽינוּ וְעַל כָּל יִשְׂרָאֵל עַמֶּֽךָ. בָּרְכֵֽנוּ אָבִֽינוּ, כֻּלָּֽנוּ כְּאֶחָד, בְּאוֹר פָּנֶֽיךָ; כִּי בְאוֹר פָּנֶֽיךָ נָתַֽתָּ לָּֽנוּ, יְיָ אֱלֹהֵֽינוּ, תּוֹרַת חַיִּים וְאַהֲבַת חֶֽסֶד, וּצְדָקָה וּבְרָכָה וְרַחֲמִים, וְחַיִּים וְשָׁלוֹם. וְטוֹב בְּעֵינֶֽיךָ לְבָרֵךְ אֶת עַמְּךָ יִשְׂרָאֵל בְּכָל עֵת וּבְכָל שָׁעָה בִּשְׁלוֹמֶֽךָ. בָּרוּךְ אַתָּה, יְיָ, הַמְבָרֵךְ אֶת עַמּוֹ יִשְׂרָאֵל בַּשָּׁלוֹם.

After the *Amidah* add the following meditation:

אֱלֹהַי, נְצֹר לְשׁוֹנִי מֵרָע, וּשְׂפָתַי מִדַּבֵּר מִרְמָה, וְלִמְקַלְלַי נַפְשִׁי תִדּוֹם, וְנַפְשִׁי כֶּעָפָר לַכֹּל תִּהְיֶה. פְּתַח לִבִּי בְּתוֹרָתֶֽךָ, וּבְמִצְוֹתֶֽיךָ תִּרְדּוֹף נַפְשִׁי; וְכֹל הַחוֹשְׁבִים עָלַי רָעָה, מְהֵרָה הָפֵר עֲצָתָם וְקַלְקֵל מַחֲשַׁבְתָּם. עֲשֵׂה לְמַֽעַן שְׁמֶֽךָ, עֲשֵׂה לְמַֽעַן יְמִינֶֽךָ, עֲשֵׂה לְמַֽעַן קְדֻשָּׁתֶֽךָ, עֲשֵׂה לְמַֽעַן תּוֹרָתֶֽךָ. לְמַֽעַן יֵחָלְצוּן

שׁים שׁלום refers directly to the priestly blessing which ends with the word שׁלום. This paragraph, which was recited daily in the Temple as part of the priestly blessing, has come down to us with occasional variations. In the ninth century Siddur of Rav Amram Gaon, for example, the reading is אהבה וחסד instead of אהבת חסד. In place of תורת חיים, Maimonides and other authorities read תורה וחיים.

For all these acts may thy name, our King, be blessed and exalted forever and ever.

All the living shall ever thank thee and sincerely praise thy name, O God, who art always our salvation and help. Blessed art thou, O Lord, Beneficent One, to whom it is fitting to give thanks.

Priestly blessing recited by Reader:

Our God and God of our fathers, bless us with the threefold blessing written in thy Torah by thy servant Moses and spoken by Aaron and his sons the priests, thy holy people, as it is said: "May the Lord bless you and protect you; may the Lord countenance you and be gracious to you; may the Lord favor you and grant you peace."

O grant peace and a life of happiness and blessedness, a life of grace, kindness and mercy, to us and to all Israel thy people. Bless us all alike, our Father, with the light of thy countenance. Truly, by the light of thy countenance thou hast given us, Lord our God, a Torah of life and lovingkindness, uprightness and blessedness, mercy, life and peace. May it please thee to bless us and all thy people Israel with thy peace at all times and at all hours. Blessed art thou, O Lord, who blessest thy people Israel with peace.

After the Amidah add the following meditation:

My God, guard my tongue from evil, and my lips from speaking falsehood. May my soul be silent to those who insult me; be my soul lowly to all as the dust. Open my heart to thy Torah, that my soul may follow thy commands. Speedily defeat the counsel of all those who plan evil against me, and upset their design. Do it for the glory of thy name; do it for the sake of thy power; do it for the sake of thy holiness; do it for the sake of thy

---

אלהי נצור is phrased in singular, because it was originally designed as an individual meditation. The first sentence is derived from Psalm 34:14, where the text reads: נצור לשונך מרע, ושפתיך מדבר מרמה ("keep your tongue from evil, and your lips from speaking falsehood").

The phrase עושה שלום במרומיו is from the book of Job (25:2).

יְדִידֶיךָ, הוֹשִׁיעָה יְמִינְךָ וַעֲנֵנִי. יִהְיוּ לְרָצוֹן אִמְרֵי פִי וְהֶגְיוֹן לִבִּי
לְפָנֶיךָ, יְיָ, צוּרִי וְגוֹאֲלִי. עֹשֶׂה שָׁלוֹם בִּמְרוֹמָיו, הוּא יַעֲשֶׂה
שָׁלוֹם עָלֵינוּ וְעַל כָּל יִשְׂרָאֵל, וְאִמְרוּ אָמֵן.

יְהִי רָצוֹן מִלְּפָנֶיךָ, יְיָ אֱלֹהֵינוּ וֵאלֹהֵי אֲבוֹתֵינוּ, שֶׁיִּבָּנֶה בֵּית
הַמִּקְדָּשׁ בִּמְהֵרָה בְיָמֵינוּ; וְתֵן חֶלְקֵנוּ בְּתוֹרָתֶךָ. וְשָׁם נַעֲבָדְךָ
בְּיִרְאָה, כִּימֵי עוֹלָם וּכְשָׁנִים קַדְמוֹנִיּוֹת. וְעָרְבָה לַיְיָ מִנְחַת
יְהוּדָה וִירוּשָׁלָיִם, כִּימֵי עוֹלָם וּכְשָׁנִים קַדְמוֹנִיּוֹת.

הַלֵּל

בָּרוּךְ אַתָּה, יְיָ אֱלֹהֵינוּ, מֶלֶךְ הָעוֹלָם, אֲשֶׁר קִדְּשָׁנוּ בְּמִצְוֹתָיו
וְצִוָּנוּ לִקְרֹא אֶת הַהַלֵּל.

תהלים קיג

הַלְלוּיָהּ; הַלְלוּ, עַבְדֵי יְיָ, הַלְלוּ אֶת שֵׁם יְיָ. יְהִי שֵׁם יְיָ
מְבֹרָךְ, מֵעַתָּה וְעַד עוֹלָם. מִמִּזְרַח שֶׁמֶשׁ עַד מְבוֹאוֹ, מְהֻלָּל שֵׁם
יְיָ. רָם עַל כָּל גּוֹיִם יְיָ, עַל הַשָּׁמַיִם כְּבוֹדוֹ. מִי כַּיְיָ אֱלֹהֵינוּ,
הַמַּגְבִּיהִי לָשָׁבֶת. הַמַּשְׁפִּילִי לִרְאוֹת בַּשָּׁמַיִם וּבָאָרֶץ. מְקִימִי
מֵעָפָר דָּל, מֵאַשְׁפֹּת יָרִים אֶבְיוֹן. לְהוֹשִׁיבִי עִם נְדִיבִים, עִם
נְדִיבֵי עַמּוֹ. מוֹשִׁיבִי עֲקֶרֶת הַבַּיִת, אֵם הַבָּנִים שְׂמֵחָה; הַלְלוּיָהּ.

הלל consists of Psalms 113–118. It is called הלל המצרי ("Egyptian
Hallel") because Psalm 114 refers to the exodus from Egypt. On Purim, the
reading of the *Megillah* takes the place of *Hallel*. On *Rosh Hashanah* and *Yom
Kippur*, *Hallel* is omitted because the High Holydays are not intended for
jubilation. Similarly, *Hallel* is not recited in the house of a mourner during

Torah. That thy beloved may be rescued, save with thy right hand
and answer me. May the words of my mouth and the meditation
of my heart be pleasing before thee, O Lord, my Stronghold and
my Redeemer.[1] May he who creates peace in his high heavens
create peace for us and for all Israel, Amen.

May it be thy will, Lord our God and God of our fathers, that
the Temple be speedily rebuilt in our days, and grant us a share
in thy Torah. There we will serve thee with reverence, as in the
days of old and as in former years. Then the offering of Judah
and Jerusalem will be pleasing to the Lord, as in the days of old
and as in former years.[2]

HALLEL

Blessed art thou, Lord our God, King of the universe, who
hast sanctified us with thy commandments and commanded us to
recite the *Hallel*.
Psalm 113

Praise the Lord! Praise, you servants of the Lord, praise the
name of the Lord. Blessed be the name of the Lord henceforth
and forever. From the rising of the sun to its setting, the Lord's
name is to be praised. High above all nations is the Lord; above
the heavens is his glory. Who is like the Lord our God, enthroned
on high, looking down upon heaven and earth? He raises the poor
out of the dust, and lifts the needy out of the dunghill, to seat
them with princes, with the princes of his people. He turns the
barren housewife into a happy mother of children. Praise the Lord!

---

shiv'ah. On *Rosh Ḥodesh*, a minor festival, *Hallel* is recited in abridged form,
the first eleven verses of Psalms 115 and 116 being omitted. This so-called
"half-*Hallel*" is likewise used on the last six days of *Pesaḥ* by reason of the
following tradition. When the Egyptians were drowning in the Red Sea on the
seventh day of *Pesaḥ*, God restrained the angels from singing his praise, saying: "How can you sing hymns while my creatures are drowning in the sea?"
(Megillah 10b). In order not to make *Ḥol ha-Mo'ed Pesaḥ* appear as more
important than the seventh day of *Pesaḥ*, the *Hallel* is abridged throughout
the last six days.

---

[1] *Psalms* 60:7; 19:15.   [2] *Malachi* 3:4.

תהלים קיד

בְּצֵאת יִשְׂרָאֵל מִמִּצְרָיִם, בֵּית יַעֲקֹב מֵעַם לֹעֵז. הָיְתָה יְהוּדָה לְקָדְשׁוֹ, יִשְׂרָאֵל מַמְשְׁלוֹתָיו. הַיָּם רָאָה וַיָּנֹס; הַיַּרְדֵּן יִסֹּב לְאָחוֹר. הֶהָרִים רָקְדוּ כְאֵילִים, גְּבָעוֹת כִּבְנֵי צֹאן. מַה לְּךָ הַיָּם כִּי תָנוּס; הַיַּרְדֵּן, תִּסֹּב לְאָחוֹר. הֶהָרִים, תִּרְקְדוּ כְאֵילִים; גְּבָעוֹת, כִּבְנֵי צֹאן. מִלִּפְנֵי אָדוֹן חוּלִי אָרֶץ, מִלִּפְנֵי אֱלוֹהַּ יַעֲקֹב. הַהֹפְכִי הַצּוּר אֲגַם מָיִם, הַחַלָּמִישׁ לְמַעְיְנוֹ-מָיִם.

תהלים קטו, א–א

לֹא לָנוּ, יְיָ, לֹא לָנוּ, כִּי לְשִׁמְךָ תֵּן כָּבוֹד, עַל חַסְדְּךָ, עַל אֲמִתֶּךָ. לָמָּה יֹאמְרוּ הַגּוֹיִם, אַיֵּה נָא אֱלֹהֵיהֶם. וֵאלֹהֵינוּ בַשָּׁמָיִם; כֹּל אֲשֶׁר חָפֵץ עָשָׂה. עֲצַבֵּיהֶם כֶּסֶף וְזָהָב, מַעֲשֵׂה יְדֵי אָדָם. פֶּה לָהֶם וְלֹא יְדַבֵּרוּ, עֵינַיִם לָהֶם וְלֹא יִרְאוּ. אָזְנַיִם לָהֶם וְלֹא יִשְׁמָעוּ, אַף לָהֶם וְלֹא יְרִיחוּן. יְדֵיהֶם וְלֹא יְמִישׁוּן, רַגְלֵיהֶם וְלֹא יְהַלֵּכוּ; לֹא יֶהְגּוּ בִּגְרוֹנָם. כְּמוֹהֶם יִהְיוּ עֹשֵׂיהֶם, כֹּל אֲשֶׁר בֹּטֵחַ בָּהֶם. יִשְׂרָאֵל, בְּטַח בַּייָ; עֶזְרָם וּמָגִנָּם הוּא. בֵּית אַהֲרֹן, בִּטְחוּ בַייָ; עֶזְרָם וּמָגִנָּם הוּא. יִרְאֵי יְיָ, בִּטְחוּ בַייָ; עֶזְרָם וּמָגִנָּם הוּא.

Psalm 114, one of the finest lyrics in literature, alludes to the dividing of the Red Sea and the Jordan. The sea and the river are personified and represented as awe-struck by the presence of the Lord. ההרים רקדו is a poetical description of the earthquake which accompanied the giving of the Torah. הצור אגם מים alludes to the miraculous supply of water in the wilderness (*Exodus* 17:6; *Numbers* 20:11).

Psalm 114

When Israel went out of Egypt, Jacob's household from a people of strange speech, Judah became God's sanctuary, Israel his dominion. The sea beheld and fled; the Jordan turned backward; the mountains skipped like rams, and the hills like lambs. What ails you, O sea, that thus you flee? Why, O Jordan, do you turn backward? You mountains, why do you skip like rams? You hills, why do you leap like lambs? Tremble, O earth, at the Lord's presence, at the presence of the God of Jacob, who turns the rock into a pool of water, the flint into a flowing fountain.

Psalm 115:1-11

Not for our sake, O Lord, not for our sake, but for thy name's sake grant glory, because of thy kindness and thy truth. Why should the heathen say: "Where is their God?" Our God is in the heavens! He does whatever he pleases. Their idols are but silver and gold, the work of human hands. They have a mouth, but they cannot speak; they have eyes, but they cannot see; they have ears, but they cannot hear; they have a nose, but they cannot smell; they have hands, but they cannot feel; they have feet, but they cannot walk; nor can they make a sound with their throat. Those who make them shall become like them, whoever trusts in them. O Israel, trust in the Lord! He is your help and your shield. House of Aaron, trust in the Lord! He is your help and your shield. You who revere the Lord, trust in the Lord! He is your help and your shield.

Psalm 115 appeals to God to raise his people from their degradation. Their restoration would vindicate the honor of his name. כמוהם יהיו עושיהם that is, men become like the objects of their worship. עזרם ומגנם הוא is the response of the choir.

הלל

Psalm 116 is a song of thanksgiving on being saved from imminent danger. The psalmist's experiences pass through the stages of suffering, prayer, deliverance and public thanksgiving.

Psalm 115:12-18

The Lord who has remembered us will bless; he will bless the house of Israel; he will bless the house of Aaron; he will bless those who revere the Lord, small and great alike. May the Lord increase you, both you and your children. May you be blessed by the Lord, Creator of heaven and earth. The heaven is the Lord's heaven, but the earth he has given to mankind. The dead cannot praise the Lord, none of those who sink into silence. We will bless the Lord henceforth and forever. Praise the Lord!

Psalm 116:1-11

I love the Lord, for he hears my supplications. Because he has inclined his ear to me, I will call upon him as long as I live. The pangs of death encircled me; the agony of the grave seized me; I was in distress and sorrow. But I called upon the name of the Lord: "O Lord, save my life!" Gracious is the Lord, and righteous; our God is merciful. The Lord protects the simple; when I was brought low, he saved me. Be again at rest, O my soul, for the Lord has dealt kindly with you. Thou hast delivered my soul from death, my eyes from tears and my feet from stumbling. I shall walk before the Lord in the world of life. I trust even when I cry out: "I am greatly afflicted." [I have faith] even when I say in haste: "All men are deceitful."

Psalm 116:12-19

What can I render to the Lord for all his kind acts toward me? I will take the cup of deliverance, and will call upon the name of the Lord. My vows to the Lord I will pay in the presence of all his people. Grievous in the sight of the Lord is the death of his faithful followers. O Lord, I am indeed thy servant; I am thy servant, the son of thy servant; thou hast removed my chains. To thee I offer thanksgiving, and call upon the name of the Lord. My vows to the Lord I will pay in the presence of all his people, in the courts of the Lord's house, in the midst of Jerusalem. Praise the Lord!

תהלים קיז

הַלְלוּ אֶת יְיָ, כָּל גּוֹיִם; שַׁבְּחוּהוּ, כָּל הָאֻמִּים. כִּי גָבַר עָלֵינוּ
חַסְדּוֹ, וֶאֱמֶת יְיָ לְעוֹלָם; הַלְלוּיָהּ.

Responsively

תהלים קיח

כִּי לְעוֹלָם חַסְדּוֹ.	הוֹדוּ לַייָ כִּי טוֹב
כִּי לְעוֹלָם חַסְדּוֹ.	יֹאמַר נָא יִשְׂרָאֵל
כִּי לְעוֹלָם חַסְדּוֹ.	יֹאמְרוּ נָא בֵית אַהֲרֹן
כִּי לְעוֹלָם חַסְדּוֹ.	יֹאמְרוּ נָא יִרְאֵי יְיָ

מִן הַמֵּצַר קָרָאתִי יָּהּ, עָנָנִי בַמֶּרְחָב יָהּ. יְיָ לִי, לֹא אִירָא;
מַה יַּעֲשֶׂה לִי אָדָם. יְיָ לִי בְּעֹזְרָי, וַאֲנִי אֶרְאֶה בְשֹׂנְאָי. טוֹב
לַחֲסוֹת בַּייָ מִבְּטֹחַ בָּאָדָם. טוֹב לַחֲסוֹת בַּייָ מִבְּטֹחַ בִּנְדִיבִים.
כָּל גּוֹיִם סְבָבוּנִי; בְּשֵׁם יְיָ, כִּי אֲמִילַם. סַבּוּנִי גַם סְבָבוּנִי; בְּשֵׁם
יְיָ, כִּי אֲמִילַם. סַבּוּנִי כִדְבֹרִים, דֹּעֲכוּ כְּאֵשׁ קוֹצִים; בְּשֵׁם יְיָ,
כִּי אֲמִילַם. דָּחֹה דְחִיתַנִי לִנְפֹּל, וַייָ עֲזָרָנִי. עָזִּי וְזִמְרָת יָהּ, וַיְהִי
לִי לִישׁוּעָה. קוֹל רִנָּה וִישׁוּעָה בְּאָהֳלֵי צַדִּיקִים; יְמִין יְיָ עֹשָׂה
חָיִל. יְמִין יְיָ רוֹמֵמָה, יְמִין יְיָ עֹשָׂה חָיִל. לֹא אָמוּת כִּי אֶחְיֶה,
וַאֲסַפֵּר מַעֲשֵׂי יָהּ. יַסֹּר יִסְּרַנִּי יָּהּ, וְלַמָּוֶת לֹא נְתָנָנִי. פִּתְחוּ לִי
שַׁעֲרֵי צֶדֶק; אָבֹא בָם, אוֹדֶה יָהּ. זֶה הַשַּׁעַר לַייָ, צַדִּיקִים
יָבֹאוּ בוֹ.

Psalm 117 is the shortest chapter in the Bible. Its two verses are an
invitation to all nations to join in acknowledging God.

Psalm 118 is intended for alternating choirs. The last nine verses, from
אודך to הודו לה׳, are spoken twice when the *Hallel* is recited, because they
do not follow the arrangement of synonymous parallelism of the previous
verses. Each of the last nine verses expresses a new thought.

Psalm 117

Praise the Lord, all you nations; laud him, all you peoples! For great is his kindness toward us; the Lord's truth endures forever.

Responsively

Psalm 118:1-4

Give thanks to the Lord, for he is good;

His mercy endures forever.

Let Israel say:

His mercy endures forever.

Let the house of Aaron say:

His mercy endures forever.

Let those who revere the Lord say:

His mercy endures forever.

Psalm 118:5-29

Out of distress I called upon the Lord; he answered me by setting me free. The Lord is with me; I have no fear. What can man do to me? The Lord is my helper; I shall see the defeat of my foes. It is better to seek refuge in the Lord than to trust in man. It is better to seek refuge in the Lord than to trust in princes. The heathen were all swarming round me; relying on the Lord, I routed them. Swarming round me, they beset me; relying on the Lord, I routed them. They swarmed like bees about me, but they were extinguished like a fire of thorns; relying on the Lord, I surely routed them. You did thrust at me that I might fall, but the Lord helped me. The Lord is my strength and my song; he has delivered me indeed. A joyful shout of triumph rings in the tents of the righteous: "The right hand of the Lord does valiantly. The Lord's right hand triumphs; the Lord's right hand does valiantly!" I shall not die, but live to recount the deeds of the Lord. The Lord has indeed punished me, but he has not left me to die. Open for me the gates of righteousness, that I may enter and praise the Lord. This is the gateway of the Lord; the righteous alone may enter.

Each verse is chanted twice:

אוֹדְךָ כִּי עֲנִיתָנִי, וַתְּהִי לִי לִישׁוּעָה.

אֶבֶן מָאֲסוּ הַבּוֹנִים, הָיְתָה לְרֹאשׁ פִּנָּה.

מֵאֵת יְיָ הָיְתָה זֹּאת; הִיא נִפְלָאת בְּעֵינֵינוּ.

זֶה הַיּוֹם עָשָׂה יְיָ, נָגִילָה וְנִשְׂמְחָה בוֹ.

Responsively

אָנָּא יְיָ, הוֹשִׁיעָה נָּא.

אָנָּא יְיָ, הוֹשִׁיעָה נָּא.

אָנָּא יְיָ, הַצְלִיחָה נָּא.

אָנָּא יְיָ, הַצְלִיחָה נָּא.

Each verse is chanted twice:

בָּרוּךְ הַבָּא בְּשֵׁם יְיָ; בֵּרַכְנוּכֶם מִבֵּית יְיָ.

אֵל יְיָ וַיָּאֶר לָנוּ, אִסְרוּ חַג בַּעֲבֹתִים, עַד קַרְנוֹת הַמִּזְבֵּחַ.

אֵלִי אַתָּה וְאוֹדֶךָּ, אֱלֹהַי אֲרוֹמְמֶךָּ.

הוֹדוּ לַיְיָ כִּי טוֹב, כִּי לְעוֹלָם חַסְדּוֹ.

———

יְהַלְלוּךָ, יְיָ אֱלֹהֵינוּ, כָּל מַעֲשֶׂיךָ, וַחֲסִידֶיךָ; צַדִּיקִים עוֹשֵׂי
רְצוֹנֶךָ, וְכָל עַמְּךָ בֵּית יִשְׂרָאֵל, בְּרִנָּה יוֹדוּ וִיבָרְכוּ, וִישַׁבְּחוּ
וִיפָאֲרוּ, וִירוֹמְמוּ וְיַעֲרִיצוּ, וְיַקְדִּישׁוּ וְיַמְלִיכוּ אֶת שִׁמְךָ מַלְכֵּנוּ.
Reader: כִּי לְךָ טוֹב לְהוֹדוֹת, וּלְשִׁמְךָ נָאֶה לְזַמֵּר, כִּי מֵעוֹלָם עַד
עוֹלָם אַתָּה אֵל. בָּרוּךְ אַתָּה, יְיָ, מֶלֶךְ מְהֻלָּל בַּתִּשְׁבָּחוֹת.

Full-*Kaddish* is here recited by the Reader.

רות, chanted on the second day, page 303.

———

יהללוך, mentioned in Pesaḥim 118a, is similar to ישתבח in its phrase-
ology. Like ישתבח, which follows the recital of *Pesuké d'Zimra*, יהללוך concludes the recital of the *Hallel* psalms.

Each verse is chanted twice:

I thank thee because thou hast answered me
And hast been my salvation.

The stone which the builders rejected
Has become the chief cornerstone.

This is the Lord's doing;
It is marvelous in our eyes.

This is the day which the Lord has made;
Let us be glad and rejoice on it.

Responsively

We implore thee, O Lord, save us!
We implore thee, O Lord, save us!
We implore thee, O Lord, prosper us!
We implore thee, O Lord, prosper us!

Each verse is chanted twice:

Blessed be he who comes in the name of the Lord;
We bless you from the house of the Lord.

The Lord is God who has given us light;
Link the dance with boughs, up to the altar-horns.

Thou art my God, and I thank thee;
Thou art my God, and I extol thee.

Give thanks to the Lord, for he is good;
His mercy endures forever.

All thy works praise thee, Lord our God; thy righteous followers who do thy will, and all thy people the house of Israel, joyously thank and bless, praise and glorify, extol and revere, sanctify and acclaim thy name, our King. It is good indeed to render thanks to thee; it is pleasant to sing praises to thy name, for thou art God from eternity to eternity. Blessed art thou, O Lord, King extolled with praises.

Full-Kaddish is here recited by the Reader.
Ruth, chanted on the second day, page 304.

קְרִיאַת הַתּוֹרָה

אֵין כָּמוֹךָ בָאֱלֹהִים, אֲדֹנָי, וְאֵין כְּמַעֲשֶׂיךָ. מַלְכוּתְךָ מַלְכוּת
כָּל עֹלָמִים, וּמֶמְשַׁלְתְּךָ בְּכָל דֹּר וָדֹר. יְיָ מֶלֶךְ, יְיָ מָלָךְ, יְיָ
יִמְלֹךְ לְעֹלָם וָעֶד. יְיָ עֹז לְעַמּוֹ יִתֵּן, יְיָ יְבָרֵךְ אֶת עַמּוֹ בַשָּׁלוֹם.

אַב הָרַחֲמִים, הֵיטִיבָה בִרְצוֹנְךָ אֶת צִיּוֹן, תִּבְנֶה חוֹמוֹת
יְרוּשָׁלָיִם. כִּי בְךָ לְבַד בָּטָחְנוּ, מֶלֶךְ אֵל רָם וְנִשָּׂא, אֲדוֹן
עוֹלָמִים.

וַיְהִי בִּנְסֹעַ הָאָרֹן וַיֹּאמֶר מֹשֶׁה: קוּמָה יְיָ, וְיָפֻצוּ אֹיְבֶיךָ,
וְיָנֻסוּ מְשַׂנְאֶיךָ מִפָּנֶיךָ. כִּי מִצִּיּוֹן תֵּצֵא תוֹרָה, וּדְבַר יְיָ
מִירוּשָׁלָיִם. בָּרוּךְ שֶׁנָּתַן תּוֹרָה לְעַמּוֹ יִשְׂרָאֵל בִּקְדֻשָּׁתוֹ.

The next verse is recited three times.
On Sabbath, it is omitted until בֶּאֱמֶת יֶשַׁע (page 163)

יְיָ, יְיָ אֵל רַחוּם וְחַנּוּן, אֶרֶךְ אַפַּיִם, וְרַב חֶסֶד וֶאֱמֶת. נֹצֵר
חֶסֶד לָאֲלָפִים, נֹשֵׂא עָוֹן וָפֶשַׁע וְחַטָּאָה, וְנַקֵּה.

רִבּוֹנוֹ שֶׁל עוֹלָם, מַלֵּא מִשְׁאֲלוֹת לִבִּי לְטוֹבָה, וְהָפֵק רְצוֹנִי
וְתֵן שְׁאֵלָתִי, לִי עַבְדְּךָ בֶּן אֲמָתֶךָ, וְזַכֵּנִי (וְאֶת אִשְׁתִּי וּבָנַי וּבְנוֹתַי)
לַעֲשׂוֹת רְצוֹנְךָ בְּלֵבָב שָׁלֵם. וּמַלְּטֵנוּ מִיֵּצֶר הָרָע, וְתֵן חֶלְקֵנוּ
בְּתוֹרָתֶךָ, וְזַכֵּנוּ שֶׁתִּשְׁרֶה שְׁכִינָתְךָ עָלֵינוּ, וְהוֹפַע עָלֵינוּ רוּחַ
חָכְמָה וּבִינָה, רוּחַ עֵצָה וּגְבוּרָה, רוּחַ דַּעַת וְיִרְאַת יְיָ. וְכֵן יְהִי
רָצוֹן מִלְּפָנֶיךָ, יְיָ אֱלֹהֵינוּ וֵאלֹהֵי אֲבוֹתֵינוּ, שֶׁתְּזַכֵּנוּ לַעֲשׂוֹת
מַעֲשִׂים טוֹבִים בְּעֵינֶיךָ וְלָלֶכֶת בְּדַרְכֵי יְשָׁרִים לְפָנֶיךָ. וְקַדְּשֵׁנוּ

TORAH READING

There is no God like thee, O Lord, and there are no deeds like thine. Thy kingdom is an everlasting kingdom; thy dominion endures through all generations. The Lord is King; the Lord was King; the Lord shall be King forever and ever. The Lord will give strength to his people, the Lord will bless his people with peace.[1]

Merciful Father, may it be thy will to favor Zion with thy goodness; mayest thou rebuild the walls of Jerusalem. Truly, in thee alone we trust, high and exalted King and God, eternal Lord.

And it came to pass, whenever the ark started, Moses would say: "Arise, O Lord, and let thy enemies be scattered; let those who hate thee flee before thee." Truly out of Zion shall come forth Torah, and the word of the Lord out of Jerusalem.[2]

Blessed be he who in holiness gave the Torah to his people Israel

The next verse is recited three times.
On Sabbath, it is omitted until "thy saving truth" (page **164**).

The Lord, the Lord is a merciful and gracious God, slow to anger and abounding in kindness and truth. He keeps kindness to the thousandth generation, forgiving iniquity and transgression and sin, and acquitting the penitent.[3]

Lord of the universe, fulfill the prayers of my heart for happiness; grant my petition and my request; enable me to do thy will with a perfect heart; deliver us from the evil impulse. Grant us a share in thy Torah; make us worthy of thy divine presence; bestow on us the spirit of wisdom and understanding, the spirit of counsel and courage, the spirit of knowledge and piety. May it be thy will, Lord our God and God of our fathers, to enable us to perform deeds that please thee, and to walk before thee in the

---

[1]*Psalms* 86:8; 145:13; 29:11.   [2]*Numbers* 10:35; *Isaiah* 2:3.   [3]*Exodus* **34:6-7.**

בְּמִצְוֹתֶיךָ, כְּדֵי שֶׁנִּזְכֶּה לְחַיִּים טוֹבִים וַאֲרֻכִּים וּלְחַיֵּי הָעוֹלָם
הַבָּא; וְתִשְׁמְרֵנוּ מִמַּעֲשִׂים רָעִים וּמִשָּׁעוֹת רָעוֹת הַמִּתְרַגְּשׁוֹת
לָבֹא לָעוֹלָם. וְהַבּוֹטֵחַ בַּיָי חֶסֶד יְסוֹבְבֶנּוּ. אָמֵן.

יִהְיוּ לְרָצוֹן אִמְרֵי פִי וְהֶגְיוֹן לִבִּי לְפָנֶיךָ, יְיָ, צוּרִי וְגוֹאֲלִי.

Three times:

וַאֲנִי תְפִלָּתִי לְךָ, יְיָ, עֵת רָצוֹן; אֱלֹהִים, בְּרָב־חַסְדֶּךָ, עֲנֵנִי
בֶּאֱמֶת יִשְׁעֶךָ.

זוהר, ויקהל

בְּרִיךְ שְׁמֵהּ דְּמָרֵא עָלְמָא, בְּרִיךְ כִּתְרָךְ וְאַתְרָךְ. יְהֵא
רְעוּתָךְ עִם עַמָּךְ יִשְׂרָאֵל לְעָלַם, וּפֻרְקַן יְמִינָךְ אַחֲזֵי לְעַמָּךְ
בְּבֵית מִקְדְּשָׁךְ; וּלְאַמְטוֹיֵי לָנָא מִטּוּב נְהוֹרָךְ, וּלְקַבֵּל צְלוֹתָנָא
בְּרַחֲמִין. יְהֵא רַעֲוָא קֳדָמָךְ, דְּתוֹרִיךְ לָן חַיִּין בְּטִיבוּתָא;
וְלֶהֱוֵא אֲנָא פְּקִידָא בְּגוֹ צַדִּיקַיָּא, לְמִרְחַם עֲלַי וּלְמִנְטַר יָתִי
וְיָת כָּל דִּי לִי וְדִי לְעַמָּךְ יִשְׂרָאֵל. אַנְתְּ הוּא זָן לְכֹלָּא וּמְפַרְנֵס
לְכֹלָּא, אַנְתְּ הוּא שַׁלִּיט עַל כֹּלָּא; אַנְתְּ הוּא דְּשַׁלִּיט עַל
מַלְכַיָּא, וּמַלְכוּתָא דִּילָךְ הִיא. אֲנָא עַבְדָּא דְקֻדְשָׁא בְּרִיךְ
הוּא, דְּסָגִדְנָא קַמֵּהּ וּמִקַּמָּא דִּיקַר אוֹרַיְתֵהּ בְּכָל עִדָּן וְעִדָּן.
לָא עַל אֱנָשׁ רָחִצְנָא, וְלָא עַל בַּר אֱלָהִין סָמִכְנָא, אֶלָּא
בֶּאֱלָהָא דִשְׁמַיָּא, דְּהוּא אֱלָהָא קְשׁוֹט, וְאוֹרַיְתֵהּ קְשׁוֹט,

<hr>

בְּרִיךְ שְׁמֵיהּ is taken from the *Zohar*, the fundamental book of *Kabbalah*, which was first made known in the thirteenth century and ascribed to Rabbi Simeon ben Yoḥai of the second century. Written in the form of a commentary on the five books of Moses, it is based on the principle that the biblical narratives contain a higher truth than what they ostensibly express. Soon after its first appearance in Spain through the efforts of Rabbi Moses de Leon, its influence spread among the Jewish people with remarkable speed. The Zohar introduces this inspiring and uplifting prayer as follows: "When the Torah is taken out to be read before the congregation, the heavenly gates of mercy are opened and the divine love is aroused; therefore one should recite: בְּרִיךְ שְׁמֵיהּ..." The term בַּר אֱלָהִין ("angel") is found in Daniel 3:25.

paths of the upright. Sanctify us with thy commandments, that we may merit the long and blessed life of the world to come; guard us from evil deeds, and from evil times which assail the world.

May kindness surround him who trusts in the Lord. Amen.

May the words of my mouth and the meditation of my heart be pleasing before thee, O Lord, my Stronghold and my Redeemer.

Three times:

I offer my prayer to thee, O Lord, at a time of grace. O God, in thy abundant kindness, answer me with thy saving truth.[1]

Zohar, Wayyakhel

Blessed be the name of the Lord of the universe! Blessed be thy crown and thy dominion. May thy good will ever abide with thy people Israel. Reveal thy saving power to thy people in thy sanctuary; bestow on us the good gift of thy light, and accept our prayer in mercy. May it be thy will to prolong our life in happiness.

Let me also be counted among the righteous, so that thou mayest have compassion on me and shelter me and mine and all that belong to thy people Israel. Thou art he who nourishes and sustains all; thou art he who rules over all; thou art he who rules over kings, for dominion is thine. I am the servant of the Holy One, blessed be he, before whom and before whose glorious Torah I bow at all times. Not in man do I put my trust, nor do I rely on any angel, but only in the God of heaven who is the God of

---

Truth is one of the pillars upon which the world rests. He who utters a falsehood is like one who removes the foundation of the world. On the other hand, he who is careful to speak the truth is like one who builds the foundation of the world. Our sages tell a story of a city where the inhabitants were so scrupulous about speaking the truth that the angel of death had no control over them.

There are the proud who think they know the truth about everything. They consider very few people their equals in wisdom, and disregard what others have to say. They imagine that whatever they find difficult to understand cannot possibly be intelligible to anyone else. They rely so much upon their own understanding that they ignore all who disagree with them.

Whoever would attain the trait of cleanness must be free from the taint

[1] *Psalm* 69:14.

וּנְבִיאוֹהִי קְשׁוֹט, וּמַסְגֵּא לְמֶעְבַּד טַבְוָן וּקְשׁוֹט. בֵּהּ אֲנָא רָחֵץ,
וְלִשְׁמֵהּ קַדִּישָׁא יַקִּירָא אֲנָא אָמַר תֻּשְׁבְּחָן. יְהֵא רַעֲוָא קֳדָמָךְ,
דְּתִפְתַּח לִבָּאי בְּאוֹרַיְתָא, וְתַשְׁלֵם מִשְׁאֲלִין דְּלִבָּאי, וְלִבָּא
דְכָל עַמָּךְ יִשְׂרָאֵל, לְטָב וּלְחַיִּין וְלִשְׁלָם.

Two *Sifré Torah* are taken from the ark.

Reader and Congregation:

שְׁמַע יִשְׂרָאֵל, יְיָ אֱלֹהֵינוּ, יְיָ אֶחָד.

Reader and Congregation:

אֶחָד אֱלֹהֵינוּ, גָּדוֹל אֲדוֹנֵינוּ, קָדוֹשׁ שְׁמוֹ.

Reader:

גַּדְּלוּ לַייָ אִתִּי, וּנְרוֹמְמָה שְׁמוֹ יַחְדָּו.

Congregation:

לְךָ יְיָ הַגְּדֻלָּה וְהַגְּבוּרָה וְהַתִּפְאֶרֶת וְהַנֵּצַח וְהַהוֹד, כִּי כֹל
בַּשָּׁמַיִם וּבָאָרֶץ; לְךָ, יְיָ, הַמַּמְלָכָה וְהַמִּתְנַשֵּׂא לְכֹל לְרֹאשׁ.
רוֹמְמוּ יְיָ אֱלֹהֵינוּ, וְהִשְׁתַּחֲווּ לַהֲדֹם רַגְלָיו, קָדוֹשׁ הוּא. רוֹמְמוּ
יְיָ אֱלֹהֵינוּ, וְהִשְׁתַּחֲווּ לְהַר קָדְשׁוֹ, כִּי קָדוֹשׁ יְיָ אֱלֹהֵינוּ.

עַל הַכֹּל יִתְגַּדַּל וְיִתְקַדַּשׁ, וְיִשְׁתַּבַּח וְיִתְפָּאַר, וְיִתְרוֹמַם
וְיִתְנַשֵּׂא שְׁמוֹ שֶׁל מֶלֶךְ מַלְכֵי הַמְּלָכִים, הַקָּדוֹשׁ בָּרוּךְ הוּא,
בָּעוֹלָמוֹת שֶׁבָּרָא, הָעוֹלָם הַזֶּה וְהָעוֹלָם הַבָּא, כִּרְצוֹנוֹ וְכִרְצוֹן

---

of pride. He must realize that pride is a form of blindness which prevents even a man of understanding from seeing his own shortcomings. He who is envious neither benefits himself nor injures the one he envies. He injures only himself. There are people so foolish that when they see a neighbor in luck, they begin to brood and are so upset and distressed that even the good which they possess no longer affords them pleasure. Of them the wise Solomon said: "Envy makes the bones rot".

Pride is an exaggerated sense of our own importance and an inward belief

truth, whose Torah is truth and whose Prophets are truth, and
who performs many deeds of goodness and truth. In him I put my
trust, and to his holy and glorious name I utter praises. May it
be thy will to open my heart to thy Torah, and to fulfill the wishes
of my heart and the heart of all thy people Israel for happiness,
life and peace.

Two Sifré Torah are taken from the ark.

Reader and Congregation:

Hear, O Israel, the Lord is our God, the Lord is One.[1]

Reader and Congregation:

One is our God. Great is our Lord. Holy is his name.

Reader:

Exalt the Lord with me, and let us extol his name together.[2]

Congregation:

Thine, O Lord, is the greatness and the power, the glory and
the victory and the majesty; for all that is in heaven and on earth
is thine; thine, O Lord, is the kingdom, and thou art supreme over
all. Exalt the Lord our God, and worship at his footstool; holy is
he. Exalt the Lord our God, and worship at his holy mountain,
for holy is the Lord our God.

Magnified and hallowed, praised and glorified, exalted and extolled above all, be the name of the supreme King of kings, the
Holy One, blessed be he, in the worlds which he has created—
this world and the world to come—in accordance with his desire

---

that we deserve praise. Whenever a man believes he is gifted in any way, he
is in danger of falling a victim to pride. There is the vain man who, because
he considers himself unique and distinguished, deems it proper to assume a
dignified bearing when he walks, when he sits, when he stands up, whenever
he speaks and whatever he does. He walks leisurely, with measured step; he
sits upright; he rises slowly; he speaks only with those of high rank, and even
among them he utters only short sentences in an oracular fashion. In all his
behavior he displays solemn pomp, as though his flesh were made of lead and
his bones of stone. (*Mesillath Yesharim*).

---

[1]*Deuteronomy* 6:4.   [2]*Psalm* 34:4.

יְרֵאָיו, וְכִרְצוֹן כָּל בֵּית יִשְׂרָאֵל. צוּר הָעוֹלָמִים, אֲדוֹן כָּל
הַבְּרִיּוֹת, אֱלוֹהַּ כָּל הַנְּפָשׁוֹת, הַיּוֹשֵׁב בְּמֶרְחֲבֵי מָרוֹם, הַשּׁוֹכֵן
בִּשְׁמֵי שְׁמֵי קֶדֶם; קְדֻשָּׁתוֹ עַל הַחַיּוֹת, וּקְדֻשָּׁתוֹ עַל כִּסֵּא
הַכָּבוֹד. וּבְכֵן יִתְקַדַּשׁ שִׁמְךָ בָּנוּ, יְיָ אֱלֹהֵינוּ, לְעֵינֵי כָּל חָי.
וְנֹאמַר לְפָנָיו שִׁיר חָדָשׁ, כַּכָּתוּב: שִׁירוּ לֵאלֹהִים, זַמְּרוּ שְׁמוֹ,
סֹלּוּ לָרֹכֵב בָּעֲרָבוֹת, בְּיָהּ שְׁמוֹ, וְעִלְזוּ לְפָנָיו. וְנִרְאֵהוּ עַיִן
בְּעַיִן בְּשׁוּבוֹ אֶל נָוֵהוּ, כַּכָּתוּב: כִּי עַיִן בְּעַיִן יִרְאוּ בְּשׁוּב יְיָ צִיּוֹן.
וְנֶאֱמַר: וְנִגְלָה כְּבוֹד יְיָ, וְרָאוּ כָל בָּשָׂר יַחְדָּו, כִּי פִּי יְיָ דִּבֵּר.

Reader:

אַב הָרַחֲמִים, הוּא יְרַחֵם עַם עֲמוּסִים, וְיִזְכֹּר בְּרִית
אֵיתָנִים, וְיַצִּיל נַפְשׁוֹתֵינוּ מִן הַשָּׁעוֹת הָרָעוֹת, וְיִגְעַר בְּיֵצֶר הָרָע
מִן הַנְּשׂוּאִים, וְיָחֹן אוֹתָנוּ לִפְלֵיטַת עוֹלָמִים, וִימַלֵּא מִשְׁאֲלוֹתֵינוּ
בְּמִדָּה טוֹבָה, יְשׁוּעָה וְרַחֲמִים.

The first *Torah* being placed upon the reading desk, the Reader says:

וְיַעֲזֹר וְיָגֵן וְיוֹשִׁיעַ לְכָל הַחוֹסִים בּוֹ, וְנֹאמַר אָמֵן. הַכֹּל הָבוּ
גֹדֶל לֵאלֹהֵינוּ, וּתְנוּ כָבוֹד לַתּוֹרָה. כֹּהֵן, קְרָב; יַעֲמֹד (פְּלוֹנִי
בֶּן פְּלוֹנִי) הַכֹּהֵן. בָּרוּךְ שֶׁנָּתַן תּוֹרָה לְעַמּוֹ יִשְׂרָאֵל בִּקְדֻשָּׁתוֹ.

תּוֹרַת יְיָ תְּמִימָה, מְשִׁיבַת נָפֶשׁ; עֵדוּת יְיָ נֶאֱמָנָה, מַחְכִּימַת
פֶּתִי. פִּקּוּדֵי יְיָ יְשָׁרִים, מְשַׂמְּחֵי לֵב; מִצְוַת יְיָ בָּרָה, מְאִירַת
עֵינָיִם. יְיָ עֹז לְעַמּוֹ יִתֵּן; יְיָ יְבָרֵךְ אֶת עַמּוֹ בַשָּׁלוֹם. הָאֵל תָּמִים
דַּרְכּוֹ; אִמְרַת יְיָ צְרוּפָה, מָגֵן הוּא לְכָל הַחוֹסִים בּוֹ.

Congregation and Reader:

וְאַתֶּם הַדְּבֵקִים בַּיְיָ אֱלֹהֵיכֶם, חַיִּים כֻּלְּכֶם הַיּוֹם.

and the desire of those who revere him, and of all the house of Israel. He is the eternal Stronghold, the Lord of all creatures, the God of all souls, who dwells in the wide extended heights, who inhabits the ancient high heavens; whose holiness is above the celestial beings and above the throne of glory. Now, thy name, Lord our God, shall be sanctified among us in the sight of all the living. Let us sing a new song before him, as it is written: "Sing to God, praise his name; extol him who is above the heavens, whose name is Lord, and exult before him." May we see him eye to eye when he returns to his abode, as it is written: "For they shall see eye to eye when the Lord returns to Zion." And it is said: "Then the glory of the Lord shall be revealed, and all shall see it together; for thus has the Lord promised."

Reader.

May the merciful Father have compassion on the people who have been upheld by him, and remember the covenant with the patriarchs; may he deliver us from evil times, and check the evil impulse in those who have been tended by him; may he graciously grant us everlasting deliverance, and in his goodness fulfill our petitions for salvation and mercy.

The first Torah being placed upon the reading desk, the Reader says:

May he help, shield and save all who trust in him; and let us say, Amen. Let us all ascribe greatness to our God, and give honor to the Torah. Let the *Kohen* come forward. (*the Reader names the first person called to the Torah.*) Blessed be he who in his holiness gave the Torah to his people Israel.

The Lord's Torah is perfect, refreshing the soul; the Lord's testimony is trustworthy, teaching the simple man wisdom. The Lord's precepts are right, gladdening the heart; the Lord's commandment is clear, enlightening the eyes. The Lord will give strength to his people; the Lord will bless his people with peace. The way of God is perfect; the word of the Lord is pure; he is a shield to all who trust in him.

Congregation and Reader:

And you who cling to the Lord your God are all alive today.

בִּרְכוֹת הַתּוֹרָה

The person called to the Torah recites:

בָּרְכוּ אֶת יְיָ הַמְבֹרָךְ.

Congregation responds:

בָּרוּךְ יְיָ הַמְבֹרָךְ לְעוֹלָם וָעֶד.

He repeats the response and continues:

בָּרוּךְ אַתָּה, יְיָ אֱלֹהֵינוּ, מֶלֶךְ הָעוֹלָם, אֲשֶׁר בָּחַר בָּנוּ מִכָּל הָעַמִּים, וְנָתַן לָנוּ אֶת תּוֹרָתוֹ. בָּרוּךְ אַתָּה, יְיָ, נוֹתֵן הַתּוֹרָה.

The Torah is read; then he recites:

בָּרוּךְ אַתָּה, יְיָ אֱלֹהֵינוּ, מֶלֶךְ הָעוֹלָם, אֲשֶׁר נָתַן לָנוּ תּוֹרַת אֱמֶת וְחַיֵּי עוֹלָם נָטַע בְּתוֹכֵנוּ. בָּרוּךְ אַתָּה, יְיָ, נוֹתֵן הַתּוֹרָה.

בִּרְכַּת הַגּוֹמֵל

One who has come safely through a dangerous experience recites:

בָּרוּךְ אַתָּה, יְיָ אֱלֹהֵינוּ, מֶלֶךְ הָעוֹלָם, הַגּוֹמֵל לְחַיָּבִים טוֹבוֹת, שֶׁגְּמָלַנִי כָּל טוֹב.

Congregation responds:

מִי שֶׁגְּמָלְךָ כָּל טוֹב, הוּא יִגְמָלְךָ כָּל טוֹב סֶלָה.

The father of a *Bar-Mitzvah* pronounces the following blessing:

בָּרוּךְ שֶׁפְּטָרַנִי מֵעָנְשׁוֹ שֶׁל זֶה.

ברכות התורה, the two blessings pronounced over the Torah, contain forty words which are said to allude to the forty days spent by Moses on Mount Sinai. These benedictions are quoted in the Talmud (Berakhoth 11b; 49b).

TORAH BLESSINGS

The person called to the Torah recites:

Bless the Lord who is blessed.

Congregation responds:

Blessed be the Lord who is blessed forever and ever.

He repeats the response and continues:

Blessed art thou, Lord our God, King of the universe, who hast chosen us from all peoples, and hast given us thy Torah. Blessed art thou, O Lord, Giver of the Torah.

The Torah is read; then he recites:

Blessed art thou, Lord our God, King of the universe, who hast given us the Torah of truth, and hast planted everlasting life in our midst. Blessed art thou, O Lord, Giver of the Torah.

THANKSGIVING

One who has come safely through a dangerous experience recites:

Blessed art thou, Lord our God, King of the universe, who bestowest favors on the undeserving, and hast shown me every kindness.

Congregation responds:

May he who has shown you every kindness ever deal kindly with you.

The father of a Bar-Mitzvah pronounces the following blessing:

Blessed be he who has relieved me of the responsibility for this boy.

ברכת הגומל is based on a talmudic statement to the effect that all who escape serious danger arising from illness, imprisonment or a perilous voyage, must offer thanks to God (Berakhoth 54b). This is derived from Psalm 107, where thanksgiving is offered on occasions such as these.

On behalf of each person called to the Torah:

מִי שֶׁבֵּרַךְ אֲבוֹתֵינוּ, אַבְרָהָם יִצְחָק וְיַעֲקֹב, הוּא יְבָרֵךְ
אֶת... שֶׁעָלָה לִכְבוֹד הַמָּקוֹם וְלִכְבוֹד הַתּוֹרָה וְלִכְבוֹד
הָרֶגֶל. הַקָּדוֹשׁ בָּרוּךְ הוּא יִשְׁמְרֵהוּ וְיַצִּילֵהוּ מִכָּל צָרָה
וְצוּקָה וּמִכָּל נֶגַע וּמַחֲלָה, וְיִשְׁלַח בְּרָכָה וְהַצְלָחָה בְּכָל
מַעֲשֵׂה יָדָיו, וְיִזְכֶּה לַעֲלוֹת לָרֶגֶל עִם כָּל יִשְׂרָאֵל אֶחָיו;
וְנֹאמַר אָמֵן.

On the occasion of naming a new-born daughter:

מִי שֶׁבֵּרַךְ אֲבוֹתֵינוּ, אַבְרָהָם יִצְחָק וְיַעֲקֹב, מֹשֶׁה וְאַהֲרֹן,
דָּוִד וּשְׁלֹמֹה, הוּא יְבָרֵךְ אֶת הָאִשָּׁה הַיּוֹלֶדֶת...* וְאֶת בִּתָּהּ
שֶׁנּוֹלְדָה לָהּ; וְיִקָּרֵא שְׁמָהּ בְּיִשְׂרָאֵל...* וְיִזְכּוּ לְגַדְּלָהּ
לְחֻפָּה וּלְמַעֲשִׂים טוֹבִים; וְנֹאמַר אָמֵן.

On behalf a sick man:

מִי שֶׁבֵּרַךְ אֲבוֹתֵינוּ, אַבְרָהָם יִצְחָק וְיַעֲקֹב, מֹשֶׁה
וְאַהֲרֹן, דָּוִד וּשְׁלֹמֹה, הוּא יְרַפֵּא אֶת הַחוֹלֶה...* הַקָּדוֹשׁ
בָּרוּךְ הוּא יִמָּלֵא רַחֲמִים עָלָיו לְהַחֲלִימוֹ וּלְרַפֹּאתוֹ,
לְהַחֲזִיקוֹ וּלְהַחֲיוֹתוֹ, וְיִשְׁלַח לוֹ מְהֵרָה רְפוּאָה שְׁלֵמָה,
רְפוּאַת הַנֶּפֶשׁ וּרְפוּאַת הַגּוּף; וְנֹאמַר אָמֵן.

On behalf of a sick woman:

מִי שֶׁבֵּרַךְ אֲבוֹתֵינוּ, אַבְרָהָם יִצְחָק וְיַעֲקֹב, מֹשֶׁה
וְאַהֲרֹן, דָּוִד וּשְׁלֹמֹה, הוּא יְרַפֵּא אֶת הַחוֹלָה...* הַקָּדוֹשׁ
בָּרוּךְ הוּא יִמָּלֵא רַחֲמִים עָלֶיהָ לְהַחֲלִימָהּ וּלְרַפֹּאתָהּ,
לְהַחֲזִיקָהּ וּלְהַחֲיוֹתָהּ, וְיִשְׁלַח לָהּ מְהֵרָה רְפוּאָה שְׁלֵמָה,
רְפוּאַת הַנֶּפֶשׁ וּרְפוּאַת הַגּוּף; וְנֹאמַר אָמֵן.

*The name is given.

On behalf of each person called to the Torah:

He who blessed our fathers Abraham, Isaac and Jacob, may he bless...* who has come up to honor God, the Torah and the festival. May the Holy One, blessed be he, protect and deliver him from all distress and illness, and bless all his efforts with success; may he live to celebrate festivals in Jerusalem among all Israel his brethren; and let us say, Amen.

On the occasion of naming a new-born daughter:

He who blessed our fathers Abraham, Isaac and Jacob, Moses and Aaron, David and Solomon. may he bless the mother...* and her new-born daughter, whose name in Israel shall be...* May they raise her for the marriage canopy and for a life of good deeds; and let us say, Amen.

On behalf of a sick man:

He who blessed our fathers Abraham, Isaac and Jacob, Moses and Aaron, David and Solomon, may he heal...* who is ill. May the Holy One, blessed be he, have mercy and speedily restore him to perfect health, both spiritual and physical; and let us say, Amen.

On behalf of a sick woman:

He who blessed our fathers Abraham, Isaac and Jacob, Moses and Aaron, David and Solomon, may he heal...* who is ill. May the Holy One, blessed be he, have mercy and speedily restore her to perfect health, both spiritual and physical; and let us say, Amen.

* *The name is given.*

אַקְדָמוּת

Chanted on the first day of *Shavuoth* before the reading of the **Torah**

אַקְדָמוּת מִלִּין וְשָׁרָיוּת שׁוּתָא

אַוְלָא שָׁקֵלְנָא הַרְמָן וּרְשׁוּתָא.

בְּבָבֵי תְּרֵי וּתְלָת דְּאֶפְתַּח בְּנַקְשׁוּתָא

בְּבָרֵי דְבָרֵי וְטָרֵי עֲדֵי לְקַשְׁשׁוּתָא.

גְּבוּרָן עָלְמִין לֵהּ וְלָא סְפֵק פְּרִישׁוּתָא

גְּוִיל אִלּוּ רְקִיעֵי קְנֵי כָּל חוּרְשָׁתָא.

דְּיוֹ אִלּוּ יַמֵּי וְכָל מֵי כְנִישׁוּתָא

דָּיְרֵי אַרְעָא סָפְרֵי וְרָשְׁמֵי רַשְׁוָתָא.

הֲדַר מָרֵא שְׁמַיָּא וְשַׁלִּיט בְּיַבֶּשְׁתָּא

הֲקֵם עָלְמָא יְחִידַאי וְכַבְּשֵׁהּ בְּכַבְּשׁוּתָא.

וּבְלָא לֵאוּ שַׁכְלְלֵהּ וּבְלָא תְשָׁשׁוּתָא

וּבְאָתָא קַלִּילָא דְּלֵית בַּהּ מְשָׁשׁוּתָא.

זַמִּן כָּל עֲבִדְתֵּהּ בְּהַךְ יוֹמֵי שִׁתָּא

זְהוֹר יְקָרֵהּ עֲלִי עֲלֵי כָרְסְיֵהּ דְּאֶשָּׁתָא.

חֲיָל אֶלֶף אַלְפִין וְרִבּוֹא לְשַׁמְּשׁוּתָא

חַדְתִּין נְבוֹט לְצַפְרִין סַגִּיאָה טְרָשׁוּתָא.

טְפֵי יְקִידִין שְׂרָפִין כְּלוּל גַּפֵּי שִׁתָּא

טְעֵם עַד יִתְיְהֵב לְהוֹן שְׁתִיקִין בְּאַדִּשְׁתָּא.

אקדמות was composed by Rabbi Meir ben Isaac of France, who lived in the eleventh century. The poem, written in Aramaic, consists of ninety verses alphabetically arranged. Its acrostic comprises, in addition to a twofold alphabet, the names of the author and his father as well as a short petition: מאיר ביר רבי יצחק, יגדל בתורה ובמעשים טובים אמן, וחזק ואמץ. There are ten syllables to each verse,

AKDAMUTH

Chanted on the first day of Shavuoth before the reading of the Torah

Before reciting the Ten Commandments,
I first ask permission and approval

To start with two or three stanzas in fear
Of God who creates and ever sustains.

He has endless might, not to be described
Were the skies parchment, were all the reeds quills,

Were the seas and all waters made of ink,
Were all the world's inhabitants made scribes.

The glorious Lord of heaven and earth,
Alone, formed the world, veiled in mystery.

Without exertion did he perfect it,
Only by a light sign, without substance.

He accomplished all his work in six days;
His glory ascended a throne of fire.

Millions of legions are at his service;
Fresh each morning they flourish with great faith.

More glowing are the six-winged seraphim,
Who keep silence till leave is given them.

---

and one rhyme (תא) runs through the entire hymn. Recited on the first day of
Shavuoth when the *kohen* is called to the Torah, this mystical poem deals with
the indescribable greatness of the Creator, the excellence of the Torah and the
future hope of Israel.

עדי לקששותא is taken from Isaiah 46:4 (ועד זקנה... אני אסבל).

אתא קלילא refers to the mystic idea that the creation of the world was
brought about by means of the Hebrew letter ה.

חדתין נבוט... a paraphrase of the verse חדשים לבקרים, רבה אמונתך (Lamentations 3:23). According to a midrashic statement, there are countless numbers
of angels who come into being daily; they praise God and vanish immediately
after the performance of their task.

יְקַבְּלוּן דֵּן מִן דֵּן שָׁוֵי דְּלָא בְשַׁשְׁתָּא
יְקַר מְלֵי כָּל אַרְעָא לְתַלְוֹתֵי קְדוּשְׁתָּא.
בְּקָל מִן קֳדָם שַׁדַּי כְּקָל מֵי נְפִישׁוּתָא
כְּרוּבִין קֳבֵל גַּלְגְּלִין מְרוֹמְמִין בְּאוּשָׁתָּא.
לְמֶחֱזֵי בְּאַנְפָּא עֵין כְּוָת גִּירֵי קַשְׁתָּא
לְכָל אֲתַר דְּמִשְׁתַּלְּחִין זְרִיזִין בְּאַשְׁוָתָא.
מְבָרְכִין בְּרִיךְ יְקָרֵהּ בְּכָל לִשָּׁן לְחִישׁוּתָא
מֵאֲתַר בֵּית שְׁכִינְתֵּהּ דְּלָא צְרִיךְ בְּחִישׁוּתָא.
נְהִים כָּל חֵיל מְרוֹמָא מְקַלְּסִין בַּחֲשַׁשְׁתָּא
נְהִירָא מַלְכוּתֵהּ לְדָר וָדָר לְאַפְרַשְׁתָּא.
סְדִירָא בְהוֹן קְדוּשְׁתָּא וְכַד חָלְפָא שַׁעֲתָא
סִיּוּמָא דִלְעָלַם וְאוֹף לָא לִשְׁבוּעֲתָא.
עֲדַב יְקַר אַחֲסַנְתֵּהּ חֲבִיבִין דִּבְקַבְעֲתָא
עָבְדִין לֵהּ חֲטִיבָא בִּדְנַח וּשְׁקַעְתָּא.
פְּרִישָׁן לְמָנָתֵהּ לְמֶעְבַּד לֵהּ רְעוּתָא
פְּרִישׁוּתֵהּ שְׁבָחֵהּ יְחַוּוֹן בְּשָׁעוּתָא.
צְבִי וְחַמֵּד וְרַגֵּג דִּילְאוֹן בְּלָעוּתָא
צְלוֹתְהוֹן בְּכֵן מְקַבֵּל וְהַנְיָא בְעוּתָא.
קְטִירָא לְחֵי עָלְמָא בְּתָגָא בִּשְׁבוּעֲתָא
קַבֵּל יְקַר טוֹטַפְתָּא יְתִיבָא בִקְבִיעוּתָא.
רְשִׁימָא הִיא גוּפָא בְּחָכְמְתָא וּבְדַעְתָּא
רְבוּתְהוֹן דְּיִשְׂרָאֵל קְרָאֵי בִּשְׁמַעְתָּא.
שְׁבַח רִבּוֹן עָלְמָא אֲמִירָא דַכְוָתָא
שְׁפַר עֲלֵי לְחַוּוֹיֵהּ בְּאַפֵּי מַלְכְוָתָא.

Without delay they call to one another:
"God's majestic splendor fills the whole earth!"

Like a mighty thunder, like ocean's roar,
The cherubim and the spheres rise loudly

To gaze at the rainbowlike appearance.
Wherever sent, they hasten anxiously,

Whispering praise in each tongue: "Blessed be
His glory in his entire universe."

All the heavenly hosts shout praise in awe:
"His glory shines forever and ever!"

Their hymn is timed; when the hour is gone,
They shall at no period chant it again.

Dear to him are the people of Israel,
Acclaiming him each morning and evening.

They are dedicated to do his will;
His wonders, his praises, they declare hourly.

He desires them to toil in the Torah,
So that their prayer be well accepted,

Bound up in the crown of the Eternal,
Securely set near the precious frontlet.

His frontlet is most skilfully inscribed:
"Great is Israel who proclaims God's Oneness."

The praise of the world's Lord, in pure homage,
I am pleased to declare before the kings.

יקר מלי... contains the essential part of the *Kedushah*, derived from Isaiah 6:3.

סיומא דלעלם that is, they are silent forever; they do not chant even after seven years. The reference is to the midrashic statement to the effect that whenever the daily angels do not chant their hymns at the exact moment, they disappear in the stream of fire known as *Dinur*.

עדב יקר אחסנתיה the lot of his precious heritage [Israel]. This refers to the talmudic passage (Ḥullin 91b) to the effect that Israel sings God's praises at all times, while the angels are limited in this respect.

קטירא לחי עלמא refers to the mystic idea that God's *tefillin* contain an inscription in praise of Israel.

תָּאִין וּמִתְכַּנְּשִׁין כְּחֵזוּ אַדְנָתָא

תְּמֵהִין וְשָׁיְלִין לֵהּ בְּעֵסֶק אָתְוָתָא.

מְנָן וּמָאן הוּא רְחִימָךְ שַׁפִּירָא בְּרֵוָתָא

אֲרוּם בְּגִינֵהּ סָפֵית מְדוֹר אַרְיָוָתָא.

יְקָרָא וְיָאֶה אַתְּ אִין תְּעָרְבִי לְמַרְוָתָא

רְעוּתֵךְ נַעֲבֵד לִיךְ בְּכָל אַתְרְוָתָא.

בְּחָכְמְתָא מְתִיבְתָּא לְהוֹן קְצָת לְהוֹדָעוּתָא

יְדַעְתּוּן חַכְּמִין לֵהּ בְּאִשְׁתְּמוֹדָעוּתָא.

רְבוּתְכוֹן מָה חֲשִׁיבָא קֳבֵל הַהִיא שְׁבַחְתָּא

רְבוּתָא דְּיַעֲבֵד לִי כַּד מַטְיָא יְשׁוּעָתָא.

בְּמֵיתֵי לִי נְהוֹרָא וְתַחֲפֵי לְכוֹן בַּהֲתָא

יְקָרֵהּ כַּד אִתְגְּלֵי בְּתָקְפָּא וּבְגֵיוָתָא.

יְשַׁלֵּם גְּמֻלַיָּא לְסַנְאֵי וְנַגְוָתָא

צִדְקָתָא לְעַם חֲבִיב וְסַגִּיא זַכְוָתָא.

חֲדוּ שְׁלֵמָא בְּמֵיתֵי וּמָנֵי דַכְיָתָא

קְרְיְתָא דִירוּשְׁלֵם כַּד יְכַנֵּשׁ גַּלְוָתָא.

יְקָרֵהּ מַטִּיל עֲלַהּ בְּיוֹמֵי וְלֵילְוָתָא

גְּנוּנֵהּ לְמֶעֱבַּד בַּהּ בְּתוּשְׁבְּחָן כְּלִילָתָא.

דְּזָהוֹר עֲנָנַיָּא לְמִשְׁפַּר כִּילָתָא

לְפוּמֵהּ דַּעֲבִידְתָּא עֲבִידָן מְטַלַּלְתָּא.

בְּתַכְתְּקֵי דְּהַב פִּזָּא וְשֶׁבַע מַעֲלָתָא

תְּחִימִין צַדִּיקֵי קֳדָם רַב פָּעֳלָתָא.

וְרֵוֵיהוֹן דָּמֵה לְשַׁבְעָא חֶדְוָתָא

רְקִיעָא בְּזֵהוֹרֵהּ וְכוֹכְבֵי זִיוָתָא.

They come and gather like the surging waves,
Wondering and asking about the signs:

Whence and who is your beloved, O fair one?
For whom do you die in the lions' den?

Most precious are you; if you merge with us,
We will do your will in all the regions.

With wisdom I answer them concisely:
You must recognize and acknowledge him!

Of what value is your glory compared
With all that God will do for me in due time,

When light will come to me and shame to you,
When he will reveal himself in great might?

He will repay the foes in all the isles;
Triumph to the dear and upright people!

Perfect joy, pure delight, will come into
Jerusalem when he will gather the exiles.

His glory will shield Zion day and night,
While his tent for praise will be made in it

Under a splendid canopy of bright clouds.
For each godly man a booth will be made,

Furnished with a gold throne of seven steps.
The righteous will be arrayed before God,

Their sight resembling sevenfold delight,
The brilliant sky and the luminous stars—

תאין ומתכנשין alludes to the medieval public disputations on the relative merits of Judaism and other religions, with particular emphasis upon the Messianic idea.

וכן היו אומות and onwards is based upon the *Sifré*, section 343: תמהין ושילין העולם שאלים את ישראל ואומרים להם: „מה דודך מדוד" שכך אתם מומתים עליו, שכך אתם נהרגים עליו?... כולכם נאים, כולכם גבורים, בואו והתערבו עמנו. וישראל אומרים להם: נאמר לכם מקצת שבחו, ואתם מכירים אותו ...

הֲדָרָא דְּלָא אֶפְשַׁר לְמִפְרַט בְּשִׂפְוָתָא
וְלָא אִשְׁתְּמַע וְחָמֵי נְבִיאָן חֶזְוָתָא.

בְּלָא שָׁלְטָא בֵּהּ עֵין בְּגוֹ עֵדֶן גִּנְתָא
מְטַיְּלֵי בֵּי חִנְגָּא לְבַהֲדֵי דִשְׁכִינְתָּא.

עֲלֵהּ רָמְזֵי דֵּן הוּא בְּרַם בְּאֲמְתָּנוּתָא
שַׂבַּרְנָא לֵהּ בְּשִׁבְיָן תְּקוֹף הֵמְנוּתָא.

יַדְבַּר לָן עָלְמִין עַלֵמִין מְדַמּוּתָא
מְנָת דִּילָן דְּמִלְּקַדְמִין פָּרֵשׁ בַּאֲרָמוּתָא.

טְלוּלֵהּ דְּלִוְיָתָן וְתוֹר טוּר רָמוּתָא
וְחַד בְּחַד כִּי סָבִיךְ וְעָבֵד קְרָבוּתָא.

בְּקַרְנוֹהִי מְנַגַּח בְּהֵמוֹת בְּרַבְרְבוּתָא
יְקַרְטַע נוּן לְקַבְלֵהּ בְּצִיצוֹי בִּגְבוּרְתָּא.

מְקָרֵב לֵהּ בָּרְיֵהּ בְּחַרְבֵּהּ רַבְרְבָתָא
אֲרִסְטוֹן לְצַדִּיקֵי יְתַקֵּן וְשֵׁרוּתָא.

מְסַחֲרִין עֲלֵי תַכֵּי דְכַדְכֹּד וְגוּמַרְתָא
נְגִידִין קַמֵּיהוֹן אֲפַרְסְמוֹן נַהֲרָתָא.

וּמִתְפַּנְּקִין וְרָווֹ בְּכַסֵּי רְוָיָתָא
חֲמַר מְרַת דְּמִבְּרֵאשִׁית נְטִיר בֵּי נַעֲוָתָא.

זַכָּאִין כַּד שְׁמַעְתּוּן שְׁבַח דָּא שִׁירָתָא
קְבִיעִין כֵּן תֶּהֱווֹן בְּהַנְהוּ חֲבוּרָתָא.

וְתִזְכּוּן דִּי תֵיתְבוּן בְּעֵלָּא דָרָתָא
אֲרֵי תְצִיתוּן לְמִלּוֹי דְּנָפְקִין בְּהַדְרָתָא.

מְרוֹמָם הוּא אֱלָהִין בְּקַדְמָא וּבַתְרַיְתָא
צְבִי וְאִתְרְעִי בָן וּמְסַר לָן אוֹרַיְתָא.

A splendor that no language can describe,
That was not heard of nor viewed by prophets.

No eye has penetrated Paradise,
Where the righteous dance in presence of God,

Reverently pointing out: "This is he
For whom we looked in exile with firm faith!

He now gently guides us eternally,
Granting us the share long reserved for us."

Leviathan contends with Behemoth;
They are locked in combat with each other.

Behemoth gores mightily with its horns;
The sea-monster counters with potent fins.

The Creator slays them with his great sword,
And prepares a banquet for the righteous,

Who sit in rows at tables of precious stones,
While before them there flow streams of balsam,

And they indulge themselves and drink full cups
Of the precious old wine preserved in vats.

You upright, having heard this hymn of praise,
May you be in that blissful company!

You will merit to sit in the first row
If you will obey God's majestic words.

God, exalted from beginning to end,
Was pleased with us and gave us the Torah.

טלולה דלויתן is a description of the contest between the legendary monsters, Leviathan and Behemoth, which ends with the destruction of both. In kabbalistic literature the Leviathan is identified with evil which will disappear in Messianic times. It has been suggested that the midrashic passages concerning the Messianic banquet convey the thought that this will be the last feast, after which there will be no bodily needs. There are some who conceive the Messianic banquet in a spiritual sense.

מקרב... בריה בחרביה a paraphrase of the verse העושו יגש חרבו (Job 40:19) in a description of Behemoth.

קְרִיאַת הַתּוֹרָה לְשָׁבוּעוֹת

FOR THE FIRST DAY

שמות יט—כ

בַּחֹדֶשׁ הַשְּׁלִישִׁי לְצֵאת בְּנֵי־יִשְׂרָאֵל מֵאֶרֶץ מִצְרָיִם בַּיּוֹם
הַזֶּה בָּאוּ מִדְבַּר סִינָי: וַיִּסְעוּ מֵרְפִידִים וַיָּבֹאוּ מִדְבַּר
סִינַי וַיַּחֲנוּ בַּמִּדְבָּר וַיִּחַן־שָׁם יִשְׂרָאֵל נֶגֶד הָהָר: וּמֹשֶׁה
עָלָה אֶל־הָאֱלֹהִים וַיִּקְרָא אֵלָיו יְהֹוָה מִן־הָהָר לֵאמֹר כֹּה
תֹאמַר לְבֵית יַעֲקֹב וְתַגֵּיד לִבְנֵי יִשְׂרָאֵל: אַתֶּם רְאִיתֶם
אֲשֶׁר עָשִׂיתִי לְמִצְרָיִם וָאֶשָּׂא אֶתְכֶם עַל־כַּנְפֵי נְשָׁרִים
וָאָבִא אֶתְכֶם אֵלָי: וְעַתָּה אִם־שָׁמוֹעַ תִּשְׁמְעוּ בְּקֹלִי וּשְׁמַרְתֶּם
אֶת־בְּרִיתִי וִהְיִיתֶם לִי סְגֻלָּה מִכָּל־הָעַמִּים כִּי־לִי כָּל־
הָאָרֶץ: וְאַתֶּם תִּהְיוּ־לִי מַמְלֶכֶת כֹּהֲנִים וְגוֹי קָדוֹשׁ אֵלֶּה
הַדְּבָרִים אֲשֶׁר תְּדַבֵּר אֶל־בְּנֵי יִשְׂרָאֵל:٭ וַיָּבֹא מֹשֶׁה וַיִּקְרָא
לְזִקְנֵי הָעָם וַיָּשֶׂם לִפְנֵיהֶם אֵת כָּל־הַדְּבָרִים הָאֵלֶּה אֲשֶׁר
צִוָּהוּ יְהֹוָה: וַיַּעֲנוּ כָל־הָעָם יַחְדָּו וַיֹּאמְרוּ כֹּל אֲשֶׁר־דִּבֶּר
יְהֹוָה נַעֲשֶׂה וַיָּשֶׁב מֹשֶׁה אֶת־דִּבְרֵי הָעָם אֶל־יְהֹוָה: וַיֹּאמֶר
יְהֹוָה אֶל־מֹשֶׁה הִנֵּה אָנֹכִי בָּא אֵלֶיךָ בְּעַב הֶעָנָן בַּעֲבוּר
יִשְׁמַע הָעָם בְּדַבְּרִי עִמָּךְ וְגַם־בְּךָ יַאֲמִינוּ לְעוֹלָם וַיַּגֵּד
מֹשֶׁה אֶת־דִּבְרֵי הָעָם אֶל־יְהֹוָה: וַיֹּאמֶר יְהֹוָה אֶל־מֹשֶׁה
לֵךְ אֶל־הָעָם וְקִדַּשְׁתָּם הַיּוֹם וּמָחָר וְכִבְּסוּ שִׂמְלֹתָם: וְהָיוּ
נְכֹנִים לַיּוֹם הַשְּׁלִישִׁי כִּי ׀ בַּיּוֹם הַשְּׁלִשִׁי יֵרֵד יְהֹוָה לְעֵינֵי
כָל־הָעָם עַל־הַר סִינָי: וְהִגְבַּלְתָּ אֶת־הָעָם סָבִיב לֵאמֹר
הִשָּׁמְרוּ לָכֶם עֲלוֹת בָּהָר וּנְגֹעַ בְּקָצֵהוּ כָּל־הַנֹּגֵעַ בָּהָר

TORAH READING FOR SHAVUOTH

For the First Day

Exodus 19, 20

In the third month after their departure from the land of Egypt, on the same day, the people of Israel came to **the** wilderness of Sinai. They had set out from Rephidim, entered **the** wilderness of Sinai and encamped in the desert: there Israel was encamped in front of the mountain. Moses went up the mountain to God; then the Lord called to him and said: Thus shall you say to the house of Jacob, tell the people of Israel: You have seen for yourselves how I treated the Egyptians and how I did bear you on eagle's wings and brought you here to myself. Now then, if you hearken to my voice and keep my covenant, you shall be my own out of all the peoples; indeed, all the earth is mine. But you shall be to me a kingdom, a holy nation. These are the words which you shall speak to the people of Israel.*

Then Moses came, summoned the elders of the people and set before them all these words which the Lord had commanded him. The people all answered together and said: Everything the Lord has spoken we will do. Then Moses brought back the words of the people to the Lord. And the Lord said to Moses: Behold, I am coming to you in a thick cloud so that the people may hear when I speak to you, that they may always have faith in you also. When Moses, then, had told the Lord the words of the people, the Lord said to Moses: Go to the people and sanctify them today and tomorrow; let them wash their garments, and be ready for the third day; for on the third day the Lord will come down on Mount Sinai before the eyes of all the people. Set limits for the people all around the mountain, saying: Take care not to go up the mountain, or even to touch its edge; if anyone touches the mountain he

---

ביום הזה, on the same day, refers to the first day of the month. The seeming redundance in מדבר סיני ויחנו במדבר is explained by Ramban to the effect that as soon as the Israelites came to the wilderness and found themselves in front of the mountain where the revelation was to take place they gladly en-

מוֹת יוּמָת: לֹא־תִגַּע בּוֹ יָד כִּי־סָקוֹל יִסָּקֵל אוֹ־יָרֹה יִיָּרֶה
אִם־בְּהֵמָה אִם־אִישׁ לֹא יִחְיֶה בִּמְשֹׁךְ הַיֹּבֵל הֵמָּה יַעֲלוּ
בָהָר: ‏٭‏ וַיֵּרֶד מֹשֶׁה מִן־הָהָר אֶל־הָעָם וַיְקַדֵּשׁ אֶת־הָעָם
וַיְכַבְּסוּ שִׂמְלֹתָם: וַיֹּאמֶר אֶל־הָעָם הֱיוּ נְכֹנִים לִשְׁלֹשֶׁת
יָמִים אַל־תִּגְּשׁוּ אֶל־אִשָּׁה: וַיְהִי בַיֹּום הַשְּׁלִישִׁי בִּהְיֹת
הַבֹּקֶר וַיְהִי קֹלֹת וּבְרָקִים וְעָנָן כָּבֵד עַל־הָהָר וְקֹל שֹׁפָר
חָזָק מְאֹד וַיֶּחֱרַד כָּל־הָעָם אֲשֶׁר בַּמַּחֲנֶה: וַיּוֹצֵא מֹשֶׁה
אֶת־הָעָם לִקְרַאת הָאֱלֹהִים מִן־הַמַּחֲנֶה וַיִּתְיַצְּבוּ בְּתַחְתִּית
הָהָר: וְהַר סִינַי עָשַׁן כֻּלּוֹ מִפְּנֵי אֲשֶׁר יָרַד עָלָיו יְהוָה בָּאֵשׁ
וַיַּעַל עֲשָׁנוֹ כְּעֶשֶׁן הַכִּבְשָׁן וַיֶּחֱרַד כָּל־הָהָר מְאֹד: וַיְהִי קוֹל
הַשֹּׁפָר הוֹלֵךְ וְחָזֵק מְאֹד מֹשֶׁה יְדַבֵּר וְהָאֱלֹהִים יַעֲנֶנּוּ
בְקוֹל: ‏٭‏ וַיֵּרֶד יְהוָה עַל־הַר סִינַי אֶל־רֹאשׁ הָהָר וַיִּקְרָא
יְהוָה לְמֹשֶׁה אֶל־רֹאשׁ הָהָר וַיַּעַל מֹשֶׁה: וַיֹּאמֶר יְהוָה אֶל־
מֹשֶׁה רֵד הָעֵד בָּעָם פֶּן־יֶהֶרְסוּ אֶל־יְהוָה לִרְאוֹת וְנָפַל
מִמֶּנּוּ רָב: וְגַם הַכֹּהֲנִים הַנִּגָּשִׁים אֶל־יְהוָה יִתְקַדָּשׁוּ פֶּן־
יִפְרֹץ בָּהֶם יְהוָה: וַיֹּאמֶר מֹשֶׁה אֶל־יְהוָה לֹא־יוּכַל הָעָם
לַעֲלֹת אֶל־הַר סִינָי כִּי־אַתָּה הַעֵדֹתָה בָּנוּ לֵאמֹר הַגְבֵּל
אֶת־הָהָר וְקִדַּשְׁתּוֹ: וַיֹּאמֶר אֵלָיו יְהוָה לֶךְ־רֵד וְעָלִיתָ אַתָּה
וְאַהֲרֹן עִמָּךְ וְהַכֹּהֲנִים וְהָעָם אַל־יֶהֶרְסוּ לַעֲלֹת אֶל־יְהוָה
פֶּן־יִפְרָץ־בָּם: וַיֵּרֶד מֹשֶׁה אֶל־הָעָם וַיֹּאמֶר אֲלֵהֶם:

וַיְדַבֵּר אֱלֹהִים אֵת כָּל־הַדְּבָרִים הָאֵלֶּה לֵאמֹר: אָנֹכִי
יְהוָה אֱלֹהֶיךָ אֲשֶׁר הוֹצֵאתִיךָ מֵאֶרֶץ מִצְרַיִם מִבֵּית עֲבָדִים:
לֹא יִהְיֶה לְךָ אֱלֹהִים אֲחֵרִים עַל־פָּנָי לֹא תַעֲשֶׂה־לְךָ פֶסֶל ׀
וְכָל־תְּמוּנָה אֲשֶׁר בַּשָּׁמַיִם ׀ מִמַּעַל וַאֲשֶׁר בָּאָרֶץ מִתַּחַת

shall be put to death. No hand shall touch him, for he shall be stoned or shot. Such one, man or beast, shall not live. Only when the ram's horn is sounded may they go up to the mountain.*

Then Moses came down from the mountain to the people; he sanctified the people, and they washed their garments. He said to the people: Be ready for the third day; approach no woman. On the morning of the third day there were peals of thunder and lightning, and a heavy cloud over the mountain, and a very loud trumpet blast; all the people in the camp trembled. Moses led the people out of the camp to meet God, and they stationed themselves at the foot of the mountain. Mount Sinai was all wrapped in smoke, for the Lord descended on it in fire; the smoke rose from it as though from a furnace, and the whole mountain trembled violently. The trumpet blast grew louder and louder; Moses spoke and God answered him by a voice.

The Lord came down to Mount Sinai, to the top of the mountain; the Lord then summoned Moses to the top of the mountain, and Moses went up. Then the Lord said to Moses: Go down and warn the people not to break through toward the Lord to gaze, else many of them will fall dead. The priests, too, who approach the Lord, shall sanctify themselves, lest the Lord may break out upon them. Moses said to the Lord: The people cannot go up to Mount Sinai, for thou didst warn us, saying: Set limits around the mountain and sanctify it. The Lord said to him again: Go down now, then come up again with Aaron; but the priests and the people must not break through to come up to the Lord, lest he may break out upon them. So Moses went **down** to the people and told them this.

God spoke all these words, saying:

1. I am the Lord your God, who brought you out of the land of Egypt, out of the house of slavery.

2. You shall have no other gods beside me. You shall not make for yourself any idols in the shape of anything that is in heaven above, or that is on the earth below, or that is in the water under

camped in the desert, without seeking a more comfortable spot. The whole section has been described as one of the most awe-inspiring regions on the face of the earth. Here they remained eleven months (compare Numbers 30:11-12).

וַאֲשֶׁ֣ר בַּמַּ֣יִם ׀ מִתַּ֣חַת לָאָ֑רֶץ לֹֽא־תִשְׁתַּחֲוֶ֥ה לָהֶ֖ם וְלֹ֣א
תָֽעָבְדֵ֑ם כִּ֣י אָֽנֹכִ֞י יְהוָ֤ה אֱלֹהֶ֙יךָ֙ אֵ֣ל קַנָּ֔א פֹּ֠קֵד עֲוֹ֨ן אָבֹ֧ת
עַל־בָּנִ֛ים עַל־שִׁלֵּשִׁ֥ים וְעַל־רִבֵּעִ֖ים לְשֹׂנְאָֽי׃ וְעֹ֥שֶׂה חֶ֙סֶד֙
לַֽאֲלָפִ֑ים לְאֹֽהֲבַ֖י וּלְשֹׁמְרֵ֥י מִצְוֹתָֽי׃   לֹ֥א תִשָּׂ֛א
אֶת־שֵֽׁם־יְהוָ֥ה אֱלֹהֶ֖יךָ לַשָּׁ֑וְא כִּ֣י לֹ֤א יְנַקֶּה֙ יְהוָ֔ה אֵ֥ת אֲשֶׁר־
יִשָּׂ֥א אֶת־שְׁמ֖וֹ לַשָּֽׁוְא׃

זָכ֛וֹר אֶת־י֥וֹם הַשַּׁבָּ֖ת לְקַדְּשׁ֑וֹ שֵׁ֤שֶׁת יָמִים֙ תַּֽעֲבֹד֙ וְעָשִׂ֣יתָ
כָּל־מְלַאכְתֶּֽךָ׃ וְי֙וֹם֙ הַשְּׁבִיעִ֔י שַׁבָּ֖ת ׀ לַֽיהוָ֣ה אֱלֹהֶ֑יךָ לֹֽא
תַֽעֲשֶׂ֣ה כָל־מְלָאכָ֡ה אַתָּ֣ה ׀ וּבִנְךָ֣ וּבִתֶּ֡ךָ עַבְדְּךָ֣ וַֽאֲמָֽתְךָ֩
וּבְהֶמְתֶּ֙ךָ֙ וְגֵֽרְךָ֔ אֲשֶׁ֖ר בִּשְׁעָרֶ֑יךָ כִּ֣י שֵֽׁשֶׁת־יָמִ֞ים עָשָׂ֣ה יְהוָ֗ה
אֶת־הַשָּׁמַ֣יִם וְאֶת־הָאָ֗רֶץ אֶת־הַיָּם֙ וְאֶת־כָּל־אֲשֶׁר־בָּ֔ם
וַיָּ֖נַח בַּיּ֣וֹם הַשְּׁבִיעִ֑י עַל־כֵּ֗ן בֵּרַ֧ךְ יְהוָ֛ה אֶת־י֥וֹם הַשַּׁבָּ֖ת
וַֽיְקַדְּשֵֽׁהוּ׃   כַּבֵּ֥ד אֶת־אָבִ֖יךָ וְאֶת־אִמֶּ֑ךָ לְמַ֙עַן֙ יַֽאֲרִכ֣וּן
יָמֶ֔יךָ עַ֚ל הָֽאֲדָמָ֔ה אֲשֶׁר־יְהוָ֥ה אֱלֹהֶ֖יךָ נֹתֵ֥ן לָֽךְ׃   לֹ֥א
תִּרְצָֽ֖ח׃   לֹ֣א תִּנְאָֽ֑ף׃   לֹ֣א תִּגְנֹֽ֒ב׃   לֹֽא־
תַֽעֲנֶ֥ה בְרֵֽעֲךָ֖ עֵ֥ד שָֽׁקֶר׃   לֹ֥א תַחְמֹ֖ד בֵּ֣ית
רֵעֶ֑ךָ   לֹֽא־תַחְמֹ֞ד אֵ֣שֶׁת רֵעֶ֗ךָ וְעַבְדּ֤וֹ וַֽאֲמָתוֹ֙ וְשׁוֹר֣וֹ
וַֽחֲמֹר֔וֹ וְכֹ֖ל אֲשֶׁ֥ר לְרֵעֶֽךָ׃ *

וְכָל־הָעָם֩ רֹאִ֨ים אֶת־הַקּוֹלֹ֜ת וְאֶת־הַלַּפִּידִ֗ם וְאֵת֙ ק֣וֹל הַשֹּׁפָ֔ר
וְאֶת־הָהָ֖ר עָשֵׁ֑ן וַיַּ֤רְא הָעָם֙ וַיָּנֻ֔עוּ וַיַּֽעַמְד֖וּ מֵֽרָחֹֽק׃ וַיֹּֽאמְרוּ֙
אֶל־מֹשֶׁ֔ה דַּבֵּר־אַתָּ֥ה עִמָּ֖נוּ וְנִשְׁמָ֑עָה וְאַל־יְדַבֵּ֥ר עִמָּ֛נוּ
אֱלֹהִ֖ים פֶּן־נָמֽוּת׃ וַיֹּ֙אמֶר מֹשֶׁ֣ה אֶל־הָעָם֮ אַל־תִּירָאוּ֒ כִּ֗י
לְבַֽעֲבוּר֙ נַסּ֣וֹת אֶתְכֶ֔ם בָּ֖א הָֽאֱלֹהִ֑ים וּבַֽעֲב֗וּר תִּהְיֶ֧ה יִרְאָת֛וֹ
עַל־פְּנֵיכֶ֖ם לְבִלְתִּ֥י תֶֽחֱטָֽאוּ׃ וַיַּֽעֲמֹ֥ד הָעָ֖ם מֵֽרָחֹ֑ק וּמֹשֶׁה֙
נִגַּ֣שׁ אֶל־הָ֣עֲרָפֶ֔ל אֲשֶׁר־שָׁ֖ם הָֽאֱלֹהִֽים׃   וַיֹּ֥אמֶר

the earth. You shall not bow down to them nor worship them; for I, the Lord your God, am a zealous God, punishing children for the sins of their fathers, down to the third or fourth generation of those who hate me, but showing kindness to the thousandth generation of those who love me and keep my commandments.

3. You shall not utter the name of the Lord your God in vain; for the Lord will not hold guiltless anyone who utters his name in vain.

4. Remember the Sabbath day to keep it holy. Six days you shall labor and do all your work; but on the seventh day, which is a day of rest in honor of the Lord your God, you shall not do any work, neither you, nor your son, nor your daughter, nor your male or female servant, nor your cattle, nor the stranger who is within your gates; for in six days the Lord made the heavens, the earth, the sea, and all that they contain, and rested on the seventh day; therefore the Lord blessed the Sabbath day and hallowed it.

5. Honor your father and your mother, that you may live long in the land which the Lord your God is giving you.

6. You shall not murder.

7. You shall not commit adultery.

8. You shall not steal.

9. You shall not testify falsely against your neighbor.

10. You shall not covet your neighbor's house; you shall not covet your neighbor's wife, nor his servant, male or female, nor his ox, nor his ass, nor anything that belongs to your neighbor

All the people witnessed the thunder and lightning, the blast of the trumpet and the mountain smoking; the people saw this and trembled; they stood at a distance, and said to Moses: You speak to us, and we will listen; but let not God speak to us lest we die. But Moses said to the people: Fear not, for God has come to test you, so that you may revere him and refrain from sinfulness. The people remained at a distance, while Moses approached the cloud where God was.

... לשנאי The penalty of man's sins will be shared by his immediate descendants only if they too hate the ways of God; but the benefits of a man's good deeds will extend indefinitely.

יְהֹוָה אֶל־מֹשֶׁה כֹּה תֹאמַר אֶל־בְּנֵי יִשְׂרָאֵל אַתֶּם רְאִיתֶם
כִּי מִן־הַשָּׁמַיִם דִּבַּרְתִּי עִמָּכֶם: לֹא תַעֲשׂוּן אִתִּי אֱלֹהֵי
כֶסֶף וֵאלֹהֵי זָהָב לֹא תַעֲשׂוּ לָכֶם: מִזְבַּח אֲדָמָה תַּעֲשֶׂה־
לִּי וְזָבַחְתָּ עָלָיו אֶת־עֹלֹתֶיךָ וְאֶת־שְׁלָמֶיךָ אֶת־צֹאנְךָ וְאֶת־
בְּקָרֶךָ בְּכָל־הַמָּקוֹם אֲשֶׁר אַזְכִּיר אֶת־שְׁמִי אָבוֹא אֵלֶיךָ
וּבֵרַכְתִּיךָ: וְאִם־מִזְבַּח אֲבָנִים תַּעֲשֶׂה־לִּי לֹא־תִבְנֶה אֶתְהֶן
גָּזִית כִּי חַרְבְּךָ הֵנַפְתָּ עָלֶיהָ וַתְּחַלְלֶהָ: וְלֹא־תַעֲלֶה
בְמַעֲלֹת עַל־מִזְבְּחִי אֲשֶׁר לֹא־תִגָּלֶה עֶרְוָתְךָ עָלָיו:

Both *Sifré Torah* being placed upon the desk, the Reader says:

יִתְגַּדַּל וְיִתְקַדַּשׁ שְׁמֵהּ רַבָּא בְּעָלְמָא דִּי בְרָא כִרְעוּתֵהּ;
וְיַמְלִיךְ מַלְכוּתֵהּ, בְּחַיֵּיכוֹן וּבְיוֹמֵיכוֹן וּבְחַיֵּי דְכָל בֵּית
יִשְׂרָאֵל, בַּעֲגָלָא וּבִזְמַן קָרִיב, וְאִמְרוּ אָמֵן.

יְהֵא שְׁמֵהּ רַבָּא מְבָרַךְ לְעָלַם וּלְעָלְמֵי עָלְמַיָּא.

יִתְבָּרַךְ וְיִשְׁתַּבַּח, וְיִתְפָּאַר וְיִתְרוֹמַם, וְיִתְנַשֵּׂא וְיִתְהַדָּר,
וְיִתְעַלֶּה וְיִתְהַלָּל שְׁמֵהּ דְּקֻדְשָׁא, בְּרִיךְ הוּא, לְעֵלָּא מִן כָּל
בִּרְכָתָא וְשִׁירָתָא, תֻּשְׁבְּחָתָא וְנֶחֱמָתָא, דַּאֲמִירָן בְּעָלְמָא,
וְאִמְרוּ אָמֵן.

The first *Torah* is then raised and the Congregation says:

וְזֹאת הַתּוֹרָה אֲשֶׁר שָׂם מֹשֶׁה לִפְנֵי בְּנֵי יִשְׂרָאֵל, עַל פִּי יְיָ
בְּיַד מֹשֶׁה.

עֵץ חַיִּים הִיא לַמַּחֲזִיקִים בָּהּ, וְתֹמְכֶיהָ מְאֻשָּׁר. דְּרָכֶיהָ
דַרְכֵי נֹעַם, וְכָל נְתִיבוֹתֶיהָ שָׁלוֹם. אֹרֶךְ יָמִים בִּימִינָהּ;
בִּשְׂמֹאלָהּ עֹשֶׁר וְכָבוֹד. יְיָ חָפֵץ לְמַעַן צִדְקוֹ, יַגְדִּיל תּוֹרָה
וְיַאְדִּיר.

Then the Lord said to Moses: Thus shall you say to the people
of Israel: You have seen for yourselves that I have spoken to you
from heaven. Do not make anything to rank with me; you must
not make for yourselves any gods of silver or of gold. An altar o
earth you shall make for me, and upon it you shall sacrifice your
burnt offerings and peace-offerings, your sheep and your oxen. In
whatever place I choose for the remembrance of my name I will
ome to you and bless you. If you make an altar of stone for met
do not build it of cut stone, for if you put your tool to it you dese-
crate it. You shall not go up by steps to my altar, lest your na-
kedness be exposed thereon.

Both Sifré Torah being placed upon the desk, the Reader says:

Glorified and sanctified be God's great name throughout the
world which he has created according to his will. May he establish
his kingdom, hastening his salvation and the coming of his Messiah, in your lifetime and during your days, and within the life of
the entire house of Israel, speedily and soon; and say, Amen.

May his great name be blessed forever and to all eternity.

Blessed and praised, glorified and exalted, extolled and honored,
adored and lauded be the name of the Holy One, blessed be he,
beyond all the blessings and hymns, praises and consolations that
are ever spoken in the world; and say, Amen.

The first Torah is then raised and the Congregation says:

This is the Torah which Moses placed before the children of
Israel. It is in accordance with the Lord's command through
Moses.

It is a tree of life to those who take hold of it, and happy
are those who support it. Its ways are pleasant ways, and all its
paths are peace. Long life is in its right hand, and in its left hand
are riches and honor. The Lord was pleased, for the sake of his
righteousness, to render the Torah great and glorious.

מן השמים דברתי עמכם ("I have spoken to you from heaven") brings to mind
Deuteronomy 4:36 which reads: "Out of heaven he let you hear his voice,
and on earth he let you see his great fire." Quoting a tannaitic Midrash
(Mekhilta), Rashi comments: God's glory was in heaven but his fire and
power he made to be felt on earth (כבודי בשמים, ואש וגבורתו על הארץ).

The following section is then read fron the second *Torah*.

במדבר כח, כו–לא

וּבְי֣וֹם הַבִּכּוּרִ֗ים בְּהַקְרִֽיבְכֶ֞ם מִנְחָ֤ה חֲדָשָׁה֙ לַֽיהֹוָ֔ה בְּשָׁבֻעֹֽתֵיכֶ֑ם מִֽקְרָא־קֹ֙דֶשׁ֙ יִהְיֶ֣ה לָכֶ֔ם כָּל־מְלֶ֥אכֶת עֲבֹדָ֖ה לֹ֥א תַעֲשֽׂוּ׃ וְהִקְרַבְתֶּ֨ם עוֹלָ֜ה לְרֵ֤יחַ נִיחֹ֙חַ֙ לַֽיהֹוָ֔ה פָּרִ֧ים בְּנֵֽי־בָקָ֛ר שְׁנַ֖יִם אַ֣יִל אֶחָ֑ד שִׁבְעָ֥ה כְבָשִׂ֖ים בְּנֵ֥י שָׁנָֽה׃ וּמִנְחָתָ֔ם סֹ֖לֶת בְּלוּלָ֣ה בַשָּׁ֑מֶן שְׁלֹשָׁ֣ה עֶשְׂרֹנִ֗ים לַפָּ֤ר הָֽאֶחָד֙ שְׁנֵ֣י עֶשְׂרֹנִ֔ים לָאַ֖יִל הָֽאֶחָֽד׃ עִשָּׂרוֹן֙ עִשָּׂר֔וֹן לַכֶּ֣בֶשׂ הָֽאֶחָ֑ד לְשִׁבְעַ֖ת הַכְּבָשִֽׂים׃ שְׂעִ֥יר עִזִּ֛ים אֶחָ֖ד לְכַפֵּ֥ר עֲלֵיכֶֽם׃ מִלְּבַ֞ד עֹלַ֤ת הַתָּמִיד֙ וּמִנְחָת֔וֹ תַּעֲשׂ֑וּ תְּמִימִ֥ם יִֽהְיוּ־לָכֶ֖ם וְנִסְכֵּיהֶֽם׃

The second *Torah* is then raised and the Congregation says וזאת התורה.

בָּרוּךְ אַתָּה, יְיָ אֱלֹהֵינוּ, מֶלֶךְ הָעוֹלָם, אֲשֶׁר בָּחַר בִּנְבִיאִים טוֹבִים, וְרָצָה בְדִבְרֵיהֶם הַנֶּאֱמָרִים בֶּאֱמֶת. בָּרוּךְ אַתָּה, יְיָ, הַבּוֹחֵר בַּתּוֹרָה, וּבְמֹשֶׁה עַבְדּוֹ, וּבְיִשְׂרָאֵל עַמּוֹ, וּבִנְבִיאֵי הָאֱמֶת וָצֶדֶק.

יחזקאל א

וַיְהִ֣י ׀ בִּשְׁלֹשִׁ֣ים שָׁנָ֗ה בָּֽרְבִיעִי֙ בַּחֲמִשָּׁ֣ה לַחֹ֔דֶשׁ וַאֲנִ֥י בְתֽוֹךְ־הַגּוֹלָ֖ה עַל־נְהַר־כְּבָ֑ר נִפְתְּחוּ֙ הַשָּׁמַ֔יִם וָאֶרְאֶ֖ה מַרְא֥וֹת אֱלֹהִֽים׃ בַּחֲמִשָּׁ֖ה לַחֹ֑דֶשׁ הִ֚יא הַשָּׁנָ֣ה הַחֲמִישִׁ֔ית לְגָל֖וּת הַמֶּ֥לֶךְ יוֹיָכִֽין׃ הָיֹ֣ה הָיָ֣ה דְבַר־יְ֠הֹוָ֠ה אֶל־יְחֶזְקֵ֨אל בֶּן־בּוּזִ֧י הַכֹּהֵ֛ן בְּאֶ֥רֶץ כַּשְׂדִּ֖ים עַל־נְהַר־כְּבָ֑ר וַתְּהִ֥י עָלָ֛יו שָׁ֖ם יַד־יְהֹוָֽה׃ וָאֵ֡רֶא וְהִנֵּה֩ ר֨וּחַ סְעָרָ֜ה בָּאָ֣ה מִן־הַצָּפ֗וֹן עָנָ֤ן גָּדוֹל֙ וְאֵ֣שׁ מִתְלַקַּ֔חַת וְנֹ֥גַהּ ל֖וֹ סָבִ֑יב וּמִ֨תּוֹכָ֔הּ כְּעֵ֥ין הַחַשְׁמַ֖ל מִתּ֥וֹךְ הָאֵֽשׁ׃ וּמִ֨תּוֹכָ֔הּ דְּמ֖וּת אַרְבַּ֣ע חַיּ֑וֹת וְזֶה֙ מַרְאֵֽיהֶ֔ן דְּמ֥וּת אָדָ֖ם לָהֵֽנָּה׃ וְאַרְבָּעָ֥ה פָנִ֖ים לְאֶחָ֑ת וְאַרְבַּ֥ע כְּנָפַ֖יִם

The following section is then read from the second Torah.

Numbers 28:26-31

On the day of first fruits, when you present a new meal-offering to the Lord at your Feast of Weeks, you shall have a holy assembly; you shall do no hard work. You shall present a burnt offering for a sweet savor to the Lord; two young bullocks, one ram, and seven yearling lambs, with their meal-offering of fine flour mixed with oil—three tenths of an *ephah* for each bullock, two tenths for the ram, and one tenth for each of the seven lambs. One goat shall be offered to make atonement for you. You shall offer these in addition to the regular daily burnt offering with its meal-offering. You shall have them unblemished, with their drink-offerings.

The second Torah is then raised and the Congregation says v'zoth ha-Torah.

Blessed art thou, Lord our God, King of the universe, who hast chosen good prophets, and hast been pleased with their words which were truthfully spoken. Blessed art thou, O Lord, who hast chosen the Torah and thy servant Moses, thy people Israel and the true and righteous prophets.

Ezekiel 1

It was in the thirtieth year, on the fifth day of the fourth month, as I was among the exiles at the river Kebar, that the heavens opened and I saw visions of God. On the fifth day of the month, in the fifth year of king Jehoiachin's exile, the word of the Lord came to the priest Ezekiel, the son of Buzi, in the land of the Chaldeans, at the river Kebar; the hand of the Lord was upon him there.

I saw a storm-wind coming from the north, a huge cloud and flashing fire with a radiance encircling it, and out of its midst there was a luster like that of electrum, from the midst of the fire. Out of it appeared the forms of four creatures, and this was their appearance: They had the form of a man, each with four faces and

---

Ezekiel prophesied in Babylon for a period of twenty-two years, having been taken into captivity eleven years before the fall of Jerusalem. According to Rabbi David Kimhi and other commentators, *the thirtieth year* refers to the last jubilee kept prior to the Babylonian Captivity. The august vision was designed to prepare Ezekiel for his prophetic activity. In a state of ecstasy,

לָאַחַת לָהֶם: וְרַגְלֵיהֶם רֶגֶל יְשָׁרָה וְכַף רַגְלֵיהֶם כְּכַף
רֶגֶל עֵגֶל וְנֹצְצִים כְּעֵין נְחֹשֶׁת קָלָל: וְיָדוֹ אָדָם מִתַּחַת
כַּנְפֵיהֶם עַל אַרְבַּעַת רִבְעֵיהֶם וּפְנֵיהֶם וְכַנְפֵיהֶם לְאַרְבַּעְתָּם:
חֹבְרֹת אִשָּׁה אֶל־אֲחוֹתָהּ כַּנְפֵיהֶם לֹא־יִסַּבּוּ בְלֶכְתָּן
אִישׁ אֶל־עֵבֶר פָּנָיו יֵלֵכוּ: וּדְמוּת פְּנֵיהֶם פְּנֵי אָדָם וּפְנֵי
אַרְיֵה אֶל־הַיָּמִין לְאַרְבַּעְתָּם וּפְנֵי־שׁוֹר מֵהַשְּׂמֹאול
לְאַרְבַּעְתָּן וּפְנֵי־נֶשֶׁר לְאַרְבַּעְתָּן: וּפְנֵיהֶם וְכַנְפֵיהֶם פְּרֻדוֹת
מִלְמָעְלָה לְאִישׁ שְׁתַּיִם חֹבְרוֹת אִישׁ וּשְׁתַּיִם מְכַסּוֹת אֵת
גְּוִיֹּתֵיהֶנָה: וְאִישׁ אֶל־עֵבֶר פָּנָיו יֵלֵכוּ אֶל אֲשֶׁר יִהְיֶה־
שָּׁמָּה הָרוּחַ לָלֶכֶת יֵלֵכוּ לֹא יִסַּבּוּ בְּלֶכְתָּן: וּדְמוּת הַחַיּוֹת
מַרְאֵיהֶם כְּגַחֲלֵי־אֵשׁ בֹּעֲרוֹת כְּמַרְאֵה הַלַּפִּדִים הִיא
מִתְהַלֶּכֶת בֵּין הַחַיּוֹת וְנֹגַהּ לָאֵשׁ וּמִן־הָאֵשׁ יוֹצֵא בָרָק:
וְהַחַיּוֹת רָצוֹא וָשׁוֹב כְּמַרְאֵה הַבָּזָק: וָאֵרֶא הַחַיּוֹת וְהִנֵּה
אוֹפַן אֶחָד בָּאָרֶץ אֵצֶל הַחַיּוֹת לְאַרְבַּעַת פָּנָיו: מַרְאֵה
הָאוֹפַנִּים וּמַעֲשֵׂיהֶם כְּעֵין תַּרְשִׁישׁ וּדְמוּת אֶחָד לְאַרְבַּעְתָּן
וּמַרְאֵיהֶם וּמַעֲשֵׂיהֶם כַּאֲשֶׁר יִהְיֶה הָאוֹפַן בְּתוֹךְ הָאוֹפָן:
עַל־אַרְבַּעַת רִבְעֵיהֶן בְּלֶכְתָּם יֵלֵכוּ לֹא יִסַּבּוּ בְּלֶכְתָּן:
וְגַבֵּיהֶן וְגֹבַהּ לָהֶם וְיִרְאָה לָהֶם וְגַבֹּתָם מְלֵאֹת עֵינַיִם
סָבִיב לְאַרְבַּעְתָּן: וּבְלֶכֶת הַחַיּוֹת יֵלְכוּ הָאוֹפַנִּים אֶצְלָם
וּבְהִנָּשֵׂא הַחַיּוֹת מֵעַל הָאָרֶץ יִנָּשְׂאוּ הָאוֹפַנִּים: עַל אֲשֶׁר
יִהְיֶה־שָּׁם הָרוּחַ לָלֶכֶת יֵלֵכוּ שָׁמָּה הָרוּחַ לָלֶכֶת וְהָאוֹפַנִּים
יִנָּשְׂאוּ לְעֻמָּתָם כִּי רוּחַ הַחַיָּה בָּאוֹפַנִּים: בְּלֶכְתָּם יֵלֵכוּ
וּבְעָמְדָם יַעֲמֹדוּ וּבְהִנָּשְׂאָם מֵעַל הָאָרֶץ יִנָּשְׂאוּ הָאוֹפַנִּים
לְעֻמָּתָם כִּי רוּחַ הַחַיָּה בָּאוֹפַנִּים: וּדְמוּת עַל־רָאשֵׁי
הַחַיָּה רָקִיעַ כְּעֵין הַקֶּרַח הַנּוֹרָא נָטוּי עַל־רָאשֵׁיהֶם
מִלְמָעְלָה: וְתַחַת הָרָקִיעַ כַּנְפֵיהֶם יְשָׁרוֹת אִשָּׁה אֶל־

four wings. Their legs were straight, the soles of their feet like the soles of calf's feet; they sparkled like burnished bronze. Under their wings, on their four sides, were human hands. As for their four faces and wings—their wings touched one another; their faces never turned as they moved; each moved straight forward. The four of them had the face of a man and the face of a lion on the right, and the face of an ox and the face of an eagle on the left. The wings of the four of them were outstretched, one pair being linked to those of the next creature, and the other pair covering the body. Each went straight forward; wherever the spirit meant to go, they went, not turning as they went. The appearance of the living creatures was like coals of fire, burning like torches; it flashed up and down among the creatures; and there was brightness to the fire, and out of the fire flashed lightning. The creatures ran to and fro like lightning.

As I looked at the creatures, lo! There was a wheel on the ground beside each of the four creatures. The color of the wheels was like topaz, and all four had the same shape, arranged as if one wheel were within another. When they moved, they moved in any direction that their four sides faced, never turning as they moved. As for their rings, they were high and awesome. The four had rings full of eyes round about. Whenever the creatures moved, the wheels moved with them, and whenever the creatures rose from earth, the wheels rose with them; wherever the spirit meant to go, they went, and the wheels rose along with them; for a living spirit was in the wheels. When those went, these went; when those stood, these stood; and when those rose from the earth, the wheels rose along with them; for a living spirit was in the wheels.

Over the heads of the creatures there was the semblance of a firmament which looked like awesome ice, spread out over their heads. Under the firmament their wings were level, the one toward the other; each creature had two wings covering its body.

Ezekiel saw approaching from the north a glowing storm-cloud, which resolved itself into a group of four living creatures, arranged symmetrically in a square. Every one had four faces: a human face looking outwards, the face of a lion on the right, the face of an ox on the left, and the face of an eagle looking inwards to the center of the square. Every one had also four wings, two of

אֲחוֹתָהּ לְאִישׁ שְׁתַּיִם מְכַסּוֹת לָהֵנָּה וּלְאִישׁ שְׁתַּיִם מְכַסּוֹת
לָהֵנָּה אֵת גְּוִיֹּתֵיהֶם: וָאֶשְׁמַע אֶת־קוֹל כַּנְפֵיהֶם כְּקוֹל
מַיִם רַבִּים כְּקוֹל־שַׁדַּי בְּלֶכְתָּם קוֹל הֲמֻלָּה כְּקוֹל מַחֲנֶה
בְּעָמְדָם תְּרַפֶּינָה כַנְפֵיהֶן: וַיְהִי־קוֹל מֵעַל לָרָקִיעַ אֲשֶׁר
עַל־רֹאשָׁם בְּעָמְדָם תְּרַפֶּינָה כַנְפֵיהֶן: וּמִמַּעַל לָרָקִיעַ
אֲשֶׁר עַל־רֹאשָׁם כְּמַרְאֵה אֶבֶן־סַפִּיר דְּמוּת כִּסֵּא וְעַל
דְּמוּת הַכִּסֵּא דְּמוּת כְּמַרְאֵה אָדָם עָלָיו מִלְמָעְלָה: וָאֵרֶא ׀
כְּעֵין חַשְׁמַל כְּמַרְאֵה־אֵשׁ בֵּית־לָהּ סָבִיב מִמַּרְאֵה מָתְנָיו
וּלְמַעְלָה וּמִמַּרְאֵה מָתְנָיו וּלְמַטָּה רָאִיתִי כְּמַרְאֵה־אֵשׁ וְנֹגַהּ
לוֹ סָבִיב: כְּמַרְאֵה הַקֶּשֶׁת אֲשֶׁר יִהְיֶה בֶעָנָן בְּיוֹם הַגֶּשֶׁם
כֵּן מַרְאֵה הַנֹּגַהּ סָבִיב הוּא מַרְאֵה דְּמוּת כְּבוֹד־יְהֹוָה
וָאֶרְאֶה וָאֶפֹּל עַל־פָּנַי וָאֶשְׁמַע קוֹל מְדַבֵּר:

וַתִּשָּׂאֵנִי רוּחַ וָאֶשְׁמַע אַחֲרַי קוֹל רַעַשׁ גָּדוֹל בָּרוּךְ כְּבוֹד־
יְהֹוָה מִמְּקוֹמוֹ:

Continue with the blessings after the *Haftarah*, page 205.

FOR THE SECOND DAY

On a weekday begin with כל הבכור, page 197.

דברים יד, כב–טז, יז

עַשֵּׂר תְּעַשֵּׂר אֵת כָּל־תְּבוּאַת זַרְעֶךָ הַיֹּצֵא הַשָּׂדֶה שָׁנָה
שָׁנָה: וְאָכַלְתָּ לִפְנֵי ׀ יְהֹוָה אֱלֹהֶיךָ בַּמָּקוֹם אֲשֶׁר־יִבְחַר
לְשַׁכֵּן שְׁמוֹ שָׁם מַעְשַׂר דְּגָנְךָ תִּירֹשְׁךָ וְיִצְהָרֶךָ וּבְכֹרֹת
בְּקָרְךָ וְצֹאנֶךָ לְמַעַן תִּלְמַד לְיִרְאָה אֶת־יְהֹוָה אֱלֹהֶיךָ כָּל־
הַיָּמִים: וְכִי־יִרְבֶּה מִמְּךָ הַדֶּרֶךְ כִּי לֹא תוּכַל שְׂאֵתוֹ
כִּי־יִרְחַק מִמְּךָ הַמָּקוֹם אֲשֶׁר יִבְחַר יְהֹוָה אֱלֹהֶיךָ לָשׂוּם
שְׁמוֹ שָׁם כִּי יְבָרֶכְךָ יְהֹוָה אֱלֹהֶיךָ: וְנָתַתָּה בַּכָּסֶף וְצַרְתָּ
הַכֶּסֶף בְּיָדְךָ וְהָלַכְתָּ אֶל־הַמָּקוֹם אֲשֶׁר יִבְחַר יְהֹוָה

Whenever they moved, I heard their wings sound like the sound of many waters, like the thunder of the Almighty, a sound of tumult like the sound of a host; when they stood still, they dropped their wings.

Above the firmament over their heads was the semblance of a throne, colored like a sapphire, and on the throne-like appearance was the semblance of a human form. From the waist upward I saw something glowing like electrum or fire round about; from the waist downward there was something resembling fire, while all around it there was brightness, resembling the bow that is in the cloud on the day of rain. Such was the appearance of the brightness round about, such was the appearance of what resembled the glory of the Lord. When I saw it, I fell upon my face; then I heard the voice of one speaking.

Then a wind lifted me up, and I heard behind me a mighty sound: Blessed be the glory of the Lord from his abode.

Continue with the blessings after the Haftorah, page 206.

FOR THE SECOND DAY
On a weekday commence with kol ha-bchor, page 198.
Deuteronomy 14:22-16:17

You shall tithe all the produce of your seed which comes forth from the field every year. Then you shall eat in the presence of the Lord your God, in the place which the Lord your God chooses as the abiding place for his name, your tithe of the grain, wine and oil, as well as the firstlings of your herd and flock, that you may learn always to revere the Lord your God. If, however, the journey is too much for you, if you cannot carry the tithe, because the place which the Lord your God chooses for his presence is too far away and the Lord your God has blessed you [with a rich harvest] you may turn the tithe into money and carry the purse in your hand when you go to the place which the Lord your God chooses.

---

which were stretched out to meet those of the two living creatures on either side. The other pairs of wings covered the bodies of the living creatures, and under these wings were human hands. The whole group was pervaded with glowing fire, from which lightnings shot forth... Overawed by the sight, Ezekiel fell upon his face, and he heard a divine voice addressing him.

אֱלֹהֶיךָ בּוֹ: וְנָתַתָּה הַכֶּסֶף בְּכֹל אֲשֶׁר־תְּאַוֶּה נַפְשְׁךָ בַּבָּקָר
וּבַצֹּאן וּבַיַּיִן וּבַשֵּׁכָר וּבְכֹל אֲשֶׁר תִּשְׁאָלְךָ נַפְשֶׁךָ וְאָכַלְתָּ
שָּׁם לִפְנֵי יְהוָה אֱלֹהֶיךָ וְשָׂמַחְתָּ אַתָּה וּבֵיתֶךָ: וְהַלֵּוִי
אֲשֶׁר־בִּשְׁעָרֶיךָ לֹא תַעַזְבֶנּוּ כִּי אֵין לוֹ חֵלֶק וְנַחֲלָה
עִמָּךְ: מִקְצֵה ׀ שָׁלֹשׁ שָׁנִים תּוֹצִיא אֶת־כָּל־מַעְשַׂר
תְּבוּאָתְךָ בַּשָּׁנָה הַהִוא וְהִנַּחְתָּ בִּשְׁעָרֶיךָ: וּבָא הַלֵּוִי
כִּי אֵין־לוֹ חֵלֶק וְנַחֲלָה עִמָּךְ וְהַגֵּר וְהַיָּתוֹם וְהָאַלְמָנָה אֲשֶׁר
בִּשְׁעָרֶיךָ וְאָכְלוּ וְשָׂבֵעוּ לְמַעַן יְבָרֶכְךָ יְהוָה אֱלֹהֶיךָ בְּכָל־
מַעֲשֵׂה יָדְךָ אֲשֶׁר תַּעֲשֶׂה:* מִקֵּץ שֶׁבַע־שָׁנִים תַּעֲשֶׂה
שְׁמִטָּה: וְזֶה דְּבַר הַשְּׁמִטָּה שָׁמוֹט כָּל־בַּעַל מַשֵּׁה יָדוֹ
אֲשֶׁר יַשֶּׁה בְּרֵעֵהוּ לֹא־יִגֹּשׂ אֶת־רֵעֵהוּ וְאֶת־אָחִיו כִּי־קָרָא
שְׁמִטָּה לַיהוָה: אֶת־הַנָּכְרִי תִּגֹּשׂ וַאֲשֶׁר יִהְיֶה לְךָ אֶת־
אָחִיךָ תַּשְׁמֵט יָדֶךָ: אֶפֶס כִּי לֹא יִהְיֶה־בְּךָ אֶבְיוֹן כִּי־בָרֵךְ
יְבָרֶכְךָ יְהוָה בָּאָרֶץ אֲשֶׁר יְהוָה אֱלֹהֶיךָ נֹתֵן־לְךָ נַחֲלָה
לְרִשְׁתָּהּ: רַק אִם־שָׁמוֹעַ תִּשְׁמַע בְּקוֹל יְהוָה אֱלֹהֶיךָ
לִשְׁמֹר לַעֲשׂוֹת אֶת־כָּל־הַמִּצְוָה הַזֹּאת אֲשֶׁר אָנֹכִי מְצַוְּךָ
הַיּוֹם: כִּי־יְהוָה אֱלֹהֶיךָ בֵּרַכְךָ כַּאֲשֶׁר דִּבֶּר־לָךְ וְהַעֲבַטְתָּ
גּוֹיִם רַבִּים וְאַתָּה לֹא תַעֲבֹט וּמָשַׁלְתָּ בְּגוֹיִם רַבִּים וּבְךָ
לֹא יִמְשֹׁלוּ: כִּי־יִהְיֶה בְךָ אֶבְיוֹן מֵאַחַד אַחֶיךָ בְּאַחַד
שְׁעָרֶיךָ בְּאַרְצְךָ אֲשֶׁר־יְהוָה אֱלֹהֶיךָ נֹתֵן לָךְ לֹא תְאַמֵּץ
אֶת־לְבָבְךָ וְלֹא תִקְפֹּץ אֶת־יָדְךָ מֵאָחִיךָ הָאֶבְיוֹן: כִּי־פָתֹחַ
תִּפְתַּח אֶת־יָדְךָ לוֹ וְהַעֲבֵט תַּעֲבִיטֶנּוּ דֵּי מַחְסֹרוֹ אֲשֶׁר
יֶחְסַר לוֹ: הִשָּׁמֶר לְךָ פֶּן־יִהְיֶה דָבָר עִם־לְבָבְךָ בְלִיַּעַל
לֵאמֹר קָרְבָה שְׁנַת־הַשֶּׁבַע שְׁנַת הַשְּׁמִטָּה וְרָעָה עֵינְךָ
בְּאָחִיךָ הָאֶבְיוֹן וְלֹא תִתֵּן לוֹ וְקָרָא עָלֶיךָ אֶל־יְהוָה וְהָיָה
בְךָ חֵטְא: נָתוֹן תִּתֵּן לוֹ וְלֹא־יֵרַע לְבָבְךָ בְּתִתְּךָ לוֹ כִּי

You may then spend the money on whatever your heart desires, oxen or sheep, wine or strong drink, or anything else you would enjoy; there you shall eat in the presence of the Lord your God and rejoice, you and your household. Nor shall you neglect the Levite who is within your gates, for he has no share or heritage with you.

At the end of every three years you shall bring out all the tithe of your produce for that year and deposit it within your gates; then the Levite who has no share or heritage with you, and also the alien, the orphan and the widow who belong to your community, may come and eat and be satisfied; so that the Lord your God may bless you in all that you do.*

At the end of every seven years you shall grant a release. The release shall be observed like this: Every creditor shall relax his claim on what he has lent his neighbor. He must not press his neighbor, his brother, for a remission has been proclaimed in honor of the Lord. You may press a foreigner for payment, but you shall remit any claim you have on your brother. Indeed, there should be no one among you in need, since the Lord your God will bless you abundantly in the land he is giving you to possess. If you but hearken to the voice of the Lord your God and carefully observe all this commandment which I command you this day, you will lend to many nations and borrow from none, you will rule over many nations and none will rule over you, since the Lord your God will bless you as he promised. If one of your brethren is in need in any community of yours within your country which the Lord your God is giving you, you must not harden your heart nor close your hand against your needy brother. Instead, you shall open your hand to him and freely lend him enough to meet his needs. Be on your guard lest a base thought enters your mind, and you say: "The seventh year, the year of release, is near"—and you grudge help to your needy brother and give him nothing. He will cry to the Lord against you and you will be guilty. You must give to him freely; you must not begrudge it when you give him

---

לא יהיה בך אביון (there should be no one among you in need) is obviously intended to prevent pauperism. The presence of poor and destitute people should remind us how far we fall short in our aims at the higher good.

בִּגְלַל ׀ הַדָּבָר הַזֶּה יְבָרֶכְךָ יְהוָֹה אֱלֹהֶיךָ בְּכָל־מַעֲשֶׂךָ
וּבְכֹל מִשְׁלַח יָדֶךָ: כִּי לֹא־יֶחְדַּל אֶבְיוֹן מִקֶּרֶב הָאָרֶץ עַל־
כֵּן אָנֹכִי מְצַוְּךָ לֵאמֹר פָּתֹחַ תִּפְתַּח אֶת־יָדְךָ לְאָחִיךָ לַעֲנִיֶּךָ
וּלְאֶבְיֹנְךָ בְּאַרְצֶךָ: כִּי־יִמָּכֵר לְךָ אָחִיךָ הָעִבְרִי אוֹ
הָעִבְרִיָּה וַעֲבָדְךָ שֵׁשׁ שָׁנִים וּבַשָּׁנָה הַשְּׁבִיעִת תְּשַׁלְּחֶנּוּ
חָפְשִׁי מֵעִמָּךְ: וְכִי־תְשַׁלְּחֶנּוּ חָפְשִׁי מֵעִמָּךְ לֹא תְשַׁלְּחֶנּוּ
רֵיקָם: הַעֲנֵיק תַּעֲנִיק לוֹ מִצֹּאנְךָ וּמִגָּרְנְךָ וּמִיִּקְבֶךָ אֲשֶׁר
בֵּרַכְךָ יְהוָֹה אֱלֹהֶיךָ תִּתֶּן־לוֹ: וְזָכַרְתָּ כִּי עֶבֶד הָיִיתָ בְּאֶרֶץ
מִצְרַיִם וַיִּפְדְּךָ יְהוָֹה אֱלֹהֶיךָ עַל־כֵּן אָנֹכִי מְצַוְּךָ אֶת־
הַדָּבָר הַזֶּה הַיּוֹם: וְהָיָה כִּי־יֹאמַר אֵלֶיךָ לֹא אֵצֵא מֵעִמָּךְ
כִּי אֲהֵבְךָ וְאֶת־בֵּיתֶךָ כִּי־טוֹב לוֹ עִמָּךְ: וְלָקַחְתָּ אֶת־
הַמַּרְצֵעַ וְנָתַתָּה בְאָזְנוֹ וּבַדֶּלֶת וְהָיָה לְךָ עֶבֶד עוֹלָם וְאַף
לַאֲמָתְךָ תַּעֲשֶׂה־כֵּן: לֹא־יִקְשֶׁה בְעֵינֶךָ בְּשַׁלֵּחֲךָ אֹתוֹ
חָפְשִׁי מֵעִמָּךְ כִּי מִשְׁנֶה שְׂכַר שָׂכִיר עֲבָדְךָ שֵׁשׁ שָׁנִים
וּבֵרַכְךָ יְהוָֹה אֱלֹהֶיךָ בְּכֹל אֲשֶׁר תַּעֲשֶׂה:

כָּל־הַבְּכוֹר אֲשֶׁר יִוָּלֵד בִּבְקָרְךָ וּבְצֹאנְךָ הַזָּכָר תַּקְדִּישׁ
לַיהוָֹה אֱלֹהֶיךָ לֹא תַעֲבֹד בִּבְכֹר שׁוֹרֶךָ וְלֹא תָגֹז בְּכוֹר צֹאנֶךָ:
לִפְנֵי יְהוָֹה אֱלֹהֶיךָ תֹאכֲלֶנּוּ שָׁנָה בְשָׁנָה בַּמָּקוֹם אֲשֶׁר־
יִבְחַר יְהוָֹה אַתָּה וּבֵיתֶךָ: וְכִי־יִהְיֶה בוֹ מוּם פִּסֵּחַ אוֹ
עִוֵּר כֹּל מוּם רָע לֹא תִזְבָּחֶנּוּ לַיהוָֹה אֱלֹהֶיךָ: בִּשְׁעָרֶיךָ
תֹּאכֲלֶנּוּ הַטָּמֵא וְהַטָּהוֹר יַחְדָּו כַּצְּבִי וְכָאַיָּל: רַק אֶת־
דָּמוֹ לֹא תֹאכֵל עַל־הָאָרֶץ תִּשְׁפְּכֶנּוּ כַּמָּיִם:

שָׁמוֹר אֶת־חֹדֶשׁ הָאָבִיב וְעָשִׂיתָ פֶּסַח לַיהוָֹה אֱלֹהֶיךָ כִּי
בְּחֹדֶשׁ הָאָבִיב הוֹצִיאֲךָ יְהוָֹה אֱלֹהֶיךָ מִמִּצְרַיִם לָיְלָה: וְזָבַחְתָּ
פֶּסַח לַיהוָֹה אֱלֹהֶיךָ צֹאן וּבָקָר בַּמָּקוֹם אֲשֶׁר יִבְחַר יְהוָֹה
לְשַׁכֵּן שְׁמוֹ שָׁם: לֹא־תֹאכַל עָלָיו חָמֵץ שִׁבְעַת יָמִים

something, for the Lord your God will bless you for this in all your works and in whatever you undertake. The poor will never cease to be in your land, that is why I command you to open your hand to your poor and needy brother in your land.

If your Hebrew brother, or Hebrew woman, is sold to you, he is to serve you for six years, but in the seventh year you shall dismiss him from your service, a free man. When you let him go free, you shall not send him away empty-handed; you shall furnish him liberally out of your flock, threshing floor and wine press; you shall provide him with whatever the Lord your God has blessed you. You must remember that you were once a slave yourself in the land of Egypt, and the Lord your God redeemed you. That is why I am giving you this command today. If, however, he tells you: "I will not leave your service," because he is fond of you and your household and fares well with you, you shall take an awl and thrust it through his ear into the door, and he shall then be your slave permanently. Your female slave, also, you shall treat in the same way. You must not begrudge it when you set him free from your service, since the service he has given you for six years was worth twice a hired man's wage. Then the Lord your God will bless you in everything you do.*

You shall consecrate to the Lord your God all the male firstlings of your herd and your flock. You shall not do work with a firstling ox, nor shear a firstling sheep. Year after year you and your family shall eat it before the Lord your God at the place the Lord chooses. If, however, a firstling is lame or blind or has any other serious defect, you shall not sacrifice it to the Lord your God. You shall eat it in your own community, the unclean and the clean may eat it alike, as though it were a gazelle or a deer. Only, you must not partake of its blood; you shall pour it out on the ground like water.*

Observe the month of Aviv, and keep the Passover in honor of the Lord your God, for it was in the month of Aviv that the Lord your God brought you out of Egypt by night. You shall sacrifice the Passover-offering to the Lord your God, an animal of the flock or the herd, in the place which the Lord chooses as the dwelling place of his name. You shall not eat leavened bread with it. For

תֹאכַל־עָלָיו מַצּוֹת לֶחֶם עֹנִי כִּי בְחִפָּזוֹן יָצָאתָ מֵאֶרֶץ מִצְרַיִם לְמַעַן תִּזְכֹּר אֶת־יוֹם צֵאתְךָ מֵאֶרֶץ מִצְרַיִם כֹּל יְמֵי חַיֶּיךָ:* וְלֹא־יֵרָאֶה לְךָ שְׂאֹר בְּכָל־גְּבֻלְךָ שִׁבְעַת יָמִים וְלֹא־יָלִין מִן־הַבָּשָׂר אֲשֶׁר תִּזְבַּח בָּעֶרֶב בַּיּוֹם הָרִאשׁוֹן לַבֹּקֶר: לֹא תוּכַל לִזְבֹּחַ אֶת־הַפָּסַח בְּאַחַד שְׁעָרֶיךָ אֲשֶׁר־ יְהוָֹה אֱלֹהֶיךָ נֹתֵן לָךְ: כִּי אִם־אֶל־הַמָּקוֹם אֲשֶׁר־יִבְחַר יְהוָֹה אֱלֹהֶיךָ לְשַׁכֵּן שְׁמוֹ שָׁם תִּזְבַּח אֶת־הַפֶּסַח בָּעֶרֶב כְּבוֹא הַשֶּׁמֶשׁ מוֹעֵד צֵאתְךָ מִמִּצְרָיִם: וּבִשַּׁלְתָּ וְאָכַלְתָּ בַּמָּקוֹם אֲשֶׁר יִבְחַר יְהוָֹה אֱלֹהֶיךָ בּוֹ וּפָנִיתָ בַבֹּקֶר וְהָלַכְתָּ לְאֹהָלֶיךָ: שֵׁשֶׁת יָמִים תֹּאכַל מַצּוֹת וּבַיּוֹם הַשְּׁבִיעִי עֲצֶרֶת לַיהוָֹה אֱלֹהֶיךָ לֹא תַעֲשֶׂה מְלָאכָה:* שִׁבְעָה שָׁבֻעֹת תִּסְפָּר־לָךְ מֵהָחֵל חֶרְמֵשׁ בַּקָּמָה תָּחֵל לִסְפֹּר שִׁבְעָה שָׁבֻעוֹת: וְעָשִׂיתָ חַג שָׁבֻעוֹת לַיהוָֹה אֱלֹהֶיךָ מִסַּת נִדְבַת יָדְךָ אֲשֶׁר תִּתֵּן כַּאֲשֶׁר יְבָרֶכְךָ יְהוָֹה אֱלֹהֶיךָ: וְשָׂמַחְתָּ לִפְנֵי | יְהוָֹה אֱלֹהֶיךָ אַתָּה וּבִנְךָ וּבִתֶּךָ וְעַבְדְּךָ וַאֲמָתֶךָ וְהַלֵּוִי אֲשֶׁר בִּשְׁעָרֶיךָ וְהַגֵּר וְהַיָּתוֹם וְהָאַלְמָנָה אֲשֶׁר בְּקִרְבֶּךָ בַּמָּקוֹם אֲשֶׁר יִבְחַר יְהוָֹה אֱלֹהֶיךָ לְשַׁכֵּן שְׁמוֹ שָׁם: וְזָכַרְתָּ כִּי־עֶבֶד הָיִיתָ בְּמִצְרָיִם וְשָׁמַרְתָּ וְעָשִׂיתָ אֶת־ הַחֻקִּים הָאֵלֶּה:*

חַג הַסֻּכֹּת תַּעֲשֶׂה לְךָ שִׁבְעַת יָמִים בְּאָסְפְּךָ מִגָּרְנְךָ וּמִיִּקְבֶךָ: וְשָׂמַחְתָּ בְּחַגֶּךָ אַתָּה וּבִנְךָ וּבִתֶּךָ וְעַבְדְּךָ וַאֲמָתֶךָ וְהַלֵּוִי וְהַגֵּר וְהַיָּתוֹם וְהָאַלְמָנָה אֲשֶׁר בִּשְׁעָרֶיךָ: שִׁבְעַת יָמִים תָּחֹג לַיהוָֹה אֱלֹהֶיךָ בַּמָּקוֹם אֲשֶׁר־יִבְחַר יְהוָֹה כִּי יְבָרֶכְךָ יְהוָֹה אֱלֹהֶיךָ בְּכֹל תְּבוּאָתְךָ וּבְכֹל מַעֲשֵׂה יָדֶיךָ וְהָיִיתָ אַךְ שָׂמֵחַ: שָׁלוֹשׁ פְּעָמִים | בַּשָּׁנָה יֵרָאֶה כָל־ זְכוּרְךָ אֶת־פְּנֵי | יְהוָֹה אֱלֹהֶיךָ בַּמָּקוֹם אֲשֶׁר יִבְחָר בְּחַג

seven days thereafter you shall eat unleavened bread, the bread of affliction—for you came out of the land of Egypt in haste—that you may remember the day you left the land of Egypt all the days of your life.*

For seven days no leaven shall be seen in your possession anywhere in your territory, and none of the meat which you sacrifice on the eve of the first day shall be left over until morning. You may not sacrifice the passover-offering in any of your communities which the Lord your God is giving you. Only at the place which the Lord your God chooses as the abiding place of his name you shall offer the Passover-sacrifice in the evening at sunset, the time of your departure from Egypt. You shall roast and eat it at the place the Lord your God chooses; then in the morning you may set out for home. For six days you shall eat unleavened bread, and on the seventh day there shall be a solemn assembly in honor of the Lord your God; you shall not do any sort of work.*

You shall count off seven weeks, counting them from the time the sickle is first put to the standing grain. You shall then celebrate the Feast of Weeks in honor of the Lord your God, offering him a freewill gift in proportion to the blessing which the Lord your God has bestowed on you. You shall rejoice before the Lord your God, you and your son and your daughter, your male and female servants, and the Levite who is within your gates, as well as the alien, the orphan and the widow among you, in the place the Lord your God chooses as the abiding place of his name. You must remember that you were once a slave in Egypt, so you must be careful to observe these statutes.*

You shall celebrate the Feast of Booths for seven days, when you have gathered in the produce from your threshing floor and wine press. You shall rejoice at your festival, you and your son and your daughter, your male and female servants, the Levite, the alien, the orphan and the widow who are within your gates. For seven days you shall celebrate in honor of the Lord your God at the place the Lord chooses; for the Lord your God will bless you in all your crops and all your handiwork, so that you can be altogether joyful.

Three times a year shall every male among you appear before

הַמַּצּוֹת וּבְחַג הַשָּׁבֻעוֹת וּבְחַג הַסֻּכּוֹת וְלֹא יֵרָאֶה אֶת־פְּנֵי יְהֹוָה רֵיקָם: אִישׁ כְּמַתְּנַת יָדוֹ כְּבִרְכַּת יְהֹוָה אֱלֹהֶיךָ אֲשֶׁר נָתַן־לָךְ:

Both *Sifré Torah* being placed upon the desk, the Reader says:

יִתְגַּדַּל וְיִתְקַדַּשׁ שְׁמֵהּ רַבָּא בְּעָלְמָא דִּי בְרָא כִרְעוּתֵהּ, וְיַמְלִיךְ מַלְכוּתֵהּ, וְיַצְמַח פֻּרְקָנֵהּ וִיקָרֵב מְשִׁיחֵהּ, בְּחַיֵּיכוֹן וּבְיוֹמֵיכוֹן וּבְחַיֵּי דְכָל בֵּית יִשְׂרָאֵל, בַּעֲגָלָא וּבִזְמַן קָרִיב, וְאִמְרוּ אָמֵן.

יְהֵא שְׁמֵהּ רַבָּא מְבָרַךְ לְעָלַם וּלְעָלְמֵי עָלְמַיָּא.

יִתְבָּרַךְ וְיִשְׁתַּבַּח, וְיִתְפָּאַר וְיִתְרוֹמַם, וְיִתְנַשֵּׂא וְיִתְהַדָּר, וְיִתְעַלֶּה וְיִתְהַלַּל שְׁמֵהּ דְּקֻדְשָׁא, בְּרִיךְ הוּא, לְעֵלָּא מִן כָּל בִּרְכָתָא וְשִׁירָתָא, תֻּשְׁבְּחָתָא וְנֶחֱמָתָא, דַּאֲמִירָן בְּעָלְמָא, וְאִמְרוּ אָמֵן.

The first *Torah* is then raised and the Congregation says:

וְזֹאת הַתּוֹרָה אֲשֶׁר שָׂם מֹשֶׁה לִפְנֵי בְּנֵי יִשְׂרָאֵל, עַל פִּי יְיָ בְּיַד מֹשֶׁה.

עֵץ חַיִּים הִיא לַמַּחֲזִיקִים בָּהּ, וְתֹמְכֶיהָ מְאֻשָּׁר. דְּרָכֶיהָ דַרְכֵי נֹעַם, וְכָל נְתִיבוֹתֶיהָ שָׁלוֹם. אֹרֶךְ יָמִים בִּימִינָהּ; בִּשְׂמֹאלָהּ עֹשֶׁר וְכָבוֹד. יְיָ חָפֵץ לְמַעַן צִדְקוֹ, יַגְדִּיל תּוֹרָה וְיַאְדִּיר.

The following section is then read from the second *Torah*.

במדבר כח, כו–לא

וּבְיוֹם הַבִּכּוּרִים בְּהַקְרִיבְכֶם מִנְחָה חֲדָשָׁה לַיהֹוָה בְּשָׁבֻעֹתֵיכֶם מִקְרָא־קֹדֶשׁ יִהְיֶה לָכֶם כָּל־מְלֶאכֶת עֲבֹדָה לֹא תַעֲשׂוּ: וְהִקְרַבְתֶּם עוֹלָה לְרֵיחַ נִיחֹחַ לַיהֹוָה פָּרִים בְּנֵי־בָקָר שְׁנַיִם אַיִל אֶחָד שִׁבְעָה כְבָשִׂים בְּנֵי שָׁנָה: וּמִנְחָתָם סֹלֶת בְּלוּלָה בַשֶּׁמֶן שְׁלֹשָׁה עֶשְׂרֹנִים לַפָּר

the Lord your God at the place he chooses; at the feast of unleavened bread, at the Feast of Weeks, and at the Feast of Booths.
No one shall appear before the Lord empty-handed, but each shall
give as much as he can, in proportion to the blessings which the
Lord your God has bestowed on you.

Both Sifré Torah being placed upon the desk, the Reader says:

Glorified and sanctified be God's great name throughout the
world which he has created according to his will. May he establish
his kingdom, hastening his salvation and the coming of his Messiah, in your lifetime and during your days, and within the life of
the entire house of Israel, speedily and soon; and say, Amen.

May his great name be blessed forever and to all eternity.

Blessed and praised, glorified and exalted, extolled and honored,
adored and lauded be the name of the Holy One, blessed be he,
beyond all the blessings and hymns, praises and consolations that
are ever spoken in the world; and say, Amen.

The first Torah is then raised and the Congregation says:

This is the Torah which Moses placed before the children of
Israel. It is in accordance with the Lord's command through Moses.

It is a tree of life to those who take hold of it, and happy
are those who support it. Its ways are pleasant ways, and all its
paths are peace. Long life is in its right hand, and in its left hand
are riches and honor. The Lord was pleased, for the sake of his
righteousness, to render the Torah great and glorious.

The following section is then read from the second Torah.
Numbers 28:26-31

On the day of first fruits, when you present a new meal-offering
to the Lord at your Feast of Weeks, you shall have a holy assembly;
you shall do no hard work. You shall present a burnt offering for
a sweet savor to the Lord; two young bullocks, one ram, and seven
yearling lambs, with their meal-offering of fine flour mixed with
oil—three tenths of an *ephah* for each bullock, two tenths for the

הָאֶחָד שְׁנֵי עֶשְׂרֹנִים לָאַיִל הָאֶחָד: עִשָּׂרוֹן עִשָּׂרוֹן לַכֶּבֶשׂ
הָאֶחָד לְשִׁבְעַת הַכְּבָשִׂים: שְׂעִיר עִזִּים אֶחָד לְכַפֵּר עֲלֵיכֶם:
מִלְּבַד עֹלַת הַתָּמִיד וּמִנְחָתוֹ תַּעֲשׂוּ תְּמִימִם יִהְיוּ־לָכֶם
וְנִסְכֵּיהֶם:

The second *Torah* is raised and the congregation says וזאת התורה.

בָּרוּךְ אַתָּה, יְיָ אֱלֹהֵינוּ, מֶלֶךְ הָעוֹלָם, אֲשֶׁר בָּחַר בִּנְבִיאִים
טוֹבִים, וְרָצָה בְדִבְרֵיהֶם הַנֶּאֱמָרִים בֶּאֱמֶת. בָּרוּךְ אַתָּה, יְיָ,
הַבּוֹחֵר בַּתּוֹרָה, וּבְמֹשֶׁה עַבְדּוֹ, וּבְיִשְׂרָאֵל עַמּוֹ, וּבִנְבִיאֵי הָאֱמֶת
וָצֶדֶק.

יַצִּיב פִּתְגָם, page 209.

חבקוק ב, כ–ג

וַיהוָה בְּהֵיכַל קָדְשׁוֹ הַס מִפָּנָיו כָּל־הָאָרֶץ:
תְּפִלָּה לַחֲבַקּוּק הַנָּבִיא עַל שִׁגְיֹנוֹת: יְהוָה שָׁמַעְתִּי שִׁמְעֲךָ
יָרֵאתִי יְהוָה פָּעָלְךָ בְּקֶרֶב שָׁנִים חַיֵּיהוּ בְּקֶרֶב שָׁנִים
תּוֹדִיעַ בְּרֹגֶז רַחֵם תִּזְכּוֹר: אֱלוֹהַּ מִתֵּימָן יָבוֹא וְקָדוֹשׁ
מֵהַר־פָּארָן סֶלָה כִּסָּה שָׁמַיִם הוֹדוֹ וּתְהִלָּתוֹ מָלְאָה
הָאָרֶץ: וְנֹגַהּ כָּאוֹר תִּהְיֶה קַרְנַיִם מִיָּדוֹ לוֹ וְשָׁם חֶבְיוֹן
עֻזֹּה: לְפָנָיו יֵלֶךְ דָּבֶר וְיֵצֵא רֶשֶׁף לְרַגְלָיו: עָמַד וַיְמֹדֶד
אֶרֶץ רָאָה וַיַּתֵּר גּוֹיִם וַיִּתְפֹּצְצוּ הַרְרֵי־עַד שַׁחוּ גִּבְעוֹת
עוֹלָם הֲלִיכוֹת עוֹלָם לוֹ: תַּחַת אָוֶן רָאִיתִי אָהֳלֵי כוּשָׁן
יִרְגְּזוּן יְרִיעוֹת אֶרֶץ מִדְיָן: הֲבִנְהָרִים חָרָה יְהוָה אִם
בַּנְּהָרִים אַפֶּךָ אִם־בַּיָּם עֶבְרָתֶךָ כִּי תִרְכַּב עַל־סוּסֶיךָ

הפטרה, signifying completion, includes those portions of the Prophets recited immediately after the reading of the Torah. Usually, though not always, the *Haftarah* passage contains some reference to an occasion described in the section read from the Torah.

ram, and one tenth for each of the seven lambs. One goat shall be offered to make atonement for you. You shall offer these in addition to the regular daily burnt offering with its meal-offering. You shall have them unblemished, with their drink-offerings.

The second Torah is raised and the Congregation says v'zoth ha-Torah.

Blessed art thou, Lord our God, King of the universe, who hast chosen good prophets, and hast been pleased with their words which were truthfully spoken. Blessed art thou, O Lord, who hast chosen the Torah and thy servant Moses, thy people Israel and the true and righteous prophets.

Habakkuk 2:20-3

The Lord is in his holy temple; be silent before him, all the earth!

A prayer of the prophet Habakkuk; upon *shigyonoth.* O Lord, I have heard the report of thee and I am afraid; O Lord, revive thy work throughout the years; in the course of years make it known that amid thy wrath thou dost remember to be merciful.

God comes from Teman, the Holy One—from Mount Paran. His majesty covers the heavens, the earth is full of his praise. His radiance appears like the light, rays flash from his side, and there he veils his glory. The pestilence strides before him, fiery bolts go forth at his feet. He stands firm and shakes the earth, he looks and makes the nations quake. The ancient hills are shattered, the everlasting mountains sink low, where he walked long ago.

I see the tents of Cushan in affliction; the curtains of the land of Midian do tremble. Is thy wrath, O Lord, against the rivers? Is thy wrath kindled against the rivers, is thy anger against the sea, that thou ridest on thy horses, on thy chariots of victory?

The prayer of Ḥabakkuk is one of the most brilliant poems in the Bible. It refers to older theophanies, or manifestations of God. What God did then, the prophet prays that he will do again. The power which God revealed on Israel's behalf at the dawn of history he can manifest again. Ḥabakkuk magnificently concludes with words expressive of complete confidence in God.

The phrase על שׁגיונות has been variously interpreted. According to the Septuagint, it means to the accompaniment of stringed instruments. The phrase למנצח בנגינותי, reminiscent of the inscription at the beginning of many of the Psalms, is here placed at the end of the poem.

מֶרְכְּבֹתֶיךָ יְשׁוּעָה: עֶרְיָה תֵעוֹר קַשְׁתֶּךָ שְׁבֻעוֹת מַטּוֹת אֹמֶר סֶלָה נְהָרוֹת תְּבַקַּע־אָרֶץ: רָאוּךָ יָחִילוּ הָרִים זֶרֶם מַיִם עָבָר נָתַן תְּהוֹם קוֹלוֹ רוֹם יָדֵיהוּ נָשָׂא: שֶׁמֶשׁ יָרֵחַ עָמַד זְבֻלָה לְאוֹר חִצֶּיךָ יְהַלֵּכוּ לְנֹגַהּ בְּרַק חֲנִיתֶךָ: בְּזַעַם תִּצְעַד־אָרֶץ בְּאַף תָּדוּשׁ גּוֹיִם: יָצָאתָ לְיֵשַׁע עַמֶּךָ לְיֵשַׁע אֶת־מְשִׁיחֶךָ מָחַצְתָּ רֹּאשׁ מִבֵּית רָשָׁע עָרוֹת יְסוֹד עַד־צַוָּאר סֶלָה: נָקַבְתָּ בְמַטָּיו רֹאשׁ פְּרָזָו יִסְעֲרוּ לַהֲפִיצֵנִי עֲלִיצֻתָם כְּמוֹ־לֶאֱכֹל עָנִי בַּמִּסְתָּר: דָּרַכְתָּ בַיָּם סוּסֶיךָ חֹמֶר מַיִם רַבִּים: שָׁמַעְתִּי וַתִּרְגַּז בִּטְנִי לְקוֹל צָלֲלוּ שְׂפָתַי יָבוֹא רָקָב בַּעֲצָמַי וְתַחְתַּי אֶרְגָּז אֲשֶׁר אָנוּחַ לְיוֹם צָרָה לַעֲלוֹת לְעַם יְגוּדֶנּוּ: כִּי־תְאֵנָה לֹא־תִפְרָח וְאֵין יְבוּל בַּגְּפָנִים כִּחֵשׁ מַעֲשֵׂה־זַיִת וּשְׁדֵמוֹת לֹא־עָשָׂה אֹכֶל גָּזַר מִמִּכְלָה צֹאן וְאֵין בָּקָר בָּרְפָתִים: וַאֲנִי בַּיהוָה אֶעְלוֹזָה אָגִילָה בֵּאלֹהֵי יִשְׁעִי: יְהוָה אֲדֹנָי חֵילִי וַיָּשֶׂם רַגְלַי כָּאַיָּלוֹת וְעַל־בָּמוֹתַי יַדְרִכֵנִי לַמְנַצֵּחַ בִּנְגִינוֹתָי:

בָּרוּךְ אַתָּה, יְיָ אֱלֹהֵינוּ, מֶלֶךְ הָעוֹלָם, צוּר כָּל הָעוֹלָמִים, צַדִּיק בְּכָל הַדּוֹרוֹת, הָאֵל הַנֶּאֱמָן, הָאוֹמֵר וְעוֹשֶׂה, הַמְדַבֵּר וּמְקַיֵּם, שֶׁכָּל דְּבָרָיו אֱמֶת וָצֶדֶק.

נֶאֱמָן אַתָּה הוּא, יְיָ אֱלֹהֵינוּ, וְנֶאֱמָנִים דְּבָרֶיךָ, וְדָבָר אֶחָד מִדְּבָרֶיךָ אָחוֹר לֹא יָשׁוּב רֵיקָם, כִּי אֵל מֶלֶךְ נֶאֱמָן וְרַחֲמָן אָתָּה. בָּרוּךְ אַתָּה, יְיָ, הָאֵל הַנֶּאֱמָן בְּכָל דְּבָרָיו.

רַחֵם עַל צִיּוֹן, כִּי הִיא בֵּית חַיֵּינוּ, וְלַעֲלוּבַת נֶפֶשׁ תּוֹשִׁיעַ בִּמְהֵרָה בְיָמֵינוּ. בָּרוּךְ אַתָּה, יְיָ, מְשַׂמֵּחַ צִיּוֹן בְּבָנֶיהָ.

Thou dost uncover thy bow, sworn are the rods of thy word; thou dost cleave the earth with rivers. The mountains have seen thee, and they tremble; the tempest of waters flows over; the deep utters its voice, and lifts its hands on high. The sun and moon stand still in their habitation at the light of thy arrows as they speed, at the flash of thy glittering spear. Thou dost bestride the earth in fury, threshing the nations in anger.

Thou comest forth for the deliverance of thy people, for the deliverance of thy anointed. Thou dost crush the head of the evil household, uncovering the foundation even unto the neck. Thou hast pierced with his own rods the head of the warriors who came as a whirlwind to scatter me; their joy was to devour the poor secretly. Thou hast trodden the sea with thy horses, the surging of mighty waters. I hear, and my body trembles, my lips quiver at the sound; rotteness enters into my bones, and as I stand I shiver. I will quietly wait for the day of trouble which will come upon the people who would assail us.

Though the fig tree may not blossom, though no fruit is on the vine, though the olive crop has failed, though the fields yield no food, though the flock is cut from the fold and there is no herd in the stalls, yet I will rejoice in the Lord, I will exult in the God who saves me. The Lord God is my strength; he makes my feet swift as the feet of hinds; he makes me tread upon my heights.

For the Choirmaster: On stringed instruments.

Blessed art thou, Lord our God, King of the universe, Creator of all the worlds, righteous in all generations, faithful God, who sayest and performest, who speakest and fulfillest, for all thy words are true and just.

Faithful art thou, Lord our God, and faithful are thy words; no word of thine returns unfulfilled, for thou art a faithful and merciful God and King. Blessed art thou, O Lord God, who art faithful in all thy words.

Have compassion on Zion, for it is the source of our life; save the humbled soul speedily in our days. Blessed art thou, O Lord, who makest Zion rejoice in her children.

שִׂמְּחֵנוּ, יְיָ אֱלֹהֵינוּ, בְּאֵלִיָּהוּ הַנָּבִיא עַבְדֶּךָ, וּבְמַלְכוּת בֵּית דָּוִד מְשִׁיחֶךָ. בִּמְהֵרָה יָבֹא, וְיָגֵל לִבֵּנוּ; עַל כִּסְאוֹ לֹא יֵשֶׁב זָר, וְלֹא יִנְחֲלוּ עוֹד אֲחֵרִים אֶת כְּבוֹדוֹ, כִּי בְשֵׁם קָדְשְׁךָ נִשְׁבַּעְתָּ לּוֹ, שֶׁלֹּא יִכְבֶּה נֵרוֹ לְעוֹלָם וָעֶד. בָּרוּךְ אַתָּה, יְיָ, מָגֵן דָּוִד.

On Sabbath add the bracketed words.

עַל הַתּוֹרָה, וְעַל הָעֲבוֹדָה, וְעַל הַנְּבִיאִים, [וְעַל יוֹם הַשַּׁבָּת הַזֶּה] וְעַל יוֹם חַג הַשָּׁבֻעוֹת הַזֶּה שֶׁנָּתַתָּ לָּנוּ, יְיָ אֱלֹהֵינוּ, [לִקְדֻשָּׁה וְלִמְנוּחָה] לְשָׂשׂוֹן וּלְשִׂמְחָה, לְכָבוֹד וּלְתִפְאָרֶת.

עַל הַכֹּל, יְיָ אֱלֹהֵינוּ, אֲנַחְנוּ מוֹדִים לָךְ, וּמְבָרְכִים אוֹתָךְ; יִתְבָּרַךְ שִׁמְךָ בְּפִי כָּל חַי תָּמִיד לְעוֹלָם וָעֶד. בָּרוּךְ אַתָּה, יְיָ, מְקַדֵּשׁ [הַשַּׁבָּת וְ]יִשְׂרָאֵל וְהַזְּמַנִּים.

We have always regarded the Torah as the heritage of the entire people. Lack of time does not exempt us from study. Even one quarter of an hour devoted daily to the study of some ethical work will bring spiritual refreshment. The daily reading of a page or two from some inspiring book should present no difficulty to anyone, since some of these books are available in the vernacular.

Let us never forget that the nations who oppressed Israel have suffered extinction. Let us ever remember that we have an important role to play in the spiritual regeneration of the world. When a people never tires of affirming the truth for which it stands, an enlightened world cannot but feel impelled to probe the nature of that truth, and ultimately to vow allegiance to it. We must continue to face the world as a separate and indivisible group. Joined one to the other, we gain fullness of stature and become complete personalities (*Rabbi Jonah Eybeshitz, Yaarath Dvash*).

Gladden us, Lord our God, with the appearance of thy servant Elijah the prophet, and with the rule of the house of David thy anointed. May he soon come and bring joy to our heart. Let no stranger occupy David's throne; let others no longer possess themselves of his glory, for thou didst promise him by his holy name that his light would never go out. Blessed art thou, O Lord, Shield of David.

On Sabbath add the bracketed words.

We thank thee for the Torah, for the worship, for the Prophets [for this Sabbath day] and for this day, the Feast of Weeks, which thou hast given us, Lord our God, [for holiness and rest], for joy and gladness, for glory and beauty.

We thank and bless thee, Lord our God, for all things; be thy name ever blessed by every living being. Blessed art thou, O Lord, who hallowest [the Sabbath] and Israel and the festivals.

Israel is like a single body, sensitive to the pain felt by any of its parts. One sinful Jew does harm to the entire body of his people. When a group of men are sailing in a boat, none of them has a right to bore a hole even under his own seat, for it might result in the sinking of all his companions.

Judaism emphasizes the duties, rights and privileges of every individual. All are equal before the majesty of justice; the weak and the strong, the poor and the rich, the native and the stranger. The decision of the judge must be rendered with utmost impartiality. The Sefer Torah is considered the most sacred possession of the Jew. Now, if the parchment is sanctified by what is written on it, how much more sanctified does a man become when his lifeblood absorbs the living words of the Torah. Knowledge of the Torah is the noblest human ideal. There is no joy greater, no contentment deeper than that gained by an understanding of the principles of the Torah (*Rabbi Israel Meir, Ḥafetz Ḥayyim*).

יַצִּיב פִּתְגָּם

Chanted on the second day of *Shavuoth* after the first verse of the *Haftarah*.

יַצִּיב פִּתְגָּם לְאָת וּדְגָם, בְּרִבּוֹ רִבְבָן עִירִין.

עָנֵה אֲנָא בְּמִנְיָנָא, דְּפָסְלִין אַרְבְּעָא טוּרִין.

קָדָמוֹהִי לְגוֹ מְוֹהִי, נָגֵד וְנָפֵק נְהַר דְּנוּרִין.

בְּטוּר תַּלְגָּא נְהוֹר שְׁרָגָא, וְזִקִּין דְּנוּר וּבְעוּרִין.

בְּרָא וּסְכָא מָה בַּחֲשׁוֹכָא, וְעִמֵּהּ שַׁרְיָן נְהוֹרִין.

רְחִיקִין צָפָא בְּלָא שְׁטִיפָא, וְגַלְיָן לֵהּ דְּמִטַּמְּרִין.

בָּעֵית מִנֵּהּ יָת הוּרְמָנֵהּ, וּבָתְרוֹהִי עֲדֵי גְּבִרִין.

יָדְעֵי הִלְכְתָא וּמַתְנִיתָא וְתוֹסֶפְתָּא, סִפְרָא וְסִפְרִין.

מֶלֶךְ חַיָּא לְעָלְמַיָּא, יְמַגֵּן עַם לְהוֹן מְשַׁחֲרִין.

אֲמִיר עֲלֵיהוֹן כְּחָלָא יְהוֹן, וְלָא יִתִמְנוּן הֵיךְ עַפְרִין.

יְחַוְּרוּן כְּעָן לְהוֹן בִּקְעָן, יְטוּפוּן נַעֲוֹהִי חַמְרִין.

רְעוּתְהוֹן הַב וְאַפֵּיהוֹן צְהַב, יְנַהֲרוּן כְּנַהַר צַפְרִין.

לִי הַב תְּקוֹף וְעֵינַךְ זְקוֹף, חֲזִי עָרְדָּ דְּבָד כָּפְרִין.

וִיהוֹן כְּתַבְנָא בְּגוֹ לִבְנָא, כְּאַבְנָא יִשְׁתְּקוּן חַפְרִין.

יְהוֹנָתָן גְּבַר עִנְוְתָן, בְּכֵן לֵהּ נַמְטֵי אַפְרִין.

פתגם יציב has been attributed to Rashi's grandson *Rabbenu Tam*, whose name acrostic (יעקב ברבי מאיר) appears in the first twelve lines of the poem. The last three lines, however, which bear the acrostic לוי, are considered as a later addition. (*Zunz, Literatur geschichte*, page 266; *Davidson*, והפיוט השירה אוצר, II, 420). פתגם יציב is recited as the introduction to the Haftarah of the second day Shavuoth.

YATSIV PITHGAM

Chanted on the second day of Shavuoth after the first verse of the Haftarah

True is the praise of God
Uttered by myriads of angels.
I too acclaim the codes of law
Carved in four rows or *Turim.*
Before him, into the waters,
Flows a river of fire.
On a mountain of snow shines
A light—sparks and flames are there.
He creates, he sees through the dark,
And with him dwells the light.
He sees far with naught to clog,
Things secret are clear to him.
I ask approval first of him,
Then I ask it of men
Versed in Halakhah, Mishnah,
Tosefta, Sifra, and Sifré.
May the King who lives forever
Shield the people who seek him,
Who were told to be countless
Like sand and dust of the earth.
May their valleys be white with flocks,
May their presses flow with wine.
Grant their desires, let their faces
Sparkle like the morning star.
Grant me strength, raise thy eyes
And see thy foes who deny thee.
Let them be like straw inside bricks,
As dumb as stone and abashed.
To Moses, the meekest of men,
Let us give thanks.

On Sabbath, during the Minḥah service, the following passage is read.

במדבר ד, כא–לג

וַיְדַבֵּ֥ר יְהֹוָ֖ה אֶל־מֹשֶׁ֥ה לֵּאמֹֽר: נָשֹׂ֗א אֶת־רֹ֛אשׁ בְּנֵ֥י גֵרְשׁ֖וֹן
גַּם־הֵ֑ם לְבֵ֥ית אֲבֹתָ֖ם לְמִשְׁפְּחֹתָֽם: מִבֶּן֩ שְׁלֹשִׁ֨ים שָׁנָ֜ה
וָמַ֗עְלָה עַ֛ד בֶּן־חֲמִשִּׁ֥ים שָׁנָ֖ה תִּפְקֹ֣ד אוֹתָ֑ם כָּל־הַבָּא֙ לִצְבֹ֣א
צָבָ֔א לַעֲבֹ֥ד עֲבֹדָ֖ה בְּאֹ֥הֶל מוֹעֵֽד: זֹ֚את עֲבֹדַ֣ת מִשְׁפְּחֹ֣ת
הַגֵּרְשֻׁנִּ֔י לַעֲבֹ֖ד וּלְמַשָּֽׂא:* וְנָשְׂא֞וּ אֶת־יְרִיעֹ֤ת הַמִּשְׁכָּן֙ וְאֶת־
אֹ֣הֶל מוֹעֵ֔ד מִכְסֵ֕הוּ וּמִכְסֵ֛ה הַתַּ֥חַשׁ אֲשֶׁר־עָלָ֖יו מִלְמָ֑עְלָה
וְאֶת־מָסַ֕ךְ פֶּ֖תַח אֹ֥הֶל מוֹעֵֽד: וְאֵת֩ קַלְעֵ֨י הֶֽחָצֵ֜ר וְאֶת־מָסַ֣ךְ ׀
פֶּ֣תַח ׀ שַׁ֣עַר הֶחָצֵ֗ר אֲשֶׁר֙ עַל־הַמִּשְׁכָּ֤ן וְעַל־הַמִּזְבֵּ֙חַ֙ סָבִ֔יב
וְאֵת֙ מֵֽיתְרֵיהֶ֔ם וְאֶת־כָּל־כְּלֵ֖י עֲבֹדָתָ֑ם וְאֵ֨ת כָּל־אֲשֶׁ֧ר יֵעָשֶׂ֛ה
לָהֶ֖ם וְעָבָֽדוּ: עַל־פִּ֨י אַהֲרֹ֜ן וּבָנָ֗יו תִּֽהְיֶה֙ כָּל־עֲבֹדַת֙ בְּנֵ֣י
הַגֵּ֣רְשֻׁנִּ֔י לְכָל־מַשָּׂאָ֖ם וּלְכֹ֣ל עֲבֹדָתָ֑ם וּפְקַדְתֶּ֤ם עֲלֵהֶם֙
בְּמִשְׁמֶ֔רֶת אֵ֖ת כָּל־מַשָּׂאָֽם: זֹ֗את עֲבֹדַת֙ מִשְׁפְּחֹ֣ת בְּנֵ֣י
הַגֵּ֣רְשֻׁנִּ֔י בְּאֹ֖הֶל מוֹעֵ֑ד וּמִ֨שְׁמַרְתָּ֔ם בְּיַד֙ אִֽיתָמָ֔ר בֶּֽן־אַהֲרֹ֖ן
הַכֹּהֵֽן:* בְּנֵ֣י מְרָרִ֔י לְמִשְׁפְּחֹתָ֖ם לְבֵית־אֲבֹתָ֑ם תִּפְקֹ֥ד
אֹתָֽם: מִבֶּן֩ שְׁלֹשִׁ֨ים שָׁנָ֜ה וָמַ֗עְלָה וְעַ֛ד בֶּן־חֲמִשִּׁ֥ים שָׁנָ֖ה
תִּפְקְדֵ֑ם כָּל־הַבָּא֙ לַצָּבָ֔א לַעֲבֹ֕ד אֶת־עֲבֹדַ֖ת אֹ֥הֶל מוֹעֵֽד:
וְזֹאת֙ מִשְׁמֶ֣רֶת מַשָּׂאָ֔ם לְכָל־עֲבֹדָתָ֖ם בְּאֹ֣הֶל מוֹעֵ֑ד קַרְשֵׁי֙
הַמִּשְׁכָּ֔ן וּבְרִיחָ֖יו וְעַמּוּדָ֥יו וַאֲדָנָֽיו: וְעַמּוּדֵ֧י הֶחָצֵ֣ר סָבִ֗יב
וְאַדְנֵיהֶ֔ם וִיתֵדֹתָ֖ם וּמֵֽיתְרֵיהֶ֑ם לְכָל־כְּלֵיהֶ֖ם וּלְכֹ֣ל עֲבֹדָתָ֑ם
וּבְשֵׁמֹ֣ת תִּפְקְד֔וּ אֶת־כְּלֵ֖י מִשְׁמֶ֥רֶת מַשָּׂאָֽם: זֹ֣את עֲבֹדַ֗ת
מִשְׁפְּחֹת֙ בְּנֵ֣י מְרָרִ֔י לְכָל־עֲבֹֽדָתָ֖ם בְּאֹ֣הֶל מוֹעֵ֑ד בְּיַד֙ אִֽיתָמָ֔ר
בֶּֽן־אַהֲרֹ֖ן הַכֹּהֵֽן:

On Sabbath, during the Minḥah Service, the following passage is read.
Numbers 4:21-33

The Lord spoke to Moses, saying: Take a census of the Gershonites also by ancestral households and families. From thirty years old up to fifty years old you shall number them, all who can enter for service, to do the work in the tent of meeting. This is the service of the families of the Gershonites, what they must do and what they must carry.

They shall carry the curtains of the tabernacle, the tent of meeting with its covering and the covering of seal-skin that is on top of it, and the curtain at the entrance of the tent of meeting. Also the hangings of the court, the curtain at the entrance of the court that encloses both the tabernacle and the altar, together with their ropes, and all the objects needed for their service; whatever needs to be done with these things they shall do. The service of the Gershonites shall be entirely under the direction of Aaron and his sons, in regard to what they must carry and what they must do; you shall assign to their charge all that they, the Gershonites, are to carry. This, then, is the service of the Gershonites in the tent of meeting, and they shall be under the supervision of Ithamar, son of Aaron the priest.

As for the Merarites, you shall number them by their families and ancestral houses. From thirty years old up to fifty years old you shall number them, every one that can enter the service, to do the work of the tent of meeting. This is what they are charged to carry throughout their service in the tent of meeting; the boards of the tabernacle with its bars, columns and pedestals, and the columns of the court round about with their pedestals, pegs and ropes, with all the equipment needed for their service; you shall assign by name the objects which they are required to carry. This, then, is the service of the families of the Merarites, throughout their service in the tent of meeting under the supervision of Ithamar, son of Aaron the priest."

The Levites were divided into three families, as descended from Levi's three sons: Gershon, Kohath, and Merari. Moses and Aaron belonged to the Kohath family. The Levites assisted the priests by performing subordinate tasks connected with the worship services.

The following three paragraphs are recited on Sabbaths only.

יְקוּם פֻּרְקָן מִן שְׁמַיָּא, חִנָּא וְחִסְדָּא וְרַחֲמֵי, וְחַיֵּי אֲרִיכֵי
וּמְזוֹנֵי רְוִיחֵי וְסִיַּעְתָּא דִשְׁמַיָּא, וּבַרְיוּת גּוּפָא וּנְהוֹרָא מַעַלְיָא,
זַרְעָא חַיָּא וְקַיָּמָא, זַרְעָא דִּי לָא יִפְסָק וְדִי לָא יִבְטַל מִפִּתְגָּמֵי
אוֹרַיְתָא, לְמָרָנָן וְרַבָּנָן, חֲבוּרָתָא קַדִּישָׁתָא דִּי בְּאַרְעָא
דְיִשְׂרָאֵל וְדִי בְּבָבֶל; לְרֵישֵׁי כַלֵּי וּלְרֵישֵׁי גַלְוָתָא, וּלְרֵישֵׁי
מְתִיבָתָא וּלְדַיָּנֵי דִי בָבָא; לְכָל תַּלְמִידֵיהוֹן וּלְכָל תַּלְמִידֵי
תַלְמִידֵיהוֹן, וּלְכָל מָן דְּעָסְקִין בְּאוֹרַיְתָא. מַלְכָּא דְעָלְמָא
יְבָרֵךְ יַתְהוֹן, יַפִּישׁ חַיֵּיהוֹן וְיַסְגֵּא יוֹמֵיהוֹן וְיִתֵּן אַרְכָה לִשְׁנֵיהוֹן,
וְיִתְפָּרְקוּן וְיִשְׁתֵּיזְבוּן מִן כָּל עָקָא וּמִן כָּל מַרְעִין בִּישִׁין. מָרָן
דִי בִשְׁמַיָּא יְהֵא בְסַעֲדְּהוֹן כָּל זְמַן וְעִדָּן, וְנֹאמַר אָמֵן.

When praying in private, omit the following two paragraphs.

יְקוּם פֻּרְקָן מִן שְׁמַיָּא, חִנָּא וְחִסְדָּא וְרַחֲמֵי, וְחַיֵּי אֲרִיכֵי
וּמְזוֹנֵי רְוִיחֵי וְסִיַּעְתָּא דִשְׁמַיָּא, וּבַרְיוּת גּוּפָא וּנְהוֹרָא מַעַלְיָא,
זַרְעָא חַיָּא וְקַיָּמָא, זַרְעָא דִּי לָא יִפְסָק וְדִי לָא יִבְטַל מִפִּתְגָּמֵי
אוֹרַיְתָא, לְכָל קְהָלָא קַדִּישָׁא הָדֵן, רַבְרְבַיָּא עִם זְעֵרַיָּא,
טַפְלָא וּנְשַׁיָּא. מַלְכָּא דְעָלְמָא יְבָרֵךְ יַתְכוֹן, יַפִּישׁ חַיֵּיכוֹן וְיַסְגֵּא
יוֹמֵיכוֹן וְיִתֵּן אַרְכָה לִשְׁנֵיכוֹן, וְתִתְפָּרְקוּן וְתִשְׁתֵּיזְבוּן מִן כָּל
עָקָא וּמִן כָּל מַרְעִין בִּישִׁין. מָרָן דִי בִשְׁמַיָּא יְהֵא בְסַעֲדְּכוֹן
כָּל זְמַן וְעִדָּן, וְנֹאמַר אָמֵן.

יְקוּם פֻּרְקָן, the prayer in Aramaic, was composed in Babylonia where Aramaic remained the daily language of the Jews for more than a thousand years, until the ninth century when Arabic became the popular language. The first *Yekum Purkan*, recited in behalf of Babylonian and Palestinian

The following three paragraphs are recited on Sabbath only.

May salvation arise from heaven. May grace, kindness and mercy—long life, ample sustenance and divine aid; physical health, perfect vision, and healthy children who will never neglect the study of the Torah—be granted to our scholars and teachers, to the holy societies that are in the land of Israel and in the land of Babylon, to the heads of the academies and the chiefs of the captivity, to the presidents of the colleges and the judges of the towns, to their disciples and the disciples of their disciples and to all who study the Torah, May the King of the universe bless them, prolong their lives, increase their days and add to their years; may they be saved and delivered from all distress and disease. May our Lord who is in heaven be their help at all times; and let us say, Amen.

When praying in private, omit the following two paragraphs.

May salvation arise from heaven. May grace, kindness and mercy—long life, ample sustenance and divine aid; physical health, perfect vision and healthy children who will never neglect the study of the Torah—be granted to this entire congregation, great and small, women and children. May the King of the universe bless you, prolong your lives, increase your days and add to your years; may you be saved and delivered from all distress and disease. May our Lord who is in heaven be your help at all times; and let us say, Amen.

scholars and leaders, was of late amplified by the addition of ודי בכל ארעת נלותנא ("and that are in all the lands of our diaspora") in order to make the whole passage applicable to our own times (Baer's Siddur, page 229). Curiously enough, *Yekum Purkan* is not included in the Babylonian *Siddurim* of Amram Gaon and Saadyah Gaon, but is mentioned in Maḥzor Vitry which has come down to us from France. רישי כלה refers to the heads of the semi-annual conventions of the Babylonian scholars which were held during the months of *Adar* and *Elul*. The second *Yekum Purkan*, phrased like the first, is a prayer for the congregation, similar in content to the Hebrew paragraph מי שברך, which singles out those who contribute toward the maintenance of the synagogue as well as to charity.

מִי שֶׁבֵּרַךְ אֲבוֹתֵינוּ אַבְרָהָם יִצְחָק וְיַעֲקֹב, הוּא יְבָרֵךְ אֶת
כָּל הַקָּהָל הַקָּדוֹשׁ הַזֶּה עִם כָּל קְהִלּוֹת הַקֹּדֶשׁ, הֵם וּנְשֵׁיהֶם
וּבְנֵיהֶם וּבְנוֹתֵיהֶם וְכֹל אֲשֶׁר לָהֶם, וּמִי שֶׁמְּיַחֲדִים בָּתֵּי כְנֵסִיּוֹת
לִתְפִלָּה, וּמִי שֶׁבָּאִים בְּתוֹכָם לְהִתְפַּלֵּל, וּמִי שֶׁנּוֹתְנִים נֵר
לַמָּאוֹר, וְיַיִן לְקִדּוּשׁ וּלְהַבְדָּלָה, וּפַת לָאוֹרְחִים וּצְדָקָה לָעֲנִיִּים,
Reader וְכָל מִי שֶׁעוֹסְקִים בְּצָרְכֵי צִבּוּר בֶּאֱמוּנָה. הַקָּדוֹשׁ בָּרוּךְ
הוּא יְשַׁלֵּם שְׂכָרָם, וְיָסִיר מֵהֶם כָּל מַחֲלָה, וְיִרְפָּא לְכָל גּוּפָם,
וְיִסְלַח לְכָל עֲוֹנָם, וְיִשְׁלַח בְּרָכָה וְהַצְלָחָה בְּכָל מַעֲשֵׂה
יְדֵיהֶם, עִם כָּל יִשְׂרָאֵל אֲחֵיהֶם, וְנֹאמַר אָמֵן.

תְּפִלָּה בִשְׁלוֹמָהּ שֶׁל מַלְכוּת

The Reader takes the Torah and recites:

הַנּוֹתֵן תְּשׁוּעָה לַמְּלָכִים וּמֶמְשָׁלָה לַנְּסִיכִים, מַלְכוּתוֹ
מַלְכוּת כָּל עוֹלָמִים; הַפּוֹצֶה אֶת דָּוִד עַבְדּוֹ מֵחֶרֶב רָעָה,
הַנּוֹתֵן בַּיָּם דֶּרֶךְ, וּבְמַיִם עַזִּים נְתִיבָה, הוּא יְבָרֵךְ וְיִשְׁמוֹר וְיִנְצוֹר
וְיַעֲזוֹר וִירוֹמֵם וִיגַדֵּל וִינַשֵּׂא לְמַעְלָה

אֶת הַנָּשִׂיא וְאֶת מִשְׁנֵהוּ

וְאֶת כָּל שָׂרֵי הָאָרֶץ הַזֹּאת.

מֶלֶךְ מַלְכֵי הַמְּלָכִים בְּרַחֲמָיו יְחַיֵּם וְיִשְׁמְרֵם, וּמִכָּל צָרָה
וְיָגוֹן וָנֶזֶק יַצִּילֵם. מֶלֶךְ מַלְכֵי הַמְּלָכִים בְּרַחֲמָיו יִתֵּן בְּלִבָּם
וּבְלֵב כָּל יוֹעֲצֵיהֶם וְשָׂרֵיהֶם לַעֲשׂוֹת טוֹבָה עִמָּנוּ וְעִם כָּל
יִשְׂרָאֵל. בִּימֵיהֶם וּבְיָמֵינוּ תִּוָּשַׁע יְהוּדָה, וְיִשְׂרָאֵל יִשְׁכּוֹן
לָבֶטַח, וּבָא לְצִיּוֹן גּוֹאֵל. וְכֵן יְהִי רָצוֹן, וְנֹאמַר אָמֵן.

הנותן תשועה has undergone some verbal variations in the course of time
The custom to pray for the welfare of the government is based on Jeremiah.
29:7 ("Seek the welfare of the country where I have sent you into exile; pray

May he who blessed our fathers, Abraham, Isaac and Jacob, bless this entire congregation and all other congregations—their wives, their sons and daughters, and all that belongs to them. May he bless those who dedicate synagogues for worship and those who enter therein to pray, those who provide lamps for lighting and wine for Kiddush and Havdalah and those who give food to the transient guests and charity to the poor, as well as all those who faithfully occupy themselves with the needs of the community. May the Holy One, blessed be he, grant them their reward, remove from them all sickness, preserve them in good health, and forgive all their sins; may he bless and prosper their work and the work of all Israel their brethren; and let us say, Amen.

PRAYER FOR THE GOVERNMENT

The Reader takes the Torah and recites:

He who granted victory to kings and dominion to princes, his kingdom is a kingdom of all ages; he who delivered his servant David from the evil sword, he who opened a road through the sea, a path amid the mighty waters—may he bless and protect, help and exalt

THE PRESIDENT AND THE VICE-PRESIDENT

AND ALL THE OFFICERS OF THIS COUNTRY.

May the supreme King of kings, in his mercy, sustain them and deliver them from all distress and misfortune. May the supreme King of kings, in his mercy, inspire them and all their counselors and aides to deal kindly with us and with all Israel. In their days and in our days Judah shall be saved, Israel shall dwell in security, and a redeemer shall come to Zion. May this be the will of God; and let us say, Amen.

---

to the Lord for it, for your welfare depends on its welfare"). This prayer is composed of excerpts from Psalms 145:13; 144:10; Isaiah 43:16; Jeremiah 23:6; Isaiah 59:20. Abudarham wrote in the fourteenth century: "It is the custom to bless the king and to pray to God that he may give him victory."

תְּפִלָּה לִשְׁלוֹם מְדִינַת יִשְׂרָאֵל

אָבִינוּ שֶׁבַּשָּׁמַיִם, צוּר יִשְׂרָאֵל וְגוֹאֲלוֹ, בָּרֵךְ אֶת מְדִינַת יִשְׂרָאֵל, רֵאשִׁית צְמִיחַת גְּאֻלָּתֵנוּ. הָגֵן עָלֶיהָ בְּאֶבְרַת חַסְדֶּךָ, וּפְרוֹשׂ עָלֶיהָ סֻכַּת שְׁלוֹמֶךָ; וּשְׁלַח אוֹרְךָ וַאֲמִתְּךָ לְרָאשֶׁיהָ, שָׂרֶיהָ וְיוֹעֲצֶיהָ, וְתַקְּנֵם בְּעֵצָה טוֹבָה מִלְּפָנֶיךָ.

חַזֵּק אֶת יְדֵי מְגִנֵּי אֶרֶץ קָדְשֵׁנוּ, וְהַנְחִילֵם אֱלֹהֵינוּ יְשׁוּעָה, וַעֲטֶרֶת נִצָּחוֹן תְּעַטְּרֵם; וְנָתַתָּ שָׁלוֹם בָּאָרֶץ, וְשִׂמְחַת עוֹלָם לְיוֹשְׁבֶיהָ.

וְאֶת אַחֵינוּ, כָּל בֵּית יִשְׂרָאֵל, פְּקָד־נָא בְּכָל אַרְצוֹת פְּזוּרֵיהֶם, וְתוֹלִיכֵם מְהֵרָה קוֹמְמִיּוּת לְצִיּוֹן עִירֶךָ, וְלִירוּשָׁלַיִם מִשְׁכַּן שְׁמֶךָ, כַּכָּתוּב בְּתוֹרַת מֹשֶׁה עַבְדֶּךָ: אִם יִהְיֶה נִדַּחֲךָ בִּקְצֵה הַשָּׁמָיִם, מִשָּׁם יְקַבֶּצְךָ יְיָ אֱלֹהֶיךָ וּמִשָּׁם יִקָּחֶךָ. וֶהֱבִיאֲךָ יְיָ אֱלֹהֶיךָ אֶל הָאָרֶץ אֲשֶׁר יָרְשׁוּ אֲבֹתֶיךָ, וִירִשְׁתָּהּ.

וְיַחֵד לְבָבֵנוּ לְאַהֲבָה וּלְיִרְאָה אֶת שְׁמֶךָ, וְלִשְׁמוֹר אֶת כָּל דִּבְרֵי תוֹרָתֶךָ. הוֹפַע בַּהֲדַר גְּאוֹן עֻזֶּךָ עַל כָּל יוֹשְׁבֵי תֵבֵל אַרְצֶךָ, וְיֹאמַר כֹּל אֲשֶׁר נְשָׁמָה בְאַפּוֹ: יְיָ אֱלֹהֵי יִשְׂרָאֵל מֶלֶךְ, וּמַלְכוּתוֹ בַּכֹּל מָשָׁלָה. אָמֵן סֶלָה.

PRAYER FOR THE WELFARE OF THE STATE OF ISRAEL

Our Father who art in heaven, Protector and Redeemer of Israel, bless thou the State of Israel which marks the dawn of our deliverance. Shield it beneath the wings of thy love; spread over it thy canopy of peace; send thy light and thy truth to its leaders, officers and counselors, and direct them with thy good counsel.

O God, strengthen the defenders of our Holy Land; grant them salvation and crown them with victory. Establish peace in the land, and everlasting joy for its inhabitants.

Remember our brethren, the whole house of Israel, in all the lands of their dispersion. Speedily let them walk upright to Zion thy city, to Jerusalem thy dwelling-place, as it is written in the Torah of thy servant Moses: "Even if you are dispersed in the uttermost parts of the world, from there the Lord your God will gather and fetch you. The Lord your God will bring you into the land which your fathers possessed, and you shall possess it."[1]

Unite our heart to love and revere thy name, and to observe all the precepts of thy Torah. Shine forth in thy glorious majesty over all the inhabitants of thy world. Let everything that breathes proclaim: "The Lord God of Israel is King; his majesty rules over all." Amen.

---

[1] *Deuteronomy* 30:4-5.

MEMORIAL SERVICE
(YIZKOR)

Meditation

O Lord, let me know my end, the number of days that I have left; let me know how short-lived I am. Thou hast made my days no longer than a span; my lifetime is as nothing in thy sight. Every man, at his best, is an empty breath. Man walks about as a mere shadow, making much ado about vanity; he heaps up riches and knows not who will possess them.

What then can I expect, O Lord? My hope is in thee! Save me from all my sins; let me not become an object of reproach. I am unable to speak, I do not open my mouth, for it is thou who hast done it to me. Relieve me from thy stroke, for I may waste underneath thy blows.

Hear my prayer, O Lord, listen to my cry, answer thou my tears; for I am but a guest of thine, a sojourner, like all my forefathers. Have mercy upon me that I may recover my strength before I depart to be no more.[1]

Responsively

O Lord, thou hast been our shelter in every generation.

From eternity to eternity thou art God.

Thou turnest man to dust, saying: Return, O man.

A thousand years to thee are like a day that passes.

Thou sweepest men away, and they sleep.

They are like grass that grows in the morning.

It flourishes in the morning, and withers in the evening.

The length of our life is seventy years, or eighty.

Our life, filled with sorrow, is soon over and we flit away.

O teach us how to make the most of each day, how to be wise.

May thy favor, Lord our God, rest upon us and direct our deeds.

I lift my eyes to the hills; whence will my help come?

---

[1] *Psalm* 39:5–14.

My help comes from the Lord who made heaven and earth.

He will not let your foot slip; he who keeps you does not slumber. The Guardian of Israel neither slumbers nor sleeps.

The Lord is your guardian; the Lord is your shelter. The sun shall never hurt you in the day, nor the moon by night.

The Lord shall keep you from all evil; he shall keep your soul. The Lord will guard you as you come and go, now and ever.[1]

Congregation:

The Lord is my shepherd; I am not in want. He makes me lie down in green meadows; he leads me beside refreshing streams. He restores my life; he guides me by righteous paths for his own sake. Even though I walk through the darkest valley, I fear no harm; for thou art with me. Thy rod and thy staff—they comfort me. Thou spreadest a feast for me in the presence of my enemies. Thou hast perfumed my head with oil; my cup overflows. Only goodness and kindness shall follow me all the days of my life; I shall dwell in the house of the Lord forever.[2]

Rabbi:

Merciful Father, we lift our hearts up to thee as we recall with tearful tenderness the men and women who are no longer with us in the land of the living. Grant peace of mind to those in our midst who bear deep wounds in their hearts today. May consolation come to them soon. May they find comfort in knowing that death is the wish of some, the relief of many, and the end of all. It places all mortals on the same level. Death separates, but it also unites. It reunites whom it separates. May the memory of our departed inspire us to live nobly and charitably, and to animate with cheerfulness all those who surround us. O Lord, let us all find sustaining hope in thee who hast been our source of strength and comfort throughout the ages. Amen.

---

[1]*Psalm* 90; **121.**   [2]*Psalm* **23.**

הַזְכָּרַת נְשָׁמוֹת

Recited on the second day

Responsively

יְיָ, מָה אָדָם וַתֵּדָעֵהוּ, בֶּן־אֱנוֹשׁ וַתְּחַשְּׁבֵהוּ.

אָדָם לַהֶבֶל דָּמָה, יָמָיו כְּצֵל עוֹבֵר.

בַּבֹּקֶר יָצִיץ וְחָלָף, לָעֶרֶב יְמוֹלֵל וְיָבֵשׁ.

לִמְנוֹת יָמֵינוּ כֵּן הוֹדַע, וְנָבִא לְבַב חָכְמָה.

שְׁמָר־תָּם וּרְאֵה יָשָׁר, כִּי אַחֲרִית לְאִישׁ שָׁלוֹם.

אַךְ אֱלֹהִים יִפְדֶּה נַפְשִׁי מִיַּד שְׁאוֹל, כִּי יִקָּחֵנִי סֶלָה.

כָּלָה שְׁאֵרִי וּלְבָבִי, צוּר לְבָבִי וְחֶלְקִי אֱלֹהִים לְעוֹלָם.

וְיָשֹׁב הֶעָפָר עַל הָאָרֶץ כְּשֶׁהָיָה, וְהָרוּחַ תָּשׁוּב אֶל הָאֱלֹהִים אֲשֶׁר נְתָנָהּ.

תהלים צא

יֹשֵׁב בְּסֵתֶר עֶלְיוֹן, בְּצֵל שַׁדַּי יִתְלוֹנָן.

אֹמַר לַיְיָ, מַחְסִי וּמְצוּדָתִי, אֱלֹהַי אֶבְטַח בּוֹ.

כִּי הוּא יַצִּילְךָ מִפַּח יָקוּשׁ, מִדֶּבֶר הַוּוֹת.

בְּאֶבְרָתוֹ יָסֶךְ לָךְ, וְתַחַת כְּנָפָיו תֶּחְסֶה; צִנָּה וְסֹחֵרָה אֲמִתּוֹ.

לֹא תִירָא מִפַּחַד לָיְלָה, מֵחֵץ יָעוּף יוֹמָם.

מִדֶּבֶר בָּאֹפֶל יַהֲלֹךְ, מִקֶּטֶב יָשׁוּד צָהֳרָיִם.

הזכרת נשמות is an ancient custom mentioned in the Midrash and in Maḥzor Vitry, page 173. According to the *Kol Bo* (an abridgment of the fourteenth century work ארחות חיים by Rabbi Aaron ha-Kohen of France), the *Yizkor* service was originally confined to the Day of Atonement in order to stir the people to repentance: וזה שנהגו להזכיר המתים, לפי שהוכרת המיתה שוברת לבו של אדם ומכניעה יצרו.

In order not to disturb the participants in the memorial service, it is customary to send out those whose parents are still alive.

MEMORIAL SERVICE

Recited on the second day

Responsively

O Lord, what is man that thou shouldst notice him?
What is mortal man that thou shouldst consider him?
Man is like a breath;
His days are like a passing shadow.
He flourishes and grows in the morning;
He fades and withers in the evening.
O teach us how to number our days,
That we may attain a heart of wisdom.
Mark the innocent, look upon the upright;
For there is a future for the man of peace.
Surely God will free me from the grave;
He will receive me indeed.
My flesh and my heart fail,
Yet God is my strength forever.
The dust returns to the earth as it was,
But the spirit returns to God who gave it.[1]

Psalm 91

He who dwells in the shelter of the Most High
Abides under the protection of the Almighty.
I say of the Lord: "He is myrefuge and my fortress,
My God, in whom I trust."
He saves you from the fowler's snare
And from the destructive pestilence.
With his pinions he will cover you,
And under hsi wings you will find refuge;
His faithfulness is a shield and buckler.
Fear not the terror of the night,
Nor the arrow that flies by day.
Nor the pestilence that stalks in darkness,
Nor the destruction that ravages at noon.

---

[1] *Psalms* 144:3-4; 90:6,12; 37:37; 49:16; 73:26; *Ecclesiastes* 12:7.

עerror

יִפֹּל מִצִּדְּךָ אֶלֶף, וּרְבָבָה מִימִינֶךָ; אֵלֶיךָ לֹא יִגָּשׁ.

רַק בְּעֵינֶיךָ תַבִּיט, וְשִׁלֻּמַת רְשָׁעִים תִּרְאֶה.

כִּי אַתָּה, יְיָ, מַחְסִי; עֶלְיוֹן שַׂמְתָּ מְעוֹנֶךָ.

לֹא תְאֻנֶּה אֵלֶיךָ רָעָה, וְנֶגַע לֹא יִקְרַב בְּאָהֳלֶךָ.

כִּי מַלְאָכָיו יְצַוֶּה לָּךְ, לִשְׁמָרְךָ בְּכָל דְּרָכֶיךָ.

עַל כַּפַּיִם יִשָּׂאוּנְךָ, פֶּן תִּגֹּף בָּאֶבֶן רַגְלֶךָ.

עַל שַׁחַל וָפֶתֶן תִּדְרֹךְ, תִּרְמֹס כְּפִיר וְתַנִּין.

כִּי בִי חָשַׁק וַאֲפַלְּטֵהוּ; אֲשַׂגְּבֵהוּ כִּי יָדַע שְׁמִי.

יִקְרָאֵנִי וְאֶעֱנֵהוּ, עִמּוֹ אָנֹכִי בְצָרָה, אֲחַלְּצֵהוּ וַאֲכַבְּדֵהוּ.

אֹרֶךְ יָמִים אַשְׂבִּיעֵהוּ, וְאַרְאֵהוּ בִּישׁוּעָתִי.

In memory of a father:

יִזְכּוֹר אֱלֹהִים נִשְׁמַת אָבִי מוֹרִי .... שֶׁהָלַךְ לְעוֹלָמוֹ. בַּעֲבוּר שֶׁאֲנִי נוֹדֵר צְדָקָה בַּעֲדוֹ, בִּשְׂכַר זֶה, תְּהֵא נַפְשׁוֹ צְרוּרָה בִּצְרוֹר הַחַיִּים עִם נִשְׁמוֹת אַבְרָהָם יִצְחָק וְיַעֲקֹב, שָׂרָה רִבְקָה רָחֵל וְלֵאָה, וְעִם שְׁאָר צַדִּיקִים וְצִדְקָנִיּוֹת שֶׁבְּגַן עֵדֶן. אָמֵן.

In memory of a mother:

יִזְכּוֹר אֱלֹהִים נִשְׁמַת אִמִּי מוֹרָתִי .... שֶׁהָלְכָה לְעוֹלָמָהּ. בַּעֲבוּר שֶׁאֲנִי נוֹדֵר צְדָקָה בַּעֲדָהּ, בִּשְׂכַר זֶה, תְּהֵא נַפְשָׁהּ צְרוּרָה בִּצְרוֹר הַחַיִּים עִם נִשְׁמוֹת אַבְרָהָם יִצְחָק וְיַעֲקֹב, שָׂרָה רִבְקָה רָחֵל וְלֵאָה, וְעִם שְׁאָר צַדִּיקִים וְצִדְקָנִיּוֹת שֶׁבְּגַן עֵדֶן. אָמֵן.

* The name of the deceased is supplied.

Though a thousand fall at your side,
And a myriad at your right hand,
It shall not come near you.
Only with your eyes will you gaze,
And see the reward of evil men.
Thou, O Lord, art my refuge!
When you have made the Most High your shelter,
No disaster shall befall you, or come near your tent.
For he will give his angels charge over you,
To guard you in all your ways.
They will bear you upon their hands,
Lest you strike your foot against a stone.
You can tread on lion and asp;
You can trample young lion and serpent.
"He clings to me, so I deliver him;
I set him safe, because he loves me.
When he calls upon me, I will answer him;
I will be with him in trouble;
I will rescue him and bring him to honor.
With long life will I satisfy him,
And let him see my saving power."

In memory of a father:

May God remember the soul of my respected father . . .* who has passed to his eternal rest. I pledge charity in his behalf and pray that his soul be kept among the immortal souls of Abraham, Isaac, Jacob, Sarah, Rebekah, Rachel, Leah, and all the righteous men and women in paradise. Amen.

In memory of a mother:

May God remember the soul of my respected mother . . .* who has passed to her eternal rest. I pledge charity in her behalf and pray that her soul be kept among the immortal souls of Abraham, Isaac, Jacob, Sarah, Rebekah, Rachel, Leah, and all the righteous men and women in paradise. Amen.

The name of the deceased is supplied.

In memory of Jewish martyrs:

יִזְכּוֹר אֱלֹהִים נִשְׁמוֹת הַקְּדוֹשִׁים וְהַטְּהוֹרִים שֶׁנֶּהֶרְגוּ, שֶׁנִּשְׁחֲטוּ וְשֶׁנִּשְׂרְפוּ, וְשֶׁנִּטְבְּעוּ וְשֶׁנֶּחְנְקוּ עַל קְדוּשׁ הַשֵּׁם. בַּעֲבוּר שֶׁנּוֹדְרִים צְדָקָה בְּעַד הַזְכָּרַת נִשְׁמוֹתֵיהֶם, בִּשְׂכַר זֶה, תִּהְיֶינָה נַפְשׁוֹתֵיהֶם צְרוּרוֹת בִּצְרוֹר הַחַיִּים עִם נִשְׁמוֹת אַבְרָהָם יִצְחָק וְיַעֲקֹב, שָׂרָה רִבְקָה רָחֵל וְלֵאָה, וְעִם שְׁאָר צַדִּיקִים וְצִדְקָנִיּוֹת שֶׁבְּגַן עֵדֶן, וְנֹאמַר אָמֵן.

For a man:

אֵל מָלֵא רַחֲמִים, שׁוֹכֵן בַּמְּרוֹמִים, הַמְצֵא מְנוּחָה נְכוֹנָה תַּחַת כַּנְפֵי הַשְּׁכִינָה, בְּמַעֲלוֹת קְדוֹשִׁים וּטְהוֹרִים כְּזֹהַר הָרָקִיעַ מַזְהִירִים, אֶת נִשְׁמַת . . . . שֶׁהָלַךְ לְעוֹלָמוֹ. בַּעֲבוּר שֶׁנָּדְרוּ צְדָקָה בְּעַד הַזְכָּרַת נִשְׁמָתוֹ, בְּגַן עֵדֶן תְּהֵא מְנוּחָתוֹ. לָכֵן בַּעַל הָרַחֲמִים יַסְתִּירֵהוּ בְּסֵתֶר כְּנָפָיו לְעוֹלָמִים, וְיִצְרוֹר בִּצְרוֹר הַחַיִּים אֶת נִשְׁמָתוֹ. יְיָ הוּא נַחֲלָתוֹ; וְיָנוּחַ עַל מִשְׁכָּבוֹ בְּשָׁלוֹם, וְנֹאמַר אָמֵן.

For a woman:

אֵל מָלֵא רַחֲמִים, שׁוֹכֵן בַּמְּרוֹמִים, הַמְצֵא מְנוּחָה נְכוֹנָה תַּחַת כַּנְפֵי הַשְּׁכִינָה, בְּמַעֲלוֹת קְדוֹשִׁים וּטְהוֹרִים כְּזֹהַר הָרָקִיעַ מַזְהִירִים, אֶת נִשְׁמַת . . . . שֶׁהָלְכָה לְעוֹלָמָהּ. בַּעֲבוּר שֶׁנָּדְרוּ צְדָקָה בְּעַד הַזְכָּרַת נִשְׁמָתָהּ, בְּגַן עֵדֶן תְּהֵא מְנוּחָתָהּ. לָכֵן בַּעַל הָרַחֲמִים יַסְתִּירֶהָ בְּסֵתֶר כְּנָפָיו לְעוֹלָמִים, וְיִצְרוֹר בִּצְרוֹר הַחַיִּים אֶת נִשְׁמָתָהּ. יְיָ הוּא נַחֲלָתָהּ; וְתָנוּחַ עַל מִשְׁכָּבָהּ בְּשָׁלוֹם, וְנֹאמַר אָמֵן.

*The name of the deceased is supplied.

In memory of Jewish martyrs:

May God remember the souls of the saintly martyrs who have been slaughtered, burned, drowned or strangled for their loyalty to God. We pledge charity in their memory and pray that their souls be kept among the immortal souls of Abraham, Isaac, Jacob, Sarah, Rebekah, Rachel, Leah, and all the righteous men and women in paradise; and let us say, Amen.

For a man:

Merciful God in heaven, grant perfect repose to the soul of . . . * who has passed to his eternal habitation; may he be under thy divine wings among the holy and pure who shine bright as the sky; may his place of rest be in paradise. Merciful One, O keep his soul forever alive under thy protective wings. The Lord being his heritage, may he rest in peace; and let us say, Amen.

For a woman:

Merciful God in heaven, grant perfect repose to the soul of . . . * who has passed to her eternal habitation; may she be under thy divine wings among the holy and pure who shine bright as the sky; may her place of rest be in paradise. Merciful One, O keep her soul forever alive under thy protective wings. The Lord being her heritage, may she rest in peace; and let us say, Amen.

* *The name of the deceased is supplied.*

אל מלא רחמים, the most soulful of the memorial prayers, is recited aloud. Twenty-two versions of אל מלא רחמים are listed in Davidson's *Thesaurus of Mediaeval Hebrew Poetry*. The traditional reading המצא מנוחה . . . את נשמת is correct on the basis of Job 34:11; 37:13.

אַב הָרַחֲמִים, שׁוֹכֵן מְרוֹמִים, בְּרַחֲמָיו הָעֲצוּמִים, הוּא
יִפְקֹד בְּרַחֲמִים הַחֲסִידִים וְהַיְשָׁרִים וְהַתְּמִימִים, קְהִלּוֹת הַקֹּדֶשׁ
שֶׁמָּסְרוּ נַפְשָׁם עַל קְדֻשַּׁת הַשֵּׁם, הַנֶּאֱהָבִים וְהַנְּעִימִים בְּחַיֵּיהֶם,
וּבְמוֹתָם לֹא נִפְרָדוּ. מִנְּשָׁרִים קַלּוּ, וּמֵאֲרָיוֹת גָּבֵרוּ, לַעֲשׂוֹת
רְצוֹן קוֹנָם וְחֵפֶץ צוּרָם. יִזְכְּרֵם אֱלֹהֵינוּ לְטוֹבָה עִם שְׁאָר
צַדִּיקֵי עוֹלָם, וְיִנְקֹם נִקְמַת דַּם עֲבָדָיו הַשָּׁפוּךְ, כַּכָּתוּב בְּתוֹרַת
מֹשֶׁה אִישׁ הָאֱלֹהִים: הַרְנִינוּ, גוֹיִם, עַמּוֹ, כִּי דַם עֲבָדָיו יִקּוֹם,
וְנָקָם יָשִׁיב לְצָרָיו, וְכִפֶּר אַדְמָתוֹ עַמּוֹ. וְעַל יְדֵי עֲבָדֶיךָ
הַנְּבִיאִים כָּתוּב לֵאמֹר: וְנִקֵּיתִי דָּמָם, לֹא נִקֵּיתִי, וַיְיָ שֹׁכֵן בְּצִיּוֹן.
וּבְכִתְבֵי הַקֹּדֶשׁ נֶאֱמַר: לָמָה יֹאמְרוּ הַגּוֹיִם אַיֵּה אֱלֹהֵיהֶם, יִוָּדַע
בַּגּוֹיִם לְעֵינֵינוּ נִקְמַת דַּם עֲבָדֶיךָ הַשָּׁפוּךְ. Reader וְאוֹמֵר: כִּי
דֹרֵשׁ דָּמִים אוֹתָם זָכָר, לֹא שָׁכַח צַעֲקַת עֲנָוִים. וְאוֹמֵר: יָדִין
בַּגּוֹיִם, מָלֵא גְוִיּוֹת, מָחַץ רֹאשׁ עַל אֶרֶץ רַבָּה, מִנַּחַל בַּדֶּרֶךְ
יִשְׁתֶּה, עַל כֵּן יָרִים רֹאשׁ.

אַשְׁרֵי יוֹשְׁבֵי בֵיתֶךָ; עוֹד יְהַלְלוּךָ סֶּלָה.
אַשְׁרֵי הָעָם שֶׁכָּכָה לּוֹ; אַשְׁרֵי הָעָם שֶׁיְיָ אֱלֹהָיו.

In some congregations the following piyyut is chanted before reciting אַשְׁרֵי.

יָהּ אֵלִי וְגוֹאֲלִי, אֶתְיַצְּבָה לִקְרָאתֶךָ.
הָיָה וְיִהְיֶה, הָיָה וְהֹוֶה, כָּל גּוֹי אַדְמָתֶךָ.
וְלַתּוֹדָה, וְלָעוֹלָה, וְלַמִּנְחָה, וְלַחַטָּאת, וְלָאָשָׁם, וְלַשְּׁלָמִים,
וְלַמִּלּוּאִים, כָּל קָרְבְּנֶיךָ.
זְכוֹר נִלְאָה, אֲשֶׁר נָשָׂאָה, וַהֲשִׁיבָהּ לְאַדְמָתֶךָ.
סֶלָה אֲהַלְלֶךָ, בְּאַשְׁרֵי יוֹשְׁבֵי בֵיתֶךָ.

May the merciful Father who dwells on high, in his infinite mercy, remember those saintly, upright and blameless souls, the holy communities who offered their lives for the sanctification of the divine name. They were lovely and amiable in their life, and were not parted in their death. They were swifter than eagles and stronger than lions to do the will of their Master and the desire of their Stronghold. May our God remember them favorably among the other righteous of the world; may he avenge the blood of his servants which has been shed, as it is written in the Torah of Moses, the man of God: "O nations, make his people joyful! He avenges the blood of his servants, renders retribution to his foes, and provides atonement for his land and his people." And by thy servants, the prophets, it is written: "I will avenge their blood which I have not yet avenged; the Lord dwells in Zion." And in the holy writings it is written: "Why should the nations say, 'Where then is their God?' Let the vengeance for thy servants' blood that is shed be made known among the nations in our sight." And it is written: "The avenger of bloodshed remembers them; he does not forget the cry of the humble." And it is further written: "He will execute judgment upon the nations and fill [the battle-field] with corpses; he will shatter the [enemy's] head over all the wide earth. From the brook by the wayside he will drink; then he will lift up his head triumphantly."

Happy are those who dwell in thy house; they are ever praising thee. Happy the people that is so situated; happy the people whose God is the Lord.

דַּק עַל דַּק, עַד אֵין נִבְדַּק, וְלִתְבוּנָתוֹ אֵין חֵקֶר.

הָאֵל נוֹרָא, בְּאַחַת סְקִירָה, בֵּין טוֹב לָרַע יְבַקֵּר. וְלַתּוֹדָה...

אֲדוֹן צְבָאוֹת, בְּרֹב פְּלָאוֹת, חִבֵּר כָּל אָהֳלוֹ.

בִּנְתִיבוֹת לֵב לְבָלֵּב, הַצּוּר תָּמִים פָּעֳלוֹ. וְלַתּוֹדָה...אַשְׁרֵי.

תהלים קמה

תְּהִלָּה לְדָוִד

אֲרוֹמִמְךָ, אֱלֹהַי הַמֶּלֶךְ, וַאֲבָרְכָה שִׁמְךָ לְעוֹלָם וָעֶד.

בְּכָל יוֹם אֲבָרְכֶךָּ, וַאֲהַלְלָה שִׁמְךָ לְעוֹלָם וָעֶד.

גָּדוֹל יְיָ וּמְהֻלָּל מְאֹד, וְלִגְדֻלָּתוֹ אֵין חֵקֶר.

דּוֹר לְדוֹר יְשַׁבַּח מַעֲשֶׂיךָ, וּגְבוּרֹתֶיךָ יַגִּידוּ.

הֲדַר כְּבוֹד הוֹדֶךָ, וְדִבְרֵי נִפְלְאֹתֶיךָ אָשִׂיחָה.

וֶעֱזוּז נוֹרְאוֹתֶיךָ יֹאמֵרוּ, וּגְדֻלָּתְךָ אֲסַפְּרֶנָּה.

זֵכֶר רַב טוּבְךָ יַבִּיעוּ, וְצִדְקָתְךָ יְרַנֵּנוּ.

חַנּוּן וְרַחוּם יְיָ, אֶרֶךְ אַפַּיִם וּגְדָל־חָסֶד.

טוֹב יְיָ לַכֹּל, וְרַחֲמָיו עַל כָּל מַעֲשָׂיו.

יוֹדוּךָ יְיָ כָּל מַעֲשֶׂיךָ, וַחֲסִידֶיךָ יְבָרְכוּכָה.

כְּבוֹד מַלְכוּתְךָ יֹאמֵרוּ, וּגְבוּרָתְךָ יְדַבֵּרוּ.

לְהוֹדִיעַ לִבְנֵי הָאָדָם גְּבוּרֹתָיו, וּכְבוֹד הֲדַר מַלְכוּתוֹ.

מַלְכוּתְךָ מַלְכוּת כָּל עֹלָמִים, וּמֶמְשַׁלְתְּךָ בְּכָל דּוֹר וָדֹר.

סוֹמֵךְ יְיָ לְכָל הַנֹּפְלִים, וְזוֹקֵף לְכָל הַכְּפוּפִים.

עֵינֵי כֹל אֵלֶיךָ יְשַׂבֵּרוּ, וְאַתָּה נוֹתֵן לָהֶם אֶת אָכְלָם בְּעִתּוֹ.

פּוֹתֵחַ אֶת יָדֶךָ, וּמַשְׂבִּיעַ לְכָל חַי רָצוֹן.

צַדִּיק יְיָ בְּכָל דְּרָכָיו, וְחָסִיד בְּכָל מַעֲשָׂיו.

קָרוֹב יְיָ לְכָל קֹרְאָיו, לְכֹל אֲשֶׁר יִקְרָאֻהוּ בֶאֱמֶת.

רְצוֹן יְרֵאָיו יַעֲשֶׂה, וְאֶת שַׁוְעָתָם יִשְׁמַע וְיוֹשִׁיעֵם.

שׁוֹמֵר יְיָ אֶת כָּל אֹהֲבָיו, וְאֵת כָּל הָרְשָׁעִים יַשְׁמִיד.

Psalm 145

A hymn of praise by David.

I extol thee, my God the King,
And bless thy name forever and ever.
Every day I bless thee
And praise thy name forever and ever.
Great is the Lord and most worthy of praise;
His greatness is unsearchable.
One generation to another praises thy works;
They recount thy mighty acts.
On the splendor of thy glorious majesty
And on thy wondrous deeds I meditate.
They speak of thy awe-inspiring might,
And I tell of thy greatness.
They spread the fame of thy great goodness,
And sing of thy righteousness.
Gracious and merciful is the Lord,
Slow to anger and of great kindness.
The Lord is good to all,
And his mercy is over all his works.
All thy works praise thee, O Lord,
And thy faithful followers bless thee.
They speak of thy glorious kingdom,
And talk of thy might,
To let men know thy mighty deeds,
And the glorious splendor of thy kingdom.
Thy kingdom is a kingdom of all ages,
And thy dominion is for all generations.
The Lord upholds all who fall,
And raises all who are bowed down.
The eyes of all look hopefully to thee,
And thou givest them their food in due season.
Thou openest thy hand,
And satisfiest every living thing with favor.
The Lord is righteous in all his ways,
And gracious in all his deeds.
The Lord is near to all who call upon him
To all who call upon him sincerely.
He fulfills the desire of those who revere him;
He hears their cry and saves them.
The Lord preserves all who love him,
But all the wicked he destroys.

תְּהִלַּת יְיָ יְדַבֶּר־פִּי; וִיבָרֵךְ כָּל בָּשָׂר שֵׁם קָדְשׁוֹ לְעוֹלָם וָעֶד.
וַאֲנַחְנוּ נְבָרֵךְ יָהּ מֵעַתָּה וְעַד עוֹלָם; הַלְלוּיָהּ.

The Reader takes the *Torah* and says:

יְהַלְלוּ אֶת שֵׁם יְיָ, כִּי נִשְׂגָּב שְׁמוֹ לְבַדּוֹ—

Congregation:

הוֹדוֹ עַל אֶרֶץ וְשָׁמָיִם. וַיָּרֶם קֶרֶן לְעַמּוֹ, תְּהִלָּה לְכָל
חֲסִידָיו, לִבְנֵי יִשְׂרָאֵל עַם קְרוֹבוֹ; הַלְלוּיָהּ.

On Sabbath:

תהלים כט

מִזְמוֹר לְדָוִד. הָבוּ לַיְיָ, בְּנֵי אֵלִים, הָבוּ לַיְיָ כָּבוֹד וָעֹז.
הָבוּ לַיְיָ כְּבוֹד שְׁמוֹ, הִשְׁתַּחֲווּ לַיְיָ בְּהַדְרַת קֹדֶשׁ. קוֹל יְיָ עַל
הַמָּיִם, אֵל הַכָּבוֹד הִרְעִים, יְיָ עַל מַיִם רַבִּים. קוֹל יְיָ בַּכֹּחַ,
קוֹל יְיָ בֶּהָדָר, קוֹל יְיָ שֹׁבֵר אֲרָזִים, וַיְשַׁבֵּר יְיָ אֶת אַרְזֵי הַלְּבָנוֹן.
וַיַּרְקִידֵם כְּמוֹ עֵגֶל, לְבָנוֹן וְשִׂרְיוֹן כְּמוֹ בֶן־רְאֵמִים. קוֹל יְיָ חֹצֵב
לַהֲבוֹת אֵשׁ. קוֹל יְיָ יָחִיל מִדְבָּר, יָחִיל יְיָ מִדְבַּר קָדֵשׁ. קוֹל יְיָ
יְחוֹלֵל אַיָּלוֹת, וַיֶּחֱשֹׂף יְעָרוֹת, וּבְהֵיכָלוֹ כֻּלּוֹ אֹמֵר כָּבוֹד. יְיָ
לַמַּבּוּל יָשָׁב, וַיֵּשֶׁב יְיָ מֶלֶךְ לְעוֹלָם. יְיָ עֹז לְעַמּוֹ יִתֵּן, יְיָ יְבָרֵךְ
אֶת עַמּוֹ בַשָּׁלוֹם.

On festivals occurring on weekdays:

תהלים כד

לְדָוִד מִזְמוֹר. לַיְיָ הָאָרֶץ וּמְלוֹאָהּ, תֵּבֵל וְיֹשְׁבֵי בָהּ. כִּי הוּא
עַל יַמִּים יְסָדָהּ, וְעַל נְהָרוֹת יְכוֹנְנֶהָ. מִי יַעֲלֶה בְהַר יְיָ, וּמִי
יָקוּם בִּמְקוֹם קָדְשׁוֹ. נְקִי כַפַּיִם וּבַר לֵבָב, אֲשֶׁר לֹא נָשָׂא לַשָּׁוְא
נַפְשִׁי, וְלֹא נִשְׁבַּע לְמִרְמָה. יִשָּׂא בְרָכָה מֵאֵת יְיָ, וּצְדָקָה מֵאֱלֹהֵי
יִשְׁעוֹ. זֶה דּוֹר דֹּרְשָׁיו, מְבַקְשֵׁי פָנֶיךָ, יַעֲקֹב, סֶלָה. שְׂאוּ שְׁעָרִים

My mouth speaks the praise of the Lord;
Let all creatures bless his holy name forever and ever.
    [1]We will bless the Lord henceforth and forever.
    Praise the Lord!

The Reader takes the Torah and says:

Let them praise the name of the Lord, for his name alone is exalted —

Congregation:

Hodo al erets v'shomoyim, va-yorem keren l'ammo,
T'hillo l'chol chasidov, livney yisro-eyl am k'rovo. Hallelu-yoh.[2]

On Sabbath:

Psalm 29

A psalm of David. Give to the Lord, heavenly beings, give to the Lord honor and glory. Give to the Lord the glory due to his name; worship the Lord in holy array. The voice of the Lord peals across the waters; it is the God of glory thundering! The Lord is over the vast waters. The voice of the Lord is mighty; the voice of the Lord is majestic. The voice of the Lord breaks the cedars; the Lord shatters the cedars of Lebanon. He makes Lebanon and Sirion leap like a calf, like a wild ox. The voice of the Lord strikes flames of fire; the voice of the Lord causes the desert to tremble; the Lord causes the desert of Kadesh to tremble. The voice of the Lord whirls the oaks, and strips the woods bare; in his palace everything says: "Glory." The Lord sat enthroned at the flood; the Lord remains King forever. The Lord will give strength to his people; the Lord will bless his people with peace.

On festivals occurring on weekday:

Psalm 24

A psalm of David. The earth and its fullness belong to the Lord, the entire world and its inhabitants. For it is he who has founded it upon the seas, and established it on the floods. Who may ascend the Lord's mountain? Who may stand within his holy place? He who has clean hands and a pure heart; he who strives not after vanity and swears not deceitfully. He will receive a blessing from the Lord, and justice from his saving God. Such is the generation of those who are in quest of him, who seek the presence of the God of Jacob. Raise your heads, O gates, raise yourselves,

---

[1]*Psalm* 115:18.   [2]*Psalm* 148:13-14.

רָאשֵׁיכֶם, וְהִנָּשְׂאוּ פִּתְחֵי עוֹלָם, וְיָבוֹא מֶלֶךְ הַכָּבוֹד. מִי זֶה מֶלֶךְ
הַכָּבוֹד, יְיָ עִזּוּז וְגִבּוֹר, יְיָ גִּבּוֹר מִלְחָמָה. שְׂאוּ שְׁעָרִים רָאשֵׁיכֶם,
וּשְׂאוּ פִּתְחֵי עוֹלָם, וְיָבֹא מֶלֶךְ הַכָּבוֹד. מִי הוּא זֶה מֶלֶךְ
הַכָּבוֹד, יְיָ צְבָאוֹת הוּא מֶלֶךְ הַכָּבוֹד, סֶלָה.

While the *Torah* is being placed in the ark:

וּבְנֻחֹה יֹאמַר: שׁוּבָה, יְיָ, רִבְבוֹת אַלְפֵי יִשְׂרָאֵל. קוּמָה יְיָ
לִמְנוּחָתֶךָ, אַתָּה וַאֲרוֹן עֻזֶּךָ. כֹּהֲנֶיךָ יִלְבְּשׁוּ צֶדֶק, וַחֲסִידֶיךָ
יְרַנֵּנוּ. בַּעֲבוּר דָּוִד עַבְדֶּךָ, אַל תָּשֵׁב פְּנֵי מְשִׁיחֶךָ. כִּי לֶקַח טוֹב
נָתַתִּי לָכֶם, תּוֹרָתִי אַל תַּעֲזֹבוּ. עֵץ חַיִּים הִיא לַמַּחֲזִיקִים בָּהּ,
וְתֹמְכֶיהָ מְאֻשָּׁר. דְּרָכֶיהָ דַרְכֵי נֹעַם, וְכָל נְתִיבוֹתֶיהָ שָׁלוֹם.
הֲשִׁיבֵנוּ יְיָ אֵלֶיךָ, וְנָשׁוּבָה; חַדֵּשׁ יָמֵינוּ כְּקֶדֶם.

Reader:

יִתְגַּדַּל וְיִתְקַדַּשׁ שְׁמֵהּ רַבָּא בְּעָלְמָא דִי בְרָא כִרְעוּתֵהּ;
וְיַמְלִיךְ מַלְכוּתֵהּ בְּחַיֵּיכוֹן וּבְיוֹמֵיכוֹן, וּבְחַיֵּי דְכָל בֵּית יִשְׂרָאֵל
בַּעֲגָלָא וּבִזְמַן קָרִיב, וְאִמְרוּ אָמֵן.

יְהֵא שְׁמֵהּ רַבָּא מְבָרַךְ לְעָלַם וּלְעָלְמֵי עָלְמַיָּא.

יִתְבָּרַךְ וְיִשְׁתַּבַּח, וְיִתְפָּאַר וְיִתְרוֹמַם, וְיִתְנַשֵּׂא וְיִתְהַדָּר,
וְיִתְעַלֶּה וְיִתְהַלָּל שְׁמֵהּ דְּקֻדְשָׁא, בְּרִיךְ הוּא, לְעֵלָּא מִן
כָּל בִּרְכָתָא וְשִׁירָתָא, תֻּשְׁבְּחָתָא וְנֶחֱמָתָא, דַּאֲמִירָן בְּעָלְמָא,
וְאִמְרוּ אָמֵן.

שאו שערים ראשיכם The ancient gates of Zion are poetically called on to
raise their heads, in token of reverence to God. Different parts of this psalm
were sung by different choirs at the time when David brought the ark to
Mount Zion.

סלה marks a pause or a transition between one thought and another. It
occurs seventy-one times in the Psalms and is not found in the prophetical

you ancient doors, that the glorious King may come in. Who, then, is the glorious King? The Lord strong and mighty, the Lord strong in battle. Raise your heads, O gates, raise yourselves, you ancient doors, that the glorious King may come in. Who, then, is the glorious King? The Lord of hosts, he is the glorious King.

While the Torah is being placed in the ark:

When the ark rested, Moses would say: "Return, O Lord, to the myriads of Israel's families." Arise, O Lord, for thy resting place, thou and thy glorious ark. May thy priests be clothed in righteousness; may thy faithful followers shout for joy. For the sake of thy servant David, reject not thy anointed. I give you good instruction; forsake not my Torah. It is a tree of life to those who take hold of it, and happy are those who support it. Its ways are ways of pleasantness, and all its paths are peace. Turn us to thee, O Lord, and let us return; renew our days as of old.[1]

Reader.

Glorified and sanctified be God's great name throughout the world which he has created according to his will. May he establish his kingdom in your lifetime and during your days, and within the life of the entire house of Israel, speedily and soon; and say, Amen.

May his great name be blessed forever and to all eternity.

Blessed and praised, glorified and exalted, extolled and honored, adored and lauded be the name of the Holy One, blessed be he, beyond all the blessings and hymns, praises and consolations that are ever spoken in the world; and say, Amen.

---

writings. The precise significance and derivation of סלה have been much discussed. According to some, סלה is an abbreviation of סב למעלה השר, a direction to the singer to return to the beginning and repeat. Others connect it with the verb סלל ("to lift, to cast up"), a direction to the orchestra to strike in with loud music while the singer's voice is hushed. The word סלה, as used in the *Shemoneh Esreh* and other prayers, invariably means *forever* in keeping with the rendering of the Targum (לעלמין).

---

[1] *Numbers* 10:36; *Psalm* 132:8–10; *Proverbs* 4:2; 3:18, 17; *Lamentations* 5:21.

מוּסָף לְיוֹם טוֹב

The *Amidah* is recited in silent devotion while standing, facing east.

כִּי שֵׁם יְיָ אֶקְרָא, הָבוּ גֹדֶל לֵאלֹהֵינוּ.

אֲדֹנָי, שְׂפָתַי תִּפְתָּח, וּפִי יַגִּיד תְּהִלָּתֶךָ.

בָּרוּךְ אַתָּה, יְיָ אֱלֹהֵינוּ וֵאלֹהֵי אֲבוֹתֵינוּ, אֱלֹהֵי אַבְרָהָם, אֱלֹהֵי יִצְחָק, וֵאלֹהֵי יַעֲקֹב, הָאֵל הַגָּדוֹל הַגִּבּוֹר וְהַנּוֹרָא, אֵל עֶלְיוֹן, גּוֹמֵל חֲסָדִים טוֹבִים, וְקֹנֵה הַכֹּל, וְזוֹכֵר חַסְדֵי אָבוֹת, וּמֵבִיא גוֹאֵל לִבְנֵי בְנֵיהֶם לְמַעַן שְׁמוֹ בְּאַהֲבָה.

מֶלֶךְ עוֹזֵר וּמוֹשִׁיעַ וּמָגֵן. בָּרוּךְ אַתָּה, יְיָ, מָגֵן אַבְרָהָם.

אַתָּה גִבּוֹר לְעוֹלָם, אֲדֹנָי; מְחַיֵּה מֵתִים אַתָּה, רַב לְהוֹשִׁיעַ.

מְכַלְכֵּל חַיִּים בְּחֶסֶד, מְחַיֵּה מֵתִים בְּרַחֲמִים רַבִּים, סוֹמֵךְ נוֹפְלִים, וְרוֹפֵא חוֹלִים, וּמַתִּיר אֲסוּרִים, וּמְקַיֵּם אֱמוּנָתוֹ לִישֵׁנֵי עָפָר. מִי כָמוֹךָ, בַּעַל גְּבוּרוֹת, וּמִי דוֹמֶה לָּךְ, מֶלֶךְ מֵמִית וּמְחַיֶּה וּמַצְמִיחַ יְשׁוּעָה.

וְנֶאֱמָן אַתָּה לְהַחֲיוֹת מֵתִים. בָּרוּךְ אַתָּה, יְיָ, מְחַיֵּה הַמֵּתִים.

When the Reader repeats the *Shemoneh Esreh*, the following *Kedushah* is said.

נַעֲרִיצְךָ וְנַקְדִּישְׁךָ כְּסוֹד שִׂיחַ שַׂרְפֵי קֹדֶשׁ, הַמַּקְדִּישִׁים שִׁמְךָ בַּקֹּדֶשׁ, כַּכָּתוּב עַל יַד נְבִיאֶךָ: וְקָרָא זֶה אֶל זֶה וְאָמַר:

מוּסָף לְיוֹם טוֹב corresponds to the additional sacrifices offered in the Temple during the three pilgrim festivals, prescribed in Numbers 28:16-31; 29:12-39.

MUSAF FOR FESTIVALS

The Amidah is recited in silent devotion while standing, facing east.

When I proclaim the name of the Lord, give glory to our God![1]
O Lord, open thou my lips, that my mouth may declare thy praise.[2]

Blessed art thou, Lord our God and God of our fathers, God of Abraham, God of Isaac and God of Jacob; great, mighty and revered God, sublime God, who bestowest lovingkindness, and art Master of all things; who rememberest the good deeds of our fathers, and who wilt graciously bring a redeemer to their children's children for the sake of thy name.

O King, Supporter, Savior and Shield! Blessed art thou, O Lord, Shield of Abraham.

Thou, O Lord, art mighty forever; thou revivest the dead; thou art powerful to save.

Thou sustainest the living with kindness, and revivest the dead with great mercy; thou supportest all who fall, and healest the sick; thou settest the captives free, and keepest faith with those who sleep in the dust. Who is like thee, Lord of power? Who resembles thee, O King? Thou bringest death and restorest life, and causest salvation to flourish.

Thou art faithful to revive the dead. Blessed art thou, O Lord, who revivest the dead.

When the Reader repeats the *Shemoneh Esreh*, the following *Kedushah* is said.

We revere and sanctify thee in the words of the assembly of holy seraphim who hallow thy name in the sanctuary, as it is written by thy prophet: "They keep calling to one another:

כי שם precedes the *Amidahs* of *Musaf* and *Minḥah* only. In *Shaharith* and *Ma'ariv* this verse is omitted, because there it would interrupt the connection between the benediction גאל ישראל and the *Amidah*.

[1] *Deuteronomy* 32:3. [2] *Psalm* 51:17.

קָדוֹשׁ, קָדוֹשׁ, קָדוֹשׁ יְיָ צְבָאוֹת;

מְלֹא כָל הָאָרֶץ כְּבוֹדוֹ.

כְּבוֹדוֹ מָלֵא עוֹלָם; מְשָׁרְתָיו שׁוֹאֲלִים זֶה לָזֶה אַיֵּה מְקוֹם

כְּבוֹדוֹ, לְעֻמָּתָם בָּרוּךְ יֹאמֵרוּ—

בָּרוּךְ כְּבוֹד יְיָ מִמְּקוֹמוֹ.

מִמְּקוֹמוֹ הוּא יִפֶן בְּרַחֲמִים, וְיָחֹן עַם הַמְיַחֲדִים שְׁמוֹ; עֶרֶב

וָבֹקֶר, בְּכָל יוֹם תָּמִיד, פַּעֲמַיִם בְּאַהֲבָה שְׁמַע אוֹמְרִים—

שְׁמַע יִשְׂרָאֵל, יְיָ אֱלֹהֵינוּ, יְיָ אֶחָד.

הוּא אֱלֹהֵינוּ, הוּא אָבִינוּ, הוּא מַלְכֵּנוּ, הוּא מוֹשִׁיעֵנוּ, וְהוּא

יַשְׁמִיעֵנוּ בְּרַחֲמָיו שֵׁנִית לְעֵינֵי כָּל חַי: לִהְיוֹת לָכֶם לֵאלֹהִים—

אֲנִי יְיָ אֱלֹהֵיכֶם.

Reader:

אַדִּיר אַדִּירֵנוּ, יְיָ אֲדֹנֵינוּ, מָה אַדִּיר שִׁמְךָ בְּכָל הָאָרֶץ.

וְהָיָה יְיָ לְמֶלֶךְ עַל כָּל הָאָרֶץ, בַּיּוֹם הַהוּא יִהְיֶה יְיָ אֶחָד וּשְׁמוֹ

אֶחָד.

וּבְדִבְרֵי קָדְשְׁךָ כָּתוּב לֵאמֹר:

יִמְלֹךְ יְיָ לְעוֹלָם, אֱלֹהַיִךְ צִיּוֹן לְדֹר וָדֹר; הַלְלוּיָהּ.

לְדוֹר וָדוֹר נַגִּיד גָּדְלֶךָ, וּלְנֵצַח נְצָחִים קְדֻשָּׁתְךָ נַקְדִּישׁ,

וְשִׁבְחֲךָ אֱלֹהֵינוּ מִפִּינוּ לֹא יָמוּשׁ לְעוֹלָם וָעֶד, כִּי אֵל מֶלֶךְ

גָּדוֹל וְקָדוֹשׁ אָתָּה. בָּרוּךְ אַתָּה, יְיָ, הָאֵל הַקָּדוֹשׁ.

אַתָּה קָדוֹשׁ וְשִׁמְךָ קָדוֹשׁ, וּקְדוֹשִׁים בְּכָל יוֹם יְהַלְלוּךָ סֶּלָה.

בָּרוּךְ אַתָּה, יְיָ, הָאֵל הַקָּדוֹשׁ.

שמע ישראל and the concluding words of the *Shema* were inserted here in the
fifth century, when special government officials were posted in the synagogues
to prevent the congregational proclamation of God's Oneness. Toward the end
of the service, when the spies had left, the *Shema* was thus recited in an
abridged form.

Holy, holy, holy is the Lord of hosts;
The whole earth is full of his glory."[1]

His glory fills the universe; his ministering angels ask one another: "Where is his glorious place?" They say to one another: "Blessed —

Blessed be the glory of the Lord from his abode."[2]

From his abode may he turn with compassion and be gracious to the people who acclaim his Oneness evening and morning, twice every day, and with tender affection recite the Shema —

"Hear, O Israel, the Lord is our God, the Lord is One."[3]

He is our God; he is our Father; he is our King; he is our Deliverer. He will again in his mercy proclaim to us in the presence of all the living:". . . to be your God —

I am the Lord your God."[4]

Reader:

Our God Almighty, our Lord Eternal, how glorious is thy name over all the world! The Lord shall be King over all the earth; on that day the Lord shall be One, and his name One.[5]

And in thy holy Scriptures it is written:
The Lord shall reign forever,
Your God, O Zion, for all generations.
Praise the Lord![6]

Reader:

Through all generations we will declare thy greatness; to all eternity we will proclaim thy holiness; thy praise, our God, shall never depart from our mouth, for thou art a great and holy God and King. Blessed art thou, O Lord, holy God.

Thou art holy and thy name is holy, and **holy** beings praise thee daily, Blessed art thou, O Lord, holy God.

---

[1]*Isaiah* 6:3. [2]*Ezekiel* 3:12. [3]*Deuteronomy* 6:4. [4]*Numbers* 15:41., [5]*Psalm* 8:10; *Zechariah* 14:9. [6]*Psalm* 146:10.

אַתָּה בְחַרְתָּנוּ מִכָּל הָעַמִּים, אָהַבְתָּ אוֹתָנוּ וְרָצִיתָ בָּנוּ,
וְרוֹמַמְתָּנוּ מִכָּל הַלְּשׁוֹנוֹת, וְקִדַּשְׁתָּנוּ בְּמִצְוֹתֶיךָ, וְקֵרַבְתָּנוּ
מַלְכֵּנוּ לַעֲבוֹדָתֶךָ, וְשִׁמְךָ הַגָּדוֹל וְהַקָּדוֹשׁ עָלֵינוּ קָרָאתָ.

וַתִּתֶּן־לָנוּ, יְיָ אֱלֹהֵינוּ, בְּאַהֲבָה, (שַׁבָּתוֹת לִמְנוּחָה וּ)מוֹעֲדִים
לְשִׂמְחָה, חַגִּים וּזְמַנִּים לְשָׂשׂוֹן, אֶת יוֹם (הַשַּׁבָּת הַזֶּה וְאֶת יוֹם)
חַג הַשָּׁבֻעוֹת הַזֶּה, זְמַן מַתַּן תּוֹרָתֵנוּ, (בְּאַהֲבָה) מִקְרָא קֹדֶשׁ,
זֵכֶר לִיצִיאַת מִצְרָיִם.

וּמִפְּנֵי חֲטָאֵינוּ גָּלִינוּ מֵאַרְצֵנוּ וְנִתְרַחַקְנוּ מֵעַל אַדְמָתֵנוּ, וְאֵין
אֲנַחְנוּ יְכוֹלִים לַעֲלוֹת וְלֵרָאוֹת וּלְהִשְׁתַּחֲוֹת לְפָנֶיךָ, וְלַעֲשׂוֹת
חוֹבוֹתֵינוּ בְּבֵית בְּחִירָתֶךָ, בַּבַּיִת הַגָּדוֹל וְהַקָּדוֹשׁ שֶׁנִּקְרָא שִׁמְךָ
עָלָיו, מִפְּנֵי הַיָּד שֶׁנִּשְׁתַּלְּחָה בְּמִקְדָּשֶׁךָ. יְהִי רָצוֹן מִלְּפָנֶיךָ, יְיָ
אֱלֹהֵינוּ וֵאלֹהֵי אֲבוֹתֵינוּ, מֶלֶךְ רַחֲמָן, שֶׁתָּשׁוּב וּתְרַחֵם עָלֵינוּ
וְעַל מִקְדָּשְׁךָ בְּרַחֲמֶיךָ הָרַבִּים, וְתִבְנֵהוּ מְהֵרָה וּתְגַדֵּל כְּבוֹדוֹ.
אָבִינוּ מַלְכֵּנוּ, גַּלֵּה כְּבוֹד מַלְכוּתְךָ עָלֵינוּ מְהֵרָה, וְהוֹפַע
וְהִנָּשֵׂא עָלֵינוּ לְעֵינֵי כָּל חָי, וְקָרֵב פְּזוּרֵינוּ מִבֵּין הַגּוֹיִם,
וּנְפוּצוֹתֵינוּ כַּנֵּס מִיַּרְכְּתֵי אָרֶץ; וַהֲבִיאֵנוּ לְצִיּוֹן עִירְךָ בְּרִנָּה,
וְלִירוּשָׁלַיִם בֵּית מִקְדָּשְׁךָ בְּשִׂמְחַת עוֹלָם, וְשָׁם נַעֲשֶׂה לְפָנֶיךָ
אֶת קָרְבְּנוֹת חוֹבוֹתֵינוּ, תְּמִידִים כְּסִדְרָם וּמוּסָפִים כְּהִלְכָתָם.
(וְאֶת מוּסַף יוֹם הַשַּׁבָּת הַזֶּה) וְאֶת מוּסַף יוֹם חַג הַשָּׁבֻעוֹת הַזֶּה,

<hr>

אתה בחרתנו (thou hast chosen us) is a passage based on many biblical
expressions that keep reminding the people of Israel that they have been chosen
by God to be a beacon of light and truth to the nations of the earth: "You are
a people holy to the Lord your God, who has chosen you from all the nations on
the face of the earth to be his own possession . . ." (Deuteronomy 14:2). However
much they may have fallen short of their duty, however much they may have
neglected to remain faithful to their sacred task, they have not been deposed

Thou didst choose us from among all peoples; thou didst love and favor us; thou didst exalt us above all tongues and sanctify us with thy commandments. Thou, our King, didst draw us near to thy service and call us by thy great and holy name.

Thou, Lord our God, hast graciously given us (Sabbaths for rest,) holidays for gladness and festive seasons for joy: (this Sabbath day and) this Feast of Weeks, our Festival of the Giving of the Torah, a holy convocation in remembrance of the exodus from Egypt.

Because of our sins we were exiled from our country and banished far from our land. We cannot go up as pilgrims to worship thee, to perform our duties in thy chosen House, the great and holy Temple which was called by thy name, on account of the hand that was let loose on thy sanctuary. May it be thy will, Lord our God and God of our fathers, merciful King, in thy abundant love again to have mercy on us and on thy sanctuary; rebuild it speedily and magnify its glory.

Our Father, our King, speedily reveal thy glorious majesty to us; shine forth and be exalted over us in the sight of all the living. Unite our scattered people from among the nations; gather our dispersed from the far ends of the earth. Bring us to Zion thy city with ringing song, to Jerusalem thy sanctuary with everlasting joy. There we will prepare in thy honor our obligatory offerings, the regular daily offerings and the additional offerings, according to rule. The *Musaf* of (this Sabbath and that of) this Feast of Weeks

---

from the office to which they were appointed. The biblical term *am segullah* (God's own people) does not imply Israel's exclusive possession of divine love and favor. On the contrary, it means that God has exclusive claim to Israel's service. The most cherished ideal of Israel is that of universal brotherhood (S. R. Hirsch). Israel's character as the chosen people does not involve the inferiority of other nations. "It was the *noblesse oblige* of the God-appointed worker for the entire human race" (Gudemann, *Das Judenthum*). The selection of Israel and the Oneness of God are closely related concepts which blend into one aspiration and ideal for a united mankind. Only in Israel did the ethical monotheism exist; and wherever else it is found later on, it has been derived directly or indirectly from Israel. The term *election* of Israel expresses a historical fact. Israel feels itself chosen, not as a master but as a servant.

נַעֲשֶׂה וְנַקְרִיב לְפָנֶיךָ בְּאַהֲבָה כְּמִצְוַת רְצוֹנֶךָ, כְּמוֹ שֶׁכָּתַבְתָּ
עָלֵינוּ בְּתוֹרָתֶךָ עַל יְדֵי מֹשֶׁה עַבְדֶּךָ, מִפִּי כְבוֹדֶךָ, כָּאָמוּר:

On Sabbath:

(וּבְיוֹם הַשַּׁבָּת, שְׁנֵי כְבָשִׂים בְּנֵי שָׁנָה תְּמִימִם, וּשְׁנֵי עֶשְׂרֹנִים
סֹלֶת מִנְחָה בְּלוּלָה בַשֶּׁמֶן וְנִסְכּוֹ. עֹלַת שַׁבַּת בְּשַׁבַּתּוֹ, עַל עֹלַת
הַתָּמִיד וְנִסְכָּהּ.)

וּבְיוֹם הַבִּכּוּרִים, בְּהַקְרִיבְכֶם מִנְחָה חֲדָשָׁה לַיְיָ,
בְּשָׁבֻעֹתֵיכֶם, מִקְרָא קֹדֶשׁ יִהְיֶה לָכֶם, כָּל מְלֶאכֶת עֲבֹדָה לֹא
תַעֲשׂוּ. וְהִקְרַבְתֶּם עֹלָה לְרֵיחַ נִיחֹחַ לַיְיָ: פָּרִים בְּנֵי בָקָר שְׁנַיִם,
אַיִל אֶחָד, שִׁבְעָה כְבָשִׂים בְּנֵי שָׁנָה.

וּמִנְחָתָם וְנִסְכֵּיהֶם כִּמְדֻבָּר: שְׁלֹשָׁה עֶשְׂרֹנִים לַפָּר, וּשְׁנֵי
עֶשְׂרֹנִים לָאָיִל, וְעִשָּׂרוֹן לַכֶּבֶשׂ, וְיַיִן כְּנִסְכּוֹ, וְשָׂעִיר לְכַפֵּר,
וּשְׁנֵי תְמִידִים כְּהִלְכָתָם.

The law of *bikkurim* is stated in the Torah as follows: "When you have
come into the land which the Lord your God is giving you as a heritage, and
have occupied it and settled it, you shall take some first fruits of the various
products of the soil... and put them in a basket; you shall go to the place,
which the Lord your God chooses... The priest shall receive the basket from you
and shall set it in front of the altar of the Lord..." (Deuteronomy 26:1-11).

The general laws regarding the sacrifices proper to the feast days were given
at Sinai (Leviticus 23) and repeated with certain details in Numbers, chapter 28.
The generation to whom they were spoken at Sinai had passed away; hence
their repetition in the book of Numbers to the younger generation. The Sabbath
offering is double that of ordinary days.

The word קָרְבָּן (sacrifice) occurs about eighty times in our Hebrew Bible,
particularly in the books of Leviticus and Numbers. In the prophetical books it is
mentioned on four occasions (Ezekiel 20:28; 40:43; Nehemiah 10:35; 13:31).
The sacrificial system symbolized self-surrender and devotion to the will of
God. The daily offering (*tamid*) symbolized Israel's pledge of unbroken service

---

ומנחתם... כמדובר refers to Numbers 29:41-61.

we will prepare and present in thy honor with love, according to thy command, as thou hast prescribed for us in thy Torah through thy servant Moses, as it is said:

On Sabbath:

(On the Sabbath day, two perfect yearling male lambs and two-tenths of an *ephah* of fine flour mixed with oil as a meal-offering, and the libation. This is the burnt-offering of each Sabbath, in addition to the daily burnt-offering and its libation.)[1]

On the day of the first-fruits, when you bring a meal-offering from the new grain to the Lord, in your Feast of Weeks, you shall hold a sacred assembly; you shall do no work. You shall present a burnt-offering, as a soothing savor, to the Lord: two young bullocks, one ram, and seven yearling male lambs.[2]

Their meal-offering and their libations were as specified: three tenths of an *ephah* [of fine flour] for each bullock, two-tenths for the ram, one-tenth for each lamb; wine according to their requisite libations. Moreover, a he-goat was offered to make atonement in addition to the two regular daily offerings.

---

to God. The fragrant smoke of incense rising towards heaven was a natural symbol of prayer ascending to God, as seen from Psalm 141:2 ("Let my prayer rise like incense before thee"). Hebrew worship in ancient times was essentially social. A sacrifice was a public ceremony. Sacrificial worship was coordinated with knowledge of the Torah and with the performance of good deeds. Prayer is now designated as עֲבוֹדָה שֶׁבַּלֵּב, service of the heart.

וּתְחֱזֶינָה עֵינֵינוּ (may our eyes behold) is paralleled by Micah 4:11 (וְתַחַז בְּצִיּוֹן עֵינֵינוּ). "Thy divine presence" (שְׁכִינָה), signifying the majestic presence of God among human beings, is used to express the immanence of God and his omnipresence. We are told that the *Shekhinah* is where people gather to worship. The *Shekhinah* is everywhere (Bava Bathra 25a). According to a midrashic statement, anyone who receives his fellow men kindly is regarded as though he had received the *Shekhinah*. The presence of the *Shekhinah* is felt where sacred study and prayer occur. However, the *Shekhinah* does not rest amidst gloom, laziness, frivolity, or idle talk.

[1] *Numbers* 28:9-10. [2] *Numbers* 28:26-27.

On Sabbath:

(יִשְׂמְחוּ בְמַלְכוּתְךָ שׁוֹמְרֵי שַׁבָּת וְקוֹרְאֵי עֹנֶג, עַם מְקַדְּשֵׁי
שְׁבִיעִי, כֻּלָּם יִשְׂבְּעוּ וְיִתְעַנְּגוּ מִטּוּבֶךָ; וְהַשְּׁבִיעִי רָצִיתָ בּוֹ
וְקִדַּשְׁתּוֹ, חֶמְדַּת יָמִים אוֹתוֹ קָרָאתָ, זֵכֶר לְמַעֲשֵׂה בְרֵאשִׁית.)

אֱלֹהֵינוּ וֵאלֹהֵי אֲבוֹתֵינוּ, מֶלֶךְ רַחֲמָן, רַחֵם עָלֵינוּ; טוֹב
וּמֵטִיב, הִדָּרֶשׁ־לָנוּ; שׁוּבָה אֵלֵינוּ בַּהֲמוֹן רַחֲמֶיךָ בִּגְלַל אָבוֹת
שֶׁעָשׂוּ רְצוֹנֶךָ; בְּנֵה בֵיתְךָ כְּבַתְּחִלָּה, וְכוֹנֵן מִקְדָּשְׁךָ עַל מְכוֹנוֹ,
וְהַרְאֵנוּ בְּבִנְיָנוֹ וְשַׂמְּחֵנוּ בְּתִקּוּנוֹ, וְהָשֵׁב כֹּהֲנִים לַעֲבוֹדָתָם,
וּלְוִיִם לְשִׁירָם וּלְזִמְרָם, וְהָשֵׁב יִשְׂרָאֵל לִנְוֵיהֶם; וְשָׁם נַעֲלֶה
וְנֵרָאֶה וְנִשְׁתַּחֲוֶה לְפָנֶיךָ בְּשָׁלֹשׁ פַּעֲמֵי רְגָלֵינוּ, כַּכָּתוּב בְּתוֹרָתֶךָ:
שָׁלֹשׁ פְּעָמִים בַּשָּׁנָה יֵרָאֶה כָל זְכוּרְךָ אֶת פְּנֵי יְיָ אֱלֹהֶיךָ
בַּמָּקוֹם אֲשֶׁר יִבְחָר, בְּחַג הַמַּצּוֹת וּבְחַג הַשָּׁבֻעוֹת וּבְחַג הַסֻּכּוֹת;
וְלֹא יֵרָאֶה אֶת פְּנֵי יְיָ רֵיקָם. אִישׁ כְּמַתְּנַת יָדוֹ, כְּבִרְכַּת יְיָ
אֱלֹהֶיךָ אֲשֶׁר נָתַן לָךְ.

וְהַשִּׂיאֵנוּ, יְיָ אֱלֹהֵינוּ, אֶת בִּרְכַּת מוֹעֲדֶיךָ לְחַיִּים וּלְשָׁלוֹם,
לְשִׂמְחָה וּלְשָׂשׂוֹן, כַּאֲשֶׁר רָצִיתָ וְאָמַרְתָּ לְבָרְכֵנוּ. אֱלֹהֵינוּ
וֵאלֹהֵי אֲבוֹתֵינוּ, (רְצֵה בִמְנוּחָתֵנוּ) קַדְּשֵׁנוּ בְּמִצְוֹתֶיךָ וְתֵן חֶלְקֵנוּ
בְּתוֹרָתֶךָ, שַׂבְּעֵנוּ מִטּוּבֶךָ, וְשַׂמְּחֵנוּ בִּישׁוּעָתֶךָ, וְטַהֵר לִבֵּנוּ
לְעָבְדְּךָ בֶּאֱמֶת; וְהַנְחִילֵנוּ, יְיָ אֱלֹהֵינוּ, (בְּאַהֲבָה וּבְרָצוֹן)
בְּשִׂמְחָה וּבְשָׂשׂוֹן, (שַׁבָּת וּ)מוֹעֲדֵי קָדְשֶׁךָ, וְיִשְׂמְחוּ בְךָ יִשְׂרָאֵל
מְקַדְּשֵׁי שְׁמֶךָ. בָּרוּךְ אַתָּה, יְיָ, מְקַדֵּשׁ (הַשַּׁבָּת וְ)יִשְׂרָאֵל
וְהַזְּמַנִּים.

רְצֵה, יְיָ אֱלֹהֵינוּ, בְּעַמְּךָ יִשְׂרָאֵל וּבִתְפִלָּתָם; וְהָשֵׁב אֶת
הָעֲבוֹדָה לִדְבִיר בֵּיתֶךָ, וְאִשֵּׁי יִשְׂרָאֵל וּתְפִלָּתָם בְּאַהֲבָה
תְקַבֵּל בְּרָצוֹן, וּתְהִי לְרָצוֹן תָּמִיד עֲבוֹדַת יִשְׂרָאֵל עַמֶּךָ.

Those who keep the Sabbath and call it a delight shall rejoice in thy kingdom; all the people who hallow the seventh day shall fully enjoy thy goodness. Thou wast pleased with the seventh day and didst hallow it; the most desirable of days didst thou call it—in remembrance of the creation.

———

Our God and God of our fathers, merciful King, have pity on us; thou art good and beneficent, answer our entreaty. In thy abundant mercy, return to us for the sake of our fathers who performed thy will. Rebuild thy Temple as of yore, and set up thy sanctuary on its site. Grant that we may see it rebuilt; gladden us by its restoration. Restore Kohanim to their service, Levites to their song and music, and Israelites to their homes. There we will go up to present ourselves and worship before thee at our three pilgrim seasons, as it is written in thy Torah: Three times a year shall all your males appear before the Lord your God in the place which he will choose: on the Feast of Unleavened Bread, on the Feast of Weeks, and on the Feast of Tabernacles; they shall not appear before the Lord empty-handed. Every man shall offer what he can afford, according as the Lord your God has blessed you.[1]

Bestow on us, Lord our God, the blessings of thy festivals for life and peace, for joy and gladness, as thou didst promise to bless us. Our God and God of our Fathers, (be pleased with our rest) sanctify us with thy commandments and grant us a share in thy Torah; satisfy us with thy goodness and gladden us with thy help; purify our heart to serve thee sincerely. In thy gracious love, Lord our God, grant us thy holy (Sabbath and) festivals for gladness and joy; may Israel who sanctifies thy name rejoice in thee. Blessed art thou, O Lord, who hallowest (the Sabbath and) Israel and the festivals.

Be pleased, Lord our God, with thy people Israel and with their prayer; restore the worship to thy innermost sanctuary; speedily accept Israel's offerings and prayer with gracious love. May the worship of thy people Israel be ever pleasing to thee.

———

[1] *Deuteronomy* 16:16-17.

When *kohanim* chant the priestly blessing:

Congregation:

וְתֶעֱרַב עָלֶיךָ עֲתִירָתֵנוּ כְּעוֹלָה וּכְקָרְבָּן; אָנָּא, רַחוּם, בְּרַחֲמֶיךָ הָרַבִּים הָשֵׁב שְׁכִינָתְךָ לְצִיּוֹן עִירֶךָ, וְסֵדֶר הָעֲבוֹדָה לִירוּשָׁלָיִם. וְתֶחֱזֶינָה עֵינֵינוּ בְּשׁוּבְךָ לְצִיּוֹן בְּרַחֲמִים, וְשָׁם נַעֲבָדְךָ בְּיִרְאָה כִּימֵי עוֹלָם וּכְשָׁנִים קַדְמוֹנִיּוֹת.

Reader:

בָּרוּךְ אַתָּה, יְיָ, שֶׁאוֹתְךָ לְבַדְּךָ בְּיִרְאָה נַעֲבוֹד.

When *kohanim* do not chant the priestly blessing:

וְתֶחֱזֶינָה עֵינֵינוּ בְּשׁוּבְךָ לְצִיּוֹן בְּרַחֲמִים. בָּרוּךְ אַתָּה, יְיָ, הַמַּחֲזִיר שְׁכִינָתוֹ לְצִיּוֹן.

מוֹדִים אֲנַחְנוּ לָךְ, שָׁאַתָּה הוּא יְיָ אֱלֹהֵינוּ וֵאלֹהֵי אֲבוֹתֵינוּ לְעוֹלָם וָעֶד. צוּר חַיֵּינוּ, מָגֵן יִשְׁעֵנוּ אַתָּה הוּא. לְדוֹר וָדוֹר נוֹדֶה לְךָ, וּנְסַפֵּר תְּהִלָּתֶךָ, עַל חַיֵּינוּ הַמְּסוּרִים בְּיָדֶךָ, וְעַל נִשְׁמוֹתֵינוּ הַפְּקוּדוֹת לָךְ, וְעַל נִסֶּיךָ שֶׁבְּכָל יוֹם עִמָּנוּ, וְעַל נִפְלְאוֹתֶיךָ וְטוֹבוֹתֶיךָ שֶׁבְּכָל עֵת, עֶרֶב וָבֹקֶר וְצָהֳרָיִם. הַטּוֹב כִּי לֹא כָלוּ רַחֲמֶיךָ, וְהַמְרַחֵם כִּי לֹא תַמּוּ חֲסָדֶיךָ, כִּי מֵעוֹלָם קִוִּינוּ לָךְ.

Congregation:

מוֹדִים אֲנַחְנוּ לָךְ, שָׁאַתָּה הוּא יְיָ אֱלֹהֵינוּ וֵאלֹהֵי אֲבוֹתֵינוּ. אֱלֹהֵי כָל בָּשָׂר, יוֹצְרֵנוּ, יוֹצֵר בְּרֵאשִׁית, בְּרָכוֹת וְהוֹדָאוֹת לְשִׁמְךָ הַגָּדוֹל וְהַקָּדוֹשׁ עַל שֶׁהֶחֱיִיתָנוּ וְקִיַּמְתָּנוּ. כֵּן תְּחַיֵּינוּ וּתְקַיְּמֵנוּ, וְתֶאֱסוֹף גָּלֻיּוֹתֵינוּ לְחַצְרוֹת קָדְשֶׁךָ לִשְׁמֹר חֻקֶּיךָ וְלַעֲשׂוֹת רְצוֹנֶךָ, וּלְעָבְדְּךָ בְּלֵבָב שָׁלֵם, עַל שֶׁאֲנַחְנוּ מוֹדִים לָךְ. בָּרוּךְ אֵל הַהוֹדָאוֹת.

מודים דרבנן is a composite of variants suggested by several rabbis of the Talmud (Sotah 40a). It is recited by the congregation in an undertone, while

When kohanim chant the priestly blessing:
Congregation:

May our prayer please thee as burnt-offering and sacrifice. Merciful God, in thy abundant love restore thy divine presence to Zion, and the order of service to Jerusalem. May our eyes behold thy return in mercy to Zion. There we will serve thee with reverence, as in the days of old and as in former years.

Reader

Blessed art thou, O Lord, whom alone we serve with reverence.

When kohanim do not chant the priestly blessing:

May our eyes behold thy return in mercy to Zion. Blessed art thou, O Lord, who restorest thy divine presence to Zion.

We ever thank thee, who art the Lord our God and the God of our fathers. Thou art the strength of our life and our saving shield. In every generation we will thank thee and recount thy praise—for our lives which are in thy charge, for our souls which are in thy care, for thy miracles which are daily with us, and for thy continual wonders and favors— evening, morning and noon. Beneficent One, whose mercies never fail, Merciful One, whose kindnesses never cease, thou hast always been our hope.

Congregation:

We thank thee, who art the Lord our God and the God of our fathers. God of all mankind, our Creator and Creator of the universe, blessings and thanks are due to thy great and holy name, because thou has kept us alive and sustained us; mayest thou ever grant us life and sustenance. O gather our exiles to thy holy courts to observe thy laws to do thy will, and to serve thee with a perfect heart. For this we thank thee. Blessed be God to whom all thanks are due.

the Reader repeats aloud the eighteenth benediction of the *Shemoneh Esreh* prayer. In the fourteenthcentury commentary of Rabbi David Abudarham it is explained that the congregation recites *Modim d'Rabbanan* because an expression of thanks is authentic when made in person rather than through a messenger or *sheliah tsibbur.*

In order to link the people closely together, the sages sought to bring various forms of Hebrew prayer into harmonious union. The formula "who healest all creatures and doest wonders" is a combination of two readings reported by the rabbis of the Talmud (Berakhoth 60b). Likewise, *Modim d'Rabbanan* is the combined result of several phrases suggested by several sages.

וְעַל כֻּלָּם יִתְבָּרַךְ וְיִתְרוֹמַם שִׁמְךָ, מַלְכֵּנוּ, תָּמִיד לְעוֹלָם וָעֶד.

וְכֹל הַחַיִּים יוֹדוּךָ סֶּלָה, וִיהַלְלוּ אֶת שִׁמְךָ בֶּאֱמֶת, הָאֵל, יְשׁוּעָתֵנוּ וְעֶזְרָתֵנוּ סֶלָה. בָּרוּךְ אַתָּה, יְיָ, הַטּוֹב שִׁמְךָ, וּלְךָ נָאֶה לְהוֹדוֹת.

When *kohanim* do not chant the priestly blessing:

(אֱלֹהֵינוּ וֵאלֹהֵי אֲבוֹתֵינוּ, בָּרְכֵנוּ בַבְּרָכָה הַמְשֻׁלֶּשֶׁת בַּתּוֹרָה, הַכְּתוּבָה עַל יְדֵי מֹשֶׁה עַבְדֶּךָ, הָאֲמוּרָה מִפִּי אַהֲרֹן וּבָנָיו, כֹּהֲנִים עַם קְדוֹשֶׁךָ, כָּאָמוּר: יְבָרֶכְךָ יְיָ וְיִשְׁמְרֶךָ. יָאֵר יְיָ פָּנָיו אֵלֶיךָ וִיחֻנֶּךָּ. יִשָּׂא יְיָ פָּנָיו אֵלֶיךָ, וְיָשֵׂם לְךָ שָׁלוֹם.)

When *kohanim* chant the priestly blessing:
Congregation:

יְהִי רָצוֹן מִלְּפָנֶיךָ, יְיָ אֱלֹהֵינוּ וֵאלֹהֵי אֲבוֹתֵינוּ, שֶׁתְּהֵא הַבְּרָכָה הַזֹּאת שֶׁצִּוִּיתָ לְבָרֵךְ אֶת עַמְּךָ יִשְׂרָאֵל, בְּרָכָה שְׁלֵמָה, וְלֹא יִהְיֶה בָּהּ שׁוּם מִכְשׁוֹל וְעָוֹן מֵעַתָּה וְעַד עוֹלָם.

ברכת כהנים, known as נשיאת כפים, was part of the daily service in the Temple. Every morning and evening, before the thank-offering, the priests raised their hands aloft and pronounced the priestly blessing from a special platform (דוכן); hence the term "duchenen." The introductory prayer (יהי רצון) and the concluding prayer recited by the *kohanim* are given in the Talmud (Sotah 39b).

In Israel, the priestly blessing is chanted daily by the *kohanim* in the synagogues; in the Diaspora, it is chanted only on festivals. Those of priestly descent remove their shoes, wash their hands, and ascend the platform (*dukhan*) in front of the ark. Then they face the congregation and, with fingers stretched in a symbolical arrangement underneath the *tallith* covering their face, they repeat the priestly benediction word for word after

For all these acts, may thy name, our King, be blessed and exalted forever and ever.

All the living shall ever thank thee and sincerely praise thy name, O God, who art always our salvation and help. Blessed art thou, O Lord, Beneficent One, to whom it is fitting to give thanks.

When kohanim do not chant the priestly blessing:

(Our God and God of our fathers, bless us with the threefold blessing written in thy Torah by thy servant Moses and spoken by Aaron and his sons the priests, thy holy people, as it is said: "May the Lord bless you and protect you; may the Lord countenance you and be gracious to you; may the Lord favor you and grant you peace.")[1]

When kohanim chant the priestly blessing:

Congregation:

May it be thy will, Lord our God and God of our fathers, that this blessing which thou hast commanded to pronounce upon thy people Israel may be a perfect blessing, forever free from stumbling and iniquity.

---

the *ḥazzan*, or cantor. The worshipers refrain from looking at the *kohanim* during the repetition of the fifteen majestic words of which, the priestly benediction is composed, to indicate that they emanate from the heavenly spheres and to concentrate on their deep significance. The *kohanim* cover their faces, so as not to cause any distraction by their physical appearance.

The priestly benediction consists of three double clauses of increasing length and intensity, in each of which the Divine Name is used. In Leviticus 9:22, we are told that Aaron, having discharged the priestly duties, lifted up his hands toward the people and blessed them. His benediction seems to have been pronounced from the top of the altar, or from its ledge, since he is said to have come down after the blessing.

---

[1] *Numbers* 6:24-26.

Reader:

אֱלֹהֵינוּ וֵאלֹהֵי אֲבוֹתֵינוּ, בָּרְכֵנוּ בַבְּרָכָה הַמְשֻׁלֶּשֶׁת בַּתּוֹרָה,
הַכְּתוּבָה עַל יְדֵי מֹשֶׁה עַבְדֶּךָ, הָאֲמוּרָה מִפִּי אַהֲרֹן וּבָנָיו

כֹּהֲנִים

Congregation:

עַם קְדוֹשֶׁךָ, כָּאָמוּר.

Kohanim:

בָּרוּךְ אַתָּה, יְיָ אֱלֹהֵינוּ, מֶלֶךְ הָעוֹלָם, אֲשֶׁר קִדְּשָׁנוּ
בִּקְדֻשָּׁתוֹ שֶׁל אַהֲרֹן וְצִוָּנוּ לְבָרֵךְ אֶת עַמּוֹ יִשְׂרָאֵל בְּאַהֲבָה.

Congregation:	Kohanim:
יְבָרֶכְךָ יְיָ מִצִּיּוֹן, עֹשֵׂה שָׁמַיִם וָאָרֶץ.	יְבָרֶכְךָ
יְיָ אֲדֹנֵינוּ, מָה אַדִּיר שִׁמְךָ בְּכָל הָאָרֶץ.	יְהֹוָה
שָׁמְרֵנִי, אֵל, כִּי חָסִיתִי בָךְ.	וְיִשְׁמְרֶךָ.

רִבּוֹנוֹ שֶׁל עוֹלָם, אֲנִי שֶׁלָּךְ וַחֲלוֹמוֹתַי שֶׁלָּךְ; חֲלוֹם חָלַמְתִּי
וְאֵינִי יוֹדֵעַ מַה הוּא. יְהִי רָצוֹן מִלְּפָנֶיךָ, יְיָ אֱלֹהַי וֵאלֹהֵי אֲבוֹתַי,
שֶׁיִּהְיוּ כָּל חֲלוֹמוֹתַי עָלַי וְעַל כָּל יִשְׂרָאֵל לְטוֹבָה, בֵּין שֶׁחָלַמְתִּי
עַל עַצְמִי וּבֵין שֶׁחָלַמְתִּי עַל אֲחֵרִים וּבֵין שֶׁחָלְמוּ אֲחֵרִים עָלָי;
אִם טוֹבִים הֵם, חַזְּקֵם וְאַמְּצֵם, וְיִתְקַיְּמוּ בִי וּבָהֶם כַּחֲלוֹמוֹת
שֶׁל יוֹסֵף הַצַּדִּיק; וְאִם צְרִיכִים רְפוּאָה, רְפָאֵם כְּחִזְקִיָּהוּ מֶלֶךְ
יְהוּדָה מֵחָלְיוֹ, וּכְמִרְיָם הַנְּבִיאָה מִצָּרַעְתָּהּ, וּכְנַעֲמָן מִצָּרַעְתּוֹ,
וּכְמֵי מָרָה עַל יְדֵי מֹשֶׁה רַבֵּנוּ, וּכְמֵי יְרִיחוֹ עַל יְדֵי אֱלִישָׁע.
וּכְשֵׁם שֶׁהָפַכְתָּ אֶת קִלְלַת בִּלְעָם הָרָשָׁע מִקְּלָלָה לִבְרָכָה, כֵּן
תַּהֲפֹךְ כָּל חֲלוֹמוֹתַי עָלַי וְעַל כָּל יִשְׂרָאֵל לְטוֹבָה, וְתִשְׁמְרֵנִי
וּתְחָנֵּנִי וְתִרְצֵנִי. אָמֵן.

רִבּוֹנוֹ שֶׁל עוֹלָם, silently recited, is derived from Berakhoth 55b.

Our God and God of our fathers, bless us with the threefold blessing written in thy Torah by thy servant Moses and spoken by Aaron and his sons

THE KOHANIM—

THY HOLY PEOPLE.

Blessed art thou, Lord our God, King of the universe, who hast sanctified us with the holiness of Aaron, and commanded us to bless thy people Israel with love.

יְבָרֶכְךָ May the Lord, who made heaven and earth, bless you from Zion.

יְיָ Lord our God, how glorious is thy name over all the world!

וְיִשְׁמְרֶךָ Protect me, O God, for I place my trust in thee.[1]

Lord of the universe, I am thine and my dreams are thine. I have dreamt a dream and I do not know what it is. May it be thy will, Lord my God and God of my fathers, to confirm all good dreams concerning myself and all the people of Israel for happiness; may they be fulfilled like the dreams of Joseph. But if they require amending, heal them as thou didst heal Hezekiah king of Judah from his illness, Miriam the prophetess from her leprosy and Naaman from his leprosy. Sweeten them as the waters of Marah were sweetened by Moses, and the waters of Jericho by Elisha. Even as thou didst turn the curse of wicked Balaam into a blessing, mayest thou turn all my dreams into happiness for myself and for all Israel. Protect me; be gracious to me and favor me. Amen.

---

[1] *Psalms* 134:3; 8:10; 16:1.

יָאֵר   אֱלֹהִים יְחָנֵּנוּ וִיבָרְכֵנוּ; יָאֵר פָּנָיו אִתָּנוּ סֶלָה.

יְהֹוָה   יְיָ יְיָ, אֵל רַחוּם וְחַנּוּן, אֶרֶךְ אַפַּיִם וְרַב חֶסֶד וֶאֱמֶת.

פְּנֵה   פְּנֵה אֵלַי וְחָנֵּנִי, כִּי יָחִיד וְעָנִי אָנִי.

אֵלֶיךָ   אֵלֶיךָ, יְיָ, נַפְשִׁי אֶשָּׂא.

וִיחֻנֶּךָ.   הִנֵּה כְעֵינֵי עֲבָדִים אֶל יַד אֲדוֹנֵיהֶם, כְּעֵינֵי שִׁפְחָה אֶל יַד גְּבִרְתָּהּ, כֵּן עֵינֵינוּ אֶל יְיָ אֱלֹהֵינוּ עַד שֶׁיְּחָנֵּנוּ.
רִבּוֹנוֹ שֶׁל עוֹלָם...

יִשָּׂא   יִשָּׂא בְרָכָה מֵאֵת יְיָ, וּצְדָקָה מֵאֱלֹהֵי יִשְׁעוֹ. וּמְצָא חֵן וְשֵׂכֶל טוֹב בְּעֵינֵי אֱלֹהִים וְאָדָם.

יְהֹוָה   יְיָ, חָנֵּנוּ, לְךָ קִוִּינוּ, הֱיֵה זְרֹעָם לַבְּקָרִים, אַף יְשׁוּעָתֵנוּ בְּעֵת צָרָה.

פָּנָיו   אַל תַּסְתֵּר פָּנֶיךָ מִמֶּנִּי בְּיוֹם צַר לִי; הַטֵּה אֵלַי אָזְנֶךָ, בְּיוֹם אֶקְרָא מַהֵר עֲנֵנִי.

אֵלֶיךָ   אֵלֶיךָ נָשָׂאתִי אֶת עֵינַי, הַיֹּשְׁבִי בַּשָּׁמָיִם.

וְיָשֵׂם   וְשָׂמוּ אֶת שְׁמִי עַל בְּנֵי יִשְׂרָאֵל, וַאֲנִי אֲבָרְכֵם.

לְךָ   לְךָ, יְיָ, הַגְּדֻלָּה וְהַגְּבוּרָה וְהַתִּפְאֶרֶת וְהַנֵּצַח וְהַהוֹד, כִּי כֹל בַּשָּׁמַיִם וּבָאָרֶץ; לְךָ, יְיָ, הַמַּמְלָכָה וְהַמִּתְנַשֵּׂא לְכֹל לְרֹאשׁ.

שָׁלוֹם.   שָׁלוֹם שָׁלוֹם לָרָחוֹק וְלַקָּרוֹב, אָמַר יְיָ, וּרְפָאתִיו.

יְהִי רָצוֹן מִלְּפָנֶיךָ, יְיָ אֱלֹהַי וֵאלֹהֵי אֲבוֹתַי, שֶׁתַּעֲשֶׂה לְמַעַן קְדֻשַּׁת חֲסָדֶיךָ וְגֹדֶל רַחֲמֶיךָ הַפְּשׁוּטִים, וּלְמַעַן טָהֳרַת שֵׁמְךָ הַגָּדוֹל הַגִּבּוֹר וְהַנּוֹרָא, בֶּן עֶשְׂרִים וּשְׁתַּיִם אוֹתִיּוֹת, הַיּוֹצֵא

יהי רצון is taken from שערי ציון, a collection of prayers and customs published by Rabbi Nathan Hanover in the seventeenth century. The four mystifying words (אנקת״ם, פסת״ם, פספסי״ם, דיונסי״ם), which are often inserted in this passage, allude to specific phrases and words that are contained therein, namely: אנקת תם, פסת תם, (כתונת) פסים, נסים. The word דיונסים seems to signify *God's miracles* (דיו=שדי).

יָאֵר May God be gracious to us and bless us and countenance us.

יְיָ It is the Lord, the Lord, a God merciful and gracious, slow to anger, rich in kindness and faithfulness.

פְּנֵה Turn to me and be gracious to me, for I am lonely and afflicted.

אֵלֶיךָ Towards thee I direct my desire.

וִיחָנֵּךְ As the eyes of servants look to the hand of their master, and as a maid's eyes to the hand of her mistress, so our eyes look to our God, till he take pity on us.[1]

Lord of the universe …

יִשָּׂא He will receive a blessing from the Lord, and justice from God his Deliverer. You shall find favor and good will with God and man alike.

יְיָ O Lord, be gracious to us; we have waited for thee; be thou their strength every morning, our salvation in time of distress.

פְּנֵה Hide not thy face from me in my day of trouble; incline thy ear to me; answer me speedily when I call.

אֵלֶיךָ To thee I raise my eyes, O thou who art enthroned in heaven.[2]

וְשָׂמוּ So shall they put my name upon the children of Israel, and I will bless them.

לְךָ Thine, O Lord, is the greatness, the power, the glory, the triumph, and the majesty; for all that is in heaven and on earth is thine; thine, O Lord, is the kingdom, and thou art supreme over all.

שָׁלוֹם "Peace, peace, to the far and the near," says the Lord, "I will heal him."[3]

May it be thy will, Lord my God and God of my fathers, to act for the sake of thy holy kindness and thy widespread abundant mercy. For the sake of the purity of thy great, mighty and revered

---

[1] *Psalm* 67:2; *Exodus* 34:6; *Psalms* 25:16; 25:1; 123:2. [2] *Psalm* 24:5; *Proverbs* 3:4; *Isaiah* 33:2; *Psalms* 102:3; 123:1. [3] *Numbers* 6:27; *I Chronicles* 29:11; *Isaiah* 57:19.

מִן הַפְּסוּקִים שֶׁל בִּרְכַּת כֹּהֲנִים הָאֲמוּרָה מִפִּי אַהֲרֹן וּבָנָיו
עַם קְדוֹשֶׁךָ, שֶׁתִּהְיֶה קָרוֹב לִי בְּקָרְאִי לָךְ. וְיִהְיוּ דְבָרַי נִשְׁמָעִים
לַעֲבוֹדָתֶךָ, וְתִשְׁמַע תְּפִלָּתִי, נַאֲקָתִי וְאַנְקָתִי, תָּמִיד כְּשֵׁם
שֶׁשָּׁמַעְתָּ אֶנְקַת יַעֲקֹב תְּמִימֶךָ, הַנִּקְרָא אִישׁ תָּם. וְתִתֶּן־לִי
וּלְכָל נַפְשׁוֹת בֵּיתִי מְזוֹנוֹתֵינוּ וּפַרְנָסָתֵנוּ בְּרֶוַח וְלֹא בְצִמְצוּם,
בְּהֶתֵּר וְלֹא בְאִסּוּר, בְּנַחַת וְלֹא בְצַעַר, מִתַּחַת יָדְךָ הָרְחָבָה,
כְּשֵׁם שֶׁנָּתַתָּ פִּסַּת פַּת לֶחֶם לֶאֱכֹל וּבֶגֶד לִלְבֹּשׁ לְיַעֲקֹב אָבִינוּ,
הַנִּקְרָא אִישׁ תָּם. וְתִתְּנֵנוּ לְאַהֲבָה, לְחֵן וּלְחֶסֶד וּלְרַחֲמִים
בְּעֵינֶיךָ וּבְעֵינֵי כָל רוֹאֵינוּ כְּשֵׁם שֶׁנָּתַתָּ אֶת יוֹסֵף צַדִּיקֶךָ, בְּשָׁעָה
שֶׁהִלְבִּישׁוֹ אָבִיו כְּתֹנֶת פַּסִּים, לְחֵן וּלְחֶסֶד וּלְרַחֲמִים בְּעֵינֶיךָ
וּבְעֵינֵי כָל רוֹאָיו. וְתַעֲשֶׂה עִמִּי נִפְלָאוֹת וְנִסִּים וּלְטוֹבָה אוֹת
וְתַצְלִיחֵנִי בִּדְרָכַי, וְתֵן בְּלִבִּי בִּינָה לְהָבִין, לְהַשְׂכִּיל וּלְקַיֵּם
אֶת כָּל דִּבְרֵי תַלְמוּד תּוֹרָתֶךָ וְסוֹדוֹתֶיהָ, וְתַצִּילֵנִי מִשְּׁגִיאוֹת.
וּתְטַהֵר רַעְיוֹנַי וְלִבִּי לַעֲבוֹדָתֶךָ וּלְיִרְאָתֶךָ, וְתַאֲרִיךְ יָמֵי

<table>
<tr><td align="right">For Parents</td><td align="center">For Family</td></tr>
<tr><td align="right">(וִימֵי אָבִי וְאִמִּי)</td><td align="center">(וִימֵי אִשְׁתִּי וּבָנַי וּבְנוֹתַי)</td></tr>
</table>

בְּטוֹב וּבִנְעִימוֹת, בְּרֹב עֹז וְשָׁלוֹם, אָמֵן.

אַדִּיר בַּמָּרוֹם, שׁוֹכֵן בִּגְבוּרָה, אַתָּה שָׁלוֹם וְשִׁמְךָ שָׁלוֹם; יְהִי
רָצוֹן שֶׁתָּשִׂים עָלֵינוּ וְעַל כָּל עַמְּךָ בֵּית יִשְׂרָאֵל חַיִּים וּבְרָכָה
לְמִשְׁמֶרֶת שָׁלוֹם.

Kohanim:

רִבּוֹנוֹ שֶׁל עוֹלָם, עָשִׂינוּ מַה שֶּׁגָּזַרְתָּ עָלֵינוּ; אַף אַתָּה עֲשֵׂה
עִמָּנוּ כְּמוֹ שֶׁהִבְטַחְתָּנוּ. הַשְׁקִיפָה מִמְּעוֹן קָדְשְׁךָ, מִן הַשָּׁמַיִם,
וּבָרֵךְ אֶת עַמְּךָ אֶת יִשְׂרָאֵל, וְאֵת הָאֲדָמָה אֲשֶׁר נָתַתָּה לָנוּ,
כַּאֲשֶׁר נִשְׁבַּעְתָּ לַאֲבוֹתֵינוּ, אֶרֶץ זָבַת חָלָב וּדְבָשׁ.

אדיר במרום is quoted in Berakhoth 55b, רבונו של עולם in Sotah 39a.

name that is contained in the priestly blessing spoken by Aaron and his sons the priests, thy holy people, be thou near to me when I call upon thee. May my words be heard that I may worship thee; ever hear my prayer as thou didst hear the prayer of Jacob whose faith in thee was perfect.

Grant me and all my family a generous, honest and congenial living derived from thy own generous hand, as thou didst grant food and clothing to our father Jacob who was a man of perfect faith. Favor us with thy lovingkindness and mercy, and the good-will of all the people we meet, as thou didst favor thy righteous Joseph when his father invested him with a colorful tunic. Grant me thy wondrous deeds, a bounteous token, and prosper my ways. Inspire me to understand and discern and fulfill all thy Torah and its implications. Save me from errors and purify my thinking that I may serve thee. Prolong my life and the life of all my family amidst abundant happiness, strength and peace. Amen.

Supreme and mighty art thou on high; thou art peace and thy name is Peace. May it be thy will to grant life and blessedness and enduring peace to us and to all thy people, the house of Israel.

Kohanim:

Lord of the universe, we have performed what thou hast decreed for us; do thou, too, fulfill what thou hast promised us. "Look down from heaven, thy holy habitation, and bless thy people Israel and the land thou hast given us—as thou didst promise to our fathers—a land abounding in milk and honey."[1]

היוצא מן הפסוקים that is, God's name consisting of twenty-two letters (as many as in the Hebrew alphabet) is implied in the priestly blessing, according to kabbalistic works. The Talmud (Kiddushin 71a) speaks of two names, consisting of twelve and forty-two letters, respectively. Whereupon Maimonides writes: "Every intelligent person knows that one word of forty-two letters is impossible; but it was a phrase of several words that had such a meaning as to convey a correct notion of the essence of God" (*Guide* 1:62). The Kabbalah describes this name in fourteen words, each of which represents the initials of three divine attributes, as for example, אב"ג, ית"ץ, קר"ע, שט"ן meaning: אל ברוך גדול, יוצר תקיף צדיק, קדוש רם עליון, שר טוב נגיד.

[1] *Deuteronomy* 26:15.

שִׂים שָׁלוֹם, טוֹבָה וּבְרָכָה, חֵן וָחֶסֶד וְרַחֲמִים, עָלֵינוּ וְעַל
כָּל יִשְׂרָאֵל עַמֶּךָ. בָּרְכֵנוּ אָבִינוּ, כֻּלָּנוּ כְּאֶחָד, בְּאוֹר פָּנֶיךָ;
כִּי בְאוֹר פָּנֶיךָ נָתַתָּ לָּנוּ, יְיָ אֱלֹהֵינוּ, תּוֹרַת חַיִּים וְאַהֲבַת חֶסֶד,
וּצְדָקָה וּבְרָכָה וְרַחֲמִים, וְחַיִּים וְשָׁלוֹם. וְטוֹב בְּעֵינֶיךָ לְבָרֵךְ
אֶת עַמְּךָ יִשְׂרָאֵל בְּכָל עֵת וּבְכָל שָׁעָה בִּשְׁלוֹמֶךָ. בָּרוּךְ
אַתָּה, יְיָ, הַמְבָרֵךְ אֶת עַמּוֹ יִשְׂרָאֵל בַּשָּׁלוֹם.

After the *Amidah* add the following meditation:

אֱלֹהַי, נְצֹר לְשׁוֹנִי מֵרָע, וּשְׂפָתַי מִדַּבֵּר מִרְמָה; וְלִמְקַלְלַי
נַפְשִׁי תִדּוֹם, וְנַפְשִׁי כֶּעָפָר לַכֹּל תִּהְיֶה. פְּתַח לִבִּי בְּתוֹרָתֶךָ,
וּבְמִצְוֹתֶיךָ תִּרְדּוֹף נַפְשִׁי; וְכָל הַחוֹשְׁבִים עָלַי רָעָה, מְהֵרָה
הָפֵר עֲצָתָם וְקַלְקֵל מַחֲשַׁבְתָּם. עֲשֵׂה לְמַעַן שְׁמֶךָ, עֲשֵׂה לְמַעַן
יְמִינֶךָ, עֲשֵׂה לְמַעַן קְדֻשָּׁתֶךָ, עֲשֵׂה לְמַעַן תּוֹרָתֶךָ. לְמַעַן
יֵחָלְצוּן יְדִידֶיךָ, הוֹשִׁיעָה יְמִינְךָ וַעֲנֵנִי. יִהְיוּ לְרָצוֹן אִמְרֵי פִי
וְהֶגְיוֹן לִבִּי לְפָנֶיךָ, יְיָ, צוּרִי וְגוֹאֲלִי. עֹשֶׂה שָׁלוֹם בִּמְרוֹמָיו,
הוּא יַעֲשֶׂה שָׁלוֹם עָלֵינוּ וְעַל כָּל יִשְׂרָאֵל, וְאִמְרוּ אָמֵן.

יְהִי רָצוֹן מִלְּפָנֶיךָ, יְיָ אֱלֹהֵינוּ וֵאלֹהֵי אֲבוֹתֵינוּ, שֶׁיִּבָּנֶה בֵּית
הַמִּקְדָּשׁ בִּמְהֵרָה בְיָמֵינוּ, וְתֵן חֶלְקֵנוּ בְּתוֹרָתֶךָ. וְשָׁם נַעֲבָדְךָ
בְּיִרְאָה, כִּימֵי עוֹלָם וּכְשָׁנִים קַדְמוֹנִיּוֹת. וְעָרְבָה לַיְיָ מִנְחַת
יְהוּדָה וִירוּשָׁלָיִם, כִּימֵי עוֹלָם וּכְשָׁנִים קַדְמוֹנִיּוֹת.

Reader's full-Kaddish, page 17.

אלהי נצור suggests a variety of Jewish ethical ideas, such as the following:
According to Rabbi Akiva, the most comprehensive precept in the Torah
is the command: "You shall love your neighbor as yourself" (Leviticus

O grant peace, happiness, blessing, grace, kindness and mercy to us and to all Israel thy people. Bless us all alike, our Father, with the light of thy countenance; indeed, by the light of thy countenance thou hast given us, Lord our God, a Torah of life, lovingkindness, charity, blessing, mercy, life and peace. May it please thee to bless thy people Israel with peace at all times and hours. Blessed art thou, O Lord, who blessest thy people Israel with peace.

After the Amidah add the following meditation:

My God, guard my tongue from evil, and my lips from speaking falsehood. May my soul be silent to those who insult me; be my soul lowly to all as the dust. Open my heart to thy Torah, that my soul may follow thy commands. Speedily defeat the counsel of all those who plan evil against me and upset their design. Do it for the glory of thy name; do it for the sake of thy power; do it for the sake of thy holiness; do it for the sake of thy Torah. That thy beloved may be rescued, save with thy right hand and answer me. May the words of my mouth and the meditation of my heart be pleasing before thee, O Lord, my Stronghold and my Redeemer. May he who creates peace in his high heavens create peace for us and for all Israel, Amen.

May it be thy will, Lord our God and God of our fathers, that the Temple be speedily rebuilt in our days, and grant us a share in thy Torah. There we will serve thee with reverence, as in the days of old and as in former years. Then the offering of Judah and Jerusalem will be pleasing to the Lord, as in the days of old and as in former years.

Reader's full-Kaddish, page 18.

19:18). Several talmudic proverbial sayings are to the effect that it is easy to acquire an enemy, but difficult to win a friend; he who turns his enemy into a friend is the bravest hero. The greater the man, the humbler he is. A person can forget in two years what he has learned in twenty. In prosperity, people feel brotherly to one another. He who studies but does not review his work is like one who sows but does not reap. Pay special attention to the poor, for it is from them that knowledge will come. Men should be careful not to give their wives any cause for tears, for God counts their tears.

אֵין כֵּאלֹהֵינוּ, אֵין כַּאדוֹנֵינוּ, אֵין כְּמַלְכֵּנוּ, אֵין כְּמוֹשִׁיעֵנוּ.

מִי כֵאלֹהֵינוּ, מִי כַאדוֹנֵינוּ, מִי כְמַלְכֵּנוּ, מִי כְמוֹשִׁיעֵנוּ.

נוֹדֶה לֵאלֹהֵינוּ, נוֹדֶה לַאדוֹנֵינוּ, נוֹדֶה לְמַלְכֵּנוּ, נוֹדֶה לְמוֹשִׁיעֵנוּ.

בָּרוּךְ אֱלֹהֵינוּ, בָּרוּךְ אֲדוֹנֵינוּ, בָּרוּךְ מַלְכֵּנוּ, בָּרוּךְ מוֹשִׁיעֵנוּ.

אַתָּה הוּא אֱלֹהֵינוּ, אַתָּה הוּא אֲדוֹנֵינוּ, אַתָּה הוּא מַלְכֵּנוּ, אַתָּה הוּא מוֹשִׁיעֵנוּ.

אַתָּה הוּא שֶׁהִקְטִירוּ אֲבוֹתֵינוּ לְפָנֶיךָ אֶת קְטֹרֶת הַסַּמִּים.

מסכת כריתות ו, א

פִּטּוּם הַקְּטֹרֶת: הַצֳּרִי, וְהַצִּפֹּרֶן, הַחֶלְבְּנָה וְהַלְּבוֹנָה. מִשְׁקַל שִׁבְעִים שִׁבְעִים מָנֶה; מוֹר וּקְצִיעָה, שִׁבֹּלֶת נֵרְדְּ וְכַרְכֹּם, מִשְׁקַל שִׁשָּׁה עָשָׂר שִׁשָּׁה עָשָׂר מָנֶה; הַקֹּשְׁטְ שְׁנֵים עָשָׂר, וְקִלּוּפָה שְׁלשָׁה, וְקִנָּמוֹן תִּשְׁעָה, בֹּרִית כַּרְשִׁינָה תִּשְׁעָה קַבִּין; יֵין קַפְרִיסִין סְאִין תְּלָתָא וְקַבִּין תְּלָתָא; וְאִם אֵין לוֹ יֵין קַפְרִיסִין, מֵבִיא חֲמַר חִוַּרְיָן עַתִּיק; מֶלַח סְדוֹמִית רֹבַע הַקָּב; מַעֲלֶה עָשָׁן כָּל שֶׁהוּא. רַבִּי נָתָן אוֹמֵר: אַף כִּפַּת הַיַּרְדֵּן כָּל שֶׁהוּא. וְאִם נָתַן בָּהּ דְּבַשׁ, פְּסָלָהּ; וְאִם חִסַּר אַחַת מִכָּל סַמָּנֶיהָ, חַיָּב מִיתָה. רַבָּן שִׁמְעוֹן בֶּן גַּמְלִיאֵל אוֹמֵר: הַצֳּרִי אֵינוֹ אֶלָּא שְׂרָף הַנּוֹטֵף מֵעֲצֵי הַקְּטָף. בֹּרִית כַּרְשִׁינָה, שֶׁשָּׁפִין בָּהּ אֶת הַצִּפֹּרֶן כְּדֵי שֶׁתְּהֵא נָאָה; יֵין קַפְרִיסִין, שֶׁשּׁוֹרִין בּוֹ אֶת הַצִּפֹּרֶן כְּדֵי שֶׁתְּהֵא עַזָּה. וַהֲלֹא מֵי רַגְלַיִם יָפִין לָהּ, אֶלָּא שֶׁאֵין מַכְנִיסִין מֵי רַגְלַיִם בָּעֲזָרָה מִפְּנֵי הַכָּבוֹד.

EN KELOHENU

There is none like our God; there is none like our Lord; there is none like our King; there is none like our Deliverer.

Who is like our God? Who is like our Lord? Who is like our King? Who is like our Deliverer?

Let us give thanks to our God; let us give thanks to our Lord; let us give thanks to our King; let us give thanks to our Deliverer.

Blessed be our God; blessed be our Lord; blessed be our King; blessed be our Deliverer.

Thou art our God; thou art our Lord; thou art our King; thou art our Deliverer.

Thou art he to whom our fathers offered the fragrant incense.

Talmud Kerithoth 6a

The incense was composed of the following eleven kinds of spices: balm, onycha, galbanum, and frankincense, seventy minas' weight of each; myrrh, cassia, spikenard, and saffron, sixteen minas' weight of each; twelve minas of costus; three minas of an aromatic bark; nine minas of cinnamon. [Added to the spices were] nine *kavs* of Karsina lye; three *seahs* and three *kavs* of Cyprus wine—if Cyprus wine could not be obtained, strong white wine might be substituted for it—a fourth of a *kav* of Sodom salt, and a minute quantity of *ma'aleh ashan* [a smoke-producing ingredient]. Rabbi Nathan says: A minute quantity of Jordan amber was also required. If one added honey to the mixture, he rendered the incense unfit for sacred use; and if he left out any of its ingredients, he was subject to the penalty of death.

Rabbi Simeon ben Gamaliel says: The balm required for the incense is a resin exuding from the balsam trees. Why was Karsina lye used? To refine the onycha. Why was Cyprus wine employed? To steep the onycha in it so as to make it more pungent. Though *mei raglayim* might have been good for that purpose, it was not decent to bring it into the Temple.

is limited to seven benedictions instead of the nineteen benedictions contained in the regular *Shemoneh Esreh*, in order to bring the blessings to a total of nineteen. *En Kelohenu* was composed during the period of the Geonim.

משנה תמיד ז, ד

הַשִּׁיר שֶׁהָיוּ הַלְוִיִּם אוֹמְרִים בְּבֵית הַמִּקְדָּשׁ.

בַּיּוֹם הָרִאשׁוֹן הָיוּ אוֹמְרִים: לַיָי הָאָרֶץ וּמְלוֹאָהּ, תֵּבֵל וְיֹשְׁבֵי בָהּ.

בַּשֵּׁנִי הָיוּ אוֹמְרִים: גָּדוֹל יְיָ וּמְהֻלָּל מְאֹד, בְּעִיר אֱלֹהֵינוּ, הַר קָדְשׁוֹ.

בַּשְּׁלִישִׁי הָיוּ אוֹמְרִים: אֱלֹהִים נִצָּב בַּעֲדַת אֵל, בְּקֶרֶב אֱלֹהִים יִשְׁפֹּט.

בָּרְבִיעִי הָיוּ אוֹמְרִים: אֵל נְקָמוֹת יְיָ, אֵל נְקָמוֹת הוֹפִיעַ.

בַּחֲמִישִׁי הָיוּ אוֹמְרִים: הַרְנִינוּ לֵאלֹהִים עוּזֵּנוּ, הָרִיעוּ לֵאלֹהֵי יַעֲקֹב.

בַּשִּׁשִּׁי הָיוּ אוֹמְרִים: יְיָ מָלָךְ, גֵּאוּת לָבֵשׁ; לָבֵשׁ יְיָ, עֹז הִתְאַזָּר; אַף תִּכּוֹן תֵּבֵל, בַּל תִּמּוֹט.

בַּשַּׁבָּת הָיוּ אוֹמְרִים: מִזְמוֹר שִׁיר לְיוֹם הַשַּׁבָּת. מִזְמוֹר שִׁיר לֶעָתִיד לָבֹא, לְיוֹם שֶׁכֻּלּוֹ שַׁבָּת וּמְנוּחָה, לְחַיֵּי הָעוֹלָמִים.

מסכת מגילה כח, ב

תָּנָא דְבֵי אֵלִיָּהוּ: כָּל הַשּׁוֹנֶה הֲלָכוֹת בְּכָל יוֹם, מֻבְטָח לוֹ שֶׁהוּא בֶן עוֹלָם הַבָּא, שֶׁנֶּאֱמַר: הֲלִיכוֹת עוֹלָם לוֹ. אַל תִּקְרָא הֲלִיכוֹת, אֶלָּא הֲלָכוֹת.

מסכת ברכות סד, א

אָמַר רַבִּי אֶלְעָזָר, אָמַר רַבִּי חֲנִינָא: תַּלְמִידֵי חֲכָמִים מַרְבִּים שָׁלוֹם בָּעוֹלָם, שֶׁנֶּאֱמַר: וְכָל בָּנַיִךְ לִמּוּדֵי יְיָ, וְרַב שְׁלוֹם

יום שכלו שבת, "the great Sabbath," a symbolic description of the world to come, a foretaste of which is offered by the weekly Sabbath.

תנא דבי אליהו, a midrashic collection of mysterious authorship, consists of two parts: *Seder Eliyyahu Rabba* (thirty-one chapters) and *Seder Eliyyahu Zuta* (twenty-five chapters). According to the Talmud (Kethuboth 106a), Elijah

Mishnah Tamid 7:4

Following are the psalms which the Levites used to recite in the Temple.

On Sunday they used to recite: "The earth and its entire contents belong to the Lord, the world and its inhabitants."[1]

On Monday they used to recite: "Great is the Lord, and most worthy of praise, in the city of our God, his holy mountain."[2]

On Tuesday they used to recite: "God stands in the divine assembly; in the midst of the judges he gives judgment."[3]

On Wednesday they used to recite: "God of retribution, Lord God of retribution, appear!"[4]

On Thursday they used to recite: "Sing aloud to God our strength; shout for joy to the God of Jacob."[5]

On Friday they used to recite: "The Lord is King; he is robed in majesty; the Lord is robed, he has girded himself with strength; thus the world is set firm and cannot be shaken."[6]

On the Sabbath they used to recite: "A song for the Sabbath day."[7] It is a song for the hereafter, for the day which will be all Sabbath and rest in life everlasting.

Talmud Megillah 28b

It was taught in the school of Elijah: Whoever studies traditional laws every day is assured of life in the world to come, for it is said: "His ways are eternal."[4] Read not here *halikhoth* [ways] but *halakhoth* [traditional laws].

Talmud Berakhoth 64a

Rabbi Elazar said in the name of Rabbi Ḥanina: Scholars increase peace throughout the world, for it is said: "All your children shall be taught of the Lord, and great shall be the peace

frequently visited Rabbi Anan (third century) and taught him *Seder Eliyyahu.* This work, which has been named "the jewel of aggadic literature," repeatedly emphasizes the importance of diligence in the study of the Torah.

[1] *Psalm* 24.   [2] *Psalm* 48.   [3] *Psalm* 82.   [4] *Psalm* 94.   [5] *Psalm* 81.   [6] *Psalm* 93.
[7] *Psalm* 92.   [8] *Habakkuk* 3:6.

בָּנֶיךָ. אַל תִּקְרָא בָּנָיִךְ, אֶלָּא בּוֹנָיִךְ. שָׁלוֹם רָב לְאֹהֲבֵי תוֹרָתֶךָ,
וְאֵין לָמוֹ מִכְשׁוֹל. יְהִי שָׁלוֹם בְּחֵילֵךְ, שַׁלְוָה בְּאַרְמְנוֹתָיִךְ.

Reader לְמַעַן אַחַי וְרֵעָי, אֲדַבְּרָה נָּא שָׁלוֹם בָּךְ. לְמַעַן בֵּית יְיָ
אֱלֹהֵינוּ, אֲבַקְשָׁה טוֹב לָךְ. יְיָ עֹז לְעַמּוֹ יִתֵּן, יְיָ יְבָרֵךְ אֶת עַמּוֹ
בַשָּׁלוֹם.

קַדִּישׁ דְּרַבָּנָן

Mourners:

יִתְגַּדַּל וְיִתְקַדַּשׁ שְׁמֵהּ רַבָּא בְּעָלְמָא דִּי בְרָא כִרְעוּתֵהּ;
וְיַמְלִיךְ מַלְכוּתֵהּ בְּחַיֵּיכוֹן וּבְיוֹמֵיכוֹן, וּבְחַיֵּי דְכָל בֵּית יִשְׂרָאֵל
בַּעֲגָלָא וּבִזְמַן קָרִיב, וְאִמְרוּ אָמֵן.

יְהֵא שְׁמֵהּ רַבָּא מְבָרַךְ לְעָלַם וּלְעָלְמֵי עָלְמַיָּא.

יִתְבָּרַךְ וְיִשְׁתַּבַּח, וְיִתְפָּאַר וְיִתְרוֹמַם, וְיִתְנַשֵּׂא וְיִתְהַדָּר,
וְיִתְעַלֶּה וְיִתְהַלָּל שְׁמֵהּ דְּקֻדְשָׁא, בְּרִיךְ הוּא, לְעֵלָּא מִן כָּל
בִּרְכָתָא וְשִׁירָתָא, תֻּשְׁבְּחָתָא וְנֶחֱמָתָא, דַּאֲמִירָן בְּעָלְמָא,
וְאִמְרוּ אָמֵן.

עַל יִשְׂרָאֵל וְעַל רַבָּנָן, וְעַל תַּלְמִידֵיהוֹן וְעַל כָּל תַּלְמִידֵי
תַלְמִידֵיהוֹן, וְעַל כָּל מָן דְּעָסְקִין בְּאוֹרַיְתָא, דִּי בְאַתְרָא הָדֵן
וְדִי בְכָל אֲתַר וַאֲתַר, יְהֵא לְהוֹן וּלְכוֹן שְׁלָמָא רַבָּא, חִנָּא
וְחִסְדָּא וְרַחֲמִין, וְחַיִּין אֲרִיכִין, וּמְזוֹנֵי רְוִיחֵי, וּפֻרְקָנָא מִן קֳדָם
אֲבוּהוֹן דְּבִשְׁמַיָּא וְאַרְעָא, וְאִמְרוּ אָמֵן.

יְהֵא שְׁלָמָא רַבָּא מִן שְׁמַיָּא, וְחַיִּים טוֹבִים, עָלֵינוּ וְעַל כָּל
יִשְׂרָאֵל, וְאִמְרוּ אָמֵן.

עֹשֶׂה שָׁלוֹם בִּמְרוֹמָיו, הוּא יַעֲשֶׂה שָׁלוֹם עָלֵינוּ וְעַל כָּל
יִשְׂרָאֵל, וְאִמְרוּ אָמֵן.

of your children."[1] Read not here *banayikh* [your children], but *bonayikh* [your builders—scholars are the true builders of peace].

Abundant peace have they who love thy Torah, and there is no stumbling for them. Peace be within your walls, and security within your palaces. In behalf of my brethren and friends, let me pronounce peace for you. For the sake of the house of the Lord our God, I will seek your good. The Lord will give strength to his people; the Lord will bless his people with peace.[2]

KADDISH D'RABBANAN

Mourners:

Glorified and sanctified be God's great name throughout the world which he has created according to his will. May he establish his kingdom in your lifetime and during your days, and within the life of the entire house of Israel, speedily and soon; and say, Amen.

May his great name be blessed forever and to all eternity.

Blessed and praised, glorified and exalted, extolled and honored, adored and lauded be the name of the Holy One, blessed be he, beyond all the blessings and hymns, praises and consolations that are ever spoken in the world; and say, Amen.

[We pray] for Israel, for our teachers and their disciples and the disciples of their disciples, and for all who study the Torah, here and everywhere. May they have abundant peace, loving-kindness, ample sustenance and salvation from their Father who is in heaven; and say, Amen.

May there be abundant peace from heaven, and happy life, for us and for all Israel; and say, Amen.

He who creates peace in his celestial heights, may he in his mercy create peace for us and for all Israel; and say, Amen.

---

[1] *Isaiah* 54:13.   [2] *Psalms* 119:165; 122:7–9; 29:10.

עָלֵינוּ לְשַׁבֵּחַ לַאֲדוֹן הַכֹּל, לָתֵת גְּדֻלָּה לְיוֹצֵר בְּרֵאשִׁית,
שֶׁלֹּא עָשָׂנוּ כְּגוֹיֵי הָאֲרָצוֹת, וְלֹא שָׂמָנוּ כְּמִשְׁפְּחוֹת הָאֲדָמָה;
שֶׁלֹּא שָׂם חֶלְקֵנוּ כָּהֶם, וְגֹרָלֵנוּ כְּכָל הֲמוֹנָם. וַאֲנַחְנוּ כּוֹרְעִים
וּמִשְׁתַּחֲוִים וּמוֹדִים לִפְנֵי מֶלֶךְ מַלְכֵי הַמְּלָכִים, הַקָּדוֹשׁ בָּרוּךְ
הוּא, שֶׁהוּא נוֹטֶה שָׁמַיִם וְיוֹסֵד אָרֶץ, וּמוֹשַׁב יְקָרוֹ בַּשָּׁמַיִם
מִמַּעַל, וּשְׁכִינַת עֻזּוֹ בְּגָבְהֵי מְרוֹמִים. הוּא אֱלֹהֵינוּ, אֵין עוֹד;
אֱמֶת מַלְכֵּנוּ, אֶפֶס זוּלָתוֹ, כַּכָּתוּב בְּתוֹרָתוֹ: וְיָדַעְתָּ הַיּוֹם
וַהֲשֵׁבֹתָ אֶל לְבָבֶךָ, כִּי יְיָ הוּא הָאֱלֹהִים בַּשָּׁמַיִם מִמַּעַל וְעַל
הָאָרֶץ מִתָּחַת, אֵין עוֹד.

עַל כֵּן נְקַוֶּה לְּךָ, יְיָ אֱלֹהֵינוּ, לִרְאוֹת מְהֵרָה בְּתִפְאֶרֶת עֻזֶּךָ,
לְהַעֲבִיר גִּלּוּלִים מִן הָאָרֶץ, וְהָאֱלִילִים כָּרוֹת יִכָּרֵתוּן; לְתַקֵּן
עוֹלָם בְּמַלְכוּת שַׁדַּי, וְכָל בְּנֵי בָשָׂר יִקְרְאוּ בִשְׁמֶךָ, לְהַפְנוֹת
אֵלֶיךָ כָּל רִשְׁעֵי אָרֶץ. יַכִּירוּ וְיֵדְעוּ כָּל יוֹשְׁבֵי תֵבֵל, כִּי לְךָ
תִּכְרַע כָּל בֶּרֶךְ, תִּשָּׁבַע כָּל לָשׁוֹן. לְפָנֶיךָ, יְיָ אֱלֹהֵינוּ, יִכְרְעוּ
וְיִפֹּלוּ, וְלִכְבוֹד שִׁמְךָ יְקָר יִתֵּנוּ, וִיקַבְּלוּ כֻלָּם אֶת עֹל מַלְכוּתֶךָ,
וְתִמְלוֹךְ עֲלֵיהֶם מְהֵרָה לְעוֹלָם וָעֶד. כִּי הַמַּלְכוּת שֶׁלְּךָ הִיא,
וּלְעוֹלְמֵי עַד תִּמְלוֹךְ בְּכָבוֹד, כַּכָּתוּב בְּתוֹרָתֶךָ: יְיָ יִמְלֹךְ
לְעֹלָם וָעֶד. Reader וְנֶאֱמַר: וְהָיָה יְיָ לְמֶלֶךְ עַל כָּל הָאָרֶץ;
בַּיּוֹם הַהוּא יִהְיֶה יְיָ אֶחָד וּשְׁמוֹ אֶחָד.

MOURNERS' KADDISH

יִתְגַּדַּל וְיִתְקַדַּשׁ שְׁמֵהּ רַבָּא בְּעָלְמָא דִּי בְרָא כִרְעוּתֵהּ;
וְיַמְלִיךְ מַלְכוּתֵהּ בְּחַיֵּיכוֹן וּבְיוֹמֵיכוֹן, וּבְחַיֵּי דְכָל בֵּית יִשְׂרָאֵל
בַּעֲגָלָא וּבִזְמַן קָרִיב, וְאִמְרוּ אָמֵן.

יְהֵא שְׁמֵהּ רַבָּא מְבָרַךְ לְעָלַם וּלְעָלְמֵי עָלְמַיָּא.

ALENU

It is our duty to praise the Master of all, to exalt the Creator of the universe, who has not made us like the nations of the world and has not placed us like the families of the earth; who has not designed our destiny to be like theirs, nor our lot like that of all their multitude. We bend the knee and bow and acknowledge before the supreme King of kings, the Holy One, blessed be he, that it is he who stretched forth the heavens and founded the earth. His seat of glory is in the heavens above; his abode of majesty is in the lofty heights. He is our God, there is none else; truly, he is our King, there is none besides him, as it is written in his Torah: "You shall know this day, and reflect in your heart, that it is theL ord who is God in the heavens above and on the earth beneath, there is none else."[1]

We hope therefore, Lord our God, soon to behold thy majestic glory, when the abominations shall be removed from the earth, and the false gods exterminated; when the world shall be perfected under the reign of the Almighty, and all mankind will call upon thy name, and all the wicked of the earth will be turned to thee. May all the inhabitants of the world realize and know that to thee every knee must bend, every tongue must vow allegiance. May they bend the knee and prostrate themselves before thee, Lord our God, and give honor to thy glorious name; may they all accept the yoke of thy kingdom, and do thou reign over them speedily forever and ever. For the kingdom is thine, and to all eternity thou wilt reign in glory, as it is written in thy Torah: "The Lord shall be King forever and ever."[2] And it is said: "The Lord shall be King over all the earth; on that day the Lord shall be One, and his name One."[3]

MOURNERS' KADDISH

Glorified and sanctified be God's great name throughout the world which he has created according to his will. May he establish his kingdom in your lifetime and during your days, and within the life of the entire house of Israel, speedily and soon; and say, Amen.

May his great name be blessed forever and to all eternity.

---

[1] *Deuteronomy* 4:39. [2] *Exodus* 15:18. [4] *Zechariah* 14:9.

יִתְבָּרַךְ וְיִשְׁתַּבַּח, וְיִתְפָּאַר וְיִתְרוֹמַם, וְיִתְנַשֵּׂא וְיִתְהַדָּר,
וְיִתְעַלֶּה וְיִתְהַלָּל שְׁמֵהּ דְּקֻדְשָׁא, בְּרִיךְ הוּא, לְעֵלָּא מִן כָּל
בִּרְכָתָא וְשִׁירָתָא, תֻּשְׁבְּחָתָא וְנֶחֱמָתָא, דַּאֲמִירָן בְּעָלְמָא,
וְאִמְרוּ אָמֵן.

יְהֵא שְׁלָמָא רַבָּא מִן שְׁמַיָּא, וְחַיִּים, עָלֵינוּ וְעַל כָּל יִשְׂרָאֵל,
וְאִמְרוּ אָמֵן.

עֹשֶׂה שָׁלוֹם בִּמְרוֹמָיו, הוּא יַעֲשֶׂה שָׁלוֹם עָלֵינוּ וְעַל כָּל
יִשְׂרָאֵל, וְאִמְרוּ אָמֵן.

אַל תִּירָא מִפַּחַד פִּתְאֹם, וּמִשֹּׁאַת רְשָׁעִים כִּי תָבֹא. עֻצוּ
עֵצָה וְתֻפָר, דַּבְּרוּ דָבָר וְלֹא יָקוּם, כִּי עִמָּנוּ אֵל. וְעַד זִקְנָה
אֲנִי הוּא, וְעַד שֵׂיבָה אֲנִי אֶסְבֹּל; אֲנִי עָשִׂיתִי וַאֲנִי אֶשָּׂא, וַאֲנִי
אֶסְבֹּל וַאֲמַלֵּט

שִׁיר הַכָּבוֹד

Recited in responsive form
The ark is opened.

אַנְעִים זְמִירוֹת וְשִׁירִים אֶאֱרֹג, כִּי אֵלֶיךָ נַפְשִׁי תַעֲרֹג.

נַפְשִׁי חִמְּדָה בְּצֵל יָדֶךָ, לָדַעַת כָּל רָז סוֹדֶךָ.

מִדֵּי דַבְּרִי בִּכְבוֹדֶךָ, הוֹמֶה לִבִּי אֶל דּוֹדֶיךָ.

עַל כֵּן אֲדַבֵּר בְּךָ נִכְבָּדוֹת, וְשִׁמְךָ אֲכַבֵּד בְּשִׁירֵי יְדִידוֹת.

אֲסַפְּרָה כְבוֹדְךָ וְלֹא רְאִיתִיךָ, אֲדַמְּךָ אֲכַנְּךָ וְלֹא יְדַעְתִּיךָ.

בְּיַד נְבִיאֶיךָ בְּסוֹד עֲבָדֶיךָ, דִּמִּיתָ הֲדַר כְּבוֹד הוֹדֶךָ.

אנעים זמירות is attributed to Rabbi Judah of Regensburg (ר' יהודה החסיד),
who was a philosopher and poet, saint and mystic. Each line in this alphabetical poem contains sixteen syllables, as in the *Hymn of Oneness* (שיר היחוד).
The alphabetical sequence begins with the fifth line.

Blessed and praised, glorified and exalted, extolled and honored, adored and lauded be the name of the Holy One, blessed be he, beyond all the blessings and hymns, praises and consolations that are ever spoken in the world; and say, Amen.

May there be abundant peace from heaven, and a good life, for us and for all Israel; and say, Amen.

He who creates peace in his celestial heights, may he create peace for us and for all Israel; and say, Amen.

Be not afraid of sudden terror, nor of the storm that strikes the wicked. Form your plot—it shall fail; lay your plan—it shall not prevail! For God is with us. Even to your old age I will be the same; when you are gray-headed, still I will sustain you; I have made you, and I will bear you; I will sustain you and save you.[1]

HYMN OF GLORY

Recited in responsive form

The ark is opened.

I sing hymns and compose songs
Because my soul longs for thee.

My soul desires thy shelter,
To know all thy mystery.

When I speak of thy glory,
My heart yearns after thy love.

Hence I utter thy glories,
And offer thee songs of love.

I tell thy praise, though I have not seen thee;
I describe thee, though I have not known thee.

Through thy prophets amidst thy worshipers
Didst thou show forth thy majestic splendor.

בסוד עבדיך has been mistranslated: "in the mystic utterance of thy servants." However, the poet uses בסוד עבדיך in the sense of בסוד קדושים (Psalm 89:8) which is rendered "in the council of the holy ones."

---

[1] *Proverbs* 3:25; *Isaiah* 8:10; 46:4.

גְּדֻלָּתְךָ וּגְבוּרָתֶךָ, כֵּנּוּ לְתֹקֶף פְּעֻלָּתֶךָ.

דִּמּוּ אוֹתְךָ וְלֹא כְּפִי יֶשְׁךָ, וַיְשַׁוּוּךָ לְפִי מַעֲשֶׂיךָ.

הִמְשִׁילוּךָ בְּרֹב חֶזְיוֹנוֹת, הִנְּךָ אֶחָד בְּכָל דִּמְיוֹנוֹת.

וַיֶּחֱזוּ בְךָ זִקְנָה וּבַחֲרוּת, וּשְׂעַר רֹאשְׁךָ בְּשֵׂיבָה וְשַׁחֲרוּת.

זִקְנָה בְּיוֹם דִּין וּבַחֲרוּת בְּיוֹם קְרָב, כְּאִישׁ מִלְחָמוֹת יָדָיו לוֹ רָב.

חָבַשׁ כּוֹבַע יְשׁוּעָה בְּרֹאשׁוֹ, הוֹשִׁיעָה לּוֹ יְמִינוֹ וּזְרוֹעַ קָדְשׁוֹ.

טַלְלֵי אוֹרוֹת רֹאשׁוֹ נִמְלָא, וּקְוֻצּוֹתָיו רְסִיסֵי לָיְלָה.

יִתְפָּאֵר בִּי כִּי חָפֵץ בִּי, וְהוּא יִהְיֶה לִי לַעֲטֶרֶת צְבִי.

כֶּתֶם טָהוֹר פָּז דְּמוּת רֹאשׁוֹ, וְחַק עַל מֵצַח כְּבוֹד שֵׁם קָדְשׁוֹ.

לְחֵן וּלְכָבוֹד צְבִי תִפְאָרָה, אֻמָּתוֹ לוֹ עִטְרָה עֲטָרָה.

מַחְלְפוֹת רֹאשׁוֹ כְּבִימֵי בְחֻרוֹת, קְוֻצּוֹתָיו תַּלְתַּלִּים שְׁחוֹרוֹת.

נְוֵה הַצֶּדֶק צְבִי תִפְאַרְתּוֹ, יַעֲלֶה נָּא עַל רֹאשׁ שִׂמְחָתוֹ.

סְגֻלָּתוֹ תְּהִי בְיָדוֹ עֲטֶרֶת, וּצְנִיף מְלוּכָה צְבִי תִפְאָרֶת.

עֲמוּסִים נְשָׂאָם עֲטֶרֶת עִנְּדָם, מֵאֲשֶׁר יָקְרוּ בְעֵינָיו כִּבְּדָם.

פְּאֵרוֹ עָלַי וּפְאֵרִי עָלָיו, וְקָרוֹב אֵלַי בְּקָרְאִי אֵלָיו.

צַח וְאָדוֹם לִלְבוּשׁוֹ אָדֹם, פּוּרָה בְּדָרְכוֹ בְּבוֹאוֹ מֵאֱדוֹם.

קֶשֶׁר תְּפִלִּין הֶרְאָה לֶעָנָו, תְּמוּנַת יְיָ לְנֶגֶד עֵינָיו.

רוֹצֶה בְּעַמּוֹ עֲנָוִים יְפָאֵר, יוֹשֵׁב תְּהִלּוֹת בָּם לְהִתְפָּאֵר.

לְפִי מעשיך **that is, the human intellect cannot conceive the essence of God, but only his acts.**

על מצח **the plate on Aaron's forehead, upon which was engraved: "Holy to the Lord" (Exodus 28:36).** עטרה **hymns of praise.** נוה הצדק **Jerusalem.**

צבי תפארת . . . **Isaiah 62:3; 46:3; 43:4; Song of Songs 5:10; Isaiah 63:1-3.**

פארו עלי **the** *tefillin* **containing the words** ה' אחד, **"the Lord is One."**

Thy greatness and thy power
They traced in thy mighty work.

> They imaged thee, not as thou art really;
> They described thee by thy acts only.

They depicted thee in countless visions;
Despite all comparisons thou art One.

> They saw in thee both old age and young age,
> With the hair of thy head now grey, now black:

Age in judgment day, youth in time of war,
As a warrior whose hands fight for him,

> A helmet of triumph tied on his head,
> His holy right arm bringing victory;

As though his head is drenched with dew of light,
And his locks are filled with drops of the night.

> He glories in me, he delights in me;
> My crown of beauty he shall ever be.

His head is like pure gold; on the forehead
He engraved his glorious holy name.

> For grace and glory, beauty and splendor,
> His own people has made a crown for him.

The locks of his head are such as in youth;
His curls, forming countless ringlets, are black.

> May his splendid Temple of righteousness
> Be prized by him above his highest joy.

May his people be a crown in his hand,
A royal diadem of great beauty.

> Borne by him, he uplifted and crowned them;
> Being precious to him, he honored them.

His glory rests on me, and mine on him;
He is near to me when I call to him.

> Dazzling he is and ruddy, his clothes red,
> When from treading Edom's winepress he comes.

Meek Moses was shown symbolic tefillin
When the Lord's image was before his eyes.

> Pleased with his people, he glorifies them;
> Enthroned in glories, he glories in them.

רֹאשׁ דְּבָרְךָ אֱמֶת, קוֹרֵא מֵרֹאשׁ דּוֹר וָדוֹר, עַם דּוֹרְשְׁךָ דְּרוֹשׁ.

שִׁית הֲמוֹן שִׁירַי נָא עָלֶיךָ, וְרִנָּתִי תִּקְרַב אֵלֶיךָ.

תְּהִלָּתִי תְּהִי לְרֹאשְׁךָ עֲטֶרֶת, וּתְפִלָּתִי תִּכּוֹן קְטֹרֶת.

תִּיקַר שִׁירַת רָשׁ בְּעֵינֶיךָ, כַּשִּׁיר יוּשַׁר עַל קָרְבָּנֶיךָ.

בִּרְכָתִי תַעֲלֶה לְרֹאשׁ מַשְׁבִּיר, מְחוֹלֵל וּמוֹלִיד צַדִּיק כַּבִּיר.

וּבְבִרְכָתִי תְנַעֲנַע לִי רֹאשׁ, וְאוֹתָהּ קַח לְךָ כִּבְשָׂמִים רֹאשׁ.

יֶעֱרַב נָא שִׂיחִי עָלֶיךָ, כִּי נַפְשִׁי תַעֲרֹג אֵלֶיךָ.

לְךָ, יְיָ, הַגְּדֻלָּה וְהַגְּבוּרָה וְהַתִּפְאֶרֶת וְהַנֵּצַח וְהַהוֹד, כִּי כֹל בַּשָּׁמַיִם וּבָאָרֶץ. לְךָ, יְיָ, הַמַּמְלָכָה וְהַמִּתְנַשֵּׂא לְכֹל לְרֹאשׁ. מִי יְמַלֵּל גְּבוּרוֹת יְיָ, יַשְׁמִיעַ כָּל תְּהִלָּתוֹ.

MOURNERS' KADDISH

הַיּוֹם שַׁבַּת קֹדֶשׁ, שֶׁבּוֹ הָיוּ הַלְוִיִּם אוֹמְרִים בְּבֵית הַמִּקְדָּשׁ:

תהלים צב

מִזְמוֹר שִׁיר לְיוֹם הַשַּׁבָּת. טוֹב לְהֹדוֹת לַיְיָ, וּלְזַמֵּר לְשִׁמְךָ עֶלְיוֹן. לְהַגִּיד בַּבֹּקֶר חַסְדֶּךָ, וֶאֱמוּנָתְךָ בַּלֵּילוֹת. עֲלֵי עָשׂוֹר וַעֲלֵי נָבֶל, עֲלֵי הִגָּיוֹן בְּכִנּוֹר. כִּי שִׂמַּחְתַּנִי יְיָ בְּפָעֳלֶךָ; בְּמַעֲשֵׂי יָדֶיךָ אֲרַנֵּן. מַה גָּדְלוּ מַעֲשֶׂיךָ, יְיָ; מְאֹד עָמְקוּ מַחְשְׁבֹתֶיךָ. אִישׁ בַּעַר לֹא יֵדָע, וּכְסִיל לֹא יָבִין אֶת זֹאת. בִּפְרֹחַ רְשָׁעִים כְּמוֹ עֵשֶׂב, וַיָּצִיצוּ כָּל פֹּעֲלֵי אָוֶן, לְהִשָּׁמְדָם עֲדֵי עַד. וְאַתָּה מָרוֹם לְעֹלָם, יְיָ. כִּי הִנֵּה אֹיְבֶיךָ, יְיָ, כִּי הִנֵּה אֹיְבֶיךָ יֹאבֵדוּ, יִתְפָּרְדוּ כָּל פֹּעֲלֵי אָוֶן. וַתָּרֶם כִּרְאֵים קַרְנִי; בַּלֹּתִי בְּשֶׁמֶן רַעֲנָן. וַתַּבֵּט

בְּרֵאשִׁית בָּרָא אֱלֹהִים alludes to רֹאשׁ דְּבָרְךָ אֱמֶת, the first three words of the Torah, whose final letters spell אֱמֶת.

Thy chief word is truth, Creator of all;
Care for thy people who seek thee forever.
O set my abundant songs before thee;
May my ringing cry come near to thee.
May my praise be deemed a crown for thy head;
Let my prayer rise like incense before thee.
Let a poor man's song be precious to thee
As the song that was sung at the offerings.
May my blessings rise to God who sustains,
Creates and brings forth, the Just, the Mighty.
As for my prayer, nod thy approval,
And accept it as the choicest incense.
May my meditation be sweet to thee,
For all my being is yearning for thee.

Thine, O Lord, is the greatness and the power, the glory and the victory and the majesty; for all that is in heaven and on earth is thine; thine, O Lord, is the kingdom, and thou art supreme over all. Who can describe the mighty deeds of the Lord, or utter all his praise?[1]

Mourners' Kaddish.

This is the holy Sabbath day of the week, on which the Levites in the Temple used to recite:

Psalm 92

A psalm, a song for the Sabbath day. It is good to give thanks to the Lord, and to sing praises to thy name, O Most High; to proclaim thy goodness in the morning, and thy faithfulness at night, with a ten-stringed lyre and a flute, to the sound of a harp. For thou, O Lord, hast made me glad through thy work; I sing for joy at all that thou hast done. How great are thy works, O Lord! How very deep are thy designs! A stupid man cannot know, a fool cannot understand this. When the wicked thrive like grass, and all evildoers flourish, it is that they may be destroyed forever. But thou, O Lord, art supreme for evermore. For lo, thy enemies, O Lord, for lo, thy enemies shall perish; all evildoers shall be dispersed. But thou hast exalted my power exceedingly;

I am anointed with fresh oil. My eye has gazed on my foes; my

---

[1]*Chronicles* 29:11; *Psalm* 106:2.

עֵינִי בְּשׁוּרָי, בַּקָּמִים עָלַי מְרֵעִים תִּשְׁמַעְנָה אָזְנָי. צַדִּיק כַּתָּמָר
יִפְרָח. כְּאֶרֶז בַּלְּבָנוֹן יִשְׂגֶּה. שְׁתוּלִים בְּבֵית יְיָ, בְּחַצְרוֹת אֱלֹהֵינוּ
יַפְרִיחוּ. Reader עוֹד יְנוּבוּן בְּשֵׂיבָה, דְּשֵׁנִים וְרַעֲנַנִּים יִהְיוּ.
לְהַגִּיד כִּי יָשָׁר יְיָ; צוּרִי, וְלֹא עַוְלָתָה בּוֹ.

MOURNERS' KADDISH

יִתְגַּדַּל וְיִתְקַדַּשׁ שְׁמֵהּ רַבָּא בְּעָלְמָא דִי בְרָא כִרְעוּתֵהּ;
וְיַמְלִיךְ מַלְכוּתֵהּ בְּחַיֵּיכוֹן וּבְיוֹמֵיכוֹן, וּבְחַיֵּי דְכָל בֵּית יִשְׂרָאֵל
בַּעֲגָלָא וּבִזְמַן קָרִיב, וְאִמְרוּ אָמֵן.

יְהֵא שְׁמֵהּ רַבָּא מְבָרַךְ לְעָלַם וּלְעָלְמֵי עָלְמַיָּא.

יִתְבָּרַךְ וְיִשְׁתַּבַּח, וְיִתְפָּאַר וְיִתְרוֹמַם, וְיִתְנַשֵּׂא וְיִתְהַדָּר,
וְיִתְעַלֶּה וְיִתְהַלָּל שְׁמֵהּ דְּקֻדְשָׁא, בְּרִיךְ הוּא, לְעֵלָּא מִן כָּל
בִּרְכָתָא וְשִׁירָתָא, תֻּשְׁבְּחָתָא וְנֶחֱמָתָא, דַּאֲמִירָן בְּעָלְמָא,
וְאִמְרוּ אָמֵן.

יְהֵא שְׁלָמָא רַבָּא מִן שְׁמַיָּא, וְחַיִּים, עָלֵינוּ וְעַל כָּל יִשְׂרָאֵל,
וְאִמְרוּ אָמֵן.

עֹשֶׂה שָׁלוֹם בִּמְרוֹמָיו, הוּא יַעֲשֶׂה שָׁלוֹם עָלֵינוּ וְעַל כָּל
יִשְׂרָאֵל, וְאִמְרוּ אָמֵן.

THE KADDISH

The essential part of the Kaddish consists of the congregational response: "May his great name be blessed forever and ever." Around this response, which is found almost verbatim in Daniel 2:20, the whole Kaddish developed. Originally, it was recited at the close of sermons delivered in Aramaic, the language spoken by the Jews for about a thousand years after the Babylonian captivity. Hence the Kaddish was composed in Aramaic, the language in which the religious discourses were held. At a later period the Kaddish was introduced into the liturgy to mark the conclusion of sections of the service or of the reading of the biblical and talmudic passages.

ears have heard my enemies' doom. The righteous will flourish like the palm tree; they will grow like a cedar in Lebanon. Planted in the house of the Lord, they shall flourish in the courts of our God. They shall yield fruit even in old age; vigorous and fresh they shall be, to proclaim that the Lord is just! He is my Strong hold, and there is no wrong in him.

MOURNERS' KADDISH

Glorified and sanctified be God's great name throughout the world which he has created according to his will. May he establish his kingdom, hastening his salvation and the coming of his Messiah, in your lifetime and during your days, and within the life of the entire house of Israel, speedily and soon; and say, Amen.

May his great name be blessed forever and to all eternity.

Blessed and praised, glorified and exalted, extolled and honored, adored and lauded be the name of the Holy One, blessed be he beyond all the blessings and hymns, praises and consolations that are ever spoken in the world; and say, Amen.

May there be abundant peace from heaven, and a good life, for us and for all Israel; and say, Amen.

He who creates peace in his celestial heights, may he create peace for us and for all Israel; and say, Amen.

The Kaddish contains no reference to the dead. The earliest allusion to the Kaddish as a mourners' prayer is found in Maḥzor Vitry, dated 1208, where it is said plainly: "The lad rises and recites Kaddish." One may safely assume that since the Kaddish has as its underlying thought the hope for the redemption and ultimate healing of suffering mankind, the power of redeeming the dead from the sufferings of *Gehinnom* came to be ascribed in the course of time to the recitation of this sublime doxology. Formerly the Kaddish was recited the whole year of mourning, so as to rescue the soul of one's parents from the torture of *Gehinnom* where the wicked are said to spend no less than twelve months. In order not to count one's own parents among the wicked, the period for reciting the Kaddish was later reduced to eleven months.

עושה שלום, which repeats in Hebrew the thought expressed in the preceding Aramaic paragraph, seems to have been added from the meditation recited at the end of the *Shemoneh Esreh*. The same sentence is also added at the end of the grace recited after meals.

שִׁיר שֶׁל יוֹם

The following six psalms are recited on the respective days of the week.

On Sundays:

הַיּוֹם יוֹם רִאשׁוֹן בַּשַּׁבָּת, שֶׁבּוֹ הָיוּ הַלְוִיִּם אוֹמְרִים
בְּבֵית הַמִּקְדָּשׁ:

תהלים כד

לְדָוִד מִזְמוֹר. לַיְיָ הָאָרֶץ וּמְלוֹאָהּ, תֵּבֵל וְיֹשְׁבֵי בָהּ. כִּי הוּא
עַל יַמִּים יְסָדָהּ, וְעַל נְהָרוֹת יְכוֹנְנֶהָ. מִי יַעֲלֶה בְהַר יְיָ, וּמִי
יָקוּם בִּמְקוֹם קָדְשׁוֹ. נְקִי כַפַּיִם וּבַר לֵבָב, אֲשֶׁר לֹא נָשָׂא לַשָּׁוְא
נַפְשִׁי, וְלֹא נִשְׁבַּע לְמִרְמָה. יִשָּׂא בְרָכָה מֵאֵת יְיָ, וּצְדָקָה מֵאֱלֹהֵי
יִשְׁעוֹ. זֶה דּוֹר דֹּרְשָׁיו, מְבַקְשֵׁי פָנֶיךָ יַעֲקֹב, סֶלָה. שְׂאוּ שְׁעָרִים
רָאשֵׁיכֶם, וְהִנָּשְׂאוּ פִּתְחֵי עוֹלָם, וְיָבוֹא מֶלֶךְ הַכָּבוֹד. מִי זֶה
מֶלֶךְ הַכָּבוֹד, יְיָ עִזּוּז וְגִבּוֹר, יְיָ גִּבּוֹר מִלְחָמָה. שְׂאוּ שְׁעָרִים
רָאשֵׁיכֶם, וּשְׂאוּ פִּתְחֵי עוֹלָם, וְיָבֹא מֶלֶךְ הַכָּבוֹד. Reader מִי
הוּא זֶה מֶלֶךְ הַכָּבוֹד, יְיָ צְבָאוֹת הוּא מֶלֶךְ הַכָּבוֹד, סֶלָה.

Mourners' Kaddish.

On Mondays:

הַיּוֹם יוֹם שֵׁנִי בַּשַּׁבָּת, שֶׁבּוֹ הָיוּ הַלְוִיִּם אוֹמְרִים
בְּבֵית הַמִּקְדָּשׁ:

תהלים מח

שִׁיר מִזְמוֹר לִבְנֵי קֹרַח. גָּדוֹל יְיָ וּמְהֻלָּל מְאֹד, בְּעִיר אֱלֹהֵינוּ,
הַר קָדְשׁוֹ. יְפֵה נוֹף, מְשׂוֹשׂ כָּל הָאָרֶץ הַר צִיּוֹן, יַרְכְּתֵי צָפוֹן,
קִרְיַת מֶלֶךְ רָב. אֱלֹהִים בְּאַרְמְנוֹתֶיהָ נוֹדַע לְמִשְׂגָּב. כִּי הִנֵּה

שיר של יום, the Psalm of the Day, was chanted by the Levites each day during the Temple service (Mishnah Tamid 7:4). According to the Talmud, the daily psalms were intended to recall the incidents of the six days of creation (Rosh Hashanah 31a).

PSALM OF THE DAY

The following six psalms are recited on the respective days of the week.

On Sundays:

Psalm 24

A psalm of David. The earth and its fullness belong to the Lord, the entire world and its inhabitants. For it is he who has founded it upon the seas, and established it on the floods. Who may ascend the Lord's mountain? Who may stand within his holy place? He who has clean hands and a pure heart; he who strives not after vanity and swears not deceitfully. He will receive a blessing from the Lord, and justice from his saving God. Such is the generation of those who are in quest of him, who seek the presence of the God of Jacob. Raise your heads, O gates, raise yourselves, you ancient doors, that the glorious King may come in. Who, then, is the glorious King? The Lord strong and mighty, the Lord strong in battle. Raise your heads, O gates, raise yourselves, you ancient doors, that the glorious King may come in. Who, then, is the glorious King? The Lord of hosts, he is the glorious King.

Mourners' Kaddish.

On Mondays:

This is the second day of the week, on which the Levites in the Temple used to recite:

Psalm 48

A song, a psalm of the Korahites. Great is the Lord, and highly to be praised, in the city of our God, his holy mountain. Beautiful in elevation, the joy of the whole earth, on the northern slope, is Mount Zion, the city of the great King. God in her palaces has made himself known as a stronghold. For lo, the kings assembled

---

מזמור a poem sung to the accompaniment of musical instruments in the Temple service.

שאו שערים ראשיכם The ancient gates of Zion are poetically commanded to raise their heads, in token of reverence to God whose entrance is an act of condescension. Different parts of this psalm were sung by different choirs of singers at the time when David brought the ark to Mount Zion.

בני קרח descendants of Korah, a division of Levites who sang in the Temple.

הַמְּלָכִים נוֹעֲדוּ, עָבְרוּ יַחְדָּו. הֵמָּה רָאוּ, כֵּן תָּמָהוּ, נִבְהֲלוּ
נֶחְפָּזוּ. רְעָדָה אֲחָזָתַם שָׁם, חִיל כַּיּוֹלֵדָה. בְּרוּחַ קָדִים תְּשַׁבֵּר
אֳנִיּוֹת תַּרְשִׁישׁ. כַּאֲשֶׁר שָׁמַעְנוּ, כֵּן רָאִינוּ בְּעִיר יְיָ צְבָאוֹת, בְּעִיר
אֱלֹהֵינוּ; אֱלֹהִים יְכוֹנְנֶהָ עַד עוֹלָם, סֶלָה. דִּמִּינוּ אֱלֹהִים
חַסְדֶּךָ, בְּקֶרֶב הֵיכָלֶךָ. כְּשִׁמְךָ אֱלֹהִים, כֵּן תְּהִלָּתְךָ עַל קַצְוֵי
אֶרֶץ; צֶדֶק מָלְאָה יְמִינֶךָ. יִשְׂמַח הַר צִיּוֹן, תָּגֵלְנָה בְּנוֹת יְהוּדָה,
לְמַעַן מִשְׁפָּטֶיךָ. סֹבּוּ צִיּוֹן וְהַקִּיפוּהָ, סִפְרוּ מִגְדָּלֶיהָ. שִׁיתוּ
לִבְּכֶם לְחֵילָה, פַּסְּגוּ אַרְמְנוֹתֶיהָ, לְמַעַן תְּסַפְּרוּ לְדוֹר אַחֲרוֹן.
Reader כִּי זֶה אֱלֹהִים אֱלֹהֵינוּ עוֹלָם וָעֶד; הוּא יְנַהֲגֵנוּ עַל מוּת.

Mourners' Kaddish.

On Tuesdays:

הַיּוֹם יוֹם שְׁלִישִׁי בַּשַּׁבָּת, שֶׁבּוֹ הָיוּ הַלְוִיִּם אוֹמְרִים
בְּבֵית הַמִּקְדָּשׁ:

תהלים פב

מִזְמוֹר לְאָסָף. אֱלֹהִים נִצָּב בַּעֲדַת אֵל, בְּקֶרֶב אֱלֹהִים
יִשְׁפֹּט. עַד מָתַי תִּשְׁפְּטוּ עָוֶל, וּפְנֵי רְשָׁעִים תִּשְׂאוּ סֶלָה. שִׁפְטוּ
דָל וְיָתוֹם, עָנִי וָרָשׁ הַצְדִּיקוּ. פַּלְּטוּ דַל וְאֶבְיוֹן, מִיַּד רְשָׁעִים
הַצִּילוּ. לֹא יָדְעוּ וְלֹא יָבִינוּ, בַּחֲשֵׁכָה יִתְהַלָּכוּ; יִמּוֹטוּ כָּל
מוֹסְדֵי אָרֶץ. אֲנִי אָמַרְתִּי אֱלֹהִים אַתֶּם, וּבְנֵי עֶלְיוֹן כֻּלְּכֶם.
אָכֵן כְּאָדָם תְּמוּתוּן, וּכְאַחַד הַשָּׂרִים תִּפֹּלוּ. Reader קוּמָה
אֱלֹהִים, שָׁפְטָה הָאָרֶץ; כִּי אַתָּה תִנְחַל בְּכָל הַגּוֹיִם.

Mourners' Kaddish.

המה ראו they saw the impregnable might of Zion and were terrified.

אניות תרשיש the great seagoing vessels that made the long voyage to Tarshish, a seacoast city in Spain (or Carthage).

כאשר שמענו כן ראינו that is, history has repeated itself. We have now experienced events similar to those which occurred in the past. This psalm celebrates the escape of Jerusalem from a threatened invasion by the armies of various confederate kings.

themselves, they invaded together. They saw [her defense] and were amazed; they were terrified, they fled in haste. Panic seized them, anguish as of a woman in travail. With the east wind thou breakest the ships of Tarshish. As we have heard, so have we seen now in the city of the Lord of hosts, in the city of our God; may God establish it forever. We meditate on thy kindness, O God, within thy temple. Like thy name, O God, thy fame shall extend to the ends of the earth; thy right hand is full of justice. Let Mount Zion be glad, let the towns of Judah rejoice, because of thy judgments. Walk about Zion, go round her, count her towers, mark well her ramparts, go through her palaces, that you may tell a later generation that such is God, our God, forever and ever. He will guide us eternally.

Mourners' Kaddish.

On Tuesday:

This is the third day of the week, on which the Levites in the Temple used to recite:

Psalm 82

A psalm of Asaph. God stands in the divine assembly; in the midst of the judges he gives judgment. "How long will you judge unjustly, and show partiality toward the wicked? Do justice to the poor and fatherless; deal righteously with the afflicted and destitute. Rescue the poor and needy; save them from the hand of the wicked." But they neither know nor understand; they walk about in darkness; all the foundations of the earth are shaken. I thought you were angels, that you were all sons of the Most High. Yet you shall die as men do, and fall like any prince. Arise, O God, rule the earth, for thou hast dominion over all the nations.

Mourners' Kaddish.

... סובו ציון that is, after the miraculous deliverance of Zion, its inhabitants can now freely walk around and contemplate the safety of the walls and towers and palaces so lately menaced with destruction.

... נצב בעדת אל God takes his stand in the assembly summoned by him, and denounces the wickedness and partiality of judges. He reminds them of their duties, and declares that because they are ignorant and corrupt human society is undermined.

... אני אמרתי I appointed you as judges and thus invested you with authority of administering divine justice; however, your high title will not exempt you from punishment. You shall die like common men, and fall like any other prince.

קומה The psalmist pleads that God should act as judge over all peoples, since the human judges have failed so miserably.

On Wednesdays:

הַיּוֹם יוֹם רְבִיעִי בַּשַּׁבָּת, שֶׁבּוֹ הָיוּ הַלְוִיִּם אוֹמְרִים
בְּבֵית הַמִּקְדָּשׁ:

תהלים צד: צה, א–ג

אֵל נְקָמוֹת, יְיָ, אֵל נְקָמוֹת, הוֹפִיעַ. הִנָּשֵׂא, שֹׁפֵט הָאָרֶץ,
הָשֵׁב גְּמוּל עַל גֵּאִים. עַד מָתַי רְשָׁעִים, יְיָ, עַד מָתַי רְשָׁעִים
יַעֲלֹזוּ. יַבִּיעוּ יְדַבְּרוּ עָתָק, יִתְאַמְּרוּ כָּל פֹּעֲלֵי אָוֶן. עַמְּךָ יְיָ
יְדַכְּאוּ, וְנַחֲלָתְךָ יְעַנּוּ. אַלְמָנָה וְגֵר יַהֲרֹגוּ, וִיתוֹמִים יְרַצֵּחוּ.
וַיֹּאמְרוּ לֹא יִרְאֶה יָּהּ, וְלֹא יָבִין אֱלֹהֵי יַעֲקֹב. בִּינוּ בֹּעֲרִים
בָּעָם, וּכְסִילִים מָתַי תַּשְׂכִּילוּ. הֲנֹטַע אֹזֶן הֲלֹא יִשְׁמָע, אִם
יֹצֵר עַיִן הֲלֹא יַבִּיט. הֲיֹסֵר גּוֹיִם הֲלֹא יוֹכִיחַ, הַמְלַמֵּד אָדָם
דָּעַת. יְיָ יֹדֵעַ מַחְשְׁבוֹת אָדָם, כִּי הֵמָּה הָבֶל. אַשְׁרֵי הַגֶּבֶר
אֲשֶׁר תְּיַסְּרֶנּוּ יָּהּ, וּמִתּוֹרָתְךָ תְלַמְּדֶנּוּ. לְהַשְׁקִיט לוֹ מִימֵי רָע,
עַד יִכָּרֶה לָרָשָׁע שָׁחַת. כִּי לֹא יִטֹּשׁ יְיָ עַמּוֹ, וְנַחֲלָתוֹ לֹא יַעֲזֹב.
כִּי עַד צֶדֶק יָשׁוּב מִשְׁפָּט, וְאַחֲרָיו כָּל יִשְׁרֵי לֵב. מִי יָקוּם לִי
עִם מְרֵעִים, מִי יִתְיַצֵּב לִי עִם פֹּעֲלֵי אָוֶן. לוּלֵי יְיָ עֶזְרָתָה לִּי,
כִּמְעַט, שָׁכְנָה דוּמָה נַפְשִׁי. אִם אָמַרְתִּי מָטָה רַגְלִי, חַסְדְּךָ יְיָ
יִסְעָדֵנִי. בְּרֹב שַׂרְעַפַּי בְּקִרְבִּי, תַּנְחוּמֶיךָ יְשַׁעַשְׁעוּ נַפְשִׁי.
הַיְחָבְרְךָ כִּסֵּא הַוּוֹת, יֹצֵר עָמָל עֲלֵי חֹק. יָגוֹדּוּ עַל נֶפֶשׁ צַדִּיק,
וְדָם נָקִי יַרְשִׁיעוּ. וַיְהִי יְיָ לִי לְמִשְׂגָּב, וֵאלֹהַי לְצוּר מַחְסִי. וַיָּשֶׁב
עֲלֵיהֶם אֶת אוֹנָם, וּבְרָעָתָם יַצְמִיתֵם; יַצְמִיתֵם יְיָ אֱלֹהֵינוּ.

לְכוּ נְרַנְּנָה לַיְיָ, נָרִיעָה לְצוּר יִשְׁעֵנוּ. נְקַדְּמָה פָנָיו בְּתוֹדָה,

---

אל נקמות is repeated for emphasis. The psalmist appeals to God to punish
the arrogant who contemptuously declare that God is indifferent to the sufferings of his people. He then turns to argue with those who foolishly agree
with their oppressors and think that God will not defent them. He who gave
others the power to hear and see can surely himself hear and see. God knows

This is the fourth day of the week, on which the Levites in the Temple used to recite:

Psalms 94; 95:1–3

God of retribution, Lord God of retribution, appear! Arise, thou judge of the earth, render to the arrogant what they deserve. How long shall the wicked, O Lord, how long shall the wicked exult? They bluster, they speak arrogantly; all the evildoers act boastfully. They crush thy people, O Lord, and afflict thy heritage. The widow and the stranger they slay, and the fatherless they murder. And they think the Lord does not see, the God of Jacob does not observe. Consider, you most stupid of the people; you fools, when will you understand? He who sets the ear, does he not hear? He who forms the eye, does he not see? He who punishes nations, shall he not punish you? He who teaches man knowledge? The Lord knows the inner thoughts of men; indeed, they are futile. Happy is the man whom thou dost instruct, O Lord, and teachest him out of thy Torah, granting him relief in days of adversity, till a pit is dug for the wicked. Indeed, the Lord will not abandon his people, nor forsake his heritage. For judgment shall again conform with justice, and all the upright in heart will follow it. Who rises up for me against the ungodly? Who stands up for me against the wrongdoers? If the Lord had not been my help, I would have soon dwelt in the silent grave. When I think my foot is slipping, thy goodness, O Lord, holds me up. When my cares are many within me, thy comforts cheer me. Can one in the seat of wickedness have fellowship with thee—one who frames evil by law? They band themselves against the life of the righteous, and condemn innocent blood. But the Lord is my stronghold; my God is the rock of my safety. He will requite them for their crime, and destroy them for their wickedness; the Lord our God will destroy them.

Come, let us sing to the Lord; let us acclaim our saving Stronghold. Let us approach him with thanksgiving; let us acclaim him

---

the evil thoughts of the wicked, and eventually the righteous will be vindicated when the day of retribution comes. It is unthinkable that God would abandon his people to the ravages of lawless judges and tyrannical rulers.

בִּזְמָרוֹת נָרִיעַ לוֹ. Reader כִּי אֵל גָּדוֹל יְיָ, וּמֶלֶךְ גָּדוֹל עַל כָּל אֱלֹהִים.

Mourners' Kaddish.

On Thursdays:

הַיּוֹם יוֹם חֲמִישִׁי בַּשַּׁבָּת, שֶׁבּוֹ הָיוּ הַלְוִיִּם אוֹמְרִים בְּבֵית הַמִּקְדָּשׁ:

תהלים פא

לַמְנַצֵּחַ עַל הַגִּתִּית לְאָסָף. הַרְנִינוּ לֵאלֹהִים עוּזֵּנוּ, הָרִיעוּ לֵאלֹהֵי יַעֲקֹב. שְׂאוּ זִמְרָה וּתְנוּ תֹף, כִּנּוֹר נָעִים עִם נָבֶל. תִּקְעוּ בַחֹדֶשׁ שׁוֹפָר, בַּכֶּסֶה לְיוֹם חַגֵּנוּ. כִּי חֹק לְיִשְׂרָאֵל הוּא, מִשְׁפָּט לֵאלֹהֵי יַעֲקֹב. עֵדוּת בִּיהוֹסֵף שָׂמוֹ, בְּצֵאתוֹ עַל אֶרֶץ מִצְרָיִם; שְׂפַת לֹא יָדַעְתִּי אֶשְׁמָע. הֲסִירוֹתִי מִסֵּבֶל שִׁכְמוֹ, כַּפָּיו מִדּוּד תַּעֲבֹרְנָה. בַּצָּרָה קָרָאתָ וָאֲחַלְּצֶךָּ, אֶעֶנְךָ בְּסֵתֶר רַעַם; אֶבְחָנְךָ עַל מֵי מְרִיבָה, סֶלָה. שְׁמַע עַמִּי וְאָעִידָה בָּךְ, יִשְׂרָאֵל אִם תִּשְׁמַע לִי. לֹא יִהְיֶה בְךָ אֵל זָר, וְלֹא תִשְׁתַּחֲוֶה לְאֵל נֵכָר. אָנֹכִי יְיָ אֱלֹהֶיךָ הַמַּעַלְךָ מֵאֶרֶץ מִצְרָיִם; הַרְחֶב־פִּיךָ וַאֲמַלְאֵהוּ. וְלֹא שָׁמַע עַמִּי לְקוֹלִי, וְיִשְׂרָאֵל לֹא אָבָה לִי. וָאֲשַׁלְּחֵהוּ בִּשְׁרִירוּת לִבָּם, יֵלְכוּ בְּמוֹעֲצוֹתֵיהֶם. לוּ עַמִּי שֹׁמֵעַ לִי, יִשְׂרָאֵל בִּדְרָכַי יְהַלֵּכוּ. כִּמְעַט אוֹיְבֵיהֶם אַכְנִיעַ, וְעַל צָרֵיהֶם אָשִׁיב יָדִי. מְשַׂנְאֵי יְיָ יְכַחֲשׁוּ לוֹ, וִיהִי עִתָּם לְעוֹלָם. Reader וַיַּאֲכִילֵהוּ מֵחֵלֶב חִטָּה, וּמִצּוּר דְּבַשׁ אַשְׂבִּיעֶךָ.

Mourners' Kaddish.

למנצח occurs in the titles of fifty-five psalms, and refers to the use of the psalm in the Temple services. The word means the conductor of the Temple choir, who trained the choir and led the music.

על הגתית occurs in the titles of three psalms. According to the Targum, *Gittith* was a harp used by the Philistines of Gath. Since the Hebrew word *gath* means "a winepress," *Gittith* may mean a melody sung at vintage festivals.

בחדש is rendered by the Targum and the Talmud: *Rosh Ḥodesh Tishri*, that is *Rosh Hashanah*. Metal trumpets, and not a *shofar*, were used on all other occasions of *Rosh Ḥodesh*.

with songs of praise. For the Lord is a great God, a King supreme above all powers.   *Mourners' Kaddish.*

On Thursday:

This is the fifth day of the week, on which the Levites in the Temple used to recite: *Psalm 81*

For the Choirmaster, upon the *Gittith;* a psalm of Asaph.

Sing aloud to God our strength; shout for joy to the God of Jacob. Raise the chorus, sound the drum, the sweet harp and the lute. Sound the shofar at the new moon, the time designated for our feast day. This is a statute for Israel, an ordinance of the God of Jacob. He made it a law in Joseph, when he went forth against the land of Egypt. I heard an unfamiliar speech: "I have removed the burden from your shoulder; your hands are relieved from the heavy basket. In trouble you called, and I saved you; I answered you from the thunder cloud; I tested you at the waters of Meribah. Hear, my people, while I warn you; O Israel, if you would only listen to me! You shall have no strange god; you shall worship no foreign god. I am the Lord your God, who brought you up from the land of Egypt; open your mouth, and I will fill it. But my people did not listen to my voice; Israel would have none of me. So I left them to their own stubbornness, that they might follow their own devices. If only my people would listen to me, if Israel would only walk in my ways! I would soon subdue their foes, and turn my hand against their oppressors. Those who hate the Lord would cringe before them, and their time would be forever. I would feed them with the finest of wheat, and with honey from the rock would I satisfy them.

Mourners' Kaddish.

בכסה ליום חגנו is traditionally interpreted to refer to Rosh Hashanah, the festival that occurs at the beginning of the month of *Tishri.*

יהוסף is a synonym for Israel, so called from the favored son of Israel. In Psalm 77:16, Jacob and Joseph are named as the fathers of the entire people of Israel.

שפת לא ידעתי . . . The psalmist represents Israel as quoting the following words of God, heard for the first time after the exodus from Egypt.

מי מריבה refers to Exodus 17:7; Numbers 20:13.

הרחב פיך . . . God will abundantly supply your needs as long as you are faithful to him.

משנאי ה' . . . God's enemies are the enemies of his people, and he would compel them to pay homage to Israel. Israel's national existence and prosperity would know no end.

On Fridays:

הַיּוֹם יוֹם שִׁשִּׁי בַּשַּׁבָּת, שֶׁבּוֹ הָיוּ הַלְוִיִּם אוֹמְרִים בְּבֵית הַמִּקְדָּשׁ:

תהלים צג

יְיָ מָלָךְ, גֵּאוּת לָבֵשׁ; לָבֵשׁ יְיָ, עֹז הִתְאַזָּר; אַף תִּכּוֹן תֵּבֵל,
בַּל תִּמּוֹט. נָכוֹן כִּסְאֲךָ מֵאָז, מֵעוֹלָם אָתָּה. נָשְׂאוּ נְהָרוֹת, יְיָ,
נָשְׂאוּ נְהָרוֹת קוֹלָם, יִשְׂאוּ נְהָרוֹת דָּכְיָם. מִקֹּלוֹת מַיִם רַבִּים,
אַדִּירִים מִשְׁבְּרֵי יָם, אַדִּיר בַּמָּרוֹם יְיָ. Reader עֵדֹתֶיךָ נֶאֶמְנוּ
מְאֹד: לְבֵיתְךָ נַאֲוָה קֹדֶשׁ, יְיָ, לְאֹרֶךְ יָמִים.

Mourners' Kaddish.

בְּטֶרֶם כָּל יְצִיר נִבְרָא.	אֲדוֹן עוֹלָם אֲשֶׁר מָלַךְ
אֲזַי מֶלֶךְ שְׁמוֹ נִקְרָא.	לְעֵת נַעֲשָׂה בְחֶפְצוֹ כֹּל
לְבַדּוֹ יִמְלוֹךְ נוֹרָא.	וְאַחֲרֵי כִּכְלוֹת הַכֹּל
וְהוּא יִהְיֶה בְּתִפְאָרָה.	וְהוּא הָיָה וְהוּא הֹוֶה
לְהַמְשִׁיל לוֹ לְהַחְבִּירָה.	וְהוּא אֶחָד וְאֵין שֵׁנִי
וְלוֹ הָעֹז וְהַמִּשְׂרָה.	בְּלִי רֵאשִׁית בְּלִי תַכְלִית
וְצוּר חֶבְלִי בְּעֵת צָרָה.	וְהוּא אֵלִי וְחַי גּוֹאֲלִי
מְנָת כּוֹסִי בְּיוֹם אֶקְרָא.	וְהוּא נִסִּי וּמָנוֹס לִי
בְּעֵת אִישַׁן וְאָעִירָה.	בְּיָדוֹ אַפְקִיד רוּחִי
יְיָ לִי וְלֹא אִירָא.	וְעִם רוּחִי גְּוִיָּתִי

אדון עולם treats of God's omnipotence and providence. This noble hymn
has been attributed to various poets, particularly to Solomon ibn Gabirol
who flourished in Spain during the eleventh century. It has been part of the
morning service since the fifteenth century. It is composed of ten lines, each
of which consists of twelve syllables. A single rhyme runs through it.

282 *Psalm of the Day*

On Fridays:

This is the first day of the week, on which the Levites in the Temple used to recite:

Psalm 93

The Lord is King; he is robed in majesty; the Lord is robed, he has girded himself with strength; thus the world is set firm and cannot be shaken. Thy throne stands firm from of old, thou art from all eternity. The floods have lifted up, O Lord, the floods have lifted up their voice; the floods lift up their mighty waves. But above the sound of many waters, mighty breakers of the sea, the Lord on high stands supreme. Thy testimonies are very sure; holiness befits thy house, O Lord, for all time.

ADON OLAM

He is the eternal Lord who reigned
Before any being was created.
At the time when all was made by his will,
He was at once acknowledged as King.
And at the end, when all shall cease to be,
The revered God alone shall still be King.
He was, he is, and he shall be
In glorious eternity.
He is One, and there is no other
To compare to him, to place beside him.
He is without beginning, without end;
Power and dominion belong to him.
He is my God, my living Redeemer,
My stronghold in times of distress.
He is my guide and my refuge,
My share of bliss the day I call.
To him I entrust my spirit
When I sleep and when I wake.
As long as my soul is with my body
The Lord is with me; I am not afraid.

קִדּוּשָׁא רַבָּה לְיוֹם טוֹב

On Sabbath:

(וְשָׁמְרוּ בְנֵי יִשְׂרָאֵל אֶת הַשַּׁבָּת, לַעֲשׂוֹת אֶת הַשַּׁבָּת לְדֹרֹתָם בְּרִית עוֹלָם. בֵּינִי וּבֵין בְּנֵי יִשְׂרָאֵל אוֹת הִיא לְעוֹלָם, כִּי שֵׁשֶׁת יָמִים עָשָׂה יְיָ אֶת הַשָּׁמַיִם וְאֶת הָאָרֶץ, וּבַיּוֹם הַשְּׁבִיעִי שָׁבַת וַיִּנָּפַשׁ. עַל כֵּן בֵּרַךְ יְיָ אֶת יוֹם הַשַּׁבָּת וַיְקַדְּשֵׁהוּ.)

אֵלֶּה מוֹעֲדֵי יְיָ, מִקְרָאֵי קֹדֶשׁ, אֲשֶׁר תִּקְרְאוּ אוֹתָם בְּמוֹעֲדָם.
וַיְדַבֵּר מֹשֶׁה אֶת מֹעֲדֵי יְיָ אֶל בְּנֵי יִשְׂרָאֵל.
סָבְרֵי מָרָנָן וְרַבּוֹתַי.
בָּרוּךְ אַתָּה, יְיָ אֱלֹהֵינוּ, מֶלֶךְ הָעוֹלָם, בּוֹרֵא פְּרִי הַגָּפֶן.

Before the evening and morning meals on Sabbaths and festivals, *Kiddush* (Sanctification) is recited over wine, the symbol of joy, for it is "wine that cheers man's heart" (Psalm 104:15). The use of wine in connection with the *Kiddush* is spoken of in the Talmud, where the biblical command "remember the Sabbath" is interpreted to mean "remember it over wine" (Pesaḥim 106a). Wine is metaphorically represented as the essence of goodness. Israel is likened to a vine brought from Egypt and planted in Eretz Yisrael, where it took deep root and prospered (Psalm 80:9-11). When wine is not available, the *Kiddush* is recited over two loaves of bread (*leḥem mishneh*) that commemorate the double portion of manna that was gathered on Fridays.

The origin of the *Kiddush* is traced back to the early period of the Second Temple, and is attributed to the men of the Great Assembly, who flourished at that time.

The morning *Kiddush* for Sabbaths and festivals is called *Kiddusha Rabbah* (the great *Kiddush*) by way of inversion, since it is of later origin and of less importance than the *Kiddush* that is recited in the evening (Pesaḥim 106a). Similarly, the Hebrew expression סַגִּי נְהוֹר, "rich of light," is a euphemism for blind. Rashi, however, explains the phrase *Kiddusha Rabbah* to mean the short benediction over wine, בּוֹרֵא פְּרִי הַגֶּפֶן, since it is used in every *Kiddush* (וְקָרֵי לֵיהּ קִידּוּשָׁא רַבָּה דְּאָכְלוּהוּ קִידּוּשֵׁי קָאָמְרֵי לֵיהּ).

The afternoon service known as *Minḥah* is one of the three daily services mentioned in Daniel 6:11. It consists of *Ashré* (Psalm 145), *Amidah* and *Alenu*. When there is a *minyan* (a quorum of ten adult males), the leader repeats the *Amidah* (standing prayer) aloud, reciting the *Kedushah* and the *Kaddishim*. On Sabbaths and on fast days a section of the Torah is read after the *Amidah*. The term *Minḥah* has been connected with Elijah's prayer at the hour of the

MORNING KIDDUSH FOR FESTIVALS

On Sabbath:

(The children of Israel shall keep the Sabbath, observing the Sabbath throughout their generations as an everlasting covenant. It is a sign between me and the children of Israel forever, that in six days the Lord made the heavens and the earth, and on the seventh day he ceased from work and rested.

Therefore the Lord blessed the Sabbath day and hallowed it.)

These are the Lord's festivals, holy convocations, which you shall proclaim in their proper season.

Moses announced the Lord's festivals, to the children of Israel.

Blessed art thou, Lord our God, King of the universe, who createst the fruit of the vine.

"evening offering" (I Kings 18:36); hence its importance is stressed in the Talmud (Berakhoth 6b).

According to traditional lore, the patriarchs Abraham, Isaac and Jacob were the authors of *Shaḥarith*, *Minḥah* and *Ma'ariv* (morning, afternoon and evening prayers), respectively. The Talmud distinguishes between *Minḥah Gedolah, Minḥah Ketannah,* and *Pelag Minḥah;* from 12:30 to sunset, from 3:30 to sunset, and from 4:45 to sunset, respectively (Berakhoth 26b). The third meal on Sabbaths is eaten between *Minḥah* and *Ma'ariv.*

The term *minḥah* occurs in the Bible in the sense of gift and meal-offering. It is only in talmudic literature that the word denotes afternoon service. *Shaḥarith* and *Minḥah* correspond to the daily sacrifice (*Tamid*) that was offered in the Temple each morning and each afternoon beginning at 12:30. Hence, *Minḥah* may be recited at any time from 12:30 p.m. to sunset. For the sake of convenience, the *Minḥah* service was postponed in the nineteenth century to very near sunset, so that it might be followed by the *Ma'ariv* service after a short interval.

Uva l'Tsiyyon (a redeemer shall come to Zion), consisting of biblical quotations accompanied by the paraphrase of the Targum, has been designed to enable every Jew to have a daily share in the study of the Torah (*Rashi,* Sotah 49a).

It is referred to as *Kedushah d'sidra* because the threefold repetition *holy, holy, holy* from Isaiah 6:3 forms here part of a series of other biblical verses. On Sabbaths and festivals, when the Torah and the Prophets are publicly recited at great length, the reading of *Uva l'Tsiyyon* is postponed from the morning to the afternoon service.

מִנְחָה לְיוֹם טוֹב

אַשְׁרֵי יוֹשְׁבֵי בֵיתֶךָ; עוֹד יְהַלְלוּךָ סֶּלָה.

אַשְׁרֵי הָעָם שֶׁכָּכָה לּוֹ; אַשְׁרֵי הָעָם שֶׁיְיָ אֱלֹהָיו.

תהלים קמה

תְּהִלָּה לְדָוִד

אֲרוֹמִמְךָ, אֱלוֹהַי הַמֶּלֶךְ, וַאֲבָרְכָה שִׁמְךָ לְעוֹלָם וָעֶד.

בְּכָל יוֹם אֲבָרְכֶךָּ, וַאֲהַלְלָה שִׁמְךָ לְעוֹלָם וָעֶד.

גָּדוֹל יְיָ וּמְהֻלָּל מְאֹד, וְלִגְדֻלָּתוֹ אֵין חֵקֶר.

דּוֹר לְדוֹר יְשַׁבַּח מַעֲשֶׂיךָ, וּגְבוּרֹתֶיךָ יַגִּידוּ.

הֲדַר כְּבוֹד הוֹדֶךָ וְדִבְרֵי נִפְלְאֹתֶיךָ אָשִׂיחָה.

וֶעֱזוּז נוֹרְאֹתֶיךָ יֹאמֵרוּ, וּגְדֻלָּתְךָ אֲסַפְּרֶנָּה.

זֵכֶר רַב טוּבְךָ יַבִּיעוּ, וְצִדְקָתְךָ יְרַנֵּנוּ.

חַנּוּן וְרַחוּם יְיָ, אֶרֶךְ אַפַּיִם וּגְדָל־חָסֶד.

טוֹב יְיָ לַכֹּל, וְרַחֲמָיו עַל כָּל מַעֲשָׂיו.

יוֹדוּךָ יְיָ כָּל מַעֲשֶׂיךָ, וַחֲסִידֶיךָ יְבָרְכוּכָה.

כְּבוֹד מַלְכוּתְךָ יֹאמֵרוּ, וּגְבוּרָתְךָ יְדַבֵּרוּ.

לְהוֹדִיעַ לִבְנֵי הָאָדָם גְּבוּרֹתָיו, וּכְבוֹד הֲדַר מַלְכוּתוֹ.

מַלְכוּתְךָ מַלְכוּת כָּל עֹלָמִים, וּמֶמְשַׁלְתְּךָ בְּכָל דּוֹר וָדֹר.

סוֹמֵךְ יְיָ לְכָל הַנֹּפְלִים, וְזוֹקֵף לְכָל הַכְּפוּפִים.

עֵינֵי כֹל אֵלֶיךָ יְשַׂבֵּרוּ, וְאַתָּה נוֹתֵן לָהֶם אֶת אָכְלָם בְּעִתּוֹ.

Happy are those who dwell in thy house;
They are ever praising thee.
Happy the people that is so situated;
Happy the people whose God is the Lord.[1]

Psalm 145

A hymn of praise by David.

I extol thee, my God the King,
And bless thy name forever and ever.
Every day I bless thee,
And praise thy name forever and ever.
Great is the Lord and most worthy of praise;
His greatness is unsearchable.
One generation to another praises thy works;
They recount thy mighty acts.
On the splendor of thy glorious majesty
And on thy wondrous deeds I meditate.
They speak of thy awe-inspiring might,
And I tell of thy greatness.
They spread the fame of thy great goodness,
And sing of thy righteousness.
Gracious and merciful is the Lord,
Slow to anger and of great kindness.
The Lord is good to all,
And his compassion is over all his works.
All thy works praise thee, O Lord,
And thy faithful followers bless thee.
They speak of thy glorious kingdom,
And talk of thy might,
To let men know thy mighty deeds,
And the glorious splendor of thy kingdom.
Thy kingdom is a kingdom of all ages,
And thy dominion is for all generations.
The Lord upholds all who fall,
And raises all who are bowed down.
The eyes of all look hopefully to thee,
And thou givest them their food in due season.

[1] *Psalms* 84:5; 144:15.

פּוֹתֵחַ אֶת יָדֶךָ, וּמַשְׂבִּיעַ לְכָל חַי רָצוֹן.

צַדִּיק יְיָ בְּכָל דְּרָכָיו, וְחָסִיד בְּכָל מַעֲשָׂיו.

קָרוֹב יְיָ לְכָל קֹרְאָיו, לְכֹל אֲשֶׁר יִקְרָאֻהוּ בֶאֱמֶת.

רְצוֹן יְרֵאָיו יַעֲשֶׂה, וְאֶת שַׁוְעָתָם יִשְׁמַע וְיוֹשִׁיעֵם.

שׁוֹמֵר יְיָ אֶת כָּל אֹהֲבָיו, וְאֵת כָּל הָרְשָׁעִים יַשְׁמִיד.

תְּהִלַּת יְיָ יְדַבֶּר־פִּי; וִיבָרֵךְ כָּל בָּשָׂר שֵׁם קָדְשׁוֹ לְעוֹלָם וָעֶד.

Reader וַאֲנַחְנוּ נְבָרֵךְ יָהּ מֵעַתָּה וְעַד עוֹלָם; הַלְלוּיָהּ.

וּבָא לְצִיּוֹן גּוֹאֵל, וּלְשָׁבֵי פֶשַׁע בְּיַעֲקֹב, נְאֻם יְיָ. וַאֲנִי, זֹאת בְּרִיתִי אוֹתָם, אָמַר יְיָ: רוּחִי אֲשֶׁר עָלֶיךָ, וּדְבָרַי אֲשֶׁר שַׂמְתִּי בְּפִיךָ לֹא יָמוּשׁוּ מִפִּיךָ וּמִפִּי זַרְעֲךָ, וּמִפִּי זֶרַע זַרְעֲךָ, אָמַר יְיָ, מֵעַתָּה וְעַד עוֹלָם. וְאַתָּה קָדוֹשׁ, יוֹשֵׁב תְּהִלּוֹת יִשְׂרָאֵל. וְקָרָא זֶה אֶל זֶה וְאָמַר: קָדוֹשׁ, קָדוֹשׁ, קָדוֹשׁ יְיָ צְבָאוֹת, מְלֹא כָל הָאָרֶץ כְּבוֹדוֹ. וּמְקַבְּלִין דֵּן מִן דֵּן וְאָמְרִין: קַדִּישׁ בִּשְׁמֵי מְרוֹמָא עִלָּאָה, בֵּית שְׁכִינְתֵּהּ; קַדִּישׁ עַל אַרְעָא, עוֹבַד גְּבוּרְתֵּהּ; קַדִּישׁ לְעָלַם וּלְעָלְמֵי עָלְמַיָּא יְיָ צְבָאוֹת; מַלְיָא כָל אַרְעָא זִיו יְקָרֵהּ. וַתִּשָּׂאֵנִי רוּחַ, וָאֶשְׁמַע אַחֲרַי קוֹל רַעַשׁ גָּדוֹל: בָּרוּךְ כְּבוֹד יְיָ מִמְּקוֹמוֹ. וּנְטָלַתְנִי רוּחָא, וּשְׁמָעֵת בַּתְרַי קָל זִיעַ סַגִּיא דִי מְשַׁבְּחִין וְאָמְרִין: בְּרִיךְ יְקָרָא דַיְיָ מֵאֲתַר בֵּית שְׁכִינְתֵּהּ. יְיָ יִמְלֹךְ לְעֹלָם וָעֶד. יְיָ מַלְכוּתֵהּ קָאֵם לְעָלַם וּלְעָלְמֵי עָלְמַיָּא. יְיָ אֱלֹהֵי אַבְרָהָם יִצְחָק וְיִשְׂרָאֵל אֲבוֹתֵינוּ, שָׁמְרָה־זֹּאת לְעוֹלָם, לְיֵצֶר מַחְשְׁבוֹת לְבַב עַמֶּךָ, וְהָכֵן לְבָבָם אֵלֶיךָ. וְהוּא רַחוּם, יְכַפֵּר עָוֹן וְלֹא יַשְׁחִית, וְהִרְבָּה לְהָשִׁיב אַפּוֹ, וְלֹא יָעִיר כָּל חֲמָתוֹ. כִּי אַתָּה, אֲדֹנָי, טוֹב וְסַלָּח וְרַב חֶסֶד לְכָל קֹרְאֶיךָ.

Thou openest thy hand,
And satisfiest every living thing with favor.
The Lord is righteous in all his ways,
And gracious in all his deeds.
The Lord is near to all who call upon him,
To all who call upon him sincerely.
He fulfills the desire of those who revere him;
He hears their cry and saves them.
The Lord preserves all who love him,
But all the wicked he destroys.
My mouth speaks the praise of the Lord;
Let all creatures bless his holy name forever and ever.
[1]We will bless the Lord henceforth and forever.
Praise the Lord!

A redeemer shall come to Zion and to those in Jacob who turn from transgression, says the Lord. As for me, this is my covenant with them, says the Lord: My spirit it is which shall be upon you; and my words which I have put in your mouth shall not depart from your mouth, nor from the mouth of your children, nor from the mouth of your children's children, says the Lord, henceforth and forever.[2]

Thou, holy God, art enthroned amidst the praises of Israel.[3] They keep calling to one another: "Holy, holy, holy is the Lord of hosts; the whole earth is full of his glory."[4] *They receive it from one another, and say: "Holy in the highest heavens, his divine abode; holy upon earth, his work of might; holy forever and to all eternity is the Lord of hosts; the whole earth is full of his radiant glory."* Then a wind lifted me up, and I heard behind me a mighty sound: "Blessed be the glory of the Lord from his abode."[5] *Then a wind lifted me up and I heard behind me a great moving sound of those who uttered praises, saying: "Blessed be the glory of the Lord from the place of his divine abode."* The Lord shall reign forever and ever.[6] *The Lord's kingship is established forever and to all eternity.*

Lord God of Abraham, Isaac and Israel our fathers, keep the mind and purpose of thy people ever in this spirit, and direct their heart to thyself.[7] He, being merciful, forgives iniquity, and does not destroy; frequently he turns his anger away, and does not stir up all his wrath. For thou, O Lord, art good and forgiving, and exceedingly kind to all who call upon thee. Thy righteousness

*The words in italics are the Targum paraphrase of the preceding verse.

---

[1] *Psalm* 115:18.   [2] *Isaiah* 59:20–21.   [3] *Psalm* 22:4.   [4] *Isaiah* 6:3.   [5] *Ezekiel* 3:12.   [6] *Exodus* 15:18.   [7] *I Chronicles* 29:18.

צִדְקָתְךָ צֶדֶק לְעוֹלָם, וְתוֹרָתְךָ אֱמֶת. תִּתֵּן אֱמֶת לְיַעֲקֹב, חֶסֶד
לְאַבְרָהָם, אֲשֶׁר נִשְׁבַּעְתָּ לַאֲבֹתֵינוּ מִימֵי קֶדֶם. בָּרוּךְ יְיָ, יוֹם יוֹם
יַעֲמָס־לָנוּ, הָאֵל יְשׁוּעָתֵנוּ, סֶלָה. יְיָ צְבָאוֹת עִמָּנוּ, מִשְׂגָּב לָנוּ
אֱלֹהֵי יַעֲקֹב, סֶלָה. יְיָ צְבָאוֹת, אַשְׁרֵי אָדָם בֹּטֵחַ בָּךְ. יְיָ
הוֹשִׁיעָה; הַמֶּלֶךְ יַעֲנֵנוּ בְיוֹם קָרְאֵנוּ. בָּרוּךְ הוּא אֱלֹהֵינוּ שֶׁבְּרָאָנוּ
לִכְבוֹדוֹ, וְהִבְדִּילָנוּ מִן הַתּוֹעִים, וְנָתַן לָנוּ תּוֹרַת אֱמֶת, וְחַיֵּי
עוֹלָם נָטַע בְּתוֹכֵנוּ; הוּא יִפְתַּח לִבֵּנוּ בְּתוֹרָתוֹ. וְיָשֵׂם בְּלִבֵּנוּ
אַהֲבָתוֹ וְיִרְאָתוֹ, לַעֲשׂוֹת רְצוֹנוֹ וּלְעָבְדוֹ בְּלֵבָב שָׁלֵם, לְמַעַן
לֹא נִיגַע לָרִיק, וְלֹא נֵלֵד לַבֶּהָלָה. יְהִי רָצוֹן מִלְּפָנֶיךָ, יְיָ
אֱלֹהֵינוּ וֵאלֹהֵי אֲבוֹתֵינוּ, שֶׁנִּשְׁמוֹר חֻקֶּיךָ בָּעוֹלָם הַזֶּה, וְנִזְכֶּה
וְנִחְיֶה וְנִרְאֶה, וְנִירַשׁ טוֹבָה וּבְרָכָה, לִשְׁנֵי יְמוֹת הַמָּשִׁיחַ וּלְחַיֵּי
הָעוֹלָם הַבָּא. לְמַעַן יְזַמֶּרְךָ כָבוֹד וְלֹא יִדֹּם; יְיָ אֱלֹהַי, לְעוֹלָם
אוֹדֶךָ. בָּרוּךְ הַגֶּבֶר אֲשֶׁר יִבְטַח בַּיְיָ, וְהָיָה יְיָ מִבְטַחוֹ. בִּטְחוּ
בַיְיָ עֲדֵי עַד, כִּי בְּיָהּ יְיָ צוּר עוֹלָמִים. Reader וְיִבְטְחוּ בְךָ יוֹדְעֵי
שְׁמֶךָ, כִּי לֹא עָזַבְתָּ דֹרְשֶׁיךָ, יְיָ. יְיָ חָפֵץ לְמַעַן צִדְקוֹ, יַגְדִּיל
תּוֹרָה וְיַאְדִּיר.

Reader:

יִתְגַּדַּל וְיִתְקַדַּשׁ שְׁמֵהּ רַבָּא בְּעָלְמָא דִי בְרָא כִרְעוּתֵהּ;
וְיַמְלִיךְ מַלְכוּתֵהּ בְּחַיֵּיכוֹן וּבְיוֹמֵיכוֹן, וּבְחַיֵּי דְכָל בֵּית יִשְׂרָאֵל,
בַּעֲגָלָא וּבִזְמַן קָרִיב, וְאִמְרוּ אָמֵן.

יְהֵא שְׁמֵהּ רַבָּא מְבָרַךְ לְעָלַם וּלְעָלְמֵי עָלְמַיָּא.

יִתְבָּרַךְ וְיִשְׁתַּבַּח, וְיִתְפָּאַר וְיִתְרוֹמַם, וְיִתְנַשֵּׂא וְיִתְהַדָּר,
וְיִתְעַלֶּה וְיִתְהַלָּל שְׁמֵהּ דְּקֻדְשָׁא, בְּרִיךְ הוּא, לְעֵלָּא מִן כָּל
בִּרְכָתָא וְשִׁירָתָא, תֻּשְׁבְּחָתָא וְנֶחֱמָתָא, דַּאֲמִירָן בְּעָלְמָא,
וְאִמְרוּ אָמֵן.

Amidah, page 299. On Sabbath the *Torah* is read.

is eternal, and thy Torah is truth.[1] Thou wilt show grace to Jacob, love to Abraham, as thou hast sworn to our fathers from days of old.[2] Blessed be the Lord who day by day bears our burden; God is ever our salvation. The Lord of hosts is with us; the God of Jacob is our stronghold. Lord of hosts, happy is the man who trusts in thee. O Lord, save us; may the King answer us when we call.[3]

Blessed be our God who has created us for his glory, and has separated us from those who go astray; who has given us the Torah of truth and planted eternal life in our midst. May he open our heart to his Torah; may he set in our heart love and reverence for him to do his will and serve him with a perfect heart, so that we shall not labor in vain, nor rear children for disaster. May it be thy will, Lord our God and God of our fathers, that we keep thy laws in this world, and thus be worthy to live to see and share the happiness and blessing in the Messianic days and in the life of the world to come. May my soul sing praise to thee, and not be silent; Lord my God, I will thank thee forever.[4] Blessed is the man who trusts in the Lord; the Lord will be his protection. Trust in the Lord forever and ever, for the Lord God is an everlasting stronghold. Those who know thy name put their trust in thee, for thou hast not forsaken those who seek thee, O Lord.[5]

The Lord was pleased, because of his righteousness, to make his Torah great and glorious.[6]

Reader:

Glorified and sanctified be God's great name throughout the world which he has created according to his will. May he establish his kingdom in your lifetime and during your days, and within the life of the entire house of Israel, speedily and soon; and say, Amen.

May his great name be blessed forever and to all eternity.

Blessed and praised, glorified and exalted, extolled and honored, adored and lauded be the name of the Holy One, blessed be he, beyond all the blessings and hymns, praises and consolations that are ever spoken in the world; and say, Amen.

---

[1] *Psalms* 78:38; 86:5; 119:142.   [2] *Micah* 7:20.   [3] *Psalms* 68:20; 46:8; 84:13; 20:10.   [4] *Psalm* 30:13.   [5] *Jeremiah* 17:7; *Isaiah* 26:4; *Psalm* 9:11.   [6] *Isaiah* 42:21.

וַאֲנִי תְפִלָּתִי לְךָ, יְיָ, עֵת רָצוֹן; אֱלֹהִים, בְּרָב־חַסְדֶּךָ, עֲנֵנִי בֶּאֱמֶת יִשְׁעֶךָ.

קְרִיאַת הַתּוֹרָה

The ark is opened.

Reader and Congregation:

וַיְהִי בִּנְסֹעַ הָאָרֹן וַיֹּאמֶר מֹשֶׁה: קוּמָה יְיָ, וְיָפֻצוּ אֹיְבֶיךָ, וְיָנֻסוּ מְשַׂנְאֶיךָ מִפָּנֶיךָ. כִּי מִצִּיּוֹן תֵּצֵא תוֹרָה, וּדְבַר יְיָ מִירוּשָׁלָיִם. בָּרוּךְ שֶׁנָּתַן תּוֹרָה לְעַמּוֹ יִשְׂרָאֵל בִּקְדֻשָּׁתוֹ.

זוהר, ויקהל

בְּרִיךְ שְׁמֵהּ דְּמָרֵא עָלְמָא, בְּרִיךְ כִּתְרָךְ וְאַתְרָךְ. יְהֵא רְעוּתָךְ עִם עַמָּךְ יִשְׂרָאֵל לְעָלַם, וּפֻרְקַן יְמִינָךְ אַחֲזֵי לְעַמָּךְ בְּבֵית מִקְדְּשָׁךְ; וּלְאַמְטוֹיֵי לָנָא מִטּוּב נְהוֹרָךְ, וּלְקַבֵּל צְלוֹתָנָא בְּרַחֲמִין. יְהֵא רַעֲוָא קֳדָמָךְ, דְּתוֹרִיךְ לָן חַיִּין בְּטִיבוּתָא; וּלְהֶוֵא אֲנָא פְקִידָא בְּגוֹ צַדִּיקַיָּא, לְמִרְחַם עֲלַי וּלְמִנְטַר יָתִי וְיָת כָּל דִּי לִי וְדִי לְעַמָּךְ יִשְׂרָאֵל. אַנְתְּ הוּא זָן לְכֹלָּא וּמְפַרְנֵס לְכֹלָּא; אַנְתְּ הוּא שַׁלִּיט עַל כֹּלָּא; אַנְתְּ הוּא דְשַׁלִּיט עַל מַלְכַיָּא, וּמַלְכוּתָא דִּילָךְ הִיא. אֲנָא עַבְדָּא דְקֻדְשָׁא בְּרִיךְ הוּא, דְּסָגִדְנָא קַמֵּהּ וּמִקַּמָּא דִּיקַר אוֹרַיְתֵהּ בְּכָל עִדָּן וְעִדָּן. לָא עַל אֱנָשׁ רָחִצְנָא, וְלָא עַל בַּר אֱלָהִין סָמִכְנָא, אֶלָּא בֵּאֱלָהָא דִשְׁמַיָּא, דְּהוּא אֱלָהָא קְשׁוֹט, וְאוֹרַיְתֵהּ קְשׁוֹט, וּנְבִיאוֹהִי קְשׁוֹט, וּמַסְגֵּא לְמֶעְבַּד טַבְוָן וּקְשׁוֹט. בֵּהּ אֲנָא רָחֵץ, וְלִשְׁמֵהּ קַדִּישָׁא יַקִּירָא אֲנָא אָמַר תֻּשְׁבְּחָן. יְהֵא רַעֲוָא קֳדָמָךְ, דְּתִפְתַּח לִבָּאִי בְּאוֹרַיְתָא, וְתַשְׁלֵם מִשְׁאֲלִין דְּלִבָּאִי, וְלִבָּא דְכָל עַמָּךְ יִשְׂרָאֵל, לְטַב וּלְחַיִּין וְלִשְׁלָם.

I offer my prayer to thee, O Lord, at a time of grace. O God, in thy abundant kindness, answer me with thy saving truth.[1]

READING OF THE TORAH

The ark is opened.

Reader and Congregation.

And it came to pass, whenever the ark started, Moses would say: "Arise, O Lord, and let thy enemies be scattered; let those who hate thee flee before thee."[2] Truly out of Zion shall come forth Torah, and the word of the Lord out of Jerusalem.[3]

Blessed be he who in holiness gave the Torah to his people Israel

Zohar, Wayyakhel

Blessed be the name of the Lord of the universe! Blessed be thy crown and thy dominion. May thy good will ever abide with thy people Israel. Reveal thy saving power to thy people in thy sanctuary; bestow on us the good gift of thy light, and accept our prayer in mercy. May it be thy will to prolong our life in happiness.

Let me also be counted among the righteous, so that thou mayest have compassion on me and shelter me and mine and all that belong to thy people Israel. Thou art he who nourishes and sustains all; thou art he who rules over all; thou art he who rules over kings, for dominion is thine. I am the servant of the Holy One, blessed be he, before whom and before whose glorious Torah I bow at all times. Not in man do I put my trust, nor do I rely on any angel, but only in the God of heaven who is the God of truth, whose Torah is truth and whose Prophets are truth, and who performs many deeds of goodness and truth. In him I put my trust, and to his holy and glorious name I utter praises. May it be thy will to open my heart to thy Torah, and to fulfill the wishes of my heart and the heart of all thy people Israel for happiness, life and peace.

---

[1] *Psalm* 69:14.   [2] *Numbers* 10:35;   [3] *Isaiah* 2:3.

The Reader takes the Torah and says:

גַּדְּלוּ לַיָי אִתִּי, וּנְרוֹמְמָה שְׁמוֹ יַחְדָּו.

Congregation:

לְךָ יְיָ הַגְּדֻלָּה וְהַגְּבוּרָה וְהַתִּפְאֶרֶת וְהַנֵּצַח וְהַהוֹד, כִּי כֹל
בַּשָּׁמַיִם וּבָאָרֶץ; לְךָ, יְיָ, הַמַּמְלָכָה וְהַמִּתְנַשֵּׂא לְכֹל לְרֹאשׁ.
רוֹמְמוּ יְיָ אֱלֹהֵינוּ, וְהִשְׁתַּחֲווּ לַהֲדֹם רַגְלָיו, קָדוֹשׁ הוּא. רוֹמְמוּ
יְיָ אֱלֹהֵינוּ, וְהִשְׁתַּחֲווּ לְהַר קָדְשׁוֹ, כִּי קָדוֹשׁ יְיָ אֱלֹהֵינוּ.

Reader:

אַב הָרַחֲמִים, הוּא יְרַחֵם עַם עֲמוּסִים, וְיִזְכֹּר בְּרִית
אֵיתָנִים, וְיַצִּיל נַפְשׁוֹתֵינוּ מִן הַשָּׁעוֹת הָרָעוֹת, וְיִגְעַר בְּיֵצֶר הָרָע
מִן הַנְּשׂוּאִים, וְיָחֹן אוֹתָנוּ לִפְלֵיטַת עוֹלָמִים, וִימַלֵּא מִשְׁאֲלוֹתֵינוּ
בְּמִדָּה טוֹבָה, יְשׁוּעָה וְרַחֲמִים.

The Torah is placed on the desk. The Reader unrolls it and says:

וְתִגָּלֶה וְתֵרָאֶה מַלְכוּתוֹ עָלֵינוּ בִּזְמַן קָרוֹב, וְיָחֹן פְּלֵיטָתֵנוּ
וּפְלֵיטַת עַמּוֹ בֵּית יִשְׂרָאֵל לְחֵן וּלְחֶסֶד, לְרַחֲמִים וּלְרָצוֹן,
וְנֹאמַר אָמֵן. הַכֹּל הָבוּ גֹדֶל לֵאלֹהֵינוּ, וּתְנוּ כָבוֹד לַתּוֹרָה. כֹּהֵן,
קְרָב; יַעֲמֹד (פלוני בן פלוני) הַכֹּהֵן. בָּרוּךְ שֶׁנָּתַן תּוֹרָה לְעַמּוֹ
יִשְׂרָאֵל בִּקְדֻשָּׁתוֹ.

Congregation: and Reader

וְאַתֶּם הַדְּבֵקִים בַּיְיָ אֱלֹהֵיכֶם, חַיִּים כֻּלְּכֶם הַיּוֹם.

Torah reading page 211

The person called to the Torah recites:

בָּרְכוּ אֶת יְיָ הַמְבֹרָךְ.

Congregation responds:

בָּרוּךְ יְיָ הַמְבֹרָךְ לְעוֹלָם וָעֶד.

He repeats the response and continues:

בָּרוּךְ אַתָּה, יְיָ אֱלֹהֵינוּ, מֶלֶךְ הָעוֹלָם, אֲשֶׁר בָּחַר בָּנוּ מִכָּל
הָעַמִּים, וְנָתַן לָנוּ אֶת תּוֹרָתוֹ. בָּרוּךְ אַתָּה, יְיָ, נוֹתֵן הַתּוֹרָה.

The Reader takes the Torah and says:

Exalt the Lord with me, and let us extol his name together.[1]

Congregation:

Thine, O Lord, is the greatness and the power, the glory and the victory and the majesty; for all that is in heaven and on earth is thine; thine, O Lord, is the kingdom, and thou art supreme over all.[2] Exalt the Lord our God, and worship at his footstool; holy is he. Exalt the Lord our God, and worship at his holy mountain, for holy is the Lord our God.[3]

Reader:

May the merciful Father have compassion on the people who have been upheld by him, and remember the covenant with the patriarchs; may he deliver us from evil times, and check the evil impulse in those who have been tended by him; may he graciously grant us everlasting deliverance, and in his goodness fulfill our petitions for salvation and mercy.

The Torah is placed on the desk. The Reader unrolls it and says:

May his kingdom soon be revealed and made visible to us; may he be gracious to our remnant, the remnant of his people, the house of Israel, granting them grace and kindness, mercy and favor; and let us say, Amen. Let us all ascribe greatness to our God, and give honor to the Torah. Let the *Kohen* come forward [*the Reader names the first person called to the Torah*]. Blessed be he who in his holiness gave the Torah to his people Israel.

Congregation and Reader:

And you who cling to the Lord your God are all alive today.[4]

Torah   reading   page   212

The person called to the Torah recites:

Bless the Lord who is blessed.

Congregation responds:

Blessed be the Lord who is blessed forever and ever.

He repeats the response and continues:

Blessed art thou, Lord our God, King of the universe, who hast chosen us from all peoples, and hast given us thy Torah. Blessed art thou, O Lord, Giver of the Torah.

---

[1] *Psalm* **34**:4.   [2] *I Chronicles* 29:11.   [3] *Psalm* 99:5, 9.   [4] *Deuteronomy* 4:4.

The Torah is read; then he recites:

בָּרוּךְ אַתָּה, יְיָ אֱלֹהֵינוּ, מֶלֶךְ הָעוֹלָם, אֲשֶׁר נָתַן לָנוּ תּוֹרַת
אֱמֶת וְחַיֵּי עוֹלָם נָטַע בְּתוֹכֵנוּ. בָּרוּךְ אַתָּה, יְיָ, נוֹתֵן הַתּוֹרָה.

When the Torah is raised, the Congregation recites:

וְזֹאת הַתּוֹרָה אֲשֶׁר שָׂם מֹשֶׁה לִפְנֵי בְּנֵי יִשְׂרָאֵל, עַל פִּי יְיָ
בְּיַד מֹשֶׁה.

עֵץ חַיִּים הִיא לַמַּחֲזִיקִים בָּהּ, וְתֹמְכֶיהָ מְאֻשָּׁר. דְּרָכֶיהָ דַרְכֵי
נֹעַם, וְכָל נְתִיבוֹתֶיהָ שָׁלוֹם. אֹרֶךְ יָמִים בִּימִינָהּ; בִּשְׂמֹאלָהּ
עֹשֶׁר וְכָבוֹד. יְיָ חָפֵץ לְמַעַן צִדְקוֹ, יַגְדִּיל תּוֹרָה וְיַאְדִּיר.

The Reader takes the Torah and says:

יְהַלְלוּ אֶת שֵׁם יְיָ, כִּי נִשְׂגָּב שְׁמוֹ לְבַדּוֹ—

Congregation:

הוֹדוֹ עַל אֶרֶץ וְשָׁמָיִם. וַיָּרֶם קֶרֶן לְעַמּוֹ, תְּהִלָּה לְכָל
חֲסִידָיו, לִבְנֵי יִשְׂרָאֵל עַם קְרוֹבוֹ; הַלְלוּיָהּ.

תהלים כד

לְדָוִד מִזְמוֹר. לַיְיָ הָאָרֶץ וּמְלוֹאָהּ, תֵּבֵל וְיֹשְׁבֵי בָהּ. כִּי הוּא
עַל יַמִּים יְסָדָהּ, וְעַל נְהָרוֹת יְכוֹנְנֶהָ. מִי יַעֲלֶה בְהַר יְיָ, וּמִי
יָקוּם בִּמְקוֹם קָדְשׁוֹ. נְקִי כַפַּיִם וּבַר לֵבָב, אֲשֶׁר לֹא נָשָׂא לַשָּׁוְא
נַפְשִׁי, וְלֹא נִשְׁבַּע לְמִרְמָה. יִשָּׂא בְרָכָה מֵאֵת יְיָ, וּצְדָקָה מֵאֱלֹהֵי
יִשְׁעוֹ. זֶה דּוֹר דֹּרְשָׁיו, מְבַקְשֵׁי פָנֶיךָ, יַעֲקֹב, סֶלָה. שְׂאוּ שְׁעָרִים
רָאשֵׁיכֶם, וְהִנָּשְׂאוּ פִּתְחֵי עוֹלָם, וְיָבוֹא מֶלֶךְ הַכָּבוֹד. מִי זֶה מֶלֶךְ
הַכָּבוֹד, יְיָ עִזּוּז וְגִבּוֹר, יְיָ גִּבּוֹר מִלְחָמָה. שְׂאוּ שְׁעָרִים רָאשֵׁיכֶם,
וּשְׂאוּ פִּתְחֵי עוֹלָם, וְיָבֹא מֶלֶךְ הַכָּבוֹד. מִי הוּא זֶה מֶלֶךְ
הַכָּבוֹד, יְיָ צְבָאוֹת הוּא מֶלֶךְ הַכָּבוֹד, סֶלָה.

The Torah is read; then he recites:

Blessed art thou, Lord our God, King of the universe, who hast given us the Torah of truth, and hast planted everlasting life in our midst. Blessed art thou, O Lord, Giver of the Torah.

When the Torah is raised, the Congregation recites:

This is the Torah which Moses placed before the children of Israel. It is in accordance with the Lord's command through Moses.[1]

It is a tree of life to those who take hold of it, and happy are those who support it. Its ways are pleasant ways, and all its paths are peace. Long life is in its right hand, and in its left hand are riches and honor. The Lord was pleased, for the sake of his righteousness, to render the Torah great and glorious.[2]

The Reader takes the Torah and says:

Let them praise the name of the Lord, for his name alone is exalted—

Congregation:

His majesty is above earth and heaven. He has raised the honor of his people, the glory of his faithful followers, the children of Israel, the people near to him. Praise the Lord![3]

Psalm 24

A psalm of David. The earth and its fullness belong to the Lord, the entire world and its inhabitants. For it is he who has founded it upon the seas, and established it on the floods. Who may ascend the Lord's mountain? Who may stand within his holy place? He who has clean hands and a pure heart; he who strives not after vanity and swears not deceitfully. He will receive a blessing from the Lord, and justice from his saving God. Such is the generation of those who are in quest of him, who seek the presence of the God of Jacob. Raise your heads, O gates, raise yourselves, you ancient doors, that the glorious King may come in. Who, then, is the glorious King? The Lord strong and mighty, the Lord strong in battle. Raise your heads, O gates, raise yourselves, you ancient doors, that the glorious King may come in. Who, then, is the glorious King? The Lord of hosts, he is the glorious King.

---

[1] *Deuteronomy* 4:44; *Numbers* 9:23.   [2] *Proverbs* 3:18, 17, 16; *Isaiah* 42:21. *Psalm* 148:13–14.

מנחה ליום טוב

297

While the *Torah* is being placed in the ark:

וּבְנֻחֹה יֹאמַר: שׁוּבָה, יְיָ, רִבְבוֹת אַלְפֵי יִשְׂרָאֵל. קוּמָה יְיָ לִמְנוּחָתֶךָ, אַתָּה וַאֲרוֹן עֻזֶּךָ. כֹּהֲנֶיךָ יִלְבְּשׁוּ צֶדֶק, וַחֲסִידֶיךָ יְרַנֵּנוּ. בַּעֲבוּר דָּוִד עַבְדֶּךָ, אַל תָּשֵׁב פְּנֵי מְשִׁיחֶךָ. כִּי לֶקַח טוֹב נָתַתִּי לָכֶם, תּוֹרָתִי אַל תַּעֲזֹבוּ. עֵץ חַיִּים הִיא לַמַּחֲזִיקִים בָּהּ, וְתֹמְכֶיהָ מְאֻשָּׁר. דְּרָכֶיהָ דַרְכֵי נֹעַם, וְכָל נְתִיבוֹתֶיהָ שָׁלוֹם. הֲשִׁיבֵנוּ יְיָ אֵלֶיךָ, וְנָשׁוּבָה; חַדֵּשׁ יָמֵינוּ כְּקֶדֶם.

Reader:

יִתְגַּדַּל וְיִתְקַדַּשׁ שְׁמֵהּ רַבָּא בְּעָלְמָא דִי בְרָא כִרְעוּתֵהּ; וְיַמְלִיךְ מַלְכוּתֵהּ בְּחַיֵּיכוֹן וּבְיוֹמֵיכוֹן, וּבְחַיֵּי דְכָל בֵּית יִשְׂרָאֵל בַּעֲגָלָא וּבִזְמַן קָרִיב, וְאִמְרוּ אָמֵן.

יְהֵא שְׁמֵהּ רַבָּא מְבָרַךְ לְעָלַם וּלְעָלְמֵי עָלְמַיָּא.

יִתְבָּרַךְ וְיִשְׁתַּבַּח, וְיִתְפָּאַר וְיִתְרוֹמַם, וְיִתְנַשֵּׂא וְיִתְהַדָּר, וְיִתְעַלֶּה וְיִתְהַלָּל שְׁמֵהּ דְּקֻדְשָׁא, בְּרִיךְ הוּא, לְעֵלָּא מִן כָּל בִּרְכָתָא וְשִׁירָתָא, תֻּשְׁבְּחָתָא וְנֶחֱמָתָא, דַּאֲמִירָן בְּעָלְמָא, וְאִמְרוּ אָמֵן.

שאו שערים ראשיכם The ancient gates of Zion are poetically called on to raise their heads, in token of reverence to God. Different parts of this psalm were sung by different choirs at the time when David brought the ark to Mount Zion.

סלה marks a pause or a transition between one thought and another. It occurs seventy-one times in the Psalms and is not found in the prophetical

While the Torah is being placed in the ark:

When the ark rested, Moses would say: "Return, O Lord to the myriads of Israel's families." Arise, O Lord, for thy resting place, thou and thy glorious ark. May thy priests be clothed in righteousness; may thy faithful followers shout for joy. For the sake of thy servant David, reject not thy anointed. I give you good instruction; forsake not my Torah. It is a tree of life to those who take hold of it, and happy are those who support it. Its ways are ways of pleasantness, and all its paths are peace. Turn us to thee, O Lord, and let us return; renew our days as of old.

Reader.

Glorified and sanctified be God's great name throughout the world which he has created according to his will. May he establish his kingdom in your lifetime and during your days, and within the life of the entire house of Israel, speedily and soon; and say, Amen.

May his great name be blessed forever and to all eternity.

Blessed and praised, glorified and exalted, extolled and honored, adored and lauded be the name of the Holy One, blessed be he, beyond all the blessings and hymns, praises and consolations that are ever spoken in the world; and say, Amen.

---

writings. The precise significance and derivation of סלה have been much discussed. According to some, סלה is an abbreviation of סב למעלה השר, a direction to the singer to return to the beginning and repeat. Others connect it with the verb סלל ("to lift, to cast up"), a direction to the orchestra to strike in with loud music while the singer's voice is hushed. The word סלה, as used in the *Shemoneh Esreh* and other prayers, invariably means *forever* in keeping with the rendering of the Targum (לעלמין).

כִּי שֵׁם יְיָ אֶקְרָא, הָבוּ גֹדֶל לֵאלֹהֵינוּ.

אֲדֹנָי, שְׂפָתַי תִּפְתָּח, וּפִי יַגִּיד תְּהִלָּתֶךָ.

בָּרוּךְ אַתָּה, יְיָ אֱלֹהֵינוּ וֵאלֹהֵי אֲבוֹתֵינוּ, אֱלֹהֵי אַבְרָהָם,
אֱלֹהֵי יִצְחָק, וֵאלֹהֵי יַעֲקֹב, הָאֵל הַגָּדוֹל הַגִּבּוֹר וְהַנּוֹרָא, אֵל
עֶלְיוֹן, גּוֹמֵל חֲסָדִים טוֹבִים, וְקוֹנֵה הַכֹּל, וְזוֹכֵר חַסְדֵי אָבוֹת,
וּמֵבִיא גוֹאֵל לִבְנֵי בְנֵיהֶם לְמַעַן שְׁמוֹ בְּאַהֲבָה.

מֶלֶךְ עוֹזֵר וּמוֹשִׁיעַ וּמָגֵן. בָּרוּךְ אַתָּה, יְיָ, מָגֵן אַבְרָהָם.

אַתָּה גִבּוֹר לְעוֹלָם, אֲדֹנָי: מְחַיֵּה מֵתִים אַתָּה, רַב לְהוֹשִׁיעַ.

מְכַלְכֵּל חַיִּים בְּחֶסֶד, מְחַיֵּה מֵתִים בְּרַחֲמִים רַבִּים, סוֹמֵךְ
נוֹפְלִים, וְרוֹפֵא חוֹלִים, וּמַתִּיר אֲסוּרִים, וּמְקַיֵּם אֱמוּנָתוֹ לִישֵׁנֵי
עָפָר. מִי כָמוֹךָ, בַּעַל גְּבוּרוֹת, וּמִי דּוֹמֶה לָךְ, מֶלֶךְ מֵמִית
וּמְחַיֶּה וּמַצְמִיחַ יְשׁוּעָה.

וְנֶאֱמָן אַתָּה לְהַחֲיוֹת מֵתִים. בָּרוּךְ אַתָּה, יְיָ, מְחַיֵּה הַמֵּתִים.

When the Reader repeats the *Shemoneh Esreh*, the following *Kedushah* is said.

נְקַדֵּשׁ אֶת שִׁמְךָ בָּעוֹלָם כְּשֵׁם שֶׁמַּקְדִּישִׁים אוֹתוֹ בִּשְׁמֵי מָרוֹם,
כַּכָּתוּב עַל יַד נְבִיאֶךָ: וְקָרָא זֶה אֶל זֶה וְאָמַר:

קָדוֹשׁ, קָדוֹשׁ, קָדוֹשׁ יְיָ צְבָאוֹת: מְלֹא כָל הָאָרֶץ כְּבוֹדוֹ.
לְעֻמָּתָם בָּרוּךְ יֹאמֵרוּ—

בָּרוּךְ כְּבוֹד יְיָ מִמְּקוֹמוֹ.

וּבְדִבְרֵי קָדְשְׁךָ כָּתוּב לֵאמֹר:

יִמְלֹךְ יְיָ לְעוֹלָם, אֱלֹהַיִךְ צִיּוֹן לְדֹר וָדֹר; הַלְלוּיָהּ.

Reader:

לְדוֹר וָדוֹר נַגִּיד גָּדְלֶךָ, וּלְנֵצַח נְצָחִים קְדֻשָּׁתְךָ נַקְדִּישׁ,
וְשִׁבְחֲךָ אֱלֹהֵינוּ מִפִּינוּ לֹא יָמוּשׁ לְעוֹלָם וָעֶד, כִּי אֵל מֶלֶךְ
גָּדוֹל וְקָדוֹשׁ אָתָּה. בָּרוּךְ אַתָּה, יְיָ, הָאֵל הַקָּדוֹשׁ.

When I proclaim the name of the Lord, give glory to our God![1]

O Lord, open thou my lips, that my mouth may declare thy praise.[2]

Blessed art thou, Lord our God and God of our fathers, God of Abraham, God of Isaac and God of Jacob; great, mighty and revered God, sublime God, who bestowest lovingkindness, and art Master of all things; who rememberest the good deeds of our fathers, and who wilt graciously bring a redeemer to their children's children for the sake of thy name.

O King, Supporter, Savior and Shield! Blessed art thou, O Lord, Shield of Abraham.

Thou, O Lord, art mighty forever; thou revivest the dead; thou art powerful to save.

Thou sustainest the living with kindness, and revivest the dead with great mercy; thou supportest all who fall, and healest the sick; thou settest the captives free, and keepest faith with those who sleep in the dust. Who is like thee, Lord of power? Who resembles thee, O King? Thou bringest death and restorest life, and causest salvation to flourish.

Thou art faithful to revive the dead. Blessed art thou, O Lord, who revivest the dead.

When the Reader repeats the *Shemoneh Esreh*, the following *Kedushah* is said.

We sanctify thy name in this world even as they sanctify it in the highest heavens, as it is written by thy prophet: "They keep calling to one another:

> Holy, holy, holy is the Lord of hosts;
> The whole earth is full of his glory."[3]

Those opposite them say: Blessed—
Blessed be the glory of the Lord from his abode.[4]
And in thy Holy Scriptures it is written:

> The Lord shall reign forever,
> Your God, O Zion, for all generations.
> Praise the Lord![5]

---

[1] *Deuteronomy* 32:3.　[2] *Psalm* 51:17.　[3] *Isaiah* 6:3.　[4] *Ezekiel* 3:12.　[5] *Psalm* 146:10.

אַתָּה קָדוֹשׁ וְשִׁמְךָ קָדוֹשׁ, וּקְדוֹשִׁים בְּכָל יוֹם יְהַלְלוּךָ סֶּלָה.
בָּרוּךְ אַתָּה, יְיָ, הָאֵל הַקָּדוֹשׁ.

אַתָּה בְחַרְתָּנוּ מִכָּל הָעַמִּים, אָהַבְתָּ אוֹתָנוּ וְרָצִיתָ בָּנוּ,
וְרוֹמַמְתָּנוּ מִכָּל הַלְּשׁוֹנוֹת, וְקִדַּשְׁתָּנוּ בְּמִצְוֹתֶיךָ, וְקֵרַבְתָּנוּ
מַלְכֵּנוּ לַעֲבוֹדָתֶךָ, וְשִׁמְךָ הַגָּדוֹל וְהַקָּדוֹשׁ עָלֵינוּ קָרָאתָ.

וַתִּתֶּן־לָנוּ, יְיָ אֱלֹהֵינוּ, בְּאַהֲבָה, (שַׁבָּתוֹת לִמְנוּחָה וּ)מוֹעֲדִים
לְשִׂמְחָה, חַגִּים וּזְמַנִּים לְשָׂשׂוֹן, אֶת יוֹם (הַשַּׁבָּת הַזֶּה וְאֶת יוֹם)
חַג הַשָּׁבוּעוֹת הַזֶּה, זְמַן מַתַּן תּוֹרָתֵנוּ, (בְּאַהֲבָה) מִקְרָא קֹדֶשׁ,
זֵכֶר לִיצִיאַת מִצְרָיִם.

אֱלֹהֵינוּ וֵאלֹהֵי אֲבוֹתֵינוּ, יַעֲלֶה וְיָבֹא, וְיַגִּיעַ וְיֵרָאֶה, וְיֵרָצֶה
וְיִשָּׁמַע, וְיִפָּקֵד וְיִזָּכֵר, זִכְרוֹנֵנוּ וּפִקְדוֹנֵנוּ, וְזִכְרוֹן אֲבוֹתֵינוּ,
וְזִכְרוֹן מָשִׁיחַ בֶּן־דָּוִד עַבְדֶּךָ, וְזִכְרוֹן יְרוּשָׁלַיִם עִיר קָדְשֶׁךָ,
וְזִכְרוֹן כָּל עַמְּךָ בֵּית יִשְׂרָאֵל לְפָנֶיךָ, לִפְלֵיטָה וּלְטוֹבָה, לְחֵן
וּלְחֶסֶד וּלְרַחֲמִים, לְחַיִּים וּלְשָׁלוֹם, בְּיוֹם חַג הַשָּׁבוּעוֹת הַזֶּה.
זָכְרֵנוּ, יְיָ אֱלֹהֵינוּ, בּוֹ לְטוֹבָה, וּפָקְדֵנוּ בוֹ לִבְרָכָה, וְהוֹשִׁיעֵנוּ
בוֹ לְחַיִּים; וּבִדְבַר יְשׁוּעָה וְרַחֲמִים חוּס וְחָנֵּנוּ, וְרַחֵם עָלֵינוּ
וְהוֹשִׁיעֵנוּ, כִּי אֵלֶיךָ עֵינֵינוּ, כִּי אֵל מֶלֶךְ חַנּוּן וְרַחוּם אָתָּה.

וְהַשִּׂיאֵנוּ, יְיָ אֱלֹהֵינוּ, אֶת בִּרְכַּת מוֹעֲדֶיךָ לְחַיִּים וּלְשָׁלוֹם,
לְשִׂמְחָה וּלְשָׂשׂוֹן, כַּאֲשֶׁר רָצִיתָ וְאָמַרְתָּ לְבָרְכֵנוּ. אֱלֹהֵינוּ

אתה קדוש, the third benediction of the *Amidah*, is designated in the Talmud
as קדוש השם (Sanctification of the Name). In public worship, the *Kedushah* is
inserted between the second and third benedictions when the reader repeats
the *Amidah*. The reason why the *Kedushah* is recited in public only is that it
is written: "I shall be sanctified among the children of Israel" (Leviticus 22:32),
implying that only in the midst of the required quorum of ten male adults
(*minyan*) is the *Kedushah* to be recited (Berakhoth 21b). The nucleus of the
Kedushah is composed of three biblical verses (Isaiah 6:3; Ezekiel 3:12; Psalms
146:10). To this nucleus various additions were composed throughout the first
millenium, some of which were adopted by all the rituals and finally became

Thou art holy and thy name is holy, and holy beings praise thee daily, Blessed art thou, O Lord, holy God.

Thou didst choose us from among all peoples; thou didst love and favor us; thou didst exalt us above all tongues and sanctify us with thy commandments. Thou, our King, didst draw us near to thy service and call us by thy great and holy name.

Thou, Lord our God, hast graciously given us (Sabbaths for rest) holidays for gladness, festive seasons for joy: (this Sabbath day and) this Feast of Weeks, our Festival of the Giving of the Torah, a holy convocation in remembrance of the exodus from Egypt.

Our God and God of our fathers, may the remembrance of us, of our fathers, of Messiah the son of David thy servant, of Jerusalem thy holy city, and of all thy people the house of Israel, ascend and come and be accepted before thee for deliverance and happiness, for grace, kindness and mercy, for life and peace, on this day of the Feast of Weeks.

Remember us this day, Lord our God, for happiness; be mindful of us for blessing; save us to enjoy life. With a promise of salvation and mercy spare us and be gracious to us; have pity on us and save us, for we look to thee, for thou art a gracious and merciful God and King.

Bestow on us, Lord our God, the blessings of thy festivals for life and peace, for joy and gladness, as thou didst promise to bless us. Our God and God of our Fathers, (be pleased with our rest)

standardized. Maḥzor Vitry (page 66) gives נקדש את שמך (we sanctify thy name) as the introduction to the weekday *Kedushah*. The Ashkenazic Nusaḥ, however, has it for the weekday, Sabbath, and Holyday שחרית and מנחה services.

The prayer יעלה ויבא is based on the following passage in the Torah: "On your feasts and new moon festivals you shall sound the trumpets...they will serve as a reminder of you before your God" (Numbers 10:10). In the synagogues, it is customary to call out *Yaaleh v'Yavo* before the *Amidah* on the eve of *Rosh Ḥodesh* as a reminder to the congregation to insert this prayer in the proper place. Recited for the prosperity of the people and for deliverance and happiness, kindness and mercy, life and peace, *Yaaleh v'Yavo* refers also to Jerusalem, Messiah, and Israel.

וֵאלֹהֵי אֲבוֹתֵינוּ, (רְצֵה בִמְנוּחָתֵנוּ) קַדְּשֵׁנוּ בְּמִצְוֹתֶיךָ וְתֵן חֶלְקֵנוּ בְּתוֹרָתֶךָ, שַׂבְּעֵנוּ מִטּוּבֶךָ, וְשַׂמְּחֵנוּ בִּישׁוּעָתֶךָ, וְטַהֵר לִבֵּנוּ לְעָבְדְּךָ בֶּאֱמֶת; וְהַנְחִילֵנוּ, יְיָ אֱלֹהֵינוּ, (בְּאַהֲבָה וּבְרָצוֹן) בְּשִׂמְחָה וּבְשָׂשׂוֹן, (שַׁבָּת וּ)מוֹעֲדֵי קָדְשֶׁךָ, וְיִשְׂמְחוּ בְךָ יִשְׂרָאֵל מְקַדְּשֵׁי שְׁמֶךָ. בָּרוּךְ אַתָּה, יְיָ, מְקַדֵּשׁ (הַשַּׁבָּת וְ)יִשְׂרָאֵל וְהַזְּמַנִּים.

רְצֵה, יְיָ אֱלֹהֵינוּ, בְּעַמְּךָ יִשְׂרָאֵל וּבִתְפִלָּתָם; וְהָשֵׁב אֶת הָעֲבוֹדָה לִדְבִיר בֵּיתֶךָ, וְאִשֵּׁי יִשְׂרָאֵל וּתְפִלָּתָם בְּאַהֲבָה תְקַבֵּל בְּרָצוֹן, וּתְהִי לְרָצוֹן תָּמִיד עֲבוֹדַת יִשְׂרָאֵל עַמֶּךָ.

וְתֶחֱזֶינָה עֵינֵינוּ בְּשׁוּבְךָ לְצִיּוֹן בְּרַחֲמִים. בָּרוּךְ אַתָּה, יְיָ, הַמַּחֲזִיר שְׁכִינָתוֹ לְצִיּוֹן.

מוֹדִים אֲנַחְנוּ לָךְ, שָׁאַתָּה הוּא יְיָ אֱלֹהֵינוּ וֵאלֹהֵי אֲבוֹתֵינוּ לְעוֹלָם וָעֶד. צוּר חַיֵּינוּ, מָגֵן יִשְׁעֵנוּ אַתָּה הוּא. לְדוֹר וָדוֹר נוֹדֶה לְּךָ, וּנְסַפֵּר תְּהִלָּתֶךָ, עַל חַיֵּינוּ הַמְּסוּרִים בְּיָדֶךָ, וְעַל נִשְׁמוֹתֵינוּ הַפְּקוּדוֹת לָךְ, וְעַל נִסֶּיךָ שֶׁבְּכָל יוֹם עִמָּנוּ, וְעַל נִפְלְאוֹתֶיךָ וְטוֹבוֹתֶיךָ שֶׁבְּכָל עֵת, עֶרֶב וָבֹקֶר וְצָהֳרָיִם. הַטּוֹב כִּי לֹא כָלוּ רַחֲמֶיךָ, וְהַמְרַחֵם כִּי לֹא תַמּוּ חֲסָדֶיךָ, מֵעוֹלָם קִוִּינוּ לָךְ.

When the Reader repeats the Amidah, the Congregation responds here by saying:

(מוֹדִים אֲנַחְנוּ לָךְ, שָׁאַתָּה הוּא יְיָ אֱלֹהֵינוּ וֵאלֹהֵי אֲבוֹתֵינוּ. אֱלֹהֵי כָל בָּשָׂר, יוֹצְרֵנוּ, יוֹצֵר בְּרֵאשִׁית, בְּרָכוֹת וְהוֹדָאוֹת לְשִׁמְךָ הַגָּדוֹל וְהַקָּדוֹשׁ עַל שֶׁהֶחֱיִיתָנוּ וְקִיַּמְתָּנוּ. כֵּן תְּחַיֵּנוּ וּתְקַיְּמֵנוּ, וְתֶאֱסוֹף גָּלֻיוֹתֵינוּ לְחַצְרוֹת קָדְשֶׁךָ לִשְׁמוֹר חֻקֶּיךָ וְלַעֲשׂוֹת רְצוֹנֶךָ, וּלְעָבְדְּךָ בְּלֵבָב שָׁלֵם, עַל שֶׁאֲנַחְנוּ מוֹדִים לָךְ. בָּרוּךְ אֵל הַהוֹדָאוֹת.)

sanctify us with thy commandments and grant us a share in thy Torah; satisfy us with thy goodness and gladden us with thy help; purify our heart to serve thee sincerely. In thy gracious love, Lord our God, grant us thy holy (Sabbath and) festivals for gladness and joy; may Israel who sanctifies thy name rejoice in thee. Blessed art thou, O Lord, who hallowest (the Sabbath and) Israel and the festivals.

Be pleased, Lord our God, with thy people Israel and with their prayer; restore the worship to thy most holy sanctuary; accept Israel's offerings and prayer with gracious love. May the worship of thy people Israel be ever pleasing to thee.

May our eyes behold thy return in mercy to Zion. Blessed art thou, O Lord, who restorest thy divine presence to Zion.

We ever thank thee, who art the Lord our God and the God of our fathers. Thou art the strength of our life and our saving shield. In every generation we will thank thee and recount thy praise—for our lives which are in thy charge, for our souls which are in thy care, for thy miracles which are daily with us, and for thy continual wonders and favors—evening, morning and noon. Beneficent One, whose mercies never fail, Merciful One, whose kindnesses never cease, thou hast always been our hope.

While the Reader recites Modim, the Congregation reads:

(We thank thee, who art the Lord our God and the God of our fathers. God of all mankind, our Creator and Creator of the universe, blessings and thanks are due to thy great and holy name, because thou hast kept us alive and sustained us; mayest thou ever grant us life and sustenance. O gather our exiles to thy holy courts to observe thy laws, to do thy will, and to serve thee with a perfect heart. For this we thank thee. Blessed be God to whom all thanks are due.)

וְעַל כֻּלָּם יִתְבָּרַךְ וְיִתְרוֹמַם שִׁמְךָ, מַלְכֵּנוּ, תָּמִיד לְעוֹלָם וָעֶד.

וְכֹל הַחַיִּים יוֹדוּךָ סֶּלָה, וִיהַלְלוּ וִיבָרְכוּ אֶת שִׁמְךָ הַגָּדוֹל בֶּאֱמֶת, לְעוֹלָם כִּי טוֹב. הָאֵל, יְשׁוּעָתֵנוּ וְעֶזְרָתֵנוּ סֶלָה. בָּרוּךְ אַתָּה, יְיָ, הַטּוֹב שִׁמְךָ, וּלְךָ נָאֶה לְהוֹדוֹת.

שָׁלוֹם רָב עַל יִשְׂרָאֵל עַמְּךָ תָּשִׂים לְעוֹלָם, כִּי אַתָּה הוּא מֶלֶךְ אָדוֹן לְכָל הַשָּׁלוֹם, וְטוֹב בְּעֵינֶיךָ לְבָרֵךְ אֶת עַמְּךָ יִשְׂרָאֵל בְּכָל עֵת וּבְכָל שָׁעָה בִּשְׁלוֹמֶךָ. בָּרוּךְ אַתָּה, יְיָ, הַמְבָרֵךְ אֶת עַמּוֹ יִשְׂרָאֵל בַּשָּׁלוֹם.

After the *Amidah* add the following meditation:

אֱלֹהַי נְצֹר לְשׁוֹנִי מֵרָע, וּשְׂפָתַי מִדַּבֵּר מִרְמָה; וְלִמְקַלְלַי נַפְשִׁי תִדּוֹם, וְנַפְשִׁי כֶּעָפָר לַכֹּל תִּהְיֶה. פְּתַח לִבִּי בְּתוֹרָתֶךָ, וּבְמִצְוֹתֶיךָ תִּרְדּוֹף נַפְשִׁי; וְכֹל הַחוֹשְׁבִים עָלַי רָעָה, מְהֵרָה הָפֵר עֲצָתָם וְקַלְקֵל מַחֲשַׁבְתָּם. עֲשֵׂה לְמַעַן שְׁמֶךָ, עֲשֵׂה לְמַעַן יְמִינֶךָ, עֲשֵׂה לְמַעַן קְדֻשָּׁתֶךָ, עֲשֵׂה לְמַעַן תּוֹרָתֶךָ. לְמַעַן יֵחָלְצוּן יְדִידֶיךָ, הוֹשִׁיעָה יְמִינְךָ וַעֲנֵנִי. יִהְיוּ לְרָצוֹן אִמְרֵי פִי וְהֶגְיוֹן לִבִּי לְפָנֶיךָ, יְיָ, צוּרִי וְגוֹאֲלִי. עֹשֶׂה שָׁלוֹם בִּמְרוֹמָיו, הוּא יַעֲשֶׂה שָׁלוֹם עָלֵינוּ וְעַל כָּל יִשְׂרָאֵל, וְאִמְרוּ אָמֵן.

יְהִי רָצוֹן מִלְּפָנֶיךָ, יְיָ אֱלֹהֵינוּ וֵאלֹהֵי אֲבוֹתֵינוּ, שֶׁיִּבָּנֶה בֵּית הַמִּקְדָּשׁ בִּמְהֵרָה בְיָמֵינוּ; וְתֵן חֶלְקֵנוּ בְּתוֹרָתֶךָ. וְשָׁם נַעֲבָדְךָ בְּיִרְאָה, כִּימֵי עוֹלָם וּכְשָׁנִים קַדְמוֹנִיּוֹת. וְעָרְבָה לַיְיָ מִנְחַת יְהוּדָה וִירוּשָׁלָיִם, כִּימֵי עוֹלָם וּכְשָׁנִים קַדְמוֹנִיּוֹת.

אלהי נצור is phrased in singular, because it was originally designed as an individual meditation. The first sentence is derived from Psalm 34:14, where

For all these acts may thy name, our King, be blessed and exalted forever and ever.

All the living shall ever thank thee and sincerely praise thy name, O God, who art always our salvation and help. Blessed art thou, O Lord, Beneficent One, to whom it is fitting to give thanks.

O grant abundant peace to Israel thy people forever, for thou art the King and Lord of all peace. May it please thee to bless thy people Israel with peace at all times and at all hours. * Blessed art thou, O Lord, who blessest thy people Israel with peace.

After the Amidah add the following meditation:

My God, guard my tongue from evil, and my lips from speaking falsehood. May my soul be silent to those who insult me; be my soul lowly to all as the dust. Open my heart to thy Torah, that my soul may follow thy commands. Speedily defeat the counsel of all those who plan evil against me, and upset their design. Do it for the glory of thy name; do it for the sake of thy power; do it for the sake of thy holiness; do it for the sake of thy Torah. That thy beloved may be rescued, save with thy right hand and answer me. May the words of my mouth and the meditation of my heart be pleasing before thee, O Lord, my Stronghold and my Redeemer.[1] May he who creates peace in his high heavens create peace for us and for all Israel, Amen.

May it be thy will, Lord our God and God of our fathers, that the Temple be speedily rebuilt in our days, and grant us a share in thy Torah. There we will serve thee with reverence, as in the days of old and as in former years. Then the offering of Judah and Jerusalem will be pleasing to the Lord, as in the days of old and as in former years.[2]

---

the text reads: נצור לשונך מרע. ושפתיך מדבר מרמה ("keep your tongue from evil, and your lips from speaking falsehood").

The phrase עושה שלום במרומיו is from the book of Job (25:2).

---

[1] *Psalms* 60:7; 19:15.   [2] *Malachi* 3:4.

Reader:

יִתְגַּדַּל וְיִתְקַדַּשׁ שְׁמֵהּ רַבָּא בְּעָלְמָא דִּי בְרָא כִרְעוּתֵהּ;
וְיַמְלִיךְ מַלְכוּתֵהּ בְּחַיֵּיכוֹן וּבְיוֹמֵיכוֹן, וּבְחַיֵּי דְכָל בֵּית יִשְׂרָאֵל,
בַּעֲגָלָא וּבִזְמַן קָרִיב, וְאִמְרוּ אָמֵן.

יְהֵא שְׁמֵהּ רַבָּא מְבָרַךְ לְעָלַם וּלְעָלְמֵי עָלְמַיָּא.

יִתְבָּרַךְ וְיִשְׁתַּבַּח, וְיִתְפָּאַר וְיִתְרוֹמַם, וְיִתְנַשֵּׂא וְיִתְהַדָּר,
וְיִתְעַלֶּה וְיִתְהַלָּל שְׁמֵהּ דְּקֻדְשָׁא, בְּרִיךְ הוּא, לְעֵלָּא מִן כָּל
בִּרְכָתָא וְשִׁירָתָא, תֻּשְׁבְּחָתָא וְנֶחֱמָתָא, דַּאֲמִירָן בְּעָלְמָא,
וְאִמְרוּ אָמֵן.

תִּתְקַבֵּל צְלוֹתְהוֹן וּבָעוּתְהוֹן דְּכָל בֵּית יִשְׂרָאֵל קֳדָם אֲבוּהוֹן
דִּי בִשְׁמַיָּא, וְאִמְרוּ אָמֵן.

יְהֵא שְׁלָמָא רַבָּא מִן שְׁמַיָּא, וְחַיִּים, עָלֵינוּ וְעַל כָּל יִשְׂרָאֵל,
וְאִמְרוּ אָמֵן.

עֹשֶׂה שָׁלוֹם בִּמְרוֹמָיו, הוּא יַעֲשֶׂה שָׁלוֹם עָלֵינוּ וְעַל כָּל
יִשְׂרָאֵל, וְאִמְרוּ אָמֵן.

עָלֵינוּ לְשַׁבֵּחַ לַאֲדוֹן הַכֹּל, לָתֵת גְּדֻלָּה לְיוֹצֵר בְּרֵאשִׁית,
שֶׁלֹּא עָשָׂנוּ כְּגוֹיֵי הָאֲרָצוֹת, וְלֹא שָׂמָנוּ כְּמִשְׁפְּחוֹת הָאֲדָמָה;
שֶׁלֹּא שָׂם חֶלְקֵנוּ כָּהֶם, וְגוֹרָלֵנוּ כְּכָל הֲמוֹנָם. וַאֲנַחְנוּ כּוֹרְעִים
וּמִשְׁתַּחֲוִים וּמוֹדִים לִפְנֵי מֶלֶךְ מַלְכֵי הַמְּלָכִים, הַקָּדוֹשׁ בָּרוּךְ
הוּא, שֶׁהוּא נוֹטֶה שָׁמַיִם וְיוֹסֵד אָרֶץ, וּמוֹשַׁב יְקָרוֹ בַּשָּׁמַיִם
מִמַּעַל, וּשְׁכִינַת עֻזּוֹ בְּגָבְהֵי מְרוֹמִים. הוּא אֱלֹהֵינוּ, אֵין עוֹד;
אֱמֶת מַלְכֵּנוּ, אֶפֶס זוּלָתוֹ, כַּכָּתוּב בְּתוֹרָתוֹ: וְיָדַעְתָּ הַיּוֹם
וַהֲשֵׁבֹתָ אֶל לְבָבֶךָ, כִּי יְיָ הוּא הָאֱלֹהִים בַּשָּׁמַיִם מִמַּעַל וְעַל
הָאָרֶץ מִתָּחַת, אֵין עוֹד.

Reader:

Glorified and sanctified be God's great name throughout the world which he has created according to his will. May he establish his kingdom in your lifetime and during your days, and within the life of the entire house of Israel, speedily and soon; and say, Amen.

May his great name be blessed forever and to all eternity.

Blessed and praised, glorified and exalted, extolled and honored, adored and lauded be the name of the Holy One, blessed be he, beyond all the blessings and hymns, praises and consolations that are ever spoken in the world; and say, Amen.

May the prayers and supplications of the whole household of Israel be accepted by their Father who is in heaven; and say, Amen.

May there be abundant peace from heaven, and life, for us and for all Israel; and say, Amen.

He who creates peace in his celestial heights, may he create peace for us and for all Israel; and say, Amen.

ALENU

It is our duty to praise the Master of all, to exalt the Creator of the universe, who has not made us like the nations of the world and has not placed us like the families of the earth; who has not designed our destiny to be like theirs, nor our lot like that of all their multitude. We bend the knee and bow and acknowledge before the supreme King of kings, the Holy One, blessed be he, that it is he who stretched forth the heavens and founded the earth. His seat of glory is in the heavens above; his abode of majesty is in the lofty heights. He is our God, there is none else; truly, he is our King, there is none besides him, as it is written in his Torah: "You shall know this day, and reflect in your heart, that it is the Lord who is God in the heavens above and on the earth beneath, there is none else."[1]

---

[1]*Deuteronomy* 4:39.

עַל כֵּן נְקַוֶּה לְּךָ, יְיָ אֱלֹהֵינוּ, לִרְאוֹת מְהֵרָה בְּתִפְאֶרֶת עֻזֶּךָ,
לְהַעֲבִיר גִּלּוּלִים מִן הָאָרֶץ, וְהָאֱלִילִים כָּרוֹת יִכָּרֵתוּן; לְתַקֵּן
עוֹלָם בְּמַלְכוּת שַׁדַּי, וְכָל בְּנֵי בָשָׂר יִקְרְאוּ בִשְׁמֶךָ, לְהַפְנוֹת
אֵלֶיךָ כָּל רִשְׁעֵי אָרֶץ. יַכִּירוּ וְיֵדְעוּ כָּל יוֹשְׁבֵי תֵבֵל, כִּי לְךָ
תִּכְרַע כָּל בֶּרֶךְ, תִּשָּׁבַע כָּל לָשׁוֹן. לְפָנֶיךָ, יְיָ אֱלֹהֵינוּ, יִכְרְעוּ
וְיִפֹּלוּ, וְלִכְבוֹד שִׁמְךָ יְקָר יִתֵּנוּ, וִיקַבְּלוּ כֻלָּם אֶת עֹל מַלְכוּתֶךָ,
וְתִמְלוֹךְ עֲלֵיהֶם מְהֵרָה לְעוֹלָם וָעֶד. כִּי הַמַּלְכוּת שֶׁלְּךָ הִיא,
וּלְעוֹלְמֵי עַד תִּמְלוֹךְ בְּכָבוֹד, כַּכָּתוּב, בְּתוֹרָתֶךָ: יְיָ יִמְלֹךְ
לְעֹלָם וָעֶד. Reader וְנֶאֱמַר: וְהָיָה יְיָ לְמֶלֶךְ עַל כָּל הָאָרֶץ;
בַּיּוֹם הַהוּא יִהְיֶה יְיָ אֶחָד וּשְׁמוֹ אֶחָד.

MOURNERS' KADDISH

יִתְגַּדַּל וְיִתְקַדַּשׁ שְׁמֵהּ רַבָּא בְּעָלְמָא דִּי בְרָא כִרְעוּתֵהּ;
וְיַמְלִיךְ מַלְכוּתֵהּ בְּחַיֵּיכוֹן וּבְיוֹמֵיכוֹן, וּבְחַיֵּי דְכָל בֵּית יִשְׂרָאֵל
בַּעֲגָלָא וּבִזְמַן קָרִיב, וְאִמְרוּ אָמֵן.

יְהֵא שְׁמֵהּ רַבָּא מְבָרַךְ לְעָלַם וּלְעָלְמֵי עָלְמַיָּא.

יִתְבָּרַךְ וְיִשְׁתַּבַּח, וְיִתְפָּאַר וְיִתְרוֹמַם, וְיִתְנַשֵּׂא וְיִתְהַדָּר,
וְיִתְעַלֶּה וְיִתְהַלָּל שְׁמֵהּ דְּקֻדְשָׁא, בְּרִיךְ הוּא, לְעֵלָּא מִן כָּל
בִּרְכָתָא וְשִׁירָתָא, תֻּשְׁבְּחָתָא וְנֶחֱמָתָא, דַּאֲמִירָן בְּעָלְמָא,
וְאִמְרוּ אָמֵן.

יְהֵא שְׁלָמָא רַבָּא מִן שְׁמַיָּא, וְחַיִּים, עָלֵינוּ וְעַל כָּל יִשְׂרָאֵל,
וְאִמְרוּ אָמֵן.

עֹשֶׂה שָׁלוֹם בִּמְרוֹמָיו, הוּא יַעֲשֶׂה שָׁלוֹם עָלֵינוּ וְעַל כָּל
יִשְׂרָאֵל, וְאִמְרוּ אָמֵן.

We hope therefore, Lord our God, soon to behold thy majestic glory, when the abominations shall be removed from the earth, and the false gods exterminated; when the world shall be perfected under the reign of the Almighty, and all mankind will call upon thy name, and all the wicked of the earth will be turned to thee. May all the inhabitants of the world realize and know that to thee every knee must bend, every tongue must vow allegiance. May they bend the knee and prostrate themselves before thee, Lord our God, and give honor to thy glorious name; may they all accept the yoke of thy kingdom, and do thou reign over them speedily forever and ever. For the kingdom is thine, and to all eternity thou wilt reign in glory, as it is written in thy Torah: "The Lord shall be King forever and ever."[1] And it is said: "The Lord shall be King over all the earth; on that day shall the Lord be One and his name One.[2]"

MOURNERS' KADDISH

Glorified and sanctified be God's great name throughout the world which he has created according to his will. May he establish his kingdom, hastening his salvation and the coming of his Messiah, in your lifetime and during your days, and within the life of the entire house of Israel, speedily and soon; and say, Amen.

May his great name be blessed forever and to all eternity.

Blessed and praised, glorified and exalted, extolled and honored, adored and lauded be the name of the Holy One, blessed be he, beyond all the blessings and hymns, praises and consolations that are ever spoken in the world; and say, Amen.

May there be abundant peace from heaven, and a good life, for us and for all Israel; and say, Amen.

He who creates peace in his celestial heights, may he create peace for us and for all Israel; and say, Amen.

---

[1] *Exodus* 15:18.   [2] *Zechariah* 14:9.

רות

א

וַיְהִי בִּימֵי שְׁפֹט הַשֹּׁפְטִים וַיְהִי רָעָב בָּאָרֶץ וַיֵּלֶךְ אִישׁ
מִבֵּית לֶחֶם יְהוּדָה לָגוּר בִּשְׂדֵי מוֹאָב הוּא וְאִשְׁתּוֹ וּשְׁנֵי
בָנָיו: וְשֵׁם הָאִישׁ אֱלִימֶלֶךְ וְשֵׁם אִשְׁתּוֹ נָעֳמִי וְשֵׁם שְׁנֵי־
בָנָיו ׀ מַחְלוֹן וְכִלְיוֹן אֶפְרָתִים מִבֵּית לֶחֶם יְהוּדָה וַיָּבֹאוּ
שְׂדֵי־מוֹאָב וַיִּהְיוּ־שָׁם: וַיָּמָת אֱלִימֶלֶךְ אִישׁ נָעֳמִי וַתִּשָּׁאֵר
הִיא וּשְׁנֵי בָנֶיהָ: וַיִּשְׂאוּ לָהֶם נָשִׁים מֹאֲבִיּוֹת שֵׁם הָאַחַת
עָרְפָּה וְשֵׁם הַשֵּׁנִית רוּת וַיֵּשְׁבוּ שָׁם כְּעֶשֶׂר שָׁנִים: וַיָּמֻתוּ
גַם־שְׁנֵיהֶם מַחְלוֹן וְכִלְיוֹן וַתִּשָּׁאֵר הָאִשָּׁה מִשְּׁנֵי יְלָדֶיהָ
וּמֵאִישָׁהּ: וַתָּקָם הִיא וְכַלֹּתֶיהָ וַתָּשָׁב מִשְּׂדֵי מוֹאָב כִּי
שָׁמְעָה בִּשְׂדֵה מוֹאָב כִּי־פָקַד יְהוָה אֶת־עַמּוֹ לָתֵת לָהֶם
לָחֶם: וַתֵּצֵא מִן־הַמָּקוֹם אֲשֶׁר הָיְתָה־שָׁמָּה וּשְׁתֵּי כַלֹּתֶיהָ
עִמָּהּ וַתֵּלַכְנָה בַדֶּרֶךְ לָשׁוּב אֶל־אֶרֶץ יְהוּדָה: וַתֹּאמֶר נָעֳמִי

The book of Ruth forms part of the synagogue service on *Shavuoth*, the
festival commemorating the Revelation at Mount Sinai, for the following
two reasons: the festival is described both as חג הבכורים (festival of the first
fruits) and זמן מתן תורה (festival of giving the Torah). The harvest figures
prominently in the story of Ruth, who accepted the law of life prescribed in

312

R U T H

I

In the days when the judges ruled there was a famine in the land, and a man of Bethlehem in Judah went to reside in the country of Moab, along with his wife and his two sons. The man's name was Elimelech, his wife's name was Naomi, and his two sons were called Mahlon and Chilion; they were Ephrathites of Bethlehem in Judah. They arrived in the country of Moab and stayed there.

Elimelech the husband of Naomi died, and she was left with her two sons, who married Moabite women, one named Orpah, and the other Ruth. They stayed there about ten years. Both Mahlon and Chilion died, so that the woman was bereft of her two children and her husband. She then set out with her daughters-in-law to return home from the country of Moab, for she had heard in the land of Moab that the Lord had remembered his people and given them bread.

She set out from the place where she was, along with her daughters-in-law; but, as they went on the way to return to the land of Judah, Naomi said to her two daughters-in-law:

---

the Torah when she accompanied her mother-in-law Naomi, married Boaz and became the ancestress of King David.

It is generally agreed that the book of Ruth is one of the most delightful stories ever written. It contains a beautiful example of filial devotion and demonstrates the reward for its practice by an alien, who has been better to Naomi her mother-in-law than seven sons. In Ruth we find a daughter clinging to her parent with true-hearted affection, being ready and willing to share Naomi's distress and loneliness. She is favored by God and men, and chosen by the influential Boaz of Bethlehem to be his wife. The young lonely widow of the first chapter is changed into a joyful mother of children in the last chapter. Her boy grows up to become the ancestor of the royal house of David.

לִשְׁתֵּי כַלּלֹתֶיהָ לָכֵנָה שֹּׁבְנָה אִשָּׁה לְבֵית אִמָּהּ יַעֲשֶׂה יְהֹוָה
עִמָּכֶם חֶסֶד כַּאֲשֶׁר עֲשִׂיתֶם עִם־הַמֵּתִים וְעִמָּדִי: יִתֵּן יְהֹוָה
לָכֶם וּמְצֶאןָ מְנוּחָה אִשָּׁה בֵּית אִישָׁהּ וַתִּשַּׁק לָהֶן וַתִּשֶּׂאנָה
קוֹלָן וַתִּבְכֶּינָה: וַתֹּאמַרְנָה לָּהּ כִּי־אִתָּךְ נָשׁוּב לְעַמֵּךְ:
וַתֹּאמֶר נָעֳמִי שֹׁבְנָה בְנֹתַי לָמָּה תֵלַכְנָה עִמִּי הַעוֹד־לִי
בָנִים בְּמֵעַי וְהָיוּ לָכֶם לַאֲנָשִׁים: שֹׁבְנָה בְנֹתַי לֵכְןָ כִּי
זָקַנְתִּי מִהְיוֹת לְאִישׁ כִּי אָמַרְתִּי יֶשׁ־לִי תִקְוָה גַּם הָיִיתִי
הַלַּיְלָה לְאִישׁ וְגַם יָלַדְתִּי בָנִים: הֲלָהֵן ׀ תְּשַׂבֵּרְנָה עַד
אֲשֶׁר יִגְדָּלוּ הֲלָהֵן תֵּעָגֵנָה לְבִלְתִּי הֱיוֹת לְאִישׁ אַל בְּנֹתַי
כִּי־מַר־לִי מְאֹד מִכֶּם כִּי־יָצְאָה בִי יַד־יְהֹוָה: וַתִּשֶּׂנָה קוֹלָן
וַתִּבְכֶּינָה עוֹד וַתִּשַּׁק עָרְפָּה לַחֲמוֹתָהּ וְרוּת דָּבְקָה־בָּהּ:
וַתֹּאמֶר הִנֵּה שָׁבָה יְבִמְתֵּךְ אֶל־עַמָּהּ וְאֶל־אֱלֹהֶיהָ שׁוּבִי
אַחֲרֵי יְבִמְתֵּךְ: וַתֹּאמֶר רוּת אַל־תִּפְגְּעִי־בִי לְעָזְבֵךְ לָשׁוּב
מֵאַחֲרָיִךְ כִּי אֶל־אֲשֶׁר תֵּלְכִי אֵלֵךְ וּבַאֲשֶׁר תָּלִינִי אָלִין עַמֵּךְ
עַמִּי וֵאלֹהַיִךְ אֱלֹהָי: בַּאֲשֶׁר תָּמוּתִי אָמוּת וְשָׁם אֶקָּבֵר
כֹּה יַעֲשֶׂה יְהֹוָה לִי וְכֹה יֹסִיף כִּי הַמָּוֶת יַפְרִיד בֵּינִי וּבֵינֵךְ:
וַתֵּרֶא כִּי־מִתְאַמֶּצֶת הִיא לָלֶכֶת אִתָּהּ וַתֶּחְדַּל לְדַבֵּר אֵלֶיהָ:
וַתֵּלַכְנָה שְׁתֵּיהֶם עַד־בּוֹאָנָה בֵּית לָחֶם וַיְהִי כְּבֹאָנָה בֵּית

The good qualities of Ruth are described as follows: she was careful to ask permission; she worked steadily, not resting during the hot hours of the day. She acknowledged herself an alien, destitute of right or claims; but Boaz commended the wisdom and affection which had brought her to take refuge under the protecting wings of the God of Israel.

In *Midrash Ruth*, Elimelech is described unfavorably and his name is interpreted as meaning "to me belongs royalty." He left Eretz Yisrael during the famine because he was afraid that the people might apply to him for help. Interpreting the very first words of the book of Ruth, the Midrash

"Go back, each of you, to your mother's house. May the Lord treat you kindly, as you have treated the dead and myself. May the Lord grant that each of you find rest in the home of a husband." Then she kissed them; but they wept loudly and said to her: "No, we will go back with you to your people." Naomi said: "Turn back, my daughters, why should you go with me? Have I other sons in my womb to be your husbands? Turn back, my daughters, go your way; I am too old to have a husband. If I were to say that I had hope, if I even had a husband this night and bore sons, would you wait on till they were grown? Would you let this restrain you from marrying? No, my daughters, my plight is too bitter, worse than yours, for the hand of the Lord has gone forth against me." Again they wept aloud; Orpah kissed her mother-in-law goodby, but Ruth clung to her.

Then she said: "Look, your sister-in-law has gone back to her people and to her gods; go back with your sister-in-law." But Ruth said: "Entreat me not to leave you and to turn back from following you; wherever you go, I will go; wherever you stay, I will stay; your people shall be my people, and your God shall be my God; wherever you die, I will die, and there I will be buried. [I swear], may the Lord do so and so to me, and worse, if anything but death part you and me." When Naomi saw that she was determined to go with her, she said no more.

The two went on till they reached Bethlehem. When they

---

tries to show that the famine occurred at a time when the people judged their judges, who perverted justice and were held responsible by the citizens.

The names of the persons mentioned in the book of Ruth seem to describe the characters of Naomi (pleasant), Maḥlon (sickly), Chilion (wasting away), Orpah (turning her back on Naomi), Ruth (friend), Boaz (nimble, fleet). Naomi's bitterness ("call me Marah") yields to hope and gratitude.

לֶחֶם וַתֵּהֹם כָּל־הָעִיר עֲלֵיהֶן וַתֹּאמַרְנָה הֲזֹאת נָעֳמִי׃
וַתֹּאמֶר אֲלֵיהֶן אַל־תִּקְרֶאנָה לִי נָעֳמִי קְרֶאןָ לִי מָרָא כִּי־
הֵמַר שַׁדַּי לִי מְאֹד׃ אֲנִי מְלֵאָה הָלַכְתִּי וְרֵיקָם הֱשִׁיבַנִי
יְהֹוָה לָמָּה תִקְרֶאנָה לִי נָעֳמִי וַיהֹוָה עָנָה בִי וְשַׁדַּי הֵרַע־
לִי׃ וַתָּשָׁב נָעֳמִי וְרוּת הַמּוֹאֲבִיָּה כַלָּתָהּ עִמָּהּ הַשָּׁבָה
מִשְּׂדֵי מוֹאָב וְהֵמָּה בָּאוּ בֵּית לֶחֶם בִּתְחִלַּת קְצִיר שְׂעֹרִים׃

ב

וּלְנָעֳמִי מוֹדַע לְאִישָׁהּ אִישׁ גִּבּוֹר חַיִל מִמִּשְׁפַּחַת אֱלִימֶלֶךְ
וּשְׁמוֹ בֹּעַז׃ וַתֹּאמֶר רוּת הַמּוֹאֲבִיָּה אֶל־נָעֳמִי אֵלְכָה־נָּא
הַשָּׂדֶה וַאֲלַקֳטָה בַשִּׁבֳּלִים אַחַר אֲשֶׁר אֶמְצָא־חֵן בְּעֵינָיו
וַתֹּאמֶר לָהּ לְכִי בִתִּי׃ וַתֵּלֶךְ וַתָּבוֹא וַתְּלַקֵּט בַּשָּׂדֶה אַחֲרֵי
הַקֹּצְרִים וַיִּקֶר מִקְרֶהָ חֶלְקַת הַשָּׂדֶה לְבֹעַז אֲשֶׁר מִמִּשְׁפַּחַת
אֱלִימֶלֶךְ׃ וְהִנֵּה־בֹעַז בָּא מִבֵּית לֶחֶם וַיֹּאמֶר לַקּוֹצְרִים
יְהֹוָה עִמָּכֶם וַיֹּאמְרוּ לוֹ יְבָרֶכְךָ יְהֹוָה׃ וַיֹּאמֶר בֹּעַז לְנַעֲרוֹ
הַנִּצָּב עַל־הַקּוֹצְרִים לְמִי הַנַּעֲרָה הַזֹּאת׃ וַיַּעַן הַנַּעַר הַנִּצָּב
עַל־הַקּוֹצְרִים וַיֹּאמַר נַעֲרָה מוֹאֲבִיָּה הִיא הַשָּׁבָה עִם־נָעֳמִי
מִשְּׂדֵי מוֹאָב׃ וַתֹּאמֶר אֲלַקֳטָה־נָּא וְאָסַפְתִּי בָעֳמָרִים אַחֲרֵי
הַקּוֹצְרִים וַתָּבוֹא וַתַּעֲמוֹד מֵאָז הַבֹּקֶר וְעַד־עַתָּה זֶה שִׁבְתָּהּ

Bethlehem-Judah was but a short distance from Moab, which was
a fertile country in the early biblical period. Only a famine could have in-
duced a Hebrew to migrate into this foreign land where he would have no
right of citizenship.

The women-servants of Boaz are referred to as going over the ground
after the reapers. Much would be wasted if this supplementary work were
not performed, since the manner of reaping was quite slovenly in those primi-

arrived in Bethlehem, the whole town was astir over them. The women said: "Is this Naomi?" But she said to them: "Do not call me Naomi; call me Mara, for the Lord has made it very bitter for me; I went away full, and the Lord has brought me back empty-handed. Why do you call me Naomi? The Lord has turned against me; and the Almighty has brought disaster on me.

So Naomi returned with her Moabite daughter-in-law, Ruth, who accompanied her back from the country of Moab. They arrived in Bethlehem at the beginning of the barley harvest.

II

Naomi had a kinsman on her husband's side, a brave man of wealth, who belonged to the family of Elimelech; his name was Boaz. Now, Ruth the Moabitess said to Naomi: "Let me go to the field and glean ears of grain behind a reaper with whom I may find favor." So Naomi said to her: "Go, my daughter." When she went and gleaned in the field after the harvesters, she happened to come upon that part of the field which belonged to Boaz, of the family of Elimelech. Just then Boaz came from Bethlehem and said to the harvesters: "The Lord be with you!" They replied: "May the Lord bless you!" Then Boaz asked the foreman of the reapers: "Whose girl is this?" The foreman replied: "It is the Moabite girl who came back with Naomi from the country of Moab; she asked to be allowed to glean and gather among the sheaves behind the reapers. She came and has continued working from early morning until now, with scarcely a moment's rest inside the house."

---

tive times. The young men are the harvesters from all parts of the country, and are apt to be loose in conduct.

The harvesters in the Near East still dip their bread in vinegar and

הַבַּ֫יִת מְעָט: וַיֹּ֫אמֶר בֹּ֫עַז אֶל־ר֗וּת הֲל֧וֹא שָׁמַ֣עַתְּ בִּתִּ֗י
אַל־תֵּלְכִי֙ לִלְקֹט֙ בְּשָׂדֶ֣ה אַחֵ֔ר וְגַ֛ם לֹ֥א תַעֲבוּרִ֖י מִזֶּ֑ה וְכֹ֥ה
תִדְבָּקִ֖ין עִם־נַעֲרֹתָֽי: עֵינַ֜יִךְ בַּשָּׂדֶ֤ה אֲשֶׁר־יִקְצֹרוּן֙ וְהָלַ֣כְתְּ
אַחֲרֵיהֶ֔ן הֲל֥וֹא צִוִּ֛יתִי אֶת־הַנְּעָרִ֖ים לְבִלְתִּ֣י נָגְעֵ֑ךְ וְצָמִ֗ת
וְהָלַכְתְּ֙ אֶל־הַכֵּלִ֔ים וְשָׁתִ֕ית מֵאֲשֶׁ֥ר יִשְׁאֲב֖וּן הַנְּעָרִֽים: וַתִּפֹּל֙
עַל־פָּנֶ֔יהָ וַתִּשְׁתַּ֖חוּ אָ֑רְצָה וַתֹּ֣אמֶר אֵלָ֗יו מַדּוּעַ֩ מָצָ֨אתִי חֵ֤ן
בְּעֵינֶ֨יךָ֙ לְהַכִּירֵ֔נִי וְאָנֹכִ֖י נָכְרִיָּֽה: וַיַּ֤עַן בֹּ֙עַז֙ וַיֹּ֣אמֶר לָ֔הּ הֻגֵּ֨ד
הֻגַּ֜ד לִ֗י כֹּ֤ל אֲשֶׁר־עָשִׂית֙ אֶת־חֲמוֹתֵ֔ךְ אַחֲרֵ֖י מ֣וֹת אִישֵׁ֑ךְ
וַתַּֽעַזְבִ֞י אָבִ֣יךְ וְאִמֵּ֗ךְ וְאֶ֙רֶץ֙ מֽוֹלַדְתֵּ֔ךְ וַתֵּ֣לְכִ֔י אֶל־עַ֕ם אֲשֶׁ֥ר
לֹא־יָדַ֖עַתְּ תְּמ֣וֹל שִׁלְשֽׁוֹם: יְשַׁלֵּ֥ם יְהוָ֖ה פָּעֳלֵ֑ךְ וּתְהִ֨י
מַשְׂכֻּרְתֵּ֜ךְ שְׁלֵמָ֗ה מֵעִ֤ם יְהוָה֙ אֱלֹהֵ֣י יִשְׂרָאֵ֔ל אֲשֶׁר־בָּ֖את
לַחֲס֥וֹת תַּֽחַת־כְּנָפָֽיו: וַ֠תֹּאמֶר אֶמְצָא־חֵ֨ן בְּעֵינֶ֤יךָ אֲדֹנִי֙ כִּ֣י
נִֽחַמְתָּ֔נִי וְכִ֥י דִבַּ֖רְתָּ עַל־לֵ֣ב שִׁפְחָתֶ֑ךָ וְאָנֹכִי֙ לֹ֣א אֶֽהְיֶ֔ה כְּאַחַ֖ת
שִׁפְחֹתֶֽךָ: וַיֹּ֩אמֶר֩ לָ֨ה בֹ֜עַז לְעֵ֣ת הָאֹ֗כֶל גֹּ֤שִֽׁי הֲלֹם֙ וְאָכַ֣לְתְּ
מִן־הַלֶּ֔חֶם וְטָבַ֥לְתְּ פִּתֵּ֖ךְ בַּחֹ֑מֶץ וַתֵּ֙שֶׁב֙ מִצַּ֣ד הַקֹּֽצְרִ֔ים
וַיִּצְבָּט־לָ֣הּ קָלִ֔י וַתֹּ֥אכַל וַתִּשְׂבַּ֖ע וַתֹּתַֽר: וַתָּ֖קָם לְלַקֵּ֑ט וַיְצַו֩
בֹּ֨עַז אֶת־נְעָרָ֜יו לֵאמֹ֗ר גַּ֣ם בֵּ֧ין הָֽעֳמָרִ֛ים תְּלַקֵּ֖ט וְלֹ֥א
תַכְלִימֽוּהָ: וְגַ֛ם שֹׁל־תָּשֹׁ֥לּוּ לָ֖הּ מִן־הַצְּבָתִ֑ים וַעֲזַבְתֶּ֛ם

---

find it very refreshing. Parched corn is their favorite food. The ears of grain,
when not quite ripe, are roasted on an iron plate, or are thrust in small bundles into a fire of dry grass. The crusty flavor about it makes pleasant eating.

As a special favor, Ruth is allowed to glean among the standing sheaves,
before they have been removed. The thrifty, affectionate Ruth carries to Naomi
the parched grain which remained over from her midday meal, much in the
manner of poor women taking home food from some feast which has been
given them.

Then Boaz said to Ruth: "Now listen, my daughter, do not go to glean in another field, do not leave this one, but keep here close to my girls. Keep your eyes on the field they are reaping, and follow them up; I have ordered the young men not to molest you. Whenever you are thirsty, go to the cans and drink what the young men have drawn." Then she fell on her face, bowing to the ground, and said to him: "Why have I, a foreigner, found favor with you that you should take notice of me." But Boaz answered her: "All that you have done for your mother-in-law since the death of your husband has been fully told me, and how you left your father and mother and your native land and came to a people that you did not know before. May the Lord reward you for what you have done. May you receive a rich reward from the Lord God of Israel, under whose wings you have come to take refuge!" She said: "May I prove worthy of your kindness; you have comforted me, your servant, and spoken consolingly to me, though I am not like one of your maids."

At mealtime, Boaz said to her: "Come here, eat some food; dip your bread in the vinegar." Then as she sat beside the reapers, he handed her some roasted grain; she ate till she was satisfied, and had some left over. She got up to glean, and Boaz instructed his servants, saying: "Let her glean even among the sheaves and do not scold her. Pull out even some stalks for her from the bundles and leave them for her to glean; do not rebuke her."

According to Leviticus 25:25, 47–48, if an Israelite was compelled by poverty to dispose of his property, the seller's kinsman could compel the purchaser to sell it back to him, so as to preserve each family in possession of its land.

Levirate marriage, or the obligation of marrying the deceased brother's widow, aimed at preventing the extinction of the dead man's name and was

וְלִקְּטָה וְלֹא תִגְעֲרוּ־בָֽהּ: וַתְּלַקֵּט בַּשָּׂדֶה עַד־הָעָ֑רֶב וַתַּחְבֹּט
אֵת אֲשֶׁר־לִקֵּטָה וַיְהִי כְּאֵיפָה שְׂעֹרִים: וַתִּשָּׂא וַתָּבוֹא
הָעִיר וַתֵּרֶא חֲמוֹתָהּ אֵת אֲשֶׁר־לִקֵּטָה וַתּוֹצֵא וַתִּתֶּן־לָהּ
אֵת אֲשֶׁר־הוֹתִרָה מִשָּׂבְעָֽהּ: וַתֹּאמֶר לָהּ חֲמוֹתָהּ אֵיפֹה
לִקַּטְתְּ הַיּוֹם וְאָנָה עָשִׂית יְהִי מַכִּירֵךְ בָּר֑וּךְ וַתַּגֵּד לַחֲמוֹתָהּ
אֵת אֲשֶׁר־עָשְׂתָה עִמּוֹ וַתֹּאמֶר שֵׁם הָאִישׁ אֲשֶׁר עָשִׂיתִי
עִמּוֹ הַיּוֹם בֹּֽעַז: וַתֹּאמֶר נָעֳמִי לְכַלָּתָהּ בָּרוּךְ הוּא לַֽיהוָה
אֲשֶׁר לֹא־עָזַב חַסְדּוֹ אֶת־הַחַיִּים וְאֶת־הַמֵּתִים וַתֹּאמֶר לָהּ
נָעֳמִי קָרוֹב לָנוּ הָאִישׁ מִגֹּאֲלֵנוּ הֽוּא: וַתֹּאמֶר רוּת הַמּוֹאֲבִיָּה
גַּם ׀ כִּי־אָמַר אֵלַי עִם־הַנְּעָרִים אֲשֶׁר־לִי תִּדְבָּקִין עַד אִם־
כִּלּוּ אֵת כָּל־הַקָּצִיר אֲשֶׁר־לִֽי: וַתֹּאמֶר נָעֳמִי אֶל־רוּת
כַּלָּתָהּ טוֹב בִּתִּי כִּי תֵצְאִי עִם־נַעֲרוֹתָיו וְלֹא יִפְגְּעוּ־בָךְ
בְּשָׂדֶה אַחֵֽר: וַתִּדְבַּק בְּנַעֲרוֹת בֹּעַז לְלַקֵּט עַד־כְּלוֹת
קְצִיר־הַשְּׂעֹרִים וּקְצִיר הַֽחִטִּים וַתֵּשֶׁב אֶת־חֲמוֹתָֽהּ:

ג

וַתֹּאמֶר לָהּ נָעֳמִי חֲמוֹתָהּ בִּתִּי הֲלֹא אֲבַקֶּשׁ־לָךְ מָנוֹחַ
אֲשֶׁר יִֽיטַב־לָֽךְ: וְעַתָּה הֲלֹא בֹעַז מֹֽדַעְתָּנוּ אֲשֶׁר הָיִית אֶת־
נַעֲרוֹתָיו הִנֵּה־ה֛וּא זֹרֶה אֶת־גֹּרֶן הַשְּׂעֹרִים הַלָּֽיְלָה:
וְרָחַצְתְּ ׀ וָסַכְתְּ וְשַׂמְתְּ שִׂמְלֹתֵךְ עָלַיִךְ וְיָרַדְתְּי הַגֹּרֶן אַל־
תִּוָּדְעִי לָאִישׁ עַד כַּלֹּתוֹ לֶאֱכֹל וְלִשְׁתּֽוֹת: וִיהִי בְשָׁכְבוֹ
וְיָדַעַתְּ אֶת־הַמָּקוֹם אֲשֶׁר יִשְׁכַּב־שָׁם וּבָאת וְגִלִּית מַרְגְּלֹתָיו

---

designed to save the property belonging to a family from being dispersed
among other families. The firstborn son of the levirate marriage was con-

So she gleaned in the field until evening. Then she beat
out what she had gleaned, and it was about an ephah of barley. She took it up and went into the town, and her mother-
in-law saw what she had gleaned. Then Ruth brought out and
gave her what she had left over from lunch. Her mother-in-
law asked her: "Where did you glean today? Where did you
work? May the man who took notice of you be blessed!" So
she told her mother-in-law with whom she had worked, and
said: "The man's name with whom I worked today is Boaz."
And Naomi said to her daughter-in-law: "May he be blessed
by the Lord, who is ever kind to the living and to the dead."
She then told her: "The man is a relative of ours, one of our
nearest kin." And Ruth the Moabitess said: "He even told me:
You shall keep close to my servants, till they have finished all
my harvesting." Naomi then said to her daughter-in-law Ruth:
"You will do well, my daughter, to accompany his maids, lest
you be molested in some other field." So she kept close to the
girls of Boaz, gleaning until the end of both barley and wheat
harvests; she lived with her mother-in-law.

III

Then her mother-in-law Naomi said to her: "My daughter,
I must seek a home for you, that you may fare well. Now there
is our kinsman Boaz, with whose maids you have been working.
Tonight he is winnowing barley in the threshing-floor. Wash
and anoint yourself; put on your best clothes and go down to
the threshing-floor. Do not make yourself known to the man
until he has finished eating and drinking. But when he lies
down, take note of the place where he lies. Then go in, uncover

---

sidered to be the son and heir of the man who died childless (Deuteronomy
25:5-10).

וְשָׁכָבְתִּ֒ וְה֕וּא יַגִּ֣יד לָ֔ךְ אֵ֖ת אֲשֶׁ֣ר תַּעֲשִׂ֑ין׃ וַתֹּ֖אמֶר אֵלֶ֑יהָ

כֹּ֛ל אֲשֶׁר־תֹּאמְרִ֥י ... אֶעֱשֶֽׂה׃ וַתֵּ֖רֶד הַגֹּ֑רֶן וַתַּ֕עַשׂ כְּכֹ֥ל

אֲשֶׁר־צִוַּ֖תָּה חֲמוֹתָֽהּ׃ וַיֹּ֨אכַל בֹּ֤עַז וַיֵּשְׁתְּ֙ וַיִּיטַ֣ב לִבּ֔וֹ וַיָּבֹ֕א

לִשְׁכַּ֕ב בִּקְצֵ֣ה הָעֲרֵמָ֑ה וַתָּבֹ֣א בַלָּ֗ט וַתְּגַ֛ל מַרְגְּלֹתָ֖יו וַתִּשְׁכָּֽב׃

וַיְהִי֙ בַּחֲצִ֣י הַלַּ֔יְלָה וַיֶּחֱרַ֥ד הָאִ֖ישׁ וַיִּלָּפֵ֑ת וְהִנֵּ֣ה אִשָּׁ֔ה

שֹׁכֶ֖בֶת מַרְגְּלֹתָֽיו׃ וַיֹּ֖אמֶר מִי־אָ֑תְּ וַתֹּ֗אמֶר אָנֹכִי֙ ר֣וּת אֲמָתֶ֔ךָ

וּפָרַשְׂתָּ֤ כְנָפֶ֙ךָ֙ עַל־אֲמָ֣תְךָ֔ כִּ֥י גֹאֵ֖ל אָֽתָּה׃ וַיֹּ֗אמֶר בְּרוּכָ֨ה

אַ֤תְּ לַֽיהוָה֙ בִּתִּ֔י הֵיטַ֛בְתְּ חַסְדֵּ֥ךְ הָאַחֲר֖וֹן מִן־הָרִאשׁ֑וֹן

לְבִלְתִּי־לֶ֗כֶת אַחֲרֵי֙ הַבַּ֣חוּרִ֔ים אִם־דַּ֖ל וְאִם־עָשִֽׁיר׃ וְעַתָּ֗ה

בִּתִּי֙ אַל־תִּ֣ירְאִ֔י כֹּ֥ל אֲשֶׁר־תֹּאמְרִ֖י אֶֽעֱשֶׂה־לָּ֑ךְ כִּ֣י יוֹדֵ֗עַ כָּל־

שַׁ֣עַר עַמִּ֔י כִּ֛י אֵ֥שֶׁת חַ֖יִל אָֽתְּ׃ וְעַתָּה֙ כִּ֣י אָמְנָ֔ם כִּ֥י אִ֛ם גֹּאֵ֖ל

אָנֹ֑כִי וְגַ֛ם יֵ֥שׁ גֹּאֵ֖ל קָר֥וֹב מִמֶּֽנִּי׃ לִ֣ינִי ׀ הַלַּ֗יְלָה וְהָיָ֤ה

בַבֹּ֙קֶר֙ אִם־יִגְאָלֵ֥ךְ טוֹב֙ יִגְאָ֔ל וְאִם־לֹ֨א יַחְפֹּ֤ץ לְגָֽאֳלֵךְ֙

וּגְאַלְתִּ֥יךְ אָנֹ֖כִי חַי־יְהוָ֑ה שִׁכְבִ֖י עַד־הַבֹּֽקֶר׃ וַתִּשְׁכַּ֤ב מַרְגְּלֹתָו֙

עַד־הַבֹּ֔קֶר וַתָּ֕קָם בטרום [בְּטֶ֛רֶם] יַכִּ֥יר אִ֖ישׁ אֶת־רֵעֵ֑הוּ וַיֹּ֙אמֶר֙ אַל־

יִוָּדַ֔ע כִּי־בָ֥אָה הָאִשָּׁ֖ה הַגֹּֽרֶן׃ וַיֹּ֗אמֶר הָ֠בִי הַמִּטְפַּ֧חַת אֲשֶׁר־

עָלַ֛יִךְ וְאֶֽחֳזִי־בָ֖הּ וַתֹּ֣אחֶז בָּ֑הּ וַיָּ֤מָד שֵׁשׁ־שְׂעֹרִים֙ וַיָּ֣שֶׁת עָלֶ֔יהָ

וַיָּבֹ֖א הָעִֽיר׃ וַתָּבוֹא֙ אֶל־חֲמוֹתָ֔הּ וַתֹּ֖אמֶר מִי־אַ֣תְּ בִּתִּ֑י

וַתַּ֨גֶּד־לָ֔הּ אֵ֛ת כָּל־אֲשֶׁ֥ר עָֽשָׂה־לָ֖הּ הָאִֽישׁ׃ וַתֹּ֕אמֶר שֵׁשׁ־

הַשְּׂעֹרִ֥ים הָאֵ֖לֶּה נָ֣תַן לִ֑י כִּ֚י אָמַ֣ר ... אַל־תָּב֥וֹאִי רֵיקָ֖ם אֶל־

חֲמוֹתֵֽךְ׃ וַתֹּ֙אמֶר֙ שְׁבִ֣י בִתִּ֔י עַ֚ד אֲשֶׁ֣ר תֵּֽדְעִ֔ין אֵ֖יךְ יִפֹּ֣ל

דָּבָ֑ר כִּ֣י לֹ֤א יִשְׁקֹט֙ הָאִ֔ישׁ כִּֽי־אִם־כִּלָּ֥ה הַדָּבָ֖ר הַיּֽוֹם׃

Grain is winnowed in the evening, to take advantage of the cool sea-wind,
which blows in Eretz Yisrael from 4 o'clock in the afternoon to half-an-hour
before sunset. The threshing floor is generally on an elevated spot. The town

his feet, and lie down; he will tell you what to do." Ruth replied:
"I will do whatever you say." So she went down to the threshing-
floor and did exactly as her mother-in-law had instructed her.

Boaz ate and drank to his heart's content, and went to lie
down at the end of the grain heap. Then she came in noise-
lessly, uncovered his feet, and lay down. In the middle of the
night, however, the man was startled and bent forward; there
was a woman lying at his feet. He asked: "Who are you?"
And she replied: "I am your servant Ruth; now spread your
robe over your servant, for you are a near kinsman." He said:
"May the Lord bless you, my daughter; this last kindness of
yours is even greater than the first, in that you have not gone
after young men, whether poor or rich. Have no fear, my
daughter; I will do for you all that you ask; all my towns-
people know that you are a good woman. Now, it is true that
I am a near kinsman, but there is a nearer kinsman than myself.
Stay as you are for tonight, and in the morning, if he will
claim you as your nearest kin, well and good; let him do a
kinsman's duty. But if he will not do his duty as a kinsman
to you, I will claim you myself, as the Lord lives. Lie down
until morning." So she lay at his feet until morning, but rose
before men could recognize one another. Boaz said: "Let it
not be known that this woman came to the threshing-floor."
Then he said to her: "Bring the mantle you are wearing and
hold it open." So she held it open, and he poured out six
measures of barley and placed the bundle on her back; then he
went into the town.

Ruth came home to her mother-in-law, who asked: "How
did you fare, my daughter?" So she told her all that the man
had done for her, saying: "He gave me these six measures of
barley, because he said: Do not come back to your mother-
in-law empty-handed." Naomi then said: "My daughter, wait
until you learn what happens, for the man will not rest till
he settles the matter today."

---

of Bethlehem, however, is situated on the summit of the mountain range,
hence it was necessary to go down to the threshing floor, which was an open
space of clean, hard, dry ground.

ד

וּבֹ֨עַז עָלָ֣ה הַשַּׁעַר֮ וַיֵּ֣שֶׁב שָׁם֒ וְהִנֵּ֨ה הַגֹּאֵ֤ל עֹבֵר֙ אֲשֶׁ֣ר דִּבֶּר־
בֹּ֔עַז וַיֹּ֛אמֶר ס֥וּרָה שְׁבָה־פֹּ֖ה פְּלֹנִ֣י אַלְמֹנִ֑י וַיָּ֖סַר וַיֵּשֵֽׁב:
וַיִּקַּ֞ח עֲשָׂרָ֧ה אֲנָשִׁ֛ים מִזִּקְנֵ֥י הָעִ֖יר וַיֹּ֣אמֶר שְׁבוּ־פֹ֑ה וַיֵּשֵֽׁבוּ:
וַיֹּ֙אמֶר֙ לַגֹּאֵ֔ל חֶלְקַת֙ הַשָּׂדֶ֔ה אֲשֶׁ֥ר לְאָחִ֖ינוּ לֶאֱלִימֶ֑לֶךְ
מָכְרָ֣ה נׇעֳמִ֔י הַשָּׁ֖בָה מִשְּׂדֵ֥ה מוֹאָֽב: וַאֲנִ֨י אָמַ֜רְתִּי אֶגְלֶ֧ה
אׇזְנְךָ֣ לֵאמֹ֗ר קְ֠נֵ֠ה נֶ֥גֶד הַיֹּשְׁבִים֮ וְנֶ֣גֶד זִקְנֵ֣י עַמִּי֒ אִם־תִּגְאַל֙
גְּאָ֔ל וְאִם־לֹ֨א יִגְאַ֜ל הַגִּ֣ידָה לִּ֗י וְאֵדַע֙ כִּ֣י אֵ֤ין זוּלָֽתְךָ֙ לִגְא֔וֹל
וְאָנֹכִ֖י אַחֲרֶ֑יךָ וַיֹּ֖אמֶר אָנֹכִ֥י אֶגְאָֽל: וַיֹּ֣אמֶר בֹּ֗עַז בְּיוֹם־
קְנוֹתְךָ֥ הַשָּׂדֶ֖ה מִיַּ֣ד נׇעֳמִ֑י וּ֠מֵאֵ֠ת ר֣וּת הַמּוֹאֲבִיָּ֤ה אֵשֶׁת־הַמֵּת֙
קָנִ֔יתִי לְהָקִ֧ים שֵׁם־הַמֵּ֖ת עַל־נַחֲלָתֽוֹ: וַיֹּ֣אמֶר הַגֹּאֵ֗ל לֹ֤א
אוּכַל֙ לִגְאׇל־לִ֔י פֶּן־אַשְׁחִ֖ית אֶת־נַחֲלָתִ֑י גְּאַל־לְךָ֤ אַתָּה֙ אֶת־
גְּאֻלָּתִ֔י כִּ֥י לֹא־אוּכַ֖ל לִגְאֹֽל: וְזֹאת֩ לְפָנִ֨ים בְּיִשְׂרָאֵ֜ל עַל־
הַגְּאֻלָּ֤ה וְעַל־הַתְּמוּרָה֙ לְקַיֵּ֣ם כׇּל־דָּבָ֔ר שָׁלַ֥ף אִ֛ישׁ נַעֲל֖וֹ
וְנָתַ֣ן לְרֵעֵ֑הוּ וְזֹ֥את הַתְּעוּדָ֖ה בְּיִשְׂרָאֵֽל: וַיֹּ֧אמֶר הַגֹּאֵ֛ל
לְבֹ֖עַז קְנֵה־לָ֑ךְ וַיִּשְׁלֹ֖ף נַעֲלֽוֹ: וַיֹּ֩אמֶר֩ בֹּ֨עַז לַזְּקֵנִ֜ים וְכׇל־
הָעָ֗ם עֵדִ֤ים אַתֶּם֙ הַיּ֔וֹם כִּ֤י קָנִ֙יתִי֙ אֶת־כׇּל־אֲשֶׁ֣ר לֶֽאֱלִימֶ֔לֶךְ
וְאֵ֛ת כׇּל־אֲשֶׁ֥ר לְכִלְי֖וֹן וּמַחְל֑וֹן מִיַּ֖ד נׇעֳמִֽי: וְגַ֣ם אֶת־ר֣וּת
הַמֹּאֲבִיָּ֣ה אֵ֨שֶׁת מַחְל֜וֹן קָנִ֧יתִי לִ֣י לְאִשָּׁ֗ה לְהָקִ֤ים שֵׁם־הַמֵּת֙
עַל־נַ֣חֲלָת֔וֹ וְלֹא־יִכָּרֵ֧ת שֵׁם־הַמֵּ֛ת מֵעִ֥ם אֶחָ֖יו וּמִשַּׁ֣עַר מְקוֹמ֑וֹ

The grain was winnowed by throwing it up with forks or shovels against
the evening breeze, which blew away the chaff, while the heavier grain fell
on the ground in a heap. The Torah forbids muzzling the oxen that are driven

IV

Boaz went up to the town gate and sat down there; and there was the near kinsman of whom Boaz had spoken, passing by. So Boaz called to him by name, saying: "Step aside and sit down here." So he stepped aside and sat down. Then Boaz picked out ten of the elders of the town, and said: "Sit down here," so they sat down. Then he said to the near kinsman: "Naomi, who has come back from the Moabite country, is putting up for sale the piece of land that belonged to our kinsman Elimelech. So I thought I would inform you, and say: Buy it in the presence of those who are sitting here, in the presence of the elders of my people. If you wish to acquire it as next of kin, redeem it; but if you will not claim it as next of kin, tell me, that I may know, for there is no one to claim it as next of kin except yourself, and I come after you." The man said: "I will redeem it." Then Boaz said: "Once you acquire the field from Naomi, you are also acquiring Ruth the Moabitess, the widow of the deceased man, so as to restore the name of the departed to his estate." The near relative replied: "I cannot take it up, lest I depreciate my own estate. Take my right of redemption yourself, for I cannot redeem it."

Now it used to be the custom in Israel that, to make binding a contract of redeeming or exchanging, one party would take off his sandal and give it to the other; this was how exchanges were attested in Israel. So when the near kinsman said to Boaz, "Acquire it for yourself," he drew off his sandal. Then Boaz said to the elders and all the people: "You are witnesses today that I have acquired from Naomi all that belonged to Elimelech, Chilion, and Mahlon. I also take Ruth the Moabitess, the widow of Mahlon, as my wife, in order to

---

over the grain spread out on a level threshing floor, open to the air (Deuteronomy 25:4). This command enjoins a kind consideration for the beasts.

עֵדִים אַתֶּם הַיּוֹם: וַיֹּאמְרוּ כָּל־הָעָם אֲשֶׁר־בַּשַּׁעַר וְהַזְּקֵנִים
עֵדִים יִתֵּן יְהֹוָה אֶת־הָאִשָּׁה הַבָּאָה אֶל־בֵּיתֶךָ כְּרָחֵל ׀
וּכְלֵאָה אֲשֶׁר בָּנוּ שְׁתֵּיהֶם אֶת־בֵּית יִשְׂרָאֵל וַעֲשֵׂה־חַיִל
בְּאֶפְרָתָה וּקְרָא־שֵׁם בְּבֵית לָחֶם: וִיהִי בֵיתְךָ כְּבֵית פֶּרֶץ
אֲשֶׁר־יָלְדָה תָמָר לִיהוּדָה מִן־הַזֶּרַע אֲשֶׁר יִתֵּן יְהֹוָה לְךָ
מִן־הַנַּעֲרָה הַזֹּאת: וַיִּקַּח בֹּעַז אֶת־רוּת וַתְּהִי־לוֹ לְאִשָּׁה
וַיָּבֹא אֵלֶיהָ וַיִּתֵּן יְהֹוָה לָהּ הֵרָיוֹן וַתֵּלֶד בֵּן: וַתֹּאמַרְנָה
הַנָּשִׁים אֶל־נָעֳמִי בָּרוּךְ יְהֹוָה אֲשֶׁר לֹא הִשְׁבִּית לָךְ גֹּאֵל
הַיּוֹם וְיִקָּרֵא שְׁמוֹ בְּיִשְׂרָאֵל: וְהָיָה לָךְ לְמֵשִׁיב נֶפֶשׁ
וּלְכַלְכֵּל אֶת־שֵׂיבָתֵךְ כִּי כַלָּתֵךְ אֲשֶׁר־אֲהֵבַתֶךְ יְלָדַתּוּ
אֲשֶׁר־הִיא טוֹבָה לָךְ מִשִּׁבְעָה בָּנִים: וַתִּקַּח נָעֳמִי אֶת־
הַיֶּלֶד וַתְּשִׁתֵהוּ בְחֵיקָהּ וַתְּהִי־לוֹ לְאֹמֶנֶת: וַתִּקְרֶאנָה לוֹ
הַשְּׁכֵנוֹת שֵׁם לֵאמֹר יֻלַּד־בֵּן לְנָעֳמִי וַתִּקְרֶאנָה שְׁמוֹ עוֹבֵד
הוּא אֲבִי־יִשַׁי אֲבִי דָוִד: וְאֵלֶּה תּוֹלְדוֹת פֶּרֶץ פֶּרֶץ הוֹלִיד
אֶת־חֶצְרוֹן: וְחֶצְרוֹן הוֹלִיד אֶת־רָם וְרָם הוֹלִיד אֶת־
עַמִּינָדָב: וְעַמִּינָדָב הוֹלִיד אֶת־נַחְשׁוֹן וְנַחְשׁוֹן הוֹלִיד אֶת־
שַׂלְמָה: וְשַׂלְמוֹן הוֹלִיד אֶת־בֹּעַז וּבֹעַז הוֹלִיד אֶת־עוֹבֵד:
וְעֹבֵד הוֹלִיד אֶת־יִשַׁי וְיִשַׁי הוֹלִיד אֶת־דָּוִד:

Mourners' Kaddish

Ploni Almoni, meaning so-and-so or such-and-such, are two words compounded into one word, *Palmoni* (Daniel 8:13), used where the man's name is unknown.

restore the name of the departed to his estate, so that the name of the deceased may not perish among his kinsmen, from the gate of his native place; you are witnesses this day." Then all the people who were at the gate, and the elders, said: "We are witnesses. May the Lord make this woman, who is coming to your house, like Rachel and Leah, who together built up the house of Israel. May you do well in Ephrathah and win fame in Bethlehem. May your house flourish like the house of Perez, whom Tamar bore to Judah, with the offspring that the Lord will give you from this girl."

So Boaz took Ruth, and she became his wife. He went in to her, and the Lord made her conceive, and she bore a son. Then the women said to Naomi: "Blessed be the Lord, who has not left you this day without a near kinsman; may he become famous in Israel. The child will revive your life and cherish you in your old age; for he is the son of your daughter-in-law, who loves you, who is better than seven sons to you." Naomi took the child, placed him on her lap, and became his nurse. The neighbor women gave him a name, saying: "A son has been born to Naomi." They named him Obed. He was the father of Jesse, the father of David.

These are the descendants of Perez: Perez was the father of Hezron, Hezron of Ram, Ram of Amminadab, Amminadab of Nahshon, Nahshon of Salmon, Salmon of Boaz, Boaz of Obed, Obed of Jesse, and Jesse of David.

Mourners' Kaddish

The shoe thrown over the land is a sign that possession is taken (Psalms 60:10; 108:10). The Hebrew word *goel* signifies the next-of-kin whose right it was to redeem his dead relative's property. It was the duty of the *goel* to marry the widow, if the relative had died childless.

עַרְבִית לְמוֹצָאֵי יוֹם טוֹב

וְהוּא רַחוּם, יְכַפֵּר עָוֹן וְלֹא יַשְׁחִית; וְהִרְבָּה לְהָשִׁיב אַפּוֹ,
וְלֹא יָעִיר כָּל חֲמָתוֹ. יְיָ, הוֹשִׁיעָה; הַמֶּלֶךְ יַעֲנֵנוּ בְיוֹם קָרְאֵנוּ.

Silent meditation:	Reader:

Reader:
בָּרְכוּ אֶת יְיָ הַמְבֹרָךְ.

Silent meditation:
יִתְבָּרַךְ וְיִשְׁתַּבַּח, וְיִתְפָּאַר וְיִתְרוֹמַם
וְיִתְנַשֵּׂא שְׁמוֹ שֶׁל מֶלֶךְ מַלְכֵי הַמְּלָכִים,
הַקָּדוֹשׁ בָּרוּךְ הוּא, שֶׁהוּא רִאשׁוֹן וְהוּא
אַחֲרוֹן, וּמִבַּלְעָדָיו אֵין אֱלֹהִים. סֹלוּ

Congregation and Reader:
בָּרוּךְ יְיָ הַמְבֹרָךְ לְעוֹלָם וָעֶד.

לָרֹכֵב בָּעֲרָבוֹת, בְּיָהּ שְׁמוֹ, וְעִלְזוּ לְפָנָיו. וּשְׁמוֹ מְרוֹמָם עַל כָּל בְּרָכָה וּתְהִלָּה. בָּרוּךְ
שֵׁם כְּבוֹד מַלְכוּתוֹ לְעוֹלָם וָעֶד. יְהִי שֵׁם יְיָ מְבֹרָךְ מֵעַתָּה וְעַד עוֹלָם.

בָּרוּךְ אַתָּה, יְיָ אֱלֹהֵינוּ, מֶלֶךְ הָעוֹלָם, אֲשֶׁר בִּדְבָרוֹ מַעֲרִיב
עֲרָבִים. בְּחָכְמָה פּוֹתֵחַ שְׁעָרִים, וּבִתְבוּנָה מְשַׁנֶּה עִתִּים,
וּמַחֲלִיף אֶת הַזְּמַנִּים, וּמְסַדֵּר אֶת הַכּוֹכָבִים בְּמִשְׁמְרוֹתֵיהֶם
בָּרָקִיעַ כִּרְצוֹנוֹ. בּוֹרֵא יוֹם וָלָיְלָה, גּוֹלֵל אוֹר מִפְּנֵי חֹשֶׁךְ וְחֹשֶׁךְ
מִפְּנֵי אוֹר, וּמַעֲבִיר יוֹם וּמֵבִיא לָיְלָה, וּמַבְדִּיל בֵּין יוֹם וּבֵין
לָיְלָה, יְיָ צְבָאוֹת שְׁמוֹ. Reader אֵל חַי וְקַיָּם, תָּמִיד יִמְלוֹךְ עָלֵינוּ,
לְעוֹלָם וָעֶד. בָּרוּךְ אַתָּה, יְיָ, הַמַּעֲרִיב עֲרָבִים.

אַהֲבַת עוֹלָם בֵּית יִשְׂרָאֵל עַמְּךָ אָהָבְתָּ; תּוֹרָה וּמִצְוֹת,
חֻקִּים וּמִשְׁפָּטִים, אוֹתָנוּ לִמַּדְתָּ; עַל כֵּן, יְיָ אֱלֹהֵינוּ, בְּשָׁכְבֵנוּ
וּבְקוּמֵנוּ נָשִׂיחַ בְּחֻקֶּיךָ, וְנִשְׂמַח בְּדִבְרֵי תוֹרָתֶךָ וּבְמִצְוֹתֶיךָ
לְעוֹלָם וָעֶד. כִּי הֵם חַיֵּינוּ וְאֹרֶךְ יָמֵינוּ, וּבָהֶם נֶהְגֶּה יוֹמָם וָלָיְלָה.
Reader וְאַהֲבָתְךָ אַל תָּסִיר מִמֶּנּוּ לְעוֹלָמִים. בָּרוּךְ אַתָּה, יְיָ,
אוֹהֵב עַמּוֹ יִשְׂרָאֵל.

EVENING SERVICE

He, being merciful, forgives iniquity, and does not destroy; frequently he turns his anger away, and does not stir up all his wrath. O Lord, save us; may the King answer us when we call.[1]

Reader:

Bless the Lord who is blessed.

Congregation and Reader:

Blessed be the Lord who is blessed forever and ever.

Silent meditation:

Blessed, praised, glorified, extolled and exalted be the name of the supreme King of kings, the Holy One, blessed be he, who is the first and the last, and besides him there is no God. Extol him who is in the heavens—Lord is his name, and rejoice before him. His name is exalted above all blessing and praise. Blessed be the name of his glorious majesty forever and ever. Let the name of the Lord be blessed henceforth and forever.

Blessed art thou, Lord our God, King of the universe, who at thy word bringest on the evenings. With wisdom thou openest the gates of heaven, and with understanding thou changest the times and causest the seasons to alternate. Thou arrangest the stars in their courses in the sky according to thy will. Thou createst day and night; thou rollest away light before darkness, and darkness before light; thou causest the day to pass and the night to come, and makest the distinction between day and night—Lord of hosts is thy name. Eternal God, mayest thou reign over us forever and ever. Blessed art thou, O Lord, who bringest on the evenings.

Thou hast loved the house of Israel thy people with everlasting love; thou hast taught us Torah and precepts, laws and judgments. Therefore, Lord our God, when we lie down and when we rise up we will speak of thy laws, and rejoice in the words of thy Torah and in thy precepts for evermore. Indeed, they are our life and the length of our days; we will meditate on them day and night. Mayest thou never take away thy love from us. Blessed art thou, O Lord. who lovest thy people Israel.

---

[1] *Psalms* 78:38; 20:10.

(When praying in private, add: אֵל מֶלֶךְ נֶאֱמָן)

דברים ו, ד–ט

שְׁמַע יִשְׂרָאֵל, יְיָ אֱלֹהֵינוּ, יְיָ אֶחָד.

בָּרוּךְ שֵׁם כְּבוֹד מַלְכוּתוֹ לְעוֹלָם וָעֶד.

וְאָהַבְתָּ אֵת יְיָ אֱלֹהֶיךָ בְּכָל לְבָבְךָ וּבְכָל נַפְשְׁךָ וּבְכָל מְאֹדֶךָ. וְהָיוּ הַדְּבָרִים הָאֵלֶּה, אֲשֶׁר אָנֹכִי מְצַוְּךָ הַיּוֹם, עַל לְבָבֶךָ. וְשִׁנַּנְתָּם לְבָנֶיךָ, וְדִבַּרְתָּ בָּם בְּשִׁבְתְּךָ בְּבֵיתֶךָ, וּבְלֶכְתְּךָ בַדֶּרֶךְ, וּבְשָׁכְבְּךָ וּבְקוּמֶךָ. וּקְשַׁרְתָּם לְאוֹת עַל יָדֶךָ, וְהָיוּ לְטֹטָפֹת בֵּין עֵינֶיךָ. וּכְתַבְתָּם עַל מְזֻזוֹת בֵּיתֶךָ וּבִשְׁעָרֶיךָ.

דברים יא, יג–כא

וְהָיָה אִם שָׁמֹעַ תִּשְׁמְעוּ אֶל מִצְוֹתַי, אֲשֶׁר אָנֹכִי מְצַוֶּה אֶתְכֶם הַיּוֹם, לְאַהֲבָה אֶת יְיָ אֱלֹהֵיכֶם, וּלְעָבְדוֹ בְּכָל לְבַבְכֶם וּבְכָל נַפְשְׁכֶם. וְנָתַתִּי מְטַר אַרְצְכֶם בְּעִתּוֹ, יוֹרֶה וּמַלְקוֹשׁ; וְאָסַפְתָּ דְגָנֶךָ, וְתִירֹשְׁךָ וְיִצְהָרֶךָ. וְנָתַתִּי עֵשֶׂב בְּשָׂדְךָ לִבְהֶמְתֶּךָ; וְאָכַלְתָּ וְשָׂבָעְתָּ. הִשָּׁמְרוּ לָכֶם פֶּן יִפְתֶּה לְבַבְכֶם, וְסַרְתֶּם וַעֲבַדְתֶּם אֱלֹהִים אֲחֵרִים, וְהִשְׁתַּחֲוִיתֶם לָהֶם. וְחָרָה אַף יְיָ בָּכֶם, וְעָצַר אֶת הַשָּׁמַיִם וְלֹא יִהְיֶה מָטָר, וְהָאֲדָמָה לֹא תִתֵּן אֶת יְבוּלָהּ; וַאֲבַדְתֶּם מְהֵרָה מֵעַל הָאָרֶץ הַטֹּבָה אֲשֶׁר יְיָ נֹתֵן לָכֶם. וְשַׂמְתֶּם אֶת דְּבָרַי אֵלֶּה עַל לְבַבְכֶם וְעַל נַפְשְׁכֶם; וּקְשַׁרְתֶּם אֹתָם לְאוֹת עַל יֶדְכֶם, וְהָיוּ לְטוֹטָפֹת בֵּין עֵינֵיכֶם. וְלִמַּדְתֶּם אֹתָם אֶת בְּנֵיכֶם לְדַבֵּר בָּם, בְּשִׁבְתְּךָ בְּבֵיתֶךָ, וּבְלֶכְתְּךָ בַדֶּרֶךְ, וּבְשָׁכְבְּךָ וּבְקוּמֶךָ. וּכְתַבְתָּם עַל מְזוּזוֹת בֵּיתֶךָ וּבִשְׁעָרֶיךָ.

לְמַעַן יִרְבּוּ יְמֵיכֶם וִימֵי בְנֵיכֶם, עַל הָאֲדָמָה אֲשֶׁר נִשְׁבַּע יְיָ לַאֲבֹתֵיכֶם לָתֵת לָהֶם, כִּימֵי הַשָּׁמַיִם עַל הָאָרֶץ.

במדבר טו, לז–מא

וַיֹּאמֶר יְיָ אֶל מֹשֶׁה לֵּאמֹר: דַּבֵּר אֶל בְּנֵי יִשְׂרָאֵל וְאָמַרְתָּ

SHEMA

(When praying in private, add: God is a faithful King.)

Deuteronomy 6:4–9

Hear, O Israel, the Lord is our God, the Lord is One.

Blessed be the name of his glorious majesty forever and ever.

You shall love the Lord your God with all your heart, and with all your soul, and with all your might. And these words which I command you today shall be in your heart. You shall teach them diligently to your children, and you shall speak of them when you are sitting at home and when you go on a journey, when you lie down and when you rise up. You shall bind them for a sign on your hand, and they shall be for frontlets between your eyes. You shall inscribe them on the doorposts of your house and on your gates.

Deuteronomy 11:13–21

And if you will carefully obey my commands which I give you today, to love the Lord your God and to serve him with all your heart and with all your soul, I will give rain for your land at the right season, the autumn rains and the spring rains, that you may gather in your grain, your wine and your oil. And I will provide grass in your fields for your cattle, and you will eat and be satisfied. Beware lest your heart be deceived, and you turn and serve other gods and worship them; for then the Lord's anger will blaze against you, and he will shut up the skies so that there will be no rain, and the land will yield no produce, and you will quickly perish from the good land which the Lord gives you. So you shall place these words of mine in your heart and in your soul, and you shall bind them for a sign on your hand, and they shall be for frontlets between your eyes. You shall teach them to your children, speaking of them when you are sitting at home and when you go on a journey, when you lie down and when you rise up. You shall inscribe them on the doorposts of your house and on your gates—

That your life and the life of your children may be prolonged in the land, which the Lord promised he would give to your fathers, as long as the sky remains over the earth.

Numbers 15:37–41

The Lord spoke to Moses, saying: Speak to the children of

אֲלֵהֶם, וְעָשׂוּ לָהֶם צִיצִת עַל כַּנְפֵי בִגְדֵיהֶם לְדֹרֹתָם, וְנָתְנוּ עַל
צִיצִת הַכָּנָף פְּתִיל תְּכֵלֶת. וְהָיָה לָכֶם לְצִיצִת, וּרְאִיתֶם אֹתוֹ
וּזְכַרְתֶּם אֶת כָּל מִצְוֹת יְיָ, וַעֲשִׂיתֶם אֹתָם; וְלֹא תָתוּרוּ אַחֲרֵי
לְבַבְכֶם וְאַחֲרֵי עֵינֵיכֶם, אֲשֶׁר אַתֶּם זֹנִים אַחֲרֵיהֶם. לְמַעַן
תִּזְכְּרוּ וַעֲשִׂיתֶם אֶת כָּל מִצְוֹתָי, וִהְיִיתֶם קְדֹשִׁים לֵאלֹהֵיכֶם.
אֲנִי יְיָ אֱלֹהֵיכֶם, אֲשֶׁר הוֹצֵאתִי אֶתְכֶם מֵאֶרֶץ מִצְרַיִם לִהְיוֹת
לָכֶם לֵאלֹהִים; אֲנִי יְיָ אֱלֹהֵיכֶם— Reader

אֱמֶת וֶאֱמוּנָה כָּל זֹאת, וְקַיָּם עָלֵינוּ כִּי הוּא יְיָ אֱלֹהֵינוּ וְאֵין
זוּלָתוֹ, וַאֲנַחְנוּ יִשְׂרָאֵל עַמּוֹ. הַפּוֹדֵנוּ מִיַּד מְלָכִים, מַלְכֵּנוּ
הַגּוֹאֲלֵנוּ מִכַּף כָּל הֶעָרִיצִים; הָאֵל הַנִּפְרָע לָנוּ מִצָּרֵינוּ,
וְהַמְשַׁלֵּם גְּמוּל לְכָל אֹיְבֵי נַפְשֵׁנוּ; הָעֹשֶׂה גְדֹלוֹת עַד אֵין חֵקֶר,
וְנִפְלָאוֹת עַד אֵין מִסְפָּר; הַשָּׂם נַפְשֵׁנוּ בַּחַיִּים, וְלֹא נָתַן לַמּוֹט
רַגְלֵנוּ; הַמַּדְרִיכֵנוּ עַל בָּמוֹת אוֹיְבֵינוּ, וַיָּרֶם קַרְנֵנוּ עַל כָּל שֹׂנְאֵינוּ;
הָעֹשֶׂה לָּנוּ נִסִּים וּנְקָמָה בְּפַרְעֹה, אוֹתוֹת וּמוֹפְתִים בְּאַדְמַת
בְּנֵי חָם; הַמַּכֶּה בְעֶבְרָתוֹ כָּל בְּכוֹרֵי מִצְרָיִם, וַיּוֹצֵא אֶת עַמּוֹ
יִשְׂרָאֵל מִתּוֹכָם לְחֵרוּת עוֹלָם. הַמַּעֲבִיר בָּנָיו בֵּין גִּזְרֵי יַם סוּף;
אֶת רוֹדְפֵיהֶם וְאֶת שׂוֹנְאֵיהֶם בִּתְהוֹמוֹת טִבַּע. וְרָאוּ בָנָיו גְּבוּרָתוֹ;
שִׁבְּחוּ וְהוֹדוּ לִשְׁמוֹ, וּמַלְכוּתוֹ בְּרָצוֹן קִבְּלוּ עֲלֵיהֶם.

מֹשֶׁה וּבְנֵי יִשְׂרָאֵל לְךָ עָנוּ שִׁירָה בְּשִׂמְחָה רַבָּה, וְאָמְרוּ כֻלָּם:
מִי כָמֹכָה בָּאֵלִם, יְיָ; מִי כָּמֹכָה נֶאְדָּר בַּקֹּדֶשׁ, נוֹרָא תְהִלֹּת,
עֹשֵׂה פֶלֶא.

מַלְכוּתְךָ רָאוּ בָנֶיךָ, בּוֹקֵעַ יָם לִפְנֵי מֹשֶׁה; זֶה אֵלִי עָנוּ
וְאָמְרוּ:   יְיָ יִמְלֹךְ לְעֹלָם וָעֶד.

וְנֶאֱמַר: כִּי פָדָה יְיָ אֶת יַעֲקֹב, וּגְאָלוֹ מִיַּד חָזָק מִמֶּנּוּ. בָּרוּךְ
אַתָּה, יְיָ, גָּאַל יִשְׂרָאֵל.

Israel and tell them to make for themselves fringes on the corners of their garments throughout their generations, and to put on the fringe of each corner a blue thread. You shall have it as a fringe, so that when you look upon it you will remember to do all the commands of the Lord, and you will not follow the desires of your heart and your eyes which lead you astray. It is for you to remember and do all my commands and be holy to your God. I am the Lord your God who brought you out of the land of Egypt to be your God; I am the Lord your God.

True and trustworthy is all this. We are certain that he is the Lord our God, and no one else, and that we Israel are his people. It is he, our King, who redeemed us from the power of despots, delivered us from the grasp of all the tyrants, avenged us upon our oppressors, and requited all our mortal enemies. He did great, incomprehensible acts and countless wonders; he kept us alive, and did not let us slip.[1] He made us tread upon the high places of our enemies, and raised our strength over all our foes. He performed for us miracles and vengeance upon Pharaoh, signs and wonders in the land of the Hamites; he smote in his wrath all the first-born of Egypt, and brought his people Israel from their midst to enduring freedom. He made his children pass between the divided parts of the Red Sea, and engulfed their pursuers and their enemies in the depths. His children beheld his might; they gave praise and thanks to his name, and willingly accepted his sovereignty.

Moses and the children of Israel sang a song to thee with great rejoicing; all of them said:

"Who is like thee, O Lord, among the mighty? Who is like thee, glorious in holiness, awe-inspiring in renown, doing wonders?"[2]

Thy children saw thy majesty as thou didst part the sea before Moses. "This is my God!" they shouted, and they said:

"The Lord shall reign forever and ever."[3]

And it is said: "Indeed, the Lord has delivered Jacob, and rescued him from a stronger power."[4] Blessed art thou, O Lord, who hast redeemed Israel.

---

[1] *Job* 9:10; *Psalm* 66:9. [2] *Exodus* 15:11. [3] *Exodus* 15:18. [4] *Jeremiah* 31:10.

הַשְׁכִּיבֵנוּ, יְיָ אֱלֹהֵינוּ, לְשָׁלוֹם, וְהַעֲמִידֵנוּ, מַלְכֵּנוּ, לְחַיִּים;
וּפְרוֹשׂ עָלֵינוּ סֻכַּת שְׁלוֹמֶךָ, וְתַקְּנֵנוּ בְּעֵצָה טוֹבָה מִלְּפָנֶיךָ,
וְהוֹשִׁיעֵנוּ לְמַעַן שְׁמֶךָ; וְהָגֵן בַּעֲדֵנוּ, וְהָסֵר מֵעָלֵינוּ אוֹיֵב, דֶּבֶר
וְחֶרֶב וְרָעָב וְיָגוֹן; וְהָסֵר שָׂטָן מִלְּפָנֵינוּ וּמֵאַחֲרֵינוּ, וּבְצֵל כְּנָפֶיךָ
תַּסְתִּירֵנוּ; כִּי אֵל שׁוֹמְרֵנוּ וּמַצִּילֵנוּ אָתָּה, כִּי אֵל מֶלֶךְ חַנּוּן
וְרַחוּם אָתָּה. Reader וּשְׁמוֹר צֵאתֵנוּ וּבוֹאֵנוּ לְחַיִּים וּלְשָׁלוֹם,
מֵעַתָּה וְעַד עוֹלָם. בָּרוּךְ אַתָּה, יְיָ, שׁוֹמֵר עַמּוֹ יִשְׂרָאֵל לָעַד.

בָּרוּךְ יְיָ לְעוֹלָם, אָמֵן וְאָמֵן. בָּרוּךְ יְיָ מִצִּיּוֹן, שֹׁכֵן יְרוּשָׁלָיִם;
הַלְלוּיָהּ. בָּרוּךְ יְיָ אֱלֹהִים, אֱלֹהֵי יִשְׂרָאֵל, עֹשֵׂה נִפְלָאוֹת לְבַדּוֹ.
וּבָרוּךְ שֵׁם כְּבוֹדוֹ לְעוֹלָם; וְיִמָּלֵא כְבוֹדוֹ אֶת כָּל הָאָרֶץ, אָמֵן
וְאָמֵן. יְהִי כְבוֹד יְיָ לְעוֹלָם; יִשְׂמַח יְיָ בְּמַעֲשָׂיו. יְהִי שֵׁם יְיָ
מְבֹרָךְ, מֵעַתָּה וְעַד עוֹלָם. כִּי לֹא יִטּשׁ יְיָ אֶת עַמּוֹ בַּעֲבוּר שְׁמוֹ
הַגָּדוֹל; כִּי הוֹאִיל יְיָ לַעֲשׂוֹת אֶתְכֶם לוֹ לְעָם. וַיַּרְא כָּל הָעָם
וַיִּפְּלוּ עַל פְּנֵיהֶם, וַיֹּאמְרוּ: יְיָ הוּא הָאֱלֹהִים, יְיָ הוּא הָאֱלֹהִים.
וְהָיָה יְיָ לְמֶלֶךְ עַל כָּל הָאָרֶץ; בַּיּוֹם הַהוּא יִהְיֶה יְיָ אֶחָד וּשְׁמוֹ
אֶחָד. יְהִי חַסְדְּךָ יְיָ עָלֵינוּ, כַּאֲשֶׁר יִחַלְנוּ לָךְ. הוֹשִׁיעֵנוּ, יְיָ
אֱלֹהֵינוּ, וְקַבְּצֵנוּ מִן הַגּוֹיִם, לְהוֹדוֹת לְשֵׁם קָדְשֶׁךָ, לְהִשְׁתַּבֵּחַ
בִּתְהִלָּתֶךָ. כָּל גּוֹיִם אֲשֶׁר עָשִׂיתָ יָבוֹאוּ וְיִשְׁתַּחֲווּ לְפָנֶיךָ, אֲדֹנָי,
וִיכַבְּדוּ לִשְׁמֶךָ. כִּי גָדוֹל אַתָּה וְעֹשֵׂה נִפְלָאוֹת; אַתָּה אֱלֹהִים
לְבַדֶּךָ. וַאֲנַחְנוּ, עַמְּךָ וְצֹאן מַרְעִיתֶךָ, נוֹדֶה לְּךָ לְעוֹלָם, לְדוֹר
וָדוֹר נְסַפֵּר תְּהִלָּתֶךָ.

בָּרוּךְ יְיָ בַּיּוֹם, בָּרוּךְ יְיָ בַּלָּיְלָה; בָּרוּךְ יְיָ בְּשָׁכְבֵנוּ, בָּרוּךְ
יְיָ בְּקוּמֵנוּ; כִּי בְיָדְךָ נַפְשׁוֹת הַחַיִּים וְהַמֵּתִים. אֲשֶׁר בְּיָדוֹ נֶפֶשׁ
כָּל חָי, וְרוּחַ כָּל בְּשַׂר אִישׁ. בְּיָדְךָ אַפְקִיד רוּחִי; פָּדִיתָה אוֹתִי,

Grant, Lord our God, that we lie down in peace, and that we rise again, O our King, to life. Spread over us thy shelter of peace, and direct us with good counsel of thy own. Save us for thy name's sake; shield us, and remove from us every enemy and pestilence, sword and famine and grief; remove the adversary from before us and from behind us; shelter us beneath the shadow of thy wings; for thou art our protecting and saving God; thou art indeed a gracious and merciful God and King. Guard thou our going out and our coming in, for life and peace, henceforth and forever. Blessed art thou, O Lord, who guardest thy people Israel forever.

Blessed be the Lord forever—Amen, Amen. Blessed from Zion be the Lord who dwells in Jerusalem. Praise the Lord! Blessed be the Lord God, the God of Israel, who alone does wonders. Blessed be his glorious name forever, and may the whole earth be filled with his glory—Amen, Amen. May the glory of the Lord be forever; may the Lord rejoice in his works. Blessed be the name of the Lord henceforth and forever. Surely, the Lord will not forsake his people by virtue of his great name, for the Lord has determined to make you into a people of his own. When all the people saw it, they fell on their faces and exclaimed: "The Lord is God! The Lord is God!" The Lord shall reign over all the earth; on that day the Lord shall be One, and his name One. May thy kindness, O Lord, rest on us, as our hope rests in thee. Lord our God, save us; gather us from the nations, that we may give thanks to thy holy name, and triumph in thy praise. All the nations whom thou hast made shall come and bow down before thee, O Lord, and shall honor thy name; for thou art great and doest wonders; thou alone art God. We thy people, the flock of thy pasture, will ever praise thee; throughout all generations we will recount thy praise.[1]

Blessed be the Lord by day; blessed be the Lord by night; blessed be the Lord when we lie down; blessed be the Lord when we rise up. In thy hand are the souls of the living and the dead, *as it is written:* "In his hand is the soul of every living thing, and the spirit of every human being."[2] Into thy hand I commit my

---

[1] *Psalms* 89:53; 135:21; 72:18–19; 104:31; 113:2; *I Samuel* 12:22; *I Kings* 18:39; *Zechariah* 14:9; *Psalms* 33:22; 106:47; 86:9–10; 79:13. [2] *Job* 12:10.

יְיָ, אֵל אֱמֶת. אֱלֹהֵינוּ שֶׁבַּשָּׁמַיִם, יַחֵד שִׁמְךָ וְקַיֵּם מַלְכוּתְךָ תָּמִיד, וּמְלוֹךְ עָלֵינוּ לְעוֹלָם וָעֶד.

יִרְאוּ עֵינֵינוּ וְיִשְׂמַח לִבֵּנוּ, וְתָגֵל נַפְשֵׁנוּ בִּישׁוּעָתְךָ בֶּאֱמֶת, בֶּאֱמֹר לְצִיּוֹן מָלַךְ אֱלֹהָיִךְ. יְיָ מֶלֶךְ, יְיָ מָלָךְ, יְיָ יִמְלֹךְ לְעוֹלָם וָעֶד. Reader. כִּי הַמַּלְכוּת שֶׁלְּךָ הִיא, וּלְעוֹלְמֵי עַד תִּמְלֹךְ בְּכָבוֹד, כִּי אֵין לָנוּ מֶלֶךְ אֶלָּא אָתָּה. בָּרוּךְ אַתָּה, יְיָ, הַמֶּלֶךְ בִּכְבוֹדוֹ תָּמִיד יִמְלֹךְ עָלֵינוּ, לְעוֹלָם וָעֶד, וְעַל כָּל מַעֲשָׂיו.

Reader:

יִתְגַּדַּל וְיִתְקַדַּשׁ שְׁמֵהּ רַבָּא בְּעָלְמָא דִי בְרָא כִרְעוּתֵהּ; וְיַמְלִיךְ מַלְכוּתֵהּ בְּחַיֵּיכוֹן וּבְיוֹמֵיכוֹן, וּבְחַיֵּי דְכָל בֵּית יִשְׂרָאֵל בַּעֲגָלָא וּבִזְמַן קָרִיב, וְאִמְרוּ אָמֵן.

יְהֵא שְׁמֵהּ רַבָּא מְבָרַךְ לְעָלַם וּלְעָלְמֵי עָלְמַיָּא.

יִתְבָּרַךְ וְיִשְׁתַּבַּח, וְיִתְפָּאַר וְיִתְרוֹמַם, וְיִתְנַשֵּׂא וְיִתְהַדָּר, וְיִתְעַלֶּה וְיִתְהַלָּל שְׁמֵהּ דְּקֻדְשָׁא, בְּרִיךְ הוּא, לְעֵלָּא מִן כָּל בִּרְכָתָא וְשִׁירָתָא, תֻּשְׁבְּחָתָא וְנֶחֱמָתָא, דַּאֲמִירָן בְּעָלְמָא, וְאִמְרוּ אָמֵן.

The *Shemoneh Esreh* is recited in silent devotion while standing, facing east.

אֲדֹנָי, שְׂפָתַי תִּפְתָּח, וּפִי יַגִּיד תְּהִלָּתֶךָ.

בָּרוּךְ אַתָּה, יְיָ אֱלֹהֵינוּ וֵאלֹהֵי אֲבוֹתֵינוּ, אֱלֹהֵי אַבְרָהָם, אֱלֹהֵי יִצְחָק, וֵאלֹהֵי יַעֲקֹב, הָאֵל הַגָּדוֹל הַגִּבּוֹר וְהַנּוֹרָא, אֵל עֶלְיוֹן, גּוֹמֵל חֲסָדִים טוֹבִים, וְקוֹנֵה הַכֹּל, וְזוֹכֵר חַסְדֵי אָבוֹת, וּמֵבִיא גוֹאֵל לִבְנֵי בְנֵיהֶם לְמַעַן שְׁמוֹ בְּאַהֲבָה.

מֶלֶךְ עוֹזֵר וּמוֹשִׁיעַ וּמָגֵן. בָּרוּךְ אַתָּה, יְיָ, מָגֵן אַבְרָהָם.

אַתָּה גִּבּוֹר לְעוֹלָם, אֲדֹנָי; מְחַיֵּה מֵתִים אַתָּה, רַב לְהוֹשִׁיעַ.

spirit; O Lord, faithful God, thou savest me.[1] Our God who art in heaven, reveal thy Oneness and establish thy kingdom forever; do thou reign over us forever and ever.

May our eyes behold, our heart rejoice, and our soul exult in thy true salvation, when it will be said to Zion: "Your God is King." The Lord is King, the Lord was King, the Lord will be King forever and ever. For the kingdom is thine, and to all eternity thou wilt reign in glory; we have no King except thee. Blessed art thou, O Lord, glorious King, who wilt reign over us and over thy entire creation forever and ever.

Reader:

Glorified and sanctified be God's great name throughout the world which he has created according to his will. May he establish his kingdom in your lifetime and during your days, and within the life of the entire house of Israel, speedily and soon; and say, Amen.

May his great name be blessed forever and to all eternity.

Blessed and praised, glorified and exalted, extolled and honored, adored and lauded be the name of the Holy One, blessed be he, beyond all the blessings and hymns, praises and consolations that are ever spoken in the world; and say, Amen.

The Shemoneh Esreh is recited in silent devotion while standing, facing east.

O Lord, open thou my lips, that my mouth may declare thy praise.[1]

Blessed art thou, Lord our God and God of our fathers, God of Abraham, God of Isaac and God of Jacob; great, mighty and revered God, sublime God, who bestowest lovingkindness, and art Master of all things; who rememberest the good deeds of our fathers, and who wilt graciously bring a redeemer to their children's children for the sake of thy name.

O King, Supporter, Savior and Shield. Blessed art thou, O Lord, Shield of Abraham.

Thou, O Lord, art mighty forever; thou revivest the dead; thou art powerful to save.

---

[1] *Psalm* 51:17.

מְכַלְכֵּל חַיִּים בְּחֶסֶד, מְחַיֶּה מֵתִים בְּרַחֲמִים רַבִּים, סוֹמֵךְ
נוֹפְלִים, וְרוֹפֵא חוֹלִים, וּמַתִּיר אֲסוּרִים, וּמְקַיֵּם אֱמוּנָתוֹ לִישֵׁנֵי
עָפָר. מִי כָמְוֹךָ, בַּעַל גְּבוּרוֹת, וּמִי דוֹמֶה לָּךְ, מֶלֶךְ מֵמִית
וּמְחַיֶּה וּמַצְמִיחַ יְשׁוּעָה.

וְנֶאֱמָן אַתָּה לְהַחֲיוֹת מֵתִים. בָּרוּךְ אַתָּה, יְיָ, מְחַיֵּה הַמֵּתִים.

אַתָּה קָדוֹשׁ וְשִׁמְךָ קָדוֹשׁ, וּקְדוֹשִׁים בְּכָל יוֹם יְהַלְלְוּךָ סֶּלָה.
בָּרוּךְ אַתָּה, יְיָ, הָאֵל הַקָּדוֹשׁ.

אַתָּה חוֹנֵן לְאָדָם דַּעַת, וּמְלַמֵּד לֶאֱנוֹשׁ בִּינָה.

אַתָּה חוֹנַנְתָּנוּ מַדַּע תּוֹרָתֶךָ, וַתְּלַמְּדֵנוּ לַעֲשׂוֹת חֻקֵּי רְצוֹנֶךָ,
וַתַּבְדֵּל, יְיָ אֱלֹהֵינוּ, בֵּין קֹדֶשׁ לְחֹל, בֵּין אוֹר לְחְשֶׁךְ, בֵּין
יִשְׂרָאֵל לָעַמִּים, בֵּין יוֹם הַשְּׁבִיעִי לְשֵׁשֶׁת יְמֵי הַמַּעֲשֶׂה. אָבִינוּ
מַלְכֵּנוּ, הָחֵל עָלֵינוּ הַיָּמִים הַבָּאִים לִקְרָאתֵנוּ לְשָׁלוֹם, חֲשׂוּכִים
מִכָּל חֵטְא, וּמְנֻקִּים מִכָּל עָוֹן, וּמְדֻבָּקִים בְּיִרְאָתֶךָ.

וְחָנֵּנוּ מֵאִתְּךָ דֵּעָה, בִּינָה וְהַשְׂכֵּל. בָּרוּךְ אַתָּה, יְיָ, חוֹנֵן
הַדָּעַת.

הֲשִׁיבֵנוּ אָבִינוּ לְתוֹרָתֶךָ, וְקָרְבֵנוּ מַלְכֵּנוּ לַעֲבוֹדָתֶךָ;
וְהַחֲזִירֵנוּ בִּתְשׁוּבָה שְׁלֵמָה לְפָנֶיךָ. בָּרוּךְ אַתָּה, יְיָ, הָרוֹצֶה
בִּתְשׁוּבָה.

סְלַח לָנוּ אָבִינוּ כִּי חָטָאנוּ, מְחַל לָנוּ מַלְכֵּנוּ כִּי פָשָׁעְנוּ, כִּי
מוֹחֵל וְסוֹלֵחַ אָתָּה. בָּרוּךְ אַתָּה, יְיָ, חַנּוּן הַמַּרְבֶּה לִסְלְחַ.

רְאֵה נָא בְעָנְיֵנוּ וְרִיבָה רִיבֵנוּ, וּגְאָלֵנוּ מְהֵרָה לְמַעַן שְׁמֶךָ,
כִּי גּוֹאֵל חָזָק אָתָּה. בָּרוּךְ אַתָּה, יְיָ, גּוֹאֵל יִשְׂרָאֵל.

רְפָאֵנוּ יְיָ וְנֵרָפֵא, הוֹשִׁיעֵנוּ וְנִוָּשֵׁעָה, כִּי תְהִלָּתֵנוּ אָתָּה:

Thou sustainest the living with kindness, and revivest the dead with great mercy; thou supportest all who fall, and healest the sick; thou settest the captives free, and keepest faith with those who sleep in the dust. Who is like thee, Lord of power? Who resembles thee, O King? Thou bringest death and restorest life, and causest salvation to flourish.

Thou art faithful to revive the dead. Blessed art thou, O Lord, who revivest the dead.

Thou art holy and thy name is holy, and holy beings praise thee daily. Blessed art thou, O Lord, holy God.

Thou favorest man with knowledge, and teachest mortals understanding.

Thou hast favored us with a knowledge of thy Torah, and taught us to perform the laws of thy will. Thou hast made a distinction, Lord our God, between the holy and the profane, between light and darkness, between Israel and the nations, between the seventh day and the six days of work. Our Father, our King, grant that the approaching days may begin for us in peace; may we be withheld from all sin, cleansed from all iniquity, and devoted to the veneration of thee.

O grant us knowledge, understanding and insight. Blessed art thou, O Lord, gracious Giver of knowledge.

Restore us, our Father, to thy Torah; draw us near, our King, to thy service; cause us to return to thee in perfect repentance. Blessed art thou, O Lord, who art pleased with repentance.

Forgive us, our Father, for we have sinned; pardon us, our King, for we have transgressed; for thou dost pardon and forgive. Blessed art thou, O Lord, who art gracious and ever forgiving.

Look upon our affliction and champion our cause; redeem us speedily for thy name's sake, for thou art a mighty Redeemer. Blessed art thou, O Lord, Redeemer of Israel.

Heal us, O Lord, and we shall be healed; save us and we shall be saved; for thou art our praise. Grant a perfect healing to all our

וְהַעֲלֵה רְפוּאָה שְׁלֵמָה לְכָל מַכּוֹתֵינוּ, כִּי אֵל מֶלֶךְ רוֹפֵא נֶאֱמָן וְרַחֲמָן אָתָּה. בָּרוּךְ אַתָּה, יְיָ, רוֹפֵא חוֹלֵי עַמּוֹ יִשְׂרָאֵל.

בָּרֵךְ עָלֵינוּ, יְיָ אֱלֹהֵינוּ, אֶת הַשָּׁנָה הַזֹּאת וְאֶת כָּל מִינֵי תְבוּאָתָהּ לְטוֹבָה, וְתֵן בְּרָכָה עַל פְּנֵי הָאֲדָמָה, וְשַׂבְּעֵנוּ מִטּוּבֶךָ, וּבָרֵךְ שְׁנָתֵנוּ כַּשָּׁנִים הַטּוֹבוֹת. בָּרוּךְ אַתָּה, יְיָ, מְבָרֵךְ הַשָּׁנִים.

תְּקַע בְּשׁוֹפָר גָּדוֹל לְחֵרוּתֵנוּ, וְשָׂא נֵס לְקַבֵּץ גָּלֻיּוֹתֵינוּ, וְקַבְּצֵנוּ יַחַד מֵאַרְבַּע כַּנְפוֹת הָאָרֶץ. בָּרוּךְ אַתָּה, יְיָ, מְקַבֵּץ נִדְחֵי עַמּוֹ יִשְׂרָאֵל.

הָשִׁיבָה שׁוֹפְטֵינוּ כְּבָרִאשׁוֹנָה, וְיוֹעֲצֵינוּ כְּבַתְּחִלָּה; וְהָסֵר מִמֶּנּוּ יָגוֹן וַאֲנָחָה; וּמְלוֹךְ עָלֵינוּ, אַתָּה יְיָ לְבַדְּךָ, בְּחֶסֶד וּבְרַחֲמִים, וְצַדְּקֵנוּ בַּמִּשְׁפָּט. בָּרוּךְ אַתָּה, יְיָ, מֶלֶךְ אוֹהֵב צְדָקָה וּמִשְׁפָּט.

וְלַמַּלְשִׁינִים אַל תְּהִי תִקְוָה, וְכָל הָרִשְׁעָה כְּרֶגַע תֹּאבֵד, וְכָל אוֹיְבֶיךָ מְהֵרָה יִכָּרֵתוּ; וְהַזֵּדִים מְהֵרָה תְעַקֵּר וּתְשַׁבֵּר וּתְמַגֵּר וְתַכְנִיעַ בִּמְהֵרָה בְיָמֵינוּ. בָּרוּךְ אַתָּה, יְיָ, שׁוֹבֵר אוֹיְבִים וּמַכְנִיעַ זֵדִים.

עַל הַצַּדִּיקִים וְעַל הַחֲסִידִים, וְעַל זִקְנֵי עַמְּךָ בֵּית יִשְׂרָאֵל וְעַל פְּלֵיטַת סוֹפְרֵיהֶם, וְעַל גֵּרֵי הַצֶּדֶק וְעָלֵינוּ, יֶהֱמוּ נָא רַחֲמֶיךָ, יְיָ אֱלֹהֵינוּ; וְתֵן שָׂכָר טוֹב לְכָל הַבּוֹטְחִים בְּשִׁמְךָ בֶּאֱמֶת, וְשִׂים חֶלְקֵנוּ עִמָּהֶם, וּלְעוֹלָם לֹא נֵבוֹשׁ, כִּי בְךָ בָּטָחְנוּ. בָּרוּךְ אַתָּה, יְיָ, מִשְׁעָן וּמִבְטָח לַצַּדִּיקִים.

wounds; for thou art a faithful and merciful God, King and Healer. Blessed art thou, O Lord, who healest the sick among thy people Israel.

Bless for us, Lord our God, this year and all its varied produce for the best. Bestow a blessing upon the face of the earth. Satisfy us with thy goodness, and bless our year like other good years. Blessed art thou, O Lord, who blessest the years.

Sound the great shofar for our freedom; lift up the banner to bring our exiles together; assemble us speedily from the four corners of the earth into our land. Blessed art thou, O Lord, who gatherest the dispersed of thy people Israel.

Restore our judges as at first, and our counselors as at the beginning; remove from us sorrow and sighing; reign thou alone over us speedily, O Lord, in kindness and mercy; clear us in righteousness and in justice. Blessed art thou, O Lord, who lovest righteousness and justice.

May the slanderers have no hope; may all wickedness perish instantly; may all thy enemies be soon cut down. Do thou speedily uproot and crush the arrogant; cast them down and humble them speedily in our days. Blessed art thou, O Lord, who breakest the enemies and humblest the arrogant.

May thy compassion, Lord our God, be aroused over the righteous and over the godly; over the leaders of thy people, the house of Israel, and over the remnant of their sages; over the true proselytes and over us. Grant a goodly reward to all who truly trust in thy name, and place our lot among them; may we never come to shame, for in thee we trust and on thy great kindness we faithfully rely. Blessed art thou, O Lord, who art the stay and trust of the righteous.

וְלִירוּשָׁלַיִם עִירְךָ בְּרַחֲמִים תָּשׁוּב, וְתִשְׁכּוֹן בְּתוֹכָהּ כַּאֲשֶׁר
דִּבַּרְתָּ, וּבְנֵה אוֹתָהּ בְּקָרוֹב בְּיָמֵינוּ בִּנְיַן עוֹלָם; וְכִסֵּא דָוִד
עַבְדְּךָ מְהֵרָה לְתוֹכָהּ תָּכִין. בָּרוּךְ אַתָּה, יְיָ, בּוֹנֵה יְרוּשָׁלָיִם.

אֶת צֶמַח דָּוִד עַבְדְּךָ מְהֵרָה תַצְמִיחַ, וְקַרְנוֹ תָּרוּם
בִּישׁוּעָתֶךָ, כִּי לִישׁוּעָתְךָ קִוִּינוּ כָּל הַיּוֹם וּמְצַפִּים לִישׁוּעָה.
בָּרוּךְ אַתָּה, יְיָ, מַצְמִיחַ קֶרֶן יְשׁוּעָה.

שְׁמַע קוֹלֵנוּ, יְיָ אֱלֹהֵינוּ; חוּס וְרַחֵם עָלֵינוּ, וְקַבֵּל בְּרַחֲמִים
וּבְרָצוֹן אֶת תְּפִלָּתֵנוּ, כִּי אֵל שׁוֹמֵעַ תְּפִלּוֹת וְתַחֲנוּנִים אָתָּה;
וּמִלְּפָנֶיךָ מַלְכֵּנוּ רֵיקָם אַל תְּשִׁיבֵנוּ, כִּי אַתָּה שׁוֹמֵעַ תְּפִלַּת
עַמְּךָ יִשְׂרָאֵל בְּרַחֲמִים. בָּרוּךְ אַתָּה, יְיָ, שׁוֹמֵעַ תְּפִלָּה.

רְצֵה, יְיָ אֱלֹהֵינוּ, בְּעַמְּךָ יִשְׂרָאֵל וּבִתְפִלָּתָם; וְהָשֵׁב אֶת
הָעֲבוֹדָה לִדְבִיר בֵּיתֶךָ, וְאִשֵּׁי יִשְׂרָאֵל וּתְפִלָּתָם בְּאַהֲבָה
תְקַבֵּל בְּרָצוֹן, וּתְהִי לְרָצוֹן תָּמִיד עֲבוֹדַת יִשְׂרָאֵל עַמֶּךָ.

וְתֶחֱזֶינָה עֵינֵינוּ בְּשׁוּבְךָ לְצִיּוֹן בְּרַחֲמִים. בָּרוּךְ אַתָּה, יְיָ,
הַמַּחֲזִיר שְׁכִינָתוֹ לְצִיּוֹן.

מוֹדִים אֲנַחְנוּ לָךְ, שָׁאַתָּה הוּא יְיָ אֱלֹהֵינוּ וֵאלֹהֵי אֲבוֹתֵינוּ
לְעוֹלָם וָעֶד. צוּר חַיֵּינוּ, מָגֵן יִשְׁעֵנוּ אַתָּה הוּא. לְדוֹר וָדוֹר
נוֹדֶה לְךָ, וּנְסַפֵּר תְּהִלָּתֶךָ, עַל חַיֵּינוּ הַמְּסוּרִים בְּיָדֶךָ, וְעַל
נִשְׁמוֹתֵינוּ הַפְּקוּדוֹת לָךְ, וְעַל נִסֶּיךָ שֶׁבְּכָל יוֹם עִמָּנוּ, וְעַל
נִפְלְאוֹתֶיךָ וְטוֹבוֹתֶיךָ שֶׁבְּכָל עֵת, עֶרֶב וָבֹקֶר וְצָהֳרָיִם. הַטּוֹב
כִּי לֹא כָלוּ רַחֲמֶיךָ, וְהַמְרַחֵם כִּי לֹא תַמּוּ חֲסָדֶיךָ,
מֵעוֹלָם קִוִּינוּ לָךְ.

Return in mercy to thy city Jerusalem and dwell in it as thou hast promised; rebuild it soon, in our days, as an everlasting structure, and speedily establish in it the throne of David. Blessed art thou, O Lord, Builder of Jerusalem.

Speedily cause the offspring of thy servant David to flourish, and let his glory be exalted by thy help, for we hopefully look to thee for deliverance all day. Blessed art thou, O Lord, who causest salvation to flourish.

Hear our voice; Lord our God, spare us, and have pity on us, accept our prayer in mercy and favor, for thou art God who hearest prayers and supplications; from thy presence, our King, dismiss us not empty-handed, for thou hearest in mercy the prayer of thy people Israel. Blessed art thou, O Lord, who hearest prayer.

Be pleased, Lord our God, with thy people Israel and with their prayer; restore the worship to thy most holy sanctuary; accept Israel's offerings and prayer with gracious love. May the worship of thy people Israel be ever pleasing to thee.

May our eyes behold thy return in mercy to Zion. Blessed art thou, O Lord, who restorest thy divine presence to Zion.

We ever thank thee, who art the Lord our God and the God of our fathers. Thou art the strength of our life and our saving shield. In every generation we will thank thee and recount thy praise—for our lives which are in thy charge, for our souls which are in thy care, for thy miracles which are daily with us, and for thy continual wonders and favors—evening, morning and noon. Beneficent One, whose mercies never fail, Merciful One, whose kindnesses never cease, thou hast always been our hope.

וְעַל כֻּלָּם יִתְבָּרַךְ וְיִתְרוֹמַם שִׁמְךָ, מַלְכֵּנוּ, תָּמִיד לְעוֹלָם וָעֶד.

וְכֹל הַחַיִּים יוֹדוּךָ סֶּלָה, וִיהַלְלוּ אֶת שִׁמְךָ בֶּאֱמֶת, הָאֵל, יְשׁוּעָתֵנוּ וְעֶזְרָתֵנוּ סֶלָה. בָּרוּךְ אַתָּה, יְיָ, הַטּוֹב שִׁמְךָ, וּלְךָ נָאֶה לְהוֹדוֹת.

שָׁלוֹם רָב עַל יִשְׂרָאֵל עַמְּךָ תָּשִׂים לְעוֹלָם, כִּי אַתָּה הוּא מֶלֶךְ אָדוֹן לְכָל הַשָּׁלוֹם, וְטוֹב בְּעֵינֶיךָ לְבָרֵךְ אֶת עַמְּךָ יִשְׂרָאֵל בְּכָל עֵת וּבְכָל שָׁעָה בִּשְׁלוֹמֶךָ. בָּרוּךְ אַתָּה, יְיָ, הַמְבָרֵךְ אֶת עַמּוֹ יִשְׂרָאֵל בַּשָּׁלוֹם.

After the *Amidah* add the following meditation:

אֱלֹהַי נְצֹר לְשׁוֹנִי מֵרָע, וּשְׂפָתַי מִדַּבֵּר מִרְמָה; וְלִמְקַלְלַי נַפְשִׁי תִדּוֹם, וְנַפְשִׁי כֶּעָפָר לַכֹּל תִּהְיֶה. פְּתַח לִבִּי בְּתוֹרָתֶךָ, וּבְמִצְוֹתֶיךָ תִּרְדּוֹף נַפְשִׁי; וְכֹל הַחוֹשְׁבִים עָלַי רָעָה, מְהֵרָה הָפֵר עֲצָתָם וְקַלְקֵל מַחֲשַׁבְתָּם. עֲשֵׂה לְמַעַן שְׁמֶךָ, עֲשֵׂה לְמַעַן יְמִינֶךָ, עֲשֵׂה לְמַעַן קְדֻשָּׁתֶךָ, עֲשֵׂה לְמַעַן תּוֹרָתֶךָ. לְמַעַן יֵחָלְצוּן יְדִידֶיךָ, הוֹשִׁיעָה יְמִינְךָ וַעֲנֵנִי. יִהְיוּ לְרָצוֹן אִמְרֵי פִי וְהֶגְיוֹן לִבִּי לְפָנֶיךָ, יְיָ, צוּרִי וְגוֹאֲלִי. עֹשֶׂה שָׁלוֹם בִּמְרוֹמָיו הוּא יַעֲשֶׂה שָׁלוֹם עָלֵינוּ וְעַל כָּל יִשְׂרָאֵל, וְאִמְרוּ אָמֵן.

יְהִי רָצוֹן מִלְּפָנֶיךָ, יְיָ אֱלֹהֵינוּ וֵאלֹהֵי אֲבוֹתֵינוּ, שֶׁיִּבָּנֶה בֵּית הַמִּקְדָּשׁ בִּמְהֵרָה בְיָמֵינוּ; וְתֵן חֶלְקֵנוּ בְּתוֹרָתֶךָ. וְשָׁם נַעֲבָדְךָ בְּיִרְאָה, כִּימֵי עוֹלָם וּכְשָׁנִים קַדְמוֹנִיּוֹת. וְעָרְבָה לַיְיָ מִנְחַת יְהוּדָה וִירוּשָׁלָיִם, כִּימֵי עוֹלָם וּכְשָׁנִים קַדְמוֹנִיּוֹת.

For all these acts may thy name, our King, be blessed and exalted forever and ever.

All the living shall ever thank thee and sincerely praise thy name, O God, who art always our salvation and help. Blessed art thou, O Lord, Beneficent One, to whom it is fitting to give thanks.

O grant abundant peace to Israel thy people forever, for thou art the King and Lord of all peace. May it please thee to bless thy people Israel with peace at all times and at all hours. Blessed art thou, O Lord, who blessest thy people Israel with peace.

After the Amidah add the following meditation:

My God, guard my tongue from evil, and my lips from speaking falsehood. May my soul be silent to those who insult me; be my soul lowly to all as the dust. Open my heart to thy Torah, that my soul may follow thy commands. Speedily defeat the counsel of all those who plan evil against me, and upset their design. Do it for the glory of thy name; do it for the sake of thy power; do it for the sake of thy holiness; do it for the sake of thy Torah. That thy beloved may be rescued, save with thy right hand and answer me. May the words of my mouth and the meditation of my heart be pleasing before thee, O Lord, my Stronghold and my Redeemer.[1] May he who creates peace in his high heavens create peace for us and for all Israel, Amen.

May it be thy will, Lord our God and God of our fathers, that the Temple be speedily rebuilt in our days, and grant us a share in thy Torah. There we will serve thee with reverence, as in the days of old and as in former years. Then the offering of Judah and Jerusalem will be pleasing to the Lord, as in the days of old and as in former years.[2]

---

[1] *Psalms* 60:7; 19:15.   [2] *Malachi* 3:4.

Reader:

יִתְגַּדַּל וְיִתְקַדַּשׁ שְׁמֵהּ רַבָּא בְּעָלְמָא דִּי בְרָא כִרְעוּתֵהּ;
וְיַמְלִיךְ מַלְכוּתֵהּ בְּחַיֵּיכוֹן וּבְיוֹמֵיכוֹן, וּבְחַיֵּי דְכָל בֵּית יִשְׂרָאֵל,
בַּעֲגָלָא וּבִזְמַן קָרִיב, וְאִמְרוּ אָמֵן.

יְהֵא שְׁמֵהּ רַבָּא מְבָרַךְ לְעָלַם וּלְעָלְמֵי עָלְמַיָּא.

יִתְבָּרַךְ וְיִשְׁתַּבַּח, וְיִתְפָּאַר וְיִתְרוֹמַם, וְיִתְנַשֵּׂא וְיִתְהַדָּר,
וְיִתְעַלֶּה וְיִתְהַלָּל שְׁמֵהּ דְּקֻדְשָׁא, בְּרִיךְ הוּא, לְעֵלָּא מִן כָּל
בִּרְכָתָא וְשִׁירָתָא, תֻּשְׁבְּחָתָא וְנֶחֱמָתָא, דַּאֲמִירָן בְּעָלְמָא,
וְאִמְרוּ אָמֵן.

תִּתְקַבַּל צְלוֹתְהוֹן וּבָעוּתְהוֹן דְּכָל בֵּית יִשְׂרָאֵל קֳדָם אֲבוּהוֹן
דִּי בִשְׁמַיָּא, וְאִמְרוּ אָמֵן.

יְהֵא שְׁלָמָא רַבָּא מִן שְׁמַיָּא, וְחַיִּים, עָלֵינוּ וְעַל כָּל יִשְׂרָאֵל,
וְאִמְרוּ אָמֵן.

עֹשֶׂה שָׁלוֹם בִּמְרוֹמָיו, הוּא יַעֲשֶׂה שָׁלוֹם עָלֵינוּ וְעַל כָּל
יִשְׂרָאֵל, וְאִמְרוּ אָמֵן.

עָלֵינוּ לְשַׁבֵּחַ לַאֲדוֹן הַכֹּל, לָתֵת גְּדֻלָּה לְיוֹצֵר בְּרֵאשִׁית,
שֶׁלֹּא עָשָׂנוּ כְּגוֹיֵי הָאֲרָצוֹת, וְלֹא שָׂמָנוּ כְּמִשְׁפְּחוֹת הָאֲדָמָה;
שֶׁלֹּא שָׂם חֶלְקֵנוּ כָּהֶם, וְגוֹרָלֵנוּ כְּכָל הֲמוֹנָם. וַאֲנַחְנוּ כּוֹרְעִים
וּמִשְׁתַּחֲוִים וּמוֹדִים לִפְנֵי מֶלֶךְ מַלְכֵי הַמְּלָכִים, הַקָּדוֹשׁ בָּרוּךְ
הוּא, שֶׁהוּא נוֹטֶה שָׁמַיִם וְיוֹסֵד אָרֶץ, וּמוֹשַׁב יְקָרוֹ בַּשָּׁמַיִם
מִמַּעַל, וּשְׁכִינַת עֻזּוֹ בְּגָבְהֵי מְרוֹמִים. הוּא אֱלֹהֵינוּ, אֵין עוֹד;
אֱמֶת מַלְכֵּנוּ, אֶפֶס זוּלָתוֹ, כַּכָּתוּב בְּתוֹרָתוֹ: וְיָדַעְתָּ הַיּוֹם
וַהֲשֵׁבֹתָ אֶל לְבָבֶךָ, כִּי יְיָ הוּא הָאֱלֹהִים בַּשָּׁמַיִם מִמַּעַל וְעַל
הָאָרֶץ מִתָּחַת, אֵין עוֹד.

Evening Service

Glorified and sanctified be God's great name throughout the world which he has created according to his will. May he establish his kingdom in your lifetime and during your days, and within the life of the entire house of Israel, speedily and soon; and say, Amen.

May his great name be blessed forever and to all eternity.

Blessed and praised, glorified and exalted, extolled and honored, adored and lauded be the name of the Holy One, blessed be he, beyond all the blessings and hymns, praises and consolations that are ever spoken in the world; and say, Amen.

May the prayers and supplications of the whole household of Israel be accepted by their Father who is in heaven; and say, Amen

May there be abundant peace from heaven, and life, for us and or all Israel; and say, Amen.

He who creates peace in his celestial heights, may he create peace for us and for all Israel; and say, ṣay, Amen.

ALENU

It is our duty to praise the Master of all, to exalt the Creator of the universe, who has not made us like the nations of the world and has not placed us like the families of the earth; who has not designed our destiny to be like theirs, nor our lot like that of all their multitude. We bend the knee and bow and acknowledge before the supreme King of kings, the Holy One, blessed be he, that it is he who stretched forth the heavens and founded the earth. His seat of glory is in the heavens above; his abode of majesty is in the lofty heights. He is our God, there is none else; truly, he is our King, there is none besides him, as it is written in his Torah: "You shall know this day, and reflect in your heart, that it is the Lord who is God in the heavens above and on the earth beneath, there is none else."[1]

---

[1] *Deuteronomy* 4:39.

עַל כֵּן נְקַוֶּה לְךָ, יְיָ אֱלֹהֵינוּ, לִרְאוֹת מְהֵרָה בְּתִפְאֶרֶת עֻזֶּךָ,
לְהַעֲבִיר גִּלּוּלִים מִן הָאָרֶץ, וְהָאֱלִילִים כָּרוֹת יִכָּרֵתוּן; לְתַקֵּן
עוֹלָם בְּמַלְכוּת שַׁדַּי, וְכָל בְּנֵי בָשָׂר יִקְרְאוּ בִשְׁמֶךָ, לְהַפְנוֹת
אֵלֶיךָ כָּל רִשְׁעֵי אָרֶץ. יַכִּירוּ וְיֵדְעוּ כָּל יוֹשְׁבֵי תֵבֵל, כִּי לְךָ
תִּכְרַע כָּל בֶּרֶךְ, תִּשָּׁבַע כָּל לָשׁוֹן. לְפָנֶיךָ, יְיָ אֱלֹהֵינוּ, יִכְרְעוּ
וְיִפֹּלוּ, וְלִכְבוֹד שִׁמְךָ יְקָר יִתֵּנוּ, וִיקַבְּלוּ כֻלָּם אֶת עֹל מַלְכוּתֶךָ,
וְתִמְלוֹךְ עֲלֵיהֶם מְהֵרָה לְעוֹלָם וָעֶד. כִּי הַמַּלְכוּת שֶׁלְּךָ הִיא,
וּלְעוֹלְמֵי עַד תִּמְלוֹךְ בְּכָבוֹד, כַּכָּתוּב, בְּתוֹרָתֶךָ: יְיָ יִמְלֹךְ
לְעֹלָם וָעֶד. Reader וְנֶאֱמַר: וְהָיָה יְיָ לְמֶלֶךְ עַל כָּל הָאָרֶץ;
בַּיּוֹם הַהוּא יִהְיֶה יְיָ אֶחָד וּשְׁמוֹ אֶחָד.

MOURNERS' KADDISH

יִתְגַּדַּל וְיִתְקַדַּשׁ שְׁמֵהּ רַבָּא בְּעָלְמָא דִי בְרָא כִרְעוּתֵהּ;
וְיַמְלִיךְ מַלְכוּתֵהּ בְּחַיֵּיכוֹן וּבְיוֹמֵיכוֹן, וּבְחַיֵּי דְכָל בֵּית יִשְׂרָאֵל
בַּעֲגָלָא וּבִזְמַן קָרִיב, וְאִמְרוּ אָמֵן.

יְהֵא שְׁמֵהּ רַבָּא מְבָרַךְ לְעָלַם וּלְעָלְמֵי עָלְמַיָּא.

יִתְבָּרַךְ וְיִשְׁתַּבַּח, וְיִתְפָּאַר וְיִתְרוֹמַם, וְיִתְנַשֵּׂא וְיִתְהַדָּר,
וְיִתְעַלֶּה וְיִתְהַלָּל שְׁמֵהּ דְּקֻדְשָׁא, בְּרִיךְ הוּא, לְעֵלָּא מִן כָּל
בִּרְכָתָא וְשִׁירָתָא, תֻּשְׁבְּחָתָא וְנֶחֱמָתָא, דַּאֲמִירָן בְּעָלְמָא,
וְאִמְרוּ אָמֵן.

יְהֵא שְׁלָמָא רַבָּא מִן שְׁמַיָּא, וְחַיִּים, עָלֵינוּ וְעַל כָּל יִשְׂרָאֵל,
וְאִמְרוּ אָמֵן.

עֹשֶׂה שָׁלוֹם בִּמְרוֹמָיו, הוּא יַעֲשֶׂה שָׁלוֹם עָלֵינוּ וְעַל כָּל
יִשְׂרָאֵל, וְאִמְרוּ אָמֵן.

We hope therefore, Lord our God, soon to behold thy majestic glory, when the abominations shall be removed from the earth, and the false gods exterminated; when the world shall be perfected under the reign of the Almighty, and all mankind will call upon thy name, and all the wicked of the earth will be turned to thee. May all the inhabitants of the world realize and know that to thee every knee must bend, every tongue must vow allegiance. May they bend the knee and prostrate themselves before thee, Lord our God, and give honor to thy glorious name; may they all accept the yoke of thy kingdom, and do thou reign over them speedily forever and ever. For the kingdom is thine, and to all eternity thou wilt reign in glory, as it is written in thy Torah: "The Lord shall be King forever and ever."[1] And it is said: "The Lord shall be King over all the earth; on that day shall the Lord be One and his name One.[2]"

MOURNERS' KADDISH

Glorified and sanctified be God's great name throughout the world which he has created according to his will. May he establish his kingdom, hastening his salvation and the coming of his Messiah, in your lifetime and during your days, and within the life of the entire house of Israel, speedily and soon; and say, Amen.

May his great name be blessed forever and to all eternity.

Blessed and praised, glorified and exalted, extolled and honored, adored and lauded be the name of the Holy One, blessed be he beyond all the blessings and hymns, praises and consolations that are ever spoken in the world; and say, Amen.

May there be abundant peace from heaven, and life, for us and for all Israel; and say, Amen.

He who creates peace in his celestial heights, may he create peace for us and for all Israel; and say, Amen.

---

[1]*Exodus* 15:18.   [2]*Zechariah* 14:9.

הַבְדָּלָה

Recited on Saturday night over a cup of wine and fragrant spices

הִנֵּה אֵל יְשׁוּעָתִי, אֶבְטַח וְלֹא אֶפְחָד, כִּי עָזִּי וְזִמְרָת יָהּ יְיָ, וַיְהִי לִי לִישׁוּעָה. וּשְׁאַבְתֶּם מַיִם בְּשָׂשׂוֹן מִמַּעַיְנֵי הַיְשׁוּעָה. לַיְיָ הַיְשׁוּעָה; עַל עַמְּךָ בִרְכָתֶךָ סֶּלָה. יְיָ צְבָאוֹת עִמָּנוּ, מִשְׂגָּב לָנוּ אֱלֹהֵי יַעֲקֹב, סֶלָה. יְיָ צְבָאוֹת, אַשְׁרֵי אָדָם בֹּטֵחַ בָּךְ. יְיָ, הוֹשִׁיעָה; הַמֶּלֶךְ יַעֲנֵנוּ בְיוֹם קָרְאֵנוּ. לַיְּהוּדִים הָיְתָה אוֹרָה וְשִׂמְחָה, וְשָׂשׂוֹן וִיקָר. כֵּן תִּהְיֶה לָנוּ. כּוֹס יְשׁוּעוֹת אֶשָּׂא, וּבְשֵׁם יְיָ אֶקְרָא.

Except on Saturday night, the *Havdalah* begins here:

סָבְרִי מָרָנָן וְרַבּוֹתַי.

בָּרוּךְ אַתָּה, יְיָ אֱלֹהֵינוּ, מֶלֶךְ הָעוֹלָם, בּוֹרֵא פְּרִי הַגָּפֶן.

(בָּרוּךְ אַתָּה, יְיָ אֱלֹהֵינוּ, מֶלֶךְ הָעוֹלָם, בּוֹרֵא מִינֵי בְשָׂמִים.

בָּרוּךְ אַתָּה, יְיָ אֱלֹהֵינוּ, מֶלֶךְ הָעוֹלָם, בּוֹרֵא מְאוֹרֵי הָאֵשׁ.)

בָּרוּךְ אַתָּה, יְיָ אֱלֹהֵינוּ, מֶלֶךְ הָעוֹלָם, הַמַּבְדִּיל בֵּין קֹדֶשׁ לְחֹל, בֵּין אוֹר לְחֹשֶׁךְ, בֵּין יִשְׂרָאֵל לָעַמִּים, בֵּין יוֹם הַשְּׁבִיעִי לְשֵׁשֶׁת יְמֵי הַמַּעֲשֶׂה. בָּרוּךְ אַתָּה, יְיָ, הַמַּבְדִּיל בֵּין קֹדֶשׁ לְחֹל.

הבדלה, marking the end of the Sabbath, is attributed to the men of the Great Assembly (Berakhoth 33a). The introductory passage הנה אל ישועתי, consisting of biblical verses, is of later origin. According to Maimonides, the symbolic use of fragrant spices during the recital of the *Havdalah* is to cheer the soul which is saddened at the departure of the Sabbath. When a festival follows immediately after the Sabbath the spices are omitted, because the soul then rejoices with the incoming holiday. The wine for the *Havdalah* is allowed to flow over as a symbol of the overflowing blessing expected in the coming week. It is customary to cup the hands around the candle and to gaze at the finger-nails. The reflection of the light on the finger-nails causes the shadow to

HAVDALAH

Recited on Saturday night over a cup of wine and fragrant spices

Behold, God is my deliverance; I will trust, and will not be afraid; truly the Lord is my strength and my song; he has delivered me indeed. Joyfully shall you draw upon the fountains of deliverance. It is for the Lord to bring help; my God, thy blessing be upon thy people. The Lord of hosts is with us; the God of Jacob is our Stronghold. Lord of hosts, happy is the man who trusts in thee. O Lord, save us; may the King answer us when we call. The Jews had light and joy, gladness and honor. So be it with us. I will take the cup of deliverance, and will call upon the name of the Lord.[1]

Except on Saturday night, the Havdalah begins here:

Blessed art thou, Lord our God, King of the universe, who createst the fruit of the vine.

(Blessed art thou, Lord our God, King of the universe, who createst various kinds of spices.

Blessed art thou, Lord our God, King of the universe, who createst the lights of fire.)

Blessed art thou, Lord our God, King of the universe, who hast made a distinction between the sacred and the profane, between light and darkness, between Israel and the other nations, between the seventh day and the six working days. Blessed art thou, O Lord, who hast made a distinction between the sacred and the profane.

---

appear on the palm of the hand, thus indicating the distinction "between light and darkness" mentioned in the *Havdalah*. A twisted candle of several wicks is used since the phrase מאורי האש ("lights of fire") is in the plural. The custom of dipping the finger in the wine and passing it over the eyes alludes to Psalm 19:9 where God's commands are described as "enlightening the eyes."

[1] *Isaiah* 12:2-3; *Psalms* 3:9; 46:12; 84:13; 20:10; *Esther* 8:16; *Psalm* 116:13.

מַעֲרָבִית לְלֵיל רִאשׁוֹן

מַעֲרָבוֹת MAARAVOTH

Poetic Insertions for the Shavuoth Evening Services

First Evening

וַיֵּרֶד אַבִּיר יַעֲקֹב, by Joseph ben Samuel Tov-Elem (Bonfils) of eleventh-century France, describes the contents of the Ten Commandments in an alphabetical acrostic. The insertion to the third paragraph (טוביה למרום עלה) continues the acrostic, but has another rhyme. The first words of the Ten Commandments are utilized in the last paragraphs. The name acrostic (יוסף) follows the alphabetic acrostic (ישועות רבות).

Reader. בָּרְכוּ אֶת יְיָ הַמְבֹרָךְ:

Cong. and Reader. בָּרוּךְ יְיָ הַמְבֹרָךְ לְעוֹלָם וָעֶד:

בָּרוּךְ אַתָּה יְיָ אֱלֹהֵינוּ מֶלֶךְ הָעוֹלָם אֲשֶׁר בִּדְבָרוֹ מַעֲרִיב עֲרָבִים
בְּחָכְמָה פּוֹתֵחַ שְׁעָרִים וּבִתְבוּנָה מְשַׁנֶּה עִתִּים וּמַחֲלִיף אֶת הַזְּמַנִּים
וּמְסַדֵּר אֶת הַכּוֹכָבִים בְּמִשְׁמְרוֹתֵיהֶם בָּרָקִיעַ כִּרְצוֹנוֹ בּוֹרֵא יוֹם וָלַיְלָה
גּוֹלֵל אוֹר מִפְּנֵי חֹשֶׁךְ וְחֹשֶׁךְ מִפְּנֵי אוֹר• וּמַעֲבִיר יוֹם וּמֵבִיא לַיְלָה
וּמַבְדִּיל בֵּין יוֹם וּבֵין לַיְלָה יְיָ צְבָאוֹת שְׁמוֹ• אֵל חַי וְקַיָּם תָּמִיד יִמְלוֹךְ
עָלֵינוּ לְעוֹלָם וָעֶד:

וַיֵּרֶד• אַבִּיר יַעֲקֹב נוֹרָא עֲלִילָה•
וַיְדַבֵּר• בִּטּוּי עֲשֶׂרֶת הַדִּבְּרוֹת בַּהֲמֻלָּה•
אָנֹכִי• גִּלָּה וְהֵאִיר לְעַמּוֹ תְּחִלָּה•
דּוֹד מַעֲבִיר יוֹם וּמֵבִיא לַיְלָה:
בָּרוּךְ אַתָּה יְיָ הַמַּעֲרִיב עֲרָבִים:

אַהֲבַת עוֹלָם בֵּית יִשְׂרָאֵל עַמְּךָ אָהַבְתָּ• תּוֹרָה וּמִצְוֹת חֻקִּים
וּמִשְׁפָּטִים אוֹתָנוּ לִמַּדְתָּ• עַל כֵּן יְיָ אֱלֹהֵינוּ בְּשָׁכְבֵנוּ וּבְקוּמֵנוּ נָשִׂיחַ

בְּחֻקֶּיךָ · וְנִשְׂמַח בְּדִבְרֵי תוֹרָתֶךָ וּבְמִצְוֹתֶיךָ לְעוֹלָם וָעֶד · כִּי הֵם חַיֵּינוּ
וְאֹרֶךְ יָמֵינוּ וּבָהֶם נֶהְגֶּה יוֹמָם וָלָיְלָה · וְאַהֲבָתְךָ אַל תָּסִיר מִמֶּנּוּ
לְעוֹלָמִים ·

לֹא יִהְיֶה לָךְ · הֶבֶל תַּבְנִית אֱלִיל נִכְלָם ·
לֹא תִשָּׂא · וְתַמִּיר קְדֻשַּׁת שֵׁם נֶעְלָם ·
זָכוֹר · וְזֵרוּזֵת מִשְׁפְּטֵי נְעַם וְסִלְסוּלָם ·
הַנּוּן יִזְכָּר לָנוּ אַהֲבַת עוֹלָם :
בָּרוּךְ אַתָּה יְיָ אוֹהֵב עַמּוֹ יִשְׂרָאֵל :

Continue with שְׁמַע (*page* 23) *till* לְךָ עָנוּ שִׁירָה (*page* 27).

טוֹבִיָּה לַמָּרוֹם עָלָה · וְהוֹרִיד דָּת כְּלוּלָה ·
בְּחַג הַשָּׁבוּעוֹת.

יָרַד צוּר בְּעַצְמוֹ · וְנָתַן עֹז לְעַמּוֹ ·
בִּרְעָמִים וּזְוָעוֹת:

כָּל עֲצֵי הַיַּעַר · אֲחָזוּם חִיל וָסַעַר ·
וְהָרִים וּגְבָעוֹת:

לִמֵּד לְעַם קְדֹשִׁים · סֵדֶר תְּקוּפוֹת וַחֳדָשִׁים ·
וְחֶשְׁבּוֹן הַשָּׁעוֹת:

מִכָּל אִם חִבְּבָם · וּלְהַר סִינַי קֵרְבָם ·
אֵל לְמוֹשָׁעוֹת:

נְשָׂאָם כְּכַנְפֵי נְשָׁרִים · שׁוֹכֵן בְּרוּם אוֹרִים ·
וּמִתַּחַת זְרֹעֹת:

סוֹרְרִים בְּעֵת שָׁמְעָם · צְבִי תִפְאֶרֶת עָם ·
יִרְגְּזוּן יְרִיעוֹת:

עֲלוּבִים חָפוּ רֹאשָׁם · וְלַהֲרִנָּה צוּר הַקְּדִישָׁם ·
בִּפְרֹעַ פְּרָעוֹת:

פְּרִישַׂת הוֹד שַׁלְמָה· וּרְקוּעַת גֹּבַהּ אֲדָמָה·
שְׁתֵּיהֶן נוֹגְעוֹת:

צַדִּיק הַר כָּפָה· עֲלֵי נָאוָה וְיָפָה·
כְּגִגִּית וְכִירִיעוֹת:

קָשְׁבוּ עַם בְּחִירִים· חֻקִּים וּמִשְׁפָּטִים יְשָׁרִים·
לְאָזֶן הַשְׁמָעַת:

רָם בְּחַסְדּוֹ שְׁמָרָם· מִכַּף כָּל צוֹרְרָם·
וּמִגְּזֵרוֹת רָעוֹת:

שָׁלַח אוֹתוֹת וּמוֹפְתִים· וְהִנְחִילָם דָּתוֹת חֲרוּתִים·
בְּחָכְמָה וּבְדֵעוֹת:

Reader. תִּפְאַרְתָּם הִגְדִּיל לְמַעֲלָה· לְתִתָּם לְשֵׁם וְלִתְהִלָּה·
כְּבִרְכַּת כּוֹס יְשׁוּעוֹת:

יְשׁוּעוֹת רַבּוֹת הֶרְאָם פּוֹדֶה וְגוֹאֵל
וְעִטְּרָם וְהִגְעָם בְּדַת יְקוּתִיאֵל·
סוֹחֲחִים רֶנֶן וְהוֹדָיָה לָאֵל·
פֵּאֲרוּ וְשִׁבְּחוּ מֹשֶׁה וּבְנֵי יִשְׂרָאֵל:

בְּגִילָה בְרִנָּה בְּשִׂמְחָה רַבָּה וְאָמְרוּ כֻלָּם·

מִי כָמֹכָה בָּאֵלִים יְיָ מִי כָּמֹכָה נֶאְדָּר בַּקֹּדֶשׁ נוֹרָא תְהִלֹת עֹשֵׂה
פֶלֶא:

מַלְכוּתְךָ רָאוּ בָנֶיךָ בּוֹקֵעַ יָם לִפְנֵי מֹשֶׁה:

כַּבֵּד· הוֹרֶיךָ בְּדִבּוּר הַחֲמִישִׁי הַשְׁמִיעָם·
לֹא תִרְצָח· קְרוּצֵי חֹמֶר לְהַכְרִית בְּנָעַם·
לֹא תִנְאָף· טוֹבַת חֵן וְסָרַת טָעַם·
נֶצַח צוּר יִשְׁעֲךָ הַמְלִיכֵהוּ בְּרֹב עָם:

זֶה צוּר יִשְׁעֵנוּ פָּצוּ פֶה וְאָמְרוּ• יְיָ יִמְלֹךְ לְעֹלָם וָעֶד:
וְנֶאֱמַר כִּי פָדָה יְיָ אֶת יַעֲקֹב וּגְאָלוֹ מִיַּד חָזָק מִמֶּנּוּ:

לֹא תִגְנֹב• בְּמִסְתָּרִים לֵישֵׁב בְּמַאֲרַב חֲצֵרִים•
לֹא תַעֲנֶה• רֵעַ חָמָס הֱיוֹת עֵד שְׁקָרִים:
לֹא תַחְמֹד• שִׁפְעַת רֵעַ וַחֲפָצִים יְקָרִים•
מֶלֶךְ יִשְׂרָאֵל וְגוֹאֲלוֹ קַיָּם לְדוֹר דּוֹרִים:

בָּרוּךְ אַתָּה יְיָ מֶלֶךְ צוּר יִשְׂרָאֵל וְגוֹאֲלוֹ:

הַשְׁכִּיבֵנוּ יְיָ אֱלֹהֵינוּ לְשָׁלוֹם וְהַעֲמִידֵנוּ מַלְכֵּנוּ לְחַיִּים• וּפְרוֹשׂ עָלֵינוּ
סֻכַּת שְׁלוֹמֶךָ וְתַקְּנֵנוּ בְּעֵצָה טוֹבָה מִלְּפָנֶיךָ וְהוֹשִׁיעֵנוּ לְמַעַן שְׁמֶךָ•
וְהָגֵן בַּעֲדֵנוּ וְהָסֵר מֵעָלֵינוּ אוֹיֵב דֶּבֶר וְחֶרֶב וְרָעָב וְיָגוֹן וְהָסֵר שָׂטָן
מִלְּפָנֵינוּ וּמֵאַחֲרֵינוּ• וּבְצֵל כְּנָפֶיךָ תַּסְתִּירֵנוּ כִּי אֵל שׁוֹמְרֵנוּ וּמַצִּילֵנוּ
אָתָּה כִּי אֵל מֶלֶךְ חַנּוּן וְרַחוּם אָתָּה• וּשְׁמוֹר צֵאתֵנוּ וּבוֹאֵנוּ לְחַיִּים
וּלְשָׁלוֹם מֵעַתָּה וְעַד עוֹלָם• וּפְרוֹשׂ עָלֵינוּ סֻכַּת שְׁלוֹמֶךָ:

וְכָל הָעָם רֹאִים• וְשׁוֹמְעִים אֶת הַקּוֹלֹת•
אֲגוּדִים יַחַד לְקַבֵּל הַמּוּרוֹת וְקַלֹּת•
לְבֶטַח הוֹשִׁיבָם עוֹשֶׂה גְדוֹלֹת•
כֵּן יִפְרוֹשׂ שְׁלוֹמוֹ עַל כָּל מַקְהֵלֹת:

בָּרוּךְ אַתָּה יְיָ הַפּוֹרֵשׂ סֻכַּת שָׁלוֹם עָלֵינוּ וְעַל כָּל עַמּוֹ יִשְׂרָאֵל וְעַל
יְרוּשָׁלָיִם:

Continue with וידבר, *page* 29.

מַעֲרִבִית לְלֵיל שֵׁנִי

Second Evening

עַל הַר סִינַי ...וַיֵּרֶד, by Isaac ben Moshe of the eleventh century,
is full of praise of the Ten Commandments. It is similar to the
previous *Maaravoth* in form and structure. After the alphabetic
acrostic, the first words of the Ten Commandments are utilized.

Reader. בָּרְכוּ אֶת יְיָ הַמְבֹרָךְ:

Cong. and Reader. בָּרוּךְ יְיָ הַמְבֹרָךְ לְעוֹלָם וָעֶד:

בָּרוּךְ אַתָּה יְיָ אֱלֹהֵינוּ מֶלֶךְ הָעוֹלָם אֲשֶׁר בִּדְבָרוֹ מַעֲרִיב עֲרָבִים
בְּחָכְמָה פּוֹתֵחַ שְׁעָרִים וּבִתְבוּנָה מְשַׁנֶּה עִתִּים וּמַחֲלִיף אֶת הַזְּמַנִּים
וּמְסַדֵּר אֶת הַכּוֹכָבִים בְּמִשְׁמְרוֹתֵיהֶם בָּרָקִיעַ כִּרְצוֹנוֹ בּוֹרֵא יוֹם וָלַיְלָה
גּוֹלֵל אוֹר מִפְּנֵי חֹשֶׁךְ וְחֹשֶׁךְ מִפְּנֵי אוֹר · וּמַעֲבִיר יוֹם וּמֵבִיא לַיְלָה
וּמַבְדִּיל בֵּין יוֹם וּבֵין לַיְלָה יְיָ צְבָאוֹת שְׁמוֹ · אֵל חַי וְקַיָּם תָּמִיד יִמְלוֹךְ
עָלֵינוּ לְעוֹלָם וָעֶד:

וַיֵּרֶד · אֱלֹהִים עַל הַר סִינַי · בֵּאֵר דָּת לִנְבוֹנָיו · וַיְדַבֵּר ·
גְּדֹלוֹת וְנוֹרָאוֹת לְעֵינַי · דָּגוּל מַעֲרִיב שְׁמָשׁוֹ מִפָּנָי:
בָּרוּךְ אַתָּה יְיָ הַמַּעֲרִיב עֲרָבִים:

אַהֲבַת עוֹלָם בֵּית יִשְׂרָאֵל עַמְּךָ אָהָבְתָּ · תּוֹרָה וּמִצְוֹת חֻקִּים
וּמִשְׁפָּטִים אוֹתָנוּ לִמַּדְתָּ · עַל כֵּן יְיָ אֱלֹהֵינוּ בְּשָׁכְבֵּנוּ וּבְקוּמֵנוּ נָשִׂיחַ
בְּחֻקֶּיךָ · וְנִשְׂמַח בְּדִבְרֵי תוֹרָתֶךָ וּבְמִצְוֹתֶיךָ לְעוֹלָם וָעֶד · כִּי הֵם חַיֵּינוּ
וְאֹרֶךְ יָמֵינוּ וּבָהֶם נֶהְגֶּה יוֹמָם וָלַיְלָה · וְאַהֲבָתְךָ אַל תָּסִיר מִמֶּנּוּ
לְעוֹלָמִים:

אָנֹכִי · הָאֵל עָשָׂה פֶּלֶא · וְהוֹצֵאתִיךָ מִבֵּית כֶּלֶא · לֹא
יִהְיֶה לָךְ · וְזָדוֹן צִמְאָה לְהַעֲלָה · הִשְׁקִיתִי בְּאַהֲבָה עָלֶיךָ
לְהַגְלָה: בָּרוּךְ אַתָּה יְיָ אוֹהֵב עַמּוֹ יִשְׂרָאֵל:

Continue with שמע (page 23) *till* לך ענו שירה (page 27).

אֲיֻמָּה נִכְתָּרָה· עֲדוּיָה וּמְעֻטָּרָה·

בְּיוֹם מַתַּן תּוֹרָה:

בְּחוֹרָה מֵעֲמָמִים· בַּת שְׁלֹשֶׁת הַתְּמִימִים·

מָפוֹט וְתֵרָה:

גֻּרְרָה בְּרֹב נִסִּים· אֲדוֹן כָּל הַמַּעֲשִׂים·

בָּאָה לַמִּדְבָּרָה:

דִּבֶּר עַל לִבָּהּ· יָשֵׁב בְּכֶם רְבָבָה·

עָדָיו לְהִתְהַדְּבְּרָה:

הֵרִין לָהּ שְׁלִישִׁי· בַּחֹדֶשׁ הַשְּׁלִישִׁי·

לִיצִיאַת שֶׂה פְזוּרָה:

וְחָמְדָה בְּצִלּוֹ חֲסוֹת· וְהֵשִׁיבָה כֵן לַעֲשׂוֹת·

וְנִתְיַפְּתָה נְזוּרָה:

זִמְּנָה רָם וְאָיוֹם· וְנִתְקַדְּשָׁה לִשְׁלֹשֶׁת יוֹם·

כְּרָמִים נוֹטֵרָה:

חֲלָאִים נִתְקַשְּׁטָה· וּבְלָאוֹתֶיהָ פָּשְׁטָה·

מִמּוֹר מְקֻטָּרָה:

טָהוֹר בָּאֵשׁ וְזָהַר· יָרַד לְרֹאשׁ הָהָר·

וְנוֹדְעָזעֲה בָּרָה:

יָשְׁבָה בִנְקִיקִים· מֵחֶרְדַּת הַבְּרָקִים·

וּמִקּוֹל הַהֲבָרָה:

כֻּלְּלָה עֲדָיִים· וְנָכוֹנוּ שָׁדַיִם·

לְיוֹנָה מְסֻתָּרָה:

לֻמְּדָה בַּמֶּה לְעָבְדוֹ· בְּכָל לִבָּהּ לְכַבְּדוֹ·

וְהַדָּת נִפְתָּרָה:

מָלְאָה פִיהָ שְׂחוֹק· בְּיוֹם נְתִינַת חֹק·

בַּכֹּל מְפֹאָרָה:

נֶחְמָדִים יְרָשָׁה· לִהְיוֹת לָהּ מוֹרָשָׁה·

לִצְבִי וְתִפְאָרָה:

סִלְסוּל פְּנִינֶיהָ· חָגְרָה בְעֹז מָתְנֶיהָ·

עֵקֶב טוֹב סַחְרָהּ:

עָרְכָה שֻׁלְחָנָהּ· וּמַלְכָּה שָׁם חָנָה·

וְלִלְחוּם נִסְחָרָהּ:

פְּתוּכֵי אֵשׁ וּמַיִם· יָרְדוּ מִן הַשָּׁמַיִם·

לְדַרֶּךְ בַּחֲבוּרָהּ:

צוּרָהּ תּוֹךְ עִירִין· נוֹדַע בַּשְּׁעָרִים·

כִּי לוֹ הַגְּבוּרָה:

קְצִיעוֹת וַאֲהָלוֹת· מְבֻסֶּמֶת בְּשִׁיר וּתְהִלּוֹת·

וְחֶסֶד מְקֻשָּׁרָה:

רַבּוֹת עָשׂוּ הֲמוֹנָה· וְאַתְּ עָלִית עַל כֻּלָּנָה·

בְּזֹאת מְאֻשָּׁרָה:

שׁוֹשַׁנַּת עֲמָקִים· קִבְּלָה מִצְוֹת וְחֻקִּים·

בִּכְתָב מִדָּרָהּ:

Reader. תּוֹרָה מְנִינָם· וְשֻׁתִּים בְּרֹאשׁ בְּנִינָם·

כְּהֻנָּה מְזֹהָרָה:

לֹא תִשָּׂא· מְכוֹם שֵׁם נוֹרָא עֲלִילָה· יַחֵד שְׁמוֹ יוֹמָם
וְלַיְלָה· זָכוֹר· כְּלְכוּל עֹנֶג לְכַפְלָה· לְיוֹצְרָךְ תְּשׁוֹרֵר
כְּעוֹבְרֵי מְצוּלָה:

בְּגִילָה בְּרִנָּה בְּשִׂמְחָה רַבָּה וְאָמְרוּ כֻלָּם·

מִי כָמֹכָה בָּאֵלִים יְיָ מִי כָּמֹכָה נֶאְדָּר בַּקֹּדֶשׁ נוֹרָא תְהִלֹת עֹשֵׂה
פֶלֶא:

מַלְכוּתְךָ רָאוּ בָנֶיךָ בּוֹקֵעַ יָם לִפְנֵי מֹשֶׁה:

כַּבֵּד· מֵאָד אָבִיךָ וְאִמֶּךָ· נֶצַח יִרְבּוּ יָמֶיךָ· לֹא תִרְצָח·
סָדוּר בְּצַלְמִי וּבְגִלְמֶךָ· עֶלְיוֹן צוּרְךָ הַמְלִיכֵהוּ כִּנְאוּמֶךָ:

זֶה צוּר יִשְׁעֵנוּ פָּצוּ פֶה וְאָמְרוּ · יְיָ יִמְלֹךְ לְעֹלָם וָעֶד:
וְנֶאֱמַר כִּי פָדָה יְיָ אֶת יַעֲקֹב וּגְאָלוֹ מִיַּד חָזָק מִמֶּנּוּ:

לֹא תִנְאָף· פְּעָמוֹת חוּצוֹת וּמַחֲלִיקוֹת· צוֹדְדוֹת נְפָשׁוֹת
בְּשׁוּחוֹת עֲמֻקּוֹת· לֹא תִגְנֹב· קְבוּצוֹת זָהָב הָשׁוּקוֹת·
רַחוּם יִגְאָלֵךְ מִמְּצוּקוֹת:

בָּרוּךְ אַתָּה יְיָ מֶלֶךְ צוּר יִשְׂרָאֵל וְגוֹאֲלוֹ:

הַשְׁכִּיבֵנוּ יְיָ אֱלֹהֵינוּ לְשָׁלוֹם וְהַעֲמִידֵנוּ מַלְכֵּנוּ לְחַיִּים · וּפְרוֹשׂ עָלֵינוּ
סֻכַּת שְׁלוֹמֶךָ וְתַקְּנֵנוּ בְּעֵצָה טוֹבָה מִלְּפָנֶיךָ וְהוֹשִׁיעֵנוּ לְמַעַן שְׁמֶךָ·
וְהָגֵן בַּעֲדֵנוּ וְהָסֵר מֵעָלֵינוּ אוֹיֵב דֶּבֶר וְחֶרֶב וְרָעָב וְיָגוֹן וְהָסֵר שָׂטָן
מִלְּפָנֵינוּ וּמֵאַחֲרֵינוּ· וּבְצֵל כְּנָפֶיךָ תַּסְתִּירֵנוּ כִּי אֵל שׁוֹמְרֵנוּ וּמַצִּילֵנוּ
אָתָּה כִּי אֵל מֶלֶךְ חַנּוּן וְרַחוּם אָתָּה· וּשְׁמוֹר צֵאתֵנוּ וּבוֹאֵנוּ לְחַיִּים
וּלְשָׁלוֹם מֵעַתָּה וְעַד עוֹלָם· וּפְרוֹשׂ עָלֵינוּ סֻכַּת שְׁלוֹמֶךָ:

לֹא תַעֲנֶה· שְׁקָרִים לַעֲנוֹת בְּעֵדוּתֶיךָ· תִּרְדֹּף צֶדֶק בְּכָל
אֹרְחוֹתֶיךָ· לֹא תַחְמֹד· יְפִי צָחוֹת קִנְיַן עֲמִיתֶךָ· בְּנֵה
מִשְׁכְּנוֹת הַשָּׁלוֹם תִּשְׁכַּב וְעָרְבָה שְׁנָתֶךָ:

בָּרוּךְ אַתָּה יְיָ הַפּוֹרֵשׂ סֻכַּת שָׁלוֹם עָלֵינוּ וְעַל כָּל עַמּוֹ יִשְׂרָאֵל וְעַל
יְרוּשָׁלָיִם:

Continue with וידבר, *page* 29.

MOURNER'S KADDISH

Transliterated

Yisgaddal v'yiskaddash shmey **rabboh**
B'olmoh dee v'roh ḥir-usey,
V'yamliḥ malḥusey
B'ḥa-yeyḥon uvyo-meyḥon,
Uvḥa-yey d'ḥol beys yisro-**eyl,**
Ba-agoloh uvizman koreev
V'imru omeyn.

Y'hey shmey rabboh m'voraḥ
L'olam ul'olmey olmah-**yoh.**

Yisboraḥ v'yishtabbaḥ,
V'yispo-ar v'yisromam,
V'yisnassey v'yis-haddar,
V'yis-alleh v'yis-hallal
Shmey d'kudshoh, b'reeḥ hu,
L'eyloh min kol birḥosoh v'**shirosoh,**
Tush-b'ḥosoh v'neḥemosoh

Da-ameeron b'olmoh
V'imru omeyn.

Y'hey shlomoh rabboh min sh'mah-**yoh,**
V'ḥa-yeem, oleynu v'al kol yisro-**eyl**
V'imru omeyn.

O-seh sholom bimromov
Hu ya-aseh sholom
Oleynu v'al kol yisro-eyl
V'imru omeyn.

KADDISH D'RABBANAN

Transliterated

Yisgaddal v'yiskaddash shmey rabboh b'olmoh dee v'roh chirusey; v'yamlich malchusey, b'cha-yeychon uvyo-meychon, uvcha-yey d'chol beys yisro-eyl, ba-agoloh uvizman koreev; v'imru omeyn.

Y'hey shmey rabboh m'vorach l'olam ul'olmey olmah-yoh.

Yisborach v'yishtabbach, v'yispo-ar v'yisromam, v'yisnassey v'yis-haddar, v'yis-alleh, v'yis-hallal shmey d'kudshoh, b'reech hu, l'eyloh min kol birchosoh v'shirosoh, tush-b'chosoh v'nechemosoh, da-ameeron b'olmoh; v'imru omeyn.

Al yisro-eyl v'al rabbonon v'al talmideyhon, v'al kol talmidey salmideyhon, v'al kol mon d'oskin b'orah'yesoh, dee b'asroh hodeyn, v'dee b'chol asar va'asar, y'hey l'hon ul'chon sh'lomoh rabboh, hinnoh v'ḥisdoh v'raḥamin, v'ḥah'yin ariḥin, um'zoney r'viḥey, u'furkonoh min kodom avuhon d'vishmah'yoh v'ar'oh; v'imru omeyn.

Y'hey shlomoh rabboh min sh'mah-yoh, v'cha-yim tovim oleynu v'al kol yisro-eyl; v'imru omeyn.

O-seh sholom bimromov, hu b'rachamov ya-aseh sholom oleynu v'al kol yisro-eyl; v'imru omeyn.

FIRST DAY OF SHAVUOTH

1978	5738	Sunday	June	11
1979	5739	Friday	June	1
1980	5740	Wednesday	May	21
1981	5741	Monday	June	8
1982	5742	Friday	May	28
1983	5743	Wednesday	May	18
1984	5744	Wednesday	June	6
1985	5745	Sunday	May	26
1986	5746	Friday	June	13
1987	5747	Wednesday	June	3
1988	5748	Sunday	May	22
1989	5749	Friday	June	9
1990	5750	Wednesday	May	30
1991	5751	Sunday	May	19
1992	5752	Sunday	June	7
1993	5753	Wednesday	May	26
1994	5754	Monday	May	16
1995	5755	Sunday	June	4
1996	5756	Friday	May	24
1997	5757	Wednesday	June	11
1998	5758	Sunday	May	31
1999	5759	Friday	May	21
2000	5760	Friday	June	9
2001	5761	Monday	May	28
2002	5762	Friday	May	17
2003	5763	Friday	June	6
2004	5764	Wednesday	May	26
2005	5765	Monday	June	13
2006	5766	Friday	June	2
2007	5767	Wednesday	May	23
2008	5768	Monday	June	9
2009	5769	Friday	May	29
2010	5770	Wednesday	May	19
2011	5771	Wednesday	June	8
2012	5772	Sunday	May	27